Becoming a
MASTER STUDENT

Fifth Canadian Edition

NELSON / E D U C A T I O N

Becoming a
MASTER STUDENT

Fifth Canadian Edition

Dave Ellis

Doug Toft
Contributing Editor

Debra Dawson
The University of Western Ontario

NELSON / EDUCATION

NELSON EDUCATION

Becoming a Master Student, Fifth Canadian Edition

by Dave Ellis, Doug Toft, and Debra Dawson

Vice President, Editorial Higher Education:
Anne Williams

Executive Editor:
Laura Macleod

Senior Marketing Manager:
Amanda Henry

Managing Developmental Editor:
Sandy Matos

Photo Researcher:
Carrie McGregor

Permissions Coordinator:
Carrie McGregor

Content Production Manager:
Christine Gilbert

Production Service:
MPS Limited, a Macmillan Company

Copy Editor:
Joan Bondar

Proofreader:
Maura Brown

Indexer:
Edwin Durbin

Production Coordinator:
Ferial Suleman

Design Director:
Ken Phipps

Managing Designer:
Franca Amore

Interior Design:
Jennifer Stimson

Cover Design:
Jennifer Stimson

Cover Image:
Hanny Breunese/Flickr/ Getty Images

Compositor:
MPS Limited, a Macmillan Company

Printer:
RR Donnelley

Library and Archives Canada Cataloguing in Publication

Ellis, David B.

Becoming a master student / Dave Ellis, Debra Dawson.—5th Canadian ed.

Includes bibliographical references and index.
ISBN: 978-0-17-665293-7

1. College student orientation. 2. Study skills. I. Dawson, Debra, 1954- II. Title.

LB2343.3.E44 2012   378.1'98
C2011-907930-5

PKG ISBN-13: 978-0-17-665293-7
PKG ISBN-10: 0-17-665293-0

Brief Table of Contents

PREFACE   XIII

INTRODUCTION   **MAKING TRANSITIONS**   2

CHAPTER 1   **FIRST STEPS**   32

CHAPTER 2   **TIME**   70

CHAPTER 3   **MEMORY**   108

CHAPTER 4   **READING**   136

CHAPTER 5   **NOTES**   162

CHAPTER 6   **TESTS**   192

CHAPTER 7   **THINKING**   224

CHAPTER 8   **COMMUNICATING**   254

CHAPTER 9   **DIVERSITY**   292

CHAPTER 10   **MONEY**   318

CHAPTER 11   **HEALTH**   346

CHAPTER 12   **WHAT'S NEXT?**   382

Glossary   421

References   423

Index   427

© Peter Dazeley/Photolibrary

© photos.com

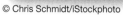
© Chris Schmidt/iStockphoto

© photos.com

Table of Contents

© aprott/iStockphoto

Making Transitions 2

Master Student Map 2

This book is worthless—if you just read it 4

Exercise 1: **Textbook Reconnaissance** 5

Get the most out of this book 6

Exercise 2: **Commitment** 7

The Discovery and Intention Journal Entry system 8

Rewrite this book 9

Discovery and Intention Statement guidelines 10

Journal Entry 1: **Recalling excellence** 11

Making the transition to postsecondary education 12

Journal Entry 2: **Plan for transition** 13

Classroom civility—what's in it for you 15

Succeeding in higher education—at any age 16

Connect to school resources 18

Connect to community resources 20

Extracurricular activities: Reap the benefits 21

Why going to college matters 22

Link to the world of work 23

You don't need this course—but you might want it 24

Ways to change a habit 25

Journal Entry 3: **Choosing your purpose** 27

The Power Processes: A User's Guide 28

Power Process: **Discover What You Want** 29

Quiz 30

1 First Steps 32

Master Student Map 32

First step: Truth is a key to mastery 33

Journal Entry 4: **Create value from this chapter** 33

Exercise 3: **Taking the First Step** 34

Exercise 4: **The Discovery Wheel** 35

Journal Entry 5: **Roll your Discovery Wheel** 39

Mastering Technology: **Supplement Your Text with Online Resources** 39

Learning Styles: Discovering how you learn 40

Journal Entry 6: **Prepare for the Learning Style Inventory** 42

Learning Style Inventory LSI-1

Take a snapshot of your learning styles LSI-2

Scoring your Inventory LSI-3

Learning Style Graph LSI-5

Cycle of Learning LSI-6

Returning to the big picture about learning styles LSI-7

Balancing your preferences LSI-8

what if ◄······· ·······► why

how ◄·············· ············►what

Using your learning style profile to succeed 43

Use the modes to learn from *any* instructor 46

Canadian employers' wish list 47

Claim your multiple intelligences 48

Exercise 5: **Develop your multiple intelligences** 48

Learning by seeing, hearing, and moving: The VAK system 51

The magic of metacognition 53

The Master Student 54

Motivation—I'm just not in the mood 57

What's stopping you from getting started on your schoolwork? 59

Attitudes, affirmations, and visualizations 60

Attitude replacements 61

Exercise 6: *Reprogram your attitude* 62

Master Student Profiles 62

Practising Critical Thinking 1 63

Power Process: *Ideas are tools* 64

Put It to Work 65

Quiz 66

Skills Snapshot 67

Master Student Profile: *Terry Beech* 68

2 Time 70

© Warren Goldswain/Shutterstock

Master Student Map 70

You've got the time 71

Journal Entry 7: *Create value from this chapter* 71

Exercise 7: *The Time Monitor/Time Plan Process* 72

Setting and achieving goals 77

Journal Entry 8: *Assess your use of time* 78

Exercise 8: *Seeing where all the time goes* 79

Exercise 9: *Create a lifeline* 79

Exercise 10: *Get real with your goals* 80

The ABC daily to-do list 81

Mastering Technology: *Use Web-Based Tools to Save Time* 83

More strategies for planning 84

Stop Procrastination NOW 86

The 7-day antiprocrastination plan 87

Practising Critical Thinking 2 88

25 ways to get the most out of now 89

Remember cultural differences 92

Beyond time management: Stay focused on what matters 94

Forget time management—just get things done 96

Exercise 11: *Master monthly calendar* 97

Gearing up: Using a long-term planner 100

Power Process: *Be Here Now* 102

Put It to Work 103

Quiz 104

Skills Snapshot 105

Master Student Profile: *Chantal Petitclerc* 106

3 Memory 108

Master Student Map 108

Take your memory out of the closet 109

Journal Entry 9: *Create value from this chapter* 109

The memory jungle 110

20 memory techniques 112

How to create a concept map 117

Practising Critical Thinking 3 119

Pay attention to your attention 120

Exercise 12: *Use Q-Cards to reinforce memory* 121

Set a trap for your memory 122

Keep your brain fit for life 122

Notable failures 123

Journal Entry 10: *Revisit your memory skills* 123

Remembering names 124

Mnemonic devices 125

Exercise 13: *Get creative* 127

Mastering Technology: *Use Your Computer to Enhance Memory* 127

Practising Critical Thinking 4 128

Exercise 14: *Move from problems to solutions* 129

Pulling it all together 130

Power Process: *Love your problems (and experience your barriers)* 131

Put It to Work 132

Quiz 133

Skills Snapshot 134

Master Student Profile: *David Suzuki* 135

© Angelo Cavalli/Digital Vision/ RF/Getty Images

Table of Contents

4 Reading 136

Master Student Map 136

Muscle Reading 137

Journal Entry 11: *Discover what you want from this chapter* 137

How Muscle Reading works 138

Phase 1: Before you read 139

Phase 2: While you read 140

Five smart ways to highlight a text 141

Phase 3: After you read 142

Muscle Reading—a leaner approach 143

Journal Entry 12: *Experimenting with Muscle Reading* 143

Read with a dictionary or laptop in your lap 144

Exercise 15: *Relax* 145

When reading is tough 146

Mastering Technology: *Find What You Want on the Internet* 147

The 21st-century researcher—using your library 148

Staying literate in the digital age 150

© photos.com

Muscle Reading for e-books 150

English as a second language 151

Reading with children underfoot 153

Practising Critical Thinking 5 155

Power Process: *Notice your pictures and let them go* 156

Put It to Work 157

Quiz 158

Skills Snapshot 159

Master Student Profile: *Eva Aariak* 160

5 Notes 162

Master Student Map 162

The note-taking process flows 163

Journal Entry 13: *Get what you want from this chapter* 163

Observe: The note-taking process flows 164

Journal Entry 14: *Create more value from lectures* 166

What to do when you miss a class 166

Record: The note-taking process flows 167

Review: The note-taking process flows 173

Journal Entry 15: *Reflect on your review habits* 174

Enrol your instructor in your education 175

Meeting with your instructor 177

When your instructor *talks fast* 177

Exercise 16: *TV note-taking* 178

Taking notes on your journey: The art of journal writing 178

Taking notes while reading 180

Note this information about your sources 181

© Goodshoot/RF/Jupiter Images

Taking notes . . . despite PowerPoint® 182

Exercise 17: *Revisit your goals* 183

Online classes—taking notes and using other review tools 184

Mastering Technology: *Your Mind, Online* 185

Power Process: *I create it all* 186

Put It to Work 187

Quiz 188

Skills Snapshot 189

Master Student Profile: *Gwonaollo Moubouyi* 190

© Yuri Arcurs/Shutterstock

6 Tests 192

Master Student Map   192

Disarm tests   193

Journal Entry 16: *Use this chapter to transform your experience of tests*   193

What to do before the test   194

Ways to predict test questions   196

Cooperative learning: Studying in groups   197

Mastering Technology: *Collaboration 2.0*   199

Students Offering Support   199

What to do during the test   200

F is for feedback, not failure   202

Words to watch for in essay questions   203

The test isn't over until . . .   203

The high costs of cheating   204

Perils of high-tech cheating   205

Let go of test anxiety   205

Have some FUN!   209

Exercise 18: *20 Things I like to do*   209

Journal Entry 17: *Notice your excuses and let them go*   210

Journal Entry 18: *Explore your feelings about tests*   210

Getting ready for math tests   211

Succeeding in science courses   214

Exercise 19: *Use learning styles for math success*   214

Eight reasons to celebrate mistakes   215

Practising Critical Thinking 6   216

Power Process: *Detach*   217

Put It to Work   218

Quiz   219

Skills Snapshot   220

Master Student Profile: *Georges Laraque*   221

© photos.com

7 Thinking 224

Master Student Map   224

Critical thinking: A survival skill   225

Journal Entry 19: *Choose to create value with this chapter*   225

Becoming a Critical Thinker   227

Four more questions for critical thinking   228

Attitudes of a critical thinker   230

Finding "aha!": Creativity fuels critical thinking   231

Tangram   231

Ways to create ideas   232

Creative ways for groups to get "unstuck"   233

Create on your feet   235

Exercise 20: *Explore emotional reactions*   235

Don't fool yourself: 15 common mistakes in logic   236

Uncovering assumptions   238

The problem of egocentric thinking   239

Gaining skill at decision making   240

Four ways to solve problems   241

"But I don't know what I want to do." Choosing your major   242

Exercise 21: *Make a trial choice of major*   244

Asking questions—Learning through inquiry   245

Practising Critical Thinking 7   246

Think critically about information on the Internet   247

Mastering Technology: *Rethinking email*   247

Exercise 22: *Translating goals into action*   248

Journal Entry 20: *Reflect on choosing a major*   248

Power Process: *Find a bigger problem*   249

Put It to Work   250

Quiz   251

Skills Snapshot   252

Master Student Profile: *Jian Ghomeshi*   253

Table of Contents

8 Communicating 254

© Pakhnyushcha/Shutterstock

Master Student Map 254

Communicating creates our world 255

Journal Entry 21: **Commit to create value from this chapter** 255

Communication—keeping the channels open 256

Exercise 23: **Practise sending or receiving** 256

Choosing to llisten 257

Choosing to speak 259

Five ways to say "I" 260

Exercise 24: **Write an "I" message** 261

Journal Entry 22: **Discover communication styles** 262

Developing emotional intelligence 263

Mastering Technology: **Setting Limits on Screen Time** 264

Managing conflict 264

Journal Entry 23: **Re-create a relationship** 266

Resolve conflicts with roommates 267

Five ways to say no . . . gracefully 267

You deserve compliments 268

7 steps to effective complaints 269

Criticism really can be constructive 269

Collaborating for success 270

Staying smart in cyberspace—safe social networking 271

Mastering Technology: **Master Students—Get Networked** 271

Text message etiquette—Five key points 272

Three phases of effective writing 273

Tools for writing group projects 278

Journal Entry 24: **Take a First Step about writing** 279

Giving credit where credit is due: Avoiding the high cost of PLAGIARISM 280

Mastering public speaking 281

Making the grade in group presentations 283

Honing your leadership skills 284

Practising Critical Thinking 8 285

Power Process: **Employ your word** 286

Put It to Work 287

Quiz 288

Skills Snapshot 289

Master Student Profile: **Neil Pasricha** 290

9 Diversity 292

Master Student Map 292

Waking up to diversity 293

Diversity in Canada 293

Journal Entry 25: **Commit to create value from this chapter** 294

Diversity is real—and valuable 295

Building relationships across cultures 297

High versus low context cultures 299

Exercise 25: **Becoming a culture learner** 301

Overcome stereotypes with critical thinking 302

Students with disabilities: Know your rights 303

Dealing with sexism and sexual harassment 305

Strategies for non-sexist communication 306

© Jeff Hunter/Getty Images

Leadership in a diverse world 307

Journal Entry 26: **Removing barriers to communication** 310

Journal Entry 27: **Reflect on the quality of a recent conversation** 311

Practising Critical Thinking 9   311
Mastering Technology: *Making Technology Accessible*   312
Power Process: *Choose your conversations and your community*   313

Put It to Work   314
Quiz   315
Skills Snapshot   316
Master Student Profile: *Trey Anthony*   317

10 Money   318

Master Student Map   318
Three paths to financial freedom   319
Journal Entry 28: *Commit to a new experience of money*   319
Exercise 26: *The Money Monitor/Money Plan*   320
No budgeting required   321
Journal Entry 29: *Reflect on your Money Monitor/Money Plan*   325
Make more money   326
Mastering Technology: *Protect Your Money Online*   327
Spend less money   328
Exercise 27: *Show me the money*   330
Managing money during tough times   330
Take charge of your credit   331
Exercise 28: *Education by the hour*   333
If you're in trouble . . .   334
Common credit terms   334
Money for the future   335
You can pay for school   336

© Retna/Photoshot

Education is worth it   336
Your learning styles and your money   337
We live like royalty   338
Free fun   338
Practising Critical Thinking 10   339
Power Process: *Risk being a fool*   340
Put It to Work   341
Quiz   342
Skills Snapshot   343
Master Student Profile: *Régine Chassagne & Edwin Farnham Butler*   344

11 Health   346

Master Student Map   346
Wake up to health   347
Journal Entry 30: *Take a First Step about your health*   347
Choose your fuel   349
Eating well with Canada's Food Guide   350
Prevent and treat eating disorders   350
Choose to exercise   351
Choose to rest   352
Choose mental health   353
Is it just me who feels stressed out?   355
Observe Yourself   355
Journal Entry 31: *Choose to be healthy*   356
Choose to stay safe   356
Choose sexual health   358
Protect against unwanted pregnancy   360

© DUSAN ZIDAR/Shutterstock

Table of Contents

Men, consider your health   364

Journal Entry 32: *Choose to break a habit*   364

Journal Entry 33: *Choose to be you*   364

Developing self-efficacy   365

Emotional pain is not a sickness   366

Suicide is no solution   367

Alcohol, tobacco, and drugs: The truth   368

Some facts . . .   369

I wouldn't bet on it   369

Exercise 29: *Addiction: How do I know . . . ?*   370

Seeing the full scope of addiction   371

Binge Drinking   372

Warning: Advertising can be dangerous to your health   373

Journal Entry 34: *Advertisements and your health*   374

Practising Critical Thinking 11   374

Journal entry 35: *Choose a new level of health*   375

Apply insights from ergonomics   375

Power Process: *Surrender*   376

Put It to Work   377

Quiz   378

Skills Snapshot   379

Master Student Profile: *Clara Hughes*   380

12 What's Next?   382

Master Student Map   382

Now that you're done—begin   383

Journal Entry 36: *Revisiting what you want and how you intend to get It*   383

". . . use the following suggestions to continue . . ."   384

Mastering Technology: *Continue Your Education at Internet University*   386

Create your career now   386

Exercise 30: *Create your career plan—now*   389

Exercise 31: *Recognize your skills*   390

Sample career plans   390

Discover your employability skills   391

Exercise 32: Assess your Employability Skills   393

Jumpstart your education with transferable skills   393

65 transferable skills   395

Use resumés and interviews to "hire" an employer   396

Looking for jobs on the Internet   398

Exercise 33: *Do something you can't*   399

Creating and using portfolios   399

Top 10 Tips to Help Ensure a Successful Job Search   400

Surviving your first day on a new job   401

Choosing schools ... again   402

Contributing: The art of selfishness   405

Service-learning: The art of learning by contributing   407

Define your values, align your actions   408

Exercise 34: *The Discovery Wheel—coming full circle*   409

Journal Entry 37: *Revisiting your Discovery Wheels*   413

Exercise 35: *This book shouts, "Use me!"*   413

Exercise 36: *Create your next semester or term*   414

Power Process: *Be it*   415

Put It to Work   416

Quiz   417

Skills Snapshot   418

Master Student Profile: *Craig and Marc Kielburger*   419

Glossary   421

References   423

Index   427

© Free the Children

WELCOME TO THE fifth Canadian edition of *Becoming a Master Student*. If you are a student about to start reading the text, you will see that I have tried to highlight more Canadian resources and information that I believe can make you successful in both school and life. This is an exciting time for you as you begin your education at the postsecondary level, and I know this book will make a difference in helping you get the most out of your studies. If you are an instructor using this book, I think you will find that I have improved the readability of the text and that it is more adaptable to your course needs.

Here are a few highlights of the new edition. To begin with, I have changed many of the master student profiles to focus on Canadians who have truly made a difference—from amazing athletes like Chantal Petitclerc to inspiring politicians such as Eva Aadriak; to creative musicians like Regine Chassagne and Edwin Farnham III of Arcade Fire; to committed activists such as Marc and Craig Kielburger; to dedicated students such as Gwenaelle Moubouyi—the stories they tell will inspire you to do more in your lives.

I have added a new chapter on money. Higher education is expensive, so learning how to handle your money is another key to your success at school. Determining how many hours to work, what type of part-time job to have, and how to use credit cards are just some of the issues discussed in Chapter 10. Also, throughout the text you will see more references to electronic tools for learning and important websites if you want more topic-specific information. The discussion of technology is now woven throughout the book rather than being in a separate chapter, as accessing and using technology is an essential learning tool for master students to employ.

Furthermore, I have updated all of the chapters in this edition and added a glossary for your reference. In the Introduction, I start with a piece on how to be successful in higher education authored by Dr. Mike Atkinson (one of Canada's top postsecondary instructors) and also in that chapter there is some convincing evidence about why postsecondary education matters for lifelong success. Procrastination is something all of us face at times throughout our lives. Chapter 1 discusses why we do this and how it can be overcome. Time management also plagues many of us, and Chapter 2 talks more about strategies for getting work done on time. Chapter 3 focuses on memory and brings you the latest information on being a self-regulated learner—an important concept if you want to succeed in school. Chapter 4's emphasis on reading has been expanded to talk more about how to use the rich resources, both digital and print, that can be found in all our libraries. Using technology to aid in note-taking is emphasized in Chapter 5. Chapter 6 focuses on test taking—a part of school whether we like it or not—and provides many new tips about how to meet with success at these tasks. Chapter 7 provides new information on how to think and solve problems effectively. There is also a discussion about how to evaluate information you read on the Internet.

Communicating effectively is essential for success, both for master students and throughout life. Chapter 8 discusses this topic and also talks about the role social networking can play in enhancing or destroying your reputation. I have expanded our discussion of diversity to focus more on the Canadian context in Chapter 9. Learning more about yourself and others is vital to your achievement in school and your success in work. Chapter 11, on health, talks about some of the new issues that are facing college and university students, such as the increase in gambling, binge drinking, and mental health problems. Addictions can have a huge impact on school achievement, so I provide information and resources on these topics. Safety issues facing LGBTQ (lesbian, gay, bisexual, transgendered, and queer or questioning) students are also addressed. The last chapter looks at what's next now that you have finished the book, and here I added in new exercises and resources. In particular, I have added 10 tips from a career counsellor for finding a job. Throughout the text, I have included new exercises, streamlined the power processes, and updated the references. I think this new edition of *Becoming a Master Student* will truly make a difference in your life, so take the time to do the exercises, visit the book's website, and enjoy reading the profiles of great Canadians.

Ancillaries

Instructor Ancillaries

The **Nelson Education Teaching Advantage (NETA)** program delivers research-based instructor resources that promote student engagement and higher-order thinking to enable the success of Canadian students and educators.

Instructors today face many challenges. Resources are limited, time is scarce, and a new kind of student has emerged: one who is juggling school with work, has gaps in his or her basic knowledge, and is immersed in technology in a way that has led to a completely new style of learning. In response, Nelson Education has gathered a group of dedicated instructors to advise us on the creation of richer and more flexible ancillaries that respond to the needs of today's teaching environments.

The members of our editorial advisory board have experience across a variety of disciplines and are recognized for their commitment to teaching. They include:

Norman Althouse
Haskayne School of Business, University of Calgary
Brenda Chant-Smith
Department of Psychology, Trent University
Scott Follows
Manning School of Business Administration, Acadia University
Jon Houseman
Department of Biology, University of Ottawa
Glen Loppnow
Department of Chemistry, University of Alberta
Tanya Noel
Department of Biology, York University
Gary Poole
Director, Centre for Teaching and Academic Growth and School of Population and Public Health, University of British Columbia
Dan Pratt
Department of Educational Studies, University of British Columbia
Mercedes Rowinsky-Geurts
Department of Languages and Literatures, Wilfrid Laurier University
David DiBattista
Department of Psychology, Brock University
Dr. Roger Fisher, PhD

In consultation with the editorial advisory board, Nelson Education has completely rethought the structure, approaches, and formats of our key textbook ancillaries. We've also increased our investment in editorial support for our ancillary authors. The result is the Nelson Education Teaching Advantage and its key components: *NETA Engagement, NETA Assessment,* and *NETA Presentation.* Each component includes one or more ancillaries prepared according to our best practices, and a document explaining the theory behind the practices.

NETA Engagement presents materials that help instructors deliver engaging content and activities to their classes. Instead of Instructor's Manuals that regurgitate chapter outlines and key terms from the text, NETA Enriched Instructor's Manuals (EIMs) provide genuine assistance to teachers. The EIMs answer questions like *What should students learn?, Why should students care?,* and *What are some common student misconceptions and stumbling blocks?* EIMs not only identify the topics that cause students the most difficulty, but also describe techniques and resources to help students master these concepts. Dr. Roger Fisher's *Instructor's Guide to Classroom Engagement (IGCE)* accompanies every Enriched Instructor's Manual. (Information about the NETA Enriched Instructor's Manual prepared for *Becoming a Master Student,* Fifth Canadian Edition is included in the description of the IRCD below.)

NETA Assessment relates to testing materials: not just Nelson's Test Banks and Computerized Test Banks, but also in-text self-tests, Study Guides and web quizzes, and homework programs like CNOW. Under *NETA Assessment,* Nelson's authors create multiple-choice questions that reflect research-based best practices for constructing effective questions and testing not just recall but also higher-order thinking. Our guidelines were developed by David DiBattista, a 3M National Teaching Fellow whose recent research as a professor of psychology at Brock University has focused on multiple-choice testing. All Test Bank authors receive training at workshops conducted by Professor DiBattista, as do the copyeditors assigned to each Test Bank. A copy of *Multiple Choice Tests: Getting Beyond Remembering,* Prof. DiBattista's guide to writing effective tests, is included with every Nelson Test Bank/Computerized Test Bank package. (Information about the NETA Test Bank prepared for *Becoming a Master Student,* Fifth Canadian Edition is included in the description of the IRCD below.)

NETA Presentation has been developed to help instructors make the best use of PowerPoint® in their classrooms. With a clean and uncluttered design developed by Maureen Stone of StoneSoup Consulting, *NETA Presentation* features slides with improved readability, more multi-media and graphic materials, activities to use in class, and tips for instructors on the Notes page. A copy of *NETA Guidelines for Classroom Presentations* by Maureen Stone is included with each set of PowerPoint® slides. (Information about the NETA PowerPoint® prepared for *Becoming a Master Student,* Fifth Canadian Edition is included in the description of the IRCD below.)

Instructor's Resource CD (IRCD)

Key instructor ancillaries are provided on the *Instructor's Resource CD* (ISBN 978-0-17-661002-9), giving instructors the ultimate tool for customizing lectures and presentations. (Downloadable Web versions are also available at **www.bams5Ce.nelson.com/faculty**) The IRCD includes:

- **NETA Engagement:** The Enriched Instructor's Manual was written by Liza Arnason, University of Ontario Institute of Technology.

It is organized according to the textbook chapters and addresses eight key educational concerns, such as typical stumbling blocks student face and how to address them. It also includes extensive teaching tips for new instructors.

- **NETA Assessment**: The Test Bank was written by Katherine Gallinger; St. Lawrence College. It includes over 200 multiple-choice questions written according to NETA guidelines for effective construction and development of higher-order questions. Also included are approximately 120 true/false questions, 30 completion questions, and 20 short-answer questions. Test Bank files are provided in Word format for easy editing and in PDF format for convenient printing, whatever your system.

  The Computerized Test Bank by ExamView® includes all the questions from the Test Bank. The easy-to-use ExamView software is compatible with Microsoft Windows and Mac. Create tests by selecting questions from the question bank, modifying these questions as desired, and adding new questions you write yourself. You can administer quizzes online and export tests to WebCT, Blackboard, and other formats.

- **NETA Presentation:** Microsoft® PowerPoint® lecture slides for every chapter have been created by Jacqueline Cottingham and Laura Jones, both from Confederation College. NETA principles of clear design and engaging content have been incorporated throughout.

- **Image Library:** This resource consists of digital copies of figures, short tables, and some photographs used in the book. Instructors may use these jpegs to create their own PowerPoint® presentations.

- **DayOne:** Day One—Prof InClass is a PowerPoint® presentation that you can customize to orient your students to the class and their text at the beginning of the course.

Nelson Education's *Becoming a Master Student* CourseMate brings course concepts to life with interactive learning and exam preparation tools that integrate with the printed textbook. Students activate their knowledge through quizzes, games, and flashcards, among many other tools. The CourseMate for *Becoming a Master Student* was written and prepared by Kay Johnson, Athabasca University.

CourseMate provides immediate feedback that enables students to connect results to the work they have just produced, increasing their learning efficiency. It encourages contact between students and faculty: You can choose to monitor your students' level of engagement with CourseMate, correlating their efforts to their outcomes. You can even use CourseMate's quizzes to practise "Just in Time" teaching by tracking results in the Engagement Tracker and customizing your lesson plans to address students' learning needs.

Watch student comprehension and engagement soar as your class engages with CourseMate. Ask your Nelson Education representative for a demo today.

Acknowledgments

I would like to take this opportunity to thank the many people who have been instrumental in developing this new edition. First, the Editorial Advisory Board (EAB) members were vital to finding out what changes were needed in the text to make our students more successful. Thank you for reading the text so thoroughly and for your insightful feedback. I think you will find many of your ideas incorporated in the new edition. Special thanks to the following EAB members:

Katherine Gallinger
St. Lawrence College
Kay Johnson
Athabasca University
Philip Jones
Algonquin College
Jeremy McQuigge
Algonquin College
Michael Sullivan
Centennial College

Next I would like to thank my Senior Developmental Editor, Sandy Matos—you were fantastic at guiding me through this process and answering all my questions. Without my research assistant, Gayle McIntyre, this book would not have happened—your keen research skills were critical in hunting down key facts for the book— and your knowledge of technology was invaluable. I also thank all of my students and the instructors I work with at the University of Western Ontario. Learning is a reciprocal process, and I learn so much from each of you every time I enter the classroom. Heartfelt gratitude is also expressed to the staff of Teaching and Learning Services who inspire me with their dedication to enhancing student learning, both inside and outside the classroom. Finally, to my family, Avery Dawson Dance and Susan Grindrod—thank you so much for putting up with so many late nights and weekends at the computer. I am truly grateful to Avery for reading the book and for talking to me about the complexity of students' lives today and to Susan for her unflagging support, patience, and can-do attitude throughout the writing of the book. You are both blessings in my life.

Making Transitions

Master Student Map

as you read, ask yourself

what if . . !

I could use the ideas in this Introduction to master any transition in my life?

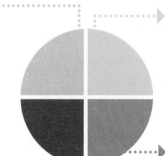

why the Introduction matters . . .

You can ease your transition to higher education and set up a lifelong pattern of success by following the strategies described here.

what is included . . .

- This book is worthless—if you just read it   4
- Get the most out of this book   6
- The Discovery and Intention Journal Entry system   8
- Discovery and Intention Statement guidelines   10
- Making the transition to postsecondary education   12
- Classroom civility—what's in it for you   15
- Succeeding in higher education—at any age   16
- Connect to school resources   18
- Connect to community resources   20
- Extracurricular activities: Reap the benefits   21
- Link to the world of work   23
- Ways to change a habit   25
- The Power Processes—a user's guide   28
- Power Process: Discover what you want   29

how

you can use this Introduction . . .

- Discover a way to interact with the book that multiplies its value.
- Use a journal to translate personal discoveries into powerful new behaviours.
- Connect with people and organizations that support your success.

MASTER STUDENTS in *action*

Students often ask me what it takes to be successful in my first-year course, thinking that there must be a "trick" or secret. There is no secret. Most students forget that they were "good enough" to be admitted in the first place, and so they have what it takes to succeed. The skills that make you a successful student are really the same ones that lead to success in any aspect of life—all it takes is time on task. Quite simply, the more time and effort you put into school, the more you get out of it. Nonetheless, here are a few suggestions from actual students that may help.

Relax . . . don't get stressed out. You need to put everything in perspective and take a deep breath from time to time. If you let stress build up, it will interfere with your ability to succeed.

Ask for help if you need it. Students often wait too long before they ask for any kind of help. Don't do this. Speak to your professor or TA, see the counselling centre, ask for academic advice. All of these services are in place to help you—use them.

Keep up with your readings and make notes before coming to class. In most courses, there is a lot of reading that you will be expected to do on your own. Lectures are not intended to cover everything in a course and reading/note taking is a very important skill you must master in your time at school. Making notes based on your reading before class provides you with a guide to what will be discussed in class. You will be better prepared to actually listen to the instructor if you have some idea where she or he is going.

Attend class. In most courses, attendance is optional. However, we offer classes for a reason—we believe that class provides an important "value added" component to the course material. Take advantage of this. Research consistently shows that the vast majority of students who come to class end up doing better on the exams than those who do not.

If you approach it as you would any other exciting opportunity, college or university can be one of the best times of your life. Work hard and challenge yourself—it will be very rewarding.

© Debra Dawson

Dr. Mike Atkinson
Introductory Psychology Professor & 3M Teaching Fellow
The University of Western Ontario

This book is worthless—
if you just read it

THE FIRST EDITION of this book began with the sentence *This book is worthless.* Many students thought this was a trick to get their attention. It wasn't. Others thought it was reverse psychology. It wasn't that, either. Still others thought it meant that the book was worthless if they didn't read it. It's more than that.

This book is worthless *even if you read it*—if reading is all you do. What was true of that first edition is true of this one. Until you take action and use the ideas in it, *Becoming a Master Student* really is worthless.

The purpose of this book is to help you make a successful transition to higher education by setting up a pattern of success that will last the rest of your life. You probably won't take action and use the ideas in this book until you are convinced that you have something to gain. That's the reason for this Introduction—to persuade you to use this book actively.

Before you stiffen up and resist this pitch, remember that you have already bought the book. Now you can get something for your money by committing yourself to take action—in other words, by committing yourself to *becoming a master student*. Here's what's in it for you.

Pitch #1: You can save money now and make more later.
Start with money. Your postsecondary education is one of the most expensive things you will ever buy. As a master student, you control the value you get out of your education, and that value can be considerable. The joy of learning aside, postsecondary school graduates make more money during their lifetimes than their non-degreed peers (Statistics Canada, 2011). It pays to be a master student.

Pitch #2: You can rediscover the natural learner in you.
As you become a master student, you will learn to gain knowledge in the most effective way possible by discovering the joyful, natural learner within you.

Children are great natural students. They quickly master complex skills, such as language, and they have fun doing it. For them, learning is a high-energy process involving experimentation, discovery, and sometimes play. Then comes school. For some students, drill and drudgery replace discovery and play. Learning can become a drag. You can use this book to reverse that process and rediscover what you knew as a child—that laughter and learning go hand in hand.

Sometimes learning does take effort, especially in college or university. As you become a master student, you will learn many ways to get the most out of that effort.

Pitch #3: You can choose from hundreds of techniques.
Becoming a Master Student is packed with hundreds of practical, nuts-and-bolts techniques. And you can begin using them immediately. For example, during the textbook reconnaissance on page 2, you can practise three powerful learning techniques in one 15-minute exercise. Even if you doze in lectures, drift during tests, or dawdle on term papers, you'll find ideas in this book that you can use to become a more effective student.

Not all of these ideas will work for you. That's why there are so many of them in *Becoming a Master Student*. You can experiment with the techniques. As you discover what works, you will develop a unique style of learning that you can use for the rest of your life.

Pitch #4: You get the best suggestions from thousands of students.
The concepts and techniques in this book are here not because learning theorists, educators, and psychologists say they work. They are here because tens of thousands of students from all kinds of backgrounds have tried them and say that they work. These are people who dreaded giving speeches, couldn't read their own notes, and fell behind in their course work. Then they figured out how to solve these problems. Now you can use their ideas.

Pitch #5: You can learn about you.
The process of self-discovery is an important theme in *Becoming a Master Student*. Throughout the book, you can use Discovery and Intention Statements for everything from organizing your desk to choosing long-term goals. Studying for an organic chemistry quiz is a lot easier with a clean desk and a clear idea of the course's importance to you.

Pitch #6: You can use a proven product.
The first four editions of this book have proved successful for hundreds of thousands of students. In schools where it was widely used, the dropout rate decreased as much as 25 percent and, in some cases, 50 percent. Student feedback has been positive. In particular, students with successful histories have praised the techniques in this book.

Pitch #7: You can learn the secret of student success. If this sales pitch still hasn't persuaded you to use this book actively, maybe it's time to reveal the secret of student success. (Provide your own drum roll here.) The secret is—that there are no secrets. Perhaps the ultimate formula is to give up formulas and keep inventing.

The strategies and tactics that successful students use are well known. You have hundreds of them at your fingertips right now, in this book. Use them. Modify them. Invent new ones. You're the authority on what works for you.

However, what makes any technique work is commitment—and action. Without them, the pages of *Becoming a Master Student* are just 1 kilogram of expensive mulch. Add your participation to the mulch, and these pages are priceless. ✳

1 exercise
Textbook Reconnaissance

Start *becoming a master student* this moment by doing a 15-minute "textbook reconnaissance." Here's how.

First, read the table of contents. Do it in three minutes or less. Next, look at every page in the book. Move quickly. Scan headlines. Look at pictures. Notice forms, charts, and diagrams. Don't forget the last few pages in back, which include extra copies of planning forms that you might find useful.

A textbook reconnaissance shows you where a course is going. It gives you the big picture. That's useful because brains work best when going from the general to the specific. Getting the big picture before you start makes it easier to recall and understand details later on.

Your textbook reconnaissance will work even better if, as you scan, you look for ideas you can use. When you find one, write the page number and a short description of it in the space below. If you run out of room, just continue your list on a separate sheet of paper. Or use Post-it® notes to flag the pages that look useful. You could even use notes in different colours to signal priority, such as green for ideas to use right away and yellow for those to apply later. The idea behind this technique is simple: It's easier to learn when you're excited, and it's easier to get excited about a course if you know it's going to be useful, interesting, or fun.

Remember, look at every page, and do it quickly. And here's another useful tip for the master student: Do it now.

Page number	Description

WWW Complete this exercise online @
www.bams5ce.nelson.com

Get the most out of this book

1. Rip 'em out. The pages of *Becoming a Master Student* are perforated because some of the information here is too important to leave in the book and some your instructor might want to see. For example, Journal Entry #3 asks you to list some important things you want to get out of your education. To keep yourself focused, you could rip that page out and post it on your bathroom mirror or some other place where you'll see it several times a day.

You can reinsert the page later by sticking it into the spine of the book. A piece of tape will hold it in place.

2. Skip around. You can use this book in several different ways. Read it straight through. Or pick it up, turn to any page, and find an idea you can use. Look for ideas you can use right now. For example, if you are about to choose a program of study or are considering changing schools, skip directly to the articles on these topics in Chapters 7 and 12, respectively.

3. If it works, use it. If it doesn't, lose it. If there are sections of the book that don't apply to you at all, skip them—unless, of course, they are assigned. Then see if you can gain value from these sections anyway. When you are committed to getting value from this book, even an idea that seems irrelevant or ineffective at first can turn out to be a powerful tool.

4. Put yourself into the book. As you read about techniques in this book, create your own scenarios, starring yourself in the title role. For example, when reading through Exercise #1: "Textbook reconnaissance," picture yourself using this technique on your world history textbook.

5. Listen to your peers. Throughout this book you will find Student Voices, short features that contain quotations from students who used *Becoming a Master Student* to promote their success. As you dig into the following chapters, think about what you would say if you could add your voice to theirs. Look for tools and techniques that can make a huge difference in your life.

6. Own this book. Right now, put your name, address, and related information on the inside cover of this book, and don't stop there. Determine what you want to get out of this educational institution and create a record of how you intend to get it by reading the Power Process and completing the Journal Entries in this Introduction. Every time your pen touches a page, you move closer to mastery of learning.

7. Do the exercises. Action makes this book work. To get the most out of an exercise, read the instructions carefully before you begin. To get the most out of this book, do most of the exercises. More important, avoid feeling guilty if you skip some. And by the way, it's never too late to go back and do the ones you skipped.

These exercises invite you to write, touch, feel, move, see, search, ponder, speak, listen, recall, choose, commit, and create. You might even sing and dance. Learning often works best when it involves action.

8. Practise critical thinking. Throughout this book are Practising Critical Thinking activities. Their purpose is to reinforce contemplation and problem solving. Note that other elements of this text, including the exercises and Journal Entries, also promote critical thinking.

9. Learn about learning styles. Check out the Learning Styles Inventory and related articles in Chapter 1. This material can help you discover your preferred learning styles and allow you to explore new styles. Then, throughout the rest of this book, you'll find suggestions for applying your knowledge of learning styles. The modes of learning can be accessed by asking four basic questions: *Why? What? How?* and *What if?*

10. Navigate through learning experiences with the Master Student Map. You can orient yourself for maximum learning every time you open this book by asking those same four questions: *Why? What? How?* and *What if?* That's the idea behind the Master Student Map included on the first page of each chapter, which includes sample answers to those questions. Remember that you can use the four-part structure of this map to cycle through several learning styles and effectively learn anything.

11. Link to the Web. Throughout this book, you'll notice reminders to visit the website for *Becoming a Master Student*:

www.bams5ce.nelson.com

Look for the Fifth Canadian Edition home page. Check regularly for articles, online exercises, and links to other useful websites.

12. Read the sidebars. Look for sidebars—short bursts of words and pictures placed between longer articles—throughout this book. These short pieces might offer an insight that transforms your experience of postsecondary education. Remember this related point: Shorter chapters in this book are just as important as longer chapters.

 **13. Practise using technology.** Read and use the Mastering Technology features as you make your way through the book. These short boxes help you apply the techniques in the book to get the most out of online learning.

14. Take this book to work. With a little tweaking in some cases, you can apply nearly all of the techniques in this book to your career. For more details, see the Put It to Work articles in each chapter. Use them to make a seamless transition from success in school to success on the job.

15. Get used to a new look and tone. This book looks different from traditional textbooks. *Becoming a Master Student* presents major ideas in magazine-style articles. You will discover lots of lists, blurbs, one-liners, pictures, charts, graphs, illustrations, and even a joke or two.

Even though this book is loaded with special features, you'll find some core elements. For example, the two pages that open each chapter include a "lead" article and an introductory Journal Entry. And at the end of each chapter you'll find a Power Process, Put It to Work article, chapter quiz, Skills Snapshot, and Master Student Profile—all noted in a toolbar at the top of the page.

Note: As a strategy for avoiding sexist language, this book alternates the use of feminine and masculine pronouns. ✳

② exercise Commitment

This book is worthless unless you actively participate in its activities and exercises. One powerful way to begin taking action is to make a commitment. Conversely, without commitment, sustained action is unlikely, and the result is again a worthless book. Therefore, in the interest of saving your valuable time and energy, this exercise gives you a chance to declare your level of involvement up front. From the choices below, choose the sentence that best reflects your commitment to using this book. Write the number in the space provided at the end of the list.

1. "Well, I'm reading this book right now, aren't I?"

2. "I will skim the book and read the interesting parts."

3. "I will read the book and think about how some of the techniques might apply to me."

4. "I will read the book, think about it, and do the exercises that look interesting."

5. "I will read the book, do some exercises, and complete some of the Journal Entries."

6. "I will read the book, do some exercises and Journal Entries, and use some of the techniques."

7. "I will read the book, do most of the exercises and Journal Entries, and use some of the techniques."

8. "I will study this book, do most of the exercises and Journal Entries, and use some of the techniques."

9. "I will study this book, do most of the exercises and Journal Entries, and experiment vigorously with most of the suggestions in order to discover what works best for me."

10. "I will use this book as if the quality of my education depends on it—doing all the exercises and Journal Entries, experimenting with most of the techniques, inventing techniques of my own, and planning to reread this book in the future."

Enter your commitment level and today's date here:

Commitment level _____ Date _____

If you selected commitment level 1 or 2, you might consider passing this book on to a friend. If your commitment level is 9 or 10, you are on your way to terrific success in school. If your level is somewhere in between, experiment with the techniques and learning strategies in this book. If you find that they work, consider returning to this exercise and raising your level of commitment.

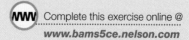 Complete this exercise online @ **www.bams5ce.nelson.com**

The Discovery and Intention Journal Entry system

One way to become a better student is to grit your teeth and try harder. There is another way. Using familiar tools and easily learned processes, the Discovery and Intention Journal Entry system can help increase your effectiveness by showing you how to focus your energy.

THE DISCOVERY and Intention Journal Entry system is a little like flying a plane. Airplanes are seldom exactly on course. Human and automatic pilots are always checking positions and making corrections. The resulting flight path looks like a zigzag. The plane is almost always flying in the wrong direction, but because of constant observation and course correction, it arrives at the right destination.

A similar system can be used by students. Most Journal Entries throughout this book are labelled as either **Discovery Statements** or **Intention Statements**—some are Discovery/Intention Statements. Each Journal Entry will contain a short set of suggestions that involve writing.

Through Discovery Statements, you can assess "where you are." These statements are a record of what you are learning about yourself as a student—both strengths and weaknesses. Discovery Statements can also be declarations of your goals, descriptions of your attitudes, statements of your feelings, transcripts of your thoughts, and chronicles of your behaviour.

Sometimes Discovery Statements chronicle a light bulb moment—a flash of insight that results when a new idea connects with your prior experiences, preferred styles of learning, or both. Perhaps a solution to a long-standing problem suddenly occurs to you, or a life-changing insight wells up from the deepest recesses of your mind. Don't let such moments disappear. Capture them in Discovery Statements.

Intention Statements can be used to alter your course. They are statements of your commitment to do a specific task or take a certain action. An intention arises out of your choice to direct your energy toward a particular goal. While Discovery Statements promote awareness, Intention Statements are blueprints for action. The two processes reinforce each other.

The purpose of this system is not to get you pumped up and excited to go out there and try harder. Rather, Discovery and Intention Statements are intended to help you focus on what you want to accomplish and how you plan to achieve your goals.

The Journal Entry process is a cycle. First, you write Discovery Statements about where you are now and where you want to be. Next, you write Intention Statements about the specific steps you will take to get there. Then, you follow up with Discovery Statements about whether you completed those steps and what you learned in the process, followed by more Intention Statements, and so on. Sometimes a statement will be long and detailed. Usually, it will be short—maybe just a line or two. With practice, the cycle will become automatic.

While Discovery Statements promote awareness, Intention Statements are blueprints for action. The two processes reinforce each other.

Don't panic when you fail to complete an intended task. Straying off course is normal. Simply make the necessary corrections. Miraculous progress might not come immediately. Do not be concerned. Stay with the cycle. Use Discovery Statements to get a clear view of your world and what you want out of it. Then use Intention Statements to direct your actions. When you notice progress, record it.

The following statement might strike you as improbable, but it is true: It often takes the same amount of energy to get what you want in school as it takes to get what you *don't* want. Sometimes getting what you don't want takes even more effort. An airplane burns the same amount of fuel flying away from its destination as it does flying toward it. It pays to stay on course.

You can use the Discovery and Intention Journal Entry system to stay on your own course and get what you want out of school. Consider the guidelines for Discovery and Intention Statements that follow, and then develop your own style. Once you get the hang of it, you might discover you can fly. ✱

Hello Author
I Agree

Rewrite this book

Some books should be preserved in pristine condition. This isn't one of them.

Something happens when you interact with your book by writing in it. *Becoming a Master Student* is about learning, and learning is an active pursuit, not a passive one. When you make notes in the margin, you can hear yourself talking with the author. When you doodle and underline, you can see the author's ideas taking shape. You can even argue with the author and come up with your own theories and explanations. In all of these ways, you become a coauthor of this book. You rewrite it to make it yours.

While you're at it, you can create symbols or codes that will help when reviewing the text later on, such as "Q" for questions or exclamation points for important ideas. You can also circle words to look up in a dictionary.

Remember, if any idea in this book doesn't work for you, you can rewrite it. Change the exercises to fit your needs. Create a new technique by combining several others. Create a technique out of thin air!

Find something you agree or disagree with on this page and write a short note in the margin about it. Or draw a diagram. Better yet, do both. Let creativity be your guide. Have fun.

Begin rewriting now.

STUDENT VOICES

I found completing the Discovery and Intention Statements very rewarding. The questions were very thought provoking and often had me thinking long after I had written an answer.

—AMY GUY

The Discovery and Intention Statements have really helped me see things that I could possibly improve on or fix when needed.

—AUBREY YOUNG

Discovery and Intention Statement guidelines

Discovery Statements

1 Record the specifics about your thoughts, feelings, and behaviour. Thoughts include inner voices. We talk to ourselves constantly in our heads. When internal chatter gets in the way, write down what you are telling yourself. If this seems difficult at first, just start writing. The act of writing can trigger a flood of thoughts.

Thoughts also include mental pictures. These are especially powerful. Picturing yourself flunking a test is like a rehearsal to do just that. One way to take away the power of negative images is to describe them in detail.

Also notice how you feel when you function well. Use Discovery Statements to pinpoint exactly where and when you learn most effectively.

In addition, observe your actions and record the facts. If you spent 90 minutes chatting online with a favourite cousin instead of reading your anatomy text, write about it and include the details, such as when you did it, where you did it, and how it felt. Record your observations quickly, as soon as you make them.

2 Use discomfort as a signal. When you approach a daunting task, such as a difficult accounting problem, notice your physical sensations—a churning stomach, perhaps, or shallow breathing or yawning. Feeling uncomfortable, bored, or tired might be a signal that you're about to do valuable work. Stick with it. Tell yourself you can handle the discomfort just a little bit longer. You will be rewarded.

You can experience those rewards at any time. Just think of a problem that poses the biggest potential barrier to your success in school. Choose a problem that you face right now, today. (Hint: It might be the thing that's distracting you from reading this article.) If you have a lot of emotion tied up in this problem, that's even better. Write a Discovery Statement about it.

3 Suspend judgment. When you are discovering yourself, be gentle. Suspend self-judgment. If you continually judge your behaviours as "bad" or "stupid" or "galactically imbecilic," sooner or later your mind will revolt. Rather than put up with the abuse, it will quit making discoveries. For your own benefit, be kind.

4 Tell the truth. Suspending judgment helps you tell the truth about yourself. "The truth will set you free" is a saying that endures for a reason. The closer you get to the truth, the more powerful your Discovery Statements will be. And if you notice that you are avoiding the truth, don't blame yourself. Just tell the truth about it.

Intention Statements

1 Make intentions positive. The purpose of writing intentions is to focus on what you want rather than what you don't want. Instead of writing "I will not fall asleep while studying accounting," write "I intend to stay awake when studying accounting."

Also avoid the word *try*. Trying is not doing. When we hedge our bets with *try*, we can always tell ourselves, "Well, I *tried* to stay awake." We end up fooling ourselves into thinking we succeeded.

2 Make intentions observable. Experiment with an idea from educational trainer Robert Mager (1975), who suggests that goals be defined through behaviours that can be observed and measured. Rather than writing "I intend to work harder on my history assignments," write "I intend to review my class notes, and I intend to make summary sheets of my reading." Then, when you review your progress, you can determine more precisely whether you have accomplished what you intended.

3 Make intentions small and keepable. Give yourself opportunities to succeed by setting goals you can meet. Break large goals into small, specific tasks that can be accomplished quickly. If you want to get a high mark in biology, ask yourself, "What can I do today?" You might choose to study biology for an extra hour. Make that your intention.

When setting your goals, anticipate self-sabotage. Be aware of what you might do, consciously or unconsciously, to undermine your best intentions. If you intend to study differential equations at 9 p.m., notice when you sit down to watch a two-hour movie that starts at 8 p.m.

Also, be careful of intentions that depend on others. If you write that you intend that your study group complete an assignment by Monday, then your success depends on the other students in the group.

4 Set timelines that include rewards.
Timelines can focus your attention. For example, if you are assigned to write an essay, break the assignment into small tasks and set a precise due date for each one. You might write "I intend to select a topic for my essay by 9 a.m. Wednesday."

Timelines are especially useful when your intention is to experiment with a technique suggested in this book. The sooner you act on a new idea, the better. Consider practising a new behaviour within four hours after you first learn about it.

Remember that you create timelines for your own benefit, not to set yourself up to feel guilty. And you can always change the timeline.

When you meet your goal on time, reward yourself. Rewards that are an integral part of a goal are powerful. For example, your reward for earning a degree might be the career you've always dreamed of. External rewards, such as a movie or an afternoon in the park, are valuable, too. These rewards work best when you're willing to withhold them. If you plan to take a nap on Sunday afternoon whether or not you've finished your English assignment, the nap is not an effective reward.

Another way to reward yourself is to sit quietly after you have finished your task and savour the feeling. One reason why success breeds success is that it feels good. ✳

journal entry 1

Discovery Statement

Recalling excellence

Welcome to the first Journal Entry in this book. You'll find Journal Entries in every chapter, all with a similar design that allows space where you can write.

In the space below, write a description of a time in your life when you learned or did something well. This experience does not have to be related to school. Describe the details of the situation, including the place, time, and people involved. Describe how you felt about it, how it looked to you, how it sounded. Describe the physical sensations you associate with the event. Also describe your emotions.

I discovered that . . .

_____

_____

_____

_____

_____

_____

_____

_____

You share one thing in common with other students at your college or university: Entering postsecondary education represents a major change in your life. You've joined a new culture with its own set of rules, both spoken and unspoken.

© Christopher Futcher/iStockphoto

Making the transition to postsecondary education

WHETHER THEY'VE JUST graduated from high school or have been out of the classroom for decades, students new to higher education immediately face many differences between secondary and postsecondary education. The sooner you understand such differences, the sooner you can deal with them. Some examples include:

- *New academic standards.* Often there are fewer tests in postsecondary education than in high school, and getting good marks might be tougher. You'll probably find that instructors expect you to study more than you did in high school. At the same time, your instructors might give you less guidance about what or how to study, and less feedback about how you are doing.

- *Responsibility for your own learning.* In postsecondary education, it is up to you to seek help if you need it. Although your instructors will be helpful if you tell them you are having difficulty learning, they expect you to take the first steps to ask for assistance. Particularly in large classes, instructors are far less likely to contact you if your grades are a problem than your teachers would be in high school.

- *Differences in teaching styles.* Instructors at colleges and universities are often steeped in their subject

matter. Many did not take courses on how to teach and might not be as interesting as some of your high school teachers. And some professors might seem more focused on research than on teaching.

- *A larger playing field.* The institution you've just joined might seem immense, impersonal, and even frightening. The sheer size of the campus, the variety of courses offered, the large number of departments— all of these can add up to a confusing array of options.

- *More students and more diversity.* The educational institution you're attending right now might enrol hundreds or thousands more students than your high school. And the diversity of these students might surprise you.

There's an opportunity that comes with all of these changes: a greater degree of freedom. Postsecondary education presents you with a new world of choices. You are now responsible for deciding what classes to take, how to structure your time, and with whom to associate. Perhaps more than ever before, you'll find that your education is your own creation. When making decisions that lead to the future of your dreams, keep the following in mind.

Decrease the unknowns. Before classes begin, get a map of the school property and walk through your first day's schedule, perhaps with a classmate or friend. Visit the classrooms and sit down in a seat and imagine yourself taking notes the next day. Visit your instructors in their offices and introduce yourself. Anything you can do to get familiar with the new routine will help.

Admit your feelings—whatever they are. Postsecondary school can be an intimidating experience for new students. People of diverse cultures, mature students, commuters, and people with disabilities can feel excluded. Anyone can feel anxious, isolated, homesick, or worried about doing well academically.

Perhaps more than ever before, you'll find that your education is your own creation.

Those emotions are common among new students, and there's nothing wrong with them. Simply admitting the truth about how you feel—to yourself and to someone else—can help you cope. And you can almost always do something constructive, no matter how you feel.

If your feelings about this transition make it hard for you to carry out the activities of daily life—going to class, working, studying, and relating to people—then get professional help. Start with a counsellor at the student health or student counselling service on your campus. The mere act of seeking help can make a difference.

Access resources. A supercharger increases the air supply to an internal combustion engine. The resulting difference in power can be dramatic. You can make just as powerful a difference in your education by using all of the resources available to students. In this case, your "air supply" includes people, clubs and organizations, and school and community services. Perhaps more than ever before, you'll find that your education is your own creation.

Of all resources, people are the most important. You can isolate yourself, study hard, and get a good education. When you make the effort to establish relationships with instructors, staff members, fellow students, and employers, you can get a great education.

Build a network of people who will personally support your success in school.

Accessing resources is especially important if you are the first person in your family to enter higher education. As a first-generation student, you are having experiences that people in your family may not understand. Talk to your family about your activities at school. If they ask how they can help you, give specific answers. Also, ask your advisor about programs for first-generation students on your campus.

Furthermore, if you used services for students with disabilities in high school, make sure you contact the centre at your new school before classes begin. If you need academic accommodation for your classes or examinations, they are the staff who will make those arrangements for you. Remember, there are many people on campus to support your success, but you need to reach out to them.

Meet with your academic counsellor. One person in particular can help you access resources and make the transition to higher education—your academic counsellor or advisor. Meet with this person regularly. Counsellors generally have a big picture of course requirements, options for choosing programs of study, and the resources available at your institution. Peer advisory programs might also be available.

journal entry

Intention Statement

Plan for transition

As a way to ease your transition to higher education, consider setting a goal to meet at least one new person each week for the next month. You could introduce yourself to someone in each of your classes, for example. You could also see your teachers during office hours and meet with your academic advisor.

List your ideas for ways to meet people in the space below.

_____

_____

_____

_____

_____

I intend to . . .

_____

_____

_____

_____

_____

_____

Learn the language of postsecondary education. Terms such as *grade point average (GPA)*, *prerequisite*, *corequisite*, *antirequisite*, *matriculation*, *registrar*, and *syllabus* might be new to you. Ease your transition to higher education by checking your school calendar for definitions of these words and others that you don't understand. Also ask your academic advisor for clarification.

Attend class. In postsecondary education, instructors generally don't take attendance. Yet you'll find that attending class is essential to your success. The amount that you pay in tuition and fees makes a powerful argument for going to classes regularly and getting your money's worth. In large part, the material that you're tested on comes from activities that take place in class.

"Showing up" for class occurs on two levels. The most visible level is being physically present in the classroom. Even more important is showing up mentally. This includes taking detailed notes, asking questions, and contributing to class discussions.

Don't assume that you already know how to study. You can cope with increased workloads and higher academic expectations by putting all of your study habits on the table and evaluating them. Keep the habits that serve you, drop those that hold you back, and adopt new ones to promote your success. Go to the sessions offered in your school by your learning skills counsellors or the advisors in your student success centre. On every page of this book, you'll find helpful suggestions to help you study.

Manage out-of-class time. Time management takes on a new meaning for students in higher education. What you do *outside* class matters as much as—or even more than—what you do in class. Instructors give you the raw materials for understanding a subject while

a class meets. You then take those materials, combine them, and *teach yourself* outside of class.

To allow for this process, schedule two hours of study time for each hour that you spend in class. Also, get a calendar that covers the entire academic year. With the syllabus for each of your courses in hand, note key events for the entire term—dates for tests, papers, and other projects. Getting a big picture of your course load makes it easier to get assignments done on time and erases the need for all-night study sessions.

Become a self-regulated learner. Psychologists use the term **self-regulation** to describe people who set specific goals, monitor their progress toward those goals, and regularly change their behaviour to produce the desired results. These people have a clear idea of their objectives and their capabilities.

Becoming a Master Student promotes self-regulation through the ongoing cycle of discovery, intention, and action. Write Discovery Statements to monitor yourself and evaluate the results you're currently creating in life. Create Intention Statements to determine exactly what you want. And use the exercises throughout the book to experience the power of putting your ideas into practice.

Take the initiative in meeting new people. Promise yourself to meet one new person each week, then write an Intention Statement describing specific ways to do this. Introduce yourself to classmates. Just before or after class is a good time to do so. Realize that most of the people in this new world of postsecondary education are waiting to be welcomed. You can help them and help yourself at the same time. ✳

 For more strategies on mastering the art of transition, visit the *Becoming a Master Student* website @
www.bams5ce.nelson.com

The topic of this article might seem like a lesson in common sense, yet some students apparently lack this characteristic. They forget the simple behaviours that create a sense of safety, mutual respect, and community in any place where people gather—including a classroom, tutoring centre, library, or instructor's office.

Classroom civility— what's in it for you

CONSIDER AN EXAMPLE: A student arrives 15 minutes late to a lecture and lets the door slam behind her. She pulls a fast-food burger out of a paper bag (hear the sound of that crackling paper). Then her cell phone rings at full volume—and she answers it. Behaviours like these send a message to everyone in the room: "I'm ignoring you."

Without civility, you lose. Even a modest lack of classroom civility creates problems for everyone. Learning gets interrupted. Trust breaks down. Your tuition dollars go down the drain. You invest hundreds of hours and thousands of dollars in getting a degree. You deserve to enter classrooms that are free of discipline problems and bullies.

Many schools have formal policies about classroom civility in their student code of conduct. Find out what policies apply to you. The consequences for violating them can be serious and may include dismissal or legal action.

With civility, you win. When you treat instructors and other students with respect, you're more likely to be treated that way in return. A respectful relationship with an instructor could turn into a favourable reference letter, a mentorship, a job referral, or a friendship that lasts for years after you graduate. Politeness pays.

Classroom civility does not mean that you have to be passive or insincere. You can present your opinions with passion and even disagree with an instructor. Just make sure you do so in a way that leaves everyone enriched rather than threatened.

The basics of classroom civility are summarized in the following suggestions. They reflect simple common sense, and they make an uncommon difference.

Be on time. If you arrive late, do not disrupt class. Close the door quietly and take a seat. When you know that you will have to leave class early, tell your instructor before class begins, and sit near an exit. If you leave class to use the bathroom or handle an emergency, do so quietly.

If you know that you're going to miss a class or be late, let your instructor know. Take the initiative to ask your instructor or another student about what you missed.

During class, participate fully. Take notes and join in discussions. Turn off your cell phone or any other electronic device that you don't need for class. Remember that sleeping, texting, or doing work for another class is a waste of your time and money. Find out what your instructor's policy is about the use of laptops in class. In any case this is not the time to do your social networking or access websites unrelated to your course.

Instructors often give assignments or make a key point at the end of a class period. Be there when it happens. Wait until class has been dismissed to pack up your notebooks and other materials.

Communicate respect. When you speak in class, begin by addressing your instructor as *Professor* or *Doctor,* or whatever the teacher prefers. Use those same salutations when addressing emails to your instructor. Remember they are far more likely to respond positively to a request if you ask respectfully.

Discussions gain value when everyone gets a chance to contribute. Show respect for others by not monopolizing class discussions. Refrain from side conversations and profanity. When presenting viewpoints that conflict with those of classmates or your instructor, combine the passion for your opinion with respect for the opinions of others. Again, all of this is even more important when communicating online. Discussions online should be respectful—attacking other students' arguments or ideas but not the individual. If working online in groups, it is probably a good idea to set group rules that will govern your behaviour online and prevent misunderstandings from occurring.

Respect gets communicated in the smallest details, such as maintaining good hygiene. Avoid making distracting noises, and cover your mouth if you yawn or cough. Also avoid wearing inappropriate clothing. And even if you meet your future spouse in class, refrain from public displays of affection.

If you disagree with a class requirement or grade that you received, talk to your instructor about it after class in a respectful way. Make an effort to find out if your school has a policy covering the issue. In a private setting, your ideas will get more attention.

See civility as a contribution. Every class you enter has the potential to become a community of people who talk openly, listen fully, share laughter, and arrive at life-changing insights. Anything you do to make that vision a reality makes everyone a winner. ✳

Succeeding in higher education— at any age

BEING AN ADULT learner puts you on a strong footing. With a rich store of life experience on which to draw, you can ask meaningful questions and more easily make connections between course work and daily life.

Any abilities that you've developed to work on teams, manage projects, meet deadlines, and solve problems are assets. Many instructors will enjoy working with you.

Following are some suggestions for returning mature students. Even if you don't fit into this category, you can look for ways to apply these ideas.

Acknowledge your concerns. Adult learners might express any of the following fears:

- I'll be the oldest person in all my classes.
- I've been out of the classroom too long.
- I'm concerned about my math, reading, and writing skills.
- I'm worried about making tuition payments.
- How will I ever make the time to study, on top of everything else I'm doing?

Those concerns are understandable. Now consider some facts. If you're returning to school after a long break from the classroom, you are part of a growing trend in Canadian postsecondary education. Recently, the Canadian Council on Learning (CCL, April 2011) reported that the participation of adults 45 to 54 increased from six percent in 1997 to 34 percent in 2002. Most individuals are there to advance their careers. If you are returning to school, look for orientation

© William Britten/iStockphoto

programs and clubs for mature students. The supports are out there, but you need to get involved.

Ease into it. If you're new to postsecondary education, consider easing into it. You can choose to attend school part-time before making a full-time commitment.

Meet with an academic advisor. In talking about what is important for mature students in postsecondary education, many people point to advising as being key for student success (McLaren, 2009). Also visit advisors to check to see if past credits for college-level courses will be counted. Even if you've never attended a post-secondary institution you may still be eligible for credits due to your life experiences. Some schools offer prior learning assessment where you can receive credit for the experiential learning or skills you may have developed through work or hobbies.

Plan your week. Many mature learners report that their number one problem is time. One solution is to plan your week. By planning ahead a week at a time, you get a bigger picture of your multiple roles as a student, an employee, and a family member.

- If your responsibilities at work or home will be heavy in the near future, then register for fewer classes next term. However, check to ensure this doesn't impact your eligibility to receive student financial aid.

- Choose recreational activities carefully, focusing on ones that relax you and recharge you the most.

- Don't load your schedule with classes that require unusually heavy amounts of reading or writing.

For more suggestions on managing time, see Chapter 2: Time.

Delegate tasks. If you have children, delegate some of the chores to them. Or start a meal exchange in your neighbourhood. Cook dinner for yourself and someone else one night each week. In return, ask that person to furnish you with a meal on another night. A similar strategy can apply to child care and other household tasks.

Get to know younger students. You share a central goal with younger students: succeeding in school. It's easier to get past the generation gap when you remember this. Consider pooling resources with younger students. Share notes, form study groups, or edit each other's essays.

Get to know other returning students. Introduce yourself to other mature learners. Being in the same classroom gives you an immediate bond. You can exchange work, home, or mobile phone numbers and build a network of mutual support. Some students adopt a buddy system, pairing up with another student in each class to complete assignments and prepare for tests. Find other mature students through contacting your mature student centre or club. Many postsecondary institutions offer special orientation programs just for mature and non-traditional students.

Seek out your financial aid offices. Find out what bursaries or other forms of financial assistance are available to support your schooling.

Find common ground with instructors. Many of your teachers might be juggling academic careers, work schedules, and family lives, too. Finding common ground gives you one more way to break the ice with instructors.

Enlist your employer's support. Employers often promote continuing education. Further education can increase your skills in a specific field while enhancing your ability to work with people. That makes you a more valuable employee or consultant.

Let your employer in on your educational plans. Point out how the skills you gain in class will help you meet work objectives. Offer informal "seminars" at work to share what you're learning in school.

Get extra mileage out of your current tasks. You can look for specific ways to merge your work and school lives. Some schools offer academic credit for work and life experience. Your company might reimburse its employees for some tuition costs or even grant time off to attend classes.

Experiment with combining tasks. For example, when you're assigned a research paper, choose a topic that relates to your current job tasks.

Look for child care. For some students, returning to class means looking for child care outside the home. Many schools offer child-care facilities at reduced rates for students.

Review your subjects before you start classes. If, for example, you've registered for trigonometry and you haven't taken a math class since high school, consider brushing up on the subject before classes begin. Also, talk with future instructors about ways to prepare for their classes.

Prepare for an academic environment. If you're used to an efficient corporate setting, school life might present some frustrations. A lack of advanced computer systems might slow down your class registration. If your computer skills are rusty consider taking a course to brush up before school begins. Many courses you take will include some online component so it is important for you to feel comfortable in this blended learning environment. Faculty members might take a little longer to return your calls or emails especially during holidays and summer breaks. Knowing the rhythm of academic life can help you plan around these possibilities.

Be willing to adopt new study habits. Rather than returning to study habits from previous school experiences, many mature learners find it more effective to treat their school assignments exactly as they would treat a project at work. They use the same tactics in the library as they do on the job, which often helps them learn more actively.

The theory of self-actualization could clarify your goals and help you get the most out of school.

Integrate class work with daily experiences.
According to psychologist Malcolm Knowles (1984), mature learners in particular look for ways to connect classroom experience with the rest of their lives. This approach can promote success in school for students of any age. You can start by remembering two words: *why* and *how. Why* prompts you to look for a purpose and benefit in what you're learning. For example, your psychology instructor lectures about Abraham Maslow's ideas on the hierarchy of human needs. Maslow (1971) stated that the need for **self-actualization** is just as important as the need for safety, security, or love. This term is about your desire to live up to your fullest potential in life; to be the best that you can be.

As you learn what Maslow meant by *self-actualization,* ask yourself why this concept would make a difference in your life. Perhaps your reason for entering postsecondary education is connected to your own quest for self-actualization, that is, for maximizing your fulfillment in life and living up to your highest potential. The theory of self-actualization could clarify your goals and help you get the most out of school.

How means looking for immediate application. Invent ways to use and test concepts in your daily life—the sooner, the better. For example, how could you restructure your life for greater self-actualization? What would you do differently on a daily basis? What would you have that you don't have now? And how would you behave differently in your moment-to-moment relationships with people?

"Publish" your schedule. After you plan your study and class sessions for the week, hang your schedule in a place where others who live with you will see it. You could make it look like an "official" document. Laminate a daily calendar, fill in your schedule with a felt-tipped pen, and post this in a high-traffic area in your house. Designate open slots in your schedule where others can sign up for "appointments" to see you. If you use an on-line calendar, print out copies to put in your school binder or on your refrigerator door, bathroom mirror, or kitchen cupboard.

Share your educational plans. The fact that you're in school will affect the key relationships in your life. Attending classes and doing homework will mean less time to spend with others. You can prepare family members and help prevent problems by discussing these issues ahead of time. You can also involve your spouse, partner, children, or close friends actively in your schooling. Offer to give them a tour of the campus, introduce them to your instructors and classmates, and encourage them to attend social events at school with you.

Take this a step further and ask the key people in your life for help. Ask them to think of ways that they can support your success in school and to commit themselves to those actions. Make your own education a joint mission that benefits everyone.

More resources are available for mature learners on the *Becoming a Master Student* website @
www.bams5ce.nelson.com

Connect to school resources

© Spencer Grant/PhotoEdit Inc.

WHEN YOU ENTERED postsecondary education, you also signed up for a world of student services. Any of them can help you succeed in school. Many of them are free.

Following are a few examples of school resources. Check your school calendar, newspaper, and website for the specific resources available to you. Your student fees pay for them. Now use them.

Academic counsellors or advisors can help you with selecting courses, choosing programs, planning your career, and adjusting in general to the culture of post-secondary education.

Alumni organizations aren't just for graduates. Alumni publications and alumni themselves can be good sources of information about the benefits and potential pitfalls of being a student at your school.

Arts resources can include museums, galleries, special libraries, and music and film recording and editing equipment. Music practise rooms are often available to all students.

Athletic facilities and *recreation centres* often include open weight rooms, swimming pools, indoor tracks, basketball courts, and racquet-sport courts available to all students.

Car-pooling maps provide information on getting across town or across the country. Connect with a car pool, and you might discover new study group partners or lifelong friends.

Chapels are usually open to students of any religion. They are quiet places to pray or meditate in peace.

Child care is sometimes made available to students at a reasonable cost through onsite daycares or preschools.

Computer labs where students can go 24 hours a day to work on projects and access the Internet are usually free. Instruction on computer use might also be offered.

Counselling services help students deal with the emotional pressures of school life, usually for free. Support is also provided for lesbian, gay, transgendered, and bisexual students. If you need help that is not available on campus, ask for a referral to an appropriate agency off campus.

A *financial aid, assistance*, or *awards office* can help students find a combination of loans, scholarships, and bursaries. It is not necessary for students to drop out of school for financial reasons when financial assistance is available.

Career services offer assistance in planning your career, and in helping you find part-time employment while you are a student and a job after you graduate. Get to know career services in first year, when you have time to explore what this service has available to support your goals.

Indigenous services are offered on most campuses and provide assistance with supporting the academic success of First Nations, Inuit, or Métis students.

Learning skills and effective writing centres are there for everyone, not just for students who are having difficulty in their courses. If you want a competitive edge to improve your academic standing, make use of these services before your first exam or assignment is due. For students whose first language is not English, making use of such centres may be essential to success.

Libraries are a key resource for student success. Academic librarians can point you toward resources that will assist in your academic research and writing. Check out your library's website to see what information and services are offered.

The ombudsperson provides safe, confidential counselling if you feel you are being treated unfairly in some way or you are having a conflict with an instructor.

They can tell you the appeal procedures for grades and suggest good techniques for problem solving.

The *registrar's office* handles information about transcripts, marks, changing programs, transferring credits, and dropping or adding classes. It also serves as a focal point for information and advice. You'll probably contact this office after you graduate when employers or other schools ask to receive transcripts of your courses and marks.

The *school calendar* lists course descriptions, requirements for graduation, and information on everything from the school's history to its marking practices.

The school newspaper provides information about activities, services, and policies. You can advertise in it for a job, a roommate, or a ride to Lethbridge. Larger schools might also have their own radio and television stations.

School security services can tell you what's safe and what's not. They can also provide information about parking, bicycle regulations, and traffic rules. Many provide a foot patrol to escort students at night back to their residence or to their cars in the evening.

Services for students with disabilities have staff members who specialize in helping students with a wide variety of disabilities make the adjustment to college or university.

Student government can help you develop skills in leadership and teamwork. If you have experience with student government, many employers will take notice.

Student health services often provide treatment for minor problems. Many offer information about alcohol and drug abuse and addiction.

Student organizations present an opportunity to explore service clubs, religious groups, sports clubs, political groups, sororities, fraternities, and programs for special populations. The last might include women's centres; students with disabilities; and gay, lesbian, transgendered, and bisexual students. As 15 percent of the students enrolled in postsecondary education come from countries outside Canada, many schools will have an international student centre and other organizations for international students. For Canadian-born students, getting involved in such centres is a great way for you to connect to new people with diverse backgrounds.

Student unions are hubs for social activities, special programs, and free entertainment. Clubs and organizations often meet there, too.

Tutoring can help, even if you think you are hopelessly stuck in a course. It is available through academic departments, or through counselling and learning skills services. ✳

Connect to community resources

© clu/iStockphoto

RESOURCES SUCH AS the following often go unused—even when people pay taxes to fund them. You can demonstrate an alternative. Taking advantage of community resources and letting others know about them is an act of service.

Arts organizations allow you to attend a play, see an independent film, hear live jazz, visit an art gallery, or groove in a poetry jam. Explore local museums, concert venues, clubs, and stadiums.

Child care is provided by both public and private organizations and may be located on your campus. Some charge for child care on a sliding scale, based on income. Girls' clubs and boys' clubs offer child care, guidance, and recreation opportunities for young people.

Coffee houses and cafés sometimes double as community gathering places. Look for notices of local events, open meetings sponsored by community organizations, live music, and more.

Community education classes are usually offered by local school boards. Use them to learn about anything from tax planning to ballroom dancing.

Consumer credit counselling can help even if you've really blown your budget. And it's usually free. Remember, no matter how bad your financial picture, you are probably in better shape than most governments.

Counselling centres in the community can assist you with a problem when you can't get help at school. Look for job and career planning services, rehabilitation offices, community outreach programs, church and social service agencies, and mental health clinics.

Distress hotlines can save your life during a crisis. Professionals or trained volunteers are often available for help 24 hours a day, whether the situation involves physical abuse, HIV AIDS, rape, potential suicide, or another emergency.

Governments (city, provincial, and federal) often have programs for students. Check the government listings in your local telephone directory.

Health care centres and clinics provide birth control, gynaecological exams, disease diagnosis and treatment, vaccinations, and care for pregnant women and sick children.

Legal aid services provide free or inexpensive assistance to low-income people.

Libraries are a treasure in any community. Even small libraries can have access to the Internet, and most employ people who are happy to help you locate information.

Local newspapers list community events and services that are free or inexpensive. Reading a local newspaper also helps you get a feel for a new city.

Local places of worship have members happy to welcome fellow worshippers who are away from home.

Local residents of your community are likely to know the cheapest restaurants, the most fascinating second-hand stores, and the best hiking spots close to town. If you are a student from out of town, cultivate friendships with local residents and with students who commute.

Local tourism offices and community information services provide information about local attractions, organizations, clubs, and businesses.

Money is sometimes available in a real emergency from the Salvation Army, the Red Cross, local churches, or a relief agency. Be prepared to document the exact nature of your need.

Multicultural centres can help you to get connected to community members from your country of origin or introduce you to new cultures.

Political parties always want volunteers. Working for a candidate you believe in is one way to learn organizational skills, meet people, and make a difference in the world.

Recreation departments of the city or county, YWCAs, YMCAs, and other organizations, provide free or inexpensive ways to exercise and have fun.

Specialty clubs and organizations promote everything from public speaking (Toastmasters) to conservation (Greenpeace).

Support groups exist for people with almost any problem, from drug addiction to cancer. You can find people with problems who meet every week to share suggestions, information, and concerns. Some examples are groups for single parents, newly widowed people, alcoholics or drug addicts, breast cancer survivors, and parents who have lost a child. ✳

Extracurricular activities: Reap the benefits

© Rob Esselment

MANY STUDENTS IN higher education are busier than they've ever been before. Often that's due to the variety of extracurricular activities available to them: athletics, student newspapers, debate teams, study groups, political action groups, and many more.

With this kind of involvement come potential benefits. People involved in extracurricular activities are often excellent students. Such activities help them bridge the worlds inside and outside the classroom. Through student organizations they develop new skills, explore possible careers, build contacts for jobs, and add experiences to their resumés. They make new friends among students and faculty, work with people from other cultures, and sharpen their skills at conflict resolution. Involvement in campus activities can ease the transition to postsecondary education. Many schools offer an Alternative Spring Break program where students have a hands-on community service learning experience during reading week that allows them to learn about new cultures, apply the knowledge they've been learning in class and work with different service agencies on a wide variety of social issues.

Getting involved in such organizations comes with some risks as well. When students don't balance extracurricular activities with class work, their success in school can suffer. They can also compromise their health by losing sleep, neglecting exercise, skipping meals, or relying on fast food. These costs are easier to avoid if you keep a few suggestions in mind:

- *Make conscious choices* about how to divide your time between schoolwork and extracurricular activities. Decide up front how many hours each week or month you can devote to student organizations. Leave room in your schedule for relaxing and for unplanned events.

- *Look to the future* when making commitments. Write down three or four of the most important goals you'd like to achieve in your lifetime. Then choose extracurricular activities that directly support those goals.

- *Create a career plan* that includes a list of skills needed for your next job. Then choose extracurricular activities to develop those skills. If you're unsure of your career choice, then get involved in campus organizations or visit the career centre to explore your options.

- *Whenever possible, develop leadership experience* by holding an office in an organization. If that's too much of a commitment, then volunteer to lead a committee or plan a special event.

- *Recognize reluctance* to follow through on a commitment. You might agree to attend meetings and find yourself forgetting them or consistently showing up late. If that happens, write a Discovery Statement about the way you're using time. Follow that with an Intention Statement about ways to keep your agreements—or consider renegotiating your agreements.

- *Say no* to activities that fail to create value for you. Avoid joining groups because you feel guilty or obligated to do so.

- *Check out the rules* before joining any student organization. Ask about dues and attendance requirements.

- *Do a trial run* by attending one or two meetings of an organization. Explain that you want to find out what the group is about before making a commitment. ✱

STUDENT VOICES

Given the opportunity to participate in Alternative Spring Break, I would tell any student to take it! The relationships, emotions, perspectives, and knowledge evoked through this program reach far beyond the scope of any textbook or lecture. Don't miss one of the most incredible experiences school has to offer!

—JULIAN RESTIVO

Why going to college matters

Many times, students wonder if it is really worth it to go to college or university. You bet it is. Over three decades of research by Ernest Pascarella and Patrick Terrenzini (2005) shows that going to college has big payoffs even beyond the skills and knowledge you will acquire. Sure you are growing up as you go through school, but beyond getting older it turns out that school makes a positive impact on many dimensions of your life. Postsecondary education adds value to your life by increasing or significantly enhancing:

Your psychosocial skills

- Self-esteem
- Leadership skills
- Independence
- Interpersonal skills

Your Attitudes and Values

- Civic and community engagement
- Openness to diversity
- Support for gender equality

Your Career and Economic Outcomes

- Job satisfaction
- Earnings
- Occupational status
- Job search abilities and skills
- Employment and career mobility

Your Quality of Life

- Better Health
- How long you will live
- Feelings of well-being
- Interest in lifelong learning
- Better consumer choices
- Savings

Of course, how much you get out of your post–secondary experience depends on what you choose to do both inside and outside the classroom. Inside the classroom you want to be as engaged in learning as you can. According to Laurie Schreiner (2010), this means being truly involved in what is going on in class—asking questions, participating in discussions with other students, and vigorously exploring ideas. You also want to try to connect what you learn in the classroom to the real world. By the way, if you do this not only will you get more out of school, you'll get higher grades too and be more likely to graduate.

So getting involved in your school work and activities outside class will only serve to enhance the benefits of your postsecondary experience. Take the time to explore new interests—try to take a broad range of courses so that you can fully develop your options. Even if you took a similar course in high school, try it again at university or in college—the courses tend to be taught differently and the opportunities to take the conversation to a greater depth are more likely at this point. Our hobbies and other interests often give us vital clues about our passions in life that can point us in the direction of careers we might explore. So use this time to join new clubs, participate in volunteer activities, and try out as many new 'hats' as possible. As most of us are likely to have multiple careers throughout our lives, it just makes sense to try to develop the broadest possible toolkit of skills and knowledge. You never know what you will need in the future. We will explore more about the value of higher education in Chapter 1.

Source: *How College Affects Students, Vol. 2, A Third Decade of Research,* by Pascarella, Ernest T., and Patrick T. Terenzini. Copyright © 2005 John Wiley & Sons. Used with permission of John Wiley & Sons, Inc.

> The suggestions in this book can help you succeed both inside and outside the classroom. Apply the techniques you gain from this course to any learning situation you encounter, whether at home, at school, or at work.

Link to the world of work

STAYING CURRENT IN the job market means continually expanding your knowledge and skills. You might change careers several times during your working life—a possibility that calls for continuous learning. As a master student, you can gain favour with employers by getting up to speed quickly on new jobs and new projects.

Starting now, read this book with a mental filter in place. Ask yourself: How can I use this idea to meet my career goals? How can I apply this technique to my current job or the next job I see for myself? The answers can help you thrive in any job, whether you work full- or part-time. To stimulate your thinking, look for the Put It to Work article located in each chapter. In addition, invent techniques of your own based on what you read and test them at work. There's no limit to the possibilities.

For example, you can use the Discovery and Intention Journal Entry system while you're in the workforce. Write Discovery Statements to note your current job skills as well as areas for improvement. Also use Discovery Statements to describe what you want from your career.

Follow up with Intention Statements that detail specifically what you want to be doing one year, five years, and ten years or more from today. Write additional Intention Statements about specific actions you can take right now to meet those career goals.

Below is a textbook reconnaissance that lists articles in this book with workplace applications. These are just a few examples. As you read, look for more.

- The skills you learn as you are *Making the transition to postsecondary education* (page 12) can help you make the transition to a new job. For example, you can decrease unknowns by working for a company on a temporary, part-time, or contract basis or you might have the opportunity to job shadow an employee for a day. These positions can lead to an offer of full-time employment. If that happens, you'll already know a lot about the company.

- The article *25 ways to get the most out of now* (page 89) is packed with ideas you can transfer to the workplace. For example, tackle difficult tasks first in the day, or at any other time when your energy peaks. Also find five-minute tasks that you can complete while waiting for a meeting to start.

- The article *20 memory techniques* (page 112) will come in handy as you learn the policies and procedures for a new job.

- Techniques presented in *Remembering names* (page 124) can help as you meet people during your job search and as you are being introduced to new coworkers.

- Use *Muscle Reading* (page 137) to keep up with journals and books in your field. This set of techniques can also help you scan websites for the information you want, keep up with ever-increasing volumes of email, and reduce mountains of inter-office memos to manageable proportions.

- The article *Record* (page 167) explains different formats for taking notes—mindmaps, concept maps, the Cornell format, and more. These are tools you can use to document what happens at work-related meetings.

- Adapt the ideas mentioned in *Cooperative learning—studying with group* (page 197) in order to cooperate more effectively with members of a project team.

- Use the thinking skills presented in *Gaining skill at decision making* (page 240) when it comes time to choose a career, weigh job offers, or make work-related decisions.

- Ideas from *Managing conflict* (page 264) can help you defuse tensions among coworkers.

- The suggestions in *Building relationships across cultures* (page 297) can assist you in adapting to the culture of a new job. Each company, large or small, develops its own culture—a set of shared values and basic assumptions. Even if you are self-employed, you can benefit by discovering and adapting to a client's corporate culture.

- Return to *Create your career now* (page 386) at any time in the future when you're redefining the kind of work that you want to do. Then hone your job-hunting skills with *Use resumés and interviews to "hire" an employer* (page 396).

- The only job security available today is the ability to transfer skills from one position to another. *Now that you're done—begin* (page 383) opens up pathways to lifelong learning. Use these suggestions to continually update your job skills and explore new areas for personal development. ✳

You don't need
this course—but you might want it

Some students don't believe they need a student success course. They might be right. These students may tell you that many schools don't even offer such a class. That's true.

Consider the benefits of taking this course anyway.

Start with a single question: What's one new thing that you could do on a regular basis to make a significant, positive difference in your life? This question might be the most important thing you ask yourself this term. The answer does not have to involve a huge behaviour change. Over weeks and months, even a small shift in the way you take notes, read a textbook, or interact with instructors can make a major difference in how well you do in school.

Students who open up to this idea experience benefits. These comments from a recent student success course evaluation are typical:

I didn't expect to get anything out of this course except an easy A. Boy, was I ever wrong. This course has changed my life!

I entered college with no confidence. Now that I have taken this class, I feel like I can succeed in any class.

This course has truly showed that I have the power to change any situation for the better.

I am now ready for the rest of my college years.

A student success course gives you dozens of strategies for creating the life of your dreams. It's possible that you might arrive at these strategies on your own, given enough time. Why wait, though? Approach this book and your course as if the quality of your education depends on them. Then wait for the benefits to unfold.

Ways to change a habit

© Warren Goldswain/Shutterstock

© Nomad_Soul/ Shutterstock

© Alberto Zornetta/Shutterstock

CONSIDER A NEW way to think about the word *habit*. Imagine for a moment that many of our most troublesome problems and even our most basic traits are just habits.

That expanding waistline that is blamed on a partner's cooking—maybe that's just a habit called overeating.

That fit of rage that a student blames on an instructor—maybe that's just the student's habit of closing the door to new ideas.

Procrastination, stress, and money shortages might just be names that we give to collections of habits—scores of simple, small, repeated behaviours that combine to create a huge result. The same goes for health, wealth, love, and many of the other things that we want from life.

One way of thinking about success is to focus on habits. Behaviours such as failing to complete reading assignments or skipping class might be habits leading to an outcome that "couldn't" be avoided—dropping out of school.

When you confront a behaviour that undermines your goals or creates a circumstance that you don't want, consider a new attitude: It's just a habit. And it can be changed.

One change in behaviour that seems insignificant at first can have effects that ripple throughout your life.

After interviewing hundreds of people, psychologists James Prochaska, John Norcross, and Carlo DiClemente (1994) identified stages that people typically go through when adopting a new behaviour. These stages take people from *contemplating* a change and making a clear *determination* to change to taking *action* and *maintaining* the new behaviour. Following are ways to help yourself move successfully through each stage.

Tell the truth

Telling the truth about any habit—from chewing our fingernails to cheating on exams—frees us. Without taking this step, our efforts to change might be as ineffective as rearranging the deck chairs on the *Titanic*. Telling the truth allows us to see what's actually sinking the ship.

When we admit what's really going on in our lives, our defences are down. We're open to accepting help from others. The support we need to change the habit has an opportunity to make an impact.

Choose and commit to a new behaviour

It often helps to choose a new habit to replace an old one. First, make a commitment to practise the new habit. Tell key people in your life about your decision to change. Set up a plan for when and how. Answer questions such as these: When will I apply the new habit? Where will I be? Who will be with me? What will I be seeing, hearing, touching, saying, or doing? Exactly how will I think, speak, or act differently?

Take the student who always snacks when he studies. Each time he sits down to read, he positions a bag of potato chips within easy reach. For him, opening a book is a cue to start chewing. Snacking is especially easy, given the place he chooses to study: the kitchen. He decides to change this habit by studying at a desk in his bedroom instead of at the kitchen table. And every time he feels the urge to bite into a potato chip, he sips a glass of water instead.

Affirm your intention

You can pave the way for a new behaviour by clearing a mental path for it. Before you apply the new behaviour, rehearse it in your mind. Mentally picture what actions you will take and in what order.

Say you are planning to improve your handwriting when taking notes. Imagine yourself in class with a new pen and a blank notebook poised before you. Notice how comfortable the pen feels in your hand. See yourself writing clearly and legibly. You can even picture how you will make individual letters—the *es, is,* and *rs.* Then, when class is over, see yourself reviewing your notes and taking pleasure in how easy they are to read.

Such scenes are more vivid if you include all of your senses. Round out your mental picture by adding sounds, textures, and colours.

You can act as if your intention is already a reality, as if the new habit is already a part of you. Experience the change you want to see—today. In some cases, this might be enough to change the old habit completely.

Start with a small change

You can sometimes rearrange a whole pattern of behaviours by changing one small habit. If you have a habit of always being late for class, and if you want to change that habit, be on time for one class. As soon as you change the old pattern by getting ready and arriving on time at one class, you'll likely find yourself arriving at all of your classes on time. You might even start arriving everywhere else on time.

Get feedback and support

This is a crucial step and a point at which many plans for change break down. It's easy to practise your new behaviour with great enthusiasm for a few days. After the initial rush of excitement, however, things can get a little tougher. We begin to find excuses for slipping back into old habits: "One more cigarette won't hurt." "I can get back to my diet tomorrow." "It's been a tough day. I deserve this beer."

One way to get feedback is to bring other people into the picture. They might be friends or family, or you might require the more focused support you can get from a support group. Ask others to remind you that you are changing your habit. If you want to stop an old behaviour, such as cramming for exams, it often works to tell everyone you know that you intend to stop. Support from others can be as simple as a quick phone call: "Hi. Have you started that outline for your research paper yet?"

You are probably the most effective source for your own support and feedback. Figure out a way to monitor your progress from charts to graphs to journals.

Practise, practise, practise—without self-judgment

Psychologists such as B. F. Skinner (1965) define learning as a stable change in behaviour that comes as a result of practice. This idea is key to changing habits. Act on your intention. If you fail or forget, let go of any self-judgment. Just keep practising the new habit and allow whatever time it takes to make a change.

Accept the feelings of discomfort that might come with a new habit. Keep practising the new behaviour, even if it feels unnatural. Trust the process. You will grow into the new behaviour. Keep practising until it becomes as natural as breathing. However, if this new habit doesn't work, simply note what happened (without guilt or blame), select a new behaviour, and begin this cycle of steps over again.

Making mistakes as you practise doesn't mean that you've failed. Even when you don't get the results you want from a new behaviour, you learn something valuable in the process. Once you understand ways to change one habit, you understand ways to change almost any habit. ✳

© photos.com

© photos.com

© photos.com

Discovery Statement

Choosing your purpose

Success is a choice—your choice. To *get* what you want, it helps to *know* what you want. That is the purpose of this Journal Entry, which has two parts.

You can begin choosing success right now by setting a date, time, and place to complete this Journal Entry. Write your choices here, then block out the time on your calendar.

Date: _____

Time: _____

Place: _____

Part 1

Select a time and place when you know you will not be disturbed for at least 20 minutes. (The library is a good place to do this.) Relax for two or three minutes, clearing your mind. Next, complete the following sentences—and then keep writing.

When you run out of things to write, stick with it just a bit longer. Be willing to experience a little discomfort. Keep writing. What you discover might be well worth the extra effort.

What I want from my education is . . .

_____

_____

_____

When I complete my education, I want to be able to . . .

_____

_____

_____

I also want . . .

_____

_____

_____

_____

_____

_____

_____

Part 2

After completing Part 1, take a short break. Reward yourself by doing something that you enjoy. Then come back to this Journal Entry.

Now, review the above list of things that you want from your education. See if you can summarize them in a one-sentence, polished statement. This will become a statement of your purpose for taking part in higher education.

Allow yourself to write many drafts of this mission statement, and review it periodically as you continue your education. With each draft, see if you can capture the essence of what you want from higher education and from your life. State it in a vivid way—a short sentence that you can easily memorize, one that sparks your enthusiasm and makes you want to get up in the morning.

You might find it difficult to express your purpose statement in one sentence. If so, write a paragraph or more. Then look for the sentence that seems most charged with energy for you.

Following are some sample purpose statements:

- My purpose for being in school is to gain skills that I can use to contribute to others.

- My purpose for being in school is to live an abundant life that is filled with happiness, health, love, and wealth.

- My purpose for being in school is to enjoy myself by making lasting friendships and following the lead of my interests.

Write at least one draft of your purpose statement below:

_____

_____

_____

_____

_____

_____

_____

_____

_____

_____

THE POWER PROCESSES

A USER'S GUIDE

A POWER PROCESS is a suggestion to shift your perspective and try on a new habit or way of seeing the world. This book includes a baker's dozen of them. Reviewers of *Becoming a Master Student* consistently refer to the power of the Power Processes. Many students point to these short, offbeat, and occasionally outrageous articles as their favourite part of the book.

Why use the Power Processes?

People operate like holograms. But just what does that mean? Holograms are three-dimensional pictures made by using lasers and a special kind of film. You can cut holographic film into tiny pieces and reproduce the entire image from any piece. Each piece contains the whole.

Scientists have observed the same principle at work in biology, physics, sociology, politics, and management. Biologists know that the chromosomes in each cell are the blueprints for that whole organism. Careful study of any one cell can show a plan for the entire body.

The hologram-like nature of human behaviour can be summed up in the word *process*. We have a natural tendency to live in patterns—to act out of habit. You can harness this idea for practical benefit. Altering a single attitude or basic behaviour is like changing the blueprint for your life. One small change can open the door to many other changes, with a cascading series of positive effects. That's the reason why the word *power* goes with the term *process*.

The Power Processes in this book offer many more examples of this approach. *Becoming a master student* means setting up patterns of success that will last the rest of your life.

How do I use the Power Processes?

Approach each Power Process with an open mind. Then experiment with it right away. See if it works for you.

Psychologists have written thousands of pages on the subject of personal change. You can find countless theories of personality, techniques for reinforcing behaviours, and other complex schemes.

As an alternative, consider that personal change is simple. Just do something differently. Now. Then see what happens.

People often make personal change more complicated. They spend years trying to enhance their self-discipline, unearth their childhood memories, search for their hidden sources of motivation, discover their higher self, and on and on.

Another option is to just change, starting today. That's the idea behind the Power Processes. You'll find 13 of them in this book:

- Discover what you want, page 29
- Ideas are tools, page 64
- Be here now, page 102
- Love your problems (and experience your barriers), page 131
- Notice your pictures and let them go, page 156
- I create it all, page 186
- Detach, page 217
- Find a bigger problem, page 249
- Employ your word, page 286
- Choose your conversations and your community, page 313
- Risk being a fool, page 340
- Surrender, page 376
- Be it, page 415

To start unleashing the power, turn the page now. ✳

DISCOVER WHAT YOU WANT

Imagine a person who walks up to a counter at the airport to buy a plane ticket for his next vacation. "Just give me a ticket," he says to the reservation agent. "Anywhere will do."

The agent stares back at him in disbelief. "I'm sorry, sir," he replies. "I'll need some more details. Just minor things—such as the name of your destination city and your arrival and departure dates."

"Oh, I'm not fussy," says the would-be vacationer. "I just want to get away. You choose for me."

Compare this with another traveller who walks up to the counter and says, "I'd like a ticket to Ixtapa, Mexico, departing on Saturday, March 23 and returning Sunday, April 7. Please give me a window seat, first class, with vegetarian meals."

Now, ask yourself which traveller is more likely to end up with a vacation that he'll enjoy.

The same principle applies in any area of life. Knowing where we want to go increases the probability that we will arrive at our destination. Discovering what we want makes it more likely that we'll attain it. Once our goals are defined precisely, our brains reorient our thinking and behaviour to align with those goals—and we're well on the way there.

The example of the traveller with no destination seems far-fetched. Before you dismiss it, do an informal experiment: Ask three other students what they want to get out of their education. Be prepared for hemming and hawing, vague generalities, and maybe even a helping of à la mode pie-in-the-sky.

What you will hear will be amazing, considering the stakes involved. Our hypothetical vacationer is about to invest a couple of weeks of his time and hundreds of dollars—all with no destination in mind. Students routinely invest years of their lives and thousands of dollars with an equally hazy idea of their destination in life.

Now suppose that you ask someone what she wants from her education and you get this answer: "I plan to get a degree in journalism with double minors in earth science and Portuguese so that I can work as a reporter covering the environment in Brazil." Chances are you've found a master student. The details of a person's vision offer a clue to mastery.

Discovering what you want greatly enhances your odds of succeeding in post-secondary education. Many students quit school simply because they are unsure about what they want from it. With well-defined goals in mind, you can look for connections between what you want and what you study. The more connections you discover, the more likely you'll stay in school—and the more likely you'll benefit from post-secondary education. For maximum clarity, write down what you want. Goals that reside strictly in your head can remain fuzzy. Writing them down brings them into sharper focus.

As you write about what you want, expand your imagination to different time frames. Define what you want to be, do, and have next week, next month, and next year. Write about what you want five years from now—and five minutes from now.

To move into action, use this book. It's filled with places to state what you want to accomplish and how you intend to go about it. Every Journal Entry and exercise exists for this purpose. Fill up those pages. With your dreams and new behaviours in hand, you might find that events fall into place almost magically. Start telling people about what you want, and you'll eventually find some who are willing to help. They might offer an idea or two or suggest a person to call or an organization to contact. The sooner you discover what you want, the sooner you can create the conditions that transform your life.

MW Complete this exercise online @
www.bams5ce.nelson.com

© aprott/iStockphoto

Name_____   Date____/____/____

1. List three common differences between secondary and postsecondary education.

2. According to the text, one way to master the transition to postsecondary education is to remind yourself that you already know how to study. True or False? Explain your answer.

3. Explain how you would respond differently to task-based compared to outcome-based instructions.

4. List two arguments for regularly attending classes in postsecondary education.

5. Define the term *self-regulation*.

6. The purpose of the Discovery and Intention Journal Entry system is to increase the amount of effort you put into succeeding in postsecondary education. True or False? Explain your answer.

7. Describe in your own words the necessary steps to complete a textbook reconnaissance.

8. List at least two benefits of discovering what you want from your education.

9. List five examples of community resources that could help you get the most from postsecondary education.

10. The process of changing habits is effective only if you concentrate on making major changes in behaviour. True or False? Explain your answer.

1 | First Steps

Master Student Map

as you read, ask yourself

what if . . .

I could create new outcomes in my life by accepting the way I am right now?

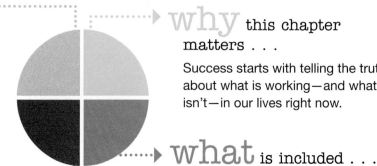

why this chapter matters . . .

Success starts with telling the truth about what is working—and what isn't—in our lives right now.

how

you can use this chapter . . .

- Experience the power of telling the truth about your current skills.
- Discover your preferred learning styles and develop new ones.
- Choose attitudes that promote your success.

what is included . . .

- First Step: Truth is a key to mastery   33
- The Discovery Wheel   35
- Learning Styles: Discovering how you learn   40
- Learning Style Inventory   LSI-1
- Using your learning style profile to succeed   43
- Claim your multiple intelligences   48
- Learning by seeing, hearing, and moving: The VAK system   51
- The Master Student   54
- Motivation—I'm just not in the mood   57
- Attitudes, affirmations, and visualizations   60
- Power Process: Ideas are tools   64
- Master Student Profile: Terry Beech   68

MASTER STUDENTS in action

At the beginning of the term, I would have said that I learned best by doing (hands-on). But now that I have grown and expanded the boundaries of my mind's learning capabilities, I learn best with a mixture of all three (watching, listening, and doing). This is because I have come to realize that all three types of learning are connected through a balance; leading one to discover the "perfect" method of learning.

—DEONDRÉ LUCAS

First Step:
Truth is a key to mastery

THE FIRST STEP technique is simple: Tell the truth about who you are and what you want. End of discussion. Now proceed to Chapter Two.

Well, it's not *quite* that simple.

The First Step is one of the most valuable tools in this book. It magnifies the power of all the other techniques. It is a key to *becoming a master student.* Urging you to tell the truth sounds like moralizing, but there is nothing moralizing about a First Step. It is a practical, down-to-earth way to change behaviour. No technique in this book has been field-tested more often or more successfully—or under tougher circumstances.

The principle of telling the truth is applied universally by people who want to turn their lives around. For members of Alcoholics Anonymous, the First Step is acknowledging that they are powerless over alcohol. For people who join Weight Watchers, the First Step is admitting how much they weigh.

It's not easy to tell the truth about ourselves. And for some of us, it's even harder to recognize our strengths. Maybe we don't want to brag. Maybe we're attached to poor self-images. The reasons don't matter. The point is that using the First Step technique in *Becoming a Master Student* means telling the truth about our positive qualities, too.

It might seem natural to judge our own shortcomings and feel bad about them. Some people believe that such feelings are necessary in order to bring about change. There is an alternative. We can discover a way to gain skill without negative feelings about the past. By taking a First Step, we can change the way things are without having to be upset about the way things have been.

Whether written or verbal, First Steps are more powerful when they are specific. For example, if you want to improve your note-taking skills, you might write, "I am an awful note taker." It would be more effective to write, "I can't read 80 percent of the notes I took in Introduction to Psychology last week, and I have no idea what was important in that class." Be just as specific about what you plan to achieve. You might declare, "I want to take legible notes that help me predict what questions will be on the final exam."

Completing the exercises in this chapter can help you tap resources you never knew you had. They are all the First Steps. It's just that simple. The truth has power.

journal entry 4

Discovery/Intention Statement

Create value from this chapter

Take five minutes to skim the Discovery Wheel exercise starting on page 35. Find one statement that describes a skill you already possess—a personal strength that will promote your success in school. Write that statement here:

_____

_____

_____

_____

The Discovery Wheel might also prompt some thoughts about skills you want to acquire. Describe one of those skills by completing the following sentence:

I discovered that . . .

_____

_____

_____

_____

Now, skim the appropriate chapter in this book for at least three articles that could help you develop this skill. For example, if you want to take more effective notes, turn to Chapter Five. List the names of your chosen articles here and a time when you will read them in more detail.

I intend to . . .

_____

_____

_____

_____

Complete the exercises in this chapter, and your courage will be rewarded. The Discovery Wheel exercise and the rest of the activities in this book can help you tap resources you never knew you had. They're all First Steps—no kidding. It's just that simple. The truth has power. ✳

③ exercise
Taking the First Step

The purpose of this exercise is to give you a chance to discover and acknowledge your own strengths, as well as areas for improvement. For many students, this is the most difficult exercise in the book. To make the exercise worthwhile, do it with courage.

Some people suggest that looking at areas for improvement means focusing on personal weaknesses. They view it as a negative approach that runs counter to positive thinking. Well, perhaps. Positive thinking is a great technique. So is telling the truth, especially when we see the whole picture—the negative aspects as well as the positive ones.

If you admit that you can't add or subtract and that's the truth, then you have taken a strong, positive First Step toward learning basic math. On the other hand, if you say that you are a terrible math student and that's not the truth, then you are programming yourself to accept unnecessary failure.

The point is to tell the truth. This exercise is similar to the Discovery Statements that appear in every chapter. The difference is that in this case, for reasons of confidentiality, you won't write down your discoveries in the book.

Be brave. If you approach this exercise with courage, you are likely to disclose some things about yourself that you wouldn't want others to read. You might even write down some truths that could get you into trouble. Do this exercise on separate sheets of paper; then hide or destroy them. Protect your privacy.

To make this exercise work, follow these suggestions:

Be specific. It is not effective to write "I can improve my communication skills." Of course you can. Instead, write down precisely what you can *do* to improve your communication skills, for example, "I can spend more time really listening while the other person is talking, instead of thinking about what I'm going to say next."

Look beyond the classroom. What goes on outside of school often has the greatest impact on your ability to be an effective student.

Be courageous. This exercise is a waste of time if it is done half-heartedly. Be willing to take risks. You might open a door that reveals a part of yourself that you didn't want to admit was there. The power of this technique is that once you know what is there, you can do something about it.

Part 1

Time yourself, and for 10 minutes write as fast as you can, completing each of the following sentences at least 10 times with anything that comes to mind. If you get stuck, don't stop. Just write something—even if it seems crazy.

- I never succeed when I . . .
- I'm not very good at . . .
- Something I'd like to change about myself is . . .

Part 2

When you have completed the first part of the exercise, review what you have written, crossing off things that don't make any sense. The sentences that remain suggest possible goals for *becoming a master student.*

Part 3

Here's the tough part. Time yourself, and for 10 minutes write as fast as you can, completing the following sentences with anything that comes to mind. As in Part 1, complete each sentence at least 10 times. Just keep writing, even if it sounds silly.

- I always succeed when I . . .
- I am very good at . . .
- Something I like about myself is . . .

Part 4

Review what you have written and circle the things that you can fully celebrate. This is a good list to keep for those times when you question your own value and worth.

4 exercise
The Discovery Wheel

The Discovery Wheel is another opportunity to tell the truth about the kind of student you are and the kind of student you want to become.

This is not a test. There are no trick questions, and the answers will only have meaning for you.

Here are two suggestions to make this exercise more effective. First, think of it as the beginning of an opportunity to change. There is another Discovery Wheel at the end of this book. You will have a chance to measure your progress, so be honest about where you are now. Second, lighten up. A little laughter can make self-evaluations a lot more effective.

Here's how the Discovery Wheel works. By the end of this exercise, you will have filled in a circle similar to the one on this page. The Discovery Wheel circle is a picture of how you see yourself as a student. The closer the shading comes to the outer edge of the circle, the higher the evaluation of a specific skill. In the example to the right, the student has rated her reading skills as low and her note-taking skills as high.

The terms *high* and *low* are not meant to reflect a negative judgment. The Discovery Wheel is not a permanent picture of who you are. It is a picture of how you view your strengths and weaknesses as a student today. To begin this exercise, read the following statements and award yourself points for each one, using the point system described below. Then add up your point total for each section and shade the Discovery Wheel on page 38 to the appropriate level.

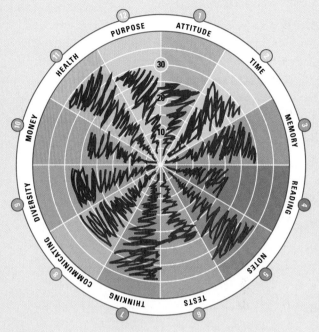

> **5 points:** This statement is always or almost always true of me.
>
> **4 points:** This statement is often true of me.
>
> **3 points:** This statement is true of me about half the time.
>
> **2 points:** This statement is seldom true of me.
>
> **1 point:** This statement is never or almost never true of me.

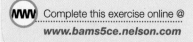

Complete this exercise online @
www.bams5ce.nelson.com

1. __4__ I enjoy learning.

2. __3__ I understand and apply the concept of multiple intelligences.

3. __5__ I connect my courses to my purpose for being in school.

4. __3__ I make a habit of assessing my personal strengths and areas for improvement.

5. __5__ I am satisfied with how I am progressing toward achieving my goals.

6. __4__ I use my knowledge of learning styles to support my success in school.

7. __4__ I am willing to consider any idea that can help me succeed in school—even if I initially disagree with that idea.

8. __3__ I regularly remind myself of the benefits I intend to get from my education.

> __3/__ **Total score (1) Attitude**

1. __3__ I set long-term goals and periodically review them.

2. __3__ I set short-term goals to support my long-term goals.

3. __2__ I write a plan for each day and each week.

4. __4__ I assign priorities to what I choose to do each day.

5. __5__ I plan regular recreation time.

6. __3__ I adjust my study time to meet the demands of individual courses.

7. __4__ I have adequate time each day to accomplish what I plan.

8. __4__ I plan review time so I don't have to cram before exams.

__28__ **Total score (2) Time**

1. __4__ I am confident of my ability to remember.

2. __4__ I can remember people's names.

3. __3__ At the end of a lecture, I can summarize what was presented.

4. __3__ I apply techniques that enhance my memory skills.

5. __2__ I can recall information when I'm under pressure.

6. __3__ I remember important information clearly and easily.

7. __2__ I can jog my memory when I have difficulty recalling.

8. __4__ I can relate new information to what I've already learned.

__25__ **Total score (3) Memory**

1. __4__ I preview and review reading assignments.

2. __3__ When reading, I ask myself questions about the material.

3. __5__ I underline or highlight important passages when reading.

4. __3__ When I read textbooks, I am alert and awake.

5. __4__ I relate what I read to my life.

6. __3__ I select a reading strategy to fit the type of material I'm reading.

7. __4__ I take effective notes when I read.

8. __3__ When I don't understand what I'm reading, I note my questions and find answers.

__29__ **Total score (4) Reading**

1. __5__ When I am in class, I focus my attention.

2. __5__ I take notes in class.

3. __4__ I am aware of various methods for taking notes and choose those that work best for me.

4. __4__ I distinguish important material and note key phrases in a lecture.

5. __5__ I copy down material that the instructor writes on the board.

6. __3__ I can put important concepts into my own words.

7. __4__ My notes are valuable for review.

8. __3__ I review class notes within 24 hours.

__33__ **Total score (5) Notes**

1. __1__ I use techniques to manage stress related to exams.

2. __3__ I manage my time during exams so that I am able to complete them.

3. __2__ I am able to predict test questions.

4. __3__ I adapt my test-taking strategy to the kind of test I'm taking.

5. __4__ I understand what essay questions ask and can answer them completely and accurately.

6. __5__ I start reviewing for tests at the beginning of the term.

7. __4__ I continue reviewing for tests throughout the term.

8. __3__ My sense of personal worth is independent of my test scores.

__25__ **Total score (6) Tests**

1. __4__ I have flashes of insight and often think of solutions to problems at unusual times.

2. __5__ I use brainstorming to generate solutions to a variety of problems.

3. __3__ When I get stuck on a creative project, I use specific methods to get unstuck.

4. __2__ I see problems and tough decisions as opportunities for learning and personal growth.

5. __4__ I am willing to consider different points of view and alternative solutions.

6. ___3___ I can detect common errors in logic.

7. ___5___ I construct viewpoints by drawing on information and ideas from many sources.

8. ___4___ As I share my viewpoints with others, I am open to their feedback.

___30___ **Total score (7) Thinking**

1. ___5___ I am candid with others about who I am, what I feel, and what I want.

2. ___4___ Other people tell me that I am a good listener.

3. ___1___ I can communicate my upset and anger without blaming others.

4. ___4___ I can make friends and create valuable relationships in a new setting.

5. ___3___ I am open to being with people I don't especially like in order to learn from them.

6. ___3___ I can effectively plan and research a large writing assignment.

7. ___3___ I create first drafts without criticizing my writing, then edit later for clarity, accuracy, and coherence.

8. ___3___ I know ways to prepare and deliver effective speeches.

___26___ **Total score (8) Communicating**

1. ___5___ I build rewarding relationships with people from backgrounds different from my own.

2. ___5___ I use critical thinking to overcome stereotypes.

3. ___4___ I point out examples of discrimination and sexual harassment and effectively respond to them.

4. ___4___ I am constantly learning ways to thrive with diversity in school and/or the workplace—attitudes and behaviours that will support my success.

5. ___3___ I can effectively resolve conflict with people from other cultures.

6. ___5___ My writing and speaking are free of sexist expressions.

7. ___3___ I take diversity into account when assuming a leadership role.

8. ___4___ I respond effectively to changing demographics in my country and community.

___36___ **Total score (9) Diversity**

1. ___3___ I am in control of my personal finances.

2. ___5___ I can access a variety of resources to finance my education.

3. ___5___ I am confident that I will have enough money to complete my education.

4. ___5___ I take on debts carefully and repay them on time.

5. ___5___ I have long-range financial goals and a plan to meet them.

6. ___5___ I make regular deposits to a savings account.

7. ___5___ I pay off the balance on credit card accounts each month.

8. ___5___ I can have fun without spending money.

___38___ **Total score (10) Money**

1. ___4___ I have enough energy to study and still fully enjoy other areas of my life.

2. ___4___ If the situation calls for it, I have enough reserve energy to put in a long day.

3. ___2___ The food I eat supports my long-term health.

4. ___1___ The way I eat is independent of my feelings of self-worth.

5. ___3___ I exercise regularly to maintain a healthy weight.

6. ___3___ My emotional health supports my ability to learn.

7. ___5___ I notice changes in my physical condition and respond effectively.

8. ___5___ I am in control of any alcohol or other drugs I put into my body.

___27___ **Total score (11) Health**

1. ___4___ I see learning as a lifelong process.

2. ___5___ I relate my studies to what I plan to do for the rest of my life.

3. ___4___ I learn by contributing to others.

4. ___3___ I have a written career plan and update it regularly.

5. ___5___ I am gaining skills to support my success in the workplace.

6. ___3___ I take responsibility for the quality of my education-and my life.

7. ___3___ I live by a set of values that translates into daily actions.

8. ___4___ I am willing to accept challenges even when I'm not sure how to meet them.

___3/___ **Total score (12) Purpose**

Filling in your Discovery Wheel

Using the total score from each category, shade in each section of the Discovery Wheel. Use different colours, if you want. For example, you could use green to denote areas you want to work on. When you have finished, complete the Journal Entry on the next page.

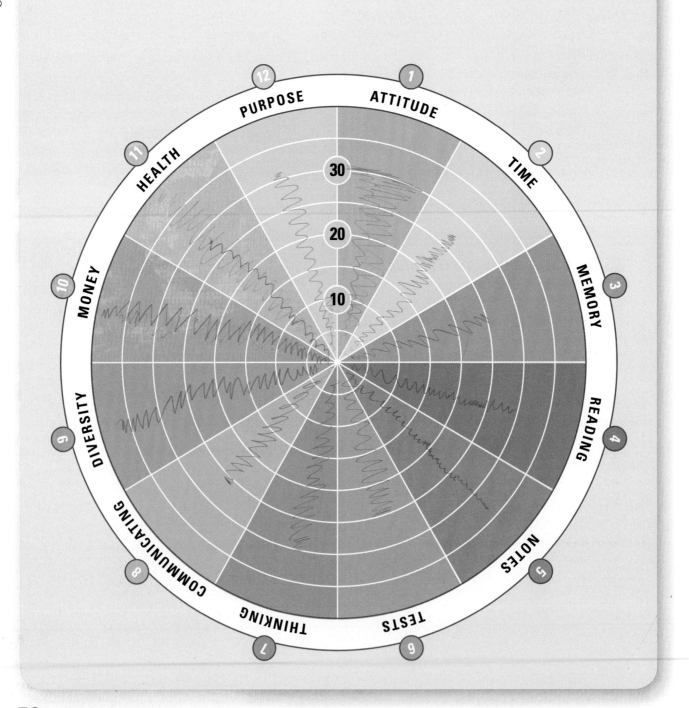

Discovery/Intention Statement

Roll your Discovery Wheel

Now that you have completed your Discovery Wheel, spend a few minutes with it. Get a sense of its weight, shape, and balance. Can you imagine running your hands around it? If you could lift it, would it feel light or heavy? How would it sound if it rolled down a hill? Would it roll very far? Would it wobble? Make your observations without judging the wheel as good or bad. Simply be with the picture you have created.

After you have spent a few minutes studying your Discovery Wheel, complete the following sentences in the space below. Don't worry if you can't think of something to write. Just put down whatever comes to mind. Remember, this is not a test.

This wheel is an accurate picture of my ability as a student because . . .

_____

_____

My self-evaluation surprises me because . . .

_____

_____

_____

The two areas in which I am strongest are . . .

_____

_____

The areas in which I want to improve are . . .

_____

_____

I want to concentrate on improving these areas because . . .

_____

_____

_____

Now, select one of your discoveries and describe how you intend to benefit from it. Complete the statement below.

To gain some practical value from this discovery, I will . . .

_____

_____

_____

mastering technology

SUPPLEMENT YOUR TEXT WITH ONLINE RESOURCES

Purchasing a textbook often gives you access to a suite of related resources, including companion websites that are regularly updated, and other digital media. One way to get your money's worth from a text is to fully use these resources, even if they are not assigned:

• To begin, check out the Student website for *Becoming a Master Student*. There you'll discover ways to take your involvement with this book to a deeper level. For example, access the website to do an online version of the Discovery Wheel exercise. Then look for videos, additional exercises, articles, PowerPoint slides, practice tests, and forms.

• Look for websites created by your instructors for specific courses. Ask them for the URLs. Check your course syllabus for more details. When your course does have a website, explore its features in detail.

• Using key words related to your course, search the Internet for related sites. Look for content that expands on topics presented in class.

• Find out if your instructors offer "virtual office hours"—times when they are willing to answer questions via email or other electronic messaging.

• Search for online homework help in specific subjects. Many schools and public libraries post such sites. Also, most academic libraries post subject guides to help students learn about and do research in specific subject areas.

• Visit your school's website. Look for lists of campus organizations, extracurricular activities, and student services.

Learning Styles: Discovering how you learn

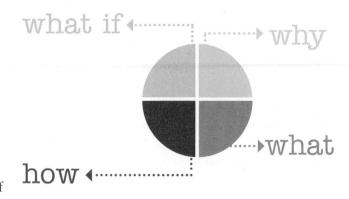

RIGHT NOW, you are investing substantial amounts of time, money, and energy in your education. What you get in return for this investment depends on how well you understand the process of learning and use it to your advantage.

If you don't understand learning, you might feel bored or confused in class. After getting a low grade, you might have no idea how to respond. Over time, frustration can mount to the point where you question the value of being in school.

Some students answer that question by dropping out of school. These students lose a chance to create the life they want. Society loses the contributions of educated workers.

You can prevent that outcome. Gain strategies for going beyond boredom and confusion. Discover new options for achieving goals, solving problems, listening more fully, speaking more persuasively, and resolving conflicts between people. Start by understanding the different ways that people create meaning from their experience and change their behaviour. In other words, learn about *how* we learn.

We learn by perceiving and processing

When we learn well, says psychologist David Kolb (1984), two things happen. First, we *perceive*—that is, we notice events and take in new experiences. Second, we *process,* or deal with, experiences in a way that helps us make sense of them.

Some people especially enjoy perceiving through *concrete experience.* They like to absorb information through their five senses. They learn by getting directly involved in new experiences. When solving problems, they rely on intuition as much as intellect. These people typically function well in unstructured classes that allow them to take initiative.

Other people favour perceiving by *abstract conceptualization.* They take in information best when they can think about it as a subject separate from themselves. They analyse, intellectualize, and create theories. Often these people take a scientific approach to problem solving and excel in traditional classrooms.

People also process experiences differently. Some people favour processing information by *reflective observation.* They prefer to stand back, watch what is going on, and think about it. They consider several points of view as they attempt to make sense of things and generate many ideas about how something happens. They value patience, good judgment, and a thorough approach to learning.

Other people like to process experience by *active experimentation.* They prefer to jump in and start doing things immediately. These people do not mind taking risks as they attempt to make sense of things; risk taking helps them learn. They are results oriented and look for practical ways to apply what they have learned.

Perceiving and processing—an example

Suppose that you get a new cell phone. It has more features than any phone you've used before. You have many options for learning how to use it. For example, you could do any of the following:

- Just get your hands on the phone right away, press some buttons, and see if you can dial a number or send a text message.
- Read the instruction manual and view help screens on the phone before you try to make a call.
- Recall experiences you've had with phones in the past and what you've learned by watching other people use their cell phones.
- Ask a friend who owns the same type of phone to coach you as you experiment with making calls and sending messages.

These actions illustrate the different ways of perceiving and processing:

1. Getting your hands on the phone right away and seeing if you can make it work is an example of learning through concrete experience.

2. Reading the manual and help screens before you use the phone is an example of learning through abstract conceptualization.

3. Recalling what you've experienced in the past is an example of learning through reflective observation.

4. Asking a friend to coach you through a hands-on activity with the phone is an example of learning through active experimentation.

Four modes of learning and four questions

Your learning style is the unique way in which you blend the possible ways of perceiving and processing experience. Learning styles can be described in many ways. To keep things simple, just think in terms of four *modes* of learning.

Mode 1 learners are concrete and reflective. They seek a purpose for new information and a personal connection with the content. They want to know that a course matters, and how it challenges or fits in with what they already know. These learners embrace new ideas that relate directly to their current interests and career plans. In summary, Mode 1 learners ask, Why learn this?

Mode 2 learners are abstract and reflective. They crave information. When learning something, they want to know the main facts, ideas, and procedures. They seek a theory to explain events and are interested in what experts have to say. Often these learners like ideas that are presented in a logical, organized way. They break a subject down into its key elements or steps and master each one in a systematic way. Mode 2 learners ask, What is the content?

Mode 3 learners are abstract and active. They hunger for an opportunity to try out what they're studying. They want to take theories and test them by putting them into practice. These learners thrive when they have well-defined tasks, guided practice, and frequent feedback. Mode 3 learners ask, How does this work?

Mode 4 learners are concrete and active. They get excited about going beyond classroom assignments. They apply what they're learning in various situations and use theories to solve real problems. Mode 4 learners ask, What if I tried this in a different setting?

The four modes—an example

Becoming a Master Student is specifically designed to move you through all four modes of learning.

At the beginning of each chapter, you complete a Journal Entry designed to connect the chapter content to your current life experience. The aim is to help you see the chapter's possible benefits and discover a purpose for reading further. You answer the Mode 1 question—*Why* learn this?

Next, you read articles that are filled with ideas and suggestions for succeeding in school and the workplace. All these readings are answers to the Mode 2 question—*What* is the content?

You also use exercises to practise new skills and facilitate feedback from your instructor and other students. These exercises are answers to the Mode 3 question—*How* does this work?

Finally, at the end of each chapter, a Put It to Work article and Skills Snapshot exercise help you apply the chapter content to different situations and choose your next step toward mastery. You discover answers to the Mode 4 question—*What if* I tried this in a different setting?

Also notice the Master Student Map at the beginning of each chapter. It presents the chapter content as answers to these four questions. For example, the Master Student Map for this chapter (page 32) suggests *why* this chapter matters: "Success starts with telling the truth about what *is* working—and what *isn't*—in our lives right now." There's a list of *what* topics are included and suggestions for *how* you can use this chapter. Finally, you're encouraged to ask, "*What if* I could create new outcomes in my life by accepting the way I am right now?"

Becoming a flexible learner

Kolb believes that effective learners are flexible. They can learn using all four modes. They consistently ask *Why? What? How?* and *What if?*—and use a full range of activities to find the answers.

Becoming a flexible learner promotes your success in school and in the workplace. By developing all four modes of learning, you can excel in many types of courses. You can learn from instructors with many different styles of teaching. You can expand your options for declaring a major and choosing a career. You can experiment with a variety of strategies and create new options for learning *anything*.

Above all, you can recover your natural gift for learning. Rediscover a world where the boundaries between learning and fun, between work and play, all disappear. While immersing yourself in new experiences, blend the sophistication of an adult with the wonder of a child. This path is one that you can travel for the rest of your life.

The following elements of this chapter are designed to help you take the next steps toward becoming a flexible learner:

■ To discover how you currently prefer to learn, take the Learning Style Inventory that follows.

■ Read the article "Using Your Learning Style Profile to Succeed" to learn ways to expand on your preferences.

■ For additional perspectives on learning styles, see the articles "Claim your Multiple Intelligences" and "Learning by Seeing, Hearing, and Moving—The VAK System."

Directions for completing the Learning Style Inventory

To help you become more aware of learning styles, Kolb developed the Learning Style Inventory (LSI). This inventory is included on the next several pages. Responding to the items in the LSI can help you discover a lot about ways you learn.

The LSI is not a test. There are no right or wrong answers. Your goal is simply to develop a profile of your current learning style. So, take the LSI quickly. You might find it useful to recall a recent time when you learned something new at school, at home, or at work. However, do not agonize over your responses.

Note that the LSI consists of twelve sentences, each with four different endings. You will read each sentence, and then write a "4" next to the ending that best describes the way you currently learn. Then you will continue ranking the other endings with a "3," "2," or "1," representing the ending that least describes you. You must rank each ending. *Do not leave any endings blank.* Use each number only once for each question.

Following are more specific directions:

1. Read the instructions at the top of page LSI-1. When you understand example A, you are ready to begin.
2. Before you write on page LSI-1, remove the sheet of paper following page LSI-2.
3. While writing on page LSI-1, press firmly so that your answers will show up on page LSI-3.
4. After you complete the twelve items on page LSI-1, go to page LSI-3. ✳

journal entry 6

Discovery Statement

Prepare for the Learning Style Inventory

As a warmup for the LSI and articles that follow, spend a minute or two thinking about times in the past when you felt successful at learning. Underline or highlight any of the following statements that describe those situations:

I was in a highly structured setting, with a lot of directions about what to do and feedback on how well I did at each step.

I was free to learn at my own pace and in my own way.

I learned as part of a small group.

I learned mainly by working alone in a quiet place.

I learned in a place where there was a lot of activity going on.

I learned by forming pictures in my mind.

I learned by *doing* something—moving around, touching something, or trying out a process for myself.

I learned by talking to myself or explaining ideas to other people.

I got the "big picture" before I tried to understand the details.

I listened to a lecture and then thought about it after class.

I read a book or article and then thought about it afterward.

I used a variety of media—such as a video, audio recording, or computer—to assist my learning.

I went beyond taking notes and wrote in a personal journal.

I was considering where to attend school and knew I had to actually set foot on each campus before choosing.

I was shopping for a car and paid more attention to how I felt about test driving each one than to the sticker prices or mileage estimates.

I was thinking about going to a movie and carefully read the reviews before choosing one.

Review the list for any patterns in the way you prefer to learn. If you see any patterns, briefly describe them here.

_____

_____

_____

_____

Learning Style Inventory

Fill in the following blanks like this example:

A. When I learn: __2__ I am happy. __3__ I am fast. __4__ I am logical. __1__ I am careful.

Remember: **4 =** Most like you **3 =** Second most like you **2 =** Third most like you **1 =** Least like you

Remove the sheet of paper following page LS-2. Press firmly while writing.

1. When I learn:	__1__ I like to deal with my feelings.	__2__ I like to think about ideas.	__3__ I like to be doing things.	__4__ I like to watch and listen.
2. I learn best when:	__4__ I listen and watch carefully.	__2__ I rely on logical thinking.	__1__ I trust my hunches and feelings.	__3__ I work hard to get things done.
3. When I am learning:	__3__ I tend to reason things out.	__4__ I am responsible about things.	__2__ I am quiet and reserved.	__1__ I have strong feelings and reactions.
4. I learn by:	__1__ feeling.	__3__ doing.	__4__ watching.	__2__ thinking.
5. When I learn:	__1__ I am open to new experiences.	__4__ I look at all sides of issues.	__3__ I like to analyze things, breaking them down into their parts.	__2__ I like to try things out.
6. When I am learning:	__4__ I am an observing person.	__3__ I am an active person.	__2__ I am an intuitive person.	__1__ I am a logical person.
7. I learn best from:	__4__ observation.	__1__ personal relationships.	__2__ rational theories.	__3__ a chance to try out and practise.
8. When I learn:	__4__ I like to see results from my work.	__1__ I like ideas and theories.	__2__ I take my time before acting.	__3__ I feel personally involved in things.
9. I learn best when:	__4__ I rely on my observations.	__1__ I rely on my feelings.	__3__ I can try things out for myself.	__2__ I rely on my ideas.
10. When I am learning:	__1__ I am a reserved person.	__2__ I am an accepting person.	__4__ I am a responsible person.	__3__ I am a rational person.
11. When I learn:	__3__ I get involved.	__4__ I like to observe.	__1__ I evaluate things.	__2__ I like to be active.
12. I learn best when:	__2__ I analyse ideas.	__1__ I am receptive and open-minded.	__3__ I am careful.	__4__ I am practical.

Take a snapshot of your learning styles

This page is intended to be completed as a culminating exercise. Before you work on this exercise, complete the Learning Styles Inventory and read the following articles:

"Learning Styles: Discovering How You Learn," page 40

"Using Your Learning Style Profile to Succeed," page 43

"Claim Your Multiple Intelligences," page 48

"Learning by Seeing, Hearing, and Moving—The VAK System," page 51

An inventory of your learning styles is just a snapshot that gives a picture of who you are today. Your answers are not right or wrong. Your score does not dictate who you can become in the future. The key questions are simply "How do I currently learn?" and "How can I become a more successful learner?"

Take a few minutes right now to complete the following sentences, describing your latest insights into the way you learn. When you finish, plan to follow up on those insights.

If someone asked me, "What do you mean by learning styles, and can you give me an example?" I'd say . . .

I would describe my current learning style(s) as . . .

If someone asked me to define intelligence, I'd say . . .

When learning well, I tend to use the following senses . . .

I apply my knowledge of learning styles and multiple intelligences by using certain strategies, such as . . .

When I study or work with people whose learning styles differ from mine, I will respond by . . .

To explore new learning styles, I will . . .

Scoring your Inventory

Now that you have taken the Learning Style Inventory, it's time to fill out the Learning Style Graph (page LSI-5) and interpret your results. To do this, please follow the next five steps.

1 First, add up all of the numbers you gave to the items marked with brown **F** letters. Then write down that total to the right in the blank next to "**Brown F**." Next, add up all of the numbers for "**Teal W**," "**Purple T**,"

and "**Orange D**," and also write down those totals in the blanks to the right.

2 Add the four totals to arrive at a GRAND TOTAL and write down that figure in the blank to the right. (*Note:* The grand total should equal 120. If you have a different amount, go back and re-add the coloured letters; it was probably just an addition error.) Now remove the next page and continue with Step 3 on page LSI-5.

scorecard

Brown F	total	18
Teal W	total	40
Purple T	total	24
Orange D	total	38
GRAND TOTAL		120

¹ F	² T	³ D	⁴ W
⁴ W	² T	¹ F	³ D
³ T	⁴ D	² W	¹ F
¹ F	³ D	⁴ W	² T
¹ F	⁴ W	³ T	² D
⁴ W	³ D	² F	¹ T
⁴ W	¹ F	² T	³ D
⁴ D	¹ T	² W	³ F
⁴ W	¹ F	³ D	² T
¹ W	² F	⁴ D	³ T
³ F	⁴ W	¹ T	² D
² T	¹ F	³ W	⁴ D

Remove this page after you have completed Steps 1 and 2 on page LSI-3. Then continue with Step 3 on page LSI-5.

Learning Style Graph

3 Remove the piece of paper that follows this page and then transfer your totals from Step 2 on page LSI-3 to the lines on the Learning Style Graph below. On the brown (F) line, find the number that corresponds to your "**Brown F**" total from page LSI-3. Then write an X on this number. Do the same for your "**Teal W**," "**Purple T**," and "**Orange D**" totals.

4 Now, pressing firmly, draw four straight lines to connect the four Xs and shade in the area to form a "kite." This is your learning style profile. Each X that you placed on these lines indicates your preference for a different aspect of learning:

Concrete Experience ("Feeling"). The number where you put your X on this line indicates your preference for learning things that have personal meaning. The higher your score on this line, the more you like to learn things that you feel are important and relevant to yourself.

Reflective Observation ("Watching"). Your number on this line indicates how important it is for you to reflect on the things you are learning. If your score is high on this line, you probably find it important to watch others as they learn about an assignment and then report on it to the class. You probably like to plan things out and take the time to make sure that you fully understand a topic.

Abstract Conceptualization ("Thinking"). Your number on this line indicates your preference for learning ideas, facts, and figures. If your score is high on this line, you probably like to absorb many concepts and gather lots of information on a new topic.

Active Experimentation ("Doing"). Your number on this line indicates your preference for applying ideas, using trial and error, and practising what you learn. If your score is high on this line, you probably enjoy hands-on activities that allow you to test out ideas to see what works.

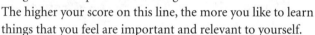

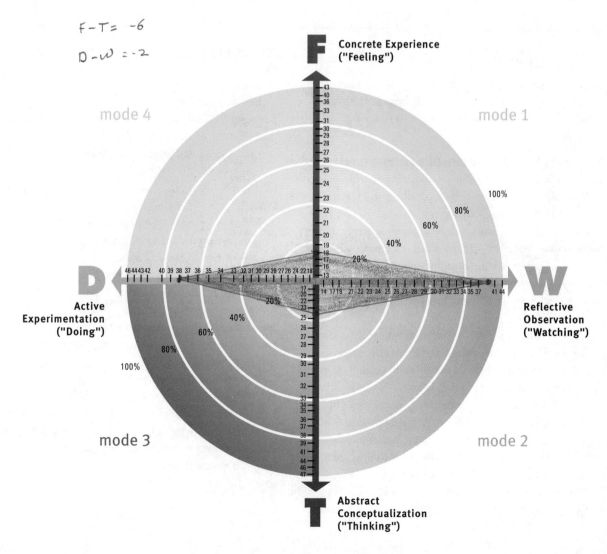

Cycle of Learning

These examples show how the learning cycle works. You're interested in something (Mode 1), so you gather information about it (Mode 2). You try out what you're learning (Mode 3), then you integrate it into your day-to-day life (Mode 4). You go through this cycle many times as one learning experience generates another.

Example 1 Learning about a historical issue

You're required to take an elective in history, and you decide to take a course on the history of immigration to Canada. Your great-grandparents came to this country as immigrants, and immigration is still taking place today. You conclude that this topic is interesting—in part, because of your family background (Mode 1: *Why?*).

Soon you're in class, and you learn that from the early years of the country's history, many Canadians have had misconceptions and fears about immigration that persist to the present day (Mode 2: *What?*).

You find yourself re-evaluating your own beliefs and assumptions. You wonder whether new immigrants in your city are experiencing some of the same stereotyping that was commonplace in earlier times. You decide to become more active in a community organization that deals firsthand with the impact of immigration policies (Mode 3: How?).

You also start to consider what it would be like to become a lawyer and devote your career to creating a system that treats all immigrants with fairness and respect. You realize that you want to make a positive difference in the lives of people who are coming to live in Canada today (Mode 4: What if?).

Example 2 Learning to use a mobile device

Learning begins with developing an interest in this technology. Maybe you want to manage your to-do lists and appointments in a way that is more efficient than writing notes to yourself on random bits of paper. Maybe you don't want to carry your laptop everywhere. Or maybe you want to store your information digitally. You conclude that this technology could help you finally get organized (Mode 1: *Why?*). Next, you learn as much as you can about the different mobile devices on the market. You visit websites, go to a computer store, and ask for a demonstration. You also talk to friends who swear by their smartphones or tablets—and those who swear never to use them—and weigh their advice and differing opinions (Mode 2: *What?*).

After you gather this information, you decide to buy your own device. You take the handwritten information from your calendar and to-do lists and enter it all into your new mobile device. This takes several hours, including the time spent learning the device's interface (Mode 3: *How?*).

Once you've conquered the mechanics of using your device, you begin to use it on a daily basis—and encounter some unexpected hassles. For one thing, tapping the screen to enter text is more tedious than you expected. . Also, your friends who stick with paper-based planning can simply open up their calendars and quickly pencil in appointments. Meanwhile, you have to turn on your device and wait for it to boot up before you can use it. Instead of feeling more organized, you end up feeling behind. You wonder what it would be like to switch back to paper-based planning. After your experiences with a mobile device, you decide to do just that. This time, however, you introduce a change in your behaviour. Instead of recording your to-do items on any scrap of paper that is lying around, you put a pen and some index cards in your pocket and carry them with you at all times. Whenever you want to make a note to yourself, you simply pull out a card and jot down your thoughts. Cards are easy to store and sort. This new system, while it seems so simple and so "low-tech," finally helps you achieve that sense of organization you've been craving (Mode 4: *What if?*).

Example 3 Thinking about the effects of the Internet

Your sociology instructor asks you to write a 2,000-word paper about the impact of the Internet on our society. As part of the assignment, you're asked to envision a society without the Internet. This interests you, since you've often wondered what it would be like to give up the Internet (Mode 1: *Why?*).

One of your first steps in writing this paper is to ask what purposes the Internet serves. You conclude that, based on the variety of content, several purposes are involved: entertainment, news and information, social networking, sports, and, of course, advertising. To research the paper, you also read two books on the history of the Internet (Mode 2: *What?*).

Still wondering how your own life would change if you were to give up the Internet, you choose to do so on a trial basis—for two weeks—and observe the effects. This change in your behaviour frees up several hours each week, which you use for reading newspapers and magazines. You find that reading a newspaper leaves you better informed about the world and that moving away from the computer screen gives you more time to actually play sports, not just watch games online. (Mode 3: *How?*).

As a result of your personal experiment with the Internet, you wonder what it would be like to give it up permanently. You choose to do this for at least six more months. You also volunteer for a campaign to adopt a more active lifestyle that encourages people to go screen free for one month each year and devote the time they save to running and playing sports.(Mode 4: *What if?*).

Remove this sheet before completing the Learning Style Graph.

This page is inserted to ensure that the other writing you do in this book doesn't show through on page LSI-7.

Remove this sheet before completing the
Learning Style Graph.

*This page is inserted to ensure that the other writing you do
in this book doesn't show through on page LSI-7.*

Returning to the big picture about learning styles

This chapter introduces many ideas about how people learn—four modes, multiple intelligences, and the VAK system. That's a lot of information! And these are just a few of the available theories. You may have heard about inventories other than the Learning Style Inventory, such as the Myers-Briggs Type Indicator® (MBTI®) Instrument.* Do an Internet search on *learning styles,* and you'll find many more.

Theories about learning styles share the following insights:

People differ in important ways.

- We can see differences as strengths—not deficits.
- Relationships improve when we take differences into account.
- Learning is continuous—it is a *process,* as well as a series of outcomes.
- We *create* knowledge rather than simply absorbing it.

- We have our own preferences for learning.
- We can often succeed by matching our activities with our preferences.
- Our preferences can expand as we experiment with new learning strategies.
- The deepest learning takes place when we embrace a variety of styles and strategies.

Remember that teachers in your life will come and go. Some will be more skilled than others. None of them will be perfect. With a working knowledge of learning styles, you can view any course as one step along a path to learning what you want, using the ways that *you* choose to learn. Along this path toward mastery, you become your own best teacher.

*MBTI and Myer-Briggs Type Indicator are registered trademarks of Consulting Psychologists Press, Inc.

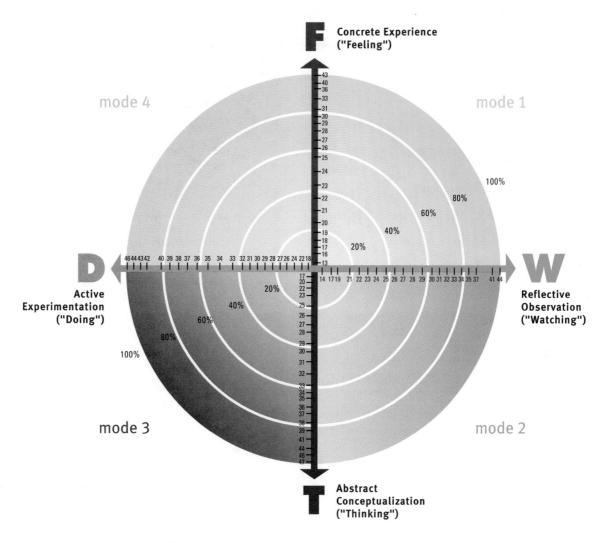

Balancing your preferences

The chart below identifies some of the natural talents as well as challenges for people who have a strong preference for any one mode of learning. For example, if most of your "kite" is in Mode 2 of the Learning Style Graph, then look at the lower right-hand corner of the following chart to see if this is an accurate description of yourself.

After reviewing the description of your preferred learning mode, read all of the sections that start with the words "People with other preferred modes." These sections explain what actions you can take to become a more balanced learner.

Concrete Experience

mode 4

Strengths:
- Getting things done
- Leadership
- Risk taking

Too much of this mode can lead to:
- Trivial improvements
- Meaningless activity

Too little of this mode can lead to:
- Work not completed on time
- Impractical plans
- Lack of motivation to achieve goals

People with other preferred modes can develop Mode 4 by:
- Making a commitment to objectives
- Seeking new opportunities
- Influencing and leading others
- Being personally involved
- Dealing with people

mode 1

Strengths:
- Imaginative ability
- Understanding people
- Recognizing problems
- Brainstorming

Too much of this mode can lead to:
- Feeling paralysed by alternatives
- Inability to make decisions

Too little of this mode can lead to:
- Lack of ideas
- Not recognizing problems and opportunities

People with other preferred modes can develop Mode 1 by:
- Being aware of other people's feelings
- Being sensitive to values
- Listening with an open mind
- Gathering information
- Imagining the implications of ambiguous situations

Active Experimentation

Reflective Observation

mode 3

Strengths:
- Problem solving
- Decision making
- Deductive reasoning
- Defining problems

Too much of this mode can lead to:
- Solving the wrong problem
- Hasty decision making

Too little of this mode can lead to:
- Lack of focus
- Reluctance to consider alternatives
- Scattered thoughts

People with other preferred modes can develop Mode 3 by:
- Creating new ways of thinking and doing
- Experimenting with fresh ideas
- Choosing the best solution
- Setting goals
- Making decisions

mode 2

Strengths:
- Planning
- Creating models
- Defining problems
- Developing theories

Too much of this mode can lead to:
- Vague ideals ("castles in the air")
- Lack of practical application

Too little of this mode can lead to:
- Inability to learn from mistakes
- No sound basis for work
- No systematic approach

People with other preferred modes can develop Mode 2 by:
- Organizing information
- Building conceptual models
- Testing theories and ideas
- Designing experiments
- Analysing quantitative data

Abstract Conceptualization

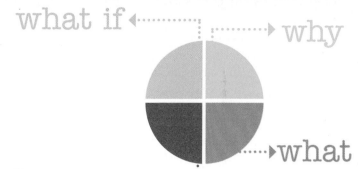

Using your learning style profile to succeed

Develop all four modes of learning

Each mode of learning highlighted in the Learning Style Inventory represents a unique blend of concrete experience, reflective observation, abstract conceptualization, and active experimentation. You can explore new learning styles simply by adopting new habits related to each of these activities. Consider the following suggestions as places to start. Also remember that any idea about learning styles will make a difference in your life only when it leads to changes in your behaviour.

To gain concrete experiences:

- See a live demonstration or performance related to your course content.
- Engage your emotions by reading a novel or seeing a video related to your course.
- Interview an expert in the subject you're learning or a master practitioner of a skill you want to gain.
- Conduct role-plays, exercises, or games based on your courses.
- Conduct an informational interview with someone in your chosen career or shadow that person for a day on the job.
- Look for a part-time job, internship, or volunteer experience that complements what you do in class.
- Deepen your understanding of another culture and extend your foreign language skills by studying abroad.

To become more reflective:

- Keep a personal journal, and write about connections among your courses.
- Form a study group to discuss and debate topics related to your courses.
- Set up a website, computer bulletin board, email listserv, or online chat room related to your major.
- Create analogies to make sense of concepts; for instance, see if you can find similarities between career planning and putting together a puzzle.

- Visit your course instructor during office hours to ask questions.
- During social events with friends and relatives, briefly explain what your courses are about.

To develop abstract thinking:

- Take notes on your reading in outline form; consider using word-processing software with an outlining feature.
- Supplement assigned texts with other books, magazine and newspaper articles, and related websites.
- Attend lectures given by your current instructors and others who teach the same subjects.
- Take ideas presented in the text or lectures and translate them into visual form—tables, charts, diagrams, and maps (see Chapter 5: Notes).
- Make hand-drawn visuals and use computer software to re-create them with more complex graphics and animation.

To become more active:

- Conduct laboratory experiments or field observations.
- Go to settings where theories are being applied or tested.
- Make predictions based on theories you learn, and then see if events in your daily life confirm your predictions.
- Try out a new behaviour described in a lecture or reading, and observe its consequences in your life.

Use the modes while choosing courses

Remember your learning style profile when you're thinking about which classes to take and how to study for each class. Look for a fit between your preferred mode of learning and your course work.

If you prefer Mode 1, for example, look for courses that sound interesting and seem worthwhile to you. If you prefer Mode 2, consider classes that centre on lectures, reading, and discussion. If you prefer Mode 3, choose courses that include demonstrations, lab sessions, role-playing, and other ways to take action. And if you enjoy Mode 4, look for courses that could apply to many situations in your life—at work, at home, and in your relationships.

You won't always be able to match your courses to your learning styles. View those situations as opportunities to practise becoming a flexible learner. By developing your skills in all four modes, you can excel in many types of courses. Also, see the sidebar "Use the modes to learn from *any* instructor" for specific strategies to make the most out of all your classes, regardless of your learning style.

Use the modes to explore your major

If you enjoy learning in Mode 1, you probably value creativity and human relationships. When choosing a major, consider the arts, English, psychology, or political science.

If Mode 2 is your preference, then you enjoy gathering information and building theories. A major related to math or science might be ideal for you.

If Mode 3 is your favourite, then you like to diagnose problems, arrive at solutions, and use technology. A major related to health care, engineering, or economics is a logical choice for you.

And if your preference is Mode 4, you probably enjoy taking the initiative, implementing decisions, teaching, managing projects, and moving quickly from planning into action. Consider a major in business or education.

As you prepare to declare a major, remain flexible. Use your knowledge of learning styles to open up possibilities rather than restrict them. Remember that regardless of your mode, you can excel at any job or major; it just may mean developing new skills in other modes.

Use the modes to explore your career

Knowing about learning styles becomes especially useful when planning your career.

People who excel at Mode 1 are often skilled at tuning in to the feelings of clients and coworkers. These people can listen with an open mind, tolerate confusion, be sensitive to people's feelings, open up to problems that are difficult to define, and brainstorm a variety of solutions. If you like Mode 1, you may be drawn to a career in counselling, social services, the ministry, or another field that centres on human relationships. You might also enjoy a career in the performing arts.

People who prefer Mode 2 like to do research and work with ideas. They are skilled at gathering data, interpreting information, and summarizing—arriving at the big picture. They may excel at careers that centre on science, math, technical communications,

or planning. Mode 2 learners may also work as college teachers, lawyers, technical writers, or journalists.

People who like Mode 3 are drawn to solving problems, making decisions, and checking on progress toward goals. Careers in medicine, engineering, information technology, or another applied science are often ideal for them.

People who enjoy Mode 4 like to influence and lead others. These people are often described as "doers" and "risk takers." They like to take action and complete projects. Mode 4 learners often excel at managing, negotiating, selling, training, and teaching. They might also work for a government agency.

Keep in mind that there is no strict match between certain learning styles and certain careers. Learning is essential to success in all careers. Also, any career can attract people with a variety of learning styles. For instance, the health care field is large enough to include people who prefer Mode 3 and become family physicians *and* people who prefer Mode 2 and become medical researchers.

Expect to encounter different styles

As higher education and the workplace become more diverse and technology creates a global marketplace, you'll meet people who differ from you in profound ways. Your fellow students and coworkers will behave in ways that express a variety of preferences for perceiving information, processing ideas, and acting on what they learn. Consider these examples:

- A roommate who's continually moving while studying—reciting facts out loud, pacing, and gesturing—probably prefers concrete experience and learning by taking action.

- A coworker who talks continually on the phone about a project may prefer to learn by listening, talking, and forging key relationships.

- A supervisor who excels at abstract conceptualization may want to see detailed project plans and budgets submitted in writing, well before a project swings into high gear.

- A study group member who always takes the initiative, manages the discussion, delegates any work involved, and follows up with everyone probably prefers active experimentation.

Differences in learning style can be a stumbling block—or an opportunity. When differences intersect, there is the potential for conflict, as well as for creativity. Succeeding with peers often means seeing the classroom and workplace as a laboratory for learning from experience. Resolving conflict and learning from mistakes are all part of the learning cycle.

Look for specific clues to another person's style

You can learn a lot about other people's styles of learning simply by observing them during the workday. Look for clues such as these:

Approaches to a task requiring learning. Some people process new information and ideas by sitting quietly and reading or writing. When learning to use a piece of equipment, such as a new computer, they'll read the instruction manual first. Others will skip the manual, unpack all the boxes, and start setting up equipment. And others might ask a more experienced colleague to guide them in person, step by step.

Word choice. Some people like to process information visually. You might hear them say, "I'll look into that" or "Give me the big picture first." Others like to solve problems verbally: "Let's talk through this problem" or "I hear you!" In contrast, some people focus on body sensations ("This product feels great") or action ("Let's run with this idea and see what happens").

Body language. Notice how often coworkers or classmates make eye contact with you and how close they sit or stand next to you. Observe their gestures, as well as the volume and tone of their voices.

Content preferences. Notice what subjects coworkers or classmates openly discuss and which topics they avoid. Some people talk freely about their feelings, their families, and even their personal finances. Others choose to remain silent on such topics and stick to work-related matters.

Process preferences. Look for patterns in the way your coworkers and classmates meet goals. When attending meetings, for example, some of them might stick closely to the agenda and keep an eye on the clock. Other people might prefer to go with the flow, even if it means working an extra hour or scrapping the agenda.

Accommodate differing styles

Once you've discovered differences in styles, look for ways to accommodate them. As you collaborate on projects with other students or coworkers, keep the following suggestions in mind:

Remember that some people want to reflect on the big picture first. When introducing a project plan, you might say, "This process has four major steps." Before explaining the plan in detail, talk about the purpose of the project and the benefits of completing each step.

Allow time for active experimentation and concrete experience. Offer people a chance to try out a new product or process for themselves—to literally get the feel of it.

Allow for abstract conceptualization. When leading a study group or conducting a training session, provide handouts that include plenty of visuals and step-by-step instructions. Visual learners and people who like to think abstractly will appreciate these handouts. Also schedule periods for questions and answers.

When planning a project, encourage people to answer key questions. Remember the four essential questions that guide learning. Answering *Why?* means defining the purpose and desired outcomes of the project. Answering *What?* means assigning major tasks, setting due dates for each task, and generating commitment to action. Answering *How?* means carrying out assigned tasks and meeting regularly to discuss things that are working well and ways to improve the project. And answering *What if?* means discussing what the team has learned from the project and ways to apply that learning to the whole class or larger organization.

When working on teams, look for ways the members can complement one another's strengths. If you're skilled at planning, find someone who excels at doing. Also seek people who can reflect on and interpret the team's experience. Pooling different styles allows you to draw on everyone's strengths.

Resolve conflict with respect for styles

When people's styles clash in educational or work settings, you have several options. One is to throw up your hands and resign yourself to personality conflicts. Another option is to recognize differences, accept them, and respect them as complementary ways to meet common goals. Taking that perspective allows you to act constructively. You might do one of the following:

Resolve conflict within yourself. In your mental pictures of classrooms and workplaces, are people all "supposed" to have the same style? Notice if you have such ideas, and gently let them go. If you *expect* to find differences in styles, you can more easily respect those differences.

Introduce a conversation about learning styles. Attend a workshop on learning styles. Then bring such training directly to your classroom or office.

Let people take on tasks that fit their learning styles. People gravitate toward the kinds of tasks they've succeeded at in the past, and that's fine. Remember, though, that learning styles are both stable and dynamic. People can broaden their styles by tackling new tasks to reinforce different modes of learning.

Rephrase complaints as requests. "This class is a waste of my time" can be recast as "Please tell me what I'll gain if I participate actively in class." "The instructor talks too fast" can become "What strategies can I use for taking notes when the instructor covers the material rapidly?"

Accept change—and occasional discomfort

Seek out chances to develop new modes of learning. If your instructor asks you to form a group to complete an assignment, avoid joining a group where everyone shares your learning style. Work on project teams with people who learn differently than you. Get together with people who both complement and challenge you.

Also look for situations where you can safely practise new skills. If you enjoy reading, for example, look for ways to express what you learn by speaking, such as leading a study group on a textbook chapter.

Discomfort is a natural part of the learning process. Allow yourself to notice any struggle with a task or lack of interest in completing it. Remember that such feelings are temporary and that you are balancing your learning preferences. By choosing to move through discomfort, you consciously expand your ability to learn in new ways. ✳

Use the modes to learn from *any* instructor

Students who experience difficulty in school might say, "My teacher doesn't get me" or "The tests are too hard for me" or "In class, we never have time for questions" or "The instructor doesn't teach to my learning style."

Such statements can become mental crutches—a set of beliefs that prevent you from taking responsibility for your education. To stay in charge of your learning, consider adopting attitudes such as the following:

I will look for the potential value in learning this information.

I can learn something useful in any situation, even if I don't like it at first.

I will experiment with this suggestion to see if it works.

No matter who's teaching a course, I am responsible for what I learn.

I will master this subject by using several modes of learning.

Remember that you can take action on such statements even if you don't fully agree with them yet. One way to change your attitudes is to adopt new behaviours, see how they work, and watch for new results in your life. This approach can be adapted to each mode:

- To develop Mode 1, ask questions that help you understand why it is important for you to learn about

a specific topic. You might also want to form a study group.

- To develop Mode 2, ask questions that help you gather enough information to understand the main points and key facts. Also, learn a new subject in stages. For example, divide a large reading assignment into sections and then read each section carefully before moving on to the next one.
- To develop Mode 3, ask questions about how a theory relates to daily life. Also, allow time to practise what you learn. You can do experiments, conduct interviews, create presentations, find a relevant work or internship experience, or even write a song that summarizes key concepts. Learn through hands-on practice.
- To develop Mode 4, ask questions about ways to apply what you have just learned to several situations. Also, seek opportunities to demonstrate your understanding. You could coach a classmate about what you have learned, present findings from your research, explain how your project works, or perform a song that someone else created.

Even when teachers don't promote all four modes of learning, you can take charge of the way you learn. In the process, you consciously direct your growth and create new options.

Canadian employers' wish list

Canadian employers want individuals from all four learning modes. Your learning style will influence not just how you prefer to learn in class but how you act in the workplace. In fact, the strengths identified in each of the modes match up well with the key employability skills identified by *The Conference Board of Canada in 2000* (2010). The Conference Board identifies three primary sets of skills they suggest you need to be successful in the workplace regardless of whether you work on your own or as part of a larger organization. First, you need to have what they call *fundamental skills*, which they see as essential to progress in the workplace. These include communication skills, your ability to manage information, use numbers and think critically, and solve problems. The next set of skills they call *personal management skills*, which they see as the skills, attitudes, and behaviour that will help you develop to your full potential. Finally, they have *teamwork skills*, which are needed to enhance the outcomes of any teamwork or project. These include skills that allow you to work well with others and to fully assist with tasks or projects that must be completed. Although we will talk more about those skills later in this book (*What's Next*), let's take a quick look at some of those skills now and see how they match up with your preferred learning style. Keep in mind that developing your skills at using all four modes is likely to be important for success in the world of work.

Concrete Experience

mode 4

Key strengths:
- Leadership skills are the strength of this mode, which means you will have developed many of the *personal management skills* of having a positive attitude, being responsible, and being adaptable that drive your leadership development.

- To get things done, you must be able to **work well with others**—a key *teamwork skill*. **Leadership** also requires that you be good at conflict resolution, motivating others, and at providing and receiving feedback.

mode 1

Key strengths:
- **Understanding people**—matches with developing the *teamwork skills* of working well with others. This includes being good at conflict management, at performing group work, at respecting diversity, and at delivering and receiving feedback.

- **Recognizing problems, brainstorming and being imaginative**—matches with acquiring *fundamental skills* that are necessary for success on the job. These skills include being able to think and solve problems and, in particular, being able to view things from many perspectives while being creative and being good at gathering needed information to help with problem solving.

Active Experimentation

Reflective Observation

Key strengths:
- **Problem solving, decision making, deductive reasoning** are all part of the *fundamental skills*. Your focus on active experimentation and abstract conceptualization makes you very good at thinking and solving problems—a key employability skill. The Conference Board suggests that individuals with this strength will be likely to use mathematics, science and technology to facilitate problem solving and decision making.

- As setting goals is key to **good decision making** you have developed your *personal management skills*, particularly in the area of being responsible so that you plan and manage your time well and are good at risk management.

mode 3

Key strengths :
- **Planning** is another of the essential *teamwork skills*. Key to this is being able to complete a project from start to finish and your ability to develop a meaningful plan to accomplish the task. Good planners are also good at setting goals and managing time and resources, which again fits into the Conference Board's *personal management skills*.

- **Problem definition** is again part of the *fundamental skills*, as is skill at analysing data. The Conference Board identifies these types of skills as being prepared to use numbers and to think and solve problems.

- **Adaptability** in being able to learn from mistakes is critical to success in creating new models. This is part of the *personal management skills* that employers are looking for.

mode 2

Abstract Conceptualization

Claim your multiple intelligences

Centre: © Tanya Constantine/Getty, clockwise from bottom left: © Vladimir Godnik/Getty, © Scott T. Baxter/Getty, © George Doyle/Getty, © Meg Takamura, © Stockbyte/ Getty, © Gregor Schuster/Getty, Tim Laman/Getty, © Doug Menuez/Getty, collage by Walter Kopec

PEOPLE OFTEN THINK that being smart means the same thing as having a high IQ, and that having a high IQ automatically leads to success. However, psychologists are finding that IQ scores do not always foretell which students will do well in academic settings—or after they graduate.

Psychologist Howard Gardner (1993) believes that no single measure of intelligence can tell us how smart we are. Instead, Gardner defines intelligence in a flexible way as "the ability to solve problems, or to create products, that are valued within one or more cultural settings." He also identifies several types of intelligence, as described below.

People using **verbal/linguistic intelligence** are adept at language skills and learn best by speaking, writing, reading, and listening. They are likely to enjoy activities such as telling stories and doing crossword puzzles.

Those using **mathematical/logical intelligence** are good with numbers, logic, problem solving, patterns, relationships, and categories. They are generally precise and methodical, and are likely to enjoy science.

When people learn visually and by organizing things spatially, they display **visual/spatial intelligence.** They think in images and pictures, and understand best by seeing the subject. They enjoy charts, graphs, maps, mazes, tables, illustrations, art, models, puzzles, and costumes.

People using **bodily/kinesthetic intelligence** prefer physical activity. They enjoy activities such as building things, woodworking, dancing, skiing, sewing, and crafts. They generally are coordinated and athletic, and would rather participate in games than just watch.

Those using **musical/rhythmic intelligence** enjoy musical expression through songs, rhythms, and musical instruments. They are responsive to various kinds of sounds, remember melodies easily, and might enjoy drumming, humming, and whistling.

People using **intrapersonal intelligence** are exceptionally aware of their own feelings and values. They are generally reserved, self-motivated, and intuitive. This type of intelligence is associated with emotional intelligence—the ability to recognize feelings and respond to them appropriately. This form of intelligence is talked about in greater detail in Chapter 8.

Outgoing people show evidence of interpersonal intelligence. They do well with cooperative learning and are sensitive to the feelings, intentions, and motivations of others. They often make good leaders.

Those using **naturalist intelligence** love the outdoors and recognize details in plants, animals, rocks, clouds, and other natural formations. These people excel in observing fine distinctions among similar items.

Each of us has **multiple intelligences** to some degree. And each of us can learn to enhance them. Experiment with learning in ways that draw on a variety of intelligences—including those that might be less familiar. When we acknowledge all of our intelligences, we can constantly explore new ways of learning. The chart on page 49 summarizes the multiple intelligences discussed in this article and suggests ways to apply them. This is not an exhaustive list or a formal inventory, so take what you find merely as points of departure. You can invent strategies of your own to cultivate different intelligences. ✶

5 exercise
Develop your multiple intelligences

Gardner's theory of multiple intelligences complements the discussion of different learning styles in this chapter. The main point is that there are many ways to gain knowledge and acquire new behaviours. You can use Gardner's concepts to explore a range of options for achieving success in school, work, and relationships.

The chart on the next page summarizes the content of "Claim Your Multiple Intelligences" and suggests ways to apply the main ideas. Instead of merely glancing through this chart, get active. Place a check mark next to any of the "Possible Characteristics" that describe you. Also check off the "Possible Learning Strategies" that you intend to use. Remember that the chart is *not* an exhaustive list or a formal inventory. Take what you find merely as points of departure. You can invent strategies of your own to cultivate different intelligences.

Type of intelligence	Possible characteristics	Possible learning strategies	Possible careers
Verbal/linguistic	❏ You enjoy writing letters, stories, and papers. ❏ You prefer to write directions rather than draw maps. ❏ You take excellent notes from textbooks and lectures. ❏ You enjoy reading, telling stories, and listening to them.	❏ Highlight, underline, and write other notes in your textbooks. ❏ Recite new ideas in your own words. ❏ Rewrite and edit your class notes. ❏ Talk to other people often about what you're studying.	Librarian, lawyer, editor, journalist, English teacher, radio or television announcer
Mathematical/logical	❏ You enjoy solving puzzles. ❏ You prefer math or science class to English class. ❏ You want to know how and why things work. ❏ You make careful step-by-step plans.	❏ Analyse tasks into a sequence of steps. ❏ Group concepts into categories and look for underlying patterns. ❏ Convert text into tables, charts, and graphs. ❏ Look for ways to quantify ideas–to express them in numerical terms.	Accountant, auditor, tax preparer, mathematician, computer programmer, statistician, economist, math or science teacher
Visual/spatial	❏ You draw pictures to give an example or clarify an explanation. ❏ You understand maps and illustrations more readily than text. ❏ You assemble things from illustrated instructions. ❏ You especially enjoy books that have a lot of illustrations.	❏ When taking notes, create concept maps, mindmaps, and other visuals (see Chapter Five). ❏ Code your notes by using different colours to highlight main topics, major points, and key details. ❏ When your attention wanders, bring it into focus it by sketching or drawing. ❏ Before you try a new task, visualize yourself doing it well.	Architect, commercial artist, fine artist, graphic designer, photographer, interior decorator, engineer, cartographer
Bodily/kinesthetic	❏ You enjoy physical exercise. ❏ You tend to avoid sitting still for long periods of time. ❏ You enjoy working with your hands. ❏ You use a lot of gestures when talking.	❏ Be active in ways that support concentration; for example, pace as you recite, read while standing up, and create flash cards. ❏ Carry materials with you and practise studying in several different locations. ❏ Create hands-on activities related to key concepts; for example, create a game based on course content. ❏ Notice the sensations involved with learning something well.	Physical education teacher, athlete, athletic coach, physical therapist, chiropractor, massage therapist, yoga teacher, dancer, choreographer, actor

(Continued)

Type of intelligence	Possible characteristics	Possible learning strategies	Possible careers
Musical/rhythmic	❏ You often sing in the car or shower. ❏ You tap your foot to the beat of a song. ❏ You play a musical instrument. ❏ You feel most engaged and productive when music is playing.	❏ During a study break, play music or dance to restore energy. ❏ Put on background music that enhances your concentration while studying. ❏ Relate key concepts to songs you know. ❏ Write your own songs based on course content.	Professional musician, music teacher, music therapist, choral director, musical instrument sales representative, musical instrument maker, piano tuner
Intrapersonal	❏ You enjoy writing in a journal and being alone with your thoughts. ❏ You think a lot about what you want in the future. ❏ You prefer individual projects to group projects. ❏ You take time to think things through before talking or taking action.	❏ Connect course content to your personal values and goals. ❏ Study a topic alone before attending a study group. ❏ Connect readings and lectures to a strong feeling or significant past experience. ❏ Keep a journal that relates your course work to events in your daily life.	Minister, priest, rabbi, professor of philosophy or religion, counselling psychologist, creator of a home-based or small business
Interpersonal	❏ You prefer group work to working alone. ❏ You have plenty of friends and regularly spend time with them. ❏ You enjoy talking and listening more than reading or writing. ❏ You thrive in positions of leadership.	❏ Form and conduct study groups early in the term. ❏ Create flash cards and use them to quiz study partners. ❏ Volunteer to give a speech or to lead group presentations on course topics. ❏ Teach the topic you're studying to someone else.	Manager, school administrator, salesperson, teacher, counselling psychologist, arbitrator, police officer, nurse, travel agent, public relations specialist, creator of a mid-size to large business
Naturalist	❏ As a child, you enjoyed collecting insects, leaves, or other natural objects. ❏ You enjoy being outdoors. ❏ You find that important insights occur during times you spend in natural surroundings. ❏ You read books and magazines on nature-related topics.	❏ During study breaks, take walks outside. ❏ Post pictures of outdoor scenes where you study and play recordings of outdoor sounds while you read. ❏ Invite classmates to discuss coursework while taking a hike or going on a camping trip. ❏ Focus on careers that hold the potential for working outdoors.	Environmental activist, park ranger, recreation supervisor, historian, museum curator, biologist, criminologist, mechanic, woodworker, construction worker, construction contractor or estimator

Learning by seeing, hearing, and moving: The VAK system

YOU CAN APPROACH the topic of learning styles with a simple and powerful system—one that focuses on just three ways of perceiving through your senses:

- Seeing, or *visual* learning
- Hearing, or *auditory* learning
- Movement, or **kinesthetic** learning

To recall this system, remember the letters *VAK*, which stand for visual, auditory, and kinesthetic. The theory is that each of us prefers to learn through one of these sense channels. And we can enrich our learning with activities that draw on the other channels.

To reflect on your VAK preferences, answer the following questions. Each question has three possible answers. Circle the answer that best describes how you would respond in the stated situation. This is not a formal inventory—just a way to prompt some self-discovery.

When you have problems spelling a word, you prefer to:

1. Look it up in the dictionary.
2. Say the word out loud several times before you write it down.
3. Write out the word with several different spellings and choose one.

You enjoy courses the most when you get to:

1. View slides, videos, and readings with plenty of charts, tables, and illustrations.
2. Ask questions, engage in small-group discussions, and listen to guest speakers.
3. Take field trips, participate in lab sessions, or apply the course content while working as a volunteer or intern.

When giving someone directions on how to drive to a destination, you prefer to:

1. Pull out a piece of paper and sketch a map.
2. Give verbal instructions.
3. Say, "I'm driving to a place near there, so just follow me."

When planning an extended vacation to a new destination, you prefer to:

1. Read colourful, illustrated brochures or articles about that place.
2. Talk directly to someone who's been there.
3. Spend a day or two at that destination on a work-related trip before taking a vacation there.

You've made a commitment to learn to play the guitar. The first thing you do is:

1. Go to a library or music store and find an instruction book with plenty of diagrams and chord charts.

2. Pull out your favourite CDs, listen closely to the guitar solos, and see if you can play along with them.
3. Buy or borrow a guitar, pluck the strings, and ask someone to show you how to play a few chords.

You've saved up enough money to lease a car. When choosing from among several new models, the most important factor in your decision is:

1. The car's appearance.
2. The information you get by talking to people who own the cars you're considering.
3. The overall impression you get by taking each car on a test drive.

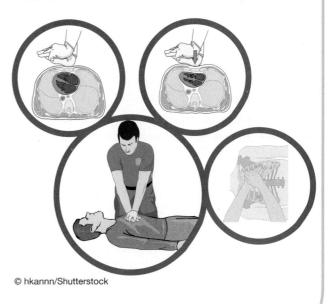

© hkannn/Shutterstock

You've just bought a new computer system—monitor, central processing unit, keyboard, DVD burner, and external speakers. When setting up the system, the first thing you do is:

1. Skim through the printed instructions that come with the equipment.
2. Call up someone with a similar system and ask her for directions.
3. Assemble the components as best as you can, see if everything works, and consult the instructions only as a last resort.

You get a scholarship to study abroad next semester, which starts in just three months. You will travel to a country where French is the most widely spoken language. To learn as much French as you can before you depart, you:

1. Buy a video-based language course that's recorded on a DVD.
2. Set up tutoring sessions with a friend who's fluent in French.
3. Sign up for a short immersion course in an environment in which you speak only French, starting with the first class.

Now take a few minutes to reflect on the meaning of your responses. All of the answers numbered "1" are examples of visual learning. The "2s" refer to auditory learning, and the "3s" illustrate kinesthetic learning. Finding a consistent pattern in your answers indicates that you prefer learning through one sense channel more than the others. Or you might find that your preferences are fairly balanced.

Listed below are suggestions for learning through each sense channel. Experiment with these examples and create more techniques of your own. Use them to build on your current preferences and develop new options for learning.

To enhance *visual* learning:

■ Preview reading assignments by looking for elements that are highlighted visually—bold headlines, charts, graphs, illustrations, and photographs.

■ When taking notes in class, leave plenty of room to add your own charts, diagrams, tables, and other visuals later.

■ Whenever an instructor writes information on a board, copy it exactly in your notes.

■ Transfer your handwritten notes to your computer. Use word processing software that allows you to format your notes in lists, add headings in different fonts, and create visuals in colour.

■ Before you begin an exam, quickly sketch a diagram on scratch paper. Use this diagram to summarize the key formulas or facts you want to remember.

■ During tests, see if you can visualize pages from your handwritten notes or images from your computer-based notes.

To enhance *auditory* learning:

■ Reinforce memory of your notes and readings by talking about them. When studying, stop often to recite key points and examples in your own words.

■ After doing several verbal summaries, record your favourite version or write it out.

■ Read difficult passages in your textbooks slowly and out loud.

■ Join study groups and create short presentations about course topics.

■ Visit your instructors during office hours to ask questions.

To enhance *kinesthetic* learning:

■ Look for ways to translate course content into three-dimensional models that you can build. While studying biology, for example, create a model of a human cell using different colours of clay.

■ Supplement lectures with trips to museums, field observations, lab sessions, tutorials, and other hands-on activities.

■ Recite key concepts from your courses while you walk or exercise.

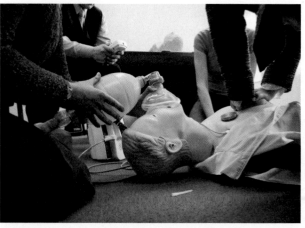

© art-4-art/iStockphoto

Intentionally set up situations in which you can learn by trial and error.

- Create a practice test and write out the answers in the room where you will actually take the exam.

One variation of the VAK system has been called VARK (Fleming, 2006). The *R* describes a preference for learning by reading and writing. People with this preference might benefit from translating charts and diagrams into statements, taking notes in lists, and converting those lists into possible items on a multiple-choice test. ✳

Reminder: Go back to page LSI-2 to complete the "Take a Snapshot of Your Learning Styles" exercise.

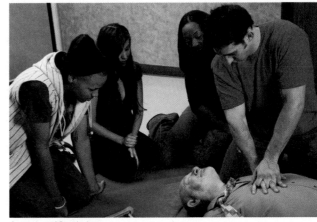
© art-4-art/iStockphoto

The magic of metacognition

It's pronounced "metta-cog-ni-shun." "Meta" means *beyond* or *above*, "**cognition**" refers to everything that goes on inside your brain—thinking, perceiving, and learning. Metacognition is thinking about thinking, learning about learning. It's your ability to stand "above" your mental processes—to observe them and to take conscious control of them.

Metacognition is one of the main benefits of higher education. Mastering this skill allows you to learn anything you want, anytime. Among other things, metacognition includes:

- *Planning*—the ability to determine your purpose, choose from alternative behaviours, predict their consequences, and monitor your progress in meeting your goals
- *Analysis*—the ability to separate a whole subject into its parts
- *Synthesis*—the ability to combine parts to form a meaningful whole
- *Application*—the ability to transfer new concepts and skills from one life situation to another

Each aspect of metacognition dovetails nicely with a mode of learning. Mode 1 involves planning—connecting the content of a course to your personal interests and goals. In Mode 2, you analyse by taking key ideas apart,

separating skills into their component steps, and learning each step in turn. In Mode 3, you synthesize—that is, combine all of the separate ideas, facts, and skills you learned to see how they work in a real-life situation. And in Mode 4, you take what you have learned in one course and apply it in other courses and outside the classroom.

Students who master metacognition can do things such as:

- state the ways that they'll benefit from learning a subject;
- describe their preferred learning styles and develop new ones;
- make accurate statements about their current abilities;
- monitor their behaviour and change their habits;
- choose and apply various strategies for reading, writing, speaking, listening, managing time, and related tasks; and
- modify strategies so that they work in several contexts.

Remember that the teachers in your life will come and go. Some are more skilled than others. None of them are perfect. With metacognition, you can view any course as one step along the path to learning what you want to learn—in the way that *you* prefer to learn it. The magic of metacognition is that you become your own best teacher.

In 1482, Leonardo da Vinci wrote a letter to a wealthy baron, applying for work. Here is an excerpt from the letter: "I can contrive various and endless means of offence and defence . . . . I have all sorts of extremely light and strong bridges adapted to be most easily carried . . . . I have methods for destroying every turret or fortress . . . . I will make covered chariots, safe and unassailable . . . . In case of need I will make big guns, mortars, and light ordnance of fine and useful forms out of the common type." And then he added, almost as an afterthought, "In times of peace I believe I can give perfect satisfaction and to the equal of any other in architecture . . . can carry out sculpture . . . and also I can do in painting whatever may be done."
The *Mona Lisa*, for example.

The Master Student

THIS BOOK is about something that cannot be taught. It's about *becoming a master student*.

Mastery means attaining a level of skill that goes beyond technique. For a master, methods and procedures are automatic responses to the needs of the task. Work is effortless; struggle evaporates. The master carpenter is so familiar with her tools, they are part of her. To a master chef, utensils are old friends. Because these masters don't have to think about the details of the process, they bring more of themselves to their work.

Mastery can lead to flashy results—an incredible painting, for example, or a gem of a short story. In basketball, mastery might result in an unbelievable shot at the buzzer. For a musician, it might be the performance of a lifetime, the moment when everything comes together. Often the result of mastery is a sense of profound satisfaction, well-being, and timelessness. Work seems self-propelled. The master is *in* control by being *out* of control. He lets go and allows the creative process to take over. That's why after a spectacular performance, it is often said of an athlete or a performer, "He was playing out of his mind."

Likewise, the master student is one who "learns out of her mind." Of course, that statement makes no sense. Mastery, in fact, doesn't make sense. It cannot be captured with words. It defies analysis. Mastery cannot be taught, only learned and experienced.

© JustASC/Shutterstock

Examine the following list of characteristics of master students in light of your own experience. The list is not complete. It merely points in a direction. Look in that direction, and you'll begin to see the endless diversity of master students. These people are old and young, male and female. They exist in every period of history.

And they come from every culture, race, and ethnic group.

Also remember to look to yourself. No one can teach us to be master students; we already *are* master students. We are natural learners by design. As students, we can discover that every day.

Following are some traits shared by master students.

Inquisitive. The master student is curious about everything. By posing questions she can generate interest in the most mundane, humdrum situations. When she is bored during a biology lecture, she thinks to herself, "I always get bored when I listen to this instructor. Why is that? Maybe it's because he reminds me of my boring Uncle Ralph, who always tells those endless fishing stories. He even looks like Uncle Ralph. Amazing! Boredom is certainly interesting." Then she asks herself, "What can I do to get value out of this lecture, even though it seems boring?" And she finds an answer.

Able to focus attention. Watch a 2-year-old at play. Pay attention to his eyes. The wide-eyed look reveals an energy and a capacity for amazement that keeps his attention absolutely focused on the here and now. The master student's focused attention has a childlike quality. The world, to a child, is always new. Because the master student can focus attention, to him the world is always new, too.

Willing to change. The unknown does not frighten the master student. In fact, she welcomes it—even the unknown in herself. We all have pictures of who we think we are, and these pictures can be useful. However, they can also prevent learning and growth. The master student is open to changes in her environment and in herself.

Able to organize and sort. The master student can take a large body of information and sift through it to discover relationships. He can play with information, organizing data by size, colour, function, timeliness, and hundreds of other categories.

Competent. Mastery of skills is important to the master student. When she learns mathematical formulas, she studies them until they become second nature. She practises until she knows them cold, then puts in a few extra minutes. She also is able to apply what she learns to new and different situations.

Joyful. More often than not, the master student is seen with a smile on his face—sometimes a smile at nothing in particular other than amazement at the world and his experience of it.

Able to suspend judgment. The master student has opinions and positions, and she is able to let go of them

when appropriate. She realizes she is more than her thoughts. She can quiet her internal dialogue and listen to an opposing viewpoint. She doesn't let judgment get in the way of learning. Rather than approaching discussions with a "Prove it to me and then I'll believe it" attitude, she asks herself, "What if this is true?" and explores possibilities.

Energetic. Notice the student with a spring in his step, the one who is enthusiastic and involved in class. When he reads, he often sits on the very edge of his chair, and he plays with the same intensity. He is a master student.

Well. Health is important to the master student, though not necessarily in the sense of being free of illness. Rather, she values her body and treats it with respect. She tends to her emotional and spiritual health, as well as her physical health.

Self-aware. The master student is willing to evaluate himself and his behaviour. He regularly tells the truth about his strengths and those aspects that could be improved.

Responsible. There is a difference between responsibility and blame, and the master student knows it well. She is willing to take responsibility for everything in her life—even for events that most people would blame on others.

For example, if a master student is served cold eggs in the cafeteria, she chooses to take responsibility for getting cold eggs. This is not the same as blaming herself for cold eggs. Rather, she looks for ways to change the situation and get what she wants. She could choose to eat breakfast earlier, or she might tell someone in the kitchen that the eggs are cold and request a change. The cold eggs might continue. Even then, the master student takes responsibility and gives herself the power to choose her response to the situation.

Willing to take risks. The master student often takes on projects with no guarantee of success. He participates in class dialogues at the risk of looking foolish. He tackles difficult essay topics. He welcomes the risk of a challenging course.

Willing to participate. Don't look for the master student on the sidelines. She's in the game. She is a player who can be counted on. She is willing to make a commitment and to follow through on it.

A generalist. The master student is interested in everything around him. He has a broad base of knowledge in many fields and can find value that is applicable to his specialties.

Willing to accept paradox. The word *paradox* comes from two Greek words, *para* (beyond) and *doxen* (opinion). A paradox is something that is beyond opinion or, more accurately, something that might seem contradictory or absurd yet might actually have meaning. For example: the master student can be committed to managing money and reaching her financial goals. At the same time, she can be totally detached from money, knowing that her real worth is independent of how much money she has. The master student recognizes the limitations of the mind and is at home with paradox. She can accept that ambiguity.

Courageous. The master student admits his fear and fully experiences it. For example, he will approach a tough exam as an opportunity to explore feelings of anxiety and tension related to the pressure to perform. He does not deny fear; he embraces it.

Self-directed. Rewards or punishments provided by others do not motivate the master student. Her motivation to learn comes from within.

Spontaneous. The master student is truly in the here and now. He is able to respond to the moment in fresh, surprising, and unplanned ways.

Relaxed about marks. Marks make the master student neither depressed nor euphoric. She recognizes that sometimes marks are important, and marks are not the only reason she studies. She does not measure her worth as a human being by the marks she receives.

Intuitive. The master student has an inner sense that cannot be explained by logic. He has learned to trust his feelings, and he works to develop this intuitive sense.

Creative. Where others see dull details and trivia, the master student sees opportunities to create. She can gather pieces of knowledge from a wide range of subjects and put them together in new ways. The master student is creative in every aspect of her life.

Willing to be uncomfortable. The master student does not place comfort first. When discomfort is necessary to reach a goal, he is willing to experience it. He can endure personal hardships and can look at unpleasant things with detachment.

Accepting. The master student accepts herself, the people around her, and the challenges that life offers.

Willing to laugh. The master student might laugh at any moment, and his sense of humour includes the ability to laugh at himself.

Going to school is a big investment. The stakes are high. It's OK to be serious about that, but you don't have to go to school on the deferred-fun program. A master student celebrates learning, and one of the best ways to do that is to have a laugh now and then.

Hungry. Human beings begin life with a natural appetite for knowledge. In some people it soon gets dulled. The master student has tapped that hunger, and it gives her a desire to learn for the sake of learning.

Willing to work. Once inspired, the master student is willing to follow through with sweat. He knows that genius and creativity are the result of persistence and work. When in high gear, the master student works with the intensity of a child at play.

Caring. A master student cares about knowledge and has a passion for ideas. She also cares about people and appreciates learning from others. She flourishes in a community that values "win-win" outcomes, cooperation, and love.

The master student in you. The master student is in all of us. By design, human beings are learning machines. We have an innate ability to learn, and all of us have room to grow and improve.

It is important to understand the difference between learning and being taught. Human beings can resist being taught anything. Carl Rogers (1969) goes so far as to say that anything that can be taught to a human being is either inconsequential or just plain harmful. What is important in education, Rogers asserts, is *learning*. And everyone has the ability to learn.

Unfortunately, people also learn to hide that ability. As they experience the pain that sometimes accompanies learning, they shut down. If a child experiences embarrassment in front of a group of people, he might learn to avoid similar situations. In doing so, he restricts his possibilities.

Some children "learn" that they are slow learners. If they learn it well enough, their behaviour comes to match that label.

As people grow older, they sometimes accumulate a growing list of ideas to defend, a catalogue of familiar experiences that discourages them from learning anything new.

Still, the master student within survives. To tap that resource, you don't need to acquire anything. You already have everything you need. Every day you can rediscover the natural learner within you. ✳

© Dana Heinemann/Shutterstock

Motivation— I'm just not in the mood

IN LARGE PART, this chapter is about your motivation to succeed in school. And a First Step in creating **motivation** is getting some definitions straight.

The terms *self-discipline*, *willpower*, and *motivation* are often used to describe something missing in ourselves. Time after time we invoke these words to explain another person's success—or our own shortcomings: "If I were more motivated, I'd get more involved in school." "Of course she got an A. She has self-discipline." "If I had more willpower, I'd lose weight." It seems that certain people are born with lots of motivation, while others miss out on it.

An alternative is to stop assuming that motivation is mysterious, determined at birth, or hard to come by. Perhaps what we call *motivation* is something that you already possess—or simply a habit that you can develop with practice. The following suggestions offer ways to do that.

Promise it. Motivation can come simply from being clear about your goals and acting on them. If you want to start a study group, you can commit yourself to inviting people and setting a time and place to meet. Promise your classmates that you'll do this, and ask them to hold you accountable. Self-discipline, willpower, motivation—none of these mysterious characteristics needs to get in your way. Just make a promise and keep your word.

Befriend your discomfort. Sometimes keeping your word means doing a task you'd rather put off. The mere thought of doing laundry, reading a chapter in a statistics book, or proofreading an essay can lead to discomfort. In the face of such discomfort, we can procrastinate. Or we can use this barrier as a means to get the job done.

Begin by investigating the discomfort. Notice the thoughts running through your head and speak them out loud: "I'd rather walk on a bed of coals than do this." "This is the last thing I want to do right now."

Also observe what's happening with your body. For example, are you breathing faster or slower than usual? Is your breathing shallow or deep? Are your shoulders tight? Do you feel any tension in your stomach?

Once you're in contact with your mind and body, stay with the discomfort a few minutes longer. Don't judge it as good or bad. Accepting the thoughts and body sensations robs them of power. They might still be there, but in time they can stop being a barrier for you.

Discomfort can be a gift—an opportunity to do valuable work on yourself. On the other side of discomfort lies mastery.

Change your mind—and your body. You can also get past discomfort by planting new thoughts in your mind or changing your physical stance. For example, instead of slumping in a chair, sit up straight or stand up. You can also get physically active by taking a short walk. Notice what happens to your discomfort.

Work with thoughts, too. Replace "I can't stand this" with "I'll feel great when this is done" or "Doing this will help me get something I want."

Sweeten the task. Sometimes it's just one aspect of a task that holds us back. We can stop procrastinating merely by changing that aspect. If distaste for our physical environment keeps us from studying, we can change that environment. Reading about social psychology might seem boring when we're alone in a dark corner of the house. Moving to a cheery, well-lit library can sweeten the task.

© Dmitriy Shironosov/Shutterstock

Talk about how bad it is. One way to get past negative attitudes is to take them to an extreme. When faced with an unpleasant task, launch into a no-holds-barred gripe session. Pull out all the stops: "There's no way I can start my income taxes now. This is terrible beyond words, an absolute disaster. This is a catastrophe of global proportions!" Griping taken this far can restore perspective. It shows how self-talk can turn inconveniences into crises.

Turn up the pressure. Sometimes motivation is a luxury. Pretend that the due date for your project has been moved up one month, one week, or one day. Raising the stress level slightly can spur you into action. Then the issue of motivation seems beside the point, and meeting the due date moves to the forefront.

Turn down the pressure. The mere thought of starting a huge task can induce anxiety. To get past this feeling, turn down the pressure by taking "baby steps." Divide a large project into small tasks. In 30 minutes or less, you could preview a book, create a rough outline for a paper, or solve two or three math problems. Careful planning can help you discover many such steps to make a big job doable.

Ask for support. Other people can become your allies in overcoming procrastination; for example, form a support group and declare what you intend to accomplish before each meeting. Then ask members to hold you accountable. If you want to begin exercising regularly, ask another person to walk with you three times weekly. People in support groups ranging from Alcoholics Anonymous to Weight Watchers know the power of this strategy.

Adopt a model. One strategy for succeeding at any task is to hang around the masters. Find someone you consider successful and spend time with her. Observe this person and use her as a model for your own behaviour. You can "try on" this person's actions and attitudes. Look for tools that feel right for you. This person can become a mentor for you.

Compare the payoffs to the costs. Behaviours such as cramming for exams or neglecting exercise have payoffs. Cramming might give us more time that's free of commitments. Neglecting exercise can give us more time to sleep.

One way to let go of such unwanted behaviours is first to celebrate them—even embrace them. We can openly acknowledge the payoffs.

Celebration can be especially powerful when we follow it up with the next step—determining the costs. For example, skipping a reading assignment can give you time to go to the movies. However, you might be unprepared for class and have twice as much to read the following week.

Maybe there is another way to get the payoff (going to the movies) without paying the cost (skipping the reading assignment). With some thoughtful weekly planning, you might choose to give up a few hours of television and end up with enough time to read the assignment *and* go to the movies.

Comparing the costs and benefits of any behaviour can fuel our motivation. We can choose new behaviours because they align with what we want most.

Do it later. At times, it's effective to save a task for later. For example, writing a resumé can wait until you've taken the time to analyse your job skills and map out your career goals. This is not a lack of motivation—it's planning.

When you do choose to do a task later, turn this decision into a promise. Estimate how long the task will take and schedule a specific date and time for it on your calendar.

Motivation can come simply from being clear about your goals and acting on them.

Heed the message. Sometimes lack of motivation carries a message that's worth heeding. An example is the student who studies accounting but seizes every chance to be with children. His chronic reluctance to read accounting textbooks might not be a problem.

Instead, it might reveal his desire to study elementary education. His original career choice might have come from the belief that "real men don't teach kindergarten."

In such cases, an apparent lack of motivation signals a deeper wisdom trying to get through.

What's stopping you from getting started on your schoolwork?

All of us sometimes have difficulty getting work done or find a million reasons to put off beginning a new task. If you have difficulty getting going on your homework or being prepared for tests, you have good company. About 70 percent of students report having chronic problems with **procrastination** (Pychyl, 2010)—putting things off until it is too late to get the task done properly. We all procrastinate, but when our behaviour starts to interfere with our success, we need to consider why. Why do we sometimes delay getting started on our essay until we don't have enough time to do a good job? Researchers have suggested a variety of reasons. Take a look at the list—later in the next chapter we will talk about strategies you can use to overcome procrastination, but for now consider if any of these reasons might apply to you. You procrastinate:

- If you give in to the immediate impulse of wanting to feel better now. Dr. Tim Pychyl from Carleton University in Ottawa suggests that this failure to self-regulate or control our own behaviour to achieve our goals interferes with many activities, from starting to exercise to stopping over-eating. As he suggests, it is easy to "give in to feel good" (2010) and avoid aversive activities like starting to study for finals.

- Because you fear failure and are pessimistic about the test outcome—the more you procrastinate the more anxious you become as deadlines loom. This is the most common reason given for procrastination (Brownlow & Reasinger, 2000).

- To protect your self-image of being a successful student, you create actual barriers to your own success—this is called self-handicapping (Brownlow & Reasinger, 2000). You avoid studying so that any poor test performance you suffer can be attributed to your lack of effort rather than lack of ability (Beck, Koons & Milgrim, 2000).

- Because you have a low level of self-esteem and just don't believe you can get it right (Brownlow & Reasinger, 2000).

- Because you are a perfectionist—if you can't get the paper done perfectly you won't finish it at all, or as a perfectionist you may set unrealistic goals for an assignment, then feel overwhelmed in meeting those goals.

- Because you have a hard time with what the task requires of you, such as a challenging new topic or having to use unfamiliar skills.

- Because you have a hard time setting goals or pursuing the goals you have.

Why does procrastination matter?
Research suggests that procrastination:

- Causes lower grades (Brownlow & Reasinger, 2000)

- Impacts your health (Pychyl, 2000)

- Makes you more dissatisfied with your courses (Brownlow & Reasinger, 2000)

- Leads to higher rates of course withdrawal (Pychyl, 2000)

- Makes you feel more negative in general (Pychyl, 2010)

So the next time you find yourself putting off studying, try to think about why that is and put into action some of the steps listed in the last article.

© Tim Pychyl and Paul Mason

Attitudes, affirmations, and visualizations

"I HAVE A BAD ATTITUDE." Some of us say this as if we were talking about having the flu. An attitude is certainly as strong as the flu, but it isn't something we have to succumb to or accept.

Some of us see our attitudes the way we see our height or eye colour: "I might not like it, but I might as well accept it."

Acceptance is certainly a worthwhile approach to things we cannot change. When it comes to attitudes, acceptance is not necessary—attitudes can change. We don't have to live our lives with an attitude that doesn't work.

Attitudes are powerful. They create behaviour. If your attitude is that you're not very interesting at a party, then your behaviour will probably match your attitude, and you might act like a bore. If your attitude is that you are fun at a party, then your behaviour is more likely to be playful. Soon you are the life of the party. All that has to change is your attitude.

Success in school starts with attitudes. Some attitudes will help you benefit from all the money and time you invest in higher education. Other attitudes will render your investment worthless. You can change your attitudes through regular practice with affirmations and visualizations.

Affirm it. An **affirmation** is a statement describing what you want. The most effective affirmations are personal, positive, and written in the present tense.

Affirmations have an almost magical power. They are used successfully by athletes and actors, executives and ballerinas, and thousands of people who have succeeded in their lives. Affirmations can change your attitudes and behaviours.

To use affirmations, first determine what you want, then describe yourself as if you already have it. To get what you want from your education, you could write,

"I, Mike Jones, am a master student. I take full responsibility for my education. I learn with joy, and I use my experiences in each course to create the life that I want."

If you decide that you want a wonderful job, you might write, "I, Susan Webster, have a wonderful job. I respect and love my colleagues, and they feel the same way about me. I look forward to going to work each day."

Effective affirmations include detail. Use brand names, people's names, and your own name. Involve all of your senses—sight, sound, smell, taste, touch. Take a positive approach. Instead of saying, "I am not fat," say, "I am slender."

Once you have written an affirmation, repeat it. Practise saying it out loud several times a day. Do this at a regular time, such as just before you go to sleep or just after you wake up. Sit in a chair in a relaxed position. Take a few deep and relaxing breaths, and then repeat your affirmation with emotion. It's also effective to look in a mirror while saying the affirmation. Keep looking and repeating until you are saying your affirmation with conviction.

Visualize it. You can improve your golf swing, tennis serve, or batting average while lying in bed. You can become a better driver, speaker, or cook while sitting silently in a chair. In line at the grocery store, you can improve your ability to type or to take tests. These goals are all possible through visualization—the technique of seeing yourself being successful.

Here's one way to begin. Choose what you want to improve. Then describe in writing what it would look like, sound like, and feel like to have that improvement in your life. If you are learning to play the piano, write down briefly what you would see, hear, and feel if you were playing skilfully. If you want to improve your relationships with your children, write down what you would

Decide what you want to improve, and write down what it would look like, sound like, and feel like to have that improvement in your life.

see, hear, and feel if you were communicating with them successfully.

Once you have a sketch of what it would be like to be successful, practise it in your imagination. Whenever you toss the basketball, it swishes through the net. Every time you invite someone out on a date, the person says yes. Each test the teacher hands back to you is graded A. Practise at least once a day. Then wait for the results to unfold in your life.

You can also use visualizations to replay errors. When you make a mistake, replay it in your imagination. After a bad golf shot, stop and imagine yourself making that same shot again, this time very successfully. If you just had a discussion with your roommate that turned into a fight, replay it successfully.

Visualizations and affirmations can restructure your attitudes and behaviours. Be clear about what you want—and then practise it. ✳

Attitude replacements

You can use affirmations to replace a negative attitude with a positive one. There are no limitations, other than your imagination and your willingness to practise. Here are some sample affirmations. Modify them to suit your individual hopes and dreams, and then practise them. The article "Attitudes, Affirmations, and Visualizations" explains ways to use these attitude replacements.

I, _____, am healthy.

I, _____, have abundant energy and vitality throughout the day.

I, _____, exercise regularly.

I, _____, work effectively with many different kinds of people.

I, _____, eat wisely.

I, _____, plan my days and use time wisely.

I, _____, have a powerful memory.

I, _____, take tests calmly and confidently.

I, _____, have a sense of self-worth that is independent of my test scores.

I, _____, am a great speller.

I, _____, fall asleep quickly and sleep soundly.

I, _____, am smart.

I, _____, am creative.

I, _____, am aware of and sensitive to other people's moods.

I, _____, have relationships that are mutually satisfying.

I, _____, work hard and contribute to other people through my job.

I, _____, know ways to play and have fun.

I, _____, focus my attention easily.

I, _____, like myself.

I, _____, am a worthwhile person even though I am _____.

I, _____, am relaxed in all situations, including _____.

I, _____, always live my life in positive ways for the highest good of all people.

WWW To hear an online version of these affirmations, link to **www.bams5ce.nelson.com**

exercise 6

Reprogram your attitude

You can employ affirmations and visualizations to successfully reprogram your attitudes and behaviours. Use this exercise to change your approach to any situation in your life.

Step 1

Pick something in your life that you would like to change. It can be related to anything—relationships, work, money, or personal skills. Below, write a brief description of what you choose to change.

_____

_____

_____

Step 2

Add more details about the change you described in Step 1. Write down how you would like the change to come about. Be outlandish. Imagine that you are about to ask your fairy godmother for a wish that you know she will grant. Be detailed in your description of your wish.

_____

_____

_____

Step 3

Here comes the fairy godmother. Use affirmations and visualizations to start yourself on the path to creating exactly what you wrote about in Step 2. Below, write at least two affirmations that describe your dream wish. Also, briefly outline a

visualization that you can use to picture your wish. Be specific, detailed, and positive.

_____

_____

_____

_____

Step 4

Put your new attitudes to work. Set up a schedule to practise them. Let the first time be right now. Then set up at least five other times and places that you intend to practise your affirmations and visualizations.

I intend to relax and practise my affirmations and visualizations for at least five minutes on the following dates and at the times and location(s) given.

Date	Time	Location
1.		
2.		
3.		
4.		
5.		

WWW Complete this exercise online @
www.bams5ce.nelson.com

Master Student Profiles

Each chapter of this text has an example of a person who embodies several qualities of a master student. As you read about these people and others like them, ask yourself: How can I apply this? Look for the timeless qualities in the people you read about. Many of the strategies used by master students from another time or place are tools that you can use today.

The master students in this book were chosen because they demonstrate unusual and effective ways to learn.

Remember that these are just 12 examples of master students (one for each chapter). You can read more about them in the Master Student Hall of Fame at **www.bams5ce.nelson.com**. Also reflect on other master students you've read about or know personally. As you meet new people, look for those who excel at learning. The master student is not a vague or remote ideal. Rather, master students are all among us.

In fact, there's one living inside your skin.

practising critical thinking

Review the article "The Master Student" in this chapter. Then skim the master student profiles throughout this book. Finally, choose one of the people profiled and describe in the space below how this person embodies the qualities of a master student.

Peter A. Facione, founder of Measured Reasons, LLC, a Los Angeles-based research and consulting company, and author of the California Critical Thinking Skills Test and the California Critical Thinking Disposition Inventory. Check out Dr. Facione's new book, *Think Critically*, for a full set of contemporary and powerful critical thinking skill-building exercises.

Source: *Critical Thinking: What It Is and Why It Counts* by Peter A. Facione. The latest version of *Critical Thinking: What It Is and Why It Counts* is available to students and faculty as a free download from www.insightassessment.com.

WWW Complete this exercise online @
www.bams5ce.nelson.com

© Edmond Van Hoorick/Digital Vision/Getty Images

IDEAS ARE TOOLS

There are many ideas in this book. When you first encounter them, don't believe any of them. Instead, think of them as tools.

For example, you use a hammer for a purpose—to drive a nail. When you use a new hammer, you might notice its shape, its weight, and its balance. You don't try to figure out whether the hammer is "right." You just use it. If it works, you use it again. If it doesn't work, you get a different hammer.

People have plenty of room in their lives for different kinds of hammers, but they tend to limit their capacity for different kinds of ideas. A new idea, at some level, is a threat to their very being—unlike a new hammer, which is simply a new hammer.

Most of us have a built-in desire to be right. Our ideas, we often think, represent ourselves.

Imagine someone defending a hammer. Picture this person holding up a hammer and declaring, "Oh, hammer, we stand on guard for thee. There are only two kinds of people in this world: people who believe in this hammer and people who don't."

That ridiculous picture makes a point. This book is not a manifesto. It's a toolbox, and tools are meant to be used.

If you read about a tool in this book that doesn't sound "right" or one that sounds a little goofy, remember that the ideas here are for using, not necessarily for believing. Suspend your judgment. Test the idea for yourself. If it works, use it. If it doesn't, don't use it.

Any tool—whether it's a hammer, a computer program, or a study technique—is designed to do a specific job. A master mechanic carries a variety of tools because no single tool works for all jobs. If you throw a tool away because it doesn't work in one situation, you won't be able to pull it out later when it's just what you need. So if an idea doesn't work for you and you are satisfied that you gave it a fair chance, don't throw it away. File it away instead. The idea might come in handy soon.

And remember, this book is not about figuring out the "right" way. Even the "ideas are tools" approach is not "right."

It's a hammer … (or maybe a saw).

 Complete this exercise online @
www.bams5ce.nelson.com

Put It to **WORK**

chapter 1

◄ ◄ ◄ ◄
- Quiz
- Skills Snapshot
- Master Student Profile

t work, you can benefit by remembering the concept of learning styles. In the workplace, people act in a variety of ways that express their preferences for perceiving information, processing ideas, and acting on what they learn.

The worker who's continually moving might prefer concrete experience over memos and meetings. She likes to learn by doing. The person who's usually on the phone might prefer to learn by listening and talking. She likes to reflect on her experiences and forge relationships.

You might have a supervisor who enjoys working with concepts as much as working with people. She might prefer to decide on a long-range goal and a detailed plan before taking action.

Discover learning styles in your workplace

You can learn a lot about your co-workers' learning styles simply by observing them during the workday. Just look for clues.

One clue is how they *approach a learning task*. Some people process new information or ideas by sitting quietly and reading or writing. When learning to use a piece of equipment, such as a new computer, they'll read the instruction manual first. Those who use a trial-and-error approach will skip the manual, unpack all the boxes, and start setting up equipment. Other coworkers might ask a more experienced colleague to guide them in person, step by step.

Another clue is *word choice*. Some people like to process information visually. You might hear them say, "I'll look into that" or "Give me the big picture first." Those who like to solve problems verbally might say, "Let's talk though this problem" or "I hear you!" In contrast, some of your co-workers express themselves using body sensations ("This product feels great") or action ("Let's run with this idea and see what happens"). In addition, notice *process preferences*—patterns in the way that your co-workers meet goals. When attending meetings, for example, some might stick closely to the agenda and keep an eye on the clock. Others might prefer to "go with the flow," even if it means working an extra hour or scrapping the agenda.

Once you've discovered such differences among your co-workers, look for ways to accommodate their learning styles.

Gear presentations to different learning styles

When you want co-workers to agree to a new procedure or promote a new product, you'll probably make a speech or give a presentation. To persuade more people, gear your presentation to several learning styles.

For example, some people want to see the overall picture first. You can start by saying "This product has four major features." Then explain the benefits of each feature in order.

© photos.com

Also allow time for verbally oriented people to ask questions and make comments. For those who prefer a hands-on approach, offer them a chance to try out the new product themselves—literally to "get the feel of it."

Finish with a handout that includes plenty of illustrations, charts, and step-by-step instructions. Visual learners and people who like to think abstractly will appreciate it.

Gear projects to different learning styles

When working on project teams, look for ways to combine complementary skills. If you're adept at planning, find someone who excels at active experimentation. Also seek people who can reflect on and interpret the team members' experiences. Pooling different learning styles allows you to draw on everyone's strengths.

Remember that a person's learning style is both stable and dynamic. People gravitate toward the kinds of tasks they've succeeded at in the past. They can also broaden their learning styles by taking on new tasks to reinforce different aspects of learning. For example, ask people who enjoy taking immediate action to step back more often and reflect on the overall purpose of a project.

QUIZ

Name_____   Date____/____/____

1. Explain three ways that you can use knowledge of your learning styles to succeed in school.

2. Define the term *mastery* as it is used in this chapter.

3. The First Step technique refers only to telling the truth about your areas for improvement. True or False? Explain your answer.

4. The four modes of learning are associated with certain questions. List the appropriate question for each mode.

5. Write an example of an effective and ineffective affirmation. Explain why you chose these examples.

6. Briefly describe how being aware of your own multiple intelligences can help you thrive in higher education.

7. According to the Power Process: "Ideas are tools." If you want the ideas in this book to work, you must believe in them. True or False? Explain your answer.

8. Explain what an affirmation is and give an example of one related to learning that you can review daily.

9. Define the word metacognition and give an example of it.

10. Explain several reasons why we all might procrastinate on occasion and three strategies of what you can do to overcome it.

Skills SNAPSHOT

The Discovery Wheel in this chapter includes a section labelled *Attitude*. For the next 10 to 15 minutes, go beyond your initial responses to that exercise. Take a snapshot of your skills as they exist today, after reading and doing this chapter.

Begin by reflecting on some recent experiences. Then take another step toward mastery by choosing to follow up on your reflections with a specific action.

SELF-AWARENESS

Three things I do well as a student are . . .

Three areas in which I'd like to improve as a student are . . .

STYLES

If asked to describe my learning style in one sentence, I would say that I am . . .

To become a more flexible learner, I could . . .

FLEXIBILITY

When I disagree with what someone else says, my first response is usually to . . .

In these situations, I could be more effective by . . .

NEXT ACTION

I'll know that I've adopted new attitudes to support my success when I'm able to say . . .

To reach that level of mastery, the most important thing I can do next is to . . .

MASTER STUDENT Profile

© Kirsty Wigglesworth/Associated Press

Canada's youngest ever elected official when he became a Nanaimo city councillor at the age of 18. He graduated from SFU in 2006 with a BBA in Business & Economics, and is currently the CEO of Hiretheworld.com.

 Find more biographical information about Terry Beech at the Master Student Hall of Fame @

www.bams5ce.nelson.com

Terry Beech
. . . is willing to work

Terry Beech remains the youngest British Columbian to win a city councillor position and the aspiring federal politician will likely hold that record for years to come, unless another successful youngster has his or her 18th birthday within seven months of a civic election.

The 27-year-old Simon Fraser University graduate packed up his Burnaby suite this week, preparing for his journey to Oxford University, where he will study for his Masters degree in entrepreneurship and electronic business. As he packs, he writes. He writes about his 1999 run for council in Nanaimo, hoping that a publisher will pick up his story. The book's revenue could help pay for his $100,000 per-year tuition.

Beech comes from a modest background. He and his family drank watered-down juice to make it last longer and they rarely had second helpings of meat at dinner because there were none. But what he lacked in "financial resources" he made up for with a pile of ingenuity and a mound of determination.

His year-long campaign grabbed the attention of his fellow citizens and his charismatic speeches charmed audiences who were impressed with his knowledge of long-standing issues in the community.

Barely out of high school, he entered public office in 1999, the same year he started classes at Malaspina University-College. At 18, he was less than half the age of every council member alongside him. Lloyd Sherry had been a councillor longer than Beech had been alive.

The youngster made it look incredibly easy, but a successful campaign takes dedication and strategy.

He found an interest in municipal politics while coaching the debate team during his senior year at John Barsby Community School in the city's south end. His orators frequently discussed local issues, then they visited council chambers to see how politicians approached the same topics. It was winter of 1998 when he learned about an 18-year-old who just became mayor in New York state.

An inspired Beech thought he had a better chance to earn one of the eight seats that flanked incumbent mayor Gary Korpan.

The voracious researcher read through 20 years of newspaper archives, learning the long-standing issues of his city. There could be no room for error. He knew the current affairs, but needed to prepare for the elders who could rely on memory.

Two fellow students from his debate team, a senior and a junior, managed his campaign. With the brain trust assembled, his team set to work.

Fall approached and the teenage strategists campaigned hard. Beech made a transparent photocopy of an election sign and borrowed an overhead projector from school. The 8 × 10 sheet of plastic translated into a 13-by-nine-foot campaign billboard after he traced the projection onto the wall of his home and painted the sign purple.

By Halloween, he and some friends bought nine pumpkins from Shady Mile Farm. They carved one letter into each of the orange holiday fruit and dropped candles inside. Slowing motorists along

Jingle Pot Road that night could read the imperative statement: VOTE BEECH.

A crowd of youngsters doled out pamphlets and candy, talking to anyone about the young man determined to represent them on council.

Then came the debates. The underdog honours graduate came into the Coast Bastion Hotel before election "fully prepared" to talk about all issues. "I was the only one who prepared a speech," he said. "I understood the issues and spoke to the crowd without being nervous. I definitely performed better than anyone there."

It took nearly an hour for Beech to leave the building because people wanted to meet the young inspiration. With a support base from the south-end community, he and his team pushed their way into the north end, distributing flyers to anyone who would take one.

The youth card worked to his advantage among the university students, but he quickly dropped the label "youth candidate," given to him by the public. Beech wrote a letter to the editor demanding people drop this condescending moniker.

"We would never talk about my age," he said of his campaign team. And the strategies paid off.

Once elected, Beech had two lives. He spent two years at Malaspina taking business and economics, before transferring to Simon Fraser University, where he finished his degree. The commute took stamina—four days in the Harbour City and three in Vancouver.

The student councillor learned to thoroughly research any decision he made during his term in office. He had to with the whole city watching.

He encourages any new candidate to know the issues of the community well before the election. "If you're a newcomer, creativity is really important. Let's face it, the incumbents have the advantage and you need to get your name out there. Between the sign, the pumpkins and my debate, people were talking about us."

Source: "Youngest councillor made win look easy," *Nanaimo Daily News*, September 5, 2008. Reprinted with permission. Retrieved from www.canada.com/nanaimodailynews/story.html?id=9b051926-d414-4c40-bcea-1acef06743ff/

2 | Time

Master Student Map

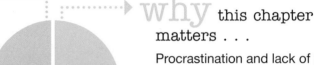

as you read, ask yourself

what if . . .

I could meet my goals with time to spare?

why this chapter matters . . .

Procrastination and lack of planning can quickly undermine your success in school.

what is included . . .

- You've got the time   71
- Setting and achieving goals   77
- The ABC daily to-do list   81
- More strategies for planning   84
- Stop procrastination NOW   86
- 25 ways to get the most out of now   89
- Beyond time management: Stay focused on what matters   94
- Gearing up: Using a long-term planner   100
- Power Process: Be here now   102
- Master Student Profile: Chantal Petitclerc   106

how you can use this chapter . . .

- Discover the details about how you currently use time.
- Set goals that make a difference in the quality of your life.
- Know exactly what to do today, this week, and this month to achieve your goals.
- Eliminate procrastination.

MASTER STUDENTS in *action*

I have found that it is essential to keep a constantly updated calendar and personal planner. Without my own planner, I would most likely draw a blank as to what I need to accomplish for the day, week, month, and beyond. I recommend that any student use both as a means of keeping organized.

—DEEANNA MOSHER

You've got the time

THE WORDS *planning* and *time management* can call forth images of restriction and control. You might visualize a prune-faced Scrooge hunched over your shoulder, stopwatch in hand, telling you what to do every minute. Bad news.

Good news: You do have enough time for the things you want to do. All it takes is learning to plan.

Time is an equal opportunity resource. All of us, regardless of gender, race, creed, or ethnicity, have exactly the same number of hours in a week. No matter how newsworthy we are, no matter how rich or poor, we get 168 hours to spend each week—no more, no less.

Time is also an unusual commodity. It cannot be saved. You can't stockpile time like wood for the stove or food for the winter. It can't be seen, felt, touched, tasted, or smelled. You can't sense time directly. Even scientists and philosophers find it hard to describe. Because time is so elusive, it is easy to ignore. That doesn't bother time at all. Time is perfectly content to remain hidden until you are nearly out of it. And when you are out of it, you are out of it.

Time is a non-renewable resource. If you're out of wood, you can chop some more. If you're out of money, you can earn a little extra. If you're out of love, there is still hope. If you're out of health, it can often be restored. But when you're out of time, that's it. When this minute is gone, it's gone.

Time seems to pass at varying speeds. Sometimes it crawls and sometimes it's faster than a speeding bullet. On Friday afternoons, classroom clocks can creep. After you've worked a 10-hour day, reading the last few pages of an economics assignment can turn minutes into hours. A year in school can stretch out to an eternity.

At the other end of the spectrum, time flies. There are moments when you are so absorbed in what you're doing that hours disappear like magic.

Approach time as if you are in control. Sometimes it seems that your friends control your time, that your boss controls your time, that your instructors or your parents or your kids or somebody else controls your time. Maybe that is not true. When you say you don't have enough time, you might really be saying that you are not spending the time you *do* have in the way that you want.

Everything written about time management boils down to two topics. One is knowing exactly *what* you want. The other is knowing *how* to get what you want. State your wants as written goals. Then choose activities that will help you meet those goals.

Spend your most valuable resource in the way you choose. Start by observing how you use time. On the following pages, Exercise 7: The Time Monitor/Time Plan Process gives you this opportunity. ✱

journal entry 7

Discovery/Intention Statement

Create value from this chapter

Think back to a time during the past year when you rushed to finish a project or when you did not find time for an activity that was important to you. List one thing you might have done to create this outcome.

I discovered that I . . .

_____

_____

_____

Take a few minutes to skim this chapter. Find three to five articles that might help you avoid such outcomes in the future and list them below.

Title	Page number
_____	_____
_____	_____
_____	_____

If you don't have time to read these articles in depth right now, schedule a time to do so.

I intend to . . .

_____

_____

_____

_____

exercise
The Time Monitor/ Time Plan Process

The purpose of this exercise is to transform time into a knowable and predictable resource. Complete this exercise over a two-week period:

- During the first week, you *monitor* your activities to get detailed information about how you actually spend your time.
- After you analyze your first week in Journal Entry 8, you *plan* the second week.
- During the second week, you *monitor* your activity again and compare it with your plan.
- Based on everything you've learned, you *plan* again.

For this exercise, monitor your time in 15-minute intervals, 24 hours a day, for seven days. Record how much time you spend sleeping, eating, studying, attending lectures, travelling to and from class, working, watching television, listening to music, taking care of the kids, running errands—everything.

If this sounds crazy, hang on for a minute. This exercise is not about keeping track of the rest of your life in 15-minute intervals. It is an opportunity to become conscious of how you spend your time, your life. Use the Time Monitor/Time Plan process only for as long as it is helpful to do so.

When you know how your time is spent, you can find ways to adjust and manage it so that you spend your life doing the things that are most important to you. Monitoring your time is a critical first step toward putting you in control of your life.

Here's an eye opener for many students. If you think you already have a good idea of how you manage time, predict how many hours you will spend in a week on each category of activity listed in the form on page 74. (Four categories are already provided; you can add more at any time.) Make your predictions before your first week of monitoring. Write them in the margin to the left of each category. After monitoring your time for one week, see how accurate your predictions were.

Following are charts for monitoring and planning, along with instructions for using them. Some students choose to keep track of their time on calendars, campus planners, mobile apps, or software designed for this purpose. You might even develop your own form for monitoring your time.

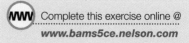 Complete this exercise online @
www.bams5ce.nelson.com

1. **Get to know the Time Monitor/Time Plan.** Look at the Time Monitor/Time Plan on page 73. Note that each day has two columns, one labelled "monitor" and the other labelled "plan." During the first week, use only the "monitor" column just like this student did.

On Monday, the student in this example got up at 6:45 a.m., showered, and got dressed. He finished this activity and began breakfast at 7:15. He put this new activity in at the time he began and drew a line just above it. He ate from 7:15 to 7:45. It took him 15 minutes to walk to class (7:45 to 8:00), and he attended classes from 8:00 to 11:00.

When you begin an activity, write it down next to the time you begin. Round off to the nearest 15 minutes. If, for example, you begin eating at 8:06, enter your starting time as 8:00. Over time, it will probably even out. In any case, you will be close enough to realize the benefits of this exercise.

Do this exercise online at www.bams5ce.nelson .com Keep your Time Monitor/Time Plan with you every minute you are awake for one week. Take a few moments every two or three hours to record what you've done. Or enter a note each time you change activities.

2. **Remember to use your Time Monitor/Time Plan.** It might be easy to forget to fill out your Time Monitor/Time Plan. One way to remember is to create a visual reminder. You can use this technique for any activity you want to remember.

Take a moment to close your eyes, and imagine that you see your Time Monitor/Time Plan. Imagine that it has arms and legs and is as big as a person. Picture the form sitting at your desk at home, in your car, in one of your classrooms, or in your favourite chair. Visualize it sitting wherever you're likely to sit. When you sit down, the Time Monitor/Time Plan will get squashed.

You can make this image more effective by adding sound effects. The Time Monitor/Time Plan might scream, "Get off me!" Or since time can be related to money, you might associate the Time Monitor/Time Plan with the sound of an old-fashioned cash register. Imagine that every time you sit down, a cash register rings to remind you it's there.

MONDAY _9_ / _12_		
Monitor		**Plan**
6:45	Get up	
	Shower	
7:00		7:00
7:15	Breakfast	
7:30		
7:45	Walk to class	
8:00	Econ 1	8:00
8:15		
8:30		
8:45		
9:00		9:00
9:15		
9:30		
9:45		
10:00	Bio 1	10:00
10:15		
10:30		
10:45		
11:00		11:00
11:15	Study	
11:30		
11:45		
12:00		12:00
12:15	Lunch	
12:30		
12:45		
1:00		1:00
1:15	Eng. Lit	
1:30		
1:45		
2:00		2:00
2:15	Coffeehouse	
2:30		
2:45		
3:00		3:00
3:15		
3:30		
3:45		
4:00		4:00
4:15	Study	
4:30		
4:45		
5:00		5:00
5:15	Dinner	
5:30		
5:45		
6:00		6:00
6:15		
6:30	Babysit	
6:45		
7:00		7:00

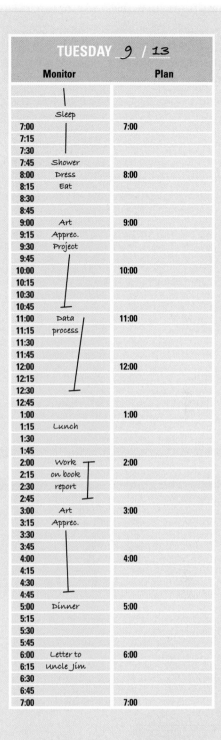

TUESDAY _9_ / _13_		
Monitor		**Plan**
	Sleep	
7:00		7:00
7:15		
7:30		
7:45	Shower	
8:00	Dress	8:00
8:15	Eat	
8:30		
8:45		
9:00	Art	9:00
9:15	Apprec.	
9:30	Project	
9:45		
10:00		10:00
10:15		
10:30		
10:45		
11:00	Data	11:00
11:15	process	
11:30		
11:45		
12:00		12:00
12:15		
12:30		
12:45		
1:00		1:00
1:15	Lunch	
1:30		
1:45		
2:00	Work	2:00
2:15	on book	
2:30	report	
2:45		
3:00	Art	3:00
3:15	Apprec.	
3:30		
3:45		
4:00		4:00
4:15		
4:30		
4:45		
5:00	Dinner	5:00
5:15		
5:30		
5:45		
6:00	Letter to	6:00
6:15	Uncle Jim	
6:30		
6:45		
7:00		7:00

3. **Evaluate the Time Monitor/Time Plan.** After you've monitored your time for one week, group your activities together by categories. The form on page 74 lists the categories "sleep," "class," "study," and "meals." Think of other categories you could add. "Grooming" might include showering, putting on make-up, brushing teeth, and getting dressed. "Travel" can include walking, driving, taking the bus, and riding your bike. Other categories might be "exercise," "entertainment," "work," "television," "domestic," and "children."

Write in the categories that work for you and then do the following:

- Guess how many hours you *think* you spent on each category of activity. List these hours in the "Estimated" column.

- List the *actual* number of hours you spent on each activity, adding up the figures from your daily time monitoring. List these hours in the "Monitored" column. Make sure that the grand total of all categories is 168 hours.

- Now take a minute, and let these numbers sink in. Compare the totals in the "Estimated" and "Monitored" columns.

Notice your reactions. You might be surprised. You might feel disappointed or even angry about where your time goes.

Use those feelings as motivation to plan your time differently. Go to the "Planned" column, and choose how much time you *want* to spend on various categories during the coming week. As you do this, allow yourself to have fun. Approach planning in the spirit of adventure. Think of yourself as an artist who's creating a new life.

In several months you might want to take another detailed look at how you spend your life. Fill in the "Monitor" and "Plan" columns on pages 75–76 simultaneously. Use a continuous cycle of monitoring and planning to get the full benefits of this exercise for the rest of your life. Let time management become more than a technique. Transform it into a habit—a constant awareness of how you spend your lifetime.

WEEK OF ___ / ___ / ___ /		
Category	**Monitored**	**Planned**
Sleep		
Class		
Study		
Meals		

MONDAY __ / __ / __ /		TUESDAY __ / __ / __ /		WEDNESDAY __ / __ / __ /	
Monitor	**Plan**	**Monitor**	**Plan**	**Monitor**	**Plan**
7:00	7:00	7:00	7:00	7:00	7:00
7:15		7:15		7:15	
7:30		7:30		7:30	
7:45		7:45		7:45	
8:00	8:00	8:00	8:00	8:00	8:00
8:15		8:15		8:15	
8:30		8:30		8:30	
8:45		8:45		8:45	
9:00	9:00	9:00	9:00	9:00	9:00
9:15		9:15		9:15	
9:30		9:30		9:30	
9:45		9:45		9:45	
10:00	10:00	10:00	10:00	10:00	10:00
10:15		10:15		10:15	
10:30		10:30		10:30	
10:45		10:45		10:45	
11:00	11:00	11:00	11:00	11:00	11:00
11:15		11:15		11:15	
11:30		11:30		11:30	
11:45		11:45		11:45	
12:00	12:00	12:00	12:00	12:00	12:00
12:15		12:15		12:15	
12:30		12:30		12:30	
12:45		12:45		12:45	
1:00	1:00	1:00	1:00	1:00	1:00
1:15		1:15		1:15	
1:30		1:30		1:30	
1:45		1:45		1:45	
2:00	2:00	2:00	2:00	2:00	2:00
2:15		2:15		2:15	
2:30		2:30		2:30	
2:45		2:45		2:45	
3:00	3:00	3:00	3:00	3:00	3:00
3:15		3:15		3:15	
3:30		3:30		3:30	
3:45		3:45		3:45	
4:00	4:00	4:00	4:00	4:00	4:00
4:15		4:15		4:15	
4:30		4:30		4:30	
4:45		4:45		4:45	
5:00	5:00	5:00	5:00	5:00	5:00
5:15		5:15		5:15	
5:30		5:30		5:30	
5:45		5:45		5:45	
6:00	6:00	6:00	6:00	6:00	6:00
6:15		6:15		6:15	
6:30		6:30		6:30	
6:45		6:45		6:45	
7:00	7:00	7:00	7:00	7:00	7:00
7:15		7:15		7:15	
7:30		7:30		7:30	
7:45		7:45		7:45	
8:00	8:00	8:00	8:00	8:00	8:00
8:15		8:15		8:15	
8:30		8:30		8:30	
8:45		8:45		8:45	
9:00	9:00	9:00	9:00	9:00	9:00
9:15		9:15		9:15	
9:30		9:30		9:30	
9:45		9:45		9:45	
10:00	10:00	10:00	10:00	10:00	10:00
10:15		10:15		10:15	
10:30		10:30		10:30	
10:45		10:45		10:45	
11:00	11:00	11:00	11:00	11:00	11:00
11:15		11:15		11:15	
11:30		11:30		11:30	
11:45		11:45		11:45	
12:00	12:00	12:00	12:00	12:00	12:00

THURSDAY ___ / ___ / ___ /		FRIDAY ___ / ___ / ___ /		SATURDAY ___ / ___ / ___ /	
Monitor	**Plan**	**Monitor**	**Plan**	**Monitor**	**Plan**
7:00	7:00	7:00	7:00		
7:15		7:15			
7:30		7:30			
7:45		7:45			
8:00	8:00	8:00	8:00		
8:15		8:15			
8:30		8:30			
8:45		8:45			
9:00	9:00	9:00	9:00		
9:15		9:15			
9:30		9:30			
9:45		9:45			
10:00	10:00	10:00	10:00		
10:15		10:15			
10:30		10:30			
10:45		10:45			
11:00	11:00	11:00	11:00		
11:15		11:15			
11:30		11:30			
11:45		11:45			
12:00	12:00	12:00	12:00		
12:15		12:15			
12:30		12:30			
12:45		12:45			
1:00	1:00	1:00	1:00		
1:15		1:15			
1:30		1:30			
1:45		1:45			
2:00	2:00	2:00	2:00		
2:15		2:15			
2:30		2:30			
2:45		2:45			
3:00	3:00	3:00	3:00	**SUNDAY ___ / ___ / ___ /**	
3:15		3:15			
3:30		3:30		**Monitor**	**Plan**
3:45		3:45			
4:00	4:00	4:00	4:00		
4:15		4:15			
4:30		4:30			
4:45		4:45			
5:00	5:00	5:00	5:00		
5:15		5:15			
5:30		5:30			
5:45		5:45			
6:00	6:00	6:00	6:00		
6:15		6:15			
6:30		6:30			
6:45		6:45			
7:00	7:00	7:00	7:00		
7:15		7:15			
7:30		7:30			
7:45		7:45			
8:00	8:00	8:00	8:00		
8:15		8:15			
8:30		8:30			
8:45		8:45			
9:00	9:00	9:00	9:00		
9:15		9:15			
9:30		9:30			
9:45		9:45			
10:00	10:00	10:00	10:00		
10:15		10:15			
10:30		10:30			
10:45		10:45			
11:00	11:00	11:00	11:00		
11:15		11:15			
11:30		11:30			
11:45		11:45			
12:00	12:00	12:00	12:00		

Many of us have vague, idealized notions of what we want out of life. These notions float among the clouds in our heads. They are wonderful, fuzzy, safe thoughts such as "I want to be a good person," "I want to be financially secure," or "I want to be happy."

Setting and achieving goals

SUCH OUTCOMES ARE great possible goals. Left in a generalized form, however, these goals can leave us confused about ways to actually achieve them. If you really want to meet a goal, translate it into specific, concrete behaviours. Find out what that goal looks like. Listen to what it sounds like. Pick it up and feel how heavy that goal is. Inspect the switches, valves, joints, cogs, and fastenings of the goal. Make your goal as real as a hammer.

There is nothing vague or fuzzy about hammers. You can see them, feel them, and hear them. They have a clear function. Goals can be every bit as real and useful.

Writing down your goals exponentially increases your chances of meeting them. Writing exposes undefined terms, unrealistic time frames, and other symptoms of fuzzy thinking. If you've been completing Intention Statements as explained in the Introduction to this book, then you've already had experience writing goals. Goals and Intention Statements both address changes you want to make in your behaviour, your values, your circumstances—or all of these. To keep track of your goals, write each one on a separate index card or key them all into a word processing file on your computer.

There are many useful methods for setting goals. The following is one of them. This method is based on writing specific goals in several time frames and areas of your life. Experiment with it and modify it as you see fit. You're also encouraged to reflect regularly on your goals. The key words to remember are specific, time, areas, and reflect. Combine the first letter of each word and you get the acronym STAR. Use this acronym STAR to remember the suggestions that follow.

Write specific goals. In writing, state your goals as observable actions or measurable results. Think in detail about how things will be different once your goals are attained. List the changes in what you'd see, feel, touch, taste, hear, be, do, or have.

Suppose that one of your goals is to become a better student by studying harder. You're headed in a powerful direction; now go for the specifics. Translate that goal into a concrete action, such as "I will study two hours for every hour I'm in class." Specific goals make clear

what actions are needed or what results are expected. Consider these examples:

Vague goal	Specific goal
Get a good education	Graduate with a B.Sc degree in engineering, with honours, by 2016
Enhance my spiritual life	Meditate for 15 minutes daily
Improve my appearance	Lose six pounds during the next six months

When stated specifically, a goal might look different to you. If you examine it closely, a goal you once thought you wanted might not be something you want after all. Or you might discover that you want to choose a new path to achieve a goal that you are sure you want.

Write goals in several time frames. To get a comprehensive vision of your future, write down:

- *Long-term goals*. Long-term goals represent major targets in your life. These goals can take 5 to 20 years to achieve. In some cases, they will take a lifetime. They can include goals in education, careers, personal relationships, travel, financial security—whatever is important to you. Consider the answers to the following questions as you create your long-term goals: What do you want to accomplish in your life? Do you want your life to make a statement? If so, what is that statement?

- *Mid-term goals*. Mid-term goals are objectives you can accomplish in one to five years. They include goals such as completing a course of study, paying off a car loan, or achieving a specific career level. These goals usually support your long-term goals.

- *Short-term goals*. Short-term goals are the ones you can accomplish in a year or less. These goals are specific achievements, such as completing a particular course or group of courses, hiking on the Bruce Trail, or organizing a family reunion. A financial goal would probably include an exact dollar amount. Whatever your short-term goals are, they will require action now or in the near future.

Write goals in several areas of life. People who set goals in only one area of life—such as their career—can find that their personal growth becomes one-sided. They could experience success at work while neglecting their health or relationships with family members and friends.

To avoid this outcome, set goals in a variety of categories. Consider what you want to experience in your:

- education
- career
- financial life
- family life
- social life
- spiritual life
- level of health

Add goals in other areas as they occur to you.

Reflect on your goals. Each week, take a few minutes to think about your goals. You can perform the following "spot checks":

- *Check in with your feelings.* Think about how the process of setting your goals felt. Consider the satisfaction you'll gain in attaining your objectives. If you don't feel a significant emotional connection with a written goal, consider letting it go or filing it away to review later.

- *Check for alignment.* Look for connections between your goals. Do your short-term goals align with your mid-term goals? Will your mid-term goals help you achieve your long-term goals? Look for a "fit" between all of your goals and your purpose for taking part in postsecondary education, as well as your overall purpose in life.

- *Check for obstacles.* All kinds of things can come between you and your goals, such as constraints on time and money. Anticipate obstacles and start looking now for workable solutions.

- *Check for immediate steps.* Here's a way to link goal setting to time management. Decide on a list of small, achievable steps you can take right away to accomplish each of your short-term goals. Write these small steps down on a daily to-do list. If you want to accomplish some of them by a certain date, enter them in a calendar that you consult daily. Then, over the coming weeks, review your to-do list and calendar. Take note of your progress and celebrate your successes.

Be SMART about your goals. Consider whether your goals are specific, measurable, attainable, relevant and time-bound, or SMART. Edwin Locke (2011) suggests that when we use SMART goals we are more likely to achieve the results we want.

- Clarity in setting goals. This is very important and by being specific, measurable, and time-bound you are more likely to have clear goals. For goals to be relevant they need to be sufficiently challenging and rewarding.

- Getting feedback on your goals allows you to clarify any uncertainties along the way and make adjustments when necessary. ✳

journal entry 8

Discovery Statement

Assess your use of time

Now that you have monitored one week, reflect on how you spend the time in your life

After one week of monitoring my time, I discovered that . . .

_____

_____

_____

I want to spend more time on . . .

_____

_____

_____

I want to spend less time on . . .

_____

_____

_____

I was surprised that I spent so much time on . . .

_____

_____

_____

I was surprised that I spent so little time on . . .

_____

_____

_____

I had strong feelings about my use of time when (describe the feeling and the situation) . . .

_____

_____

_____

exercise
Seeing where all the time goes

You've probably heard people say, "I just don't know where my time goes." Well, this chapter offers ways to find out.

First, discover the details about how you spend your lifetime by doing the Time Monitor/Time Plan process on page 72.

Next, get a big picture of those results—literally. Create a chart, diagram, or some other visual way to show the categories of activity that take up most of your time. Consider creating a pie chart like the example shown below.

Using a pie chart to display your activities is useful for at least two reasons. First, a circle is a fixed shape. It reinforces the idea that you have only a fixed amount of time to work with—24 hours per day, 168 hours per week. Second, seeing your life represented on the chart can help you adjust the size of each slice in the pie—that is, each category of activity.

After looking at the example, fill in the first blank circle with your totals from the "Monitored" column on page 74. Label this pie chart "Monitored." Then fill in the second blank circle with the totals from your "Planned" column on that page. Label this pie chart "Planned."

Create your pie chart online @
www.bams5ce.nelson.com

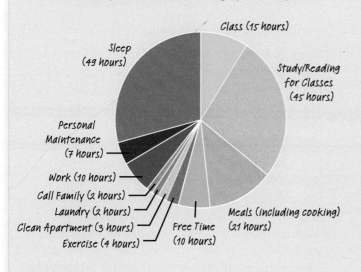

Class (15 hours)
Sleep (49 hours)
Study/Reading for Classes (45 hours)
Personal Maintenance (7 hours)
Work (10 hours)
Call Family (2 hours)
Laundry (2 hours)
Clean Apartment (3 hours)
Exercise (4 hours)
Free Time (10 hours)
Meals (including cooking) (21 hours)

exercise
Create a lifeline

On a large sheet of paper, draw a horizontal line. This line will represent your lifetime. Now add key events in your life to this line in chronological order. Examples are birth, first day at school, graduation from high school, and enrolment in higher education.

Now extend the lifeline into the future. Write down key events you would like to see occur 1 year, 5 years, and 10 or more years from now. Choose events that align with your core values. Work quickly in the spirit of a brainstorm, bearing in mind that this plan is not a final one.

Afterward, take a few minutes to review your lifeline. Select one key event for the future, and list any actions you

could take in the next month to bring yourself closer to that goal. Do the same with the other key events on your lifeline. You now have the rudiments of a comprehensive plan for your life.

Finally, extend your lifeline another 50 years beyond the year when you would reach age 100. Describe in detail what changes in the world you'd like to see as a result of the goals you attained in your lifetime.

Do this exercise online @
www.bams5ce.nelson.com

10 exercise
Get real with your goals

One way to make goals effective is to examine them up close. That's what this exercise is about. Using a process of brainstorming and evaluation, you can break a long-term goal into smaller segments until you have taken it completely apart. When you analyse a goal to this level of detail, you're well on the way to meeting it.

For this exercise, you will use a pen, extra paper, and a watch with a second hand. (A digital watch with a built-in stopwatch is even better.) Timing is an important part of the brainstorming process, so follow the stated time limits. This entire exercise takes about an hour.

Part one: Long-term goals

Brainstorm. Begin with an eight-minute brainstorm. For eight minutes, write down everything you think you want in your life. Write as fast as you can and write whatever comes into your head. Leave no thought out. Don't worry about accuracy. The object of a brainstorm is to generate as many ideas as possible. Use a separate sheet of paper for this part of the exercise.

Evaluate. After you have finished brainstorming, spend the next six minutes looking over your list. Analyse what you wrote. Read the list out loud. If something is missing, add it. Look for common themes or relationships between goals. Then select three long-term goals that are important to you—goals that will take many years to achieve. Write these goals below in the space provided.

_____

_____

_____

Before you continue, take a minute to reflect on the process you've used so far. What criteria did you use to select your top three goals? For example, list some of the core values (such as love, wealth, or happiness) underlying these goals.

Part two: Mid-term goals

Brainstorm. Read out loud the three long-term goals you selected in Part One. Choose one of them. Then brainstorm a list of goals you might achieve in the next one to five years that would lead to the accomplishment of that one long-term goal. These are mid-term goals. Spend eight minutes on this brainstorm. Remember, neatness doesn't count. Go for quantity.

Evaluate. Analyse your brainstorm of mid-term goals. Then select three that you determine to be important in meeting the long-term goal you picked. Allow yourself six minutes for this part of the exercise. Write your selections below in the space provided.

_____

_____

_____

Again, pause for reflection before going on to the next part of this exercise. Why do you see these three goals as more important than the other mid-term goals you generated? Write about your reasons for selecting these three goals.

Part three: Short-term goals

Brainstorm. Review your list of mid-term goals and select one. In another eight-minute brainstorm, generate a list of short-term goals—those you can accomplish in a year or less that will lead to the attainment of that mid-term goal. Write down everything that comes to mind. Do not evaluate or judge these ideas yet. For now, the more ideas you write down, the better.

Evaluate. Analyse your list of short-term goals. The most effective brainstorms are conducted by suspending judgment, so you might find some bizarre ideas on your list. That's fine. Now is the time to cross them out. Next, evaluate your remaining short-term goals and select three that you are willing and able to accomplish. Allow yourself six minutes for this part of the exercise. Then write your selections below in the space provided.

_____

_____

_____

The more you practise, the more effective you can be at choosing goals that have meaning for you. You can repeat this exercise, employing the other long-term goals you generated or creating new ones. By using this brainstorm and evaluation process, you can make goals come to life in the here and now.

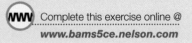 Complete this exercise online @
www.bams5ce.nelson.com

The ABC daily to-do list

One of the most effective ways to stay on track and actually get things done is to use a daily to-do list. While the Time Monitor/ Time Plan gives you a general picture of the week, your daily to-do list itemizes specific tasks you want to complete within the next 24 hours.

ONE ADVANTAGE OF keeping a daily to-do list is that you don't have to remember what to do next. It's on the list. A typical day in the life of a student is full of separate, often unrelated tasks—reading, attending lectures, reviewing notes, working at a job, writing papers, researching special projects, running errands. It's easy to forget an important task on a busy day. When that task is written down, you don't have to rely on your memory.

The following steps present one method for to-do lists. Experiment with these steps, modify them as you see fit, and invent new techniques that work for you.

Step 1 Brainstorm tasks

To get started, list all of the tasks you want to get done tomorrow. Each task will become an item on a to-do list. Don't worry about putting the entries in order or scheduling them yet. Just list everything you want to accomplish on a sheet of paper or a planning calendar, or in a notebook.

Step 2 Estimate time

For each task you wrote down in step 1, estimate how long it will take you to complete it. This can be tricky. If you allow too little time, you end up feeling rushed. If you allow too much time, you become less productive. For now, give it your best guess. Your estimates will improve with practice. Now pull out your calendar or Time Monitor/Time Plan. You've probably scheduled some hours for activities such as classes or work. This leaves the unscheduled hours for tackling your to-do lists.

Add up the time needed to complete all your to-do items. Also add up the number of unscheduled hours in your day. Then compare the two totals. The power of this step is that you can spot overload in advance. If you have eight hours' worth of to-do items but only four unscheduled hours, that's a potential problem. To solve it, proceed to step 3.

© Warren Goldswain/Shutterstock

Step 3 Rate each task by priority

To prevent overscheduling, decide which to-do items are the most important given the time you have available. One suggestion for doing this comes from the book *How to Get Control of Your Time and Your Life* by Alan Lakein (1996): Simply label each task A, B, or C.

The As on your list are those things that are the most critical. These are assignments that are coming due or jobs that need to be done immediately. Also included are activities that lead directly to your short-term goals.

The Bs on your list are important, but less so than the As. Bs might someday become As. For the present, these tasks are not as urgent as As. They can be postponed, if necessary, for another day.

The Cs do not require immediate attention. C priorities include activities such as "shop for a new blender" and "research genealogy on the Internet." Cs are often small, easy jobs with no set timeline. These, too, can be postponed.

Once you've labelled the items on your to-do list, schedule time for all of the As. The Bs and Cs can be done randomly during the day when you are in between tasks and are not yet ready to start the next A.

Step 4 Cross off tasks.

Keep your to-do list with you at all times, crossing off activities when you finish them and adding new ones

Step 1: Brainstorm tasks

Step 2: Estimate time

Step 3: Rate each task by priority

Step 4: Cross off tasks

Step 5: Evaluate

when you think of them. Crossing off tasks can be fun—a visible reward for your diligence. This step fosters a sense of accomplishment.

When using the ABC priority method, you might experience an ailment common to students: C fever. This is the uncontrollable urge to drop that A task and begin crossing Cs off your to-do list. If your history paper is due tomorrow, you might feel compelled to vacuum the rug, call your third cousin in Tulsa, and make a trip to the store for shoelaces. The reason C fever is so common is that A tasks are usually more difficult or time-consuming to achieve, with a higher risk of failure.

If you notice symptoms of C fever, ask: Does this job really need to be done now? Do I really need to organize my music collection, or might I better use this time to study for tomorrow's accounting exam? Use your to-do list to keep yourself on task, working on your As. Don't panic or berate yourself when you realize that in the last six hours, you have completed 11 Cs and not a single A. Calmly return to the As.

Step 5 Evaluate

At the end of the day, evaluate your performance. Look for A priorities you didn't complete. Look for items that repeatedly turn up as Bs or Cs on your list and never seem to get done. Consider changing these to As or dropping them altogether. Similarly, you might consider changing an A that didn't get done to a B or C priority. When you're done evaluating, start on tomorrow's to-do list. Be willing to admit mistakes. You might at first rank some items as As only to realize later that they are actually Cs. Some of the Cs that lurk at the bottom of your list day after day might really be As. When you keep a daily to-do list, you can adjust these priorities before they become problems.

The ABC system is not the only way to rank items on your to-do list. Some people prefer the "80-20" system. This is based on the idea that 80 percent of the value of any to-do list comes from only 20 percent of the tasks on that list. So on a to-do list of 10 items, find the two that will contribute most to your life, and complete those tasks without fail.

Another option is to rank items as "yes," "no," or "maybe." Do all of the tasks marked "yes." Ignore those marked "no." And put all of the "maybes" on the shelf for later. You can come back to the "maybes" at a future point and rank them as "yes" or "no."

Or you can develop your own style for to-do lists. You might find that grouping items by categories such as "errands" or "reading assignments" works best. Be creative.

In addition, there are apps you can use to help you manage your time better—check out what you can find online.

Keep in mind the power of planning a whole week or even two weeks in advance. Planning in this way can make it easier to put activities in context and see how your daily goals relate to your long-term goals. Weekly planning can also free you from feeling that you have to polish off your whole to-do list in one day. Instead, you can spread tasks out over the whole week.

In any case, make starting your own to-do list an A priority. ✳

STUDENT VOICES

Goal setting is a very real pursuit in a master student's life. Not only are goals set and strived for, they are also re-evaluated on a periodic basis. This re-evaluation process is more than an "Am I still on course?" A master student also asks, "Is this still the best course?"

—KEITH BELLOWS

USE WEB-BASED TOOLS TO SAVE TIME

Time management tools generally fall into three major categories, no matter which system or set of techniques you use:

- **Lists** of goals and planned actions for meeting those goals (to-do items).
- **Calendars** for scheduling appointments and keeping track of due dates.
- **Contact managers**—sometimes called *personal relationship managers*—for keeping track of other people's addresses, phone numbers, email addresses, and other contact information, along with notes from meetings with clients, customers, or coworkers.

Today you can choose from dozens of free online applications that fill these functions. Online applications can save you time because they're available from *any* computer that you can access, in any location—as long as it's connected to the Internet. Cell phone applications are also available to help you organize your time. If you use online or cell phone applications, you don't have to keep track of information scrawled on pieces of paper or transfer files from computer to computer. All the data you've entered from any computer are at your fingertips, at any time.

Many Web-based applications are aimed directly at students. A few of the options are described below. To find more, do an Internet search using the key words *web, tools,* and *students.*

Purpose	Application	Uses
Calendar	Google Calendar (www.google.com/calendar)	Keep track of scheduled events and share them with other people; use Tasks for your to-do list; coordinate your data with other Google online applications
Calendar	30 Boxes (30boxes.com)	Keep track of scheduled events, and share them with other people
File-syncing	Dropbox (www.dropbox.com)	Keeps your files in one place so there is no need to email yourself backups
Goal setting	43Things (www.43things.com)	List goals, and track your progress toward them as part of an online community
Goal setting	myGoals.com (www.mygoals.com)	List goals, get automatic action reminders, and choose from a library of "GoalPlans" based on expert-recommended content
Lists	Gubb (www.gubb.net)	Create and edit lists (including to-do lists), check off completed items, assign due dates to items, and send lists via email or text messaging
Lists	Remember the Milk (www.rememberthemilk.com)	Create and manage tasks online and offline, and send yourself reminders
Multipurpose	Google Docs (docs.google.com)	Create and share documents, spreadsheets, presentations, and forms
Multipurpose	Zoho (www.zoho.com)	Create and share documents, spreadsheets, presentations, and forms; create a wiki (a website that anyone can edit); send and receive email; manage to-do lists; create a calendar; chat online; and clip content (audio, video, text, and images) from the Web
Multipurpose	Yahoo (www.yahoo.com)	Send and receive email, manage contact information, take notes, and create a calendar
Multipurpose	OpenOffice (www.openoffice.org)	Create documents, spreadsheets, presentations, graphics, and databases
Multipurpose	MyNoteIt (www.mynoteit.com)	Share, edit and search notes, plan assignments with the calendar, and get things done with the task list

 Find an updated list of Web-based applications online @
www.bams5ce.nelson.com

More strategies for planning

PLANNING SETS YOU FREE. When you set goals and manage time, your life does not just happen by chance. You are on equal terms with the greatest sculptor, painter, or playwright. More than creating a work of art, you are designing a life.

Without planning, we fall prey to simply digging in—engaging in frantic activity with uncertain results. Planning replaces this behaviour with clearly defined outcomes and action steps.

An effective plan is flexible, not carved in stone. You can change your plans frequently and still preserve the advantages of planning—choosing your overall direction and taking charge of your life. And even when other people set the goal, you can choose how to achieve it.

Planning is a self-creative venture that lasts for a lifetime. Following are nine ways to get the most from this process. The first four are suggestions about goal setting. The rest cover the details of scheduling activities based on your goals.

Back up to a bigger picture. When choosing activities for the day or week, step back for a few minutes and consider your longer-range goals—what you want to accomplish in the next six months, the next year, the next five years, and beyond.

Ask whether the activities you're about to schedule actually contribute to those goals. If they do, great. If not, ask whether you can delete some items from your calendar or to-do list to make room for goal-related activities. See if you can free up at least one hour each day for doing something you love instead of putting it off to a more "reasonable" or "convenient" time.

You can back up to a bigger picture even when your goals are not precisely defined. You might suddenly sense that now is the time in your life to start a new relationship, take a long trip, or move to a new apartment or house. Pay attention to these intuitions. Allow space in your daily and weekly schedule to explore and act on your dreams.

Look boldly for things to change. It's fascinating to note the areas that are off limits when people set goals. Goals that involve money, sex, career, marriage, and other topics can easily fall into the category "I'll just have to live with this."

When creating your future, expand your thinking about what aspects of your life can be changed and what cannot. Be willing to put every facet of your life on the table. Staying open-minded can lead to a future you never dreamed was possible.

Look for what's missing—and what to maintain. Goals often arise from a sense of what's missing in our lives. Goal setting is fuelled by problems that are not resolved, projects that are incomplete, relationships we want to develop, and careers we still want to pursue.

However, not all planning has to spring from a sense of need. You can set goals to maintain things that you already have, or to keep doing the effective things that you already do. If you exercise vigorously three times each week, you can set a goal to keep exercising. If you already have a loving relationship with your spouse, you can set a goal to nurture that relationship for the rest of your life.

Think even further into the future. To have fun and unleash your creativity, set goals as far into the future as you can. The specific length of time doesn't matter. For some people, long-range planning might mean 10, 20, or even 50 years from now. For others, imagining three years feels right. Do whatever works for you.

Once you've stated your longest-range goals, work backward until you can define a next step to take. Suppose your 30-year goal is to retire and maintain your present standard of living. Ask yourself, "To do that, what financial goals do I need to achieve in 20 years? In 10 years? In 1 year? In 1 month? In 1 week?" Put the answers to these questions in writing.

Schedule fixed blocks of time first. When planning your week, start with class time and work time. These time periods are usually determined in advance, so other activities must be scheduled around them. Then schedule essential daily activities such as sleeping and eating. In addition, schedule some time each week for actions that lead directly to one of your written goals.

Set clear starting and stopping times. Tasks often expand to fill the time we allot to them. "It always takes me an hour just to settle into a reading assignment," might become a self-fulfilling prophecy.

Try scheduling a certain amount of time for a reading assignment—set a timer, and stick to it. Students often find that they can decrease study time by forcing themselves to read faster. They can usually do so without sacrificing comprehension.

A variation of this technique is called time boxing. Set aside a specific number of minutes or hours to spend on a certain task. Instead of working on that task until it's done, commit to work on it just for that specific amount of time. Then set a timer, and get to work. In effect, you're placing the task inside a definite "box"—a specific space on your daily calendar.

Time boxing is one way to overcome resistance to a task, focus your attention, and make a meaningful dent in large projects. The amount of time you choose can be relatively small—such as 10 minutes. Start with short periods, and gradually increase them.

Scheduling a fixed time can apply to other tasks. Some people find they can get up 15 minutes earlier in the morning and still feel alert throughout the day. Plan 45 minutes for a trip to the grocery store instead of an hour. Over the course of a year, those extra minutes can add up to hours.

Feeling rushed or sacrificing quality is not the goal here. The point is to push yourself a little and discover what your time requirements really are.

Schedule for flexibility and fun. Recognize that unexpected things will happen, and allow for them. Leave some holes in your schedule. Build in blocks of unplanned time. Consider setting aside time each week marked "flex time" or "open time." Use these hours for emergencies, spontaneous activities, catching up, or seizing new opportunities.

Include time for errands. The time we spend buying toothpaste, paying bills, and doing laundry is easy to overlook. These little errands can destroy a tight schedule and make us feel rushed and harried all week. Plan for them, and remember to allow for travel time between locations.

Also make room for fun. Fun is important. Brains that are constantly stimulated by new ideas and new challenges need time off to digest them. Take time to browse aimlessly through the library, stroll with no destination, ride a bike, or do other things you enjoy. It's important to "waste" time once in a while.

To maintain flexibility and fun, be realistic. Don't set yourself up for failure by telling yourself you can do a four-hour job in two hours. There are only 168 hours in a week. If you schedule 169 hours, you're sunk.

Plan for changes in your workload. You might find yourself with a lighter load of assignments to complete during the first few days or weeks of any course. This typically happens when instructors give an overview of the subject or take time to review material that you already know from another course.

Faced with this situation, some students are tempted to let early homework slide. They figure that they'll have plenty of time to catch up later. These students often get a rude surprise when the course shifts into warp speed. After reviewing the basics, instructors may cover new and more difficult material at a faster pace, piling on extra readings, writing assignments, and quizzes.

To stay on top of your workload over the entire term, plan for such a change of pace. Stay on top of your assignments right from the start. Whenever possible, work ahead. This tactic gives you an edge when the load for a course gets heavier, or when big assignments for several courses are due during the same week.

Involve others when appropriate. Sometimes the activities you schedule depend on gaining information, assistance, or direct participation from other people. If you neglect to inform others of your plans or forget to ask for their cooperation at the outset—surprise! Your schedule can crash.

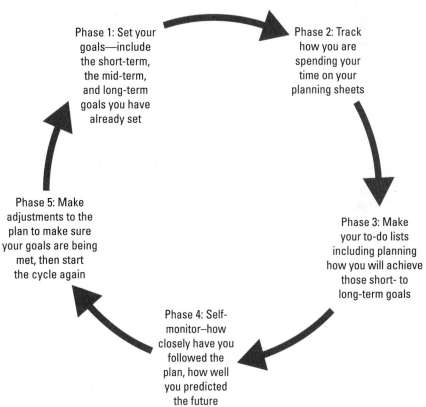

Phase 1: Set your goals—include the short-term, the mid-term, and long-term goals you have already set

Phase 2: Track how you are spending your time on your planning sheets

Phase 3: Make your to-do lists including planning how you will achieve those short- to long-term goals

Phase 4: Self-monitor—how closely have you followed the plan, how well you predicted the future

Phase 5: Make adjustments to the plan to make sure your goals are being met, then start the cycle again

The time-management cycle: pulling it all together. Statements such as these often follow a communication breakdown: "I just assumed you were going to pick up the kids from school on Tuesday." "I'm working overtime this week and hoped that you'd take over the cooking for a while."

When you schedule a task that depends on another person's involvement, let that person know—the sooner, the better. ✳

Stop Procrastination NOW

CONSIDER A BOLD IDEA: The way to begin to stop procrastinating is to choose to stop procrastinating. Giving up procrastination is actually a simple choice; people make it complicated.

Test this idea for yourself. Think of something that you've been putting off. Choose a small, specific task—one that you can complete in five minutes or less. Then do that task today.

Tomorrow, choose another task and do it. Repeat this strategy each day for one week. Notice what happens to your habit of procrastination.

If the above suggestion just doesn't work for you, then experiment with any strategy from the list below. (Just don't put it off.)

Discover the costs. Find out if procrastination keeps you from getting what you want. Clearly seeing the side effects of procrastination can help you kick the habit.

Discover your procrastination style. Psychologist Linda Sapadin (1997) identifies different styles of procrastination. For example, *dreamers* have big goals that they seldom translate into specific plans. *Worriers* focus on the worst-case scenario and are likely to talk more about problems than about solutions. *Defiers* resist new tasks or promise to do them and then don't follow through. *Overdoers* create extra work for themselves by refusing to delegate tasks and neglecting to set priorities. And *perfectionists* put off tasks for fear of making a mistake.

Awareness of your procrastination style is a key to changing your behaviour. If you exhibit the characteristics of an overdoer, for example, then say no to new projects. Also ask for help in completing your current projects.

To discover your procrastination style, observe your behaviour. Avoid judgments. Just be a scientist: Record the facts. Write Discovery Statements about specific ways you procrastinate. Follow up with Intention Statements about what to do differently.

Trick yourself into getting started. If you have a 50-page chapter to read, then grab the book and say to yourself, "I'm not really going to read this chapter right now. I'm just going to flip through the pages and scan the headings for 10 minutes." Tricks like these can get you started on a task you've been dreading.

Let feelings follow action. If you put off exercising until you feel energetic, you might wait for months. Instead, get moving now. Then watch your feelings change. After five minutes of brisk walking, you might be in the mood for a 20-minute run. This principle—action generates motivation—can apply to any task that you've put on the back burner.

Choose to work under pressure. Sometimes people thrive under pressure. As one writer puts it, "I don't do my *best* work under deadline. I do my *only* work under deadline." Used selectively, this strategy might also work for you.

Put yourself in control. If you choose to work with a due date staring you right in the face, then schedule a big block of time during the preceding week. Until then, enjoy!

Think ahead. Use the monthly calendar on page 98 or the long-term planner on page 101 to list due dates for assignments in all your courses. Using these tools, you can anticipate heavy demands on your time and take action to prevent last-minute crunches. Make *Becoming a Master Student* your home base—the first place to turn in taking control of your schedule.

Give up "someday." Procrastination rests on this vague notion: *I'll do it someday.* Other people reinforce this notion by telling you that your life will *really* start when you . . . . (Fill in the blank with phrases like *graduate* *from college, get married, have kids, get promoted,* or *retire.*) Using this logic, you could wait your whole life to start living. Avoid this fate. Take action today.

Create goals that draw you forward. A goal that grabs you by the heartstrings is an inspiration to act now. If you're procrastinating, then set some goals that excite you. Then you might wake up one day and discover that procrastination is part of your past. ✳

 Find more strategies for ending procrastination @ www.bams5ce.nelson.com

The 7-day antiprocrastination plan

Listed here are seven strategies you can use to reduce or eliminate many sources of procrastination. The suggestions are tied to the days of the week to help you remember them. Use this list to remind yourself that each day of your life presents an opportunity to stop the cycle of procrastination.

MONDAY Make it meaningful. What is important about the task you've been putting off? List all the benefits of completing it. Look at it in relation to your short-, mid-, or long-term goals. Be specific about the rewards for getting it done, including how you will feel when the task is completed. To remember this strategy, keep in mind that it starts with the letter *M*, like the word *Monday*.

TUESDAY Take it apart. Break big jobs into a series of small ones you can do in 15 minutes or less. If a long reading assignment intimidates you, divide it into two-page or three-page sections. Make a list of the sections and cross them off as you complete them so you can see your progress. Even the biggest projects can be broken down into a series of small tasks. This strategy starts with the letter *T*, so mentally tie it to *Tuesday*.

WEDNESDAY Write an intention statement. For example, if you can't get started on a term paper, you might write, "I intend to write a list of at least 10 possible topics by 9:00 p.m. I will reward myself with an hour of guilt-free recreational reading." Write your intention on an index card and carry it with you, or post it in your study area where you can see it often. In your memory, file the first word in this strategy—*write*—with *Wednesday*.

THURSDAY Tell everyone. Publicly announce your intention to get a task done. Tell a friend that you intend to learn 10 irregular French verbs by Saturday. Tell your spouse, roommate, parents, and children. Include anyone who will ask whether you've completed the assignment or who will suggest ways to get it done. Make the world your support group. Associate *tell* with *Thursday*.

FRIDAY Find a reward. Construct rewards to yourself carefully. Be willing to withhold them if you do not complete the task. Don't pick a movie as a reward for studying biology if you plan to go to the movie anyway. And when you legitimately reap your reward, notice how it feels. Remember that *Friday* is a fine day to *find* a reward. (Of course, you can find a reward on any day of the week. Rhyming *Friday* with *fine day* is just a memory trick.)

SATURDAY Settle it now. Do it now. The minute you notice yourself procrastinating, plunge into the task. Imagine yourself at a cold mountain lake, poised to dive. Gradual immersion would be slow torture. It's often less painful to leap. Then be sure to savour the feeling of having the task behind you. Link *settle* with *Saturday*.

SUNDAY Say no. When you keep pushing a task into a low-priority category, re-examine your purpose for doing it at all. If you realize that you really don't intend to do something, quit telling yourself that you will. That's procrastinating. Just say no. Then you're not procrastinating. You don't have to carry around the baggage of an undone task. *Sunday*—the last day of this seven-day plan—is a great day to finally let go and just *say* no.

STUDENT VOICES

Making lists has been one of my favourite tools to stay on track and prioritize. Not much gives me more pleasure than to cross off duties one by one and to see the number of items left to do shrink to nothing, or what can be put off until another time.

—LAURIE MURRAY

practising critical thinking

1. List five areas of your life in which you procrastinate, and describe them briefly in the first column below.
2. Look back at the articles you just read about procrastination, and pick a procrastination tool that you think might work to help you overcome each of your five procrastination areas. Write that tool in the second column.
3. In the third column, describe specifically how you will implement the procrastination tool.

Example:

Procrastination area	Potential tool	Specific plan
1. Not starting my research project.	Take It Apart	Break down the project as follows:
		Topic/thesis statement (week 1)
		Preliminary research (week 2)
		In-depth research (week 3)
		First draft (week 4)
		Revision for final version (week 5)

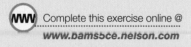

Complete this exercise online @
www.bams5ce.nelson.com

25 ways to get the most out of now

The following time-management techniques are about:

The following time-management techniques are about:

- **When to study**
- **Where to study**
- **Ways to handle the rest of the world**
- **Things to ask yourself if you get stuck**

Don't feel pressured to use all of the techniques listed below or to tackle them in order. As you read, note the suggestions you think will be helpful. Pick one technique to use now. When it becomes a habit, come back to this article and select another one. Repeat this cycle and enjoy the results as they unfold in your life.

Ferenc Szelepcsenyi/Shutterstock

When to study

1 Study difficult (or "boring") subjects first. If your chemistry problems put you to sleep, get to them first, while you are fresh. We tend to give top priority to what we enjoy studying, yet the courses we find most difficult often require the most creative energy. Save your favourite subjects for later. If you find yourself avoiding a particular subject, get up an hour earlier to study it before breakfast. With that chore out of the way, the rest of the day can be a breeze.

Continually being late with course assignments indicates a trouble area. Further action is required. Clarify your intentions about the course by writing down your feelings in a journal, talking with an instructor, or asking for help from a friend or counsellor. Consistently avoiding study tasks can also be a signal to re-examine your program of study.

2 Be aware of your best time of day. Many people learn best in daylight hours. If this is true for you, schedule study time for your most difficult subjects before nightfall.

Unless you grew up on a farm, the idea of being conscious at 4:00 a.m. might seem ridiculous. Yet many successful business people begin the day at 5:00 a.m. or earlier. Athletes and yogis use this time, too. Some writers complete their best work before 9:00 a.m.

Others experience the same benefits by staying up late. They flourish after midnight. If you aren't convinced, then experiment. When you're in a time crunch, get up early or stay up late. You might even see a sunrise.

3 Use waiting time. Five minutes waiting for a bus, 20 minutes waiting for the dentist, 10 minutes between classes—waiting time adds up fast. Have short study tasks ready to do during these periods. For example, you can carry a notebook with facts, formulas, or definitions and pull it out anywhere.

A voice recorder can help you use commuting time to your advantage. Make recordings of yourself reading your notes or find out if your instructor has made a podcast of the last class session. Then play these in a car stereo as you drive, or listen through your headphones as you ride on the bus or subway.

Where to study

4 Use a regular study area. Your body and your mind know where you are. Using the same place to study, day after day, helps train your responses. When you arrive at that particular place, you can focus your attention more quickly.

5 Study where you'll be alert. In bed, your body gets a signal. For most students, that signal is more likely to be "Time to sleep!" than "Time to study!" Just as you train your body to be alert at your desk, you also train it to slow down near your bed. For that reason, don't study where you sleep.

Easy chairs and sofas are also dangerous places to study. Learning requires energy. Give your body a message that energy is needed. Put yourself in a situation that supports this message.

Some schools offer empty classrooms as places to study. Many students report that they find themselves studying effectively in a classroom setting.

6 Use a library. Libraries are designed for learning. The lighting is perfect. The noise level is low. A wealth of material is available. Entering a library is a signal to focus the mind and get to work. Many students can get more done in a shorter time frame at the library than anywhere else. Experiment for yourself.

Ways to handle the rest of the world

7 Pay attention to your attention. Breaks in concentration are often caused by internal interruptions. Your own thoughts jump in to divert you from your studies. When this happens, notice these thoughts and let them go.

Perhaps the thought of getting something else done is distracting you. One option is to handle that other task now and study later. Or you can write yourself a note about it, or schedule a specific time to do it.

8 Agree with living mates about study time. This includes roommates, partners, and children. Make the rules clear, and be sure to follow them yourself. Explicit agreements—even written contracts—work well. One student always wears a colourful hat when he wants to study. When his wife and children see the hat, they respect his wish to be left alone.

9 Turn off the phone and stop checking your messages. The phone is the ultimate interrupter. People who wouldn't think of distracting you in person might call or text you at the worst times because they can't see that you are studying. You don't have to be a phone victim. If a simple "I can't talk, I'm studying" doesn't work, use dead silence or don't respond to the message. It's a conversation killer. Or short-circuit the whole problem: Turn it off.

Social networking can eat up your study time and if you start your homework by thinking "I'll just check Facebook" you may end up hours later no further ahead with your work. Turn social networks off of your computer while you are studying. Dr. Tim Pychyl (2010), a Canadian psychologist, has been doing work on procrastination since 1995. He warns that we need to beware of push technologies that remind of incoming emails and text messages—it is just too easy to give in to the impulse to read these messages when they are literally being pushed at us. Turn off those functions on your phones and computers to help resist the temptation to respond.

10 Learn to say no. This is a timesaver and a valuable life skill for everyone. Some people feel it is rude to refuse a request. But saying no can be done effectively and courteously. Others want you to succeed as a student. When you tell them that you can't do what they ask because you are busy educating yourself, most people will understand.

11 Hang a "do not disturb" sign on your door. Create a "do not disturb" sign. They work. Using signs can relieve you of making a decision about cutting off each interruption—a timesaver in itself.

12 Get ready the night before. Completing a few simple tasks just before you go to bed can help you get in gear the next day. If you need to make some phone calls first thing in the morning, look up those numbers and put a voice message on your cell phone as a reminder. If you need to drive to a new location, make note of the address and put it next to your car keys. If you plan to spend the next afternoon writing a paper, get your materials together: dictionary, notes, outline, paper and pencil, flash drive, laptop—whatever you need. Pack your lunch or gas up the car. Organize your briefcase or backpack.

13 Use accessing social networking sites as a reward. It is easy to waste hours of your life on these sites, so make sure that being linked in isn't more important than doing your work.

Consider letting yourself check your Facebook site as reward for an hour of studying but be careful not to let yourself be interrupted by friends who know you are online. Computers are great study tools, but they can be a huge distraction from getting your work done. If you do end up chatting with friends online during study time, make sure it is about study-related issues, not about last night's entertainment. And surfing the Net may feel like studying, but it can also be a real time waster. Again, use the Internet to reward your studying, not to begin your homework.

14 Avoid noise distractions. To promote concentration, avoid studying in front of the television and turn off the radio. Many students insist that they study better with background noise, and this might be true. Some students report good results with carefully selected and controlled music. For many others, silence is the best form of music to study by.

At times, noise levels might be out of your control. A neighbour or roommate might decide to find out how far he can turn up his music before the walls crumble. Meanwhile, your ability to concentrate on the principles of sociology goes down the drain. To avoid this scenario, schedule study sessions during periods when your living environment is usually quiet. If you live in residence, ask if study rooms are available. Or go somewhere else where it's quiet, such as the library. Some students have even found refuge in quiet cafés, self-service laundries, and places of worship.

15 Manage interruptions. Be aware of repeat offenders. Ask yourself if there are certain friends or relatives who consistently interrupt your study time. If avoiding the interrupter is impractical, send a clear message. Sometimes others don't realize that they are breaking your concentration. You can give them a gentle yet firm reminder. If this doesn't work, there are methods to make your message more effective. For more ideas, see Chapter 8: Communicating. See if you can "firewall" yourself for selected study periods each week. Find a place where you can count on being alone and working without interruption.

Sometimes interruptions still happen, though. Create a system for dealing with them. Try to make sure you get back on track as fast as possible.

Things to ask yourself if you get stuck

16 Ask: What is one task I can accomplish toward achieving my goal? This is a helpful technique to use when faced with a big, imposing job. Pick out one small accomplishment, preferably one you can complete in about five minutes; then do it. The satisfaction of getting one thing done can spur you on to get one more thing done. Meanwhile, the job gets smaller.

17 Ask: Am I being too hard on myself? If you are feeling frustrated with a reading assignment, if your attention wanders repeatedly, or if you've fallen behind on math problems that are due tomorrow, take a minute to listen to the messages you are giving yourself. Are you scolding yourself too harshly? Lighten up. Allow yourself to feel a little foolish and then get on with the task at hand. Don't add to the problem by berating yourself.

Worrying about the future is another way people beat themselves up: How will I ever get all this done? What if every paper I'm assigned turns out to be this hard? If I can't do the simple calculations now, how will I ever pass the final? Instead of promoting learning, such questions fuel anxiety.

Labelling and generalizing weaknesses are other ways people are hard on themselves. Being objective and specific will help eliminate this form of self-punishment and will likely generate new possibilities. An alternative to saying "I'm terrible in algebra" is to say "I don't understand factoring equations." This rewording suggests a plan to improve.

18 Ask: Is this a piano? Carpenters who construct rough frames for buildings have a saying they use when they bend a nail or accidentally hack a chunk out of a piece of wood: "Well, this ain't no piano." It means that perfection is not necessary. Ask yourself if what you are doing needs to be perfect. Perhaps you don't have to apply the same standards of grammar to lecture notes that you would apply to an essay. If you can complete a job 95 percent perfectly in two hours and 100 percent perfectly in four hours, ask yourself whether the additional 5 percent improvement is worth doubling the amount of time you spend.

Sometimes it is a piano. A tiny miscalculation can ruin an entire lab experiment. A misstep in solving a complex math problem can negate hours of work. Computers are notorious for turning little errors into nightmares. Accept lower standards only when appropriate.

A related suggestion is to weed out low-priority tasks. The to-do list for a large project can include dozens of items, not all of which are equally important. Some can be done later, while others could be skipped altogether, if time is short.

Apply this idea when you study. In a long reading assignment, look for pages you can skim or skip. When it's appropriate, read chapter summaries or article abstracts. As you review your notes, look for material that might not be covered on a test and decide whether you want to study it.

19 Ask: Would I pay myself for what I'm doing right now? If you were employed as a student, would you be earning your wages? Ask yourself this question when you notice that you've taken your third snack break in 30 minutes. Most students are, in fact, employed as students. They are investing in their own productivity and paying a big price for the privilege of being a student. Sometimes they don't realize that doing a mediocre job now might result in fewer opportunities in the future.

20 **Ask: Can I do just one more thing?** Ask yourself this question at the end of a long day. Almost always you will have enough energy to do just one more short task. The overall increase in your productivity might surprise you.

21 **Ask: Am I making time for things that are important but not urgent?** If we spend most of our time putting out fires, we can feel drained and frustrated. According to Stephen R. Covey (1990), this happens when we forget to take time for things that are not urgent but are truly important. Examples include exercising regularly, reading, meditating, spending quality time alone or with family members and friends, travelling, and cooking nutritious meals. Each of these can contribute directly to a long-term goal or life mission. Yet when schedules get tight, we often forgo these things, waiting for that elusive day when we'll "finally have more time."

That day won't come until we choose to make time for what's truly important. Knowing this, we can use some of the suggestions in this chapter to free up more time.

22 **Ask: Can I delegate this?** Instead of slogging through complicated tasks alone, you can draw on the talents and energy of other people. Busy executives know the value of delegating tasks to coworkers. Without delegation, many projects would flounder or die.

You can apply the same principle. Instead of doing all the housework or cooking by yourself, for example, you can assign some of the tasks to family members or roommates. Instead of driving across town to deliver a package, you can hire a delivery service to do so. All of these tactics can free up extra hours for studying.

It's not practical (or ethical) to delegate certain study tasks, such as writing essays or completing reading assignments. However, you can still draw on the ideas of others in completing such tasks. For instance, form a writing group to edit and critique each others' essays, brainstorm topics or titles, and develop lists of sources.

If you're absent from a class, find a classmate to summarize the lecture, discussion, and any upcoming assignments. Prime Ministers depend on briefings. You can use this technique, too.

23 **Ask: How did I just waste time?** Notice when time passes and you haven't accomplished what you had planned to do. Take a minute to review your actions and note the specific ways you wasted time. We tend to operate by habit, wasting time in the same ways over and over again. When you are aware of things you do that drain your time, you are more likely to catch yourself in the act next time. Observing one small quirk might save you hours. But keep this in mind: Asking you to notice how you waste time is not intended to make you feel guilty. The point is to increase your skill by getting specific information about how you use time.

24 **Ask: Could I find the time if I really wanted to?** The way people speak often rules out the option of finding more time. An alternative is to speak about time with more possibility.

Remember cultural differences

There are as many different styles for managing time as there are people. These styles vary across cultures.

In Canada and the United States, for example, business meetings typically start on time. That's also true in Scandinavian countries such as Norway and Sweden. However, travellers to Panama might find that meetings start about a half-hour late. And people who complain about late meetings while doing business in Mexico might be considered rude.

Cultural differences can get even more pronounced. In her book *Freedom and Culture*, anthropologist Dorothy Lee (1959) writes about a group of people in the Trobriand Islands east of New Guinea. Their language has no verb tenses—no distinction between past, present, and future.

The Trobrianders celebrate each event as an end in itself, not as a means to achieve some future goal. In this culture, the whole concept of time management would have little meaning.

When you study or work with people of different nationalities and ethnic backgrounds, look for differences in their approaches to time. A behaviour that you might view as rude or careless—such as showing up late for appointments—could simply result from seeing the world in a different way.

 Find more information about cultural differences in time management online @
www.bams5ce.nelson.com

The next time you're tempted to say "I just don't have time," pause for a minute. Question the truth of this statement. Could you find four more hours this week for studying? Suppose that someone offered to pay you $10,000 to find those four hours. Suppose, too, that you will get paid only if you don't lose sleep, call in sick for work, or sacrifice anything important to you. Could you find the time if vast sums of money were involved? Remember that when it comes to school, vast sums of money are involved.

25 **Ask: Am I willing to promise it?** This might be the most powerful time-management idea of all. If you want to find time for a task, promise yourself—and others—that you'll get it done.

To make this technique work, do more than say that you'll try or that you'll give it your best shot. Take an oath, as you would in court. Give it your word.

One way to accomplish big things in life is to make big promises. There's little reward in promising what's safe or predictable. No athlete promises to place seventh in the Olympic Games. Chances are that if we're not making big promises, we're not stretching ourselves.

The point of making a promise is not to chain ourselves to a rigid schedule or to impossible expectations.

We can also promise to reach goals without unbearable stress. We can keep schedules flexible and carry out our plans with ease, joy, and satisfaction.

At times we can go too far. Some promises are truly beyond us, and we might break them. However, failing to keep a promise is just that—failing to keep a promise. A broken promise is not the end of the world.

Promises can work magic. When our word is on the line, it's possible to discover reserves of time and energy we didn't know existed. Promises can push us to exceed our expectations. *

WWW Discover even more ways to get the most out of now @ **www.bams5ce.nelson.com**

For more helpful tips on how to resist procrastination, go to **www.procrastination.ca/.** On this website, Dr. Tim Pychyl talks about his recent research on this topic and provides links to his blog, comics, and podcasts. Listening to his podcasts on the way to school might just be what you need to do to get things done.

2

© Tim Pychyl and Paul Mason

Beyond time management: Stay focused on what matters

THEY SEE A person with a 50-item to-do list clutching a calendar chock full of appointments. They imagine a robot who values cold efficiency, compulsively accounts for every minute, and is too rushed to develop personal relationships. Often this image is what's behind the comment "Yeah, there are some good ideas in those time-management books, but I'll never get around to using them. Too much work."

These stereotypes about time management hold a kernel of truth. Sometimes people who pride themselves on efficiency are merely keeping busy. In their rush to check items off their to-do lists, they might be fussing over things that don't need doing—insignificant tasks that create little or no value in the first place. If this is one of your fears, relax. The point of managing time is not to overload your schedule with extra obligations. Instead, the aim is to get the important things done and still have time to be human. An effective time manager is productive and relaxed at the same time.

Discover your style

Many of the suggestions in this chapter appeal to "left-brained" people—those who thrive on making lists, scheduling events, and handling details. These suggestions might not work for people who like to see wholes and who think visually. Remember that the strategies discussed in this chapter represent just one set of options for managing time.

The trick is to discover what works for you. Do give time-management strategies a fair chance. Some might be suitable, with a few modifications. Instead of writing a conventional to-do list, for instance, you can plot your day on a mind map. (Mind maps are explained

Woman: Hill Street Studios/Getty; *clock:* Falko Matte/Shutterstock; collage by Walter Kopec

in Chapter Five: Notes.) Or write to-dos, one per Post-it® note, in any order in which tasks occur to you. Later you can edit, sort, and rank the notes, choosing which items to act on.

Strictly speaking, time cannot be managed. Time is a mystery, an abstract concept that cannot be captured in words. The minutes, hours, days, and years march on whether we manage anything or not. What we can do is manage ourselves in respect to time. A few basic principles can do that as well as a truckload of cold-blooded techniques.

Know your values. Begin by managing time from a bigger picture. Instead of thinking in terms of minutes or hours, view your life as a whole.

Given the finite space between birth and death, determine what matters most to you.

As a way to define your values, write your own obituary. Describe the ways you want to be remembered. List the contributions you intend to make during your lifetime and the kind of person you wish to become. If this exercise is too spooky, then complete the lifeline exercise on page 103 instead. Or simply write your life purpose—a sentence or short paragraph that describes what's most important to you.

Next, return to the Time Monitor/Time Plan exercise on page 72. Look at your completed Time Monitor, and place a check mark next to the activities that are directly aligned with your values. Write a Discovery Statement about how "on purpose" you were for the week. Follow it with an Intention Statement about any resulting changes in your plan for next week.

TIME

2

Focus on your own well-being first Whatever you need to do to stay healthy both mentally and physically, schedule that in first, whether that involves going to the gym regularly, playing soccer, practising mindfulness, doing yoga, or spending time with elders or friends. Bresciani, Duncan, and Huo Cao (2010) suggest that—similar to the mantra of always putting money into our own savings first and then paying the bills—this is the best way to ensure that key activities that relate to our own well-being actually occur. They suggest that you ask yourself, "How can I plan those well-being activities so there is the least likelihood of them being displaced by other tasks?" Good question. And if you don't know what those well-being activities are, they recommend starting with developing your sense of humour and including some belly laughs in each day.

Do less. Managing time is as much about dropping worthless activities as about adding new and useful ones. The idea is to weed out those actions that deliver little reward.

Decide right now to eliminate activities with a low payoff. When you add a new item to your schedule, consider dropping a current one.

Slow down. Sometimes it's useful to hurry, such as when you're late for a meeting or about to miss a train. At other times, haste is a choice that serves no real purpose. If you're speeding through the day like a launched missile, consider what would happen if you got to your next destination a little bit later than planned. Rushing to stay a step ahead might not be worth the added strain.

Handle it now A long to-do list can result from postponing decisions and procrastinating. An alternative is to handle a task or decision immediately. Answer that letter now. Make that phone call as soon as it occurs to you. Then you don't have to add the task to your calendar or to-do list.

The same idea applies when someone asks you to volunteer for a project and you realize immediately that you don't want to do it. Save time by graciously telling the truth up front. Saying "I'll think about it and get back to you" just postpones the conversation until later, when it might take more time.

Woman: Hill Street Studios/Getty; *Clock:* Falko Matte/Shutterstock; collage by Walter Kopec

Remember people. Few people on their deathbed ever say, "I wish I'd spent more time at the office." They're more likely to say, "I wish I'd spent more time with my family and friends." Life is about relationships. Make connections to all sorts of people who cross your path in the day, from your instructors, to friends, to your coach. It turns out that having multiple roles in life is one of the keys to well-being, so don't neglect the people who you value in your life (Bresciani, Duncan, & Huo Cao, 2010).

Efficiency is a concept that applies to things—not people. When it comes to maintaining and nurturing relationships, we can often benefit from loosening up our schedules. We can allow extra time for conflict management, spontaneous visits, and free-ranging conversations.

Focus on outcomes. You might feel guilty when you occasionally stray from your schedule and spend two hours napping or watching reality TV. But if you're regularly meeting your goals and leading a fulfilling life, there's probably no harm done. When managing time, the overall goal of personal effectiveness counts more than the means used to achieve it. This can be true even when your time-management style differs from that recommended by experts.

Likewise, there are many methods for planning your time. Some people prefer a written action plan that carefully details each step leading to a long-range goal. Others just note the due date for accomplishing a goal and periodically assess their progress. Either strategy can work.

Visualizing the desired outcome can be as important as having a detailed action plan. Here's an experiment. Write a list of goals you plan to accomplish over the next six months. Then create a vivid mental picture of yourself attaining them and enjoying the resulting benefits. Visualize this image several times in the next few weeks. File the list away, making a note on your calendar to review it in six months. When six months have passed, look over the list and note how many of your goals you have actually accomplished.

Buy less. Before you purchase an item, estimate how much time it will take to locate, assemble, use, repair, and maintain it. You might be able to free up hours by doing without. If the product comes with a 400-page manual or 20 hours of training, beware. Before rushing to the store to add another possession to your life, see if you can reuse or adapt something you already own. This is also a greener approach to your life.

Forget about time. Schedule "downtime"—a period when you're accountable to no one else and have nothing to accomplish—into every day. This is time to do nothing, free of guilt. Even a few minutes spent in this way can yield a sense of renewal.

Also experiment with decreasing your awareness of time. Leave your watch off for a few hours each day. Try to spend time away from clocks, computers and phones that constantly remind us of the time. Notice how often you glance at your watch, and make a conscious effort to do so less often. Trying to live fully in the present is difficult when we are always thinking about what we need to do next. So occasionally we need to focus on just being here now. You might be surprised at the insights you gain when your attention is focused on the present.

If you still want some sense of time, then use alternatives to the almighty, unforgiving clock. Measure your day with a sundial, hourglass, or egg timer. Or synchronize your activities with the rhythms of nature, for example, by rising at dawn. You can also plan activities to harmonize with the rhythms of your body. Schedule your most demanding tasks for times when you're normally most alert. Eat when you're hungry, not according to the clock. Toss out schedules when it's appropriate. Sometimes the best-laid plans are best laid to rest.

Take time to retreat from time. Create a sanctuary, a haven, a safe place in your life that's free from any hint of schedules, lists, or accomplishments. One of the most effective ways to manage time is to periodically forget about it.

Forget time management—just get things done

David Allen (2001), author of *Getting Things Done: The Art of Stress-free Productivity*, says that a lack of time is not the real issue for the people he coaches in time management. Instead, the problem is "a lack of clarity and definition about what a project really is, and what the associated next-action steps required are." Allen translates this idea into the following suggestions:

1. **Collect.** To begin, gather every unfinished project, incomplete task, misplaced object—or anything else that's nagging you—and dump it into a "bucket," or collection area. This area could be an actual bucket that's big enough to hold various objects, a file folder, a traditional in-basket, or all of these receptacles. If an item is too big to store in a bucket, write a reminder of it on an index card or a piece of paper—one item per card or sheet—so that it's easier to file later. Stick this reminder in one of your buckets.

2. **Process.** Now go to each of your buckets, one at a time. Take whatever item is at the top of the pile and ask, "Do I truly want to or need to do something about this?" If the answer is no, calmly dispose of the item. If the answer is yes, then choose immediately how to respond:

   - If you can take action on this item in two minutes or less, do so now.

   - If you're dealing with an item that can best be handled by someone else, delegate it to that person.

   - If you're dealing with an item that will take more than two minutes for you to do, write a reminder to do it later.

   Repeat the above procedure for each item in each of your buckets. The overall goal is to empty the buckets at least once each week.

3. **Organize.** Now group your reminders into appropriate lists by category. The categories are ultimately up to you, but Allen's recommendations include the following:

   - A calendar for listing actions to be completed on a specific date or at a specific time.

   - A list of current projects. A *project* is an outcome that requires two or more actions to produce.

   - A to-do list. Group the items on this list by the physical location where you will do them—for example, *at phone* or *at computer*.

4. **Review.** Every week, review your reminders and ask yourself, "What are all my current projects? And what is the *very next physical action* (such as a phone call or errand) that I can take to move each project forward?"

5. **Do.** Every day, review your calendar or lists. Based on this information and on your intuition, make moment-to-moment choices about how to spend your time.

This exercise will give you an opportunity to step back from the details of your daily schedule and get a bigger picture of your life. The more difficult it is for you to plan beyond the current day or week, the greater the benefit of this exercise.

Your basic tool is a one-month calendar. Use it to block out specific times for upcoming events, such as study group meetings, due dates for assignments, review periods before tests, and other time-sensitive tasks.

To get started, you might want to copy the blank monthly calendar on pages 98–99 onto both sides of a sheet of paper. Or make several copies of these pages and tape them together so that you can see several months at a glance.

Alternatively, you can create a calendar from a template in your word processor, or download a free calendar online.

Also, be creative. Experiment with a variety of uses for your monthly calendar. For instance, you can note day-to-day changes in your health or moods, list the places you visit while you are on holiday, or circle each day that you practise a new habit. For examples of filled-in monthly calendars, see the pages below.

Find printable copies of this monthly calendar online @ **www.bams5ce.nelson.com**

Gearing up:
Using a long-term planner

Planning a day, a week, or a month ahead is a powerful practice. Using a long-term planner—one that displays an entire quarter, a session, or a year at a glance—can yield even more benefits.

WITH A LONG-TERM PLANNER, you can eliminate a lot of unpleasant surprises. Long-term planning allows you to avoid scheduling conflicts—the kind that obligate you to be in two places at the same time three weeks from now. You can also anticipate busy periods, such as final exams, and start preparing for them now. Good-bye, all-night cram sessions. Hello, serenity.

Find a long-term planner, or make your own. Many office supply stores carry academic planners in paper form that cover an entire school year. Computer software for time management offers the same feature. You can also be creative and make your own long-term planner. A big roll of newsprint pinned to a bulletin board or taped to a wall will do nicely.

Enter scheduled dates that extend into the future. Use your long-term planner to list commitments that extend beyond the current month. Enter test dates, lab sessions, days that classes will be cancelled, and other events that will take place over this term and next term.

Create a master assignment list. Find the syllabus for each course you're currently taking. Then, in your long-term planner, enter the due dates for all of the assignments in all of your courses. This can be a powerful reality check.

The purpose of this technique is not to make you feel overwhelmed by all the things you have do. Rather, its aim is to help you take a First Step toward recognizing the demands on your time. Armed with the truth about how you use your time, you can make more accurate plans.

Include non-academic events. In addition to tracking academic commitments, you can use your long-term planner to mark significant events in your life outside of school. Include birthdays, doctor's appointments, concert dates, credit card payment due dates, and car maintenance schedules.

Use your long-term planner to divide and conquer. Big assignments such as major essays or presentations pose a special risk. When you have three months to do a project, you might say to yourself, "That looks like a lot of work, but I've got plenty of time. No problem." Two months, three weeks, and six days from now, it could suddenly be a problem.

For some people, academic life is a series of last-minute crises punctuated by periods of exhaustion. You can avoid that fate. The trick is to set due dates *before* the final due date.

When planning to write an important essay, for instance, enter the final due date in your long-term planner. Then set individual due dates for each milestone in the writing process—creating an outline, completing your research, finishing a first draft, editing the draft, and preparing the final copy. By meeting these interim due dates, you make steady progress on the assignment throughout the term. That sure beats trying to crank out all those pages at the last minute.

WWW Find printable copies of this long-term planner online @ **www.bams5ce.nelson.com**

Week of	Monday	Tuesday	Wednesday	Thursday	Friday	Saturday	Sunday
9 / 5							
9 / 12		English quiz					
9 / 19			English paper due		Speech #1		
9 / 26	Chemistry test					Skiing at the lake	
10 / 3		English quiz		Speech #2			
10 / 10			Geography project due				
10 / 17			--- No classes ---				

LONG-TERM PLANNER ___ / ___ / ___ to ___ / ___ / ___

Week of	Monday	Tuesday	Wednesday	Thursday	Friday	Saturday	Sunday
___ / ___							
___ / ___							
___ / ___							
___ / ___							
___ / ___							
___ / ___							
___ / ___							
___ / ___							
___ / ___							
___ / ___							
___ / ___							
___ / ___							
___ / ___							
___ / ___							
___ / ___							
___ / ___							
___ / ___							
___ / ___							
___ / ___							
___ / ___							
___ / ___							
___ / ___							
___ / ___							
___ / ___							
___ / ___							
___ / ___							
___ / ___							
___ / ___							
___ / ___							
___ / ___							

Name _____

TIME

2

BE HERE NOW

Being right here, right now is such a simple idea. It seems obvious. Where else can you be but where you are? When else can you be there but when you are there? The answer is that you can be somewhere else at any time—in your head. It's common for our thoughts to distract us from where we've chosen to be. When we let this happen, we lose the benefits of focusing our attention on what's important to us in the present moment.

To "be here now" means to do what you're doing when you're doing it. It means to be where you are when you're there. Students consistently report that focusing attention on the here and now is one of the most powerful tools in this book.

We all have a voice in our head that hardly ever shuts up. If you don't believe it, conduct this experiment: Close your eyes for 10 seconds, and pay attention to what is going on in your head. Please do this right now.

Notice something? Perhaps a voice in your head was saying, "Forget it. I'm in a hurry." Another might have said, "I wonder when 10 seconds is up." Another could have been saying, "What little voice? I don't hear any little voice."

That's the voice.

This voice can take you anywhere at any time—especially when you are studying. When the voice takes you away, you might appear to be studying, but your brain is at the beach.

All of us have experienced this voice, as well as the absence of it. When our inner voices are silent, time no longer seems to exist. We forget worries, aches, pains, reasons, excuses, and justifications. We fully experience the here and now. Life is magic.

Do not expect to get rid of daydreams entirely. That is neither possible nor desirable. Inner voices serve a purpose. They enable us to analyse, predict, classify, and understand events out there in the "real" world. The trick is to consciously choose when to be with your inner voice and when to let it go.

Instead of trying to force a stray thought out of your head—a futile enterprise—simply notice it. Accept it. Tell yourself, "There's that thought again." Then gently return your attention to the task at hand. That thought, or another, will come back. Your mind will drift. Simply notice again where your thoughts take you, and gently bring yourself back to the here and now.

The idea behind this Power Process is simple. When you plan for the future, plan for the future. When you listen to a lecture, listen to a lecture. When you read this book, read this book. And when you choose to daydream, daydream. Do what you're doing when you're doing it.

Be where you are when you're there. Be here now ... and now ... and now.

Learn more about this Power Process online @
www.bams5ce.nelson.com

© Alex James Bramwell/Shutterstock

Put It to WORK

*B*eing skilled at managing time will serve you in any career you choose. Here are some ways to transfer techniques from this chapter to the workplace.

Monitor work time

Use the Time Monitor/Time Plan process to analyse the way you currently use your time at work. With this awareness, you can minimize downtime and boost your productivity. Look for low-value activities to eliminate. Also note your peak periods of energy during the workday and schedule your most challenging tasks for these times.

Use a long-term planner to manage major projects at work

Besides scheduling a due date for the final product, set interim due dates—what you'll produce at key points leading up to that final date. For example, you're planning to launch a new in-house training program in one year. Set individual due dates for finishing each major component of the program—such as manuals, websites, and videos.

Avoid the perils of multi-tasking

Our effectiveness often decreases when we try to do several things at once, such as talking on a mobile phone while driving. When you get busy at work, you might feel tempted to multi-task. Yet studies indicate that multi-tasking reduces metabolic activity in the brain, lowers the ability to complete tasks efficiently, and increases the number of errors made in following a procedure (Brescani, Duncan, & Hui Cao, 2010). Turn to the Power Process: "Be Here Now" to find a solution. Plan your workday as a succession of tasks. Then give each task your full attention. Use the ABC priority system to weed out tasks of lower importance. This can give you more time to focus on the As.

© photos.com

Overcome procrastination

This problem is as widespread in the workplace as it is on any campus. Apply the suggestions from "The seven-day antiprocrastination plan" and "More ways to stop procrastination" to work tasks as well as academic tasks.

Calculate the cost of attending meetings

Meetings are a way of life for countless people in the workplace. In fact, if you're in a management or supervisory position, meetings can take up most of your workday. See if you can modify the "Education by the hour" exercise to calculate what it costs you to attend a one-hour business meeting. With this data in hand, write an Intention Statement about how you plan to get the most value out of the meetings you will attend in the future.

Use a lifeline to chart your career path

Your career plan can extend decades into the future. Below are some possible lifeline entries for a person focusing on a career in education.

May 2015	Graduate with a teaching degree
August 2016	Begin teaching high school art
September 2023	Apply to go on a savings plan to fund a personal sabbatical
September 2027	Return to school for a graduate degree in school administration
September 2029	Begin career as a high school principal
September 2033	Take a one-year sabbatical to live in New Zealand
September 2034	Return to job as a high school principal
January 2037	Begin a home-based consulting business, advising teachers and principals about ways to avoid career burnout

Do long-term planning for your organization. The strategies for long-term planning in this chapter can help you set goals for your company that extend well into the future. For example, create a lifeline for your organization, listing specific outcomes to achieve during each of the next five years.

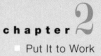

QUIZ

Name_____   Date____/____/____

1. Name three ways you can control interruptions when you study.

2. Rewrite the statement "I want to study harder" so that it becomes a specific goal.

3. The text suggests that long-term goals are important. Write one example of a long-term goal.

4. Describe a short- and mid-term goal that would help you achieve the long-term goal from question three.

5. What are at least five of the 25 ways to get the most out of now?

6. In time-management terms, what is meant by "This ain't no piano"?

7. Define "C fever" as it applies to the ABC priority method.

8. Scheduling marathon study sessions once in a while is generally an effective strategy. True or False? Explain your answer.

9. Describe at least three strategies for overcoming procrastination.

10. The Power Process: "Be Here Now" rules out planning. True or False? Explain your answer.

Skills *SNAPSHOT*

chapter 2

■ Put It to Work
■ Quiz
◀ ◀ ◀ ◀ ◀
■ Master Student Profile

The Discovery Wheel in Chapter 1, Exercise 4, includes a section labeled "Time." For the next 10 to 15 minutes, go beyond your initial responses to that exercise. Take a snapshot of your skills as they exist today, after reading and doing this chapter.

Begin by reflecting on some recent experiences. Then take the next step in your mastery of time by choosing the strategy you'd like to experiment with next.

GOALS

I would describe my ability to set specific goals as . . .

The most important goal for me to achieve during this school year is . . .

DAILY PLANNING

When setting priorities for what to do each day, the first thing I consider is . . .

I keep track of my daily to-do items by . . .

PROCRASTINATION

The kinds of tasks on which I tend to procrastinate include . . .

My strategies for overcoming procrastination currently include . . .

BALANCE

My ability to balance recreation with working and studying can be described as . . .

If I sense that I'm not making enough time for family and friends, I respond by . . .

NEXT ACTION

I'll know that I've reached a new level of mastery with planning when . . .

To reach that level of mastery, the most important thing I can do next is to . . .

MASTER STUDENT Profile

© REUTERS/Dylan Martinez

Chantal Petitclerc (1969 –) is an athlete who inspires others. After winning 21 medals in 2008, she was awarded the Lou Marsh Trophy as Canadian athlete of the year.

 Find more biographical information about Chantal Petitclerc at the Master Student Hall of Fame @

www.bams5ce.nelson.com

Chantal Petitclerc
... is optimistic

When she's racing, Chantal Petitclerc's focus is always on winning. Becoming a role model for other athletes with disabilities is just part of the prize.

"I've never seen myself as someone being on a mission," the wheelchair racer says. "I've always seen myself as an athlete trying to go fast and win a race.

"I see that there are positive effects of that. I recognize that and I'm really happy for that."

Petitclerc, 39, who won five gold medals and set three world records while competing in her final Paralympic Games this summer in Beijing, has been voted The Canadian Press female athlete of the year. She becomes the first Paralympian to receive the award since it was created in 1933.

"It's the conclusion of a season and a year that has been amazing to me, really magic," said Petitclerc. "It seems like it keeps rolling with good news for me.

"I think it's significant for me as an athlete but even more so, it's significant for my sport. That's what makes me the most happy."

[…]

On the track, the muscular Petitclerc is a machine. In Beijing she beat competitors 16 years her junior.

"Those Games were my best ever and the most challenging," said Petitclerc, who is unbeaten in 10 consecutive Paralympic races dating back to 2004 in Athens. "The field, the calibre (of athletes) was higher than ever before. My schedule was crazy."

On one night in Beijing she won two races, setting world records in each, in a span of 90 minutes.

The medal Petitclerc is most proud of is the 800 metres, which she won in world record time. Petitclerc, along with coach Peter Eriksson, devised a "kamikaze strategy" for the race.

Instead of playing it safe, Petitclerc broke from the pack almost from the start of the race. She used her strength to open up a lead that none of the other racers could cut into.

"I was very proud of that," she laughed. "I didn't play it safe. I was going for five gold. This was taking a big chance."

"To be able to decide it, and do it with 100 percent commitment, and break the world record, that was the most amazing feeling."

Petitclerc can be a menacing opponent but is considered a hero by many of the other racers.

"She's a big inspiration for me," Britain's Shelly Woods said in an interview following Petitclerc's final race in China. "She's one of my heroines.

"Racing her you want to get tough and beat her, but at the same time you are in awe of her."

Many of the voters agreed.

"It's a shame we haven't resolved to marry the Olympics and the Paralympics so greatness such as she has repeatedly demonstrated would be much more widely celebrated," said Phil Andrews of the *Guelph Mercury*.

Jim Christie of the *Globe and Mail* said Petitclerc's achievements transcend sport.

"It's not just that she beat other wheelchair athletes, it's that she pushed herself to beat the best she'd ever done and did it on the biggest stage available to her," Christie said. "She's been the icon . . . that people with disabilities don't have to be in the margins of society."

With her Paralympic career finished, Petitclerc has shifted her focus to marathon racing. She will concentrate on 10-kilometre events and half-marathons this year. By 2010 she hopes to challenge for victories at the New York, Boston, and Berlin marathons.

Once she retires, Petitclerc plans to remain involved with Paralympic sports.

"Coaching is an option," she said. "I think there is a lot to do about development for kids.

"It's hard to know where the kids are and how to reach them and how to provide them with equipment."

Petitclerc, who raced in the T54 class for wheelchair athletes with different levels of spinal cord injuries and amputations, was born in Saint-Marc-des-Carrieres, Quebec. She was 13 when she lost the use of her legs after a barn door fell on her.

Just two months after the accident, she was swimming. At age 18 she was introduced to wheelchair sports. She used a homemade wheelchair in her first competitive race and finished last.

Her first Paralympic Games was in Barcelona in 1992, where she won two bronze medals. During her career she has won 14 gold, 5 silver and 2 bronze Paralympic medals.

Petitclerc rarely spends time thinking about what her life would have been like if she hadn't lost the use of her legs.

"I know some people say your accident made you stronger, it was a good thing because it made you this champion," she said. "I prefer to think I had this personality and I had this strength. That's why I was able to bounce (back) from this accident.

"There is no way to know what would have happened with my life. I like to think I would have had a great life and I would have achieved my dreams even if I didn't have the accident. Right now this is the life I want. I wouldn't change it for anything."

Source: The Canadian Press (December 2010). "Petitclerc Voted CP's Female Athlete of the Year," TSN. Retrieved July 5, 2011, from http://www.tsn.ca/olympics/story/?id=260898&lid=headline&lpos=secStory_main

3 Memory

Master Student Map

as you read, ask yourself

what if . . .

I could use my memory to its full potential?

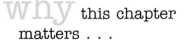

why this chapter matters . . .

Learning memory techniques can boost your skills at test taking, reading, note taking, and many other tasks.

what is included . . .

- Take your memory out of the closet   109
- The memory jungle   110
- 20 memory techniques   112
- Pay attention to your attention   120
- Set a trap for your memory   122
- Remembering names   124
- Mnemonic devices   125
- Power Process: Love your problems (and experience your barriers)   131
- Master Student Profile: David Suzuki   135

how you can use this chapter . . .

- Focus your attention.
- Make conscious choices about what to remember.
- Recall facts and ideas with more ease.

MASTER STUDENTS in *action*

Before I read the Memory chapter, I had trouble remembering what I had studied when taking a test or quiz. Visualization is by far the most useful technique I have come across in this book. While I'm taking the test, I visualize the book or paper that I had studied from. It also helps with names. I visualize something funny to go along with someone's name.

—TAUNI ALDINGER

Take your memory out of the closet

ONCE UPON A TIME, people talked about human memory as if it were a closet. You stored individual memories there like old shirts and stray socks. Remembering something was a matter of rummaging through all that stuff. If you were lucky, you found what you wanted.

This view of memory creates some problems. For one thing, closets can get crowded; things too easily disappear. Even with the biggest closet, you eventually run out of space. If you want to pack some new memories in there—well, too bad. There's no room. Brain researchers have shattered this image to bits. Memory is not a closet. It's not a place or a thing. Instead, memory is a *process*.

On a conscious level, memories appear as distinct and unconnected mental events: words, sensations, images. They can include details from the distant past—the smell of cookies baking in your grandmother's kitchen or the feel of sunlight warming your face through the window of your Grade 1 classroom. On a biological level, each of those memories involves millions of nerve cells, or **neurons**, firing chemical messages at each other. If you could observe these exchanges in real time, you'd see regions of cells all over the brain glowing with electrical charges at speeds that would put a computer to shame.

When a series of cells connects several times in a similar pattern, the result is a memory. Canadian psychologist Donald Hebb (2001) uses the aphorism "Neurons which fire together, wire together" to describe this principle. This means that memories are not really "stored." Instead, remembering is a process in which you **encode** information as links between active neurons that fire together and **decode**, or reactivate, neurons that wired together in the past. Memory is the probability that certain patterns of brain activity will occur again in the future. In effect, you re-create a memory each time you recall it.

Whenever you learn something new, your brain changes physically by growing more connections between neurons. The more you learn, the greater the number of connections. For all practical purposes, there's no limit to how many memories your brain can encode.

There's a lot you can do to wire those neural networks into place. That's where the memory techniques described in this chapter come into play. Step out of your crowded mental closet into a world of infinite possibilities. ✳

journal entry 9

Discovery/Intention Statement

Create value from this chapter

Write a sentence or two describing the way you feel when you want to remember something but have trouble doing so. Think of a specific incident in which you experienced this problem, such as trying to remember someone's name or a fact you needed during a test.

I discovered that I . . .

_____

_____

_____

Now spend five minutes skimming this chapter and find three to five memory strategies you think could be helpful. List the strategies below and note the page numbers where they are explained. Then write an Intention Statement scheduling a time to study them in more detail.

Strategy   **Page number**

_____

_____

_____

I intend to . . .

_____

_____

_____

_____

The memory jungle

© Debra Dawson

Think of your memory as a vast, overgrown jungle. This memory jungle is thick with wild plants, exotic shrubs, twisted trees, and creeping vines. It spreads over thousands of kilometres—dense, tangled, forbidding. *The more often you recall information, and the more often you put the same information into your memory, the easier it is to find.*

IMAGINE THAT THE jungle is surrounded on all sides by towering mountains. There is only one entrance to the jungle: a small meadow that is reached by a narrow pass through the mountains.

In the jungle there are animals, millions of them. The animals represent all of the information in your memory. Imagine that every thought, mental picture, or perception you ever had is represented by an animal in this jungle. Every single event ever perceived by any of your five senses—sight, touch, hearing, smell, or taste—has also passed through the meadow and entered the jungle. Some of the thought animals, such as the colour of your Grade 7 teacher's favourite sweater, are well hidden. Other thoughts, such as your mobile-phone number or the position of the reverse gear in your car, are easier to find.

There are two rules of the memory jungle. Each thought animal must pass through the meadow at the entrance to the jungle. And once an animal enters the jungle, it never leaves.

The meadow represents short-term memory. You use this kind of memory when you look up a telephone number and hold it in your memory long enough to make a call. Short-term memory appears to have a limited capacity (the meadow is small) and disappears fast (animals pass through the meadow quickly). Lots of things can lead to information not being transferred from short-term to long-term memory. For instance, just after your friend tells you his new phone number, your conversation is interrupted. If you don't have time to rehearse the new number, chances are it won't pass into long-term memory.

The jungle itself represents long-term memory. This is the kind of memory that allows you to recall information from day to day, week to week, and year to year. Remember that thought animals never leave the long-term memory jungle. The trick, though, is that although thought animals never leave long-term memory, it doesn't mean you will be able to access that specific thought animal (or memory) when you want to. The following visualizations can help you recall useful concepts about memory.

Visualization #1: A well-worn path

© Michael Atkinson

Imagine what happens as a thought, in this case we'll call it an elephant, bounds across short-term memory and into the jungle. The elephant leaves a trail of broken twigs and hoof prints that you can follow. Brain research suggests that thoughts can wear paths in the brain

(Hyden, 1969). These paths are called *neural traces*. The more well-worn the neural trace, the easier it is to retrieve (find) the thought. In other words, the more often the elephant retraces the path, the clearer the path becomes. The more often you recall information, and the more often you put the same information into your memory, the easier it is to find. When you buy a new car, for example, the first few times you try to find reverse, you have to think for a moment. After you have found reverse gear every day for a week, the path is worn into your memory. After a year, the path is so well-worn that when you dream about driving your car backward, you even dream the correct motion for putting the gear in reverse.

Visualization #2: A herd of thoughts

The second picture you can use to your advantage is the picture of many animals gathering at a clearing—like thoughts gathering at a central location in the memory. It is easier to retrieve thoughts that are grouped together, just as it is easier to find a herd of animals than it is to find a single elephant.

Pieces of information are easier to recall if you can associate them with similar information. So the organization of material is a key to successful recall of information. For example, you can more readily remember a particular player's batting average if you can associate it with other baseball statistics.

© Debra Dawson

short-term memory meadow, and review it soon after it enters the long-term memory jungle. Wear a path in your memory immediately.

Visualization #4: You are directing the animal traffic

The fourth picture is one with you in it. You are standing at the entrance to the short-term memory meadow, directing herds of thought animals as they file through the pass, across the meadow, and into your long-term memory. You are taking an active role

© Michael Atkinson

Visualization #3: Turning your back

Imagine releasing the elephant into the jungle, turning your back, and counting to 10. When you turn around, the elephant is gone. This is exactly what happens to most of the information you receive.

Generally, we can recall only 50 percent of the material we have just read. Within 24 hours, most of us can recall only about 20 percent. This means that 80 percent of the material has not been meaningfully encoded and is wandering around, lost in the memory jungle.

The remedy is simple: Review quickly. Do not take your eyes off the thought animal as it crosses the

© Michael Atkinson

in the learning process. You are paying attention. You are doing more than sitting on a rock and watching the animals file past into your brain. See what type of animal it is—think about whether you have seen it before or whether it is something new. Try to categorize the thought animals—look for similarities between what is new or different than what you have seen before (Svinicki, 2004). Connecting these new animals to those you have seen before increases the odds you will recognize them the next time you see them in the memory jungle. Practise getting the animals out of the jungle— what types of animals did you see? (Karpicke & Blunt, 2011). As you engage in this process you have taken control of your memory. ✳

Find guided visualizations based on the memory jungle online @
www.bams5ce.nelson.com

20 memory techniques

Experiment with these techniques to develop a flexible, custom-made memory system that fits your style of learning.

THE 20 TECHNIQUES are divided into four categories, each of which represents a general principle for improving memory. Briefly, the categories are:

Organize it. Organized information is easier to find.

Use your body. Learning is an active process; get all of your senses involved.

Use your brain. Work *with* your memory, not *against* it.

Recall it. This is easier when you use the other principles efficiently to notice and elaborate on incoming information.

The first three categories, which include techniques #1 through #16, are about storing information effectively. Most memory battles are won or lost here.

To get the most out of this article, first survey the following techniques by reading each heading. Then read the techniques. Next, skim them again, looking for the ones you like best. Mark those and use them.

Organize it

1 Be selective. There's a difference between gaining understanding and drowning in information. During your stay in higher education, you will be exposed to thousands of facts and ideas. No one expects you to memorize all of them. To a large degree, the art of memory is the art of selecting what to remember in the first place.

As you dig into your textbooks and notes, make choices about what is most important to learn. Imagine that you are going to create a test on the material and consider the questions you would ask.

When reading, look for chapter previews, summaries, and review questions. Pay attention to anything printed in bold type. Also notice visual elements—tables, charts, graphs, and illustrations. All of these are clues pointing to what's important. During lectures, notice what the instructor emphasizes. Anything that's presented visually—on the board, on overheads, or with PowerPoint slides—is probably crucial.

2 Categorize. One way to create meaning is to learn from the general to the specific. Before you begin your next reading assignment, skim it to locate the main idea. You can use the same techniques you

learned in Exercise #1: "Textbook reconnaissance" on page 2. If you're ever lost, step back and look at the big picture. The details might make more sense.

You can organize any list of items—even random ones—in a meaningful way to make them easier to remember. In his book *Information Anxiety*, Richard Saul Wurman (1989) proposes five principles for organizing any body of ideas, facts, or objects:

Principle	Example
Organize by **time**	Events in history or in a novel flow in chronological order.
Organize by **location**	Addresses for a large company's regional offices are grouped by province and city.
Organize by **category**	Nonfiction library materials are organized by subject categories.
Organize by **continuum**	Products rated in *Consumer's Guide* are grouped from highest in price to lowest in price, or highest in quality to lowest in quality.
Organize by **alphabet**	Entries in a book index are listed in ABC order.

3 Create associations. The data already encoded in your neural networks are arranged according to a scheme that makes sense to you. When you introduce new data, you can remember the details more effectively if you associate them with similar or related data.

Think about your favourite courses. They probably relate to subjects that you already know something about. If you know a lot about the history of 20th-century music, you'll find it easier to remember facts about music recorded since 1900. If you've already passed an advanced algebra course, you're primed to remember calculus formulas. And if you've enjoyed several novels by your favourite author, you've already cleared a memory path for another book from that writer.

Even when you're tackling a new subject, you can build a mental store of basic background information—the raw material for creating associations. Preview reading assignments, and complete those readings before you attend lectures. Before taking advanced courses, master the prerequisites. Remember, trying to recall discrete pieces of information increases the memory load and makes it more difficult to recall at a later date—the more associations you form between what you already know and what you are trying to learn, the easier it will be for you to recall that info at a later date.

Use your body

4 Learn it once, actively. Action is a great memory enhancer. You can test this theory by studying your assignments with the same energy that you bring to the dance floor or the basketball court.

You can use simple, direct methods to infuse your learning with action. When you sit at your desk, sit up straight. Sit on the edge of your chair, as if you were about to spring out of it and sprint across the room.

Also experiment with standing up when you study. It's harder to fall asleep in this position. Some people insist that their brains work better when they stand.

Pace back and forth and gesture as you recite material out loud. Use your hands. Get your whole body involved in studying.

This technique illustrates the practical advantage of knowing about learning styles. In Chapter 1, the article "Learning styles: Discovering how you learn" explains four aspects of learning: concrete experience, abstract conceptualization, active experimentation, and reflective observation. Many courses in higher education lean heavily toward abstract conceptualization, emphasizing lectures, essays, and textbook assignments. These courses might not give you the chance to act on ideas, to experiment with them, and to test them in situations outside the classroom.

So get involved in activities outside of the classroom that allow you to test what you are learning in class. For example, if you are interested in the environment, get involved with a club that takes you out into nature and see how well the theories hold up in the real world. Bring those experiences back into the classroom. Or in psychology, many of you will hear theories about how children learn. Volunteer in a daycare and see which of those theories really explains how children learn language, for example.

Your English instructor might tell you that one quality of effective writing is clear organization. To test this idea, examine the texts you come in contact with daily—newspapers, popular magazines, websites, and textbooks. Look for examples of clear organization *and* unclear organization. Then write Intention Statements about ways to organize your own writing more clearly.

Your sociology class might include a discussion about how groups of people resolve conflict. See if you can apply any of these ideas to resolving conflict in your own family. Then write Discovery Statements about your experiences.

The point behind each of these examples is the same: To remember an idea, go beyond thinking about it. *Do* something with it.

5 Relax. When you're relaxed, you absorb new information quickly and recall it with greater ease and accuracy. Students who can't recall information under the stress of a final exam often can recite the same facts later when they are relaxed.

Relaxing might seem to contradict the idea of active learning as explained in technique #4, but it doesn't. Being relaxed is not the same as being drowsy, zoned out, or asleep. Relaxation is a state of alertness, free of tension, during which your mind can play with new information, roll it around, create associations with it, and apply many of the other memory techniques. You can be active *and* relaxed.

6 Recite and repeat. When you repeat something out loud, you anchor the concept in two different senses. First, you get the physical sensation in your throat, tongue, and lips when voicing the concept. Second, you hear it. The combined result is synergistic, just as it is when you create pictures. That is, the effect of using two different senses is greater than the sum of their individual effects.

The "out loud" part is important. Reciting silently in your head can be useful—in the library, for example—but it is not as effective as making noise. Your mind can trick itself into thinking it knows something when it doesn't. Your ears are harder to fool.

The repetition part is important, too. Repetition is a common memory device because it works. It is particularly useful when you want to memorize facts—unrelated bits of information, like the capitals of the provinces or types of rocks. However, it leads to what we think of as shallow processing—where the information is stored according to its surface features like the shape of the letters or the sound of the words—information that does not really connect to the meaning of the information. So although this can be a very successful strategy for memorizing some types of information, when you can learn pieces of information without learning the meaning, this is not as effective at getting information into long-term memory. Remembering information word-for-word means you are not getting the in-depth understanding required for deep learning. You may have difficulty on a test if the instructor rewords the concept. To get the in-depth understanding required, learn the connections between the concepts. So rather than learning just the names of different rocks, try to learn why and how they differ from one another. Repetition blazes a trail through the pathways of your brain, making the information easier to find. Repeat a concept out loud until you know it, then say it five more times.

Recitation works best when you recite concepts in your own words. For example, if you want to remember that the acceleration of a falling body due to gravity at sea level equals 9.8 metres per second, you might say, "Gravity makes an object accelerate 9.8 metres per second faster for each second that it's in the air at sea level." Putting it in your own words forces you to think about it.

Have some fun with this technique. Recite by writing a song about what you're learning. Sing it in the shower. Use any style you want, ("Country, jazz, rock, or rap—when you sing out loud, learning's a snap!").

Or imitate someone. Imagine your textbook being read by Jim Carrey, Celine Dion, or Clint Eastwood, ("Go ahead, punk. Make my density equal mass over volume.").

Recite and repeat. It's a technique you can use anywhere.

7 Create pictures. Draw diagrams. Make cartoons. Use these images to connect facts and illustrate relationships. Associations within and among abstract concepts can be "seen" and recalled more easily when they are visualized. The key is to use your imagination.

For example, Boyle's law states that at a constant temperature, the volume of a confined ideal gas varies inversely with its pressure. Simply put, cutting the volume in half doubles the pressure. To remember this concept, you might picture someone "doubled over" using a bicycle pump. As she increases the pressure in the pump by decreasing the volume in the pump cylinder, she seems to be getting angrier. By the time she has doubled the pressure (and halved the volume) she is boiling ("Boyle-ing") mad.

Another reason to create pictures is that visual information is associated with a part of the brain that is different from the part that processes verbal information. When you create a picture of a concept, you are anchoring the information in a second part of your brain. This increases your chances of recalling that information.

To visualize abstract relationships effectively, create an action-oriented image, such as the person using the pump. Make the picture vivid, too. The person's face could be bright red. And involve all of your senses. Imagine how the cold metal of the pump would feel and how the person would grunt as she struggled with it.

8 Write it down. This technique is obvious, yet easy to forget. Writing a note to yourself helps you remember an idea, even if you never look at the note again.

You can extend this technique by writing down an idea not just once, but many times. Let go of the old image of being forced to write "I will not throw paper wads" 100 times on the chalkboard after school. When you choose to remember something, repetitive writing is a powerful tool.

Writing engages a different kind of memory than speaking. Writing prompts us to be more logical, coherent, and complete. Written reviews reveal gaps in knowledge that oral reviews miss, just as oral reviews reveal gaps that written reviews miss.

Another advantage of written reviews is that they more closely match the way you're asked to remember materials in school. During your studies, you'll probably take far more written exams than oral exams. Writing can be an effective way to prepare for such tests.

Finally, writing is physical. Your arm, your hand, and your fingers join in. Remember, learning is an active process—you remember what you *do*.

Use your brain

9 Engage your emotions. One powerful way to enhance your memory is to make friends with your amygdala. This is an area of your brain that lights up with extra neural activity each time you feel a strong emotion. When a topic excites love, laughter, or fear, the amygdala sends a flurry of chemical messages that say, in effect: *This information is important and useful. Don't forget it.*

You're more likely to remember course material when you relate it to a goal—whether academic, personal, or career—that you feel strongly about. This is one reason why it pays to be specific about what you want. The more goals you have and the more clearly they are defined, the more channels you create for incoming information.

You can use this strategy even when a subject seems boring at first. If you're not naturally interested in a topic, then create interest. Find a study partner in the class—if possible, someone you know and like—or form a study group. Also consider getting to know the instructor personally. When a course creates a bridge to human relationships, you engage the content in a more emotional way.

10 Overlearn. One way to fight mental fuzziness is to learn more than you need to know about a subject simply to pass a test. You can pick a subject apart, examine it, add to it, and go over it until it becomes second nature.

This technique is especially effective for problem solving. Do the assigned problems, and then do more problems. Look up additional information from a reputable source online. Find another textbook and work similar problems. Then make up your own problems and solve them. When you pretest yourself in this way, the potential rewards are speed, accuracy, and greater confidence at final exam time.

11 Escape the short-term memory trap. Short-term memory is different from the kind of memory you'll need during final exams. For example, most of us can look at an unfamiliar phone number once and remember it long enough to dial it. See if you can recall that number the next day.

Short-term memory can fade after a few minutes, and it rarely lasts more than several hours. At the end of class, take a few minutes to write down the most important points you learned in class today. This will help you solidify the memory and also give you some notes to use when it comes time to study. It's too easy to be writing notes and copying the PowerPoint® slides in class without really thinking about what the instructor is saying. If you know you are going to have to summarize your notes at the end of class, you will pay more attention. Similarly, a short review within minutes or hours of a study session can move material from short-term memory into long-term memory. That quick mini review can save you hours of study time when exams roll around.

12 **Use your times of peak energy.** Study your most difficult subjects during the times when your energy peaks. Many people can concentrate more effectively during daylight hours. The early morning hours can be especially productive, even for those who hate to get up with the sun. Observe the peaks and valleys in your energy flow during the day and adjust study times accordingly. Perhaps you will experience surges in memory power during the late afternoon or evening.

13 **Distribute learning.** As an alternative to marathon study sessions, experiment with shorter, spaced-out sessions. You might find that you can get far more done in three two-hour sessions than in one six-hour session.

For example, when you are studying for your Canadian history exam, study for an hour or two and then wash the dishes. While you are washing the dishes, part of your mind will be reviewing what you studied. Return to Canadian history for a while. Then call a friend. Even when you are deep in conversation, part of your mind will be reviewing history.

You can get more done if you take regular breaks. You can even use the breaks as mini rewards. After a productive study session, give yourself permission to log on and check your email, listen to a song, or play 10 minutes of hide-and-seek with your kids. Set a timer to remind yourself to get back on track.

Distributing your learning is a brain-friendly thing to do. You cannot absorb new information and ideas during all of your waking hours. If you overload your brain, it will find a way to shut down for a rest—whether you plan for it or not. By taking periodic breaks while studying, you allow information to sink in. During these breaks, your brain is taking the time to literally rewire itself by growing new connections between cells. Psychologists call this process *consolidation* (Siegel,

2001). But be careful to get back on task—again it is easy to start surfing the web and realize your 20 minute break has stretched to an hour.

There is an exception to the idea of allowing time for consolidation. When you are so engrossed in a textbook that you cannot put it down, when you are consumed by an idea for an essay and cannot think of anything else—keep going. The master student within you has taken over. Enjoy the ride.

14 **Be aware of attitudes.** People who think history is boring tend to have trouble remembering dates and historical events. People who believe math is difficult often have a hard time recalling mathematical equations and formulas. All of us can forget information that contradicts our opinions.

If you think a subject is boring, remind yourself that everything is related to everything else. Look for connections that relate to your own interests.

For example, consider a person who is fanatical about cars. He can rebuild a motor in a weekend and has a good time doing so. From this apparently specialized interest, she can explore a wide realm of knowledge. She can relate the workings of an engine to principles of physics, math, and chemistry. Computerized parts in newer cars can lead her to the study of data processing. She can research how the automobile industry has changed our cities and helped create suburbs, a topic that includes urban planning, sociology, business, economics, psychology, and history.

Being aware of attitudes is not the same as fighting them or struggling to give them up. Acknowledge them. Notice them. Simple awareness can deflate an attitude that is blocking your memory.

15 **Elaborate.** According to Harvard psychologist Daniel Schacter (2001), all courses in memory improvement are based on a single technique—elaboration. *Elaboration* means consciously encoding new information. Current brain research indicates that elaboration is more effective than rehearsal for long-term memory.

One way to elaborate is to ask yourself questions about incoming information: "Does this remind me of something or someone I already know?" "Is this similar to a technique that I already use?" and "Where and when can I use this information?"

When you learned to recognize Italy on a world map, your teacher probably pointed out that the country is shaped like a boot. This is a simple form of elaboration.

The same idea applies to more complex material. When you meet someone new, for example, ask yourself, "Does she remind me of someone else?" Or when reading this book, preview the material using the Master Student Map that opens each chapter.

Two other common elaborative study strategies are **graphic organizers** and **concept maps**. One example of a graphic organizer is a *topic-point-details* chart.

At the top of this chart, write the main topic of a lecture or reading assignment. In the left column, list the main points you want to remember. And in the right column, list key details related to each point. See Example 1 for the beginning of a chart based on this article:

Example 1

20 MEMORY TECHNIQUES	
Point	**Details**
1. Be selective	Choose what not to remember. Look for clues to important material.
2. Categorize	Organize by time, location, category, continuum, or alphabet.
3. Create associations	Link new facts with facts you already know.
4. Learn actively	Sit straight. Stand while studying. Recite while walking. Test those theories in the real world.
5. Relax	Release tension. Remain alert.

You could use a similar chart to prompt critical thinking about an issue. Express that issue as a question, and write it at the top. In the left column, note the opinion about the issue. In the right column, list notable facts, expert opinions, reasons, and examples that support each opinion. Example 2 in the top right column is about tax cuts as a strategy for stimulating the economy.

Sometimes you'll want to remember the main actions in a story or historical event. Create a timeline by drawing a straight line. Place points in order on that line to represent key events. Place earlier events toward the left end of the line and later events toward the right. At the bottom of this page, Example 3

Example 2

STIMULATE THE ECONOMY WITH CORPORATE TAX CUTS?	
Opinion	**Support**
Yes	Savings from tax cuts allow businesses to invest money in new equipment.
	Tax cuts encourage businesses to expand and hire new employees.
No	Least efficient way to create jobs and increase growth in the economy.
	Tax cuts create budget deficits.
Maybe	Tax cuts might work in some economic conditions.
	Budget deficits might be only temporary.

shows the start of a timeline of events relating to the history of Afghanistan since 1933.

When you want to compare or contrast two things, play with a Venn diagram. Represent each thing as a circle. Draw the circles so that they overlap. In the overlapping area, list characteristics that the two things share. In the outer parts of each circle, list the unique characteristics of each thing. Example 4 on page 117 compares the two types of journal entries included in this book—Discovery Statements and Intention Statements.

Example 3

CHRONOLOGY OF AFGHANISTAN BEGINNING WITH INDEPENDENCE FROM BRITAIN IN 1919				
● 1933 Zahir Shah rules as king for the next 4 decades.	● 1973 Coup led by Mohammed Daud. Declares country a republic.	● 1978-1979 Daud is overthrown. Power struggles occur. Soviet forces enter country.	● 1989-1996 Soviet forces leave but civil war continues. Taliban seize control of Kabul.	● 2001-2011 US, Britain launch air strikes, Taliban deposed from government, Canada joins mission, Karzai elected PM twice.

Example 4

Discovery Statements   Intention Statements

- Describe specific thoughts
- Describe specific feelings
- Describe current and past behaviours

- Are a type of journal entry
- Are based on telling the truth
- Can be written at any time on any topic
- Can lead to action

- Describe future behaviours
- Can include timelines
- Can include rewards

The graphic organizers described here are just a few of the many kinds available. To find more examples, do an Internet search. Have fun, and invent graphic organizers of your own.

Another variation on the graphic organizer is the **concept maps.** Concept mapping, pioneered by Joseph Novak and D. Bob Gowin (1984), is a tool you can use to display the organization underlying lectures, discussions, and any reading materials. A subject that you study in school might include dozens or even hundreds of concepts that you need to learn. However, learning the subject relies on a simple, underlying process: You take one new concept at a time and link it to a concept that you already understand, creating a new **proposition** which states a relationship between two or more concepts.

Concept maps take this process out of your head and puts in on paper in a visual format. You list concepts and arrange them in a meaningful order. Then you explicitly state the relationships between concepts, forming meaningful propositions.

Concept maps also promote critical thinking. Creating a concept map can alert you to gaps in your understanding—where you are missing concepts, or concepts with illogical links. They are an elaborative study strategy which we know supports effective encoding (Svinicki, 2004)—getting materials into memory—particularly when they are developed along with materials you are trying to learn.

Why do they work? Well, both concept maps and graphic organizers lead to deeper processing of material

How to create a concept map

1. **List the key concepts in the text.** Aim to express each concept in three words or less. Most concept words are nouns, including terms and proper names. At this point, you can list the concepts in any order. For ease in ranking the concepts later, write each one on a single Post-it® note.

2. **Rank the concepts so that they flow from general to specific.** On a large sheet of paper, write the main concept at the top of the page. Place the most specific concepts near the bottom. Arrange the rest of the concepts in appropriate positions throughout the middle of the page. Circle each concept.

3. **Draw lines that connect the concepts.** On these connecting lines, add words that describe the relationship between the concepts. Again, limit yourself to the fewest words needed to make an accurate link—three

words or less. Linking words are often verbs, verb phrases, or prepositions.

4. **Finally, review your map.** Look for any concepts that are repeated in several places on the map. You can avoid these repetitions by adding more links between concepts. Also look for accurate linking words and missing concepts.

As you gain facility with concept maps, you might wish to create them on a computer. Use any software with drawing capabilities. For example, the software program *Inspiration*, a visual thinking and learning tool, is specifically designed to create concept maps.

 Sample concept maps based on selected articles in this book are available online @
www.bams5ce.nelson.com

Pay attention to your attention

MANY OF THE memory glitches of everyday life result from simple absent-mindedness and a failure to concentrate. Often, the results are minor inconveniences, such as misplacing an umbrella or entering a room and forgetting why. Sometimes, though, the consequences are serious—missing an important meeting, forgetting to answer key questions on a final exam, or running a stop sign and causing an accident.

When you notice your mind heading off on an unscheduled holiday, use any of the following techniques to return to the here and now.

Reduce interference. Turn down the music—or turn it off—when you study. Find a quiet place that is free from distractions. If there's a party at your house, go to the library. If you like to snack, don't tempt yourself by studying next to the refrigerator. Two hours of studying in front of the television might be worth 10 minutes of studying where it is quiet. If you have two hours in which to study *and* watch television, it's probably better to study for an hour and then watch television for an hour. Doing one activity at a time increases your ability to remember. Research shows that when you multi-task you actually learn less than when you just pay attention to one thing (Fried, 2008). When our attention is divided, our performance suffers; so when you are studying . . . study!

Think out loud. You can also train your attention by noticing unconscious actions and making them conscious. An example is the sequence of actions you might take before you leave home for the day—grabbing your keys, turning off lights, and locking the front door. If you go through this series in a robotic trance of semi-attention, you might get to campus and wonder, Did I remember to lock the door? You can eliminate such worries by saying to yourself before you leave home, "Now I am turning out the lights . . . . Now I am checking the stove . . . . Now I am turning the lock." Instead of coasting through large portions of your life on automatic pilot, you'll wake up and pay attention.

Bring your attention to your body—or your body to attention. In any given moment, your mind can be in two or more places at once. Your body, however, is always parked in one spot and dwells contentedly in the present moment. To focus your attention instantly, simply return to your body. Notice simple sensations—the air passing in and out of your nostrils, or your clothes gently resting on your skin. Then redirect your attention to the task at hand. Another option is to bring your body to a state of attention. Stand erect or sit with a straight spine on the edge of your chair. Visualize yourself on a tennis court, poised to return a serve. Repeat this process whenever your mind drifts.

Use a concentration cheat sheet. Each time that your attention wanders during a class or meeting, make a tick mark in the margins of your note paper. Creating a visible record of your distractions is one way to reduce them. Also, the physical act of writing re-engages your attention.

Note: This technique works only if you release any self-judgment about how often your mind wanders. At first, you might end up with row after row of tick marks. That's OK. With time and consistent practice, they will decrease.

Deal with distraction. One source of distraction is an urgent task that constantly resurfaces in your mind. Perhaps there is an important phone call to make, an errand to run, or a pressing problem to solve. When time and circumstances allow, deal with the distraction by taking care of the matter as the first priority.

If that's not feasible, write a detailed Intention Statement that describes exactly what you will do to handle the distraction. With your intention safely recorded in writing, you can now zero in on studying, working, or whatever else is most important in the present moment.

Know when to get help. A condition called attention deficit/hyperactivity disorder (ADHD) interferes with the ability to concentrate. People with ADHD consistently experience negative consequences—missed due dates, low marks, poor work performance, strained relationships with friends and family, and more—as a result of being unable to focus their attention.

If you find that none of the above techniques helps you take charge of your attention, then meet with an academic advisor or counsellor and ask for help. ADHD can be reliably diagnosed and treated.

Students who do not have ADHD might also need help. Academic advising could be helpful for all students who can't concentrate. ✱

Doing one activity at a time increases your ability to remember.

12 exercise
Use Q-Cards to reinforce memory

One memory strategy you might find useful involves a special kind of flash card. It's called a *Question Card*, or *Q-Card* for short.

To create a standard flash card, you write a question on one side of an index card and its answer on the other side. Q-Cards have a question on *both* sides. Here's the trick: The question on each side of the card contains the answer to the question on the other side.

The questions you write on Q-Cards can draw on both **lower- and higher-order thinking skills**. Writing these questions forces you to encode material in different ways. You activate more areas of your brain and burn the concepts even deeper into your memory.

For example, say that you want to remember the subject of Bill 101, which made French the official language of the Province of Québec. On one side of an index card, write *What bill made French the official language of the Province of Québec?* Turn the card over and write *What did Bill 101 do?*

To get the most from Q-Cards:

- Add a picture to each side of the card. This helps you learn concepts faster and develop a more visual learning style.

- Read the questions and recite the answers out loud. Two keys to memory are repetition and novelty, so use a different voice whenever you read and recite. Whisper the first time you go through your cards, then shout or sing the next time. Doing this develops an auditory learning style.

- Carry Q-Cards with you and pull them out during waiting times. To develop a kinesthetic learning style, handle your cards often.

- Create a Q-Card for each new and important concept within 24 hours after attending a class or completing an assignment. This is your *active stack* of cards. Keep answering the questions on these cards until you learn each new concept.

- Review all of the cards from the term for a certain subject on one day each week. For example, on Monday, review all cards from biology; on Tuesday, review all cards from history. These cards make up your *review stacks*.

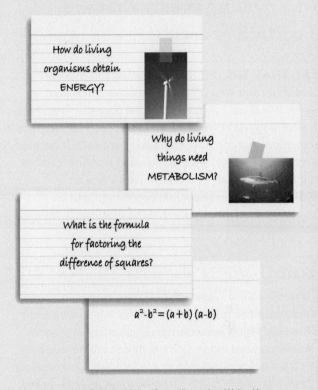

How do living organisms obtain ENERGY?

Why do living things need METABOLISM?

What is the formula for factoring the difference of squares?

$$a^2 - b^2 = (a+b)(a-b)$$

Shark and windmill © Digital Vision/Getty; *illustration:* Walter Kopec

MEMORY

3

Set a trap for your memory

When you want to remind yourself to do something, link this activity to another event you know will take place. The key is to "trap" your memory by picking events that are certain to occur.

SAY THAT YOU'RE walking to class and suddenly remember that your accounting assignment is due tomorrow. Switch your watch to the opposite wrist. Now you're "trapped." Every time you glance at your wrist and remember that you have switched your watch, it becomes a reminder that you were supposed to remember something else. (You can do the same with a ring.)

If you empty your pockets every night, put an unusual item in your pocket in the morning to remind

phone: © photos.com; door: © Ryan McVay/Photodisc Green/Getty, illustration: Walter Kopec

yourself to do something before you go to bed. For example, to remember to call your younger sister on her birthday, pick an object from the playpen—a teething toy, perhaps—and put it in your pocket. When you empty your pocket that evening and find the teething toy, you're more likely to make the call.

Everyday rituals that are seldom neglected, such as feeding a pet, listening to the weather report, and unlacing shoes—provide opportunities for setting traps. For example, tie a triple knot in your shoelace as a reminder to set the alarm for your early morning study group meeting. You can even use imaginary traps. To remember to pay your phone bill, picture your phone hanging on the front door. In your mind, create the feeling of reaching for the doorknob and grabbing the phone instead. When you get home and reach to open the front door, the image is apt to return to you.

Link two activities together, and make the association unusual. ✳

Keep your brain fit for life

Memories are encoded as physical changes in the brain. And your brain is an organ that needs regular care and exercise. Higher education gives you plenty of chances to exercise that organ. Don't let those benefits fade after you leave school. Starting now, adopt habits to keep your brain lean and fit for life. Consider these research-based suggestions from the Alzheimer's Association (2009).

Stay mentally active If you sit at a desk most of the workday, take a class. If you seldom travel, start reading maps of new locations and plan a cross-country trip. Seek out museums, theatres, concerts, and other cultural events. Even after you graduate, consider learning another language or taking up a musical instrument. Learning gives your brain a workout, much like sit-ups condition your abs.

Stay socially active Having a network of supportive friends can reduce stress levels. In turn, stress management helps to maintain connections between brain cells. Stay socially active by working, volunteering, and joining clubs.

Stay physically active Physical activity promotes blood flow to the brain. It also reduces the risk of diabetes, cardiovascular disease, and other diseases that can impair brain function.

Adopt a brain-healthy diet A diet rich in dark-skinned fruits and vegetables boosts your supply of antioxidants—natural chemicals that nourish your brain. Examples of these foods are raisins, blueberries, blackberries, strawberries, raspberries, kale, spinach, brussels sprouts, alfalfa sprouts, and broccoli. Avoid foods that are high in saturated fat and cholesterol, which may increase the risk of Alzheimer's disease.

Drink alcohol moderately, if at all A common definition of moderate consumption for people of legal drinking age is a limit of one drink per day for women and two drinks per day for men. Heavier drinking can affect memory. In fact, long-term alcoholics tend to develop conditions that impair memory. One such condition is Korsakoff's syndrome, a disorder that causes people to forget incidents immediately after they happen.

Protect your heart In general, what's good for your heart is good for your brain. Protect both organs by eating well, exercising regularly, managing your weight, staying tobacco-free, and getting plenty of sleep. These habits reduce your risk of heart attack, stroke, and other cardiovascular conditions that interfere with blood flow to the brain.

Notable failures

Sometimes you feel that no matter how hard you try, you are doomed to fail. However, keep in mind that many famous people did not meet with success initially, but later went on to fame and fortune. The adage "If at first you don't succeed, try, try again" has a lot of merit. It is often from our failures that we learn the most. So the next time you get a poor grade on a test or don't make the team you want, keep in mind that that event just might be your first step to success.

Einstein was four years old before he could speak and seven before he could read. **Beethoven**'s music teacher once said of him, "As a composer he is hopeless."

In his first professional race, cyclist **Lance Armstrong** finished last.

The first time **Jerry Seinfeld** walked onstage as a comic at a comedy club, he looked out at the audience and froze.

Susan Boyle's first appearance on British TV did not lead to fame or fortune.

Walt Disney was fired by a newspaper editor because "he lacked imagination and had no good ideas."

J.K. Rowling completed the first of the Harry Potter books while receiving welfare payments. The first agent she sent some chapters to was not at all interested in promoting her.

Emily Dickinson had only seven poems published in her lifetime.

Decca Records turned down a recording contract with the **Beatles** with an unprophetic evaluation: "We don't like their sound. Groups of guitars are on their way out."

In 1954, Jimmy Denny, manager of the Grand Ole Opry, fired **Elvis Presley** after one performance.

"I've missed more than 9,000 shots in my career," **Michael Jordan** said. "I've lost almost 300 games. Twenty-six times I've been trusted to take the game winning shot . . . and missed. I've failed over and over and over again in my life. That is why I succeed."

Spike Lee applied for graduate study at the top film schools in the U.S. Due to his scores on the Graduate Record Exam, both schools turned Lee down.

Source: Adapted from "But They Did Not Give Up," http://www.des.emory.edu/mfp/OnFailingG.html (accessed February 20, 2009).

journal entry 10

Discovery Statement

Revisit your memory skills

Take a minute to reflect on the memory techniques in this chapter. You probably use some of them already without being aware of it. In the space below, list at least three techniques you have used in the past and describe how you used them.

_____

_____

_____

_____

_____

_____

_____

_____

_____

Remembering names

ONE POWERFUL WAY to immediately practise memory techniques is to use them to remember names.

Recite and repeat in conversation. When you hear a person's name, repeat it. Immediately say it to yourself several times without moving your lips. You could also repeat the name out loud in a way that does not sound forced or artificial: "I'm pleased to meet you, Maria."

Ask the other person to recite and repeat. You can let other people help you remember their names. After you've been introduced to someone, ask that person to spell the name and pronounce it correctly for you. Most people will be flattered by the effort you're making to learn their names.

Visualize. After the conversation, construct a brief visual image of the person. For a memorable image, make it unusual. For example, imagine the name painted in hot pink fluorescent letters on the person's forehead.

© photos.com

Admit you don't know. Admitting that you can't remember someone's name can actually put people at ease. Most of them will sympathize if you say, "I'm working to remember names better. Yours is right on the tip of my tongue. What is it again?" (By the way, that's exactly what psychologists call that feeling—the "tip of the tongue" phenomenon.)

Introduce yourself again. Most of the time we assume introductions are one-shot affairs. If we miss a name the first time around, our hopes for remembering it are dashed. Instead of giving up, reintroduce yourself: "Hello, again. We met earlier. I'm Jesse, and please tell me your name again."

Use associations. Link each person you meet with one characteristic that you find interesting or unusual. For example, you could make a mental note: "Vicki Cheng—long, black hair" or "James Washington—horn-rimmed glasses."

Limit the number of new names you learn at one time. Occasionally, we find ourselves in situations where we're introduced to many people at the same time: "Dad, these are all the people in my Boy Scout troop." "Let's take a tour so you can meet all 32 people in this department."

When meeting a group of people, concentrate on remembering just two or three names. Free yourself from feeling obligated to remember everyone. Few of the people in mass introductions expect you to remember their names. Another way to avoid memory overload is to limit yourself to learning just first names. Last names can come later.

Ask for photos. In some cases, you might be able to get photos of all the people you meet. For example, a small business where you apply for a job might have a brochure with pictures of all the employees. Ask for individual or group photos and write in the names if they're not included. You can use these photos as "flash cards" as you drill yourself on names.

Go early. Consider going early to conventions, parties, and classes. Sometimes just a few people show up on time at these occasions. That's fewer names for you to remember. And as more people arrive, you can overhear them being introduced to others—an automatic review for you.

Make it a game. In situations where many people are new to one another, consider pairing up with another person and staging a contest. Challenge each other to remember as many new names as possible. Then choose an "award"—such as a movie ticket or free meal—for the person who wins.

Use technology. After you meet new people, enter their names as contacts in your email or cell phone, or add them to a database. If you get business cards, enter phone numbers, email addresses, and other contact information as well. You might even take their picture with your phone and add the picture to your contact list.

Intend to remember. The simple act of focusing your attention at key moments can do wonders for your memory. Test this idea for yourself. The next time you're introduced to someone, direct 100 percent of your attention to hearing that person's name. Do this consistently and see what happens to your ability to remember names.

The intention to remember can be more powerful than any single memory technique. Recalling names is important not just in school but is also an important skill on the job. As the section later in this chapter called *Put It to Work* suggests, many of the ideas in this chapter are essential for career success. So practise learning names now—it's a skill you will use for a lifetime. ✳

Mnemonic devices

It's pronounced *ne-mon'-ik.* The word refers to tricks that can increase your ability to recall everything from grocery lists to speeches.

Sandwich: © magicoven/Shutterstock; *Illustration:* Walter Kopec

SOME ENTERTAINERS use **mnemonic devices** to perform "impossible" feats of memory, such as recalling the names of everyone in a large audience after hearing them just once. Waiters use mnemonics to take orders from several tables without the aid of pad and pencil. Using mnemonic devices, speakers can go for hours without looking at their notes. The possibilities for students are endless.

There is a catch. Mnemonic devices have three serious limitations.

First, they don't always help you understand or digest material. Instead of encouraging critical thinking skills, mnemonics rely only on rote memorization.

Second, the mnemonic device itself is sometimes complicated to learn and time-consuming to develop. It might take more energy to create such a device than to memorize something by using a more traditional memory technique, such as repetition.

Third, mnemonic devices can be forgotten. Recalling a mnemonic device might be as hard as recalling the material itself.

In spite of their limitations, mnemonic devices can be powerful. There are five general categories: new words, creative sentences, rhymes and songs, the loci system, and the peg system.

New words **Acronyms** are words created from the initial letters of a series of words. Examples include CSIS (Canadian Security Intelligence Service), radar (radio detecting and ranging), scuba (self-contained underwater breathing apparatus), and laser (light amplification by stimulated emission of radiation). You can make up your own acronyms to recall series of facts. A common mnemonic acronym is Roy G. Biv, which has helped thousands of students remember the colours of the visible spectrum (red, orange, yellow, green, blue, indigo, and violet). IPMAT helps biology students remember the stages of cell division (interphase, prophase, metaphase, anaphase, and telophase).

Creative sentences **Acrostics** are sentences that help you remember a series of letters that stand for something. For example, the first letters of the words in the sentence "Every good boy does fine" (E, G, B, D, and F) are the music notes of the lines of the treble clef staff.

Rhymes and songs Advertising executives spend billions of dollars a year on commercials designed to burn their messages into your memory. You are programmed to remember rhymes and songs from the time you watched *Sesame Street.*

Put It to **WORK**

© Stephen Coburn/Shutterstock

You can use strategies in *Becoming a Master Student* to succeed at work. Get started by reflecting on the following case study.

Paula Chang is a nurse at a large urban hospital. Paula just joined the staff in the cardiology department, which includes 40 nurses, doctors, and other health care workers. She was hired two months after graduating with a nursing degree from a nearby university.

Among Paula's goals for her new career was to learn the names of her colleagues by the end of the first week on the job. She succeeded.

One afternoon, the department head, Dr. Frank Rangel, invited Paula into his office for an informal chat. Frank had heard several colleagues talking about Paula's ability to remember names. He wanted to congratulate her—and learn a thing or two about memory techniques from his youngest team member.

"You're the first person on my staff who's ever managed to learn so many names so quickly," said Frank. "What's your secret?"

"No secrets, honest," Paula replied. "It's all about attitude, I guess. I simply made it a priority to remember names. I remember a teacher I had in college who had anywhere from 50 to 100 students in his lecture classes. On the first day of class, he went around the room and asked each of us for our name. It took a lot of time, but then he called us by name for the rest of the semester. I remember feeling so touched by that. I promised I would do the same thing when I started my first job."

Frank smiled and said, "That's impressive. Memorizing so many names so quickly is a neat trick. But I'm just wondering: Does it really make a difference?"

"Yes, I think so," Paula said. "For one thing, I feel more confident right away about my surroundings. I feel more comfortable asking questions when I remember names."

Paula also shared an idea with Frank for future new employees. As a visual learner, she learns better by seeing photos of people and associating pictures with names. So Paula volunteered to take pictures of her colleagues to help everyone learn names.

Paula applied several strategies from this chapter:

• Create pictures.

• Engage your emotions.
• Intend to remember.

List more memory strategies that Paula could use:

_____

_____

_____

_____

Also consider the following suggestions when you want to sharpen your memory for names in the workplace. You can adapt these techniques to remembering any kind of detailed, factual information.

• Think of someone you already know who has the same first name as a new coworker. Visualize these two people standing side by side. Look for strong differences or similarities between them.

• Use rhymes or alliteration (the repetition of sounds). If Tim is slim or Sandra wears a scarf, you've got a natural "hook" for remembering their names.

• Use a new person's name every chance you get. In a meeting, for example, refer to "Jim's idea" or "Susan's question."

• Make small talk with people when you first meet them. Associate one key fact—such as a person's hometown or favourite hobby—with an image of the person's face.

QUIZ

Name_____   Date____/____/____

1. Explain when using the "recite and repeat" memory technique is a good idea.

2. Give a specific example of "setting a trap" for your memory.

3. Describe a visualization that can help you remember Boyle's law.

4. Define *acronym* and give an example.

5. What is the difference between deep and surface learning? Name at least one technique that you can use to deepen your learning.

6. Mnemonic devices are tricks that can increase your ability to:
   (a) learn complicated pieces of information
   (b) memorize mathematical equations
   (c) memorize facts and ideas
   (d) learn difficult concepts

7. Briefly describe at least three memory techniques.

8. There are five general categories of mnemonic devices given in the text. Explain two of them.

9. Briefly describe two ideas that can help you unconditionally accept a problem you're having right now.

10. Explain a strategy that can help transfer information from your short-term memory into your long-term memory.

4 Reading

Master Student Map

as you read, ask yourself

what if . . .

I could finish my reading with time to spare and easily recall the key points?

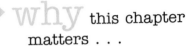

why this chapter matters . . .

Higher education requires extensive reading of complex material.

how

you can use this chapter . . .

- Analyze what effective readers do and experiment with new techniques.
- Increase your vocabulary and adjust your reading speed for different types of material.
- Comprehend difficult texts with more ease.

what is included . . .

- Muscle Reading   137
- How Muscle Reading works   138
- Read with a dictionary or laptop in your lap   144
- When reading is tough   146
- The 21st-century researcher—using your library   148
- Staying literate in the digital age   150
- English as a second language   151
- Reading with children underfoot   153
- Power Process: Notice your pictures and let them go   156
- Master Student Profile: Eva Aariak   160

> ## MASTER STUDENTS in action
>
> One night when I was reading, I had so much on my mind I reread the page probably five times. I finally just put the book down and cleared my mind. I put on some of my favourite music, and I took a fantasy trip by thinking about all my upcoming exciting things that I would be doing. When I was done, I got back to my reading with no trouble at all.
>
> **—LINDSEY GIBLIN**

Muscle Reading

WHAT IF THERE was a way you could actually spend less time on your reading and get more out of it? The Muscle Reading technique is a way to decrease difficulty and struggle by increasing energy and skill.

Picture yourself sitting at a desk, a book in your hands. Your eyes are open, and it looks as if you're reading. Suddenly your head jerks up. You blink. You realize your eyes have been scanning the page for 10 minutes, and you can't remember a single thing you have read.

Or picture this: You've had a hard day. You didn't sleep well, a co-worker called in sick, and you had to work an extra shift to cover. Dinner was late, of course, and you don't get to your books until 8 p.m. You begin a reading assignment on something called "the equity method of accounting for common stock investments." "I am preparing for the future," you tell yourself, as you plod through two paragraphs and begin the third. Suddenly, everything in the room looks different. Your head is resting on your elbow, which is resting on the equity method of accounting. The clock reads 11:00 p.m. Say good-bye to three hours.

Sometimes the only difference between a sleeping pill and a textbook is that the textbook doesn't have a warning on the label about operating heavy machinery.

Contrast this scenario with the image of an active reader. This person does the following:

- Stays alert, poses questions about what she reads, and searches for the answers.
- Recognizes levels of information within the text, separating the main points and general principles from supporting details.
- Quizzes herself about the material, makes written notes, and lists unanswered questions.
- Instantly spots key terms and takes the time to find the definitions of unfamiliar words.
- Thinks critically about the ideas in the text and looks for ways to apply them.

That sounds like a lot to do. Yet, skilled readers routinely accomplish all these things and more—while enjoying reading (Bohart, 2005).

One way to experience this kind of success is to approach reading with a system in mind. An example is Muscle Reading. You can use Muscle Reading to avoid mental mini-vacations and reduce the number of unscheduled naps during study time, even after a hard day.

This is not to say that Muscle Reading will make your education a breeze. Muscle Reading might even look like more work at first. Effective textbook reading is an active, energy-consuming, sit-on-the-edge-of-your-seat business. That's why this strategy is called Muscle Reading. ✳

journal entry 11

Discovery/Intention Statement

Discover what you want from this chapter

Recall a time when you encountered problems with reading, such as words you didn't understand or paragraphs you paused to reread more than once. Sum up the experience and how you felt about it by completing the following statement.

I discovered that I . . .

_____

_____

_____

_____

_____

Now list three to five specific reading skills you want to gain from this chapter.

I intend to . . .

_____

_____

_____

_____

_____

_____

How Muscle Reading works

All photos: © OLJ Studio/Shutterstock

MUSCLE READING is a three-phase technique you can use to extract the ideas and information you want.

Phase one includes steps to take *before* you read.

Phase two includes steps to take *while* you read.

Phase three includes steps to take *after* you read.

Each phase has three steps.

PHASE ONE:
Before you read
Step 1: **Preview**
Step 2: **Outline**
Step 3: **Question**

PHASE TWO:
While you read
Step 4: **Read**
Step 5: **Underline**
Step 6: **Answer**

PHASE THREE:
After you read
Step 7: **Recite**
Step 8: **Review**
Step 9: **Review again**

To assist your recall of Muscle Reading strategies, memorize three short sentences:

P̲ry O̲ut Q̲uestions.

R̲oot U̲p A̲nswers.

R̲ecite, R̲eview, and R̲eview again.

These three sentences correspond to the three phases of the Muscle Reading technique. Each sentence is an acrostic. The first letter of each word stands for one of the nine steps listed above.

Take a moment to invent images for each of those sentences.

For *phase one*, visualize or feel yourself prying out questions from a text. These are questions you want answered based on a brief survey of the assignment. Make a mental picture of yourself scanning the material, spotting a question, and reaching into the text to pry it out. Hear yourself saying, "I've got it. Here's my question." Then for *phase two*, get your muscles involved. Feel the tips of your fingers digging into the text as you root up the answers to your questions.

Finally, you enter *phase three*. Hear your voice reciting what you have learned. Listen to yourself making a speech or singing a song about the material as you review it.

To jog your memory, write the first letters of the Muscle Reading acrostic in a margin or at the top of your notes. Then check off the steps you intend to follow. Or write the Muscle Reading steps on index cards and then use them for bookmarks.

Muscle Reading might take a little time to learn. At first you might feel it's slowing you down. That's natural when you're gaining a new skill. Mastery comes with time and practice.

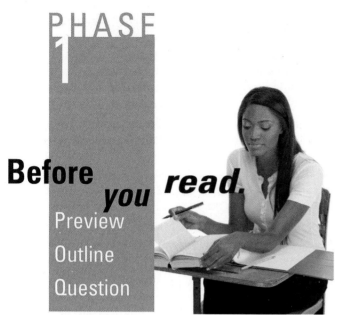

PHASE 1

Before you read.

Preview
Outline
Question

© OLJ Studio/Shutterstock

Step 1 Preview

Before you start reading, preview the entire assignment. You don't have to memorize what you preview to get value from this step. Previewing sets the stage for incoming information by warming up a space in your mental storage area.

If you are starting a new book, look over the table of contents and flip through the text page by page. If you're going to read one chapter, flip through the pages of that chapter. Even if your assignment is merely a few pages in a book, you can benefit from a brief preview of the table of contents.

Keep the preview short. If the entire reading assignment will take less than an hour, your preview might take five minutes. Previewing is also a way to get started when an assignment looks too big to handle. It is an easy way to step into the material.

Keep an eye out for summary statements. If the assignment is long or complex, read the summary first. Many textbooks have summaries in the introduction or at the end of each chapter.

Read all chapter headings and subheadings. Like the headlines in a newspaper, these are usually printed in large, bold type. Often headings are brief summaries in themselves.

When previewing, seek out familiar concepts, facts, or ideas. These items can help increase comprehension by linking new information to previously learned material. Look for ideas that spark your imagination or curiosity. Inspect drawings, diagrams, charts, tables, graphs, and photographs. Imagine what kinds of questions will show up on a test. Previewing helps to clarify your purpose for reading. Ask yourself what you will do with this material and how it can relate to your long-term goals. Are you reading just to get the main points? Key supporting details? Additional details? All of the above? Your answers will guide what you do with each step that follows.

Step 2 Outline

With complex material, take time to understand the structure of what you are about to read. Outlining actively organizes your thoughts about the assignment and can help make complex information easier to understand.

If your textbook provides chapter outlines, spend some time studying them. When an outline is not provided, sketch a brief one in the margin of your book or at the beginning of your notes on a separate sheet of paper. Later, as you read and take notes, you can add to your outline.

Headings in the text can serve as major and minor entries in your outline. For example, the heading for this article is "Phase one: Before you read," and the subheadings list the three steps in this phase. When you outline, feel free to rewrite headings so that they are more meaningful to you.

The amount of time you spend on this step will vary. For some assignments, a 10-second mental outline is all you might need. For other assignments (fiction and poetry, for example), you can skip this step altogether.

Step 3 Question

Before you begin a careful reading, determine what you want from an assignment. Then write down a list of questions, including any that resulted from your preview of the materials.

Another useful technique is to turn chapter headings and subheadings into questions. For example, if a heading is "Transference and suggestion," you can ask yourself, "What are *transference* and *suggestion*? How does *transference* relate to *suggestion*?" Make up a quiz as if you were teaching this subject to your classmates. If there are no headings, look for key sentences and turn these into questions. These sentences usually show up at the beginnings or ends of paragraphs and sections.

Have fun with this technique. Make the questions playful or creative. You don't need to answer every question that you ask. The purpose of making up questions is to get your brain involved in the assignment. Take your unanswered questions to class, where they can be springboards if there is class discussion.

Demand your money's worth from your textbook. If you do not understand a concept, write specific questions about it. The more detailed your questions, the more powerful this technique becomes.

Find examples of Phase 1 strategies online @
www.bams5ce.nelson.com

4

READING

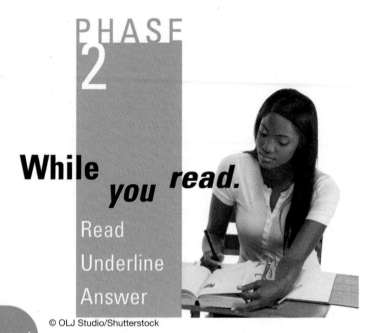

PHASE 2

While you read.

Read
Underline
Answer

Step 4 Read

You have previewed the assignment, organized it in your mind, and formulated questions. Now you are ready to begin reading.

Before you dive into the first paragraph, take a few moments to reflect on what you already know about this subject. Do this even if you think you know nothing. This technique prepares your brain to accept the information that follows.

As you read, be conscious of where you are and what you are doing. Use the Power Process: "Be here now" in Chapter Two. When you notice your attention wandering, gently bring it back to the present moment.

One way to stay focused is to avoid marathon reading sessions. Schedule breaks and set a reasonable goal for the entire session. Then reward yourself with an enjoyable activity for five or 10 minutes every hour or two.

For difficult reading, set more limited goals. Read for a half-hour and then take a break. Most students find that shorter periods of reading distributed throughout the day and week can be more effective than long sessions. You can use the following four techniques to stay focused as you read.

First, visualize the material. Form mental pictures of the concepts as they are presented. If you read that a voucher system can help control cash disbursements, picture a voucher handing out dollar bills. Using visual imagery in this way can help deepen your understanding of the text, while allowing information to be transferred into your long-term memory.

Second, read the material out loud, especially if it is complicated. Some of us remember better and understand more quickly when we hear an idea.

Third, get a "feel" for the subject. For example, let's say you are reading about a microorganism—a paramecium—in your biology text. Imagine what it would feel like to run your finger around the long, cigar-shaped body of the organism. Imagine feeling the large fold of its gullet on one side and the tickle of the hairy little cilia as they wiggle in your hand.

Fourth, remember that a goal of your reading is to answer the questions you listed during phase one. After you've identified the key questions, predict how the author will answer them. Then read to find out if your predictions were accurate.

A final note: It's easy to fool yourself about reading. Just having an open book in your hand and moving your eyes across a page doesn't mean you are reading effectively. Reading textbooks takes energy, even if you do it sitting down. There's a saying about corporation presidents: they usually wear out the front of their chairs first. Approach your reading assignment like a company president. Sit up. Keep your spine straight. Use the edge of your chair. And avoid reading in bed—except for fun.

Step 5 Underline

Deface your books. Use them up. Have fun writing in them. Indulge yourself as you never could with your secondary school books.

The purpose of marking up a book is to call out important concepts or information that you will need to review later. Underlining can save lots of time when you are studying for tests.

Underlining offers a secondary benefit. When you read with a pen or pencil in your hand, you involve your kinesthetic senses of touch and motion. Being physical with your books can help build strong neural pathways in your memory.

Avoid underlining too soon. Wait until you complete a chapter or section to make sure you know the key points. Then mark up the text. Sometimes, underlining after you read each paragraph works best.

Underline sparingly, usually less than 10 percent of the text. If you mark up too much on a page, you defeat the purpose—to flag the most important material for review.

In addition to underlining, you can mark up a text in the following ways:

- Place an asterisk (*) or an exclamation point (!) in the margin next to an especially important sentence or term.
- Circle key terms and words to look up later in a dictionary.
- Stick Post-it® notes on important sections and label them for quick referral.

- Write short definitions of key terms in the margin.
- Write a "Q" in the margin to highlight possible test questions, passages you don't understand, and questions to ask in class.
- Write personal comments in the margin—points of agreement or disagreement with the author.
- Write mini-indexes in the margin, that is, the numbers of other pages in the book where the same topic is discussed.
- Write summaries by listing the main points or key events covered in a chapter.
- Rewrite chapter titles, headings, and subheadings so that they're more meaningful to you.
- Draw diagrams, pictures, tables, or maps that translate text into visual terms.
- Number each step in a list or series of related points.

Step 6 Answer

As you read, seek out the answers to your questions and write them down. Fill in your outline. Jot down new questions and note when you don't find the answers you are looking for. Use these notes to ask questions in class, or see your instructor personally.

When you read, create an image of yourself as a person in search of the answers. You are a detective, watching for every clue, sitting erect in your straight-back chair, demanding that your textbook give you what you want—the answers.

 Find examples of Phase 2 strategies online @
www.bams5ce.nelson.com

Five smart ways to highlight a text

Underlining a text with a pen can make underlined sections—the important parts—harder to read. As an alternative, many students use coloured highlighters to flag key words and sentences.

Highlighting can be a powerful tool. It also presents a danger—the ever-present temptation to highlight too much text. Excessive highlighting leads to wasted time during reviews and can also spoil the appearance of your books. Get the most out of all that money you pay for books. Highlight in an efficient way that leaves texts readable for years to come.

Use highlighting to monitor your comprehension. Critical thinking plays a role in underlining and highlighting. When highlighting, you're making moment-by-moment decisions about what you want to remember from a text. You're also making inferences about what material might be included on an exam.

Read carefully first. Read an entire chapter or section at least once before you begin highlighting. Don't be in a hurry to mark up your book. Get to know the text first. Make two or three passes through difficult sections before you highlight.

Make choices up front about what to highlight. Perhaps you can accomplish your purposes by highlighting only certain chapters or sections of a text. When you highlight, remember to look for passages that directly answer the questions you posed during step 3 of Muscle Reading. Within these passages, highlight individual words, phrases, or sentences rather than whole paragraphs. The important thing is to choose an overall strategy before you put highlighter to paper.

Recite first. You might want to apply step 7 of Muscle Reading before you highlight. Talking about what you read—to yourself or with other people—can help you grasp the essence of a text. Recite first, then go back and highlight. You'll probably highlight more selectively.

Underline, then highlight. Underline key passages lightly in pencil. Then close your text and come back to it later. Assess your underlining. Perhaps you can highlight less than you underlined and still capture the key points.

Take your critical thinking a step further by using highlighting to check your comprehension. Stop reading periodically and look back over the sentences you've highlighted. See if you are making accurate distinctions between main points and supporting material. Highlighting too much—more than 10 percent of the text—can be a sign that you're not making this distinction and that you don't fully understand what you're reading. See the article "When reading is tough" later in this chapter for suggestions that can help.

 Find an example of smart highlighting online @
www.bams5ce.nelson.com

Read with a dictionary or laptop in your lap

A LARGE VOCABULARY makes reading more enjoyable and increases the range of materials you can explore. In addition, building your vocabulary gives you more options for self-expression when speaking or writing. When you can choose from a larger pool of words, you increase the precision and power of your thinking.

Strengthen your vocabulary by savouring words. Look up unfamiliar words. Pay special attention to words that arouse your curiosity.

Students regularly use two kinds of dictionaries: the desk dictionary and the unabridged dictionary. A desk dictionary is an easy-to-handle abridged dictionary that you normally use several times in the course of a day. Keep this book within easy reach (maybe in your lap) so you can look up unfamiliar words while reading. You can find a large, unabridged dictionary in a library or bookstore. It provides more complete information about words and definitions not included in your desk dictionary, as well as synonyms, usage notes, and word histories. Or you may prefer to use one of the many free online dictionaries such as dictionary.canadaspace.com—just be sure to check one that spells words using Canadian English. If you want to keep learning new words, there are many apps that will give you a word of the day that you can listen to on your mobile device. This is a handy way to broaden vocabulary if you are travelling to school on public transit.

Construct a word stack. When you come across an unfamiliar word, write it down in a note pad or keep a list of new words on your computer. Below the word, copy the sentence in which it was used. You can look up each word immediately, or you can look up the words later. Write the definition of each word on the back of the index card, adding the diacritical marks that tell you how to pronounce it.

Learn—even when your dictionary is across town. When you are listening to a lecture and hear

© Peter Dazeley/Photolibrary

an unusual word or when you are reading on public transit and encounter a word you don't know, you can still build your word stack. Pull out your notebook or your computer and write down the word and its sentence. Later, you can look up the definition and copy it down.

Divide words into parts. Another suggestion is to divide an unfamiliar word into syllables and look for familiar parts. This works well if you make it a point to learn common prefixes (beginning syllables) and suffixes (ending syllables). For example, the suffix -*tude* usually refers to a condition or state of being. Knowing this makes it easier to conclude that *habitude* refers to a usual way of doing something and that *similitude* means being similar or having a quality of resemblance. See an unabridged dictionary for more examples of word parts.

Infer the meaning of words from their context. You can often deduce the meaning of an unfamiliar word simply by paying attention to its context—the surrounding words, phrases, sentences, paragraphs, or images. Later you can confirm your deduction by consulting a dictionary.

Practise looking for context clues such as:

- *Definitions.* A key word might be defined right in the text. Look for phrases such as *defined as* or *in other words*. These often introduce definitions.

- *Examples.* Authors often provide examples to clarify a word meaning. If the word is not explicitly defined, then study the examples. They're often preceded by the phrases *for example, for instance,* or *such as.*

- *Lists.* When a word is listed in a series, pay attention to the other items in the series. They might define the unfamiliar word through association.

- *Comparisons.* You might find a new word surrounded by synonyms—words with a similar meaning. Look for synonyms after words such as *like* and *as.*

- *Contrasts.* A writer might use a word together with its antonym—a word or phrase with the opposite meaning. Look for phrases such as *on the contrary* and *on the other hand.* ✱

exercise
Relax

Eye strain can be the result of continuous stress. Take a break from your reading and use this exercise to release tension.

1. Sit on a chair or lie down and take a few moments to breathe deeply.

2. Close your eyes, place your palms over your eyes, and visualize a perfect field of black.

3. Continue to be aware of the blackness for two or three minutes while you breathe deeply.

4. Now remove your hands from your eyes and open your eyes slowly.

5. Relax for a minute more, then continue reading.

When reading is tough

Sometimes ordinary reading methods are not enough. Many students get bogged down in a murky reading assignment. The solution starts with a First Step: When you are confused, tell the truth about it. Successful readers monitor their understanding of reading material. They do not see confusion as a mistake or a personal shortcoming. Instead, they take it as a cue to change reading strategies and process ideas at a deeper level.

© photos.com

Read it again. Somehow, students get the idea that reading means opening a book and dutifully slogging through the text—line by line, page by page—moving in a straight line from the first word until the last. Actually, this method can be an ineffective way to read much of the published material you'll encounter in college or university.

Feel free to shake up your routine. Make several passes through any reading material. During a preview, for example, just scan the text to look for key words and highlighted material. Next, skim the entire chapter or article again, spending a little more time and taking in more than you did during your preview. Finally, read in more depth, proceeding word by word through some or all of the text.

Difficult material—such as the technical writing in science texts—is often easier the second time around. If you read an assignment and are completely lost, do not despair. Admit your confusion. Sleep on it. When you return to the assignment, regard it with fresh eyes (Bohart, 2005).

Look for essential words. If you are stuck on a paragraph, mentally cross out all of the adjectives and adverbs and read the sentence without them. Find the important words. These will usually be verbs and nouns.

Hold a mini-review. Pause briefly to summarize—either verbally or in writing—what you've read so far. Stop at the end of a paragraph and recite, in your own words, what you have just read. Jot down some notes or create a short outline or summary.

Read it out loud. Make noise. Read a passage out loud several times, each time using a different inflection and emphasizing a different part of the sentence. Be creative. Imagine that you are the author talking.

Talk to your instructor or teaching assistant. When you are stuck, admit it and make an appointment with your instructor. Most teachers welcome the opportunity to work individually with students. Be specific about your confusion. Point out the paragraph that you found toughest to understand.

Stand up. Changing positions periodically can combat fatigue. Experiment with standing as you read, especially if you get stuck on a tough passage and decide to read it out loud.

Skip around. Jump immediately to the end of the article or chapter. You might have lost the big picture, and sometimes simply seeing the conclusion or summary is all you need to put the details in context. Retrace the steps in a chain of ideas and look for examples. Absorb facts and ideas in whatever order works for you—which may be different than the author's presentation.

Take a workshop from your learning skills or student success centre. Most schools provide free workshops to students on all aspects of learning

READING

4

including textbook reading. These services are part of your tuition fee, so make good use of them. It is often the top students who use these services the most, as they are ones seeking that competitive edge in terms of grades. So be like the best and seek help—even if you don't really think you need it.

Find a tutor. Many educational institutions provide free tutoring services. If your school does not provide tutoring services, other students who have completed the course can assist you.

Use another text. Find a similar text in the library or related information online. Sometimes a concept is easier to understand if it is expressed another way.

Pretend you understand, then explain it. We often understand more than we think we do. Pretend that the material is clear as a bell and explain it to another person, or even yourself. Write down your explanation. You might be amazed by what you know.

Ask: "What's going on here?" When you feel stuck, stop reading for a moment and diagnose what's happening. At these stop points, mark your place in the margin of the page with a penciled "S" for "Stuck." If you see a pattern to your marks over several pages, this might indicate a question you want to answer before going further. Or you might discover a reading habit you'd like to change.

Stop reading. When none of the above suggestions work, do not despair. Admit your confusion and then take a break. Catch a movie, go for a walk, study another subject, or sleep on it. The concepts you've already absorbed might come together at a subconscious level as you move on to other activities. Allow some time for that process. When you return to the reading material, see it with fresh eyes. ✳

STUDENT VOICES

I never understood how valuable a dictionary was until I found out that I could access one on the Web. I made a file in my word processing program to store the words I looked up and reviewed them prior to my tests. Reading this book taught me the value of looking up words I didn't understand.
—YAHJA MAHMOUD

mastering technology

FIND WHAT YOU WANT ON THE INTERNET

At one level, searching the Internet is simple. Just go online to a search engine such as Google, or Yahoo!, look for the search box, and enter a key word or two to describe what you want to find. Then hit the enter key.

You might find exactly what you're looking for in this way. If you don't, then take your Internet searches to the next level:

Use specific key words. For example, entering firefox or safari will give you more focused results than entering web browser. Reading strategies or note-taking strategies will get more specific results than study strategies.

Use unique key words. Whenever possible, use proper names. Enter Beatles or Radiohead rather than British rock bands. If you're looking for nearby restaurants, enter restaurant and your postal code rather than the name of your city.

Start with fewer key words rather than more. Instead of ways to develop your career plan, just enter career plan. The extra words might lead to irrelevant results or narrow your search too much.

If you're looking for certain words in a certain order, use quotation marks. "Audacity of hope" will return a list of pages with that exact phrase.

Search within a site. If you're looking only for articles about college tuition from *The Globe and Mail*, then add globe and mail or globeandmail.com to the search box.

When you're not sure of a key word, add a wild card character. In most search engines, that character is the asterisk (*). If you're looking for the title of a film directed by James Cameron and just can't remember the name, enter james cameron directed *.

Look for more search options. The previous suggestions will keep you from drowning in a sea of useless search results. For academic papers, check out Google Scholar, which searches the academic literature and points you to the most highly cited articles on your topic. In addition, many search engines also offer advanced search features and explain how to use them. Look for the word advanced or more on the site's home page, and click on the link.

Experiment with meta-search engines. Meta-search engines combine results from several search engines. Examples include Yippy, Dogpile, and SurfWax.

Create your own search engine. Google allows you to customize your search engine. Go online to www.google.com/coop/cse/

NWV Discover more search strategies @ **www.bams5ce.nelson.com**

READING

4

The 21st-century researcher—using your library

© Masterfile Royalty Free

LIBRARIES HOUSE TREASURES. They include materials that will help you complete assignments, improve your writing, develop presentations, and plan your career. In addition to housing print and audio-visual publications, libraries give you access to online sources. With skills to mine all this wealth, you can acquire new knowledge for the rest of your life.

Remember that much published material is available only in print. The book—a form of information technology that's been with us for centuries—still has something to offer the 21st-century researcher.

Ask a librarian. They enjoy helping people. They chose this line of work because they enjoy helping people. They also understand that some people feel nervous about finding materials. Asking a librarian for help can save you hours. So if you can't find what you want, go ask a librarian.

Start with a reference librarian. If the library has the material that you want, this person will find it. If not, he will direct you to another source. This source might be a business, community agency, or government office.

If you have trouble finding something in your library, don't give up. Perhaps the book you want is on a cart waiting to be reshelved. A librarian can find out.

Take a tour. Libraries—from the smallest one in your hometown to the Library and Archives Canada—consist of just three basic elements:

- *Catalogues*—online databases that list all of the library's accessible sources.
- *Collections*—materials, such as periodicals (magazines and newspapers), books, pamphlets,

audiovisual materials, and materials available from other collections via interlibrary loan.

- *Computer resources*—Internet access; connections to campus-wide computer networks; and databases stored on CD-ROMs, on CDs, on DVDs, or online.

Before you start your next research project, take some time to investigate all three elements of your campus or community library. Start with a library orientation session or tour. Step into each room, and ask what's available there. Also find out whether the library houses any special collections. You might find one related to your major or another special interest.

Search the catalogue. The library catalogue is a database that lists all available materials. Some catalogues include listings for several libraries. To find materials, do a keyword search—much like using a search engine on the Internet.

The catalogue lists materials by subject, author, and title. Each listing includes a Library of Congress or Dewey decimal system number. These call numbers are used to shelve and locate materials. When you find a book by its call number, look at the materials around it on the shelf. There you will find sources of information on the same topic.

Catalogues let you see if material is on the shelf or checked out. You may even be able to put a hold on materials that are currently in circulation. Ask a librarian if you can do these things from a computer at your home or workplace.

Inspect the collection. When inspecting a library's collections, look for materials such as the following:

- *Encyclopedias.* Use leading print and online encyclopedias, such as *Encyclopedia Britannica*. Specialized encyclopedias cover many fields and include, for example, *Encyclopedia of Psychology, Encyclopedia of Asian History,* and *McGraw-Hill Encyclopedia of Science and Technology*. Note: Although Wikipedia is a very popular way to find out information online, this is not typically an acceptable source for academic writing.

- *Biographies.* Read accounts of people's lives in biographical works such as *Who's Who, Dictionary of Canadian Biography,* and *Biography Index: A Cumulative Index to Biographical Material in Books and Magazines*.

- *Critical works.* Read what scholars have to say about works of art and literature in Oxford Companion volumes (such as *Oxford Companion to Art* and *Oxford Companion to African American Literature*).

- *Statistics and government documents.* Among the many useful sources are *Statistics Canada* and *Library and Archives Canada.* For more information, go to the Internet for a complete listing of all government Internet websites: http://www.canada.gc.ca/depts/major/depind-eng.html

- *Almanacs, atlases, and gazetteers.* For population statistics and boundary changes, see the *World Almanac and Book of Facts,* the *New York Times Almanac,* or the *CIA World Factbook.*

- *Dictionaries.* Consult the *Oxford English Dictionary,* and other specialized dictionaries such as the *Penguin Dictionary of Literary Terms and Literary Theory* and the *Dictionary of the Social Sciences.*

- *Indexes and databases.* Databases contain publication information and an abstract, or sometimes the full text, of an article available for downloading or printing from your computer. Your library subscribes to many databases, which are accessible through online library catalogues or Web links.

- *Reference works in specific subject areas.* These references cover a vast range of material. Examples include the *Encyclopedia of the Biological Sciences* and the *Concise Oxford Companion to Classical Literature.* Ask a librarian for more information.

- *Periodical articles.* Find articles in periodicals (works issued periodically, such as scholarly journals, popular magazines, and newspapers) by using a periodical index. Use electronic indexes for recent works and print indexes for earlier works—especially for works written before 1980. Check to see which services your library subscribes to and the dates the indexes cover. Indexes might provide abstracts. Some indexes, such as Lexis-Nexis Academic Universe, InfoTrac, OCLC FirstSearch, provide the full text of articles (Raimes, 2004). Typically you can gain access to online articles by accessing a proxy server on your library's home page.

Access computer resources. Many libraries have access to special databases that are not available on the Internet. A reference librarian can tell you about them.

Also ask about e-books (electronic books). These free texts are delivered straight to your computer.

Inspect your finds. Once you find materials about a particular topic, inspect each one. Allow time for this step. Scan all the materials to find the most useful ones, and read them several times. Do this in a place where you can write notes—not while you're riding a stationary bike or watching TV.

With print sources, give special attention to the preface, publication data, table of contents, bibliography, glossary, endnotes, and index. (Nonprint materials, including online documents, often include similar types of information.) Also scan any headings, subheadings, and summaries. If you have time, read a chapter or section.

Then evaluate materials according to the following:

Relevance. Look for sources that deal directly with your research questions. If you're in doubt about the relevance of a particular source, ask yourself, "Will this material help me achieve the purpose of my research and support my thesis?"

Currentness. Notice the publication date of your source material (usually found in the front matter on the copyright page). If your topic is time-sensitive, set some guidelines about how current you want your sources to be.

Credibility. Scan the source for biographical information about the author. Look for education, training, and work experience that qualifies this person to publish on the topic. This is particularly important for online materials where the actual source of the material may be hard to detect. Just because it is on the Internet doesn't make the source credible. Also notice any possible sources of bias, such as political affiliations or funding sources.

You might also find that it helps to close your books, stop taking notes, and get away from your computer for a while. Digest your first impressions of the materials you've gathered. Take a walk—outdoors, if possible—and ask yourself the following questions:

- What are the main topics that these authors cover?
- What are the main problems that these authors want to solve?
- What are the authors' main areas of agreement and disagreement?
- If I could meet with these authors in person, what would I ask them?
- What personal experiences do I have with these topics?
- If I were limited to only one note card to express my thoughts on these topics, what would I write?
- If I were being interviewed about these topics on a talk show, what would I say?

The idea behind these questions is to use the work of others to get to the heart of an issue and stimulate your *own* thinking. It's amazing how many students go through higher education without doing this.

Discover the pleasures of solitary reflection, emerging insights, and sudden inspiration. A library furnished with plush chairs and wooden bookcases is a traditional setting for these experiences. Add computer technology and library skills to the mix, and you get an ideal environment for the 21st-century researcher. ✳

Staying literate in the digital age

READING BOOKS FOR pleasure is strongly linked to success in school and in the workplace. Skilled readers generally go on to higher-paying jobs and have more opportunities to advance in their careers.

However, recent research published by Life Literacy Canada (Nielsen, 2009) found that:

- Four out of ten adult Canadians have low levels of literacy—they have less than high school level of prose literacy.

- Those with higher levels of prose literacy are more likely to have higher paying jobs, better health, and higher levels of involvement with community groups.

- The Conference Board of Canada states that workplace literacy is important for creating a workforce that is better at decision-making, at teamwork, and is more productive.

If you'd like to begin or increase your leisure reading, here are a few suggestions for how to get started.

Read for pleasure. Look for fun things to read—books that are not required for your classes or job and that reflect your personal interests. Scan *The Globe and Mail* best seller lists. Look for book reviews in your local newspaper. Ask friends and instructors to recommend books. Sample a few of them.

Make time to read. Keep track of how much time you spend online or in front of the TV. Consider trading some of that time for pleasure reading.

Let books read to you. Comb your local library for audiobooks. Many are available on CD or as digital downloads.

Slow down and reflect. When you read for pleasure, forget about speed-reading. Take in the words at your own pace.

In addition, look up from the page once in awhile to think about what you've just read, or write a journal entry. In a Discovery Statement, list the main points or events that you want to remember. Also note what surprised you or led to a flash of insight. Whenever you disagree, argue with the author in writing.

In an Intention Statement, describe any follow-up action you want to take. Perhaps what you've read suggests a goal for you to achieve or an idea that you may want to use. Describe it in more detail. List the next action you could take to get started.

Make reading a social event. Good readers tend to revel in conversation, so talk about what you're reading. Also consider joining a book group. ✳

Muscle Reading for e-books

Today you can read e-books on many platforms—computers, mobile phones, and dedicated devices such as the Amazon Kindle, Kobo, Sony Reader, or iPad. Muscle your way into this new medium by using features that are not available with printed books. Though e-book features vary, see if you can do the following.

Find navigation tools To flip electronic pages, look for previous and next buttons or arrows on the right and left borders of each page. Many e-books also offer a "go to page" feature that allows you to key in a specific page number.

For a bigger picture of the text, look for a table of contents that lists chapter headings and subheadings. Note that charts, illustrations, photos, tables, diagrams, and other visuals might be listed separately.

Search Look for a search box that allows you to enter key words and find all the places in the text where those words are mentioned.

Customize page appearance For more readable text, adjust the font size or zoom in on a page.

Look for links to related information Many e-book readers will supply a definition of any word in the text. All you need to do is highlight a word and click on it. Also find out if your e-book reader will connect you to websites related to the topic of your e-book.

Mark it up Look for ways to electronically underline or highlight text. In addition, see if you can annotate the book by keying in your own notes tied to specific pages. You might be able to tag each note with a key word and then sort your notes into categories.

Print See if you can connect your e-book device to a printer. You might find it easier to study difficult passages on paper.

Sit back and listen Some e-book readers will convert highlighted text into speech.

Monitor battery life Recharge the battery for your e-book device or laptop computer so that it has enough power to last throughout your work or school day.

If you grew up speaking a language other than English, or if you grew up speaking a dialect of English that is termed nonstandard—such as a Caribbean dialect of English—you're probably called a student of English as a Second Language (ESL). ESL might not do full justice to your experience. Your cultural background as a whole might differ greatly from many of your fellow students. You might also speak *several* languages in addition to English.

English as a second language

KNOWING A LANGUAGE other than English offers advantages. You can think thoughts that are not possible in English and see the world in ways that are unique to people who speak your native language.

If you are having difficulties mastering English, experiment with the following suggestions to learn English with more success.

Many ESL/ELL students feel insecure about using English in social settings, including the classroom. Choosing not to speak, however, can delay your mastery of English and isolate you from other students.

As an alternative, make it your intention to speak up in class. List several questions beforehand, and plan to ask them. Also schedule a time to meet with your instructors during office hours to discuss any material that you find confusing. These strategies can help you build relationships while developing English skills.

In addition, start a conversation with at least one native speaker of English in each of your classes. For openers, ask about their favourite instructors or ideas for future courses to take.

Celebrate mistakes

English is a complex language. Whenever you extend your vocabulary and range of expression, the likelihood of making mistakes increases. The person who wants to master English yet seldom makes mistakes is probably being too careful. Do not look upon mistakes as a sign of weakness. Mistakes can be your best teachers—if you are willing to learn from them.

Remember that the terms *English as a Second Language* and *English Language Learner* describe a

difference—not a deficiency. The fact that you've entered a new culture and are mastering another language gives you a broader perspective than people who speak only one language. And if you currently speak two or more languages, you've already demonstrated your ability to learn.

Error	Correction
Sun is bright.	The sun is bright.
He cheerful.	He is cheerful.
I enjoy to play chess.	I enjoy playing chess.
Good gifts received everyone.	Everyone received good gifts.
I knew what would present the teachers.	I knew what the teachers would present.
I like very much burritos.	I like burritos very much.
I want that you stay.	I want you to stay.
Is raining.	It is raining.
My mother she lives in Manitoba.	My mother lives in Manitoba.
I gave the paper to she.	I gave the paper to her.
They felt safety in the car.	They felt safe in the car.
He has three car.	He has three cars.
I have helpfuls family members.	I have helpful family members.
She don't know nothing.	She knows nothing.

Analyse errors in using English

To learn from your errors, first make a list of the errors that are common to you. Ask an instructor or an English-speaking friend to help you. Next to the error, write a corrected version. For examples, see the chart above.

Learn by speaking and listening

You probably started your English studies by using textbooks. Writing and reading in English are important, but to gain greater fluency, also make it your goal to hear and speak English.

For example, listen to radio talk shows. Imitate the speaker's pronunciation by repeating phrases and sentences that you hear. During conversations, also notice the facial expressions and gestures that accompany certain English words and phrases.

If you speak English with a heavy accent, do not be concerned. Many people speak clear, accented English. Work on neutralizing your accent only if you can't be understood easily.

Take advantage of opportunities to read and hear English at the same time. For instance, turn on English subtitles when watching a film on DVD. Also, check your library for audiobooks. Check out the printed book, and follow along as you listen.

Use computer resources

Some online dictionaries allow you to hear words pronounced. They include Answers.com (www.answers.com) and Merriam-Webster Online (www.m-w.com). Other resources include online book sites with a read-aloud feature. An example is Project Gutenberg (www.gutenberg.org; search on "Audio Books"). Speaks for Itself (www.speaksforitself.com) is a free download that allows you to hear text from websites read aloud.

Also, check general websites for ESL students. A popular one is Dave's ESL Café (www.eslcafe.com), which will lead you to others.

Gain skills in note taking and testing

When taking notes, remember that you don't have to capture everything that an instructor says. To a large extent, the art of note taking consists of choosing what *not* to record. Listen for key words, main points, and important examples. Remember that instructors will often repeat these things. You'll have more than one chance to pick up on the important material. When you're in doubt, ask for repetition or clarification. For additional suggestions, see Chapter 5: Notes.

Taking tests is a related challenge. You may find that certain kinds of test questions—such as multiple-choice items—are more common in the Canada than in your native country. Chapter 6: Tests, can help you master these and many other types of tests.

When in doubt, use expressions you understand

Native speakers of English use many informal expressions that are called *slang*. You are more likely to find slang in conversations than in written English.

Native speakers also use *idioms*—colourful expressions with meanings that are not always obvious. Idioms can often be misunderstood. For instance, a "fork in the road" does not refer to an eating utensil discarded on a street.

Learning how to use slang and idioms is part of gaining fluency in English. However, these elements of the language are tricky. If you mispronounce a key word or leave one out, you can create a misunderstanding. In important situations—such as applying for a job or meeting with a teacher—use expressions you fully understand.

Create a community of English learners

Learning as part of a community can increase your mastery. For example, when completing a writing assignment in English, get together with other people who are learning the language. Read each other's papers and suggest revisions. Plan on revising your paper a number of times based on feedback from your peers.

You might feel awkward about sharing your writing with other people. Accept that feeling—and then remind yourself of everything you have to gain by learning from a group. In addition to learning English more quickly, you can raise your grades and make new friends.

Native speakers of English might be willing to assist your group. Ask your instructors to suggest someone. This person can benefit from the exchange of ideas and the chance to learn about other cultures. Most schools offer international student services that typically have English conversation classes. Effective writing programs can also be very helpful with your written submissions. Make sure you investigate the resources available on your campus.

Celebrate your gains

Every time you analyse and correct an error in English, you make a small gain. Celebrate those gains. Taken together over time, they add up to major progress in mastering English as a second language. ✳

Reading with children underfoot

© PhotoConcepts/Jupiter Images

IT IS POSSIBLE to combine effective study time and quality time with children. The following suggestions come mostly from students who are also parents. The specific strategies you use will depend on your schedule and the ages of your children.

Attend to your children first. When you first come home from school, keep your books out of sight. Spend 10 minutes with your children before you settle in to study. Give them hugs and ask about their day. Then explain that you have some work to do. Your children might reward you with 30 minutes of quiet time. A short time of full, focused attention from a parent can be more satisfying than longer periods of partial attention.

Of course, this suggestion won't work with the youngest children. If your children are infants or toddlers, schedule sessions of concentrated study for when they are asleep.

Use "pockets" of time. See if you can arrange study time at school before you come home. If you arrive at school 15 minutes earlier and stay 15 minutes later, you can squeeze in an extra half-hour of study time that day. Also look for opportunities to study in between classes.

Before you shuttle children to soccer games or dance classes, throw a book in the car. While your children are warming up for the game or changing clothes, steal another 15 minutes to read.

Plan special activities for your child. Find a regular playmate for your child. Some children can pair off with close friends and safely retreat to their rooms for hours of relatively quiet play. You can check on them occasionally and still get lots of reading done.

Another option is to take your children to a public playground. While they swing, slide, and dig in the sand, you can dig into your textbooks. Lots of physical activity will tire out your children in constructive ways. If they go to bed a little early, that's extra time for you to read.

After you set up appropriate activities for your children, don't attend to them every second, even if you're nearby as they play. Obviously, you want to break up fights, stop unsafe activity, and handle emergencies. Short of such incidents, you're free to read.

Use television responsibly. Another option is to use television as a babysitter—when you can control

A short time of full, focused attention from a parent can be more satisfying than longer periods of partial attention.

the programming. Rent a movie or show for your child to watch as you study. If you're concerned about your child becoming a "couch potato," select educational programs that keep his mind active and engaged.

See if your child can use headphones while watching television. That way, the house stays quiet while you study.

Allow for interruptions. It's possible that you'll be interrupted even if you set up special activities for your child in advance. If so, schedule the kind of studying that can be interrupted. For instance, you could write out or review flash cards with key terms and definitions. Save the tasks that require sustained attention for other times.

Plan study breaks with children. Another option is to spend 10 minutes with your children for every 50 minutes that you study. View this not as an interruption but as a study break.

Or schedule time to be with your children when you've finished studying. Let your children in on the plan: "I'll be done reading at 7:30. That gives us a whole hour to play before you go to bed."

Many children love visible reminders that "their time" is approaching. An oven timer works well for this purpose. Set it for 15 minutes of quiet time. Follow that with five minutes of show-and-tell, storybooks, or another activity with your child. Then set the timer for another 15 minutes of studying, another break, and so on.

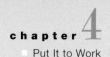
QUIZ

Name_____ Date____/____/____

1. Name the acrostic that can help you remember the steps of Muscle Reading.

2. You must complete all nine steps of Muscle Reading to get the most out of any reading assignment. True or False? Explain your answer.

3. Describe at least three strategies you can use to preview a reading assignment.

4. Briefly explain how to use headings in a text to create an outline.

5. In addition to underlining and highlighting, there are other ways to mark up a text. List three possibilities.

6. To get the most benefit from marking a book, underline at least 25 percent of the text. True or False? Explain your answer.

7. Explain at least three techniques you can use when reading is tough.

8. The Power Process in this chapter includes this sentence: "The next time you discover you are angry, disappointed, or frustrated, look to see which of your pictures aren't being fulfilled." Give an example from your own experience.

9. Define the "topic-point" method of summarizing.

10. An active reader does all of the following EXCEPT for:
    (a) Looking up unfamiliar terms and concepts
    (b) Testing herself on the material
    (c) Reading quickly, focusing in on the sound of the words
    (d) Checking for main points and supporting points

Skills SNAPSHOT

Now that you've learned about Muscle Reading, review the *Reading* section of the Discovery Wheel on page 36. Think about whether that evaluation of your reading skills is still accurate. After studying this chapter, you might want to make some major changes in the way you read. Or, perhaps you are a more effective reader than you thought you were.

In either case, take a snapshot of your current reading skills by completing the following sentences.

BEFORE YOU READ

If someone asked me how well I keep up with my assigned reading, I would say that . . .

To get the most out of a long reading assignment, I start by . . .

WHILE YOU READ

To focus my attention while I read, I . . .

When I take notes on my reading, my usual method is to . . .

AFTER YOU READ

When it's important for me to remember what I read, I . . .

When I don't understand something that I've read, I overcome confusion by . . .

NEXT ACTION

I'll know that I've reached a new level of mastery with reading when . . .

To reach that level of mastery, the most important thing I can do next is to . . .

MASTER STUDENT Profile

© REUTERS/Chris Wattie

Eva Aariak

. . . is energetic

Has a lifelong love of languages and has been a teacher, a language commissioner, and operated an arts and crafts retail store in Iqaluit. As the language commissioner, she chose the Inuktitut name for the Internet, Ikiaqqivik which means "travelling through layers."

 Find more biographical information about Eva Aariak at the Master Student Hall of Fame @

www.bams5ce.nelson.com

Eva Aariak, the second premier of Nunavut, is in Nuuk, Greenland, attending the quadrennial Inuit Circumpolar Council meeting, where delegates are discussing the European sealskin ban, the lure and threat of Arctic oil exploration, and how to make the Inuit healthy again—all worthy considerations—but Aariak is preoccupied. She has only one day between this conference and a trip to the eastern shore of James Bay to relinquish ownership of a string of islands to the Québec Cree, and she's been invited to spend that day in Toronto with the Queen. The thing is, she has a hunch about a birth.

The solution may seem obvious: put on a smile, go to the Royal York hotel, and foster alliances with power brokers. But a child is only born once, so instead she stops in Iqaluit to unpack and repack, and, as if surrendering to her mother's will, Aariak's daughter Karliin goes into labour on July 5, the one day, delivering Aariak's third and very overdue grandchild. The boy was named after Aariak's father, who died in 1985 but returns with this birth. [. . .]

She's only the fifth woman ever to lead a provincial or territorial government in Canada, and was, on her election to the 19-seat Nunavut Legislative Assembly in October 2008, its sole female MLA (a by-election has since brought in a second). A photo of that group hanging outside her office features a fraternity of suits and sealskins with Aariak seated in the middle, looking like a mascot in business casual. But Aariak is not captain by fluke. In accordance with the non-partisan, consensus-style system, MLAs held a leadership forum soon after the election and voted for the premiership by secret ballot. In other words, the boys chose her to lead. [. . .]

Nakinngaaqpit?
(Where are you coming from?)

Eva Aariak is five-foot-one, with a short, sensible haircut and several pairs of flat-soled black leather shoes, also sensible, on a rack by her front door. She is fifty-five.

She doesn't smoke cigarettes. Never has.

She has a high school equivalency diploma, and various postsecondary certificates in teaching and business management.

Her biological father is a Scottish bagpiper and a former art buyer for Canadian Arctic Producers. His name is Eric Mitchell. She didn't grow up with him but, as an adult, has nurtured their relationship.

She ate a lot of stewed rabbit and attended Anglican church as a child. She doesn't indulge in either anymore.

Her brother-in-law committed suicide.

Her mother had tuberculosis—twice.

She is a divorced single mother of three grown children and one teenage son, Jari, who lives at home and plays guitar and piano, and whose biological mother, Aariak's sister, died of an aneurysm during childbirth. . . .

She can whistle like a sandpiper.

She wonders if other premiers hem their children's pants.

The last book she read was *Eat, Pray, Love,* by Elizabeth Gilbert.

She was once head of the Baffin Regional Chamber of Commerce.

Before becoming premier, she owned and operated a high-end Inuit arts and crafts store in Iqaluit.

Her daughter Karliin, a fashion designer, represented Canada this year at the annual international fur and leather exhibition in Milan, with a sumptuous Audrey Hepburn-style seal jacket. Karliin is married to Jamal Shirley, whose grandfather, Jimmy Shirley, played guitar for Ella Fitzgerald.

Aariak is well travelled: she liked Copenhagen for the architecture, Cuba for the political history, Scotland for the castles, and Hawaii for the exotic seclusion.

[. . .]

Eva Aariak, then Eva Joseph, was among the first wave of Inuit children to earn a Western education. While some of her peers suffered abuse at church-run residential schools, Aariak's attendance at a vocational school in Fort Churchill, Manitoba, was positive. She studied the usual subjects, along with home economics and office skills, and later completed high school in Ottawa, where she lived with a family she is still close with today. She began a food and fashion program at Kemptville College, south of Ottawa, but returned north before finishing in order to marry, start a family, and try on job after job to see which one fit: teacher, home management educator, children's book coordinator, government equal employment officer, journalist, public affairs manager, translator. Many of these were in Iqaluit, a tiny city served by three levels of government, land claims bodies, and countless boards, agencies, and organizations, all hungry for educated, bilingual, reliable Inuit staff. People like Aariak. But in 2006, she switched gears and opened her own store, Malikkaat, which sells local jewellery, clothing, and art. About the only job she never held—before becoming premier—was politician. She had considered running for office for years, but family came first.

[. . .]

Inuktitut can be intimidating to non-speakers—all those long, congested words, never intended to be written but only spoken or sung; sensuous words that pop on the lips and tongue, tumble into throaty *g*'s and *q*'s, and express full sentences like *ilinniatuinnaqtunga* ("I'm only just learning"), which could describe anyone from a child to a writer, a premier or the people she governs.

Source: Gregoire, Lisa. (January 2011). "Madam Premier: How Eva Aariak is reinventing the politics of the North." *The Walrus*. Retrieved July 5, 2011, from www.walrusmagazine.com/print/2011.01-politics-madam-premier.

Master Student Map

as you read, ask yourself

what if . . .

I could take notes that remain informative and useful for weeks, months, or even years to come?

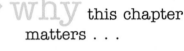

why this chapter matters . . .

Note-taking helps you remember information, and influences how well you do on tests.

what is included . . .

- The note-taking process flows   163
- Observe   164
- Record   167
- Review   173
- Enrol your instructor in your education   175
- When your instructor *talks fast*   177
- Taking notes on your journey: The art of journal writing   178
- Taking notes while reading   180
- Online classes—taking notes and using other review tools   184
- Power Process: I create it all   186
- Master Student Profile: Gwenaelle Moubouyi   190

how

you can use this chapter . . .

- Experiment with several formats for note-taking.
- Create a note-taking format that works especially well for you.
- Take effective notes in special situations—such as while reading and when instructors talk fast.

MASTER STUDENTS in *action*

Being responsible is what your career depends on—going to class, turning in assignments on time, studying for exams in advance, and, most importantly, knowing when to go out and when to stay home. Becoming a master student means setting and accomplishing goals—not to prove anything to anyone but to yourself.

—MAURICIO RUEDA

The note-taking process flows

ONE WAY TO understand note-taking is to realize that taking notes is just one part of the process. Effective note-taking consists of three parts: observing, recording, and reviewing. First, you observe an "event"—a statement by an instructor, a lab experiment, a slide show of an artist's work, or a chapter of required reading. Then you record your observations of that event; that is, you "take notes." Finally, you review what you have recorded.

Each part of the process is essential, and each depends on the others. Your observations determine what you record. What you record determines what you review. And the quality of your review can determine how effective your next observations will be. For example, if you review your notes on the Sino-Japanese War of 1894, the next day's lecture on the Boxer Rebellion of 1900 will make more sense.

Legible and speedy handwriting is also useful when taking notes. A knowledge of outlining is handy, too. A nice pen, a new notebook, and a laptop computer are all great note-taking devices. And they're all worthless— unless you participate as an energetic observer *in* class and regularly review your notes *after* class. If you take those two steps, you can turn even the most disorganized chicken scratches into a powerful tool. Sometimes note-taking looks like a passive affair, especially in large lecture classes. One person at the front of the room does most of the talking. Everyone else is seated and silent, taking notes. The lecturer seems to be doing all of the work.

Don't be deceived. Observe more closely, and you'll see some students taking notes in a way that radiates energy. They're awake and alert, poised on the edge of their seats. They're writing, a physical activity that expresses mental engagement. These students listen for levels of ideas and information, make choices about what to record, and compile materials to review. In higher education, you might spend hundreds of hours taking notes. Making them more effective is a direct investment in your success in college and beyond. Think of your notes as a textbook that *you* create—one that's more current and more in tune with your learning preferences than any textbook you could buy. ✳

journal entry 13

Discovery/Intention Statement

Get what you want from this chapter

Think about the possible benefits of improving your skills at note-taking. Recall a recent incident in which you had difficulty taking notes. Perhaps you were listening to an instructor who talked fast, or you got confused and stopped taking notes altogether. Describe the incident in the space below.

_____
_____
_____
_____

Now preview this chapter to find at least five strategies that you can use right away to help you take better notes. Sum up each of those strategies in a few words and note page numbers where you can find out more about each suggestion.

Strategy   **Page number**

_____
_____
_____
_____
_____

Reflect on your intention to experiment actively with this chapter. Describe a specific situation in which you might apply the strategies you listed above. If possible, choose a situation that will occur within the next 24 hours.

I intend to . . .

_____
_____
_____
_____

OBSERVE
The note-taking process flows

SHERLOCK HOLMES, a fictional master detective and student of the obvious, could track down a villain by observing the fold of his scarf and the mud on his shoes. In real life, a doctor can save a life by observing a mole—one a patient has always had—that undergoes a rapid change. An accountant can save a client thousands of dollars by observing the details of a spreadsheet. A student can save hours of study time by observing that she gets twice as much done at a particular time of day.

Keen observers see facts and relationships. They know ways to focus their attention on the details, then tap their creative energy to discover patterns. To sharpen your classroom observation skills, experiment with the following techniques and continue to use those that you find most valuable.

Set the stage

Complete outside assignments. Nothing is more discouraging (or boring) than sitting through a lecture about the relationship of Le Châtelier's principle to the principle of kinetics if you've never heard of Henri Louis Le Châtelier or kinetics. Instructors usually assume that students complete assignments, and they construct their lectures accordingly. The more familiar you are with a subject, the more easily you can absorb important information during class lectures.

Bring the right materials. "Can I borrow a pen?" Sound familiar? A good pen does not make you a good observer, but the lack of a pen or a notebook can be distracting enough to take the fine edge off your concentration. Make sure you have a pen, pencil, notebook, and any other materials you will need. Bring your textbook to class, especially if the lectures relate closely to the text.

If you are consistently unprepared for a class, that might be a message about your intentions concerning the course. Find out if it is. The next time you're in a frantic scramble to borrow pen and paper 37 seconds before the class begins, notice the cost. Use the borrowed pen and paper to write a Discovery Statement about your lack of preparation. Consider whether you intend to be successful in the course.

(woman) Getty, (frames) Shutterstock, collage by Walter Kopec

Ask your instructor if you are allowed to use a laptop in class. Using a laptop may allow you to access other material the instructor has provided for the course like the PowerPoint® presentation or other course materials available through your online course management program or instructor website.

Sit front and centre. Students who get as close as possible to the front and center of the classroom often do better on tests for several reasons. The closer you sit to the lecturer, the harder it is to fall asleep. The closer you sit to the front, the fewer interesting, or distracting, classmates are situated between you and the instructor. Material on the board is easier to read from up front. Also, the instructor can see you more easily when you have a question.

In addition, sound waves from the human voice begin to degrade at a distance of 2.5 to 3.5 metres. If you sit more than 4.5 metres from the speaker, your ability to hear and take effective notes might be compromised. Get close to the source of the sound. Get close to the energy.

Instructors are usually not trained to perform. While some can project their energy to a large audience, some cannot. An instructor who sounds boring from the back of the room might sound more interesting up close.

Sitting up front enables you to become a constructive force in the classroom. By returning the positive energy that an engaged instructor gives out, you can reinforce the instructor's enthusiasm and enhance your experience of the class.

Sitting close to the front is a way to commit yourself to getting what you want out of school. One reason students gravitate to the back of the classroom is that they think the instructor is less likely to call on them. Sitting in back can signal a lack of commitment. When you sit up front, you are declaring your willingness to take a risk and participate.

Conduct a short pre-class review. Arrive early, then put your brain in gear by reviewing your notes from the previous class. Scan your reading assignment. Look at the sections you have underlined. Review assigned problems and exercises. Note questions you intend to ask.

"Be here now" in class

Accept your wandering mind. The techniques in the Power Process: "Be here now" can be especially useful when your head soars into the clouds. Don't fight daydreaming. When you notice your mind wandering during class, look at this as an opportunity to refocus your attention. If thermodynamics is losing out to beach parties, let go of the beach.

Notice your writing. When you discover yourself slipping into a fantasyland, feel the weight of your pen in your hand. Notice how your notes look. Paying attention to the act of writing can bring you back to the here and now.

You also can use writing in a more direct way to clear your mind of distracting thoughts. Pause for a few seconds and write those thoughts down. If you're distracted by thoughts of errands you need to run after class, record them on a pad of paper or your mobile device. Or simply put a symbol, such as an arrow or asterisk, in your notes to mark the places where your mind started to wander. Once your distractions are out of your mind and safely stored on paper, you can gently return your attention to taking notes.

Be with the instructor. In your mind, put yourself right up front with the instructor. Imagine that you and the instructor are the only ones in the room and that the lecture is a personal conversation between the two of you. Pay attention to the instructor's body language and facial expressions. Look the instructor in the eye.

Remember that the power of this suggestion is immediately reduced by digital distractions—checking your Facebook site, browsing the Internet, or text messaging. Taking notes is a way to stay focused. The physical act of taking notes signals your mind to stay in the same room as the instructor.

Notice your environment. When you become aware of yourself daydreaming, bring yourself back to class by paying attention to the temperature in the room, the feel of your chair, or the quality of light coming through the window. Run your hand along the surface of your desk. Listen to the sound of the instructor's voice. Be in that environment. Once your attention is back in the room, you can focus on what's happening in class.

Postpone debate. When you hear something you disagree with, note your disagreement and let it go. Don't allow your internal dialogue to drown out subsequent material. If your disagreement is persistent and strong, make note of this and then move on. Internal debate can prevent you from absorbing new information. It is OK to absorb information you don't agree with. Just absorb it with the mental tag "My instructor says . . . , and I don't agree with this."

Let go of judgments about lecture styles. Human beings are judgment machines. We evaluate everything, especially other people. If another person's eyebrows are too close together (or too far apart), if she walks a certain way or speaks with an unusual accent, we instantly make up a story about her. We do this so quickly that the process is usually not a conscious one.

Don't let your attitude about an instructor's lecture style, habits, or appearance get in the way of your education. You can decrease the power of your judgments if you pay attention to them and let them go.

You can even let go of judgments about rambling, unorganized lectures. Turn them to your advantage. Take the initiative and organize the material yourself. While taking notes, separate the key points from the examples and supporting evidence. Note the places where you got confused and make a list of questions to ask.

Participate in class activities. Ask questions. Volunteer for demonstrations. Be willing to take a risk or look foolish, if that's what it takes for you to learn. Chances are, the question you think is "dumb" is also on the minds of several of your classmates. Remember, learning is an active, not a passive, activity. The more you do with the material in class, the more likely you are to recall it later. So, join in class discussions; don't treat being in class like you are watching a movie. Get active.

Relate the class to your goals. If you have trouble staying awake in a particular class, write at the top of your notes how that class relates to a specific goal. Identify the reward or payoff for reaching that goal.

Think critically about what you hear. This might seem contrary to the previously mentioned technique "Postpone debate." This is the time to list questions or write down your agreements and disagreements. After class, look up answers in your text or visit your instructor during office hours to review the material.

Watch for clues

Be alert to repetition. When an instructor repeats a phrase or an idea, make a note of it. Repetition is a signal that the instructor thinks the information is important.

Listen for introductory, concluding, and transition words and phrases. These include phrases such as "the following three factors," "in conclusion," "the most important consideration," "in addition to," and "on the other hand." These phrases and others signal relationships, definitions, new subjects, conclusions, cause and effect, and examples. They reveal the structure of the lecture. You can use these phrases to organize your notes.

Watch the board, overhead projector, or PowerPoint® presentation. If an instructor takes the time to write something down, consider the material to be important. Copy all diagrams and drawings, equations, names, places, dates, statistics, and definitions. But check first to see if any complicated diagrams are posted on the course website.

Watch the instructor's eyes. If an instructor glances at her notes and then makes a point, it is probably a signal that the information is especially important. Anything she reads from her notes is a potential test question.

Highlight the obvious clues. Instructors will often tell students point-blank that certain information is likely to appear on a test or an exam. Make stars or other special marks in your notes next to this information. Instructors are not trying to hide what's important.

Notice the instructor's interest level. If the instructor is excited about a topic, it is more likely to appear on an exam. Pay attention when she seems more animated than usual. ✳

---

journal entry 14

Discovery/Intention Statement

Create more value from lectures

Think back to the last few lectures you have attended. How do you currently observe (listen to) lectures? What specific behaviours do you have as you sit and listen? Briefly describe your responses in the space below.

I discovered that I . . .

_____

_____

_____

Now write an Intention Statement about any changes you want to make in the way you respond to lectures.

I intend to . . .

_____

_____

_____

_____

What to do when you miss a class

In most courses, you'll benefit by attending every class session. If you miss a class, try to catch up as quickly as possible.

Clarify policies on missed classes   On the first day of classes, find out about your instructors' policies on absences. See if you can make up assignments, quizzes, and tests. Also inquire about doing extra-credit assignments.

Contact a classmate   Early in the semester, identify a student in each class who seems responsible and dependable. Exchange email addresses and phone numbers. If you know you won't be in class, contact this student ahead of time. When you notice that your classmate is absent, pick up extra copies of handouts, make assignments lists, and offer copies of your notes. But don't rely too heavily on other people's notes. There is no guarantee that their notes are as good as yours.

Contact your instructor   If you miss a class, contact your instructor. Ask if she has another section of the same course that you could attend so you won't miss the lecture information. Also ask about getting handouts you might need before the next class meeting. But before contacting the instructor, make sure to check the course website for handouts or important information.

RECORD
The note-taking process flows

THE FORMAT AND STRUCTURE of your notes are more important than how fast you write or how elegant your handwriting is. The following techniques can improve the effectiveness of your notes.

General techniques for note-taking

Use key words. An easy way to sort the extraneous material from the important points is to take notes using key words. Key words or phrases contain the essence of communication. They include

- concepts, technical terms, names, and numbers
- linking words, including words that describe action, relationship, and degree (for example, *most, least,* and *faster*)

Key words evoke images and associations with other words and ideas. They trigger your memory. That makes them powerful review tools. One key word can initiate the recall of a whole cluster of ideas. A few key words can form a chain from which you can reconstruct an entire lecture.

To see how key words work, take yourself to an imaginary classroom. You are now in the middle of an anatomy lecture. Picture what the room looks like, what it feels like, how it smells. You hear the instructor say:

OK, what happens when we look directly over our heads and see a piano falling out of the sky? How do we take that signal and translate it into the action of getting out of the way? The first thing that happens is that a stimulus is generated in the neurons—receptor neurons—of the eye. Light reflected from the piano reaches our eyes. In other words, we see the piano. The receptor neurons in the eye transmit that sensory signal, the sight of the piano, to the body's nervous system. That's all they can do, pass on information. So we've got a sensory signal coming into the nervous system. But the neurons that initiate movement in our legs are effector neurons. The information from the sensory neurons must be transmitted to effector neurons or we will get squashed by the piano. There must be some kind of interconnection between receptor and effector neurons. What happens between the two? What is the connection?

Key words you might note in this example include *stimulus, generated, receptor neurons, transmit, sensory signals, nervous system, effector neurons,* and *connection.* You could reduce the instructor's 163 words to these 12 key words. With a few transitional words, your notes might look like this:

> Stimulus (piano) generated in receptor neurons (eye)
>
> Sensory signals transmitted by nervous system to effector neurons (legs)
>
> What connects receptor to effector?

Note the last key word of the lecture above—*connection.* This word is part of the instructor's question and leads to the next point in the lecture. Be on the lookout for questions like this. They can help you organize your notes and are often clues for test questions.

Use pictures and diagrams. Make relationships visual. Copy all diagrams from the board and invent your own.

A drawing of a piano falling on someone who is looking up, for example, might be used to demonstrate the relationship of receptor neurons to effector neurons. Label the eyes "receptor" and the feet "effector." This picture implies that the sight of the piano must be translated into a motor response. By connecting the explanation of the process with the unusual picture of the piano falling, you can link the elements of the process together.

Write notes in paragraphs. When it is difficult to follow the organization of a lecture or to put information into outline form, create a series of informal paragraphs. These paragraphs will contain few complete sentences. Reserve complete sentences for

RECORD

(woman) Getty, (frames) Shutterstock, collage by Walter Kopec

precise definitions, direct quotations, and important points that the instructor emphasizes by repetition or other signals—such as the phrase "This is an important point." For other material, apply the suggestions in this article for using key words.

Copy material from the board or PowerPoint® presentation Record all formulas, diagrams, and problems that the instructor writes down. Copy dates, numbers, names, places, and other facts. If it's on the board or in the presentation, put it in your notes. You can even use your own signal or code to flag that material. Anything the instructor presents can appear on a test.

Use a three-ring binder. Three-ring binders have several advantages over other kinds of notebooks. First, pages can be removed and spread out when you review. This way, you can get the whole picture of a lecture. Second, the three-ring binder format allows you to insert handouts right into your notes. Third, you can insert your own out-of-class notes in the correct order. Fourth, you can easily make additions, corrections, and revisions.

Use only one side of a piece of paper. When you use one side of a page, you can review and organize all your notes by spreading them out side by side. Most students find the benefit well worth the cost of the paper. Perhaps you're concerned about the environmental impact of consuming more paper. If so, you can use the blank side of old notes and use recycled paper.

Keep your own thoughts separate. For the most part, avoid making editorial comments in your lecture notes. The danger is that when you return to your notes, you might mistake your own idea for that of the instructor. If you want to make a comment—either a question to ask later or a strong disagreement—clearly label it as your own. Pick a symbol or code and use it in every class.

Use an "I'm lost" signal. No matter how attentive and alert you are, you might get lost and confused in a lecture. If it is inappropriate to ask a question, record in your notes that you were lost. Invent your own signal—for example, a circled question mark. When you write down your code for "I'm lost," leave space for the explanation or clarification that you will get later. The space will also be a signal that you missed something. Later, you can speak to your instructor or ask to see a fellow student's notes. As long as you are honest with yourself when you don't understand, you can stay on top of the course.

Label, number, and date all notes. Develop the habit of labelling and dating your notes at the beginning of each class. Number the page, too. Sometimes the sequence of material in a lecture is important. Write your name and phone number in each notebook in case you lose it. Class notes become more and more valuable as a term or session progresses.

Use standard abbreviations. Be consistent with your abbreviations. If you make up your own abbreviations or symbols, write a key explaining them in your notes. Avoid vague abbreviations. When you use an abbreviation such as *comm.* for *committee*, you run the risk of not being able to remember whether you meant *committee, commission, common, commit, community, communicate,* or *communist.*

One way to abbreviate is to leave out vowels. For example, *talk* becomes *tlk, said* becomes *sd, Canadian* becomes *Cdn.*

Leave blank space. Notes tightly crammed into every corner of the page are hard to read and difficult to use for review. Give your eyes a break by leaving plenty of space.

Later, when you review, you can use the blank spaces in your notes to clarify points, write questions, or add other material. Instructors often return to material covered earlier in the lecture.

Take notes in different colours. You can use colours as highly visible organizers. For example, you can signal important points with red. Or use one colour of ink for notes about the text and another colour for lecture notes. Notes that are visually pleasing can be easier to review.

Use graphic signals. The following ideas can be used with any note-taking format.

- Use brackets, parentheses, circles, and squares to group information that belongs together.

- Use stars, arrows, and underlining to indicate important points. Flag the most important points with double stars, double arrows, or double underlines.
- Use arrows and connecting lines to link related groups and to replace words such as *leads to, becomes,* and *produces.*
- Use equal signs and greater- and less-than signs to indicate compared quantities.
- Use question marks for their obvious purpose. Double question marks can signal tough questions or especially confusing points.

To avoid creating confusion with graphic symbols, use them carefully and consistently. Write a "dictionary" of your symbols in the front of your notebooks, such as the one shown below.

$[$ $]$, $( )$, $\bigcirc$, $\square$ = info that belongs together

*, ↘, = = important

**, ↘↘, ≡, !!! = extra important

> = greater than < = less than
= = equal to

⟶ = leads to, becomes
Ex: school → job → money

? = huh ?, lost

?? = big trouble, clear up immediately

Use recorders effectively. There are persuasive arguments for not using a digital recorder. Here are the main ones.

When you record a lecture, there is a strong temptation to daydream. After all, you can always listen to the lecture again later on. Unfortunately, if you let the recorder do all of the work, you are skipping a valuable part of the learning process. Actively participating in class can turn a lecture into a valuable study session.

There are more potential problems. Listening to recorded lectures can take a lot of time—more time than reviewing written notes. Recorders can't answer the questions you didn't ask in class. Also, recording devices malfunction. In fact, the unscientific Hypothesis of Recording Glitches states that the tendency of recorders to malfunction is directly proportional to

the importance of the material. With those warnings in mind, some students use a recorder effectively. For example, you can use recordings as backups to written notes. (Check with your instructor first. Some prefer not to be recorded.) Turn the recorder on, then take notes as if it weren't there. Recordings can be especially useful if an instructor speaks fast.

You could also record yourself after class, reading your written notes. Teaching the class to yourself is a powerful review tool. Instead of taping all of your notes, for example, you might record only the key facts or concepts.

Check with your instructor to see if they make podcasts of their lectures. They can be great tools for review if you listen to them on your MP3 player while traveling on the bus or just walking around campus.

The Cornell format

A note-taking system that has worked for students around the world is the *Cornell format* (Pauk & Owens, 2005). Originally developed by Walter Pauk at Cornell University during the 1950s, this approach is now taught and used in many countries.

The cornerstone of this system is what Pauk calls the *cue column*—a wide margin on the left-hand side of the paper. The cue column is the key to the Cornell format's many benefits. Here's how to use the Cornell format.

Format your paper. On each sheet of your note paper, draw a vertical line, top to bottom, about two inches from the left edge of the paper. This line creates the cue column—the space to the left of the line.

Take notes, leaving the cue column blank. As you read an assignment or listen to a lecture, take notes on the right-hand side of the paper. Fill up this column with sentences, paragraphs, outlines, charts, or drawings. Do not write in the cue column. You'll use this space later, as you do the next steps.

Condense your notes in the cue column. Think of the notes you took on the right-hand side of the paper as a set of answers. In the cue column, list potential test questions that correspond to your notes. Write one question for each major term or point.

As an alternative to questions, you can list key words from your notes. Yet another option is to pretend that your notes are a series of articles on different topics. In the cue column, write a newspaper-style headline for each "article." In any case, be brief. If you cram the cue column full of words, you defeat its purpose—to reduce the number and length of your notes.

Cue column	Notes
What are the goals of the Integrated Pan-Canadian Healthy Living Strategy?	The goals are: — to improve overall health outcomes for all Canadians. — to reduce health disparities between Canadians. — to emphasize healthy eating and physical activity to the Canadian public. — to address other healthy living priorities. Source: Health Canada, 2003.
Who is developing this strategy?	The federal, provincial, and territorial governments, together with their partners (NGOs, health specialists, First Nations, Métis and Inuit people, and others) are working together to develop the Healthy Living Strategy.

Summary
The federal and provincial/territorial governments plan to improve the health of Canadians by supporting them in making positive health choices through the Integrated Pan-Canadian Living Strategy.

Write a summary. Pauk recommends that you reduce your notes even more by writing a brief summary at the bottom of each page. This step offers you another way to engage actively with the material. It can also make your notes easier to review for tests.

Use the cue column to recite. Cover the right-hand side of your notes with a blank sheet of paper. Leave only the cue column showing. Then look at each item you wrote in the cue column and talk about it. If you wrote questions, answer each question. If you wrote key words, define each word and talk about why it's important. If you wrote headlines in the cue column, explain what each one means and offer supporting details. After reciting, uncover your notes and look for any important points you missed. Repeat this cycle of reciting and checking until you've mastered the material.

Word template for Cornell notes. If you take notes on your computer, there actually is a Word template you can use. This may be much simpler than bringing rulers and pads of paper to class. Just search online for Cornell template—it is easy to find.

Mind mapping

This system, developed by Tony Buzan (1991), can be used in conjunction with the Cornell format. In some circumstances, you might want to use **mindmaps** exclusively.

To understand mindmaps, first review the features of traditional note-taking. Outlines (explained in the next section) divide major topics into minor topics, which, in turn, are subdivided further. They organize information in a sequential, linear way.

This kind of organization doesn't reflect certain aspects of brain function, a point that has been made in discussions about "left brain" and "right brain" activities. People often use the term *right brain* when referring to creative, pattern-making, visual, intuitive brain activity. They use the term *left brain* when talking about orderly, logical, step-by-step characteristics of thought. Writing instructor Gabrielle Rico (1983) uses another metaphor. She refers to the left-brain mode as our "sign mind" (concerned with words) and the right-brain mode as our "design mind" (concerned with visuals).

A mindmap uses both kinds of brain functions. Mindmaps can contain lists and sequences and show relationships. They can also provide a picture of a subject. Mindmaps are visual patterns that can serve as a framework for recalling information. They work on both verbal and nonverbal levels.

One benefit of mindmaps is that they quickly, vividly, and accurately show the relationships between ideas. Also, mind mapping helps you think from general to specific. By choosing a main topic, you first focus on the big picture, then zero in on subordinate details. And by using only key words, you can condense a large subject into a small area on a mindmap. You can review more quickly by looking at the key words on a mindmap than by reading notes word for word.

Give yourself plenty of room. Use legal or even ledger size blank paper. If that's not available, turn regular notebook paper on its side so that you can take notes in a horizontal (instead of vertical) format. Another option is to find software that allows you to draw flow charts or diagrams. Then you can generate mindmaps on a computer.

Determine the main concept of the lecture. Write that concept in the centre of the paper and circle it, underline it, or highlight it with colour. You can also write the concept in large letters. Record concepts related to the main concept on lines that radiate outward from the centre. An alternative is to circle these concepts.

Use key words only. Whenever possible, reduce each concept to a single word per line or circle in your mindmap. Though this might seem awkward at first, it prompts you to summarize and to condense ideas to their essence. That means fewer words for you to write now and fewer to review when it's time to prepare for tests. (Using shorthand symbols and abbreviations can help.) Key words are usually nouns and verbs that communicate the bulk of the speaker's ideas. Choose words that are rich in associations and that can help you re-create the lecture.

Jazz it up. Use colour to organize your mindmap. If there are three main subjects covered in the lecture, you can record each subject in a different colour. Add symbols and other images as well.

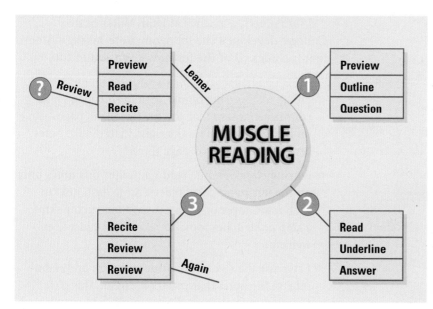

Preview
Read
Recite
Review — Leaner

MUSCLE READING

1 — Preview
Outline
Question

3 — Recite
Review
Review — Again

2 — Read
Underline
Answer

? Review

called a *heading*. These are arranged in different levels:

- In the first or "top" level of headings, note the major topics that are presented in a lecture or reading assignment.

- In the second level of headings, record the key points that relate to each topic in the first-level headings.

- In the third level of headings, record specific facts and details that support or explain each of your second-level headings. Each additional level of subordinate heading supports the ideas in the previous level of heading.

Roman numerals offer one way to illustrate the difference between levels of headings. See the following example.

Create links. One mindmap doesn't have to include all of the ideas in a book or an article. Instead, you can link mindmaps. For example, draw a mindmap that sums up the five key points in a chapter, and then make a separate, more detailed mindmap for each of those key points. Within each mindmap, include references to the other mindmaps. This helps explain and reinforce the relationships among many ideas. Some students pin several mindmaps next to each other on a bulletin board or tape them to a wall. This allows for a dramatic—and effective—look at the big picture.

There are numerous online mind mapping tools that you can use too. One of the most useful is Free Mind (http://freemind.sourceforge.net) that is easy to use and free. Try it out and see if it helps. If you are involved in group projects, then there are several other mind mapping tools that will let you work share your results with others. Two common tools are Mindomo at www.mindomo.com/ or MindMeister http://www.mindmeister.com/. Others can be found on this textbook's website.

Outlining

An outline shows the relationship between major points and supporting ideas. One benefit of taking notes in the outline format is that doing so can totally occupy your attention. You are recording ideas and also organizing them. This can be an advantage if the material has been presented in a disorganized way. Perhaps you've had negative experiences with outlining in the past. Instructors might have required you to use complex, rigid outlining formats based exclusively on Roman numerals or on some unfamiliar system. By playing with variations, you can discover the power of outlining to reveal relationships between ideas. Technically, each word, phrase, or sentence that appears in an outline is

---

The Integrated Pan-Canadian Healthy Living Strategy Will Improve the Health of All Canadians

First-level heading

I. The goal of the Integrated Pan-Canadian Healthy Living Strategy is to improve overall health outcomes for all Canadians.

Second-level heading

A. Its aim is to reduce health disparities between groups of Canadians.

B. It emphasizes healthy eating and physical activity, and their relationship to healthy weights.

II. The Healthy Living Strategy is a joint venture of the federal, provincial, and territorial governments working together with outside partners.

A. Partners include NGOs, health specialists, First Nations, Métis and Inuit people, community leaders, business people, and others.

B. All these partners have important perspectives on how best to encourage and support healthy living for Canadians. Their input has been gathered in the following ways.

Third-level heading

1. Consultation meetings with all partners.

2. Strategic roundtables with government officials and partners.

3. Written reports on the results of these consultations.

4. A national symposium on healthy living.

NOTES

You can also use other heading styles, as illustrated here.

Distinguish levels with indentations only:

First-level heading
    Second-level heading
        Third-level heading
            Fourth-level heading

Distinguish levels with bullets and dashes:

FIRST–LEVEL HEADING
    • Second-level heading
        – Third-level heading

Distinguish headings by size:

FIRST–LEVEL HEADING
Second-level heading
Third-level heading

Combining formats

Feel free to use different note-taking systems for different subjects and to combine formats. Do what works for you.

For example, combine mindmaps along with the Cornell format. You can modify the Cornell format by dividing your paper in half, reserving one half for mindmaps and the other for linear information, such as lists, graphs, and outlines, as well as equations, long explanations, and word-for-word definitions. You can incorporate a mindmap into your paragraph-style notes whenever you feel one is appropriate. Mindmaps are also useful for summarizing notes taken in the Cornell format.

John Sperry, a teacher at Utah Valley State College, developed the following note-taking system that includes all of the formats discussed in this article:

■ Fill up a three-ring binder with fresh paper. Open your notebook so that you see two blank pages—one on the left and one on the right. Plan to take notes across this entire two-page spread.

■ During class or while reading, write your notes only on the left-hand page. Place a large dash next to each main topic or point. If your instructor skips a step or switches topics unexpectedly, just keep writing.

■ Later, use the right-hand page to review and elaborate on the notes that you took earlier. This page is for anything you want. For example, add visuals such as mindmaps. Write review questions, headlines, possible test questions, summaries, outlines, mnemonics, or analogies that link new concepts to your current knowledge.

■ To keep ideas in sequence, place appropriate numbers on top of the dashes in your notes on the left-hand page. Even if concepts are presented out of order during class, they'll still be numbered correctly in your notes. ✳

 See more examples of notes in various formats online @ **www.bams5ce.nelson.com**

NOTES

5

REVIEW
The note-taking process flows

(woman) Getty, (frames) Shutterstock, collage by Walter Kopec

THINK OF REVIEWING as an integral part of note-taking rather than as an added task. To make new information useful, encode it in a way that connects to your long-term memory. The key is reviewing.

Review within 24 hours. In the last chapter, when you read the suggestion to review what you've read within 24 hours, you were asked to sound the trumpet. Well, if you have one, get it out and sound it again. This might be the most powerful note-taking technique you can use. It can save you hours of review time later in the term.

Many students are surprised that they can remember the content of a lecture in the minutes and hours after class. They are even more surprised by how well they can read the sloppiest of notes. Unfortunately, short-term memory deteriorates quickly. The good news is that if you review your notes soon enough, you can move that information from short-term to long-term memory. And you can do it in just a few minutes—often 10 minutes or less.

The sooner you review your notes, the better, especially if the class was difficult. In fact, you can start reviewing during class. When your instructor pauses to set up the overhead projector or erase the board, scan your notes. Dot the *i*s, cross the *t*s, and write out unclear abbreviations. Another way to use this technique is to get to your next class as quickly as you can. Then use the four or five minutes before the lecture begins to review the notes you just took in the previous class. If you do not get to your notes immediately after class, you can still benefit by reviewing later in the day. A review right before you go to sleep can also be valuable.

Think of the day's unreviewed notes as leaky faucets, constantly dripping, losing precious information until you shut them off with a quick review. Remember, it's possible to forget up to 80 percent of the material within 24 hours—unless you review.

Edit notes. During your first review, fix words that are illegible. Write out abbreviated words that might be unclear to you later. Make sure you can read everything. If you can't read something or don't understand something you *can* read, mark it, and make a note to ask your instructor or another student. Check to see that your notes are labelled with the date and class and that the pages are numbered. You can edit with a different coloured pen or pencil if you want to distinguish between what you wrote in class and what you filled in later.

Fill in key words in the left-hand column. This task is important if you are to get the full benefit of using the Cornell format. Using the key word principles described earlier in this chapter, go through your notes and write key words or phrases in the left-hand column.

These key words will speed up the review process later. As you read your notes and focus on extracting important concepts, your understanding of the lecture is further reinforced.

Use your key words as cues to recite. With a blank sheet of paper, cover your notes, leaving only the key words in the left-hand margin showing. Take each key word in order and recite as much as you can about the point. Then uncover your notes and look for any important points you missed.

Conduct short weekly review periods. Once a week, review all of your notes again. The review sessions don't need to take a lot of time. Even a 20-minute weekly review period is valuable. Some students find that a weekend review, say, on Sunday afternoon, helps them stay in continuous touch with the material. Scheduling regular review sessions on your calendar helps develop the habit.

If you are irritated at the sound of an instructor's voice, you're focusing on the form of her presentation. When you put aside your concern about her voice and turn your attention to the points she's making, you're focusing on content.

Personal preferences regarding an instructor's clothes, hairstyle, political views, or mannerisms can get in the way, too. When this happens, notice your response without judgment. Then gently return your attention to the class content.

Form your own opinion about each instructor. You might hear conflicting reports about instructors from other students. The same instructor could be described as a riveting speaker or as completely lacking in charisma. Decide for yourself.

Seek alternatives. You might feel more comfortable with another instructor's style or method of organizing course materials. Consider changing instructors, asking another instructor for help outside of class, or attending an additional section taught by a different instructor. You can also learn from other students, courses, tutors, study groups, books, DVDs, and tapes. You can be a master student, even when you have instructors you don't like. Your education is your own creation.

Avoid excuses. Instructors know them all. Accept responsibility for your own mistakes, and avoid thinking that you can fool the instructor. When you treat instructors honestly, you are more likely to be treated as a responsible adult in return.

Submit professional work. Prepare papers and projects as if you were submitting them to an employer. Pay attention to form. Imagine that a promotion and raise will be determined by your work. Instructors often grade hundreds of papers during a term. Your neat, orderly, well-organized paper can lift an instructor's spirits after a long night of deciphering gibberish.

Arrive early for class. You can visit with your instructor and get to know her better. You can review notes and prepare for class. Being on time demonstrates your commitment and interest.

Accept criticism. Learn from your instructors' comments about your work. It is an instructor's job to give feedback. Don't take it personally. Sometimes students ignore these comments and then get penalized on the next assignments for making the same mistakes. When you get a paper back, read the comments and then wait 24 hours to re-read them again. If you don't understand the comment or you disagree with the feedback, make an appointment to see your instructor. When you meet with the instructor or teaching assistant, ask him to explain the comments; then, ask how you can improve next time, and what are the critical elements you need to pay attention to.

Use course evaluations. In many classes you'll have an opportunity to evaluate the instructor. When you're asked to do so, respond honestly. Write about the aspects of the class that did not work well for you. Offer specific ideas for improvement. Also note what *did* work well. Formal evaluations often come late in the course, after final tests and assignments. This might lead students to gloss over evaluations or give only vague feedback. If you want your feedback to make a difference, treat this evaluation as you would an assignment.

Take further steps, if appropriate. Sometimes severe conflict develops between students and instructors. Feedback from students might not be enough to reach a resolution. In such cases, you might decide to file a complaint or ask for help from a third party, such as the department chair or an administrator. If you don't know who to complain to, check to see if you have an ombudsperson (a neutral individual who provides unbiased counsel to students).

Be prepared to document your case in writing. When talking about the instructor, offer details. Describe specific actions that created problems for the class. Stick to the facts—events that other class members can verify. Your school probably has a formal appeal procedure to use in these cases. Before you act, understand what the policies are. You are a consumer of education. You have a right and a responsibility to complain if you think you have been treated unfairly. ✳

> *You can be a master student, even when you have instructors you don't like. Your education is your own creation.*

 Discover more ways to create positive relationships with instructors online @
www.bams5ce.nelson.com

NOTES

5

Meeting with your instructor

Meeting with an instructor outside class can save hours of study time and help your grade. To get the most from these meetings, consider doing the following:

- Schedule a meeting time during the instructor's office hours or, if you are not available, ask her when else she is available.

- If you need to cancel or reschedule, let your instructor know well in advance.

- During the meeting, relax. This activity is not graded.

- Come prepared with a list of questions and any materials you'll need. During the meeting, take notes on the instructor's suggestions.

- Show the instructor your class notes to see if you're capturing essential material.

- Get feedback on outlines that you've created for papers.

- Ask about ways to prepare for upcoming exams.

- If the course is in a subject area that interests you, ask about the possibilities of declaring a major in that area and the possible careers that are associated with that major.

- Avoid questions that might offend your instructor—for example, "I missed class on Monday. Did we do anything important?"

- Ask if your instructor is willing to answer occasional short questions via email or a phone call. Ask how often they respond to email—some instructors only respond to student email once a day whereas others may be available 24/7.

- When the meeting is over, thank your instructor for making time for you.

Instead of trying to resolve a conflict with an instructor in the few minutes before or after class, schedule a time during office hours. During this meeting, state your concerns in a respectful way. Then focus on finding solutions.

When your instructor *talks fast*

Take more time to prepare for class. Familiarity with a subject increases your ability to pick up on key points. If an instructor lectures quickly or is difficult to understand, conduct a thorough preview of the material to be covered.

Be willing to make choices. When an instructor talks fast, focus your attention on key points. Instead of trying to write everything down, choose what you think is important. Occasionally, you will make a wrong choice and neglect an important point. Worse things could happen. Stay with the lecture, write down key words, and revise your notes immediately after class.

Exchange photocopies of notes with classmates. Your fellow students might write down something you missed. At the same time, your notes might help them. Exchanging photocopies can fill in the gaps.

Leave large empty spaces in your notes. Leave plenty of room for filling in information you missed. Use a symbol that signals you've missed something, so you can remember to come back to it.

See the instructor after class. Take your class notes with you and show the instructor what you missed.

Use a digital recorder. Recording a lecture gives you a chance to hear it again whenever you choose. Some recorders allow you to vary the speed of the recording. With this feature, you can perform magic and actually slow down the instructor's speech. Again remember to seek permission before you record anybody's voice.

Before class, take notes on your reading assignment. You can take detailed notes on the text before class. Leave plenty of blank space. Take these notes with you to class and simply add your lecture notes to them.

Go to the lecture again. Many classes are taught in multiple sections. That gives you the chance to hear a lecture at least twice—once in your regular class and again in another section of the class.

Ask questions—even if you're totally lost. Many instructors allow a question session. This is the time to ask about the points you missed.

There might be times when you feel so lost that you can't even formulate a question. That's OK. One option is to report this fact to the instructor. She can often guide you to a clear question. Another option is to ask a related question. This might lead you to the question you really wanted to ask.

Ask the instructor to slow down. This is the most obvious solution. If asking the instructor to slow down doesn't work, ask her to repeat what you missed. ✳

Use a journal to manage stress. Much stress has its source in negative self-talk—nagging voices in our heads that make dire predictions for the future and undermine our abilities: "This is the worst thing that could ever happen to me" or "I never finish what I start."

Getting these disempowering ideas out of your head and onto paper is one way to defuse them. Begin by listing any irrational, self-defeating beliefs you have. Then write down more reasonable, empowering beliefs and Intention Statements.

Use a journal to increase writing skills. Writing in a journal can sharpen your powers of observation. To begin with, list as many details as you can about a person or an object in your environment. Make your description as complete, vivid, and detailed as you can.

Try your hand at fiction, too. Create characters for plays or novels. Write poems, short stories, or articles that you might submit for publication.

Review your journal for writing topics. Perhaps you've already written down something that could become the basis for a research paper.

Use a journal for personal growth. Visualizations and affirmations can begin on the pages of your journal. Also write about your fears, hopes, dreams, and ambitions. In this way, a journal becomes a trusted confidant who always respects your safety and privacy. Here is a counsellor who's available anyplace, anytime—at no cost to you. ✳

Taking notes while reading

TAKING NOTES WHILE reading requires the same skills that apply to class notes: observing, recording, and reviewing. Just remember that there are two kinds of notes that apply to reading: review notes and research notes.

Review notes

Take review notes when you want more detailed notes than writing in the margin of your text allows. You might want to single out a particularly difficult section of a text and make separate notes. Or make summaries of overlapping lecture and text material. You can't underline or make notes in library books, so these sources will require separate notes, too.

To take more effective review notes, follow these suggestions:

- *Use a variety of formats.* Translate text into Cornell notes, mindmaps, or outlines. Combine these formats to create your own. Translate diagrams, charts, and other visual elements into words. Then reverse the process by translating straight text into visual elements.

- *However, don't let the creation of formats get in your way.* Even a simple list of key points and examples can become a powerful review tool.

- *Condense a passage to key quotes.* Authors embed their essential ideas in key sentences. As you read, continually ask yourself, "What's the point?" Then see if you can point to a specific sentence on the page to answer your question. Look especially at headings, subheadings, and topic sentences of paragraphs. Write these key sentences word for word in your

notes, and put them within quotation marks. Copy as few sentences as you can and still retain the core meaning of the passage.

- *Condense by paraphrasing.* Pretend that you have to summarize a chapter, article, or book on a postcard. Limit yourself to a single paragraph—or a single sentence—and use your own words. This is a great way to test your understanding of the material.

- *Take a cue from the table of contents.* Look at the table of contents in your book. Write each major heading on a piece of paper, or key those headings into a word-processing file on your computer. Include page numbers. Next, see if you can improve on the table of contents. Substitute your own headings for those that appear in the book. Turn single words or phrases into complete sentences, and use words that are meaningful to you.

- *Note special concepts in math and science.* When you read mathematical, scientific, or other technical materials, copy important formulas or equations. Re-create important diagrams, and draw your own visual representations of concepts. Also write down data that might appear on an exam.

Research notes

Take research notes when preparing to write a paper or deliver a speech. One traditional method of research is to take notes on index cards. You write one idea, fact, or quotation per card. The advantage of limiting each card to one item of information is that you can easily arrange cards according to the sequence of your outline—and ongoing changes in your outline. You can also do the same thing on your computer using presentation software such as PowerPoint® or Keynote®. Each idea this time is put on a separate slide. Similar to the index cards, you can re-organize the slides easily when you do your outline.

You can also take advantage of the software features of your word processing program that help you create tables of contents, indexes, graphics, and other elements you might want to use in your project later on.

No matter which method you use, your research notes will fall into two main categories.

The first category is information about your sources. For example, a source card for a book will show the author, title, date and place of publication, and publisher. You'll need such information later in the writing process as you create a formal list of your sources—especially sources of quotes or paraphrased material that is included in the body of your paper or presentation. By keeping track of your sources as you conduct research, you create a working bibliography. Ask your instructor about what source information to record (and also see the sidebar to this article). When recording your own ideas, simply note the source as "me."

The second category of research notes includes the actual ideas and facts that you will use to create the content of your paper or presentation. Again, if you're using index cards, write only *one* piece of information on each information card—a single quotation, fact, or concept. Doing so makes it easier for you to sort cards later.

Be sure to avoid plagiarism. When people take words or images from a source and present them as their own,

Note this information about your sources

Following are checklists of the information to record about various types of sources. Whenever possible, print out or make photocopies of each source. For books, include a copy of the title page and copyright page, both of which are found in the front matter. For magazines and scholarly journals, copy the table of contents.

For each book you consult, record the following:

☐ Author

☐ Editor (if listed)

☐ Translator (if listed)

☐ Edition number (if listed)

☐ Full title, including the subtitle

☐ Name and location of the publisher

☐ Copyright date

☐ Page numbers for passages that you quote, summarize, or paraphrase

For each article you consult, record the following:

☐ Author

☐ Editor (if listed)

☐ Translator (if listed)

☐ Full title, including the subtitle

☐ Name of the periodical

☐ Volume number

☐ Issue number

☐ Issue date

☐ Page numbers for passages that you quote, summarize, or paraphrase

For each computer-based source you consult (such as Internet documents), record the following:

☐ Author

☐ Editor (if listed)

☐ Translator (if listed)

☐ Full title of the page or article, including the subtitle

☐ Name of the organization that posted the site or published the CD-ROM

☐ Dates when the page or other document was published and revised

☐ Date when you accessed the source

☐ URL for Web pages (the uniform resource locator, or website address, which often starts with http://)

☐ Version number (for CD-ROMs)

☐ Volume, issue number, and date for online journals

Note: Computer-based sources may not list all the above information. For Web pages, at a minimum, record the date you accessed the source and the URL.

For each interview you conduct, record the following:

☐ Name of the person you interviewed

☐ Professional title of the person you interviewed

☐ Contact information for the person you interviewed— mailing address, phone number, email address

☐ Date of the interview

To assist you with recording the correct information for your references, be sure to check to see if your library offers citation management software such as RefWorks or EndNote. These types of software tools make it much easier to correctly record citation information and to automatically create bibliographies or footnotes. The method you use to write up your references will vary by the discipline you are in. It may be APA, MLA or Chicago. Again check your library website, as chances are they have citation style guides accessible through their Web pages.

Online classes— taking notes and using other review tools

© Yuri Arcurs/Shutterstock

IF YOU ARE taking an online course or a course that is heavily supported by online materials, note-taking could be a new challenge. You can print out anything that appears on a computer screen. This includes online course materials, articles, books, manuscripts, email messages, chat room sessions, and more.

One potential problem is that you might skip the note-taking process altogether. ("I can just print out everything!") You would then miss the chance to internalize a new idea by restating it in your own words— a principal benefit of note-taking.

Result: Material passes from computer to printer without ever intersecting with your brain.

To prevent this problem, find ways to engage actively with online materials. Take review notes in Cornell, mindmap, concept map, or outline format. Write Discovery and Intention Statements to capture key insights from the materials and to state ways you intend to apply them. Also talk about what you're learning. Recite key points out loud, and discuss what you read online with other students.

Of course, it's fine to print out online material. If you do, treat your printouts like textbooks, and apply the steps of Muscle Reading explained in Chapter 4. In addition, consider the following ways to create the most value from course content that's delivered online.

Do a trial run with technology. Verify your access to course websites, including online tutorials, PowerPoint® presentations, readings, quizzes, tests, assignments, bulletin boards, and chat rooms. Ask your instructors for website addresses, email addresses, and passwords. Work out any bugs when you start the course and well before that first assignment is due.

If you're planning to use a computer lab on campus, find one that meets course requirements. Remember that on-campus computer labs may not allow you to install all the software needed to access websites for your courses or textbooks.

Develop a contingency plan. Murphy's Law of Computer Crashes states that technology tends to break down at the moment of greatest inconvenience. You might not believe this piece of folklore, but it's still wise to prepare for it:

- Find a "technology buddy" in each of your classes— someone who can contact the instructor if you lose Internet access or experience other computer problems.
- Every day, make backup copies of files created for your courses.
- Keep extra printer supplies—paper and toner or ink cartridges—on hand at all times. Don't run out of necessary supplies on the day a paper is due.

Set up folders and files for easy reference. Create a separate folder for each class on your computer's hard drive. Give each folder a meaningful name, such as *biology–spring 2012.* Place all files related to a course in the appropriate folder. Doing this can save you from one of the main technology-related time wasters: searching for lost files.

Also name individual files with care. Avoid changing extensions that identify different types of files, such as .ppt for PowerPoint® presentations or .pdf for files in the Adobe Reader® portable document format. Changing extensions might lead to problems when you're looking for files later or sharing them with other users.

Take responsibility. If you register for an online course with no class meetings, you might miss the motivating presence of an instructor and classmates. Instead, manufacture your own motivation. Be clear about what you'll gain by doing well in the course. Relate course content to your major and career goals. Don't wait to be contacted by your classmates and instructor. Initiate that contact on your own.

If you feel confused about anything you're learning, ask for help right away. This is especially important when you don't see the instructor face to face in class. Some students simply drop online courses rather than seek help. E-mail or call the instructor before you make that choice. If the instructor is on campus, you might be able to arrange for a meeting during office hours.

Prevent procrastination. Courses that take place mostly or totally online can become invisible in your weekly academic schedule. This tendency reinforces the temptation to put off dealing with these courses until late in the term. You can avoid this fate:

- Early in the term, create a detailed schedule for online courses. In your calendar, list a due date for each assignment. Break big assignments into smaller steps, and schedule a due date for each step.

- Consider scheduling times in your daily or weekly calendar to complete online course work. Give these scheduled sessions the same priority as regular classroom meetings. At these times, check for online announcements relating to assignments, tests, and other course events.

- When you receive an online assignment, email any questions immediately. If you want to meet with an instructor in person, request an appointment several days in advance.

- Download or print out online course materials as soon as they're posted on the class website. These materials might not be available later in the term.

- If possible, submit online assignments early. Staying ahead of the game will help you avoid an all-nighter at the computer during finals week.

Focus your attention. Some students are used to visiting websites while watching television, listening to loud music, or using instant messaging software. When applied to online learning, these habits can reduce your learning and imperil your grades. To succeed with technology, turn off the television, quit online chat sessions, and turn down the music. Whenever you go online, stay in charge of your attention.

Ask for feedback. To get the most from online learning, request feedback from your instructor via email. When appropriate, also ask for conferences by phone or in person.

Sharing files offers another source of feedback. For example, Microsoft Word has a Track Changes feature that allows other people to insert comments into your documents and make suggested revisions. These edits are highlighted on the screen. Use such tools to get feedback on your writing from instructors and peers.

Note: Be sure to check with your instructors to see how they want students enrolled in their online courses to address and label their emails. Many teachers ask their online students to use a standard format for the subject area so they can quickly recognize emails from them.

Contact other students.
Make personal contact with at least one other student in each of your classes—especially classes that involve lots of online course work. Create study groups to share notes, quiz each other, critique papers, and do other learning tasks. This kind of support can help you succeed as an online learner. ✳

mastering technology

YOUR MIND, ONLINE

Imagine how useful—and fun—it would be to download everything you've ever read or thought and then instantly locate what you know about a particular topic. Something like this *is* possible today. Computer applications give you a variety of ways to store text and images, organize them, search them, and even share them with others when appropriate. These applications fall into three categories.

Online Notebooks Zoho Notebook, myNoteIt and similar applications allow you to "clip" images and text from various Web pages, categorize all this content, and add your own notes.

Personal Information Managers Examples of personal information managers include EverNote, Yojimbo, and DEVONThink. These applications share many features with online notebooks. However, some of them allow you to add "offline" content, such as digital photos of business cards and receipts. You can search through all this content by using tags and key words.

Browser Extensions Zotero is a Firefox extension that allows you to store Web pages, PDF files, and notes in rich-text format. This tool makes it easy to cite the sources of text and images and to convert your citations into a bibliography—a great way to avoid plagiarism.

I CREATE IT ALL

This article describes a powerful tool for times of trouble. In a crisis, "I create it all" can lead the way to solutions. "I create it all" means treating experiences, events, and circumstances in your life as if you created them.

"I create it all" is one of the most unusual and bizarre suggestions in this book. It certainly is not a belief. Use it when it works. Don't when it doesn't.

Keeping that in mind, consider how powerful this Power Process can be. It is really about the difference between two distinct positions in life: being a victim or being responsible.

A victim of circumstances is controlled by outside forces. We've all felt like victims at one time or another. Sometimes we felt helpless.

In contrast, we can take responsibility. Responsibility is "response-ability"—the ability to choose a *response* to any event. You can choose your *response* to any event, even when the event itself is beyond your control.

Many students approach grades from the position of being victims. When the student who sees the world this way gets an F, she reacts something like this: "Another F! That teacher couldn't teach her way out of a wet paper bag. She can't teach English for anything. And that textbook—how boring!"

The problem with this viewpoint is that in looking for excuses, the student is robbing herself of the power to get any grade other than an F. She's giving all of her power to a bad teacher and a boring textbook.

There is another way, called *taking responsibility*. You can recognize that you choose your grades by choosing your actions. Then you are the source, rather than the result, of the grades you get. The student who got an F could react like this:

"Another F! Oh, shoot! Well, hmmm…. What did I do to create it?"

Now, that's power. By asking, "How did I contribute to this outcome?" you are no longer the victim. This student might continue by saying, "Well, let's see. I didn't review my notes after class. That might have done it." Or "I went out with my friends the night before the test. Well, that probably helped me fulfill some of the requirements for getting an F."

The point is this: When the F is the result of your friends, the book, or the teacher, you probably can't do anything about it. However, if you *chose* the F, you can choose a different grade next time. You are in charge.

 Learn more about this Power Process online @

www.bams5ce.nelson.com

Put It to **WORK**

Developing the ability to take useful notes during meetings is one way to make yourself valued in the workplace. It might even help you get promoted. With this in mind, look for ways to apply suggestions from this chapter at work.

© Dean Mitchell/Shutterstock

Hanae Niigata is a part-time office manager for a large cardiovascular clinic. Her responsibilities include handling incoming calls, scheduling patient visits, maintaining medical records, and completing other tasks assigned by physicians and nurses.

Hanae's career focus is health care. She has worked as a home health aide and is currently enrolled in school. Her goal is to obtain a degree in nursing and work as a registered nurse.

Hanae has a reputation as a hard worker. Even in a noisy environment with frequent interruptions, she completes tasks that require attention to detail and sustained concentration. She catches errors on medical records that her co-workers tend to miss. In addition, Hanae is often the first person in the office to whom people turn when they have a problem to solve. Even in the most difficult circumstances, she can generate a list of options—including solutions that occur to no one else.

Recently, Hanae attended a 2-hour course on a new telephone system soon to be installed in her office. She was told to take detailed notes so she could teach the system to several receptionists. Hanae was shocked that the old system was being replaced. In her opinion, it was user-friendly.

As the training session began, Hanae diligently attempted to write down almost everything the instructor said. While doing so, she repeatedly found herself distracted by the thought that her manager was replacing a perfectly good phone system with some "sure-to-be-a-nightmare, high-tech garbage."

After completing the course, Hanae sat down with her manager to fill him in on the new system. As she thumbed through her notes, she realized they didn't make much sense to her, even though she had just finished writing them. She couldn't recall much of the course from memory, either, leaving her with little information to share with her manager.

Hanae routinely applies strategies from this book to many areas of her work. For example, she applies the Power Process "Be Here Now" to help her pay attention amid distractions and catch errors on medical records. In addition, she is a creative thinker and problem solver, using several strategies you will learn in Chapter 7: Thinking. But when it came to the training session, she didn't apply any of the book's note-taking strategies. List strategies that Hanae could have used to take more effective notes on the training session that she attended:

_____

_____

_____

_____

_____

When you are at work, consider using the three "As" when you take notes during a meeting. Record key details about the following:

- *Attendance*. Notice who shows up. Your employer might expect meeting notes to include a list of attendees.
- *Agreements*. The purpose of most meetings is to reach an agreement about something—a policy, project, or plan. Note each agreement. If you're not sure whether an agreement was reached, ask for clarification.
- *Actions*. During meetings, people often commit to take some type of action in the future. Record each proposed follow-up action and who agreed to do it.

Skilled meeting planners often put an agenda in writing and distribute it in advance. You can use this agenda as a way to organize your notes. However, be prepared for times when people depart from the agenda and introduce new topics.

QUIZ

Name_____ Date____/____/____

1. What are the three major steps of effective note-taking, as explained in this chapter? Summarize each step in one sentence.

2. Techniques you can use to "set the stage" for note-taking do <u>not</u> include:
   Complete outside assignments.
   Bring the right materials.
   Set aside questions in order to concentrate.
   Conduct a short preclass review.
   Sit front and centre.

3. What is an advantage of sitting in the front and centre of the classroom?

4. By the way they behave, instructors sometimes give clues that the material they are presenting is important. Describe at least three of these behaviours.

5. An effective method to postpone debate during a lecture is to ignore your own opinions and passively record the instructor's words. True or False? Explain your answer.

6. When using the Cornell system of note-taking:
   Write the main point on a line or in a box, circle, or any other shape.
   Use only Roman numerals in an outline form.
   Copy each new concept on a separate index card.
   Remember never to combine it with mind mapping.
   Draw a vertical line about two inches from the left edge of the paper.

7. Explain how key words can be used when taking notes. Then select and write down at least five key words from this chapter.

8. Reviewing within 24 hours assists short-term memory only. Long-term memory requires reviews over a longer period of time. True or False? Explain your answer.

9. Describe at least three strategies for reviewing notes.

10. Briefly define the word *responsibility* as it is used in the Power Process: "I Create It All."

Skills SNAPSHOT

The Discovery Wheel in Chapter 1 includes a section labelled *Notes*. For the next 10 to 15 minutes, go beyond your initial responses to that exercise. Take a snapshot of your skills as they exist today, after reading and doing this chapter.

Begin by reflecting on some of your recent experiences with note-taking. These experiences can include classroom notes, as well as notes on your reading assignments. Then take the next step toward mastery by committing to a specific action in the near future.

OBSERVING

If my attention wanders while taking notes, I refocus by . . .

When I strongly disagree with the opinion of a speaker or author, I respond by . . .

RECORDING

The formats I usually use to take notes are . . .

A new note-taking format that I'd like to experiment with is . . .

REVIEWING

If asked to rate the overall quality of the notes that I've taken in the last week, I would say that . . .

In general, I find my notes to be most useful when they . . .

NEXT ACTION

I'll know that I've reached a new level of mastery with note-taking when . . .

MASTER STUDENT Profile

Used with permission of
Gwen Madiba

A student who was named one of the top 100 women in Canada in 2010 in the *future leader* category. She works tirelessly for numerous volunteer agencies and organized her school's first Black History Gala.

 Find more biographical information about Gwenaelle Moubouyi at the Master Student Hall of Fame @

www.bams5ce.nelson.com

Gwenaelle Moubouyi

. . . is inspiring

Gwenaelle Moubouyi's success can be measured by her dedication and devotion to others. And her commitment to the University of Ottawa, Canada and the international community hasn't gone unnoticed.

This spring, U of O president Allan Rock nominated Moubouyi for a spot on Canada's Most Powerful Women Top 100 list, which is organized by the Women's Executive Network.

"It's very humbling to know that I was nominated," said Moubouyi. "It feels great to know that some people actually care about the work that I'm doing and that it does matter and it does make a significant difference in some people's lives. I am very, very thankful to have been nominated in this network of inspiring women in my adoptive country."

Born in Gabon, a country in West Africa, Moubouyi moved to Canada at the age of seven when her father was received a job as a diplomat. She chose the University of Ottawa for postsecondary studies because it offered a joint program that included two of her passions: Communications and sociology.

An active member of the university community, Moubouyi co-founded the program I ACT, a youth network initiative. She organized the first Congolese Student Association gala entitled Rising for Change, the New Era of Congo. She

has also been an active participant in the Ontario Task Force Against Campus Racism.

In addition, she created International Dialogues, a program to encourage dialogue between international representatives, government members and students. And, finally, she conceived and planned the first Black History Month gala, which was attended by Rock and former Governor General Michaëlle Jean.

Moubouyi also played a significant role in the university's response in the aftermath of the Haitian earthquake. This month she is organizing a fundraiser to raise money for schools and school materials in Haiti.

Apart from her immense contributions to the university community, Moubouyi has an international presence as well. She is an ambassador with Vision Gram, a non-governmental organization that works with women and children in the Congo. She has also worked with an orphanage in Gabon, launched a project for women in Senegal and worked closely with a women's rights organization in Haiti.

In addition to her recent nomination, Moubouyi was named one of 2010's young black people who inspire by *The Next Big Thing* magazine.

Moubouyi is currently working on her master's thesis in sociology, and her study theme clearly reflects her passion for Canada.

"I decided to work with Aboriginal youth and use hip-hop as a movement and a tool of social change and transformation in aboriginal communities in Nunavik and Nunavut," explained Moubouyi.

"I think our university is really a world of possibilities, and we have amazing people, and sometimes we have to look beyond our differences to appreciate our similarities."

Moubouyi aspires to be a journalist, to work in international relations and development, and to start her PhD.

"I know that seems like a lot of things at the same time and everybody always tells me 'you're all over the place,' but I believe that if you organize yourself properly and you surround yourself with good support systems, you'll be able to do it."

Everyone, however, has their limits. Despite her confidence and optimism, there has been a learning curve for Moubouyi.

"Be accountable to yourself . . . this is something I learned the hard way. Last year, I passed out in the stairs at the cafeteria. I was just doing so many things, not taking care of myself. I wanted to help here and there and I forgot about myself," she said.

"It's not wrong to put yourself first, because in order to be able to take care of the world, you have to be able to take care of yourself."

Source: Hill, Briana. (2010). "U of O student nominated for list of Canada's most powerful women." Canadian University Press Newswire. Retrieved July 5, 2011, from http://cupwire.hotink.net/articles/34838

What to do during the test

PREPARE YOURSELF FOR the test by arriving early. That often leaves time to do a relaxation exercise. While you're waiting for the test to begin and talking with classmates, avoid the question "How much did you study for the test?" This question might fuel anxious thoughts that you didn't study enough. When you enter the room, try to choose a seat near a wall and near a clock so that you have something to look at during the exam. In a large test hall, it can be difficult to look anywhere without the instructor thinking you are trying to look at other students' papers.

As you begin

Ask the instructor, proctor, or invigilator if you can use scratch paper during the test. If you use a separate sheet of paper without permission, you might appear to be cheating. If you get permission, use this paper to jot down memory aids, formulas, equations, facts, or other material you know you'll need and might forget. An alternative is to make quick notes in the margins of the test sheet. Similarly find out the rules for having any electronics on your desk. Although students can sometimes bring calculators, most schools ban mobile devices even if you are using them just to know the time. Plan on wearing a watch or take a seat in the exam room near a clock.

Pay attention to verbal directions given as a test is distributed. Then scan the whole test immediately. Evaluate the importance of each section. Notice how many marks each part of the test is worth and estimate how much time you'll need for each section, using its value as your guide. For example, don't budget 20 percent of your time for a section that is worth only 10 percent of the marks.

Read the directions slowly. Then reread them. It can be agonizing to discover that you lost marks on a test merely because you failed to follow the directions. When the directions are confusing, ask to have them clarified.

Now you are ready to begin the test. If necessary, allow yourself a minute or two of "panic" time. Notice any tension you feel, and apply one of the techniques explained in the article "Let Go of Test Anxiety" later in this chapter.

Answer the easiest, shortest questions first. This gives you the experience of success. It also stimulates associations and prepares you for more difficult questions. Pace yourself and watch the time. If you can't think of an answer, move on. Follow your time plan.

© CandyBox Images/Shutterstock

If you are unable to determine the answer to a test question, keep an eye out throughout the test for context clues that may remind you of the correct answer, or provide you with evidence to eliminate wrong answers.

Multiple choice questions

- *Answer each question in your head first.* Do this before you look at the possible answers. If you come up with an answer that you're confident is right, look for that answer in the list of choices.

- *Test each possible answer.* Remember that multiple choice questions consist of two parts: the question stem, and a list of possible answers.

- *Read all possible answers before selecting one.* Check to see if the stem includes negatives like the word NOT or NEVER. If it does, circle the word so that you pay attention to it when you try to select your response. Sometimes two answers will be similar but only one will be correct, so read the answers slowly and pay attention to subtle differences in the answers. You might want to try determining which is the worst answer if two answers are similar.

- *Don't be fooled by distractors.* These are extra pieces of information that literally distract you from finding the correct answer. Instead, look for the key points and stroke out the distractors.

- *Eliminate incorrect answers.* Cross off the answers that are clearly *not* correct. The answer you cannot eliminate is probably the best choice.

True/false questions

- *Read the entire question.* Separate the statement into its grammatical parts—individual clauses and phrases—and then test each one. If any part is false, the entire statement is false.

- *Look for qualifiers.* These include words such as *all, most, sometimes,* or *rarely.* Absolute qualifiers such as *always* or *never* generally indicate a false statement.

- *Find the devil in the details.* Double-check each number, fact, and date in a true/false statement. Look for numbers that have been transposed or facts that have been slightly altered. These are signals of a false statement.

- *Watch for negatives.* Look for words such as *not* and *cannot.* Read the sentence without these words and see if you come up with a true or false statement. Then reinsert the negative words and see if the statement makes more sense. Watch especially for sentences with two negative words. As in math operations, two negatives cancel each other out: *We cannot say that Chekov never succeeded at short story writing* means the same as *Chekov succeeded at short story writing.*

Computer-graded tests

- Make sure that the answer you mark corresponds to the question you are answering.

- Check the test booklet against the answer sheet whenever you switch sections and whenever you come to the top of a column.

- Watch for stray marks; they can look like answers.

- If you change an answer, be sure to erase the wrong answer completely, removing all pencil markings.

Open-book tests

- Carefully organize your notes, readings, and any other materials you plan to consult when writing answers. Don't be misled by thinking open-book tests are easy when they are often the most difficult. Just because you CAN bring many pieces of material with you to the test means organization is the key.

- Write down any formulas you will need on a separate sheet of paper.

- Bookmark the table of contents and index in each of your textbooks. Place Post-it® Notes and index flags or paper clips on other important pages of books (pages with tables, for instance).

- Create an informal table of contents or index for the notes you took in class.

- Predict which material will be covered on the test and highlight relevant sections in your readings and notes.

Short-answer/fill-in-the-blank tests

- Concentrate on key words and facts. Be brief.

- Over-learning material can really pay off. When you know a subject backward and forward, you can answer this type of question almost as quickly as you can write.

© photos.com

Matching tests

- Begin by reading through each column, starting with the one with fewer items. Check the number of items in each column to see if they're equal. If they're not, look for an item in one column that you can match with two or more items in the other column.

- Look for any items with similar wording and make special note of the differences between these items.

- Match words that are similar grammatically. For example, match verbs with verbs and nouns with nouns.

- When matching individual words with phrases, first read a phrase. Then look for the word that logically completes the phrase.

- Cross out items in each column when you are through with them.

Essay questions

Managing your time is crucial to answering essay questions. Note how many questions you have to answer and monitor your progress during the exam period. Writing shorter answers and completing all of the questions on an essay test will probably yield a better score than leaving some questions blank.

Find out what an essay question is asking—precisely. If a question asks you to *compare* the ideas of Sigmund Freud and Karl Marx, no matter how eloquently you *explain* them, you are on a one-way trip to No Credit City.

Before you write, make a quick outline. An outline can help speed up the writing of your detailed answer, you're less likely to leave out important facts, and if you don't have time to finish your answer, your outline could win you some points. To use test time efficiently, keep your outline brief. Focus on key words to use in your answer.

Introduce your answer by getting to the point. General statements such as "There are many interesting facets to this difficult question" can cause acute irritation for instructors marking dozens of tests.

One way to get to the point is to begin your answer with part of the question. Suppose the question is "Discuss how increasing the city police budget might or might not contribute to a decrease in street crime." Your first sentence might be "An increase in police expenditures will not have a significant effect on street crime for the following reasons." Your position is clear. You are on your way to an answer.

When you expand your answer with supporting ideas and facts, start out with the most solid points. Be brief and avoid filler sentences.

Write legibly. Marking essay questions is in large part a subjective process. Sloppy, difficult-to-read handwriting might actually lower your mark.

Write on one side of the paper only. If you write on both sides of the paper, writing will show through and obscure the writing on the other side. If necessary, use the blank side to add points you missed. Leave a generous left-hand margin and plenty of space between your answers, in case you want to add to them later.

Finally, if you have time, review your answers for grammar and spelling errors, clarity, and legibility.

Online tests

If the test is going to be online, in advance of the test ask the instructor if the test is open book or not. Ask whether you can go back to a question if you skip it.

Also ask if you can review all the questions before you begin to fill in your answers. If you must answer each question before you move on to the next question, this could be stressful to you and you will need to prepare even more thoroughly for the exam than for one that is paper based. If your instructor has not done so already, ask him to put up sample quizzes on your course management system so that you can practise completing the test online. During the actual test, you will also need to monitor your time even more carefully to ensure you complete answering all the test questions.

Finally, ask your instructor if it is possible to change your answers, and if you can print out the test and your answers before you submit the test. The printed tests are good for you to review prior to the final exam.

If your test is online, consider your test space. If it is your residence room, make sure you place a big "Do not disturb" sign on the door and that the space is quiet enough so that you can focus on the test. As with a paper-based test, have all the tools you will need to complete the test out on your desk—such as pens, calculators, or a water bottle—prior to beginning the test. ✳

F is for feedback, not failure

When some students get an F on an assignment, they interpret that letter as a message: "You are a failure." That interpretation is not accurate. Getting an F means only that you failed a test—not that you failed your life.

From now on, imagine that the letter *F* when used as a grade represents another word: *feedback*. An F is an indication that you didn't understand the material well enough. It's a message to do something differently before the next test or assignment.

If you interpret F as *failure,* you don't get to change anything. But if you interpret F as *feedback,* you can change your thinking and behaviour in ways that promote your success.

Words to watch for in essay questions

The following words are commonly found in essay test questions. If you want to do well on essay tests, study this page thoroughly. Know these words backward and forward. To heighten your awareness of them, underline the words when you see them in a test question.

Analyze: Break into separate parts and discuss, examine, or interpret each part. Then give your opinion.

Compare: Examine two or more items. Identify similarities and differences.

Contrast: Show differences. Set in opposition.

Criticize: Make judgments. Evaluate comparative worth. Criticism often involves analysis.

Define: Explain the exact meaning—usually, a meaning specific to the course or subject. Definitions are usually short.

Describe: Give a detailed account. Make a picture with words. List characteristics, qualities, and parts.

Discuss: Consider and debate or argue the pros and cons of an issue. Write about any conflict. Compare and contrast.

Explain: Make an idea clear. Show logically how a concept is developed. Give the reasons for an event.

Prove: Support with facts (especially facts presented in class or in the text).

Relate: Show the connections between ideas or events. Provide a larger context for seeing the big picture.

State: Explain precisely.

Summarize: Give a brief, condensed account. Include conclusions. Avoid unnecessary details.

Trace: Show the order of events or the progress of a subject or event.

If any of these terms are still unclear to you, consult your unabridged dictionary. A thorough knowledge of these words helps you answer essay questions in a way that best demonstrates your understanding of the course content.

 Review these key words and other helpful vocabulary terms by using the flash cards online @
www.bams5ce.nelson.com

The test isn't over until . . .

MANY STUDENTS believe that a test is over as soon as they turn in the answer sheet. Consider another point of view: You're not done with a test until you know the answer to any question that you missed—and why you missed it.

This point of view offers major benefits. Tests in many courses are cumulative. In other words, the content included on the first test is assumed to be working knowledge for the second test, mid-term, or final exam. When you discover what questions you missed and understand the reasons for lost points, you learn something—and you greatly increase your odds of achieving better scores later in the course.

To get the most value from any test, take control of what you do at two critical points: the time immediately following the test, and the time when the test is returned to you.

Immediately following the test. After finishing a test, your first thought might be to nap, snack, watch a movie online, or go out with friends to celebrate. Restrain those impulses for a short while so that you can reflect on the test. The time you invest now carries the potential to raise your marks in the future.

To begin with, sit down in a quiet place and take a few minutes to write some Discovery Statements related to your experience of taking the test. Doing this while the test is still fresh in your mind increases the value of this technique. Describe how you felt about taking the test, how effective your review strategies were, and whether you accurately predicted the questions that appeared on the test.

Follow up with an Intention Statement or two. State what, if anything, you will do differently to prepare for the next test. The more specific you are, the better. If the test revealed any gaps in your knowledge, list follow-up questions to ask in class.

When the test is returned. When a returned test includes an instructor's comments, view this document as a treasure trove of intellectual gold.

First, make sure that the point totals add up correctly and double-check for any other errors in marking. Even the best instructors make an occasional mistake.

Next, ask these questions:

- On what material did the instructor base test questions—readings, lectures, discussions, or other class activities?

- Were there questions from specific chapters that you missed more than others? If yes, then it will be important to reread those chapters and ask your instructor more questions before the final exam.
- What types of questions appeared in the test—objective (such as matching items, true/false questions, or multiple choice), short-answer, or essay?

- What types of questions did you miss?
- Can you learn anything from the instructor's comments that will help you prepare for the next test?

Also see if you can correct any answers that lost points. To do this, carefully analyse the source of your errors and find a solution. Consult the following chart for help. ✱

Source of test error	Possible solutions
Study errors—studying material that was not included on the test, or spending too little time on material that did appear on the test	• Ask your instructor about specific topics that will be included on a test. • Practise predicting test questions. • Form a study group with class members to create mock tests.
Careless errors, such as skipping or misreading directions	• Read and follow directions more carefully–especially when tests are divided into several sections with different directions. • Set aside time during the next test to proofread your answers.
Concept errors—mistakes made when you do not understand the underlying principles needed to answer a question or solve a problem	• Look for patterns in the questions you missed. • Make sure that you complete all assigned readings, attend all lectures, and show up for laboratory sessions. • Ask your instructor for help with specific questions.
Application errors—mistakes made when you understand underlying principles but fail to apply them correctly	• Rewrite your answers correctly. • When studying, spend more time on solving sample problems. • Predict application questions that will appear in future tests and practise answering them.
Test mechanics errors—missing more questions in certain parts of the test than others, changing correct answers to incorrect ones at the last minute, leaving items blank, miscopying answers from scratch paper to the answer sheet	• Set time limits for taking each section of a test and stick to them. • Proofread your test answers carefully. • Look for patterns in the kind of answers you change at the last minute. • Change answers only if you can state a clear and compelling reason to do so.

The high costs of cheating

Cheating on tests can be a tempting strategy. It offers the chance to get a good grade without having to study.

INSTEAD OF STUDYING, we could spend more time watching TV, partying, sleeping, or doing anything that seems like more fun. Another benefit is that we could avoid the risk of doing poorly on a test—which could happen even if we *do* study.

But before you rush out to make cheating a habit, remember that it also carries costs. Here are some to consider.

We learn less. While we might think that some courses offer little or no value, it is more likely that we can create value from any course. If we look deeply enough, we can discover some idea or acquire some skill to prepare us for future courses or a career after graduation.

We lose money. Getting an education costs a lot of money. Cheating sabotages our purchase. We pay full tuition without getting full value for it.

Fear of getting caught promotes stress. When we're fully aware of our emotions about cheating, we might discover intense stress. Even if we're not fully aware of our emotions, we're likely to feel some level of discomfort about getting caught.

Violating our values promotes stress. Even if we don't get caught cheating, we can feel stress about violating our own ethical standards. Stress can compromise our physical health and overall quality of life.

Cheating on tests can make it easier to violate our integrity again. Human beings become comfortable with behaviours that they repeat. Cheating is no exception.

Think about the first time you drove a car. You might have felt excited—even a little frightened. Now driving is probably second nature, and you don't give it much thought. Repeated experience with driving creates familiarity, which lessens the intense feelings you had during your first time at the wheel.

We can experience the same process with almost any behaviour. Cheating once will make it easier to cheat again. And if we become comfortable with compromising our integrity in one area of life, we might find it easier to compromise in other areas.

Cheating lowers our self-esteem. Whether or not we are fully aware of it, cheating sends us the message that we are not smart enough or responsible enough to make it on our own. We deny ourselves the celebration and satisfaction of authentic success.

In the end it is about the value of your degree. Cheating lowers that value and you end up cheating yourself out of your own education. So think twice even if you think, "Well, everyone is doing it, so who does it

harm?" An effective alternative to cheating is to become a master student. Ways to do this are described on every page of this book. ✱

Perils of high-tech cheating

Digital technology offers many blessings, but it also expands the options for cheating during a test. For example, one student loaded class notes into a Sidekick (a hand-held device) and tried to read them. Another student dictated his class notes into files stored on his iPod and tried to listen to them. At one school, students used cell phones to take photos of test questions. They sent the photos to classmates outside the testing room, who responded by text-messaging the answers (Glater, 2006).

All of these students were caught. Schools are becoming sophisticated about detecting high-tech cheating. Some install cameras in exam rooms. Others use software that monitors the programs running on students' computers during tests. And most schools simply ban all digital devices during tests.

There's no need to learn the hard way—through painful consequences—about the high costs of high-tech cheating. Using the suggestions in this chapter can help you succeed on tests *and* preserve your academic integrity.

Let go of test anxiety

If you freeze during all kinds of tests and flub questions when you know the answers, you might be suffering from test anxiety.

A LITTLE TENSION before a test is good. That tingly, butterflies-in-the-stomach feeling you get from extra adrenalin can sharpen your awareness and keep you alert. You can enjoy the benefits of a little tension while you stay confident and relaxed.

© photos.com

CHAPTER SIX TESTS **205**

Sometimes, however, tension is persistent and extreme. It causes loss of sleep, appetite, and sometimes even hair.

If it interferes with your daily life and consistently prevents you from doing your best in school, it might be test anxiety.

Symptoms of anxiety include the following (Mayo Clinic, 2007):

- Inability to concentrate
- Insomnia
- Sweating
- Shortness of breath
- Fatigue
- Irritability
- Stomach ache
- Diarrhea
- Headache

Anxiety has three elements: mental, physical, and emotional. The mental element includes your thoughts, including predictions of failure. The physical component includes physical sensations such as shallow breathing and muscle tension. The emotional element occurs when thoughts and physical sensations combine. The following techniques can help you deal with these elements of stress in *any* situation, from test anxiety to stage fright.

Dealing with thoughts

Yell "Stop!" When you notice that your mind is consumed with worries and fears, and your thoughts are spinning out of control, mentally yell "Stop!" If you're in a situation that allows it, yell it out loud.

This action is likely to bring your focus back to the present moment and allow you to redirect your thoughts. Once you've broken the cycle of worry or panic, you can use any of the following techniques.

Dispute your thoughts. Certain thoughts tend to increase test anxiety. They often boil down to this statement: *Getting a low grade on a test is a disaster.* Do the math, however: A four-year degree often involves taking about 40 courses (10 courses per year over four years for a full-time student). This means that your final grade on any one course amounts to about only 4 percent of your total grade point average.

Also consider that your final grade in any one course is usually based on more than one test. This means that a single test score is not going to make or break your college career.

This argument is not meant to convince you to stop preparing for tests. It *is* an argument to keep each test in perspective—and to dispute thoughts that only serve to create anxiety.

Visualize success. Most of us live up—or down—to our own expectations. If we spend a lot of time mentally rehearsing what it will be like to fail a test, our chances of doing so increase. Instead, you can take time to rehearse what it will be like to succeed. Be specific. Create detailed pictures, actions, and even sounds as part of your visualization. If you are able to visit the room where you will take the test, mentally rehearse while you are actually in this room.

Focus. Focus your attention on a specific object. Examine details of a painting, study the branches on a tree, or observe the face of your watch (right down to the tiny scratches in the glass). During an exam, take a few seconds to listen to the sounds of concentration—the squeaking of chairs, the scratching of pencils, the muted coughs. Touch the surface of your desk and notice the texture.

Concentrate all of your attention on one point. Don't leave room in your mind for anxiety-related thoughts.

Praise yourself. Talk to yourself in a positive way. Many of us take the first opportunity to belittle ourselves: "Way to go, dummy! You don't even know the answer to the first question on the test." We wouldn't dream of treating a friend this way, yet we do it to ourselves.

An alternative is to give yourself some encouragement. Treat yourself as if you were your own best friend. Consider telling yourself, "I am very relaxed. I am doing a great job on this test."

Consider the worst. Rather than trying to put a stop to your worrying, consider the very worst thing that could happen. Take your fear to the limit of absurdity.

Imagine the catastrophic problems that might occur if you were to fail the test. You might say to yourself, "Well, if I fail this test, I might fail the course, lose my scholarship, and get kicked out of school. Then I won't be able to get a job, so the bank will repossess my car, and I'll start drinking." Keep going until you see the absurdity of your predictions.

After you stop laughing, you can backtrack to discover a reasonable level of concern. Your worry about failing the entire course if you fail the test might be justified. At that point ask yourself: "Can I live with that?" Unless you are taking a test in parachute packing and the final question involves jumping out of a plane, the answer will almost always be yes. If the answer is no, use another technique. In fact, use several.

Dealing with the physical sensations of anxiety

Breathe. You can calm physical sensations within your body by focusing your attention on your breathing. Concentrate on the air going in and out of your lungs. Experience it as it passes through your nose and mouth.

Do this for two to five minutes. If you notice that you are taking short, shallow breaths, begin to take longer and deeper breaths. Imagine your lungs to be a pair of bagpipes. Expand your chest to bring in as much air as possible. Then listen to the plaintive chords as you slowly release the air.

Scan your body. Simple awareness is an effective technique to reduce the tension in your body.

Sit comfortably and close your eyes. Focus your attention on the muscles in your feet and notice if they are relaxed. Tell the muscles in your feet that they can relax.

Move up to your ankles and repeat the procedure. Next go to your calves and thighs and buttocks, telling each group of muscles to relax.

Do the same for your lower back, diaphragm, chest, upper back, neck, shoulders, jaw, face, upper arms, lower arms, fingers, and scalp.

Tense and relax. If you are aware of a particularly tense part of your body or if you discover tension when you're scanning your body, you can release this tension with the tense-relax method.

To do this, find a muscle that is tense and make it even more tense. If your shoulders are tense, pull them back, arch your back, and tense your shoulder muscles even more tightly. Then relax. The net result is that you can be aware of the relaxation and allow yourself to relax even more.

You can use the same procedure with your legs, arms, abdomen, chest, face, and neck. Clench your fists, tighten your jaw, straighten your legs, and tense your abdomen all at once. Then relax and pay close attention to the sensations of relaxation. By paying attention, you can learn to re-create these sensations whenever you choose.

Use guided imagery. Relax completely and take a quick fantasy trip. Close your eyes, free your body of tension, and imagine yourself in a beautiful, peaceful, natural setting. Create as much of the scene as you can. Be specific. Use all of your senses.

For example, you might imagine yourself at a beach. Hear the surf rolling in and the sea gulls calling to each other. Feel the sun on your face and the hot sand between your toes. Smell the sea breeze. Taste the salty mist from the surf. Notice the ships on the horizon and the rolling sand dunes. Use all of your senses to create a vivid imaginary trip.

Some people find that a mountain scene or a lush meadow scene works well. You can take yourself to a place you've never been or re-create an experience out of your past. Find a place that works for you and practise getting there. When you become proficient, you can return to it quickly for trips that might last only a few seconds.

With practice, you can use this technique even while you are taking a test.

Describe sensations. Focus your attention on your anxiety. If you are feeling nauseated or if you have a headache, concentrate on that feeling. Describe it to yourself. When you completely experience a physical sensation, it will often disappear. People suffering from chronic pain have used this technique successfully (Kabat-Zin, 2001).

Be with it. As you describe your anxiety in detail, don't resist it. A recent study of students who were anxious found that those who spent 10 minutes before the test writing about their fears actually did better in terms of achievement than those who just relaxed before the test. It appears that by writing about it, students were able to get rid of their fears ahead of the test and so were able to relax and better concentrate during the test (Taylor, 2011).

Exercise aerobically. This is one technique that won't work in the classroom or while you're taking a test. Yet it is an excellent way to reduce body tension. Exercise regularly during the days that you review for a test or exam. See what effect this has on your ability to focus and relax *during* the test or exam.

Do some kind of exercise that will get your heart beating at twice your normal rate and keep it beating at that rate for 15 or 20 minutes. Aerobic exercises include rapid walking, running, swimming, bicycling, basketball, and anything else that elevates your heart rate and keeps it elevated.

Find alternatives to chemicals. When faced with stress, some people turn to relief in the form of a pill, a drink, or a drug in some other form. Chemicals such as caffeine and alcohol *can* change the way you feel. They also come with costs that go beyond money. For example, drinking alcohol can relax you *and* interfere with your attention and memory. Caffeine or energy drinks might make you feel more confident in the short term. Watch what happens, though, when you start to come down from a caffeine-induced high. You might feel even more irritable than you did *before* drinking that double espresso.

6

TESTS

All lectures aside, chemicals that you take without a prescription are ineffective ways to manage anxiety. Use other techniques instead.

Dealing with emotions

Accept emotions—whatever they are. Consider our typical response to problems. If a car has a flat tire, that's a problem. The solution is to repair or replace the tire. If a bathroom faucet drips, that's a problem. The solution is to repair or replace part of the faucet.

This problem–solution approach often works well when applied to events outside us. It does not work so well, however, when applied to events *inside* us. When we define anger, sadness, fear, or any emotion as a problem, we tend to search for a solution. However, emotions respond differently than flat tires and drippy faucets.

Typical attempts to "solve" unpleasant emotions include eating, drinking, watching TV, or browsing the Internet. These are actually attempts to resist the emotions and try to make them go away. For a short time, this strategy might work. Over the long term, however, our efforts to repair or replace emotions often have the opposite effect: The emotions persist or even get stronger. Our solutions actually become part of the problem.

An alternative to problem solving is *acceptance*. We can stop seeing emotions as problems. This attitude frees us from having to search for solutions (which often fail anyway).

Acceptance means just letting our emotions be. It means releasing any resistance to emotions. This approach is a wise one, since what we *resist* usually *persists*. Our emotions are just bundles of thoughts and physical sensations. Even the most unpleasant ones fade sooner or later.

The next time you are feeling anxious before a test, simply let that feeling arise and then pass away.

Practise detachment. To *detach* means to step back from something and see it as separate from ourselves. When we detach from an emotion, we no longer identify with it. We no longer say, "*I am afraid*" or "*I am sad.*" We say something like "There's fear again" or "I feel sadness right now." Using language such as this offers us a way to step back from our internal experiences and keep them in perspective.

Before a test, you might find it especially useful to detach from your thoughts. Borrow some ideas from acceptance and commitment therapy, which is used by a growing number of therapists (Hayes, 2004). Take an anxiety-producing thought—such as *I always screw up on tests*—and do any of the following:

- Repeat the thought over and over again out loud until it becomes just a meaningless series of sounds.
- Repeat the thought while using the voice of a cartoon character such as Donald Duck or Homer Simpson.
- Rephrase the thought so that you can sing it to the tune of a nursery rhyme or the song "Happy Birthday."
- Preface the thought with "I'm having the thought that . . ." (*I'm having the thought that I always screw up on tests.*)
- Talk back to your mind by saying, "That's an interesting thought, mind; thanks a lot for sharing." Or simply say, "Thanks, mind."

Make contact with the present moment. If you feel anxious, see if you can focus your attention on a specific sight, sound, or other sensation that's happening in the present moment. Examine the details of a painting. Study the branches on a tree. Observe the face of your watch right down to the tiny scratches in the glass. During an exam, take a few seconds to listen to the sounds of squeaking chairs, the scratching of pencils, the muted coughs. Touch the surface of your desk and notice the texture. Focus all of your attention on one point—anything other than the flow of thoughts through your head. Focusing in this manner is one way to use the Power Process: "Be Here Now."

Get help

When these techniques don't work, when anxiety is serious, get help. If you become withdrawn, have frequent thoughts about death or suicide, get depressed and stay depressed for more than a few days, or have prolonged feelings of hopelessness, see a counsellor or doctor.

Depression and anxiety are common among students. Suicide is the second leading cause of death among young adults between the ages of 15 and 25. This is tragic and unnecessary. Most schools have counsellors and doctors available through student services or student health services. If not, the student health service or another office can refer you to community agencies that provide free or inexpensive counselling. You can also get emergency assistance over the phone. Most phone books contain listings for suicide prevention hotlines and other emergency services. ✳

Have some FUN!

Contrary to popular belief, finals week does not have to be a drag.

In fact, if you have used techniques in this chapter, exam week can be fun. You will have done most of your studying long before finals arrive.

When you are well prepared for tests, you can even use fun as a technique to enhance your performance. The day before a final, go for a run or play a game of basketball. Take in a movie or a concert. A relaxed brain is a more effective brain. If you have studied for a test, your mind will continue to prepare itself even while you're at the movies.

Get plenty of rest, too. There's no need to cram until 3:00 a.m. when you have reviewed material throughout the term.

On the first day of finals, you can wake up refreshed, have a good breakfast, and walk into the exam room with a smile on your face. You can also leave with a smile on your face, knowing that you are going to have a fun week. It's your reward for studying regularly throughout the term.

18 exercise
20 Things I like to do

One way to relieve tension is to mentally yell "Stop!" and substitute a pleasant daydream for the stressful thoughts and emotions you are experiencing. In order to create a supply of pleasant images to recall during times of stress, conduct an eight-minute brainstorm about things you like to do. Your goal is to generate at least 20 ideas. Time yourself and write as fast as you can in the space below.

When you have completed your list, study it. Pick out two activities that seem especially pleasant and elaborate on them by creating a mindmap. Write down all of the memories you have about that activity.

You can use these images to calm yourself in stressful situations.

No matter what you do, remember to breathe. You can relax in any moment just by making your breath slower and deeper. Practise doing this while you study math. It will come in handy at test time.

Boost study skills for math

Choose teachers with care. Whenever possible, find a math teacher whose approach to math matches your learning style. Talk with several teachers until you find one you enjoy.

Another option is to ask around. Maybe your academic advisor can recommend math teachers. Also ask classmates to name their favourite math teachers—and to explain the reasons for their choices.

In some cases, only one teacher will be offering the math course you need. The suggestions that follow can be used to learn from a teacher regardless of her teaching style.

Take math courses back to back. Approach math in the same way that you learn a foreign language. If you take a year off in between French I and French II, you won't gain much fluency. To master a language, you take courses back to back. It works the same way with math, which is a language in itself.

Form a study group. During the first week of each math course, organize a study group. Ask each member to bring five problems to group meetings, along with solutions. Also exchange contact information so that you can stay in touch via email, phone, and text messaging.

Avoid short courses. Courses that you take during summer school or another shortened term are condensed. You might find yourself doing far more reading and homework each week than you do in longer courses. If you enjoy math, the extra intensity can provide a stimulus to learn. But if math is not your favourite subject, give yourself extra time. Enrol in courses spread out over more calendar days.

Participate in class. Success in math depends on your active involvement. Attend class regularly. Complete homework assignments *when they're due*—not just before the test. If you're confused, get help right away from an instructor, tutor, or study group. Instructors' office hours, free on-campus tutoring, and classmates are just a few of the resources available to you. Also support class participation

with time for homework. Make daily contact with math.

Prepare for lab sessions. Laboratory work is crucial to many science classes. To get the most out of these sessions, be prepared. Complete required reading before you enter the lab. Also gather the materials you'll need ahead of time.

Prepare for several types of tests. Math tests often involve lists of problems to solve. Ask your instructor about what type of tests to expect. Then prepare for the tests using strategies from this chapter.

Ask questions fearlessly. It's a cliché, and it's true: In math, there are no dumb questions. Ask whatever questions will aid your understanding. Keep a running list of them, and bring the list to class.

Make your text top priority. Math courses are often text driven. Class activities closely follow the book. This fact underscores the importance of completing your reading assignments. Master one concept before going on to the next, and stay current with your reading. Be willing to read slowly and reread sections as needed.

Read actively. To get the most out of your math texts, read with paper and pencil in hand. Work out examples. Copy diagrams, formulas, and equations. Use chapter summaries and introductory outlines to organize your learning.

From time to time, stop, close your book, and mentally reconstruct the steps in solving a problem. Before you memorize a formula, understand the basic concepts behind it.

Practise solving problems. To get ready for math tests, work *lots* of problems. Find out if practice problems or previous tests are on file in the library, in the math department, or with your math teacher.

Isolate the types of problems that you find the most difficult. Practise them more often. Be sure to get help with these kinds of problems *before* exhaustion or frustration sets in.

To prepare for tests, practise working problems fast. Time yourself. This activity is a great one for math study groups.

Approach problem solving with a three-step process, as shown in the chart on the following page. During each step, apply an appropriate strategy.

1: Prepare

- Read each problem two or three times, slowly and out loud whenever possible.
- Consider creating a chart with three columns labelled *What I already know, What I want to find out,* and *What connects the two.* The third column is the place to record a formula that can help you solve the problem.
- Determine which arithmetic operations (addition, subtraction, multiplication, division) or formulas you will use to solve the problem.
- See if you can estimate the answer before you compute it.

2: Compute

- Reduce the number of unknowns as much as you can. Consider creating a separate equation to solve each unknown.
- When solving equations, carry out the algebra as far as you can before plugging in the actual numbers.
- Cancel and combine. For example, if the same term appears in both dividend and divisor, they will cancel each other out.
- Remember that it's OK to make several attempts at solving the problem before you find an answer.

3: Check

- Plug your answer back into the original equation or problem and see if it works out correctly.
- Ask yourself if your answer seems likely when compared with your estimate. For example, if you're asked to apply a discount to an item, that item should cost less in your solution.
- Perform opposite operations. If a problem involves multiplication, check your work by division; add, then subtract; factor, then multiply; find the square root, then the square; differentiate, then integrate.
- Keep units of measurement clear. Say that you're calculating the velocity of an object. If you're measuring distance in metres and time in seconds, the final velocity should be in metres per second.

Use tests to show what you know

Practise test taking. Part of preparing for any math test is rehearsal. Instead of passively reading through your text or scanning class notes, do a practice test:

- Print out a set of practice problems, and set a timer for the same length of time as your testing period.
- Whenever possible, work practice problems in the same room where you will take the actual test.
- Use only the kinds of supporting materials—such as scratch paper or lists of formulas—that will be allowed during the test.
- As you work problems, use deep breathing or another technique to enter a more relaxed state.

Ask appropriate questions. If you don't understand a test item, ask for clarification. The worst that can happen is that an instructor or proctor will politely decline to answer your question.

Write legibly. Put yourself in the instructor's place. Imagine the prospect of grading stacks of illegible answer sheets. Make your answers easy to read. If you show your work, underline key sections and circle your answer.

Do your best. There are no secrets involved in getting ready for math tests. Master some stress management techniques, do your homework, get answers to your questions, and work sample problems. If you've done those things, you're ready for the test and deserve to do well. If you haven't done all those things, just do the best you can.

Remember that your personal best can vary from test to test, and even from day to day. Even if you don't answer all test questions correctly, you can demonstrate what you *do* know right now.

During the test, notice when solutions come easily. Savour the times when you feel relaxed and confident. If you ever feel math anxiety in the future, these are the times to remember. ✳

STUDENT VOICES

The master student realizes that it is time saving to review more often and right after class rather than to initiate a marathon study session right before the test.

—MALTE STRAUSS

Succeeding in science courses

Many of the strategies that help you prepare for math tests can also help you succeed in science courses. For example, forming small study groups can be a fun way to learn these subjects.

Relating science to your career interests and daily life is also important. People in many professions—from dentists to gardeners—rely on science to do their jobs. And even if you don't choose a science-driven career, you will live in a world that's driven by technology. Understanding how scientists observe, collect data, and arrive at conclusions can help you feel more at home in this world.

In addition, use some strategies that are unique to succeeding in science courses.

Prepare for Variety   Remember that the word *science* refers to a vast range of subjects—astronomy, biology, chemistry, physics, physiology, geology, ecology, geography, and more. Most of these subjects include math as one of their tools. Beyond that, however, are key differences.

You can take advantage of this variety. Choose courses in a science that matches your personal interests and comfort level for technical subjects.

Prepare for Lab Sessions   Laboratory work is crucial to many science classes. To get the most out of these sessions, be prepared. Complete required reading before you enter the lab. Also gather the materials you'll need ahead of time.

 Find more strategies for succeeding in science online @
www.bams5ce.nelson.com

exercise 19
Use learning styles for math success

Review the articles about learning styles in Chapter 1: First Steps. Look for strategies that could promote your success in math. Modify any of the suggested strategies so that they work for you, or invent new techniques of your own.

If you're a visual learner, for example, you might colour code your notes by writing key terms and formulas in red ink.

If you like to learn by speaking and listening, consider reading key passages in your textbooks out loud. And if you're a kinesthetic learner, use "manipulatives"—such as magnetic boards with letters and numbers—when you study math.

Whatever you choose, commit to using at least one new strategy. In the space below, describe what you will do.

Eight reasons to celebrate mistakes

Most of us are haunted by the fear of failure. We dread the thought of making mistakes or being held responsible for a major breakdown. We shudder at the missteps that could cost us marks, careers, money, or even relationships.

© Gordana Sermek/Shutterstock

IT'S POSSIBLE to take an entirely different attitude toward mistakes. Rather than fearing them, we could actually celebrate them. We could marvel at our mistakes and laugh loudly when we "blow it."

A creative environment is one in which failure is not fatal. Businesses, striving to be on the cutting edge of competition, desperately seek innovative changes. They know that innovation requires taking risks, despite the chance of failure.

This is not idle talk. There are places where people actually celebrate mistakes (McGregor, Symonds, Foust, Brady & Herbst, 2006).

- The Coca-Cola Company launched a number of beverages that bombed—including Choglit, OK Soda, Surge, and New Coke. But at the company's annual meeting in 2006, chair and chief executive officer E. Neville Isdell told investors to accept failures as a way to regenerate the company.
- Scott Anthony, director of a consulting firm named Innosight, coaches companies to fumble to success by failing early and cheaply as they develop new products.
- Thomas D. Kuczmarski, a Chicago-based consultant, suggests that companies hold "failure parties" to reward mistakes that lead to better products.

Note: Nothing in this article amounts to an argument in favour of *making* mistakes in the first place. Rather, the intention is to encourage shining a light on mistakes so that we can examine them and fix them. Mistakes that are hidden cannot be corrected.

Eight solid reasons for celebrating mistakes

1 Celebration allows us to notice the mistake. Celebrating mistakes gets them out into the open. This is the opposite of covering up mistakes or blaming others for them. Hiding mistakes takes a lot of energy—energy that could be channelled into correcting errors.

2 Mistakes are valuable feedback. A manager of a major corporation once made a mistake that cost his company $100,000. He predicted that he would be fired when his boss found out. Instead, his boss responded, "Fire you? I can't afford to do that. I just spent $100,000 training you." Mistakes are part of the learning process. Not only are mistakes usually more interesting than most successes—they're often more instructive.

3 Mistakes demonstrate that we're taking risks. People who play it safe make few mistakes. Making mistakes is evidence that we're stretching to the limit of our abilities—growing, risking, and learning. Fear of making mistakes can paralyze us into inaction. Celebrating mistakes helps us move into gear and get things done.

4 Celebrating mistakes reminds us that it's OK to make them. When we celebrate, we remind ourselves that the person who made the mistake is not bad—just human. This is not a recommendation that you purposely set out to make mistakes. Mistakes are not an end in themselves. Rather, their value lies in what we learn from them. When we make a mistake, we can admit it and correct it.

Put It to *WORK*

Y ou can apply many of the techniques discussed in this chapter directly to common situations in the workplace. For example, use the test-taking strategies when you take licensing exams, certification exams, and other tests in your career field. In addition, consider the following suggestions.

Seize opportunities to learn cooperatively

Forming study groups or committees helps you develop important workplace skills. Almost every job is accomplished by the combined efforts of many people. For example, manufacturing a single car calls for the contribution of designers, welders, painters, electricians, marketing executives, computer programmers, and many others.

Perhaps you prefer to complete your assignments by working independently. However, teamwork is often required in the workplace. Joining study groups now, while you are in school, can help you expand your learning styles and succeed in the workplace.

Apply your cooperative learning skills to working on project teams

To create a successful project team at work, combine the individual skills of team members in complementary ways. Major tasks in any project include:

- *Planning*—defining the desired outcomes, setting due dates for each task, and generating commitment to action.
- *Doing*—carrying out assigned tasks.
- *Reflecting*—meeting regularly to discuss what's working well and ways to improve the next phase of the project.
- *Interpreting*—discussing what the team has learned from the project and ways to apply that learning to the whole organization.

Many people are drawn to one of these tasks more than the others. Assign tasks to people based on their strengths and preferences.

One potential trap of working in teams is that one person ends up doing most of the work. This person might feel resentful and complain. If you find yourself in this situation,

© James Peragine/Shutterstock

transform your complaint into a request. Instead of scolding team members for being lazy, request help. Ask team members to take over tasks that you've been doing. Delegate specific jobs.

Manage job stress

The same techniques that help you manage test anxiety can help you manage stress at work. Apply techniques for managing the mental and physical aspects of stress while interviewing for a job, making a presentation, doing a performance review, or carrying out any task that raises your anxiety level.

Celebrate mistakes

Recall a mistake you made at work and then write about it. In a Discovery Statement, describe what you did to create a result you didn't want ("I discovered that I tend to underestimate the number of hours projects take"). Then write an Intention Statement describing something you can do differently in the future ("I intend to keep track of my actual hours on each project so that I can give more accurate estimates").

Go for fun

Finally, see if you can adapt suggestions from "Have some FUN!" to cultivate enjoyment at work. One benefit of career planning (see Chapter 12) is finding a job that allows you to follow your interests—in other words, to have fun. Successful people often eliminate the distinction between work and play in their lives. You're more likely to excel professionally when you're having a blast at your job.

chapter 6

QUIZ

◄ ◄ ◄ ◄ ◄

▢ Put It to Work
▢ Skills Snapshot
▢ Master Student Profile

Name_____   Date____/____/____

1. Preparing for tests can include creating review tools. Name at least two of these tools.

2. When answering multiple choice questions, it is better to read all of the possible answers before answering the question in your head. True or False? Explain your answer.

3. The presence of absolute qualifiers, such as *always* or *never*, generally indicates a false statement. True or False? Explain your answer.

4. Briefly explain the differences between a daily review and a major review.

5. Define the term *study checklist*, and give three examples of what to include on such checklists.

6. Describe how using the Power Process: "Detach" differs from giving up.

7. Choose one technique for taking math and science tests, and explain how it, or some variation of it, could apply to taking a test in another subject.

8. Name at least three benefits of participating in a study group.

9. Describe at least three techniques for dealing with the thoughts connected to test anxiety.

10. Describe at least three techniques for dealing with the physical feelings connected to test anxiety.

Skills *SNAPSHOT*

Now that you've had some concrete experience with the strategies presented in this chapter, take a minute to reflect on your responses to the "Tests" section of the Discovery Wheel on page 36. Expand on those responses by completing the following sentences.

PREPARING FOR TESTS

When studying for a test, the first thing I usually do is . . .

In addition, I . . .

TAKING TESTS

One strategy that helps me with objective tests (true/false and multiple choice) is . . .

One strategy that helps me with short-answer and essay tests is . . .

MANAGING TEST ANXIETY

On the day of a test, my level of confidence is generally . . .

If I feel stressed about a test, I respond by . . .

NEXT ACTION

I'll know that I've reached a new level of mastery with tests when . . .

To reach that level of mastery, the most important thing I can do next is to . . .

MASTER STUDENT Profile

Georges Laraque
. . . is determined

© REUTERS/Andy Clark

There was a time not long ago when a meal out with Georges Laraque would have meant a gargantuan steak and some fine wine. Now it's an Öm Burger (mushrooms, sun-dried tomatoes, flax seeds, and mixed vegetables packed into a patty) accompanied by a shooter of freshly squeezed wheatgrass juice. All served at one of the two vegan restaurants in town that he co-owns.

Mr. Laraque, who before he retired from the NHL last year, was best known for his readiness to give and take beatings, now seems to be doing everything possible to shed the tough-guy image. In the past two years, he has become a vegan, a celebrity spokesman for the animal-rights group PETA, and deputy leader of the federal Green Party. On the ice, he is now more frequently seen figure skating than playing hockey. And next month he will be a panelist on CBC's Canada Reads, trying to win a literary showdown by arguing the merits of the novel *The Bone Cage*.

On the surface, the causes and activities Mr. Laraque, 34, has embraced seem worlds away from his life as a professional athlete. But the way he sees it, they are in keeping with the defiant approach to life he has taken since he was a child. "If you tell me I'm not going to make it, I'm going to make it," he said in an interview at his restaurant, Crudessence. It is an approach shaped by his experience of racism at a young age.

The son of Haitian immigrants, Mr. Laraque was the only black child on the hockey rinks of his hometown of Tracy, northeast of Montréal. He was a top player, but when it came time to select the elite teams, he somehow never made the cut. Even in the recreational house league, coaches would pass him over.

Hockey, he said, was not even his favourite sport, but the experience left him resolved to prove the bigots wrong. "I used it as a motivation. They helped me push myself to make it to the NHL," he said. "I feel that until I die, it's my job to break stereotypes."

Take the notion that vegans are a sickly, skinny bunch. "A lot of people who talk about veganism or vegetarianism are small and skinny," Mr. Laraque said, and this can turn off potential converts. At 6-foot-3, 280 pounds, Mr. Laraque is anything but malnourished. He was moved to embrace veganism in 2009 after seeing the documentary *Earthlings* about animal abuse.

He skipped team outings to steakhouses and was occasionally teased by teammates, who would give him a handful of grass and say it was dinner. He managed to cut out all animal products and maintain his size and strength, and since hanging up his skates he has added 30 pounds.

His activism caught the attention of Green Party leader Elizabeth May, and last summer Ms. May invited him to become deputy leader. He said he is too busy to consider running in the next election, whenever it comes—among other projects, he is raising money to build a hospital in earthquake-ravaged Haiti. But he plans to use his celebrity to support the campaign of his fellow Greens and help get Ms. May elected in British Columbia.

"I talk differently, a different language that people can understand and relate

(1976 -) A retired hockey player and currently the deputy leader of the Green Party.

Find more biographical information about Georges Laraque at the Master Student Hall of Fame @

www.bams5ce.nelson.com

to," he said. "Maybe people don't vote because they don't relate to politics, they find it boring. I guarantee that when I talk about the Green Party, it isn't boring."

The enforcer's turn last fall on CBC's *Battle of the Blades*, in which retired hockey pros pair with figure skaters to perform routines, could be dismissed as a stunt. But Mr. Laraque was not in it for laughs. He knew enough about figure skating to know how demanding it is. "Figure skating is an extreme sport. It's way harder and tougher than hockey," he said.

He looks at the upcoming Canada Reads debate as a similar challenge. "One of the biggest problems we have is kids becoming illiterate," he said. "People don't read any more." The book he has chosen to defend tells the story of two amateur athletes striving to make the Olympics.

And now he is free to do what he loves best: prove his doubters wrong. "You want people to be captivated by what you're saying, to be inspired," he said. "If what they get is the opposite of what they're expecting, then they remember it."

Source: "It's My Job to Break Stereotypes," Graeme Hamilton, *National Post*, January 29, 2011. Material reprinted with the express permission of National Post, a division of Postmedia Network Inc.

7 Thinking

Master Student Map

as you read, ask yourself

what if . . .

I could solve problems more creatively and make decisions in every area of life with more confidence?

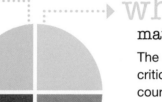

why this chapter matters . . .

The ability to think creatively and critically helps you succeed in any course.

how

you can use this chapter . . .

- Read, write, speak, and listen more effectively.
- Learn strategies to enhance your success in problem solving.
- Apply thinking skills to practical decisions, such as choosing a major.

what is included . . .

- Critical thinking: A survival skill   225
- Becoming a Critical Thinker   227
- Finding "aha!"—Creativity fuels critical thinking   231
- Ways to create ideas   232
- Don't fool yourself: 15 common mistakes in logic   236
- Uncovering assumptions   238
- Gaining skill at decision making   240
- Four ways to solve problems   241
- "But I don't know what I want to do." Choosing your major   242
- Asking questions—Learning through inquiry   245
- Think critically about information on the Internet   247
- Power Process: Find a bigger problem   249
- Master Student Profile: Jian Ghomeshi   253

MASTER STUDENTS in action

I think critical thinking is when you're presented with a problem or a scenario and you don't just go with your gut reaction. You have to look at the problem from many different angles and weigh different options before you decide what is the right answer.

—LAUREN SWIDLER

Critical thinking: A survival skill

SOCIETY DEPENDS ON persuasion. Advertisers want us to spend money on their products. Political candidates want us to "buy" their stands on the issues. Teachers want us to agree that their classes are vital to our success. Parents want us to accept their values. Authors want us to read their books. Broadcasters want us to spend our time in front of the radio or television, consuming their programs and not those of the competition. The business of persuasion has an impact on all of us.

A typical Canadian sees thousands of television commercials each year. And that's just one medium of communication. Add to that the writers and speakers who enter our lives through radio shows, magazines, books, billboards, brochures, Internet sites, and fundraising appeals—all with a product, service, cause, or opinion for us to embrace.

This leaves us with hundreds of choices about what to buy, where to go, and who to be. It's easy to lose our heads in the crosscurrent of competing ideas—unless we develop skills in critical thinking. When we think critically, we can make choices with open eyes.

Benefits of critical thinking *Critical thinking underlies reading, writing, speaking, and listening.* These are the basic elements of communication—a process that occupies most of our waking hours.

Critical thinking promotes social change. Consider that the institutions in any society—courts, governments, schools, businesses—are the products of a certain way of thinking. Any organization draws its life from certain assumptions about the way things should be done. Before the institution can change, those assumptions need to be loosened up or reinvented. In many ways, the real location of an institution is inside our heads.

Critical thinking uncovers bias and prejudice. This is a first step toward communicating with people of other races, nationalities, and cultures.

Critical thinking reveals long-term consequences. Crises occur when our thinking fails to keep pace with reality. An example is the world's ecological crisis, which arose when people polluted the earth, air, and water without considering the long-term consequences. Imagine how different our world would be if our leaders followed the First Nations practice of thinking of themselves as being the caretakers of the earth. Their thinking would then have to focus on the long-term

journal entry 19

Discovery/Intention Statement

Choose to create value with this chapter

Think back to a time when you felt unable to choose among several different solutions to a problem or several stands on a key issue in your life. In the space below, describe this experience.

I discovered that . . .

_____

_____

_____

Now scan this chapter to find useful suggestions for decision making, problem solving, and critical thinking. Note below at least four techniques that look especially promising to you.

Strategy	Page number

Finally, declare a time that you intend to explore these techniques in more detail, along with a situation coming up during this session or term in which you could apply them.

I intend to improve my thinking skills by . . .

_____

_____

_____

_____

_____

_____

THINKING

impacts of environmental destruction. Novelist Ernest Hemingway once said that anyone who wants to be a great writer must have "… a built-in, shockproof [crap] detector (Cheney, 1990)." That inelegant comment points to a basic truth: As critical thinkers, we are constantly on the lookout for thinking that's inaccurate, sloppy, or misleading.

Critical thinking is a skill that will never go out of style. Throughout history, half-truths, faulty assumptions, and other nonsense have at one time been commonly accepted as true. Examples include:

- Illness results from an imbalance in the four vital fluids: blood, phlegm, water, and bile.
- People who touch toads will get warts.
- Caucasians are inherently more intelligent than people of other races.
- Women are incapable of voting intelligently.
- Humans evolved from chimpanzees.
- We will never invent anything smaller than a transistor. (That was before the computer chip.)
- Computer technology will usher in the age of the paperless office.

The critical thinkers of history courageously challenged such ideas. These men and women pointed out that—metaphorically speaking—the emperor had no clothes.

Even in mathematics and the hard sciences, the greatest advances take place when people re-examine age-old beliefs. Scientists continually uncover things that contradict everyday certainties. For example, physics presents us with a world where solid objects are made of atoms spinning around in empty space—where matter and energy are two forms of the same substance. At a moment's notice, the world can deviate from the "laws of nature." That is because those "laws" exist in our heads—not in the world.

Critical thinking is a path to freedom from half-truths and deception. You have the right to question what you see, hear, and read. Acquiring this ability is one of the major goals of a liberal education.

Critical thinking as thorough thinking For some people, the term *critical thinking* has negative connotations. If you prefer, use *thorough thinking* instead. Both terms point to the same array of activities: sorting out conflicting claims, weighing the evidence, letting go of personal biases, and arriving at reasonable conclusions. This adds up to an ongoing conversation—a constant process, not a final product.

We live in a society that seems to value quick answers and certainty. This is often at odds with effective thinking. Thorough thinking is the ability to examine and re-examine ideas that might seem obvious. Such thinking takes time and the willingness to say three subversive words: "I don't know."

Thorough thinking is also the willingness to change our opinion as we continue to examine a problem. This calls for courage and detachment. Just ask anyone who has given up a cherished point of view in light of new evidence.

Skilled students are thorough thinkers. They distinguish between opinion and fact. They ask probing questions and make detailed observations. They uncover assumptions and define their terms. They make assertions carefully, basing them on sound logic and solid evidence. Almost everything that we call *knowledge* is a result of these activities. This means that critical thinking and learning are intimately linked.

It's been said that human beings are rational creatures. Yet no one is born a thorough thinker. This is a learned skill. Use the suggestions in this chapter to claim the thinking powers that are your birthright. The critical thinker is one aspect of the master student who lives inside you. ✱

STUDENT VOICES

The first time I tried to apply creative thinking to my schoolwork was for a term paper. It was very hard because it was something that I was not used to. But the more that I worked at it—brainstorming, focusing, questioning my conclusions—the easier it became. Now I automatically go through this process, whether I'm writing a report or choosing the best brand of peanut butter.

—SCOOTER WILLIAMS

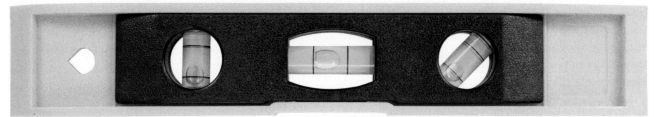

© Filimonov/Shutterstock

Becoming a Critical Thinker

Critical thinking is a path to intellectual adventure. Though there are dozens of possible approaches, the process can be boiled down to concrete steps.

STRIPPED TO ITS ESSENCE, critical thinking means asking and answering questions. The four basic questions in the Learning Styles Applications in this book—*Why? What? How?* and *What if?*—are a powerful tool for thinking. As they take you through the cycle of learning, they can also guide you in becoming a critical thinker. This article offers a variety of tools for answering those questions. For more handy implements, see *Becoming a Critical Thinker* by Vincent Ryan Ruggiero.

1 Why am I considering this issue? Critical thinking and personal passion go together. Begin critical thinking with a question that matters to you. Seek a rationale for your learning. Understand why it is important for you to think about a specific topic. You might want to arrive at a new conclusion, make a prediction, or solve a problem. By finding a personal connection with an issue, your interest in acquiring and retaining new information increases.

2 What are various points of view on this issue? Imagine Karl Marx, Cesar Chavez, and Conrad Black assembled in one room to choose the most desirable economic system. Picture Mahatma Gandhi, Lester B. Pearson, and General Romeo Dallaire lecturing at a United Nations conference on conflict resolution. Visualize Fidel Castro, Barack Obama, and Jack Layton in a discussion about distributing the world's resources equitably. When seeking out alternative points of view, let such events unfold in your mind.

One path to critical thinking is tolerance for a wide range of opinions.

Dozens of viewpoints exist on every important issue—reducing crime, ending world hunger, preventing war, educating our children, and countless other concerns. In fact, few problems allow for any single, permanent solution. Each generation produces its own answers to critical questions, based on current conditions. Our search for answers is a conversation that spans centuries. On each question, many voices are waiting to be heard.

You can take advantage of this diversity by seeking out alternative views with an open mind. When talking to another person, be willing to walk away with a new point of view—even if it's the one you brought to the table, supported with new evidence. After thinking thoroughly, you can adopt new perspectives or hold your current viewpoints in a different way.

Examining different points of view is an exercise in analysis, which you can do with the suggestions that follow.

Define terms. Imagine two people arguing about whether an employer should limit extended health care benefits to members of a family. To one person, the word *family* means a mother, father, and children; to the other person, the word *family* applies to any long-term, supportive relationship between people who live together. Chances are, the debate will go nowhere until these people realize that they're defining the same word in different ways.

Conflicts of opinion can often be resolved—or at least clarified—when we define our key terms up front. This is especially true with abstract, emotion-laden terms such as *freedom, peace, progress,* or *justice*. Blood has been shed over the meaning of these words. Define them with care.

Look for assertions. A speaker's or writer's key terms occur in a larger context called an assertion. An ***assertion*** is a complete sentence that directly answers a key question. For example, consider this sentence from the article "The Master Student" in Chapter 1: "Mastery means attaining a level of skill that goes beyond technique." This sentence is an assertion that answers an important question: How do we recognize mastery?

THINKING

7

Look for at least three viewpoints. When asking questions, let go of the temptation to settle for just a single answer. Once you have come up with an answer, say to yourself, "Yes, that is one answer. Now what's another?" Using this approach can sustain honest inquiry, fuel creativity, and lead to conceptual breakthroughs. Be prepared: The world is complicated, and critical thinking is a complex business. Some of your answers might contradict others. Resist the temptation to have all of your ideas in a neat, orderly bundle.

Practise tolerance. One path to critical thinking is tolerance for a wide range of opinions. Taking a position on important issues is natural. When we stop having an opinion on things, we've probably stopped breathing.

The problem occurs when we become so attached to our current viewpoints that we refuse to consider alternatives. Many ideas that are widely accepted in Western cultures—for example, civil liberties for people of colour, same-sex partners, and the right of women to vote—were once considered dangerous. Viewpoints that seem outlandish today might become widely accepted a century, a decade, or even a year from now. Remembering this can help us practise tolerance for differing beliefs and, in doing so, make room for new ideas that might alter our lives.

Effective understanding calls for listening without judgment.

3 How well is each point of view supported? Uncritical thinkers shield themselves from new information and ideas. As an alternative, you can follow the example of scientists, who constantly search for evidence that contradicts their theories. The following suggestions can help.

Look for logic and evidence. The aim of using logic is to make statements that are clear, consistent, and coherent. As you examine a speaker's or writer's assertions, you might find errors in logic—assertions that contradict each other or assumptions that are unfounded.

Also assess the evidence used to support points of view. Evidence comes in several forms, including facts, expert testimony, and examples. To think critically about evidence, ask questions such as:

- Are all or most of the relevant facts presented?
- Are the facts consistent with each other?
- Are facts presented accurately—or in a misleading way?
- Are enough examples included to make a solid case for the viewpoint?

- Do the examples truly support the viewpoint?
- Are the examples typical? That is, could the author or speaker support the assertion with other examples that are similar?
- Is the expert credible—truly knowledgeable about the topic?

Consider the source. Look again at that article on the problems of manufacturing cars powered by natural gas. It might have been written by an executive from an oil company. Check out the expert who disputes the connection between smoking and lung cancer. That "expert" might be the president of a tobacco company.

This is not to say that we should dismiss the ideas of people who have a vested interest in stating their opinions. Rather, we can take their self-interest into account as we consider their ideas.

© photos.com

Four more questions for critical thinking

The four main questions presented in "Becoming a Critical Thinker" offer one approach to this skill. In their classic *How to Read a Book,* Mortimer Adler and Charles Van Doren offer another approach. They list four different questions to sum up the whole task of thinking critically about a body of ideas (Adler, Mortimer, & Van Doren, 1972):

What is the writing or speech about as a whole? To answer this question, state the main topic in one sentence. Then list the related subtopics.

What is being said in detail, and how? List the main terms, assertions, and arguments. Also state what problems the writer or speaker is trying to solve.

Is it true? Examine the logic and evidence behind the ideas. Look for missing information, faulty information, and errors in reasoning. Also determine which problems were solved and which remain unsolved.

What of it? After answering the first three questions, prepare to change your thinking or behaviour as a result of encountering new ideas.

Understand before criticizing. Polished debaters can sum up their opponents' viewpoints—often better than the people who support those viewpoints themselves. Likewise, critical thinkers take the time to understand a statement of opinion before agreeing or disagreeing with it.

Effective understanding calls for listening without judgment. Enter another person's world by expressing her viewpoint in your own words. If you're conversing with that person, keep revising your summary until she agrees that you've stated her position accurately. If you're reading an article, write a short summary of it. Then scan the article again, checking to see if your synopsis is on target.

Watch for hot spots. Many people have mental "hot spots"—topics that provoke strong opinions and feelings. Examples are abortion, homosexuality, animal rights, and the environment.

To become more skilled at examining various points of view, notice your own particular hot spots. Make a clear intention to accept your feelings about these topics and to continue using critical thinking techniques.

One way to cool down our hot spots is to remember that we can change or even give up our current opinions without giving up ourselves. That's a key message behind the articles "Ideas Are Tools" and "Detach." These Power Processes remind us that human beings are much more than the sum of their current opinions.

Be willing to be uncertain. Some of the most profound thinkers have practised the art of thinking by using a magic sentence: "I'm not sure yet."

Those are words that many people do not like to hear. Our society rewards quick answers and quotable sound bites. We're under considerable pressure to utter the truth in 10 seconds or less.

In such a society, it is courageous and unusual to take the time to pause, to look, to examine, to be thoughtful, to consider many points of view—and to be unsure. When a society adopts half-truths in a blind rush for certainty, a willingness to embrace uncertainty can move us forward.

4 What if I could combine various points of view or create a new one? Finding the truth is like painting a barn door by tossing an open can of paint at it. Few people who throw at the door miss it entirely. Yet no one can cover the whole door in a single toss.

© M. Dykstra/Shutterstock

People who express a viewpoint are seeking the truth. And no reasonable person claims to cover the whole barn door—to understand the whole truth about anything. Instead, each viewpoint can be seen as one approach among many possible alternatives. If you don't think that any one opinion is complete, combine different perspectives on the issue.

Create a critical thinking "spreadsheet." When you consult authorities with different stands on an issue, you might feel confused about how to sort out, evaluate, and combine their points of view. To overcome confusion, create a critical thinking "spreadsheet." List the authorities across the top of a page and key questions down the left side. Then indicate each authority's answer to each question, along with your own answers.

For example, the following spreadsheet clarifies different points of view on the issue of whether to outlaw Ultimate Fighting.

You could state your own viewpoint by combining your answers to the questions in the spreadsheet: "I favour legalized Ultimate Fighting. While Ultimate Fighting poses dangers, so do other sports. And as with other sports, the risk of injury can be reduced when fighters get proper training."

Write about it. Thoughts can move at blinding speed. Writing slows down that process. Gaps in logic that slip by us in thought or speech are often exposed when we commit the same ideas to paper. Writing down our thoughts allows us to compare, contrast, and combine points of view more clearly—and therefore to think more thoroughly.

© R.V. Bulck/iStockphoto

THINKING

	Medical doctor	Former Ultimate Fighter	Sports journalist	Me
Is Ultimate Fighting a sport?	No	Yes	Yes	Yes
Is Ultimate Fighting dangerous?	Yes	Yes	Yes	Yes
Is Ultimate Fighting more dangerous than other sports?	Yes	No	Yes	No
Can the risk of injury be overcome by proper training?	No	No	No	Yes

Accept your changing perspectives. Researcher William Perry (1970 found that students in higher education move through stages of intellectual development. Students in earlier stages tend to think there is only one correct viewpoint on each issue, and they look to their instructors to reveal that truth. Later, students acknowledge a variety of opinions on issues and construct their own viewpoints.

Monitor changes in your thinking processes as you combine viewpoints. Distinguish between opinions that you accept from authorities and opinions that are based on your own use of logic and your search for evidence.

Also look for opinions that result from objective procedures (such as using the *Why? What? How?* and *What if?* questions in this article) and personal sources (using intuition or "gut feelings").

Remember that the process of becoming a critical thinker will take you through a variety of stages. Give yourself time, and celebrate your growing mastery. ✱

 Find more strategies for becoming a critical thinker online @ **www.bams5ce.nelson.com**

Attitudes of a critical thinker

The American Philosophical Association invited a panel of 46 scholars from Canada and the United States to come up with answers to the following two questions (Facione, 2011): "What is college/university-level critical thinking?" and "What leads us to conclude that a person is an effective critical thinker?" After two years of work, this panel concluded that critical thinkers share the attitudes summarized in the following chart.

Attitude	Sample statement
Truth-seeking	"Let's follow this idea and see where it leads, even if we feel uncomfortable with what we find out."
Open-minded	"I have a point of view on this subject, and I'm anxious to hear yours as well."
Analytical	"Taking a stand on the issue commits me to take some new action."
Systematic	"The speaker made several interesting points, and I'd like to hear some more evidence to support each one."
Self-confident	"After reading the book for the first time, I was confused. I'll be able to understand it after studying the book some more."
Inquisitive	"When I first saw that painting, I wanted to know what was going on in the artist's life when she painted it."
Mature	"I'll wait until I gather some more facts before reaching a conclusion on this issue."

THINKING

7

Finding "aha!"
Creativity fuels critical thinking

THIS CHAPTER OFFERS you a chance to practise two types of critical thinking: convergent thinking and divergent thinking. One focuses on finding a single solution to a problem, while the other asks you to consider as many viewpoints as possible.

Convergent thinking involves a narrowing-down process. Out of all the possible viewpoints on an issue or alternative solutions to a problem, you choose the one that is the most reasonable or that provides the most logical basis for action.

Some people see convergent thinking and critical thinking as the same thing. However, there's more to critical thinking. Before you choose among viewpoints, generate as many of them as possible. Open up alternatives and consider all of your options. Define problems in different ways. Keep asking questions and looking for answers. This opening-up process is called **divergent** or *creative thinking*. Creative thinking provides the basis for convergent thinking. In other words, one path toward having good ideas is to have *lots* of ideas. Then you can pick and choose from among them, combining and refining them as you see fit.

Choose when to think creatively. The key is to make conscious choices about what kind of thinking to do in any given moment. Generally speaking, creative thinking is more appropriate in the early stages of planning and problem solving. Feel free to dwell in this domain for a while. If you narrow down your options too soon, you run the risk of missing an exciting solution or of neglecting a novel viewpoint. Convergent thinking is essential, and you should save it until you have plenty of options on the table.

Remember that creative thinking and convergent thinking take place in a continuous cycle. After you've used convergent thinking to narrow down your options, you can return to creative thinking at any time to generate new ones.

Cultivate "aha!" Central to creative thinking is something called the "aha!" experience. Writer Robert Fulford has said, "Research is hard, writing is harder, but thinking is hardest of all." Aha! is the burst of creative energy heralded by the arrival of new, original thinking. It is the sudden emergence of an unfamiliar pattern, a previously undetected relationship, or an unusual combination of familiar elements. It is an exhilarating experience.

Aha! does not always result in a timeless poem or a Nobel Prize. It can be inspired by anything from playing a new riff on a guitar to figuring out why your car's fuel pump doesn't work. A nurse might notice a patient's symptom that everyone else missed. That's an aha! An accountant might discover a tax break for a client. That's an aha! A teacher might devise a way to reach a difficult student. Aha!

Follow through. The flip side of aha! is following through. Thinking is both fun and work. It is effortless and uncomfortable. It's the result of luck and persistence. It involves spontaneity and step-by-step procedures, planning and action, convergent and creative thinking.

Employers in all fields are desperately seeking those rare people who can find aha! and do something with it. The necessary skills include the ability to spot assumptions, weigh evidence, separate fact from opinion, organize thoughts, and avoid errors in logic. All of this can be demanding work. Just as often, it can be energizing and fun. ✳

Tangram

© Robwing/
Dreamstime.com

A tangram is an ancient Chinese puzzle game that stimulates the "play instinct" so critical to creative thinking. The cat figure at the left was created by rearranging seven sections of a square. Hundreds of images can be devised in this manner. Playing with tangrams allows us to see relationships we didn't notice before.

The rules of the game are simple: Use these seven pieces to create something that wasn't there before. Be sure to use all seven. You might start by mixing up the pieces and seeing whether you can put them back together to form a square.

Make your own tangram by cutting pieces like those at the left out of poster board. When you come up with a pattern you like, trace around the outside edges of it and see if a friend can discover how you did it.

Ways to create ideas

ANYONE CAN THINK creatively. Use the following techniques to generate ideas about everything, whether you're studying math problems, remodelling a house, or writing a bestseller. With practice, you can set the stage for creative leaps, jump with style, and land on your feet with brand-new ideas in hand.

Conduct a brainstorm

Brainstorming is a technique for finding solutions, creating plans, and discovering new ideas. When you are stuck on a problem, brainstorming can break through the stumbling block.

For example, if you run out of money two days before payday every week, you can brainstorm ways to make your money last longer. You can brainstorm ways to pay for your education. You can brainstorm ways to find a job.

The purpose of brainstorming is to generate as many solutions as possible. Sometimes the craziest, most outlandish ideas, while unworkable in themselves, can lead to new ways to solve problems. Use the following steps to try out the brainstorming process:

(woman) Floresco Productions/OJO Images/Getty Images; (words) Shutterstock; collage by Walter Kopec

- *Focus on a single issue or problem.* State your focus as a question. Open-ended questions that start with the words *what, how, who, where,* and *when* often make effective focusing questions.
- *Relax.* Creativity is enhanced by a state of relaxed alertness. If you are tense or anxious, use relaxation techniques such as those described in "Let Go of Test Anxiety" in Chapter 6.
- Set a time limit for your brainstorming session. Use a clock to time it to the minute. Stopwatches work well, or you may have a timer on your cell phone. Experiment with various lengths of time. Both short and long brainstorms can produce powerful results.
- *Allow all answers.* Brainstorming is based on attitudes of permissiveness and patience. Accept every idea. If it pops into your head, put it down on paper.

Quantity, not quality, is the goal. Avoid making judgments and evaluations during the brainstorming session. If you get stuck, think of an outlandish idea, and write it down. One crazy idea can unleash a flood of other, more workable solutions.

- *Brainstorm with others.* Group brainstorming is a powerful technique. Group brainstorms take on lives of their own. Assign one member of the group to write down solutions. Feed off the ideas of others, and remember to avoid evaluating or judging anyone's ideas during the brainstorm.
- After your brainstorming session, evaluate the results. Toss out any truly crazy ideas, but not before you give them a chance.

Focus and let go

Focusing and letting go are alternating parts of the same process. Intense focus taps the resources of your conscious mind. Letting go gives your subconscious mind time to work. When you focus for intense periods and then let go for a while, the conscious and subconscious parts of your brain work in harmony. In doing so, they can produce the highest-quality results.

Focusing attention means being in the here and now. To focus your attention on a project, notice when you pay attention and when your mind starts to wander. And involve all of your senses. For example, if you are having difficulty writing a paper at a computer, practise focusing by listening to the sounds as you type. Notice the feel of the keys as you strike them. When you know the sights, sounds, and sensations you associate with being truly in focus, you'll be able to repeat the experience and return to your paper more easily.

Be willing to recognize conflict, tension, and discomfort. Notice them and fully accept them, rather than fighting against them. Look for the specific thoughts and body sensations that make up the discomfort.

Allow them to come fully into your awareness, and then let them pass.

You might not be focused all of the time. Periods of inspiration might last only seconds. Be gentle with yourself when you notice that your concentration has lapsed. In fact, that might be a time to let go. "Letting go" means not forcing yourself to be creative. Practise focusing for short periods at first, then give yourself a break. Phone a friend. Get up and take a walk around the room or around your block. Take a few minutes to look out your window. Listen to some music or, better yet, sing a few songs to yourself.

You also can break up periods of focused concentration with stretches, sit-ups, or push-ups. Use relaxation and breathing exercises. Muscle tension and the lack of oxygen can inhibit self-expression. Take a nap when you are tired. Thomas Edison took frequent naps. Then the light bulb clicked on.

Cultivate creative serendipity

The word *serendipity* was coined by the English author Horace Walpole from the title of an ancient Persian fairy tale, "The Three Princes of Serendip." The princes had a knack for making lucky discoveries. Serendipity is that knack, and it involves more than luck. It is the ability to see something valuable that you weren't looking for. History is full of serendipitous people. Country doctor Edward Jenner noticed "by accident" that milkmaids seldom got smallpox. The result was his discovery that mild cases of cowpox immunized them. Penicillin was also discovered "by accident." Scottish scientist Alexander Fleming was growing bacteria in a laboratory petri dish. A spore of *Penicillium notatum,* a kind of mould, blew in the window and landed in the dish, killing the bacteria. Fleming isolated the active ingredient. A few years later, during World War II, it saved thousands of lives. Had Fleming not been alert to the possibility, the discovery might never have been made.

You can train yourself in the art of serendipity. First, keep your eyes open. You might find a solution to an accounting problem in a Saturday morning cartoon. You might discover a topic for your essay at the corner convenience store. Multiply your contacts with the world. Resolve to meet new people. Join a study or discussion group. Read. Go to plays, concerts, art shows, lectures, and movies. Watch television programs you normally wouldn't watch. Use idea files and play with data, as described below.

Finally, expect discoveries. One secret for success is being prepared to recognize "luck" when you see it.

Keep idea files

We all have ideas. People who are viewed as creative are those who treat their ideas with care. That means not only recognizing ideas, but also recording them and following up on them. One way to keep track of ideas is to write them down on a pad of paper or if you have a smartphone, use the note-taking application to record them.

Keep a journal. Journals don't have to be exclusively about your own thoughts and feelings. You can record observations about the world around you, conversations with friends, important or offbeat ideas—anything.

To fuel your creativity, read voraciously, including newspapers and magazines. Keep a clip file of interesting articles. Explore beyond mainstream journalism. There are hundreds of low-circulation specialty magazines and online news journals that cover almost any subject you can imagine.

Keep letter-sized file folders of important correspondence, magazine and news articles, and other material. You can also create idea files on a computer using word processing, outlining, or database software.

Safeguard your ideas, even if you're pressed for time. Jotting down four or five words is enough to capture the essence of an idea. You can write down one quotation in a minute or two. And if you carry a small notepad in a

Creative ways for groups to get "unstuck"

Sometimes creative thinking dies in committee. People are afraid to disagree with a forceful leader and instead keep their mouths shut. Or a long-standing group ignores new members with new ideas. The result can be "group think," where no one questions the prevailing opinion. To stimulate creative thinking in groups, try these strategies:

Put your opinion on hold.   If you're leading a meeting, ask other people to speak up first. Then look for the potential value in *any* idea. Avoid nonverbal language that signals a negative reaction, such as frowning or rolling your eyes.

Rotate group leadership.   Ask group members to take turns. This strategy can work well in groups where people have a wide range of opinions.

Divide larger groups into several teams. People might be more willing to share their ideas in a smaller group.

Assign a devil's advocate.   Give one person free permission to poke holes in any proposal.

Invite a guest expert.   A fresh perspective from someone outside the group can spark an aha!

Set up a suggestion box.   Let people submit ideas anonymously, in writing.

pocket or purse, you can record ideas while standing in line or sitting in a waiting room.

Review your files regularly. Some amusing thought that came to you in November might be the perfect solution to a problem in March.

Collect and play with data

Look from all sides at the data you collect. Switch your attention from one aspect to another. Examine each fact, and avoid getting stuck on one particular part of a problem.

Turn a problem upside down by picking a solution first and then working backward. Ask other people to look at the data. Solicit opinions.

Living with the problem invites a solution. Write down data, possible solutions, or a formulation of the problem on a notepad or your phone. Look at your ideas before you go to bed at night. Review them when you are waiting for the bus. Make them part of your life and think about them frequently.

Look for the obvious solutions or the obvious "truths" about the problem—then toss them out. Ask yourself: "Well, I know X is true, but if X were *not* true, what would happen?" Or ask the reverse: "If that *were* true, what would follow next?"

Put unrelated facts next to each other and invent a relationship between them, even if it seems absurd at first. In *The Act of Creation,* novelist Arthur Koestler (1964) says that finding a context in which to combine opposites is the essence of creativity. Make imaginary pictures with the data. Condense it. Categorize it. Put it in chronological order. Put it in alphabetical order. Put it in random order. Order it from most to least complex. Reverse all of those orders. Look for opposites.

It has been said that there are no new ideas—only new ways to combine old ideas. Creativity is the ability to discover those new combinations.

Create while you sleep

A part of our mind works as we sleep. You've experienced this directly if you've ever fallen asleep with a problem on your mind and awakened the next morning with a solution. For some of us, the solution appears in a dream or just before falling asleep or waking up.

You can experiment with this process. Ask yourself a question as you fall asleep. Keep pencil and paper or a recorder near your bed. The moment you wake up, begin writing or speaking and see if an answer to your question emerges.

Many of us have awakened from a dream with a great idea, only to fall asleep and lose it forever. To capture your ideas, keep a notebook by your bed at all times. Put the notebook where you can find it easily.

There is a story about how Benjamin Franklin used this suggestion. Late in the evenings, as he was becoming drowsy, he would sit in his rocking chair with a rock in his right hand and a metal bucket on the floor beneath the rock. The moment he fell asleep, the rock would fall from his grip into the bottom of the bucket, making a loud noise that awakened him. Having placed a pen and paper nearby, he immediately wrote down what he was thinking. Experience taught him that his thoughts at this moment were often insightful and creative.

Refine ideas and follow through

Many of us ignore this part of the creative process. How many great money-making schemes have we had that we never pursued? How many good ideas have we had for short stories that we never wrote? How many times have we said to ourselves, "You know, what they ought to do is attach two handles to one of those things, paint it orange, and sell it to police departments. They'd make a fortune." And we never realize that we are "they."

Genius resides in the follow-through—the application of perspiration to inspiration. One powerful tool you can use to follow through is the Discovery and Intention Journal Entry system. First write down your idea in a Discovery Statement, and then write what you intend to do about it in an Intention Statement. You also can explore the writing techniques discussed in Chapter 8: Communicating as a guide for refining your ideas.

Another way to refine an idea is to simplify it. And if that doesn't work, mess it up. Make it more complex.

Finally, keep a separate file in your ideas folder for your own inspirations. Return to it regularly to see if there is anything you can use. Today's defunct essay idea could be next year's A in speech class.

Create success strategies

Use creative thinking techniques to go beyond the pages of this book and create your own ways to succeed in school. Read other books on success. Interview successful people. Reflect on any of your current behaviours that help you do well in school. Change any habits that fail to serve you.

If you have created a study group with people from one of your classes, set aside time to talk about ways to succeed in any class. Challenge each other to practise your powers of invention. Test any new strategies you create and report to the group on how well they're working for you.

Trust the process

Learn to trust the creative process—even when no answers are in sight. We are often reluctant to look at problems if no immediate solution is at hand. We grow impatient and tend to avoid frustration by giving up altogether. Most of us do this to some degree with personal problems as well. If we are having difficulty with a relationship and don't see a quick resolution, we deny that the problem exists rather than facing up to it.

Trust that a solution will show up. Frustration and a feeling of being stuck are often signals that a solution is imminent.

Sometimes solutions break through in a giant AHA! More often they come in a series of little aha!s. Be aware of what your aha!s look, feel, and sound like. That sets the stage for even more flights of creative thinking. ✳

Create on your feet

A popular trend in executive offices is the "stand-up" desk—a raised working surface at which you stand rather than sit.

Standing has advantages over sitting for long periods. You can stay more alert and creative when you're on your feet. One theory is that our problem-solving ability improves when we stand, due to increased heart rate and blood flow to the brain.

Standing is great for easing lower-back pain, too. Sitting aggravates the spine and its supporting muscles.

This is a technique with tradition. If you search the Web for stand-up desks, you'll find models based on desks used by Thomas Jefferson, Winston Churchill, and writer Virginia Woolf. Consider setting your desk up on blocks or putting a box on top of your desk so that you can stand while writing, preparing speeches, or studying. Discover whether this approach works for you.

Photo courtesy of David Ellis

20 exercise Explore emotional reactions

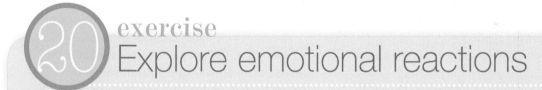

Each of us has certain "hot spots"—issues that trigger strong emotional reactions. These topics may include the long gun registry, capital punishment, the environment, and funding for welfare programs. There are many other examples, varying from person to person. Examine your own hot spots on a separate sheet of paper by writing a word or short phrase summarizing each issue about which you feel very strongly. Then describe what you typically say or do when each issue comes up in conversation.

After you have completed your list, think about what you can do to become a more effective thinker when you encounter one of these issues. For example, you could breathe deeply and count to five before you offer your own point of view. Or you might preface your opinion with an objective statement such as "There are many valid points of view on this issue. Here's the way I see it, and I'm open to your idea."

Don't fool yourself: 15 common mistakes in logic

LOGIC IS A branch of philosophy that seeks to distinguish between effective and ineffective reasoning. Students of logic look for valid steps in an *argument,* or a series of assertions. The opening assertions of the argument are the *premises,* and the final assertion is the *conclusion.*

Effective reasoning is not just an idle pastime for unemployed philosophers. Learning to think logically offers many benefits: When you think logically, you take your reading, writing, speaking, and listening skills to a higher level. You avoid costly mistakes in decision making. You can join discussions and debates with more confidence, cast your election votes with a clear head, and become a better-informed citizen. People have even improved their mental health by learning to dispute illogical beliefs (Seligman, 2002).

Over the last 2,500 years, specialists in logic have listed some classic land mines in the field of logic—common mistakes that are called *fallacies*. These fallacies are included in just about every logic textbook. Following are fifteen examples. Knowing about them before you string together a bunch of assertions can help you avoid getting fooled.

1 Jumping to conclusions. Jumping to conclusions is the only exercise that some lazy thinkers get. This fallacy involves drawing conclusions without sufficient evidence. Take the bank officer who hears about an immigrant failing to pay back a loan. After that, the officer turns down all loan applications from immigrants. This person has formed a rigid opinion on the basis of hearsay. Jumping to conclusions—also called *hasty generalization*—is at work here. Following are more examples of this fallacy:

- When I went to Mexico for spring break, I felt sick the whole time. Mexican food makes people sick.

- Google's mission is to "organize the world's information." Their employees must be on a real power trip.

© photos.com

- During a recession, more people go to the movies. People just want to sit in the dark and forget about their money problems.

2 Attacking the person. This mistake in logic is common at election time. An example is the candidate who claims that her opponent has never wanted to really live in Canada during the campaign. People who indulge in personal attacks are attempting an intellectual sleight of hand to divert our attention from the truly relevant issues.

3 Appealing to authority. A professional athlete endorses a brand of breakfast cereal. A famous musician features a beer company's product in a rock video. The promotional brochure for an advertising agency lists all of the large companies that have used its services.

In each case, the people involved are trying to win your confidence—and your dollars—by citing authorities. The underlying assumption is usually this: *Famous people and organizations buy our product. Therefore, you should buy it too.* Or: *You should accept this idea merely because someone who's well known says it's true.*

Appealing to authority is usually a substitute for producing real evidence. It invites sloppy thinking. When our only evidence for a viewpoint is an appeal to authority, it's time to think more thoroughly.

4 Pointing to a false cause. The fact that one event follows another does not necessarily mean that the two events have a cause-and-effect relationship. All we can actually say is that the events might be correlated. For example, as children's vocabularies improve, they can get more cavities. This does not mean that cavities are the result of an improved vocabulary. Instead, the increase in cavities is due to other factors, such as physical maturation and changes in diet or personal care.

THINKING

5 Thinking in all-or-nothing terms. Consider these statements: Doctors are greedy. . . . You can't trust politicians. . . . Students these days are in school just to get high-paying jobs; they lack idealism. . . . Homeless people don't want to work.

These opinions imply the word *all*. They gloss over individual differences, claiming that all members of a group are exactly alike. They also ignore key facts, for instance, that some doctors volunteer their time at free medical clinics and that many homeless people are children who are too young to work. All-or-nothing thinking is one of the most common errors in logic.

6 Basing arguments on emotion. The politician who ends every campaign speech with flag waving and slides of her hugging babies is staking her future on appeals to emotion. So is the candidate who paints a grim scenario of the disaster and ruination that will transpire unless she is elected. Get past the fluff and histrionics to see if you can uncover any worthwhile ideas.

7 Using a faulty analogy. An **analogy** states a similarity between two things or events. Some arguments rest on analogies that hide significant differences. For instance, people who say if we ban alcohol advertising then pretty soon we will ban the advertising of eggs because they contain cholesterol which is a harmful substance. Is it really fair to compare alcohol to cholesterol in terms of being harmful substances?

8 Creating a straw man. The name of this fallacy comes from the scarecrows traditionally placed in gardens to ward off birds. A scarecrow works because it looks like a man. Likewise, a person can attack ideas that *sound like* his opponent's ideas but are actually absurd. For example, some members of Parliament attacked the law legalizing same-sex marriage by saying polygamy would be allowed if same-sex partners were allowed to legally marry. In fact, supporters of this bill proposed no such thing.

9 Begging the question. Speakers and writers beg the question when their colourful language glosses over an idea that is unclear or unproven. Consider this statement: *The criminal has committed the worst crime possible.* Anyone who makes such a statement "begs" (fails to answer) a key question: What is the worst crime possible?

10 Confusing fact and opinion. Facts are statements verified by direct observation or compelling evidence that creates widespread agreement. In recent years, some politicians argued for tax cuts to corporations on the grounds that the Canadian economy needed to create more jobs. However, it's not a fact that tax cuts automatically create more jobs.

This statement is almost impossible to verify by direct observation, and there's actually evidence against it.

11 Creating a red herring. When hunters want to throw a dog off a trail, they can drag a smoked red herring (or some other food with a strong odour) over the ground in the opposite direction. This distracts the dog, who is fooled into following a false trail. Likewise, people can send our thinking on false trails by raising irrelevant issues. Case in point: In 2008, some people who opposed the presidential campaign by U.S. senator Barack Obama emphasized his middle name: Hussein. This was an irrelevant attempt to link the senator to Saddam Hussein, the dictator and former ruler of Iraq.

12 Appealing to tradition. Arguments based on an appeal to tradition take a classic form: *Our current beliefs and behaviours have a long history; therefore, they are correct.* This argument has been used to justify the divine right of kings, feudalism, witch burnings, slavery, child labour, and a host of other traditions that are now rejected in most parts of the world. Appeals to tradition ignore the fact that unsound ideas can survive for centuries before human beings realize that they are being fooled.

13 Appealing to "the people." Consider this statement: Millions of people use Wikipedia as their main source of factual information. Wikipedia must be the best reference work in the world. This is a perfect example of the *ad populum* fallacy. (In Latin, that phrase means "to the people.") The essential error is assuming that popularity, quality, and accuracy are the same.

Appealing to "the people" taps into our universal desire to be liked and to associate with a group of people who agree with us. No wonder this fallacy is also called "jumping on the bandwagon." Following are more examples:

■ *Internet Explorer is the most widely used Web browser. It must be the best one.*

■ *Dan Brown's books, including* The Da Vinci Code, *did not sell as well as the* Harry Potter *books by J. K. Rowling. I guess we know who's the better writer.*

You can refute such statements by offering a single example: Many Canadians once believed that women were inferior and therefore should not be allowed to vote. That did not make either belief right.

14 Distracting from the real issue. The fallacy of distracting from the real issue occurs when a speaker or writer makes an irrelevant statement and then draws a conclusion based on that statement. For example: *The most recent recession was*

CHAPTER SEVEN THINKING **237**

caused by people who borrowed too much money and bankers who loaned too much money. Therefore, you should never borrow money to go to school. This argument ignores the fact that a primary source of the recession was loans to finance housing—not loans to finance education. Two separate topics are mentioned, and statements about one do not necessarily apply to the other.

15 **Sliding a slippery slope.** The fallacy of sliding a slippery slope implies that if one undesired event occurs, then other, far more serious events will follow: *If we restrict our right to free speech, then all of our rights will soon be taken away. If people keep downloading music for free, pretty soon they'll demand to get everything online for free. I notice that more independent bookstores are closing; it's just a matter of time before people stop reading.* When people slide a slippery slope, they assume that different types of events have a single cause. They also assume that a particular cause will operate indefinitely. In reality, the world is far more complex. Grand predictions about the future often prove to be wrong.

Finding fallacies before they become a fatal flaw (bonus suggestions). Human beings have a long history of fooling themselves. This article presents just a partial list of logical fallacies. You can prevent them and many more by following a few suggestions:

- When outlining a paper or speech, create a two-column chart. In one column, make a list of your main points. In the other column, summarize the evidence for each point. If you have no evidence for a point, a logical fallacy may be lurking in the wings.

- Go back to some of your recent writing—assigned papers, essay tests, journal entries, and anything else you can find. Look for examples of logical fallacies. Note any patterns, such as repetition of one particular fallacy. Write an Intention Statement about avoiding this fallacy.

- Be careful when making claims about people who disagree with you. One attitude of a critical thinker is treating everyone with fairness and respect. *

Practise hunting for fallacies online @
www.bams5ce.nelson.com

STUDENT VOICES

Successful choices are a result of solving a problem, looking at pros and cons, making the decision or choice, and checking how you feel about (and how others will be affected by) this conclusion. This takes concerted effort, but a master student uses this inquisitive, analytical, and open-minded process to gain self-confidence and maturity.

—KRISTINE RUGGLES

Uncovering assumptions

Consider the following argument:

- Orca whales mate for life.
- Orca whales travel in family groups.
- Science has revealed that Orca whales are intelligent.
- Therefore, Orca whales should be saved from extinction.

One idea underlies this line of thought: Any animal that displays significant human characteristics deserves special protection.

Whether or not you agree with this argument, consider for a moment the process of making assumptions. Assumptions are assertions that guide our thinking and behaviour.

Assumptions are invisible and powerful

Often these assertions are unconscious. People can remain unaware of their most basic and far-reaching assumptions—the very ideas that shape their lives.

Spotting assumptions can be tricky, since they are usually unstated and offered without evidence. And scores of assumptions can be held at the same time. Those assumptions might even contradict each other, resulting in muddled thinking and confused behaviour. This makes uncovering assumptions a feat worthy of the greatest detective.

Assumptions drive out attitudes and actions

Letting assumptions remain in our subconscious can erect barriers to our success. Take the person who says, "I don't worry about saving money for the future. I think life is meant to be enjoyed today—not later." This statement rests on at least two assumptions: *saving money is not enjoyable,* and *we can enjoy ourselves only when we're spending money.*

It would be no surprise to find out that this person runs out of money near the end of each month and depends on cash advances from high-interest credit cards. She is shielding herself from some ideas that could erase her debt: Saving money can be a source of satisfaction, and many enjoyable activities cost nothing.

The stakes in uncovering assumptions are high. Prejudice thrives on the beliefs that certain people are inferior or dangerous due to their skin colour, ethnic background, or sexual orientation. Those beliefs have led to flawed assumptions such as *mixing the blood of the races will lead to genetically inferior offspring* and *racial integration of the armed forces will lead to the destruction of morale.*

When we remain ignorant of our assumptions, we also make it easier for people with hidden agendas to do our thinking for us. Unethical advertisers know that unchallenged assumptions are potent tools for influencing our attitudes and behaviour.

Assumptions can create conflict

Heated conflict and hard feelings often result when people argue on the level of opinions—forgetting that the real conflict lies at the level of their assumptions.

An example is the question about whether the government should fund public works programs that create jobs during a recession. People who advocate such programs might assume that creating such jobs is an appropriate task for the federal government. On the other hand, people who argue against such programs might assume that the government has no business interfering with the economy. There's little hope of resolving this conflict of opinion unless we deal with something more basic: our assumptions about the proper role of government.

Look for assumptions

You can follow a three-step method for testing the validity of any viewpoint. First, look for the assumptions—the assertions implied by that viewpoint. Second, write down these assumptions. Third, see if you can find any exceptions to them. This technique helps detect many errors in logic. ✳

The problem of egocentric thinking

Egocentric thinking results from the unfortunate fact that humans do not naturally consider the rights and needs of others. We do not naturally appreciate the point of view of others, nor the limitations in our own point of view. We become explicitly aware of egocentric thinking only if trained to do so. We do not naturally recognize our egocentric assumptions, the egocentric way we use information, the egocentric way we interpret data, the source of our egocentric concepts and ideas, the implications of our egocentricity. We do not naturally recognize our self-serving perspective.

As humans we live with the unrealistic but confident sense that we have fundamentally figured out the way things actually are, and that we have done this objectively. We naturally believe in our intuitive perceptions, however inaccurate. Instead of using intellectual standards in thinking, we often use self-centred psychological standards to determine what to believe and what to reject. Here are the most commonly used psychological standards in human thinking.

"It's true because I believe it." Innate egocentrism: I assume that what I believe is true because I have never questioned the basis for many of my beliefs.

"It's true because we believe it." Innate sociocentrism: I assume that the dominant beliefs of the groups to which I belong are true even though I have never questioned the basis for those beliefs.

"It's true because I want to believe it." Innate wish fulfillment: I believe in whatever puts me (or the groups to which I belong) in a positive light. I believe what "feels good," what does not require me to change my thinking in any significant way, what does not require me to admit I have been wrong.

"It's true because I have always believed it." Innate self-validation: I have a strong desire to maintain beliefs I have long held, even though I have not seriously considered the extent to which those beliefs are justified by the evidence.

"It's true because it is in my selfish interest to believe it." Innate selfishness: I believe whatever justifies my getting power, money or personal advantage even though these beliefs are not grounded in sound reasoning or evidence.

Source: Paul, R. & Elder, L. (2008). *The Miniature Guide to Critical Thinking Concepts and Tools.* Dillon Beach, CA: The Foundation for Critical Thinking Press.

 For more information on critical thinking, go online @ **www.bams5ce.nelson.com**

THINKING

7

Gaining skill at decision making

WE MAKE DECISIONS all of the time, whether we realize it or not. Even avoiding decisions is a form of decision making. The student who puts off studying for a test until the last minute might really be saying, "I've decided this course is not important" or "I've decided not to give this course much time."

A planned decision-making style requires you to gather information and adopt a more systematic approach that requires you to balance logical reasoning and intuition. Decide right now to apply some of the following suggestions, and you can take your overall decision making to new heights of effectiveness.

Recognize decisions. Decisions are more than wishes or desires. There's a world of difference between "I wish I could be a better student" and "I will take more powerful notes, read with greater retention, and review my class notes daily." Decisions are specific and lead to focused action. When we decide, we narrow down. We give up actions that are inconsistent with our decision. Deciding to eat fruit for dessert instead of ice cream rules out the next trip to the ice cream store.

Establish priorities. Some decisions are trivial. No matter what the outcome, your life is not affected much. Other decisions can shape your circumstances for years. Devote more time and energy to the decisions with big outcomes.

Clarify your values. When you know specifically what you want from life, making decisions becomes easier. This is especially true when you define your values precisely and put them in writing. Saying that you value education is fine. Now give that declaration some teeth. Note that you value lifelong learning as a chance to upgrade your career skills, for instance. That can make registering for next year's classes much easier.

Base your decisions on a life plan. The benefit of having long-term goals for our lives is that they provide a basis for many of our daily decisions. Being certain about what we want to accomplish this year and this month makes today's choices more clear.

Balance learning styles when making decisions. To make decisions more effectively, use all four modes of learning explained in Chapter 1: First Steps. The key is to balance reflection with action, and thinking with experience. First, take the time to think creatively, and generate many options. Then think critically about the possible consequences of each option before choosing one. Remember, however, that thinking is no substitute for experience. Act on your chosen option and notice what happens. If you're not getting the results that you want, then quickly return to creative thinking to invent new options.

Choose an overall strategy. Every time you make a decision, you choose a strategy—even when you're not aware of it. Effective decision makers can articulate and choose from among several strategies.

- *Find all of the available options and choose one deliberately.* This strategy can be the most time consuming, calling on you to gather the most information. Save this strategy for times when you have a relatively small number of options, each of which leads to noticeably different results.

- *Find all of the available options and choose one randomly.* This strategy can be risky. Save it for times when your options are basically similar and fairness is the main issue.

- *Limit the options, then choose.* For example, when deciding which search engine to use on the Internet, visit many sites and then narrow the list down to two or three that you choose.

- *Choose the first acceptable option that you find.* This strategy can work well when you have many options, and when thoroughly researching each option will take too much time or create too little benefit. For instance, when you're writing a paper and are pressed for time, write down the first five facts you find that directly support your thesis. You could look for more facts, but the extra investment of time might not produce enough usable results.

- *Choose to act on someone else's decision.* You use this strategy, for example, when you buy music based on a friend's recommendation. A more sophisticated version of this strategy is arbitration—people who are in conflict agree to act on the decision made by a third party, such as a judge, who listens to each person's case.

Use time as an ally. Sometimes we face dilemmas—situations in which any course of action leads to undesirable consequences. In such cases, consider putting a decision on hold. Wait it out. Do nothing until the circumstances change, making one alternative clearly preferable to another. Waiting is especially useful if you find yourself in a negative mood, which can affect your ability to think clearly and creatively. Wait for the mood to pass, then assess your options.

Use intuition. Some decisions seem to make themselves. A solution pops into your mind and you gain newfound clarity. Using intuition is not the same as forgetting about the decision or refusing to make it. Intuitive decisions usually arrive after we've gathered the relevant facts and faced a problem for some time.

Act on your decision. There comes a time to move from the realm of discovery and intention to the arena of action. Action is a hallmark of a true decision.

Evaluate your decision. Hindsight can be a valuable source of insight. After you act on a decision, observe the consequences over time. Reflect on how well your decision worked and what you might have done differently. Look on each individual decision as a source of feedback that will improve your overall skill at decision making.

Think choices. This final suggestion involves some creative thinking. Consider that the word *decide* derives from the same root as *suicide* and *homicide*. In the spirit of those words, a decision forever "kills" all other options. That's kind of morbid. Instead, use the word *choice*, and see if it frees up your thinking. When you *choose*, you express a preference for one option over others. However, those options remain live possibilities for the future. Choose for today, knowing that as you gain more wisdom and experience, you can choose again. ✳

Four ways to solve problems

THERE IS A vast literature on problem solving techniques. Much of it can be traced to philosopher John Dewey, who devised these steps of effective problem solving:

- Perceive a "felt difficulty" and state it clearly and concisely.
- Invent possible solutions.
- Rationally test each solution by anticipating its possible consequences.
- Act on the preferred solution, evaluate the consequences, and determine whether a new solution is needed (Dewey, 1910). Much of what you'll read about problem solving amounts to variations on Dewey's steps. Think of problem solving as a process with four P's: Define the *problem*, generate *possibilities*, create a *plan*, and *perform* your plan.

1 Define the problem. To define a problem effectively, understand what a problem is—a mismatch between what you want and what you have. Problem solving is all about reducing the gap between these two factors.

Start with what you have. Tell the truth about what's present in your life right now, without shame or blame. For example: "I often get sleepy while reading my physics assignments, and after closing the book I cannot remember what I just read."

Next, describe in detail what you want. Go for specifics: "I want to remain alert as I read about physics. I also want to accurately summarize each chapter I read."

Remember that when we define a problem in limiting ways, our solutions merely generate new problems. As Einstein said, "The world we have made is a result of the level of thinking we have done thus far.

We cannot solve problems at the same level at which we created them" (Carlzon, 1989). This idea has many applications for success in college or university. An example is the student who struggles with note-taking. The problem, she thinks, is that her notes are too sketchy. The logical solution, she decides, is to take *more* notes, and her new goal is to write down almost everything her instructors say. No matter how fast and furiously she writes, she cannot capture all of the instructors' comments.

Consider what happens when this student defines the problem in a new way. After more thought, she decides that her dilemma is not the *quantity* of her notes but their quality. She adopts a new format for taking notes, dividing her note paper into two columns. In the right-hand column she writes down only the main points of each lecture. And in the left-hand column she notes two or three supporting details for each point.

Over time, this student makes the joyous discovery that there are usually just three or four core ideas to remember from each lecture. She originally thought the solution was to take more notes. What really worked was taking notes in a new way.

2 Generate possibilities. Now put on your creative thinking hat. Open up. Brainstorm as many possible solutions to the problem as you can. As you generate possibilities, gather relevant facts. For example, when you're faced with a dilemma about what courses to take next term, get information on class times, locations, and instructors. If you haven't decided which summer job offer to accept, gather information on salary, benefits, and working conditions.

3 **Create a plan.** After rereading your problem definition and list of possible solutions, choose the solution that seems most workable. Think about specific actions that will reduce the gap between what you have and what you want. Visualize the steps you will take to make this solution a reality and arrange them in chronological order. To make your plan even more powerful, put it in writing.

4 **Perform your plan.** This step gets you off your chair and out into the world. Now you actually *do* what you have planned. Ultimately, your skill in solving problems lies in how well you perform your plan. Through the quality of your actions, you become the architect of your own success.

Note that the four P's of this problem solving process closely parallel the four key questions listed in the article "Becoming a Critical Thinker":

Define the **problem**	**What** is the problem?
Generate **possibilities**	**What if** there are several possible solutions?
Create a **plan**	**How** would this possible solution work?
Perform your plan	**Why** is one solution more workable than another?

When facing problems, experiment with these four P's, and remember that the order of steps is not absolute. Also remember that any solution has the potential to create new problems. If that happens, cycle through the four P's of problem solving again. ✳

 For more strategies for problem solving go online @ **www.bams5ce.nelson.com**

"But I don't know what I want to do." Choosing your major

© Brian A Jackson/Shutterstock, © Yuri Arcurs/Shutterstock
© Illustrart/Shutterstock

ONE DECISION that troubles many students in post-secondary education is the choice of a program of study or an academic major. Here is an opportunity to apply your skills at critical thinking, decision making, and problem solving. The following four suggestions can guide you through this process.

1 Discover options

Follow the fun. Perhaps you look forward to attending one of your classes and even like completing the assignments. This is a clue to your choice of major.

See if you can find lasting patterns in the subjects and extracurricular activities that you've enjoyed over the years. Look for a major that allows you to continue and expand on these experiences.

Also sit down with a notepad and brainstorm answers to the following questions:

- What do you enjoy doing most with your unscheduled time?
- Imagine that you're at a party and having a fascinating conversation. What is this conversation about?

- What websites do you frequently visit or have bookmarked in a Web browser?
- What kind of problems do you enjoy solving—those that involve people? Products? Ideas?
- What interests are revealed by your choices of reading material, Web blogs and other entertainment?
- What would an ideal day look like to you? Describe where you'd be, who would be with you, and what activities you'd do. Do any of these visions suggest a possible major?

THINKING

7

Questions like these are not frivolous. They can uncover a "fun factor" that energizes you to finish the work of completing a major.

Consider your abilities. In choosing an academic program, ability counts as much as interest. Einstein enjoyed playing the violin, but his love of music didn't override his choice of a career in science. In addition to considering what you enjoy, think about times and places when you excelled. List the courses that you aced, the work assignments that you mastered, and the hobbies that led to rewards or recognition. Let your choice of a program of study reflect a discovery of your passions *and* potentials.

Use formal techniques for self-discovery. Writing is a path to the kind of self-knowledge involved in choosing your major. Start with the exercises and Journal Entries in this book. Review what you've written, looking for statements about your interests and abilities.

Also consider questionnaires and inventories that are designed to correlate your interests with specific majors. Examples include the Strong Interest Inventory and the Self-Directed Search. Your student services or careers office can give you more details about these and related inventories. For some fun, take several of them and meet with an advisor to interpret the results.

Remember that there is no questionnaire, inventory, test, or formula for choosing a major or career. Likewise, there is no expert who can make these choices for you. Inventories can help you gain self-knowledge, and other people can offer valuable perspectives. However, what you *do* with all this input is entirely up to you.

Link to long-term goals. Your choice of a study program or major can fall into place once you determine what you want in life. Before you choose a major, back up to a bigger picture. List your core values, such as contributing to society, achieving financial security and professional recognition, enjoying good health, or making time for fun. Also write down specific goals that you want to accomplish 5 years, 10 years, or even 50 years from today.

Many students find that the prospect of getting what they want in life justifies all of the time, money, and day-to-day effort invested in going to school. Having a clear career goal gives you a powerful incentive for attending classes, taking part in discussions, reading textbooks, writing papers, and completing other assignments. When you see a clear connection between finishing school and creating the life of your dreams, the daily tasks of higher education become charged with meaning.

Studies indicate that the biggest factor associated with completing a degree in higher education is commitment to personal goals (Carlzon, 1989). A choice of academic major reflects those goals.

Ask other people. Key people in your life might have valuable suggestions about your choice of major. Ask for their ideas, and listen with an open mind. At the same time, distance yourself from any pressure to choose a major or career that fails to interest you. If you make a choice based solely on the expectations of other people, you could end up with a major or even a career you don't enjoy.

Gather information. Check your school's catalogue or website for a list of available majors. Here is a gold mine of information. Take a quick glance, and highlight all the majors that interest you. Then talk to students who have declared them. Also read descriptions of courses required for these majors. Chat with instructors who teach courses in these areas, and ask for copies of their course syllabi. Go to the bookstore and browse required texts.

Based on all this information, write a list of prospective programs of study. Discuss them with an academic advisor and someone at your school's career centre.

Invent a major. When choosing a major, you might not need to limit yourself to those listed in your school catalogue. Many schools now have flexible programs that allow for independent study. Through such programs you might be able to combine two existing majors or invent an entirely new one of your own.

Consider dual degrees. Many schools provide the opportunity to complete two degrees at the same time. For instance, you might combine the study of engineering with getting a business degree. Combining two degrees can allow you to expand the skills you develop and provide you with some powerful credentials in the work place. Completing a minor course of study in a complimentary area will also serve to enhance your career choices. So if you are studying business, consider a minor in French. Proficiency in French could broaden your career options not just in Canada but also abroad.

Think critically about the link between your major and your career. Your career goals might have a significant impact on your choice of major. For an overview of career planning and an immediate chance to put ideas down on paper, see Chapter 12: What's Next?

You might be able to pursue a rewarding career by choosing among *several* different majors. Even students planning to apply for law school or medical school have flexibility in their choice of majors. In addition, after graduation, many people are employed in jobs with little relationship to their major. And you might choose a career in the future that is unrelated to any currently available major.

Remember that many students who choose an "impractical" major go on to prosper in their careers.

According to the National Committee for Latin and Greek (2006), people who majored in classical civilizations and literature range from Ted Turner (founder of CNN) to Toni Morrison (winner of the Noble Prize for Literature) and J. K. Rowling (author of the Harry Potter novels).

2 Make a trial choice

Just choose—now. Don't delay the benefits of choosing a program of study. Even if you're undecided right now, you probably have an idea about what program interests you.

To verify this, do a short experiment. Search your school's calendar for a list of available programs of study or majors. Read through the list two or three times. Then pretend that you have to make a choice today. Write down the first three ideas that come to mind.

Hold onto this list, which reflects your intuition or "gut feelings," as you perform the more arduous task of researching various areas of study and careers in detail. Your research might lead to a new choice—or it might simply confirm one of the programs of study on your original list.

3 Evaluate your trial choice

When you've made a trial choice, take on the role of a scientist. Treat your choice as a hypothesis and then design a series of experiments to test it. For example:

- Visit with instructors who teach courses in the program, asking about required course work and career options in the field.

- Discuss your trial choice with an academic adviser and a career counsellor. Both individuals can provide you with key information about whether this is the right path for you.

- Enrol in a course related to your possible area of study. Remember that introductory courses might not give you a realistic picture of the workloads involved in advanced courses. To find out more about both workloads and what it takes to be successful in the program, meet informally with students who have declared the same program of study.

- Find an internship, service-learning experience, part-time job, or volunteer experience related to the program.

- Interview someone who works in a field related to the program of study or find out if your school has a job-shadowing program.

If these experiences confirm your choice of program of study, celebrate that fact. If they result in choosing a new program of study, celebrate that outcome as well.

Also remember that higher education represents a safe place to test your choice of study programs—and to change your mind. As you sort through your options, help is always available from administrators, instructors, advisers, and peers.

4 Choose again

Keep your choice of a major in perspective. There is probably no single "correct" choice. Your unique collection of skills is likely to provide the basis for majoring in several fields.

Odds are that you'll change your major at least once throughout your degree or diploma—and that you'll change careers several times during your life. One benefit of higher education is mobility. You gain the general skills and knowledge that can help you move into a new major or career field at any time.

Viewing a program of study as a one-time choice that determines your entire future can raise your stress levels. Instead, look at choosing a major as the start of a continuing path that involves discovery, choice, and passionate action.

WWW Find more strategies for choosing a major online @ *www.bams5ce.nelson.com*

21 exercise
Make a trial choice of major

This exercise presents another method for choosing a major. Look at your school's academic calendar for a list of majors, and cross out all of the programs that you already know are not right for you. You will probably eliminate well over half the list.

Now scan the remaining majors. Next to the ones that definitely interest you, write "yes." Next to majors that you're willing to consider and are still unsure about, write "maybe."

Focus on your "yes" choices. See if you can narrow them down to three majors. List those here.

Finally, write an asterisk next to the major that interests you most right now. This is your trial choice of major.

THINKING

7

Thinking is born of questions. Questions open up options that might otherwise remain unexplored. Questions wake up people and lead them to investigate more closely issues and assumptions that had previously gone unchallenged. Questions promote curiosity, create new distinctions, and multiply possibilities. Besides, instructors love them. One of the best ways to develop your relationship with an instructor is to ask a question.

Asking questions— Learning through inquiry

THERE'S A CHINESE PROVERB: "Tell me and I forget; show me and I remember; involve me and I understand." Asking questions is a way to stay involved. One of the main reasons you are in school is to ask questions—a process called *inquiry-based learning.* This process takes you beyond memorizing facts and passing tests. Asking questions turns you into a lifelong learner.

Asking questions is also a great way to improve relationships with friends and coworkers. When you ask a question, you offer a huge gift to people—an opportunity for them to speak their brilliance and for you to listen to their answers.

Students often say, "I don't know what to ask." If you have ever been at a loss for what to ask, here are some ways to construct powerful questions about any subject you study in school, or about any area of your life that you choose to examine.

Let your pen start moving. Sometimes you can access a deeper level of knowledge by taking out your pen, putting it on a piece of paper, and writing down questions—even before you know *what* to write. Don't think. Just watch the paper and notice what appears. The results might be surprising.

Ask about what's missing. Another way to invent useful questions is to notice what's missing from your life and then ask how to supply it. For example, if you want to take better notes, you can write, "What's missing is skill in note-taking. How can I gain more skill in taking notes?" Or "What's missing is time. How do I create enough time in my day to actually do the things that I say I want to do?"

Pretend to be someone else. Another way to invent questions is first to think of someone you greatly respect. Then pretend you're that person and ask the questions you think *she* would ask.

Begin a general question, then brainstorm endings. By starting with a general question and then brainstorming a long list of endings, you can invent a question that you've never asked before. For example:

What can I do when . . . ? What can I do when an instructor calls on me in class and I have no idea what to say? What can I do when an instructor doesn't show up for class on time? What can I do when I feel overwhelmed with assignments?

How can I . . . ? How can I get just the kind of courses that I want? How can I expand my career options? How can I become much more effective as a student, starting today?

When do I . . . ? When do I decide on a program of study? When do I transfer to another school? When do I meet with an instructor to discuss an upcoming essay?

Ask what else you want to know. Many times you can quickly generate questions by simply asking yourself, "What else do I want to know?" Ask this question immediately after you read a paragraph in a book or listen to someone speak.

Start from the assumption that you are brilliant, and begin asking questions that can help you unlock your brilliance.

STUDENT VOICES

A Master Student practises critical thinking. . . . She does not always accept the first answer as the only answer, and constantly questions what is put before her. I am determined to get every ounce of information, to glean and hold onto it, use it, and mature my thinking.

—LYNN LINEBERGER

Put It to *WORK*

Strategies for creative and critical thinking can assist you in developing new products and services in the workplace. Some examples follow.

© photos.com

State the obvious and go for the opposite

One way to generate a burst of creativity followed by critical thinking is to take an idea that seems obvious and state its opposite. Then see if you can find evidence to support the opposite idea.

This principle has been used with great success in business. An example comes from Jan Carlzon, former president of the Scandinavian Airline SAS. Carlzon questioned an "obvious" truth—that upper management in any company should make most of the decisions. He went for the opposite idea and allowed rank-and-file employees to make daily decisions that directly affected customers. If a customer got bumped from a flight, an SAS counter clerk could decide on the spot whether to pay the customer's hotel bill for the night or find the customer an alternative flight on a competitor's airline. After implementing this policy, SAS's business grew dramatically.

Find a smaller problem

After reading the Power Process: "Find a Bigger Problem," consider the merits of the opposite strategy. For example, you might feel overwhelmed with managing a complex, year-long project at work. One response is to give up—to quit. Another is to resign yourself to drudgery and dive into the project with a deep sigh.

"Find a smaller problem" offers an alternative: Just divide a huge project into many small jobs. Rather than worry about the project as a whole, turn your full attention to a small, specific task until it is complete. Do the same with the next small task, and the next. Just handle the details, one after another, until the project is finished.

The role of planning is critical. "Find a smaller problem" is not a suggestion to fill your days with busywork. When you plan effectively, the small jobs you do are critical to the success of the bigger project.

Experiment with the decreasing options technique

The decreasing options technique (DOT) is a decision-making strategy. It allows you to rank a large pool of ideas created by groups of people in meetings. Before you put DOT into action, go to an office supply store and get a package of several hundred adhesive dots—small stickers that can be attached to a sheet of paper. Then follow these steps:

* *Ask meeting participants to brainstorm solutions to a problem.* Permit all ideas to be expressed. Don't edit them yet. To save time, ask participants to submit ideas before the meeting takes place. That way you can summarize and post ideas ahead of time.
* *Summarize each idea in a single word or phrase on a large sheet of paper.* Write letters that are big enough to be seen across the meeting room. Place only one idea on each sheet of paper.
* *Post the sheets where all meeting participants can see them.*
* *Do an initial review of the ideas.* Ask participants if they can eliminate some ideas as obviously unworkable. Also group similar ideas together and eliminate duplications.
* *"Dot" ideas.* Give each participant a handful of sticker dots. Then ask participants to go around the room and place an adhesive dot next to the ideas that they consider most important.
* *Discuss the most important ideas.* Stand back and review the ideas. The high-priority concerns of the group will stand out clearly as the sheets with the most dots. Now you can bring these important ideas to the discussion table.

You can also use the DOT method online with bulletin boards or "virtual" meetings. Participants can use email or networking software to post their ideas and manipulate computer graphics that look like sticker dots.

chapter 7

QUIZ

Put It to Work
◄ ◄ ◄ ◄ ◄
Skills Snapshot
Master Student Profile

Name_____   Date____/____/____

1. List four questions that can guide you on your path to becoming a critical thinker.

2. Briefly describe one strategy for answering each question you listed in your response to Question 1.

3. Explain what is meant in this chapter by *aha!*

4. List and briefly describe three ways to create ideas.

5. Summarize the main steps in choosing a program of study or major.

6. According to the text, *critical thinking* and *thorough thinking* are two distinct and different activities. True or False? Explain your answer.

7. Define *all-or-nothing thinking* and give an example.

8. Explain the suggestion "watch for hot spots" and describe its connection to critical thinking.

9. Name at least one fallacy involved in this statement: "Everyone who's ever visited Toronto has agreed that it's the best city in the country."

10. List the four suggested steps for problem solving and give an example of each step.

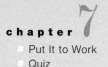
Skills *SNAPSHOT*

Now that you've experimented with some new strategies for thinking, take a few minutes to revisit your responses to the "Thinking" section of the Discovery Wheel exercise on page 37. Then complete the following sentences.

CREATIVE AND CRITICAL THINKING

When I'm asked to come up with a topic for a paper or speech, the first thing I do is . . .

When I'm asked for my opinion about a political candidate, the first thing I take into account about the candidate is . . .

APPLIED THINKING

In declaring my major, the steps I plan to take include . . .

One of the biggest problems I face right now is . . .

To come up with a solution for this problem, I will . . .

I'll know that I've reached a new level of mastery with critical and creative thinking skills when . . .

To reach that level of mastery, the most important thing I can do next is to . . .

MASTER STUDENT Profile

chapter 7

☐ Put It to Work
☐ Quiz
☐ Skills Snapshot
◄ ◄ ◄ ◄ ◄

Jian Ghomeshi

. . . is creative

© CP PHOTO/Jonathan Hayward

Follow your passions
Know who you are
Be patient and remember the big picture
You are your own brand
Ask questions and think critically

These are Jian Ghomeshi's five tips for liberal arts graduates on how to be successful. Ghomeshi, a self-described "jack of many trades, master of none" is the host of *Q*, CBC Radio's daily arts and culture show. He is also the proud holder of a Bachelor of Arts degree. At McMaster recently as the keynote speaker during Career Services' Government Career Week, he gave an inspiring talk on how to be your own brand, follow your passions and succeed in a new era. . . .

He addressed the questions some students ask, such as "what do I do with my degree?" and "will I ever need to know this in 'real life'?" His answers ranged broadly but they all emphasized the importance of pursuing your passions and following your dreams.

How did he get to where he is now? He certainly didn't follow a planned route. "If I had tried to plan, I probably wouldn't be doing what I'm doing, I probably would have messed it up," he says. Explaining the unconventional path he followed to get what he calls his 'dream gig', he encouraged the audience to follow their dreams even if they don't know where they will lead. . . . For Jian, the route to success included a combined BA in History and Political Science from York University, with a minor in women studies. Throughout his time at York he was also very involved in music as a singer, songwriter and musician. Despite being offered a scholarship to Stanford University to continue his studies in political science, after graduation he followed his heart and co-founded a band, Moxy Früvous, which was active all through the 1990s. Since then, he has mostly been working in different capacities at the CBC, as well as writing for numerous national and international newspapers.

A big believer in the liberal arts, Jian credits his own education as being largely responsible for his success. "You are always going to gain from having a sense of history and great literature. Don't feel pressure to create the perfect job. I use [my education] every day." Noting how his women studies courses helped him to develop his own sense of the world, and his sense of right and wrong, Jian commented, "I wouldn't know at the time I would be able to use what I was learning, but I did, and I do." Emphasizing number five on his list of tips, Jian added, "thinking critically got me where I am, and that's valuable."

Jian encourages students to explore their different possibilities and talents, "spread yourself out, build a wide foundation and follow all of your different passions." Who would have predicted Jian would follow the path he did? Your path can be equally unpredictable and lead to success just as great.

Source: Moody, Michelle (October 2009). "Follow Your Dreams, Be a Success." McMaster University. Retrieved July 5, 2011 from http://www.humanities.mcmaster.ca/news/Ghomeshi.html

A broadcaster who is the host of a national daily show on cultural affairs called *Q* on CBC. He is also a writer, singer, songwriter, and musician.

Find more biographical information about Jian Ghomeshi at the Master Student Hall of Fame @

www.bams5ce.nelson.com

In our daily contact with other people and the mass media, we are exposed to hundreds of messages. Yet the obstacles to receiving those messages accurately are numerous.

Communication—keeping the channels open

FOR ONE THING, only a small percentage of communication is verbal. We also send messages with our bodies and with the tone of our voices. Throw in a few other factors, such as a hot room or background noise, and it's a wonder we can communicate at all.

Written communication adds a whole other set of variables. When you speak, you supplement the meaning of your words with the power of body language and voice inflection. When you write, those nonverbal elements are absent. Instead, you depend on your skills at word choice, sentence construction, and punctuation to get your message across. The choices that you make in these areas can aid—or hinder—communication.

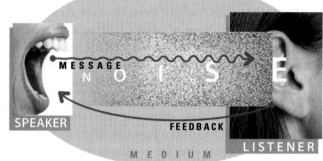

Mouth: © photos.com; ear: Andrew Blais/Shutterstock

In communication theory, the term **noise** refers to any factor that distorts meaning. When noise is present, the channels of communication start to close. Noise can be external (a lawn mower outside

exercise 23
Practise sending or receiving

The purpose of this exercise is to help you slow down the pace of communication and clearly separate the roles of sending and receiving. Begin by applying the following steps to conversations on neutral topics. With some practice, you'll be ready to use this technique in situations that could escalate into an argument.

First, find a partner, and choose a topic for a conversation. Also set a time limit for doing this exercise. You will need someone to time the exercise for you. Then complete the following steps:

1. Sit back to back with your partner. Decide which one of you will talk first. The *sender* should speak for three minutes on the topic. The partner should listen without speaking until the sender's time is up.

2. When it is the partner or *receiver's* turn, the she should first summarize what the *sender* said before they respond. The individual should take about a minute to

summarize and then will again have three minutes to talk on the topic. The partner should again listen without speaking until it is his turn.

3. Next the original *sender* will summarize what the partner said for a minute and then again have three minutes to respond.

4. Keep switching roles until each of the partners has had at least three opportunities to speak. Remember to summarize what your partner said before you begin speaking and to not interrupt when the other person is talking.

After completing these steps, reflect on the experience. How well could you summarize what your partner said? What has this exercise taught you about your current skills as a speaker and listener?

a classroom) or internal (the emotions of the sender or receiver, such as speech anxiety). To a large extent, skilful communication means reducing noise and keeping channels open.

One powerful technique for doing these crucial things is to separate the roles of sending and receiving. Communication channels get blocked when we try to send and receive messages at the same time. Instead, be aware of when you are the receiver and when you are the sender. If you are receiving (listening or reading), just receive; avoid switching into the sending (speaking or writing) mode. When you are sending, stick with it until you are finished.

Communication works best when each of us has plenty of time to receive what others send *and* the opportunity to send a complete message when it's our turn. Communication is a two-way street. When someone else talks, just listen. Then switch roles so that you can be the sender for a while. Keep this up until you do a reasonably complete job of creating shared meaning. ✳

Choosing to listen

Observe a person in a conversation who is not talking. Is he listening? Maybe. Maybe not. He might be preparing his response or daydreaming.

LISTENING IS NOT EASY. Doing it effectively requires concentration and energy. It's worth it. Listening well promotes success in school: more powerful notes, more productive study groups, and better relationships with students and instructors. A skilled listener is appreciated by friends, family, and business associates. The best salespeople and managers are the best listeners. People love a good listener. Through skilled listening, you gain more than respect. You gain insight into other people. You learn about the world and about yourself.

To be a good listener, choose to listen. Once you've made this choice, you can use the following techniques to be a more effective listener. These ideas are especially useful in times of high emotional tension.

Non-verbal listening

Much of listening is non-verbal. Here are five guidelines for effective non-verbal listening.

Be quiet. Silence is more than staying quiet while someone is speaking. Allowing several seconds to pass before you begin to talk gives the speaker time to catch his breath and gather his thoughts. He might want to continue. Someone who talks non-stop might fear he will lose the floor if he pauses.

If the message being sent is complete, this short break gives you time to form your response and helps you avoid the biggest barrier to listening—listening with your answer running. If you make up a response before the person is finished, you might miss the end of the message—which is often the main point.

In some circumstances, pausing for several seconds might be inappropriate. Ignore this suggestion completely when someone asks in a panic where to find the nearest phone to call the fire department.

Maintain eye contact. Look at the other person while he speaks. Doing so demonstrates your attentiveness and helps keep your mind from wandering. Your eyes also let you "listen" to body language and behaviour. When some of us avoid eye contact, not only do we fail to see—we fail to listen.

This idea is not an absolute. While maintaining eye contact is important in many cultures, people from some cultures are uncomfortable with sustained eye contact. Some individuals learn primarily by hearing; they can listen more effectively by turning off the visual input once in a while. Keep in mind the differences among people.

Display openness. You can communicate openness by means of your facial expression and body position. Uncross your arms and legs. Sit up straight. Face the other person and remove any physical barriers between you, such as a pile of books.

Suspend judgments. Listening and agreeing are two different activities. As listeners, our goal is to fully receive another person's message. This does not mean that we're

> *Through skilled listening, you gain more than respect. You gain insight into other people. You learn about the world and about yourself.*

obligated to agree with the message. Once you're confident that you accurately understand a speaker's point of view, you are free to agree or disagree with it. The key to effective listening is understanding *before* evaluating.

Send acknowledgments. Let the speaker know periodically that you are still there. Words and non-verbal gestures of acknowledgment convey to the speaker that you are interested and that you are receiving his message. These include "Umhum," "OK," "Yes," and head nods.

These acknowledgments do not imply your agreement. When people tell you what they don't like about you, your head nod doesn't mean that you agree. It just indicates that you are listening.

Verbal listening

Choose when to speak. When we listen to another person, we often interrupt with our own stories, opinions, suggestions, and comments. Consider the following dialogue:

"Oh, I'm so excited. I just found out that I've been nominated to be in *Who's Who in Canadian Musicians*."

"Yeah, that's neat. My Uncle Elmer got into *Who's Who in Canadian Veterinarians*. He sure has an interesting job. One time I went along when he was treating a cow and you'll never believe what happened next...."

To avoid this kind of one-sided conversation, delay your verbal responses. This does not mean that you remain totally silent while listening. It means that you wait for an *appropriate* moment to respond.

Watch your non-verbal responses, too. A look of "Who cares!" from you can deter the other person from finishing his message.

Feed back meaning. Sometimes you can help the speaker clarify her message by paraphrasing it. This does not mean parroting what another person says. Instead, briefly summarize. Feed back what you see as the essence of that person's message: "Let me see if I understood what you said . . ." or "What I'm hearing you say is. . . ." (Psychotherapist Carl Rogers (1961) referred to this technique as **reflection**.) Often, the other person will say, "No, that's not what I meant. What I said was. . . ."

There will be no doubt when you get it right. The sender will say, "Yeah, that's it," and either continue with another message or stop sending when he knows you understand.

If you don't understand the message, be persistent. Be concise. This is not a time to stop the other person by talking on and on about what you think you heard.

Listen beyond words. Be aware of non-verbal messages and behaviour. You might point out that the speaker's body language seems to be the exact opposite of his words. For example: "I noticed you said you are excited, but you look bored."

Keep in mind that the same non-verbal behaviour can have different meanings, depending on the listener's cultural background. Someone who looks bored might simply be listening in a different way.

The idea is to listen not only to the words but also to the emotion behind the words. Sometimes that emotional message is more important than the verbal content.

Listen for requests and intentions. "This class is a waste of my time." "Our instructor talks too fast." An effective way to listen to such complaints is to look for the request hidden in them.

"This class is a waste of my time" can be heard as "Please tell me what I'll gain if I participate actively in class." "The instructor talks too fast" might be asking "What strategies can I use to take notes when the instructor covers material rapidly?" We can even transform complaints into intentions. Take this complaint: "The parking lot by the residences is so dark at night that I'm afraid to go to my car." This complaint can result in having a light installed in the parking lot.

Viewing complaints as requests gives us more choices. Rather than responding with defensiveness ("What does he know anyway?"), resignation ("It's always been this way and always will be"), or indifference ("It's not my job"), we can decide whether to grant the request (do what will alleviate the other's difficulty) or help the person translate his own complaint into an action plan.

Allow emotion. In the presence of full listening, some people will share things that they feel deeply about. They might shed a few tears, cry, shake, or sob. If you feel uncomfortable when this happens, see if you can accept the discomfort for a little while longer. Emotional release can bring relief and trigger unexpected insights.

Ask for more. Full listening with unconditional acceptance is a rare gift. Many people have never experienced it. They are used to being greeted with resistance, so they habitually stop short of saying what they truly think and feel. Help them shed this habit by routinely asking, "Is there anything more you want to say about that?" This question sends the speaker a message that you truly value what she has to say.

Be careful with questions and advice. Questions are directive. They can take conversations in a new direction, which may not be where the speaker wants to go. Ask questions only to clarify the speaker's message. Later, when it's your turn to speak, you can introduce any topic that you want.

Also be cautious about giving advice. Unsolicited advice can be taken as condescending or even insulting. Skilled listeners recognize that people are different,

8

COMMUNICATING

and they do not assume that they know what's best for someone else.

Take care of yourself. People seek good listeners, and there are times when you don't want to listen. You might be distracted with your own concerns. Be honest. Don't pretend to listen. You can say, "What you're telling me is important, and I'm pressed for time right now. Can we set aside another time to talk about this?" It's OK *not* to listen.

Stay open to the adventure of listening. Receiving what another person has to say is an act of courage. Listening fully—truly opening yourself to the way another person sees the world—means taking risks. Your opinions may be challenged. You may be less certain or less comfortable than you were before.

Along with the risks come rewards. Listening in an unguarded way can take your relationships to a new depth and level of honesty. This kind of listening can open up new possibilities for thinking, feeling, and behaving. And when you practise full listening, other people are more likely to receive when it's your turn to send.

You might want to try repeating Exercise 23 but this time face your partner, sitting a comfortable distance apart. Choose a new topic. You still should not interrupt your partner when she is speaking but this time, try to ensure that you use your nonverbal listening skills. How does communication change when you use nonverbal cues like sending acknowledgments? How did the conversation feel this time? Was it any easier to summarize the information or to talk? ✴

 Find more strategies for full listening online @ **www.bams5ce.nelson.com**

Choosing to speak

You have been talking with people for most of your life, and you usually manage to get your messages across. There are times, though, when you don't. Often, these times are emotionally charged.

WE ALL HAVE this problem. Sometimes we feel wonderful or rotten or sad or scared, and we want to express it. Emotions can get in the way of the message. Described below are four techniques for delivering a message through tears, laughter, fist pounding, or hugging. They are: Replace "You" messages with **"I" messages**, avoid questions that aren't really questions, notice non-verbal messages, and notice barriers to communication.

Replace "You" messages with "I" messages. It can be difficult to disagree with someone without him becoming angry or you becoming upset. When conflict occurs, we often make statements about the other person, or "You" messages:

"You are rude."

"You make me mad."

"You must be crazy."

"You don't love me anymore."

This kind of communication results in defensiveness. The responses might be:

"I am not rude."

"I don't care."

"No, *you* are crazy."

"No, *you* don't love *me*!"

"You" messages are hard to listen to. They label, judge, blame, and assume things that might or might not be true. They demand rebuttal. Even praise can sometimes be an ineffective "You" message. "You" messages don't work.

When communication is emotionally charged, psychologist Thomas Gordon suggests that you consider limiting your statements to descriptions about yourself.[3] Replace "You" messages with "I" messages.

"You are rude" might become "I feel upset."

"You make me mad" could be "I feel angry."

"You must be crazy" can be "I don't understand."

"You don't love me anymore" could become "I'm afraid we're drifting apart."

Suppose a friend asks you to pick him up at the airport. You drive 30 kilometres and wait for the plane. No friend. You decide your friend missed his plane, so you wait three hours for the next flight. No friend. Perplexed and worried, you drive home. The next day, you see your friend downtown.

"What happened?" you ask.

"Oh, I caught an earlier flight."

"You are a rude person," you reply.

Look for the facts, the observable behaviour. Everyone will agree that your friend asked you to pick him up, that he did take an earlier flight, and that you did not receive a call from him. But the idea that he is rude is not a fact—it's a judgment.

He might go on to say, "I called your home and no one answered. My mom had a stroke and was rushed to Valley View. I caught the earliest flight I could get." Your judgment no longer fits.

When you saw your friend, you might have said, "I waited and waited at the airport. I was worried about you. I didn't get a call. I feel angry and hurt. I don't want to waste my time. Next time, you can call me when your flight arrives, and I'll be happy to pick you up."

"I" messages don't judge, blame, criticize, or insult. They don't invite the other person to counterattack with

> *Most non-verbal behaviour is unconscious. We can learn to be aware of it and choose our non-verbal messages.*

Five ways to say "I"

An "I" message can include any or all of the following five elements. Be careful when including the last two, since they can contain hidden judgments or threats.

Observations Describe the facts—the indisputable, observable realities. Talk about what you—or anyone else—can see, hear, smell, taste, or touch. Avoid judgments, interpretations, or opinions. Instead of saying, "You're a slob," say, "The pan from last night's lasagna was still on the stove this morning."

Feelings Describe your own feelings. It is easier to listen to "I feel frustrated" than to "You never help me." Stating how you feel about another's actions can be valuable feedback for that person.

Wants You are far more likely to get what you want if you *say* what you want. If someone doesn't know what you want, he doesn't have a chance to help you get it. Ask clearly. Avoid demanding or using the word *need*. Most people like to feel helpful, not obligated. Instead of saying, "Do the dishes when it's your turn, or else!" say, "I want to divide the housework fairly."

Thoughts Communicate your thoughts, and use caution. Beginning your statement with the word "I" doesn't make it an "I" message. "I think you are a slob" is a "You" judgment in disguise. Instead, say, "I'd have more time to study if I didn't have to clean up so often."

Intentions The last part of an "I" message is a statement about what you intend to do. Have a plan that doesn't depend on the other person. For example, instead of "From now on we're going to split the dishwashing evenly," you could say, "I intend to do my share of the housework and leave the rest."

more of the same. "I" messages are also more accurate. They report our own thoughts and feelings.

At first, "I" messages might feel uncomfortable or seem forced. That's OK. Use the five ways to say "I" explained below.

Finally, repeat Exercise 23 with a new topic. Again sit facing your partner and continue to use non-verbal listening skills when your partner is talking. This time, when you summarize what the sender says use "I" messages. Afterwards think about how including "I" messages changed the exchange between the two of you. When did you feel most listened to? Reflect on this exercise the next time you begin to debate a student in class. How could you make those exchanges more productive?

Remember that questions are not always questions. You've heard these "questions" before. A parent asks, "Don't you want to look nice?" Translation: "I wish you'd cut your hair, lose the blue jeans, and put on a tie." Or how about this question from a partner: "Honey, wouldn't you love to go to an exciting hockey game tonight?" Translation: "I've already bought tickets."

We use questions that aren't questions to sneak our opinions and requests into conversations. "Doesn't it upset you?" means "It upsets me," and "Shouldn't we hang the picture over here?" means "I want to hang the picture over here."

Communication improves when we say, "I'm upset" and "Let's hang the picture over here."

Choose non-verbal messages. How you say something can be more important than what you say. Your tone of voice and gestures add up to a silent message that you send. This message can support, modify, or contradict your words. Your posture, the way you dress, how often you shower, and even the poster hanging on your wall can negate your words before you say them. Most non-verbal behaviour is unconscious. We can learn to be aware of it and choose our non-verbal messages. The key is to be clear about our intention and purpose. When we know what we want to say and are committed to getting it across, our inflections, gestures, and words work together and send a unified message.

Notice barriers to sending messages. Sometimes fear stops us from sending messages. We are afraid of other people's reactions, sometimes justifiably. Being truthful doesn't mean being insensitive to the impact that our messages have on others. Tact is a virtue; letting fear prevent communication is not.

Assumptions can also be used as excuses for not sending messages. "He already knows this," we tell ourselves.

Predictions of failure can be barriers to sending, too. "He won't listen," we assure ourselves. That statement might be inaccurate. Perhaps the other person senses that we're angry and listens in a guarded way. Or perhaps he is listening and sending non-verbal messages we don't understand.

Or we might predict, "He'll never do anything about it, even if I tell him." Again, making assumptions can defeat your message before you send it.

It's easy to make excuses for not communicating. If you have fear or some other concern about sending a message, be aware of it. Don't expect the concern to go away. Realize that you can communicate even with your concerns. You can choose to make them a part of the message: "I am going to tell you how I feel, and I'm afraid that you will think it's stupid."

Talking to someone when you don't want to could be a matter of educational survival. A short talk with an adviser, a teacher, a friend, or a family member might solve a problem that could jeopardize your education.

Speak candidly. When we brood on negative thoughts and refuse to speak them out loud, we lose perspective. And when we keep joys to ourselves, we diminish our satisfaction. A solution is to share regularly what we think and feel. Psychotherapist Sidney Jourard (1971) referred to such openness and honesty as *transparency* and wrote eloquently about how it can heal and deepen relationships.

Sometimes candid speaking can save a life. For example, if you think a friend is addicted to drugs, telling her so in a supportive, nonjudgmental way is a sign of friendship.

Imagine a community in which people freely and lovingly speak their minds—without fear or defensiveness. That can be your community.

This suggestion comes with a couple of caveats. First, there is a big difference between speaking candidly about your problems and complaining about them. Complainers usually don't seek solutions. They just want everyone to know how unhappy they are. Instead, talk about problems as a way to start searching for solutions.

Second, avoid bragging. Other people are turned off by constant references to how much money you have, how great your partner is, how numerous your social successes are, or how much status your family enjoys. There is a difference between sharing excitement and being obnoxious.

Speak up! Look for opportunities to practise speaking strategies. Join class discussions or clubs on campus that focus on speaking, like "Toastmasters," Start conversations about topics that excite you. Ask for information and clarification. Ask for feedback on your skills.

Also speak up when you want support. Consider creating a team of people who help one another succeed. Such a team can develop naturally from a study group that works well. Ask members if they would be willing to accept and receive support in achieving a wide range of academic and personal goals. Meet regularly to do goal-setting exercises from this book and brainstorm success strategies.

After you have a clear statement of your goals and a plan for achieving them, let family members and friends know. This can be a good way to keep motivated, and provides an understanding for when you may not be available to them. When appropriate, let them know how they can help. You may be surprised at how often people respond to a genuine request for support. ✳

 Find more strategies for speaking online @ **www.bams5ce.nelson.com**

②④ exercise
Write an "I" message

First, pick something about school that irritates you. Then pretend that you are talking to a person who is associated with this irritation. In the space below, write down what you would say to this person as a "you" message.

Now write the same complaint as an "I" message. Include all of the elements suggested in "Five Ways to Say 'I.'"

Discovery/Intention Statement

Discover Communication Styles

The concept of *communication styles* can be useful when you want to discover sources of conflict with another person—or when you're in a conversation with someone from a different culture.

Consider the many ways in which people express themselves verbally. These characteristics can reflect an individual's preferred communication style:

- Extroversion—talking to others as a way to explore possibilities for taking action.
- Introversion—thinking through possibilities alone before talking to others.
- Dialogue—engaging in a discussion to hear many points of view before coming to a conclusion or decision.
- Debate—arguing for a particular point of view from the outset of a discussion.
- Openness—being ready to express personal thoughts and feelings early in a relationship.
- Reserve—holding back on self-expression until a deeper friendship develops.
- A faster pace of conversation—allowing people to speak quickly and forcefully while filling any gaps in conversation.
- A slower pace of conversation—allowing people to speak slowly and quietly while taking time to formulate their thoughts.

These are just a few examples of differences in communication styles. You might be able to think of others.

The point is that people with different communication styles can make negative assumptions about each other. For example, those who prefer fast-paced conversations might assume that people who talk slowly are indecisive. And people who prefer slower-paced conversations might assume that people who talk quickly are pushy and uninterested in anyone else's opinion.

Take this opportunity to think about your preferred communication styles and assumptions. Do they enhance or block your relationships with other people? Think back over the conversations you've had during the past week. Then complete the following sentences, using additional paper as needed.

I discovered that I prefer conversations that allow me to . . .

_____

_____

_____

_____

_____

I discovered that I usually feel uncomfortable in conversations when other people . . .

_____

_____

_____

_____

_____

When people do the things listed in Item 2, I tend to make certain assumptions, such as . . .

_____

_____

_____

_____

_____

As an alternative to making the assumptions listed in Item 3, I intend to . . .

_____

_____

_____

_____

_____

8

COMMUNICATING

Developing emotional intelligence

EMOTIONAL INTELLIGENCE MEANS recognizing feelings and responding to them in skillful ways. Daniel Goleman (1995), author of *Emotional Intelligence: Why It Can Matter More Than IQ,* concludes that "IQ washes out when it comes to predicting who, among a talented pool of candidates *within* an intellectually demanding profession will become the strongest leader." At that point, **emotional intelligence** starts to become more important.

If you're emotionally intelligent, you're probably described as someone with good "people skills." That's a short form for being aware of your feelings, acting in thoughtful ways, showing concern for others, resolving conflict, and making responsible decisions. You can deepen these skills with the following strategies.

Recognize three elements of emotion

Even the strongest emotion consists of just three elements: physical sensations, thoughts, and action. Usually they happen so fast that you can barely distinguish them. Separating them out is a first step toward emotional intelligence.

Imagine that you suddenly perceive a threat—such as a supervisor who's screaming at you. Immediately your heart starts beating in double time and your stomach muscles clench (physical sensations). Then thoughts race through your head: *This is a disaster. She hates me. And everyone's watching.* Finally, you take action, which could mean staring at her, yelling back, or running away.

Name your emotions

Naming your emotions is a First Step to going beyond the "fight or flight" reaction to any emotion. Naming gives you power. The second that you attach a word to an emotion, you start to gain perspective. People with emotional intelligence have a rich vocabulary to describe a wide range of emotions. For examples, do an Internet search with the key words *feeling list.* Read through the lists you find for examples of ways that you can name your feelings in the future.

Accept your emotions

Another step toward emotional intelligence is accepting your emotions—*all* of them. This can be challenging if you've been taught that some emotions are "good" while others are "bad." Experiment with another viewpoint: Emotions are complicated. They have many causes that are beyond your control, including what *other* people

do. Because you do not choose your emotional reactions from moment to moment, you cannot be held morally responsible for them. However, you can be held responsible for what you *do* in response to any emotion.

Express your emotions

One possible response to any emotion is expressing it. The key is to speak without blaming others for the way you feel. The basic tool for doing so is using "I" messages, as described on page 260.

Respond rather than react

The heart of emotional intelligence is moving from mindless reactions to mindful actions. See if you can introduce an intentional gap between sensations and thoughts on the one hand and your next action on the other hand. To do this more often:

- *Run a "mood metre."* Check in with your moods several times each day. On a pad of paper note the time of day and your emotional state at that point. Rate your mood on a scale of 1 (relaxed and positive) to 10 (very angry, very sad, or very afraid).

- *Write Discovery Statements.* In your journal, write about situations in daily life that trigger strong emotions. Describe these events—and your usual responses to them—in detail.

- *Write Intention Statements.* After seeing patterns in your emotions, you can consciously choose to behave in new ways. Instead of yelling back at the angry supervisor, for example, make it your intention to simply remain silent and breathe deeply until she finishes. Then say, "I'll wait to respond until we've both had a chance to cool down."

Make decisions with emotional intelligence

Emotional intelligence can help you make decisions. When considering a possible choice, ask yourself, "How am I likely to feel if I do this?" You can use "gut feelings" to tell when an action might violate your values or hurt someone.

Think of emotions as energy. Anger, sadness, and fear send currents of sensation through your whole body. Ask yourself how you can channel that energy into constructive action. ✳

 Learn more ways to develop emotional intelligence online @

www.bams5ce.nelson.com

COMMUNICATING

8

mastering technology

SETTING LIMITS ON SCREEN TIME

Access to wireless communication offers easy ways to procrastinate. We call it "surfing," "texting," "IMing,"— and sometimes "researching" or "working." Author Edward Hallowell (2006) coined a word to describe these activities when done compulsively—*screensucking*.

Digital devices create value. With a computer you can stream music, watch videos, listen to podcasts, scan newspapers, read books, check email, and send instant messages. With a cell phone you can be available to key people when it counts. And any of these activities can become addicting distractions.

Discover how much time you spend

online To get an accurate picture of your involvement in social networking and other online activity, use the Time Monitor/Time Plan exercise included in Chapter 2. Then make conscious choices about how much time you want to spend online and on the phone. Don't let social networking distract you from meeting personal and academic goals.

Go offline to send the message that other people matter

It's hard to pay attention to the person who is right in front of you when you're hammering out text messages or updating your Twitter stream. You can also tell when someone else is doing these things and only half-listening to you.

An alternative is to close up your devices and "be here now." When you're eating, stop answering the phone. Notice how the food tastes. When you're with a friend, close up your laptop. Hear every word he says. Instead of using a computer or cell phone to rehash the past or plan the future, rediscover where life actually takes place—in the present moment.

Developing interpersonal intelligence requires being with people and away from a computer or cell phone. People who break up with a partner through text messaging are not developing that intelligence. True friends know when to go offline to resolve a conflict. They know when to go back home and support a family member in crisis.

Managing conflict

Conflict management is one of the most practical skills you'll ever learn. Here are strategies that can help.

THE FIRST FIVE strategies below are about dealing with the *content* of a conflict—defining the problem, exploring viewpoints, and discovering solutions. The remaining strategies are about finding a *process* for resolving any conflict, no matter what the content.

To bring these strategies to life, think of ways to use them in managing a conflict that you face right now.

Focus on content

Back up to common ground. Conflict heightens the differences between people. When this happens, it's easy to forget how much we still agree with each other.

As a first step in managing conflict, back up to common ground. List all of the points on which you are *not* in conflict: "I know that we disagree about how much to spend on a new car, but we do agree that the old one

© Marc Dietrich/Shutterstock

needs to be replaced." Often, such comments put the problem in perspective and pave the way for a solution.

State the problem. Using "I" messages, as explained earlier in this chapter, state the problem. Tell people what you observe, feel, think, want, and intend to do. Allow the other people in a particular conflict to do the same.

Each person might have a different perception of the problem. That's fine. Let the conflict come into clear focus. It's hard to fix something unless people agree on what's broken.

Remember that the way you state the problem largely determines the solution. Defining the problem in a new way can open up a world of possibilities. For example, "I need a new roommate" is a problem statement that dictates one solution. "We could use some agreements about who cleans the apartment" opens up more options, such as resolving a conflict about who will wash the dishes tonight.

© Yuri Arcurs/Shutterstock

State all points of view. If you want to defuse tension or defensiveness, set aside your opinions for a moment. Take the time to understand the other points of view. Sum up those viewpoints in words that the other parties can accept. When people feel that they've been heard, they're often more willing to listen.

Ask for complete communication. In times of conflict, we often say one thing and mean another. So before responding to what the other person says, use active listening. Check to see if you have correctly received that person's message by saying, "What I'm hearing you say is. . . . Did I get it correctly?"

Focus on solutions. After stating the problem, dream up as many solutions as you can. Be outrageous. Don't hold back. Quantity—not quality—is the key. If you get stuck, restate the problem and continue brainstorming.

Next, evaluate the solutions you brainstormed. Discard the unacceptable ones. Talk about which solutions will work and how difficult they will be to implement. You might hit upon a totally new solution.

Choose one solution that is most acceptable to everyone involved, and implement it. Agree on who is going to do what by when. Then keep your agreements.

Finally, evaluate the effectiveness of your solution. If it works, pat yourselves on the back. If not, make changes or implement a new solution.

Focus on the future. Instead of rehashing the past, talk about new possibilities. Think about what you can do to prevent problems in the future. State how you intend to change, and ask others for their contributions to the solution.

Focus on process

Commit to the relationship. The thorniest conflicts usually arise between people who genuinely care for each other. Begin by affirming your commitment to the other person: "I care about you, and I want this relationship to last. So I'm willing to do whatever it takes to resolve this problem." Also ask the other person for a similar commitment.

Allow strong feelings. Permitting conflict can also mean permitting emotion. Being upset is all right. Feeling angry is often appropriate. Crying is OK. Allowing other people to see the strength of our feelings can help resolve the conflict. This suggestion can be especially useful during times when differences are so extreme that reaching common ground seems possible.

Expressing the full range of your feelings can transform the conflict. Often what's on the far side of anger is love. When we express and release resentment, we might discover genuine compassion in its place.

Notice your need to be "right." Some people approach conflict as a situation where only one person wins. That person has the "right" point of view. Everyone else loses.

When this happens, step back. See if you can approach the situation in a neutral way. Define the conflict as a problem to be solved, not as a contest to be won. Explore the possibility that you might be mistaken. There might be more than one acceptable solution. The other person might simply have a different learning style than yours. Let go of being "right," and aim for being effective at resolving conflict instead.

Sometimes this means apologizing. Conflict sometimes arises from our own errors. Others might move quickly to end the conflict when we acknowledge this fact and ask for forgiveness.

Slow down the communication. In times of great conflict, people often talk all at once. Words fly like speeding bullets, and no one listens. Chances for resolving the conflict take a nosedive.

When everyone is talking at once, choose either to listen or to talk—not both at the same time. Just send your message. Or just receive the other person's message.

Think critically about your assumptions. An inability to say no can spring from the assumption that you'll lose friends if you state what you really want. But consider this: If you cannot say no, then you are not in charge of your time. You've given that right to whoever wants to interrupt you. This is not a friendship based on equality. True friends will respect your wishes.

Plan your refusal. You might find it easier to say no when you don't have to grasp for words. Choose some key words and phrases in advance—for example, "I'd love to, but not today"; "Thanks for asking, but I have a huge test tomorrow and want to study"; or "I'd prefer not to do anything tonight, do you want to grab lunch tomorrow instead?"

When you refuse, align your verbal and nonverbal messages. Reinforce your words with a firm voice and a posture that communicates confidence.

Avoid apologies or qualifiers. People give away their power when they couch their *nos* in phrases such as "I'm sorry, but I just don't know if I want to" or "Would you get upset if I said no?"

You don't have to apologize for being in charge of your life. It's OK to say no.

Wait for the request. People who worry about saying no often give in to a request before it's actually been made. Wait until you hear a question. "Time to party!" is not a question. Nor is it a call to action. Save your response until you hear a specific request, such as "Would you go to a party with me?"

Remember that one no leads to another yes. *Yes* and *no* are complementary, not contradictory. Saying no to one activity allows you to say yes to something that's more important right now. Saying no to a movie allows you to say yes to outlining a paper or reading a textbook chapter. You can say an unqualified yes to the next social activity—and enjoy it more—after you've completed some key tasks on your to-do list. ✳

You deserve compliments

Some people find it more difficult to accept compliments than criticisms. Here are some hints for handling compliments.

Accept the compliment. People sometimes respond to praise with "Oh, it's really nothing" or "This old thing? I've had it for years." This type of response undermines both you and the person who sent the compliment.

Choose another time to deliver your own compliments. Automatically returning a compliment can appear suspiciously polite and insincere.

Let the compliment stand. Asking "Do you really think so?" questions the integrity of the message. It can also sound as if you're fishing for more compliments.

Accepting compliments is not the same as being conceited. If you're in doubt about how to respond, just smile and say, "Thank you!" This simple response affirms the compliment, along with the person who delivered it.

You are worthy and capable. Allow people to acknowledge that fact.

<blockquote>
Sometimes relationship building involves making a complaint. Whining, blaming, pouting, kicking, and spitting usually don't get results. Here are some guidelines for complaining effectively.
</blockquote>

7 steps to effective complaints

1 Go to the source. Start with the person who is most directly involved with the problem.

2 Present the facts without blaming anyone. Your complaint will carry more weight if you document the facts. Keep track of names and dates. Note what actions were promised and what results actually occurred.

3 Go up the ladder to people with more responsibility. If you don't get satisfaction at the first level, go to that person's direct supervisor. Requesting a supervisor's name will often get results. Write a letter to the company president.

4 Ask for commitments. When you find someone who is willing to solve your problem, get him to say exactly what he is going to do and when.

5 Use available support. There are dozens of groups, as well as government agencies,

© woodsy/Shutterstock

willing to get involved in resolving complaints. Contact consumer groups or the Better Business Bureau. The Internet is also a powerful tool for complaining. Lots of corporations will respond to tweets complaining of poor service and sites like consumerist.com widely publicize complaints. Trade associations can sometimes help. Ask city council members, MPPs/MLAs, and MPs. All of them want your vote, so they are usually eager to help.

6 Take legal action, if necessary. Small claims court is relatively inexpensive, and you don't have to hire a lawyer. These courts can handle cases involving small amounts of money (up to $25,000 in most provinces). Legal aid offices can sometimes answer questions.

7 Don't give up. Assume that others are on your team. Many people are out there to help you. State what you intend to do and ask for their partnership. ✳

Criticism really can be constructive

Although receiving criticism is rarely fun, it is often educational. Here are some ways to get the most value from it.

Avoid finding fault. When your mind is occupied with finding fault in others, you aren't open to hearing constructive comments about yourself.

Take it seriously. Some people laugh or joke in order to cover up their anger or embarrassment at being criticized. A humorous reaction on your part can be mistaken for a lack of concern.

React to criticism with acceptance. Most people don't enjoy pointing out another's faults. Denial, argument, or joking makes it more difficult for them to give honest feedback. You can disagree with criticism and still accept it calmly.

Keep it in perspective. Avoid blowing the criticism out of proportion. The purpose of criticism is to generate positive change and self-improvement. There's no need to overreact to it.

Listen without defensiveness. You can't hear the criticism if you're busy framing your rebuttal.

COMMUNICATING

8

Collaborating for success

COLLABORATING SIMPLY MEANS working with others to achieve a common goal. In the workplace, things get done through collaboration. For example, the Boeing 747 airplane—among the world's largest aircraft—resulted from 75,000 blueprints that were created and implemented by a complex network of teams (LaFasto, 2002).

To develop collaboration skills, take your cue from the Power Processes included throughout this book. Following are ways you can use four of the Power Processes to supercharge your next team project. Review the other Power Processes, and create more ideas of your own.

Discover what you want. To promote effective results, define your team's purpose, its expected results, and how it will be held accountable. Also ask for enough support—in terms of time, money, and other resources—to produce those results.

To define specific results, ask four questions based on the Master Student Map that begins each chapter of this book:

- Why is this project being done?
- What would a successful outcome for this project look like?
- How are we going to create a bridge from our current reality to that successful outcome?
- What if we truly made this outcome a high priority? What is the very next action that each of us would take to make it happen?

Ideas are tools. According to Frank LaFasto and Carl Larson (2002), authors of *When Teams Work Best*, the most common barrier to effective teamwork is an atmosphere of defensiveness. Teams tend to fizzle when they create new ideas that team members greet with immediate skepticism or outright rejection: *This suggestion will never work. . . . That's just not the way we do things around here. . . . We can't break with tradition. . . .* These responses are examples of "groupthink," which happens when a team automatically rules out new ideas simply because they're . . . well, new.

You can prevent this outcome by asking pointed questions before a team convenes its first meeting: Are we truly interested in change? Are we willing to act on what the team recommends? Or are we just looking for a team to reinforce our current practices?

Instead of automatically looking for what's wrong with a suggested idea, suggest that the team look for potential applications for that idea. Even a proposal that seems outlandish at first might become workable with a few modifications. In an empowered team, all ideas are welcome, problems are freely admitted, and any item is open for discussion.

Be here now. Concentration and focused attention are attributes of effective students—and effective teams. When a team tries to tackle too many problems or achieve too many goals, it gets distracted. Members can forget the team's purpose and lose their enthusiasm for the project. You can help restore focus by asking these questions: *What is the single most important goal that our team can meet?* and *What is the single most important thing we can do now to meet that goal?*

Notice your pictures and let them go. During much of the previous century, people worked in jobs with clearly defined tasks and limited responsibilities. Collaborations among employees in different departments were rare.

The concept of teamwork presents a different picture of how to operate a workplace. But old pictures die hard. Companies may give lip service to the idea of teams and yet fall back into traditional practices. Managers might set up teams but offer little training to help people function in this new working environment.

You can prepare for effective workplace practices now. While you are in school, seize opportunities to work collaboratively. Form study groups. Enrol in classes that include group projects. At the same time, keep in mind that not everyone will share your assumptions about the value of teams. By demonstrating your abilities, you can help them form new pictures. ✳

COMMUNICATING

8

Staying smart in cyberspace— safe social networking

SOCIAL NETWORKS ARE groups of people who connect with each other while they're online. These network communities can create value. Websites such as Facebook and LinkedIn are known as places to share news, photos, and personal profiles. You can also use such sites to form study groups, promote special events, and make job contacts. Microblogging services such as Twitter allow hour-by-hour and even minute-to-minute contact.

Activity in online communities can also have unexpected consequences. You might find examples of "cyberbullying"—hate speech or threats of violence. And some users find that embarrassing details from their online profiles come back to haunt them years later.

You can use simple strategies to stay in charge of your safety, reputation, and integrity any time you connect with people online.

Post only what you want made public and permanent. The Internet as a whole is a public medium. This is true of its online communities as well. Post only the kind of information about yourself that you *want* to be made public.

Friends, relatives, university administrators, potential employers, and police officers might be able to access your online profile. Don't post anything that could embarrass you later. Act today to protect the person that you want to be four or five years from now.

Remember that there is no delete key for the Internet. Websites such as the Internet Archive and its "Wayback Machine" almost guarantee that anything you post online will stay online for a long time. Anyone with Internet access can take your words and images and post them on a website or distribute them via email to

damage your reputation. In the virtual world, you never know who's following you.

To avoid unwanted encounters with members of online communities, also avoid posting the following:

- Your home address.
- Your school address.
- Your phone number.
- Your birth date.
- Your screen name for instant messaging.
- Your class schedule.
- Your financial information, such as bank account numbers, credit card numbers, your social insurance number, or information about an eBay or PayPal account.
- Information about places that you regularly go at certain times of the day.
- Information about places you plan to visit in the future.
- Provocative pictures or messages with sexual innuendos.
- Pictures of yourself at school or at work.
- To further protect your safety, don't add strangers to your list of online friends.
- Use similar caution and common sense when joining groups. Signing up for a group with a name like *Binge Drinking Forever* can have consequences for years to come.

Be honest. After you've chosen what information to post, make sure that it's accurate. False information can lead to expulsion from a community. For example,

mastering technology

MASTER STUDENTS—GET NETWORKED

Learning naturally occurs in social networks—that is, among groups of teachers and students. With technology, you can extend your network across the reach of the Internet. For example:

- Choose a topic that interests you, and search for related websites and podcasts.
- Use an RSS reader such as Google Reader, or NetNewsWire to get updated lists of articles on the websites you'd like to follow.

- Use Twitter, email, and participate in online forums to contact experts on your topic.
- Use videoconferencing websites to converse in real time with people across the world.
- Pay special attention to well-written blogs, and join the discussion by commenting on the postings.
- Create your own blog to document your learning, and welcome comments from others.

8

COMMUNICATING

MySpace administrators delete profiles of people who lie about their age (2009).

Also avoid flirting while you're online. People may not be who they say they are.

Use privacy features. Many online communities offer options for blocking messages from strangers, including instant messages and friendship invitations. Several social networking sites allow you to create both private and public profiles. (Look for a link on each site titled "Frequently Asked Questions," "Security Features," "Account Settings," or "Privacy Settings.") For further protection, review and update your list of contacts on a regular basis.

In addition, respect the privacy of other members. If you want to post something on someone's site, send a message asking for permission first.

Be cautious about meeting community members in person. Because people can give misleading or false information about themselves online, avoid meeting them in person. If you do opt for a face-to-face meeting, choose a public place, and bring along a friend you trust.

Report malicious content. If you find online content that you consider offensive or dangerous, report it to site administrators. In many online communities, you can do this anonymously. You can help prevent online forms of intolerance, prejudice, and discrimination. Set a positive counterexample by posting messages that demonstrate acceptance of diversity.

Remember netiquette. The word *etiquette* refers to common courtesy in interpersonal relationships. Its online equivalent is called **netiquette**—a set of guidelines for using computers, cell phones, or any other form of technology.

Certain kinds of exchanges can send the tone of online communications—including social networking, email messages, and blog postings—into the gutter. To promote a cordial online community, abide by the following guidelines:

- Respect others' time. People often turn to the Internet with the hope of saving time—not wasting it. You can accommodate their desires by typing concise messages. Adopt the habit of getting to your point, sticking to it, and getting to the end.

- Fine-tune the mechanics. Proofread your message for spelling and grammar—just as you would a printed message. Some email programs have built-in spell checkers as an optional tool. Give your readers the gift of clarity and precision. Use electronic communications as a chance to hone your writing skills.

- Avoid typing passages in ALL UPPERCASE LETTERS. This is the online equivalent of shouting.

- Design your messages for fast retrieval. Avoid graphics and attachments that take a long time to download, tying up your recipient's computer.

- Remember that the message is missing the emotion. When you communicate online, the people who receive your email will miss out on voice inflection and nonverbal cues that are present in face-to-face communication. Without these cues, words can be easily misinterpreted. Reread your message before sending it to be sure you have clarified what you want to say and how you feel.

The cornerstone of netiquette is to remember that the recipient on the other end is a human being. Whenever you're at a keyboard or cell phone typing messages, ask yourself one question: "Would I say this to the person's face?" ✳

 Learn more about smart social networking online @ www.bams5ce.nelson.com

Text message etiquette—Five key points

1. **Keep it short.** Limit text messages to about 150 characters. That's two to three sentences. If you go longer, your phone might split the message in two or even drop the last few words. In addition, long texts can be confusing. Send an email or make a phone call instead.

2. **Double-check the outgoing number.** If a message intended for your boyfriend or girlfriend ends up going to your boss, the results could be alarming.

3. **At work, in class and in other public places, set your phone on vibrate.** No one else wants to hear how many text messages you're getting.

4. **Keep the time in mind.** Save 2:00 a.m. text messages for special circumstances and your closest friends. A text can ring at the same volume as a phone call and wake people up.

5. **Make sure your message is appropriate for a text message.** Sometimes a phone call really is a better device for conveying information.

Three phases of effective writing

THIS SECTION OUTLINES a three-phase process for writing any essay or speech:

1. Getting ready to write
2. Writing a first draft
3. Revising your draft

   Even though the following articles lay out a step-by-step process, remember that writing is highly personal. You might go through the steps in a different order or find yourself working on several at once.

© Digital Vision/Getty Images

PHASE 1: Getting ready to write

Schedule and list-writing tasks

You can divide the ultimate goal—a finished essay—into smaller steps that you can tackle right away. Estimate how long it will take to complete each step. Start with the date your essay is due and work backward to the present. Say that the due date is December 1 and you have about three months to write the essay. Schedule November 20 as your targeted completion date, plan what you want to get done by November 1, and then list what you want to get done by October 1. To help you plan your time, many schools have online assignment planners. They will help get you organized and send you email reminders to keep you on schedule. Check out what tools are available on your school's library website.

Generate ideas for a topic

Brainstorm with a group. There's no need to create in isolation. Forget the myth of the lonely, frustrated artist hashing out his ideas alone in a dimly lit Paris café. You can harness the energy and the natural creative power of a group to assist you. For ideas about ways to brainstorm, see Chapter 7: Thinking.

Speak it. To get ideas flowing, start talking. Admit your confusion or lack of a clear idea. Then just speak. By putting your thoughts into words, you'll start thinking more clearly. To paraphrase novelist E. M. Forster, "'Speak before you think' is creation's motto." (Wurman, Leifer, & Sume, 2001).

Use free writing. Free writing, a technique championed by writing teacher Peter Elbow (1981), sends a depth probe into your creative mind. This is one way to bypass your internal censors, those little voices in your head that constantly say, "That sentence wasn't very good. Why don't you stop this before you get hurt?"

There's only one rule in free writing: Write without stopping. Set a time limit—say, 10 minutes—and keep your pencil in motion or your fingers dancing across the keyboard the whole time.

Give yourself permission to keep writing. Ignore the urge to stop and rewrite, even if you think what you've written isn't very good. There's no need to worry about spelling, punctuation, or grammar. It's OK if you stray from the initial subject. Just keep writing and let the ideas flow. Experiment with free writing as soon as your instructor assigns an essay.

Refine initial ideas

Select a topic and working title. It's easy to put off writing if you have a hard time choosing a topic. However, it is almost impossible to make a wrong choice at this stage. Just choose any subject. You can choose again later.

Using your instructor's guidelines for the essay or speech, write down a list of topics that interest you. Write as many of these as you can think of in two minutes. Then choose one. If you can't decide, use scissors to cut your list into single items, put them in a box, and pull one out. To avoid getting stuck on this step, set a precise timeline: "I will choose a topic by 4:00 p.m. on Wednesday."

The most common pitfall is selecting a topic that's too broad. "Louis Riel" is not a useful topic for your Canadian history essay. Instead, consider "Louis Riel's activities during the Northwest Rebellion." Your topic statement can function as a working title.

Write a thesis statement. Clarify what you want to say by summarizing it in one concise sentence. This sentence, called a thesis statement, refines your working title. It also helps in making a preliminary outline.

You might write a thesis statement such as "Louis Riel's activities as leader of the Métis in the Northwest Rebellion did not justify his execution for treason." A statement that's clear and to the point can make your essay easier to write. Remember, you can always rewrite your thesis statement as you learn more about your topic.

A thesis statement is different from a topic statement. Like newspaper headlines, a thesis statement makes an assertion or describes an action. It is expressed in a complete sentence, including a verb. "Diversity" is a topic. "Cultural diversity is valuable" is a thesis statement.

Consider your purpose

Effective writing flows from a purpose. Discuss the purpose of your assignment with your instructor. Also think about how you'd like your reader or listener to respond after considering your ideas. Do you want him to think differently, to feel differently, or to take a certain action?

Your writing strategy is greatly affected by how you answer these questions. If you want someone to think differently, make your writing clear and logical. Support your assertions with evidence. If you want someone to feel differently, consider crafting a story. Write about a character your audience can empathize with, and tell how he resolves a problem that they can relate to. And if your purpose is to move the reader into action, explain exactly what steps to take and offer solid benefits for doing so.

To clarify your purpose, state it in one sentence. For example, "The purpose of this essay is to define the term *success* in such a clear and convincing way that I win a scholarship from a college."

Do initial research

At this stage, the objective of your research is not to uncover specific facts about your topic. That comes later. First, you want to gain an overview of the subject. Discover the structure of your topic—its major divisions and branches. Say that you want to persuade the reader to vote for a certain candidate. You must first learn enough about this person to summarize his background and state his positions on key issues.

Outline

An outline is a kind of map. When you follow a map, you avoid getting lost. Likewise, an outline keeps you from wandering off the topic.

To start an outline, consider using the outlining features in your word processing software or you can do a search of the Internet for free outlining tools—there are lots out there. These programs allow you to record and rearrange ideas on the screen, much the way you'd write on and shuffle index cards.

Or you could gather a stack of index cards and brainstorm ideas you want to include in your essay. Write one phrase or sentence per card.

Then experiment with the cards. Group them into separate stacks, each stack representing one major category. After that, arrange the stacks in order. Finally, arrange the cards within each stack in a logical order. Rearrange them until you discover an organization that you like.

After you write the first draft of your outline, test it. Make sure that each word relates directly to your statement of purpose.

Do in-depth research

You can find information about research skills in Chapter 4: Reading and in Chapter 5: Notes. Here are some more suggestions.

You can use a computer outlining or database program to record your research. There are a number of mind mapping tools that allow you to develop your essay outline and also are useful for doing collaborative projects. Go on the Internet and search for mind mapping tools—there is lots out there to choose from and many of them are free or low cost. Most word processing packages also include features that can be used for note-taking.

Keeping track of references can also be very time consuming. Software like EndNote, RefWorks, or Zotero are great tools for organizing your references. RefWorks allows you to import references directly from databases, and it will adapt to whatever style guide you need to use for your essay such APA or MLA. As RefWorks is a Web-based tool, you can access it from anywhere you are once you have an account. It also allows you to share your references with other members of your team if you're working on a group project. Check out which e-tools your school subscribes to at the library or your writing or student success centre.

If a computer is not available, simple index cards work wonders when conducting research. Just write down one idea per card. This makes it easy to organize—and reorganize—your ideas. Organizing research cards as you create them saves time. Keep source cards separate from information cards and maintain general categories.

You can also save time in two other ways. First, copy all of the information correctly. If you haven't collected the references using a program like RefWorks, then include the source code and page number on information cards. Use the same format for all of your cards.

Sense the time to begin writing

A common mistake that beginning writers make is to hold their noses, close their eyes, and jump into the writing process with both feet first—and few facts. Avoid this temptation by gathering more information than you think you can use.

You can begin writing even before your research is complete. The act of writing creates ideas and reveals areas where more research is needed.

Finding a natural place to begin is one signal to start writing. This is not to say that the skies will suddenly open up and your completed essay will appear before your eyes. You might instead get a strong sense of how to write just one small section of your essay or speech. When this happens, write.

STUDENT VOICES

I used to have a really hard time starting my essays, but then I found out that if I started in the middle, I could write more freely. At the end of my essay I can go back and write the introductory paragraph and organize the essay. Getting rid of writer's block was a huge load off my shoulders.

—PAT WATERMEN

PHASE 2: Writing a first draft

If you've planned your writing project and completed your research, you've already done much of the hard work. Now you can relax into writing your first draft.

TO CREATE YOUR draft, gather your notes and arrange them to follow your outline. Then write about the ideas in your notes. Write in paragraphs, one idea per paragraph. If you have organized your notes logically, related facts will appear close to each other. As you complete this task, keep the following suggestions in mind.

Remember that the first draft is not for keeps

You can save quality for later, when you revise. Your goal at this point is simply to generate lots of material.

Don't worry about grammar, punctuation, or spelling as you write your first draft. Write as if you were explaining the subject to a friend. The purpose of

FIRST DRAFT

© magicoven/Shutterstock

a first draft is merely to have something to work with—period. For most of us, that's a heck of a lot better than facing a blank page. You will revise this rough draft several times, so don't be concerned if it seems rough or choppy.

Write freely

Many writers prefer to get their first draft down quickly. Their advice is just to keep writing, much as in free writing. You can pause occasionally to glance at your notes and outline. The idea is to avoid stopping to edit your work. You can save that for the next step.

Be yourself

Let go of the urge to sound "official" or "scholarly," and write in a natural voice instead. Address your thoughts not to the teacher but to an intelligent student or someone you care about. Visualize this person and choose the three or four most important things you'd say to him about the topic. This helps you avoid the temptation to write merely to impress.

The flip side of this point is that we can't really write the way we speak. Slang expressions used in everyday speech are not appropriate in academic writing.

Let your inner writer take over

There might be times when ideas come to you spontaneously—when thoughts flow from your head to your hand without conscious effort. This is a "natural high," similar to states that accomplished athletes, musicians, and artists have described. Often, those moments come just after a period of feeling stuck. Welcome getting stuck. A breakthrough is not far behind.

Ease into it

Some people find that it works well to forget the word *writing*. Instead, they ease into the task with activities that help generate ideas. You can free-associate, cluster, meditate, daydream, doodle, draw diagrams, visualize the event you want to describe, talk into a voice recorder—anything that gets you started.

Make writing a habit

The word *inspiration* is not in the working vocabulary for many professional writers. Instead of waiting for inspiration to strike, they simply make a habit of writing at a certain time each day. You can use the same strategy. Schedule a block of time to write your first draft. The very act of writing can breed inspiration.

Respect your deep mind

Part of the process of writing takes place outside our awareness. There's nothing mysterious about this. Many people report that ideas come to them while they're doing something totally unrelated to writing. Often this happens after they've been grappling with a question and have reached a point where they feel stuck. It's like the composer who said, "There I was, sitting and eating a sandwich, and all of a sudden this tune pops into my head." You can trust your deep mind. It's writing while you eat, sleep, and brush your teeth.

Get physical

Writing is physical, like running or playing tennis. You can move your body in ways that are in tune with the flow of your ideas. While working on the first draft, take breaks. Go for a walk. Speak or sing your ideas out loud. From time to time, practise relaxation techniques and breathe deeply.

Use affirmations and visualizations

Write with the idea that the finished essay or speech is inside you, waiting to be released. Affirmations and visualizations can help you with this. Imagine what your finished essay will look like. Construct a detailed mental picture of the title page and major sections. See a clean, typed copy, and speculate how it will feel to hold the essay and flip through the pages. Visualize the reaction of audience members after you've given your speech.

Then support your writing by sprinkling your self-talk with statements that affirm your abilities. For example: "I express myself clearly and persuasively." "I am using an effective process to write my essay." "I will be pleased with the results."

STUDENT VOICES

Education is a process of learning to read, write, and compute, and the result of this process is a Master Student who is capable of solving problems and who is able to think independently. What is important is not information itself, but knowing how to use that information to function in life. Furthermore, study skills and successful endeavours improve with repetition in the same way skills in sports improve with practice.

—BELLE ROYLES

PHASE 3: Revising your draft

SCHEDULE TIME FOR rewrites before you begin, and schedule at least one day in between revisions so that you can let the material sit. On Tuesday night, you might think your writing sings the song of beautiful language. On Wednesday, you will see that those same words, such as the phrase "sings the song of beautiful language," belong in the trash basket.

Ideally, a student will revise an essay two or three times, make a clean copy of those revisions, then let the last revised draft sit for at least three or four days. The brain needs that much time to disengage itself from the project. Obvious grammatical mistakes, awkward constructions, and lapses in logic are hidden from us when we are in the middle of the creative process. Give yourself time to step back, and then go over the essay one last time before starting the third phase of the writing process.

There's a difference in pace between writing a first draft and revising it. Keep in mind the saying "Write in haste, revise at leisure." When you edit and revise, slow down and take a microscope to your work. One guideline is to allow 50 percent of writing time for planning, research, and writing the first draft. Then give the remaining 50 percent to revising.

An effective way to revise your essay is to read it out loud. The eyes tend to fill in the blanks in our own writing. The combination of voice and ears forces us to pay attention to the details.

Another technique is to have a friend look over your essay. This is never a substitute for your own review, but a friend can often see mistakes you miss. Remember, when other people criticize or review your work, they're not attacking you. They're just commenting on your essay. With a little practice, you can actually learn to welcome feedback.

Reading aloud and having a friend comment on your essay are techniques that can help you in each step of rewriting explained below.

Cut

Look for excess baggage. Avoid at all costs and at all times the really, really terrible mistake of using way too many unnecessary words, a mistake that some student writers often make when they sit down to write essays for the various courses in which they participate at the fine institutions of higher learning that they are fortunate enough to attend. (Example: The previous sentence could be edited to "Avoid unnecessary words.")

Approach your rough draft as if it were a chunk of granite from which you will chisel the final product.

In the end, much of your first draft will be lying on the floor. What is left will be the clean, clear, polished product. Sometimes the revisions are painful. Sooner or later, every writer invents a phrase that is truly clever but makes no contribution to the purpose of the essay. Grit your teeth and let it go.

Note: For maximum efficiency, make the larger cuts first—sections, chapters, pages. Then go for the smaller cuts—paragraphs, sentences, phrases, words.

Keep in mind that cutting a passage means just for now, for this essay, for this assignment. You might want to keep a file of deleted writings to save for future use.

Paste

In deleting passages, you've probably removed some of the original transitions and connecting ideas from your draft. The next task is to rearrange what's left of your essay or speech so that it flows logically. Look for consistency within paragraphs and for transitions from paragraph to paragraph and section to section.

If your draft doesn't hang together, reorder your ideas. One of the best things about using a computer to edit your drafts is that it is simple to move paragraphs around. If you are afraid of losing some great ideas, you can use the track changes function in your word processing system to mark your revisions in colour until you decide what will stay and what will go. Most word processing programs have an audio guide to walk you through using this function.

Fix

Now it's time to look at individual words and phrases.

In general, rely on nouns and verbs. Using too many adjectives and adverbs weakens your message and adds unnecessary bulk to your writing. Write about the details and be specific. Also, use the active rather than the passive voice.

Instead of writing in the passive voice:
A project was initiated.
You can use the active voice:
The research team began a project.

Whenever possible, talk about things that hold your interest. Include your personal experiences and start with a bang! Consider this introduction to a speech on the subject of world hunger:

I'm very honoured to be here with you today. I intend to talk about malnutrition and starvation. First, I want to outline the extent of these problems, then I will discuss some basic assumptions concerning world hunger, and finally I will propose some solutions.

You can almost hear the snores from the audience. Following is a rewrite:

More people have died from hunger in the past five years than have been killed in all of the wars, revolutions, and murders in the past 150 years. Yet there is enough food to go around. I'm honoured to be here with you today to discuss solutions to this problem.

Though some members of an audience begin to drift during any speech, most people pay attention for at least the first few seconds. Your main points should be highlighted in the beginning sentences of your speech. Draft your introduction and then come back to it after you've written the rest of your speech. In the process of creating the main body and conclusion, your thoughts about the purpose and main points of your speech might change. You might even want to write the introduction last.

Write the main body. The main body of your speech is the content, which accounts for 70 to 90 percent of most speeches. In the main body, you develop your ideas in much the same way that you develop a written essay.

In speeches, transitions are especially important. Give your audience a signal when you change points, using meaningful pauses and verbal emphasis as well as transitional phrases: "On the other hand, until the public realizes what is happening to children in these countries. . . ." or "The second reason hunger persists is. . . ."

In long speeches, recap from time to time and preview what's to come. Use facts, descriptions, expert opinions, and statistics to hold your audience's attention.

Write the conclusion. At the end of the speech, summarize your points and draw your conclusion. You started with a bang; now finish with drama. The first and last parts of a speech are the most important. Make it clear to your audience when you've reached the end. Avoid endings such as "This is the end of my speech." A simple standby is "So in conclusion, I want to reiterate three points: First. . . ." When you are finished, stop talking.

Create speaking notes. Some professional speakers recommend writing out your speech in full, then putting key words or main points on a few index cards. Number the cards so that if you drop them, you can put

them in order again quickly. As you finish the information on each card, move it to the back of the pile. Write information clearly and in letters large enough to be seen from a distance.

The disadvantage of the index card system is that it involves card shuffling. Some speakers prefer to use standard outlined notes. You can include your speaking points within PowerPoint® and this is also a simple way to keep track of what slide you are on. Again, put notes in a large font so you can read your notes from a distance. Another option is mindmapping. Even an hour-long speech can be mapped on one sheet of paper. You can also use memory techniques to memorize the outline of your speech.

Create supporting visuals. Presentations often include visuals such as slides created with presentation software such as PowerPoint® or Keynote®. These visuals can reinforce your main points and help your audience understand how your presentation is organized. Remember to include your reference sources in your presentation. This includes your sources of both visual and textual material.

Use visuals to *complement* rather than *replace* your speaking. If you use too many visuals—or visuals that are too complex—your audience might focus on them and forget about you. To avoid this fate:

- Use fewer visuals rather than more. Save them for illustrations, photos, charts, and concepts that are hard to express in words. For a 15-minute presentation, a total of 5 to 10 slides is enough.

- Limit the amount of text on each visual. Stick to key words presented in short sentences or phrases, and in bulleted or numbered lists.

- Use a consistent set of plain fonts that are large enough for all audience members to see.

- Stick with a simple, coherent colour scheme. Use light-coloured text on a dark background, or dark text on a light background.

Overcome your fear of public speaking

You may not be able to eliminate fear of public speaking entirely, but you can take steps to reduce and manage it.

Prepare thoroughly. Research your topic thoroughly. Knowing your topic inside and out can create a baseline of confidence. To make a strong start, memorize the first four sentences that you plan to deliver, and practise them many times. Delivering them flawlessly when you're in front of an audience can build your confidence for the rest of your speech.

Accept your physical sensations. You've probably experienced physical sensations that are commonly associated with stage fright: dry mouth, a pounding

8

You might create a speech with the aim of changing the way your audience thinks or feels about a topic. Think critically about the complexity of this task. Consider your audience's *attitude system*, which has three key elements:

- *Attitudes* involve feelings of approval or disapproval.
- *Beliefs* reflect what people know—or think they know—about a topic.
- *Values* are broad, enduring principles that guide our behaviours.

Of these three elements, values are often the most resistant to change. In addition, people generally seek consistency in their attitudes, beliefs, and values.

This situation suggests a strategy for persuasion. Instead of trying to change your audience's values, see if you can persuade your audience members that one of their attitudes or beliefs *contradicts* their values. Then you can present a new attitude or belief that restores consistency to their attitude system.

Say that you are preparing to speak to a politically conservative audience about a gun registry system managed by the federal government. This proposal is not always popular with conservatives. However, many members of this political group also value law and order legislation. You could create a speech arguing that the gun control registry helps to keep Canadians safe. To analyze the audience for your next speech, create a list of attitudes, beliefs, and values to consider. To organize your thinking, fill in the following chart.

Audience attitudes toward your topic	Audience beliefs about your topic

---

heart, sweaty hands, muscle jitters, shortness of breath, and a shaky voice. One immediate way to deal with such sensations is to simply notice them. Tell yourself, "Yes, my hands are clammy. Yes, my stomach is upset. Also, my face feels numb." Trying to deny or ignore such facts can increase your fear. When you fully accept sensations, however, they start to lose power.

Focus on content, not delivery. Michael Motley, a professor at the University of California–Davis, distinguishes between two orientations to speaking. People with a ***performance orientation*** believe that the speaker must captivate the audience by using formal techniques that differ from normal conversation. In contrast, speakers with a ***communication orientation*** see public speaking simply as an extension of one-to-one conversation. The goal is not to perform but to communicate your ideas to an audience in the same ways that you would explain them to a friend.

Adopting a communication orientation can reduce your fear of public speaking. Instead of thinking about yourself, focus on your message. Your audiences are more interested in *what* you have to say than *how* you say it. Forget about giving a "speech." Just give people valuable ideas and information that they can use.

Practise your presentation

The key to successful public speaking is practice.

Use your "speaker's voice." When you practise, do so in a loud voice. Your voice sounds different when you talk loudly, and this can be unnerving. Get used to it early on.

Practise in the room in which you will deliver your speech. Hear what your voice sounds like over a sound system. If you can't practise your speech in the actual room, at least visit the site ahead of time. Also make sure that the materials you will need for your speech, such as a computer and screen, will be available when you want them.

Make a recording. Many schools have digital recording equipment available for student use. Use it while you practise, then view the finished recording to evaluate your presentation.

Listen for repeated phrases. Examples include *you know, kind of, really,* plus any little *uh*'s, *umm*'s, and *ah*'s. To get rid of these, tell yourself that you intend to notice every time they pop up in your daily speech. When you hear them, remind yourself that you don't use those words anymore.

Keep practising until you know your material inside and out. Avoid speaking word for word, as if you were reading a script. When you know your material well, you can deliver it in a natural way. Practise your presentation until you could deliver it in your sleep, then run through it a few more times.

Deliver your presentation

Before you begin, get the audience's attention. If people are still filing into the room or adjusting their seats, they're not ready to listen. Begin when all eyes are on you.

Making the grade in group presentations

When preparing group presentations, you can use three strategies for making a memorable impression.

Get organized. As soon as you get the assignment, select a group leader and exchange contact information. Schedule specific times and places for planning, researching, writing, and practising your presentation.

At your first meeting, write a to-do list including all of the tasks involved in completing the assignment. Distribute tasks fairly, paying attention to the strengths of individuals in your group. For example, some people excel at brainstorming while others prefer researching.

As you get organized, remember how your presentation will be evaluated. If the instructor doesn't give marking criteria, create your own.

One powerful way to get started is to define clearly the topic and thesis, or main point, of your presentation. Then, support your thesis by looking for the most powerful facts, quotations, and anecdotes you can find.

Get coordinated. Coordinate your presentation so that you have transitions between individual speakers. Practise making those transitions smooth.

Also practise using visuals such as flipcharts, posters, or presentation software. To give visuals their full impact, make them appropriate for the room where you will present. Make sure that text is large enough to be seen from the back of the room.

Get cooperation. Presentations that get top scores take teamwork and planning—not egos. Communicate with group members in an open and sensitive way. Contribute your ideas and be responsive to the viewpoints of other members. When you do, your group is on the way to scoring well.

 For more strategies on overcoming communication apprehension check online @
www.bams5ce.nelson.com

8

COMMUNICATING

Deal with stage fright by noticing it. Use the Power Process: "Love your problems." Tell yourself, "Yes, my hands are clammy. I notice that my stomach is slightly upset. My face feels numb." Allow these symptoms to exist. Experience them fully. When you do, they often become less persistent. Notice all of your thoughts and feelings, and then gently release them.

Project your voice. When you speak, talk loudly enough to be heard. Avoid leaning over your notes or the podium.

Maintain eye contact. When you look at people, they become less frightening. Remember, too, that it is easier for the audience to listen to someone when that person is looking at them. Find a few friendly faces around the room and imagine that you are talking to each person individually.

Notice your non-verbal communication. Only a fraction of our communication is verbal. Be aware of what your body is telling your audience. Contrived or staged gestures will look dishonest. Be natural. If you don't know what to do with your hands, notice that. Then don't do anything with them.

Notice the time. You can increase the impact of your words by keeping track of the time during your speech. Better to end early than run late. The conclusion of your speech is what is likely to be remembered, and you might lose this impact if people are looking at the clock.

Pause when appropriate. Beginners sometimes feel that they have to fill every moment with the sound of their voices. Release that expectation. Give your listeners a chance to make notes and absorb what you say.

Have fun. One way to feel at ease while speaking is to look at your audience and imagine everyone dressed as clowns. Chances are that if you lighten up and enjoy your presentation, so will they.

Reflect on your presentation

Reflect upon and review your performance. Did you finish on time? Did you cover all of the points you intended to cover? Was the audience attentive? Did you handle any nervousness effectively?

Welcome evaluation from others. Most of us find it difficult to hear criticism about our speaking. Be aware of resisting such criticism and then let go of your resistance. Listening to feedback will increase your skill. ✳

8

COMMUNICATING

EMPLOY YOUR WORD

When you give your word, you are creating—literally. The person you are is, for the most part, a result of the agreements you make. Others know who you are by your words and your commitments. And you can learn who you are by observing which commitments you choose to keep and which ones you choose to avoid.

Relationships are built on agreements. When we break a promise to be faithful to a spouse, to help a friend move to a new apartment, or to pay a bill on time, relationships are strained.

The words we use to make agreements can be placed onto several different levels. We can think of each level as one rung on a ladder—the ladder of powerful speaking. As we move up the ladder, our speaking becomes more effective.

The lowest rung on the ladder is *obligation*. Words used at this level include *I should, he ought to, someone had better,*

they need to, I must, and *I had to.* Speaking this way implies that something other than ourselves is in control of our lives. When we live at the level of obligation, we speak as if we are victims.

The next rung up is *possibility*. At this level, we examine new options. We play with new ideas, possible solutions, and alternative courses of action. As we do, we learn that we can make choices that dramatically affect the quality of our lives. We are not the victims of circumstance. Phrases that signal this level include *I might, I could, I'll consider, I hope to,* and *maybe.*

From possibility, we can move up to *preference*. Here we begin the process of choice. The words *I prefer* signal that we're moving toward one set of possibilities over another, perhaps setting the stage for eventual action.

Above preference is a rung called *passion*. Again, certain words signal this level:

I want to, I'm really excited to do that, and *I can't wait.*

Action comes with the next rung—*planning.* When people use phrases such as *I intend to, my goal is to, I plan to,* and *I'll try like mad to,* they're at the level of planning. The Intention Statements you write in this book are examples of planning.

The highest rung on the ladder is *promising.* This is where the power of your word really comes into play. At this level, it's common to use phrases such as these: *I will, I promise to, I am committed,* and *you can count on it.* Promising is where we bridge from possibility and planning to action. Promising brings with it all of the rewards of employing your word.

(WWW) Find more ways online to employ your words @
www.bams5ce.nelson.com

© Pakhnyushcha/Shutterstock

Put It to **WORK**

You can use strategies you learn in *Becoming a Master Student* to succeed at work. To discover ways in which your new communication skills can transfer to your career, reflect on the following case study.

© Sanna Lindberg/PhotoAlto Agency RF Collections/Getty Images

Mark Hyland earned a two-year college diploma in dental hygiene and then completed a B.A. in business administration. Soon after graduating, he moved back to his hometown and went to work as an office manager for his family dentist.

Mark welcomed the chance to apply the skills he'd gained in school. He ordered supplies, managed the payroll, handled the day-to-day accounting chores, and filed tax returns for the business.

Everyone in the dental office admitted that Mark's skills in these areas were superb. His communication skills were another matter, though. Several long-term patients complained that Mark's manner was condescending—even harsh—during casual conversations at the office. One day, the dentist who hired Mark overheard him talking to a patient.

"I just happened to glance at your records and noticed that you've got a lot of plaque on your upper teeth," said Mark. "Do you ever floss?"

The patient tried to make light of the situation. "Oh well," she said, "we all have our vices, and ...."

"Yeah, but it's your teeth we're talking about here," Mark said, interrupting her. "They're really stained, too, from drinking too much coffee."

The dentist winced. He feared he was about to lose a valued patient. However, he'd known Mark for years and counted his parents as friends. He wanted to meet with Mark and give him feedback, yet the dentist knew that this conversation would be awkward for both of them. He found this meeting an easy thing to put off.

Review the suggestions given in this chapter for creating "I" messages. Then write an "I" message that the dentist could use to express his concerns with Mark.

_____

_____

_____

List at least two other suggestions for managing conflict that the dentist could use.

_____

_____

_____

Finally, list two suggestions for Mark to keep in mind when talking to patients.

_____

_____

_____

In addition, consider the following strategies for communicating effectively during your first crucial year as a new employee:

- Use memory techniques to learn coworkers' names quickly.
- Be honest when you don't understand directions—and willing to ask questions.
- Be open to feedback about your performance—and be willing to change your behaviour on the basis of that feedback.
- Be willing to complete the mundane tasks that are part of almost every job—understand what it means to "pay your dues" in a constructive way.
- To gain credibility in your organization, get involved in a high-profile project, and then perform well.
- Each day, look for a simple way to demonstrate a positive attitude and strong work ethic.

QUIZ

Name_____ Date____/____/____

1. What type of tools can you use to work on group assignments together?

2. One suggested guideline for non-verbal listening is to respond frequently to the speaker. True or False? Explain your answer.

3. The suggested techniques for verbal listening include which of the following?
   (a) Parrot exactly what another person says.
   (b) Pay attention to the speaker's words and not the emotions behind the words.
   (c) Always put your own concerns aside in order to listen attentively.
   (d) Look for the requests hidden in complaints.

4. Reword the following complaint as a request: "You always interrupt when I talk!"

5. List the five parts of an "I" message (the five ways to say "I").

6. The fact that a disagreement is getting worse means that there's little hope for conflict resolution. True or False? Explain your answer.

7. Which of the following is an effective thesis statement? Explain your answer.
   (a) Two types of thinking.
   (b) Critical thinking and creative thinking go hand in hand.
   (c) The relationship between critical thinking and creative thinking.

8. Define *plagiarism* and explain ways to avoid it.

9. Describe at least three techniques for practising and delivering a speech.

10. What characteristic distinguishes the top five rungs of the ladder of powerful speaking from the bottom rung?

Skills **SNAPSHOT**

By now, you've had a chance to read this chapter and apply some of the suggestions it includes. Take a few minutes to revisit your responses to the "Communicating" section of the Discovery Wheel exercise on page 37. Then complete the following sentences.

The technique that has made the biggest difference in my skill at listening is . . .

When I hear an accomplished public speaker, the skill that I notice first and most admire is . . .

When I'm effective at managing conflict, I am remembering to . . .

I'll know that I've reached a new level of mastery with my communication skills when . . .

To reach that level of mastery, the most important thing I can do next is to . . .

MASTER STUDENT Profile

MCMULLAN CO/SIPA/Photoshot

Neil Pasricha
. . . is positive

Neil Pasricha is an author whose book *The Book of Awesome* became an international bestseller. His blog site has been named one of *PC Magazine's* Top 100 Internet sites. At 8:00 a.m. in a downtown Tim Hortons, Neil Pasricha is already busy at his laptop, writing blog entry No. 535, describing how stretching as you wake up is awesome.

 Find more biographical information about Neil Pasricha at the Master Student Hall of Fame @

www.bams5ce.nelson.com

The little joys in life—and we do mean little: bakery air, popping bubble wrap, a really cold glass of water on a hot day—have preoccupied Pasricha, a Harvard MBA and former comedy writer, since he started the blog 1000awesomethings.com in 2008 to cheer himself up during a bleak period.

Boy, did it ever work. A self-described nerd with an office job in Mississauga, he won two Webby awards, the Oscars of the Internet, for his blog last year and on April 20 his *The Book of Awesome* comes out with a good shot at the bestseller list.

His blog—some entries are nostalgic, reflective, but always positive—now gets about 40,000 visits a day, more than 11 million hits in total. His email box is regularly packed with readers' messages, spilling out their woes and thanking him for lifting their spirits. "You made me realize the sun is still shining," wrote one woman.

"The response has been overwhelming," says Pasricha, 30. "I feel like the Pied Piper of happiness."

At Indigo Books and Music, Bahram Olfati, vice-president of adult trade, was skeptical at first about Pasricha's take on the subject. "That's my nature. C'mon, it's not so easy to be happy," says Olfati. Then he read it. "Staying in the shower an extra five minutes does make me happy. It is the little things," he laughs.

"Millions of blogs don't get picked up. The ones that do," says Olfati, "genuinely connect with people's feelings. The writers' personalities come through.

They're people you could easily become friends with."

"Walking here, as I approached the intersections, the red hand kept turning to walk without me breaking stride," says Pasricha, who lives downtown. "That's awesome. It was like the universe knew I was coming."

He extracts scraps of paper from his pocket, all scribbled with germs of ideas, and rapidly scrolls through his iPhone, revealing a stream of jotted-down thoughts.

"I'm really hyper, even before my coffee. Can you tell?"

In the universe of Pasricha, he was the kid with the thick Coke-bottle glasses growing up in Whitby. "I tried and quit so many sports." He writes about that too in his blog although he finds the upside of being face-smacked with a hard-kicked soccer ball (No. 893, Orange slices at half time). He remembers being a happy-go-lucky kid, friends with everyone, even the bullies.

At Queen's University, he studied commerce but loved writing for *Golden Words,* the school humour newspaper. He'd found his calling: comedy writer. But it became draining very quickly. "I realized this could never be my full time thing."

So he put on a business suit, did a marketing stint at Procter & Gamble, Toronto; ran a Quiznos franchise in Whitby; and took off for Harvard Business School. Somewhere in there, he got married.

And then Pasricha hit what he calls his "gloom and doom phase." His marriage was rocky, and his best friend emotionally unhinged. So what did he do?

"I decided I needed to look on the bright side of life." He went to his computer and started to write about a thousand—changed at the last second from a million—awesome things. No. 1000: Broccoflower, ". . . bizarre misfit child from two of nature's most hideous vegetables."

Followed soon by "The last crummy triangle in a bag of potato chips," "Getting grass stains," "Locking people out of the car and pretending to drive away," each entry a short essay. "Slowly I was finding myself in the posts," he explains.

So when, in January 2009, his wife said she no longer loved him, he wept all weekend and then posted No. 854, Crying, why letting the big, wet tears rain down is great.

His manner is more serious, more intense now. "I think you can choose to be happy," he says, leaning forward. "It's why 11 million people have visited the site. It's why people send me message after message, thanking me, saying, 'I needed this.'"

Has he always been such a positive thinker?

"You can call it that," he says flatly. "I think these are things we all think about. You go through six green lights in a row, you think 'awesome'. We all love snow days. They're truisms. I'm just the one saying, let's focus on the positive, we need it."

Outside, the sky is a cloudless blue, the temperature unseasonably warm, the cross sign already flashing walk. "Have a great weekend," shouts Pasricha, the guru of small joys, melding into the crowd.

Source: White, Nancy J. (April 14 2010). "The 'awesome' blog is a huge hit: 40,000 Internet visits a day." Retrieved July 5, 2011 from http://www .thestar.com/printarticle/795405. Reprinted with permission of Torstar Syndication Services.

9 Diversity

Master Student Map

as you read, ask yourself

what if . . .

I could create positive relationships with people from any culture?

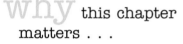

why this chapter matters . . .

You're likely to learn and work with people from many different cultures.

how

you can use this chapter . . .

- Study effectively with people from many different cultures.
- Gain skills to succeed in a multicultural workforce.
- Choose conversations that promote your success.

what is included . . .

- Waking up to diversity   293
- Diversity is real—and valuable   295
- Building relationships across cultures   297
- Overcome stereotypes with critical thinking   302
- Students with disabilities: Know your rights   303
- Dealing with sexism and sexual harassment   305
- Leadership in a diverse world   307
- Power Process: Choose your conversations and your community   313
- Master Student Profile: Trey Anthony   317

MASTER STUDENTS in *action*

You have to fill in bubbles for your race and I remember raising my hand and asking the teacher what I should put because I wasn't sure (it said to only fill in one) . . . I just said, "My father is black and my mother is white; what should I put?" She leaned over, nodded knowingly, and just tapped the Black option. . . . It was the first time I realized that despite how I might identify myself, that might not be how others perceive me.

—DANIELLA CICCONE

Waking up to diversity

THOSE OF US who can study, work, and live with people from other cultures, economic classes, and races can enjoy more success at school, on the job, and in our neighbourhood communities. Sharing in this success means learning new ways to think, speak, and act. Learning about diversity opens up a myriad of possibilities—an education in itself. At first, this can seem frightening, frustrating, or even painful. It can also be exciting, enriching, and affirming.

Canada is a mosaic of people from many different cultures and ethnicities. We currently have the highest rate of immigration among developed countries (Friesen, 2010). Recent Statistics Canada reports (2010) suggest that by 2031 over 25 percent of the population will be foreign born with about half of this population being born in Asia. By that time, nearly half of Canadians under 15 will be foreign born themselves or have a parent who was not born in Canada. Immigrants aren't expected to assimilate when they move to Canada, but rather to add their cultures into the mix.

According to a recent United Nations Human Development Report, Toronto has the second largest proportion of foreign-born residents of any city in the world. Almost half the people who live in Toronto (44 percent) were born outside Canada, with more than 90 different ethnic groups (Conway-Smith, 2004). Over 75 percent of new immigrants who arrived in Canada between 2001 and 2006 were from visible minorities (Statistics Canada, 2008). In addition, by 2031 it is also forecast that more than 70 percent of people who are visible minorities will live in either Montréal, Toronto or Vancouver (Statistics Canada, 2010). The largest visible minority group from Vancouver will be Chinese in origin (23 percent of the population) whereas in Toronto the biggest group will be South Asian (24 percent). Even outside of these cities the civic populations are changing; over 30 percent of the populations of cities such as Abbotsford, Calgary, Ottawa, and Windsor are expected to be visible minorities by 2031.

Not only in Canada but all over the globe, the cultures of the world meet daily through a growing world economy and a global network of computers. Discussions of diversity often focus on characteristics commonly linked to race—differences in skin tone, facial features, and hair texture. But grouping people according to such differences is arbitrary. We could just as easily classify them on the basis of height, weight, foot size, fingernail length, or a hundred other physical traits.

In this chapter, the word *diversity* refers to differences of any type. From this perspective, diversity can be compared to an iceberg. Only the top of an iceberg is visible; most of it is hidden under water. Likewise, only a few aspects of diversity are visible, such as obvious differences in physical appearance, language, social and economic background, and behaviour. Much remains hidden from our awareness—different ideas about relationships, decision making, and problem solving; different assumptions about the meaning of love and duty, beauty and friendship, justice and injustice; and much more.

This chapter is titled "Diversity" because that term is widely accepted. You might gain more value from thinking about *cultural competence* instead. This term

Diversity in Canada

Did you know?
- Over 80 percent of Canadians live in urban areas (Statistics Canada, 2009).
- Over 20 percent of same sex couples live in Toronto (Statistics Canada, 2009).
- 10 percent of the student population of the University of Saskatchewan is Aboriginal in origin ("The Impact", 2011).
- Over 14 percent of Canadians have a physical disability with pain and mobility disabilities being the most common (Statistics Canada, 2011).
- 6 percent of the population of Nunavut say they have no religion, with the most common religion being the Anglican faith (Statistics Canada, 2001).
- By 2031 the proportion of Montréalers of Black or Arab origin will be almost equal (Statistics Canada, 2010).
- By 2031 the largest visible minority group in Canada will be South Asian (Statistics Canada, 2010).

reminds us that even in the most culturally sensitive environment, people can fail at understanding each other and working toward shared goals. *Cultural competence* refers to gaining skills in these areas and actively using those skills in daily life.

You'll learn the most by stepping outside your comfort zone and taking risks. Get involved in a study group or campus organization with people from different countries. Keep asking yourself, "What is the next action I could take to live and work more effectively in our global village?" The answers could change your life. ✷

journal entry 25

Discovery/Intention Statement

Commit to Create Value from This Chapter

Briefly describe an incident in which you felt excluded from a group because you differed in some way from the other people. This difference could be any kind, such as hair length, style of clothing, political affiliation, religion, skin colour, sexual orientation, age, gender, economic status, or accent.

I discovered that I . . .

_____

_____

_____

_____

_____

Now, think about the opposite scenario. Recall a time when you felt included in a group of people, even though the group was diverse. Describe this incident as well.

I discovered that I . . .

_____

_____

_____

_____

_____

_____

Finally, scan this chapter for ideas that could help you change situations like the first one you described above to an environment more like the second. List at least five ideas that you intend to explore in more detail, along with their associated page numbers.

Strategy   **Page number**

_____

_____

_____

_____

_____

_____

_____

_____

_____

_____

_____

_____

We have always lived with people of different races and cultures. Many of us come from families who immigrated to Canada just recently or one or two generations ago. The things we eat, the tools we use, and the words we speak are a cultural tapestry woven by many different peoples.

Diversity is real—and valuable

THINK ABOUT A common daily routine. A typical Canadian citizen awakens in a bed (an invention from the Near East). After dressing in clothes (often designed in Italy), she slices a banana (grown in Honduras) onto her bowl (made in China) of cereal, and brews coffee (shipped from Nicaragua). After breakfast, she reads the morning newspaper (printed by a process invented in Germany on paper, which was first made in China). She then puts on her iPod® (made from components manufactured in Japan, China, and Korea) and listens to music (possibly performed by a band from Cuba).

Multiculturalism refers to ethnic diversity—and many other kinds of diversity as well. As anthropologist Dorothy Lee (1959) reminds us, culture is simply one society's solutions to perennial human problems, such as how to worship, celebrate, resolve conflict, work, think, and learn. **Culture** is a set of learned behaviours— a broader concept than race, which refers to the biological makeup of people. From this standpoint, we can speak of the culture of large corporations or the culture of the fine arts. There are the cultures of men and women; heterosexual, homosexual, and bisexual people; and older and younger people. There are differences between urban and rural dwellers, between able-bodied people and those with disabilities, and between people from two-parent families, people from single-parent families, and people from same-sex families. There are social classes based on differences in standards of living. And diversity in religion is a factor, too. This can be especially difficult to accept, since many people identify strongly with their religious faith.

Multiculturalism refers to racial and ethnic diversity— and many other kinds of diversity as well.

People can differ in countless ways—race, gender, ethnic group, sexual orientation, and more. The suggestions offered in this chapter can help you respond effectively to the many kinds of diversity you'll encounter. Higher education can help reinforce an attitude of tolerance, open-mindedness, and respect for individual differences.

Discrimination is also real. The ability to live with diversity is now more critical than ever. Racism, sexism, homophobia, and other forms of discrimination still exist, even in educational settings. The Canadian Human Rights Commission investigates complaints of discrimination and fosters public understanding and adherence to the principles of the Human Rights Act.

Consider how you would respond to these situations:

- Members of a sociology class are debating the merits of social welfare in Canada. The instructor calls on a student from the Six Nations Reserve and says, "Tell us. What's the First Nations perspective on this issue anyway?" Here the student is being stereotyped as a spokesperson for her entire ethnic group.

- Students in a mass media communications class are learning to think critically about television programs. They're talking about a situation comedy set in an urban high school. "Man, they really whitewashed that show," says one student. "It's mostly about inner-city kids, but they didn't show anybody getting into

9

DIVERSITY

trouble, doing drugs, or joining gangs." The student's comment perpetuates common racial stereotypes.

■ On the first day of the term, students taking English composition enter a class taught by a professor from India. One of the students asks the professor, "Am I in the right class? Maybe there's been a mistake. I thought this was supposed to be an English class." The student assumed that only people with white skins are qualified to teach English courses.

Forrest Toms of Training Research and Development defines racism as "prejudice plus power"—the power to define reality, to enshrine one set of biases. The operating assumption behind racism is that differences mean deficits.

Higher education can help reinforce an attitude of tolerance, open-mindedness, and respect for individual differences.

When racism lives, we all lose—even those groups with social and political power. We lose the ability to make friends and to function effectively on teams. We crush human potential. People without the skills to bridge cultures are already at a disadvantage.

Higher education offers a chance to change this. Academic environments can become cultural laboratories—places where people of diverse races and cultures can meet in an atmosphere of tolerance. Students who create alliances outside their immediate group are preparing to succeed in both school and work.

Diversity is valuable. Synergy is the idea that the whole is more than the sum of its parts. Consider some examples: A symphony orchestra consists of many different instruments; when played together, their effect is multiplied many times. A football team has members with different specialties; when their talents are combined, they can win a league championship.

Diversity in a society offers another example of synergy. It takes no more energy to believe that differences enrich us than it does to believe that differences endanger us. Embracing diversity adds value to any organization and can be far more exciting than just meeting the minimum requirements for affirmative action.

Today we are waking up not only to the *fact* of diversity but also to the *value* of diversity. Biologists tell us that diversity of animal species benefits our ecology. The same idea applies to the human species. Through education, our goal can be to see that we are all part of a complex world—that our own culture is different from, not better than, others. Knowing this, we can stop saying, "This is the way to work, learn, relate to others, and view the world." Instead, we can say, "Here is the way I have been doing it. I would also like to see your way."

The fact of diversity also represents opportunity in the workplace. Understanding cultural differences—local and international—will help you to embrace others' viewpoints that can lead to profitable solutions. Organizations that are attuned to diversity are more likely to prosper in the global marketplace.

Accepting diversity does not mean ignoring the differences among cultures so that we all become the same. Instead, we can become more like a mosaic—a piece of art in which each element maintains its individuality and blends with others to form a harmonious whole.

The more you can embrace diversity, the more friends you can make in school and the better prepared you'll be for the workforce of the 21st century. If you plan to pursue a career in health care, for example, you can prepare to work with patients from many ethnic groups. If you choose to start a business, you can prepare to sell to customers from many demographic groups. And if you plan to teach, you can prepare to assist every student who walks into your classroom.

Learning to live with diversity is a process of returning to "beginner's mind"—a place where we question our biases and assumptions. This is a magical place, a place of new beginnings and options. It takes courage to dwell in beginner's mind—courage to go outside the confines of our own culture and world view. It can feel uncomfortable at first. Yet there are lasting rewards to gain. Research shows that students who interact more frequently with those who are different than themselves grow more in terms of interpersonal development and cognition than those who don't (Schreiner, 2010). You all have school in common, so use this opportunity to meet new people and explore other points of view.

As you read the following articles, look to yourself. This chapter aims to help you examine your own biases. With self-awareness, you can go beyond them. ✳

STUDENT VOICES

A master student tries on other people's skin, and it is not judgmental. We are all different and a master student accepts that diversity.

—LYNN LINEBERGER

9

DIVERSITY

> Communicating with people of other cultures is a learned skill—a habit. According to Stephen R. Covey (1989), author of *The Seven Habits of Highly Effective People*, a habit is the point at which desire, knowledge, and skill meet. Desire is about wanting to do something. Knowledge is understanding what to do. And skill is the ability to do it.

Building relationships across cultures

DESIRE, KNOWLEDGE, AND skill are equally important for bridging gaps in cultural understanding. This article speaks to the first two factors—*desire* and *knowledge*—and also provides suggestions for gaining *skill*.

Start with self-discovery

The first step to developing diversity skills is to learn about yourself and understand the lenses through which you see the world. One way to do this is to intentionally switch lenses—that is, to consciously perceive familiar events in a new way.

For example, think of a situation in your life that involved an emotionally charged conflict among several people. Now mentally put yourself inside the skin of another person in that conflict. Ask yourself, "How would I view this situation if I were that person?" You can also learn by asking, "What if I were a person of the opposite gender? Or if I were a member of a different racial or ethnic group? Or if I were older or younger?" Do this exercise consistently, and you'll discover that we live in a world of multiple realities. There are many different ways to interpret any event—and just as many ways to respond, given our individual differences.

Also reflect on how people can have experiences of privilege *and* prejudice. For example, someone might tell you that he's more likely to be promoted at work because he's white and male—*and* that he's been looked down upon because he lives in a trailer park.

See if you can recall incidents such as these from your own life. Think of times when you were favoured because of your gender, race, or age—and times when you were excluded or ridiculed based on one of those same characteristics. In doing this, you'll discover ways to identify with a wider range of people.

Learn about other cultures

Back up your desire with knowledge. People from different cultures read differently, write differently, think differently, eat differently, and learn differently than you. Knowing this, you can be more effective with your classmates, coworkers, and neighbours.

One key to understanding styles is to look for several possible interpretations of any behaviour. For example:

- Consider the hand signal that signifies *OK* to many Canadians—thumb and index finger forming a circle. In France, that signal denotes the number zero. In Japan, it is a symbol for money. And in Brazil, it is considered an obscene gesture.

- When Canadians see a speaker who puts her hands in her pockets, they seldom attribute any meaning to this behaviour. But in many countries—such as Germany, Indonesia, and Austria—this gesture is considered rude.

- During a conversation, you might prefer having a little distance between yourself and another person. But in Iran, people may often get so close to you that you can feel their breath (Miller, 1979).

- In much of Canadian culture you are supposed to look at individuals directly when you talk to them. However, this is not true of many Aboriginal peoples or people from many Asian cultures.

These examples could be extended to cover many areas—posture, physical contact, facial expressions, and more. And the various ways of interpreting these

9

DIVERSITY

behaviours are neither right nor wrong. They simply represent differing styles in making meaning out of what we see.

You might find yourself fascinated by the styles that make up a particular culture. Consider learning as much about that culture as possible. Immerse yourself in it. Read novels, see plays, go to concerts, listen to music, look at art, take courses, and learn the language.

Look for differences between individualist and collectivist cultures

Individualist cultures flourish in Canada, the United States and Western Europe. If your family has deep roots in one of these areas, you were probably raised to value personal fulfillment and personal success. You received recognition or rewards when you stood out from your peers by earning the highest grades in your class, scoring the most points during a basketball season, or demonstrating another form of individual achievement.

In contrast, collectivist cultures value cooperation over competition. Group progress is more important than individual success. Credit for an achievement is widely shared. If you were raised in such a culture, you probably place a high value on your family and were taught to respect your elders. Collectivist cultures dominate Asia, Africa, and Latin America.

In short, individualist cultures often emphasize "I." Collectivist cultures tend to emphasize "we." Forgetting about the differences between them can strain a friendship or wreck an international business deal.

If you were raised in an individualist culture:

■ *Remember that someone from a collectivist culture may place a high value on "saving face."* This idea involves more than simply avoiding embarrassment. This person may *not* want to be singled out from other members of a group, even for a positive achievement. If you have a direct request for this person or want to share something that could be taken as a personal criticism, save it for a private conversation.

■ *Respect titles and last names.* Although Canadians often like to use first names immediately after meeting someone, in some cultures this practice is acceptable only among family members. Especially in work settings, use last names and job titles during your first meetings. Allow time for informal relationships to develop.

■ *Put messages in context.* For members of collectivist cultures, words convey only part of an intended message. Notice gestures and other nonverbal communication as well.

If you were raised in a collectivist culture, you can creatively "reverse" the above list. Keep in mind that direct questions from a Canadian student or coworker are meant not to offend but only to clarify an idea. Don't be surprised if you are called by a nickname, if no one asks about your family, or if you are rewarded for a personal achievement. In social situations, remember that indirect cues might not get another person's attention. Practise asking clearly and directly for what you want.

Reach out

If carrying out any of these suggestions feels awkward, just apply the Power Process: "Be here now." Then use the suggestions in this article. By intentionally expanding your comfort zone over time, you can break down social barriers and gain a new level of ease at being with people.

A more formal option is to arrange an intergroup dialogue—a "*facilitated*, face-to-face meeting between students from two or more social identity groups that have a history of conflict or potential conflict." Examples are Christians and Muslims, blacks and whites, and people with disabilities and those without disabilities. The goal is sustained and meaningful conversation about controversial issues (Zúñiga, 2009). Groups typically gather for two-hour meetings over 6 to 12 weeks.

Look for common ground

Students in higher education often find that they worry about many of the same things—including tuition bills, the quality of the residence food, and the shortage of on-campus parking spaces. More important, our fundamental goals as human beings—such as health, physical safety, and economic security—cross culture lines.

The key is to honour the differences among people while remembering what we have in common. Diversity is not just about our differences—it's also about our similarities. On a biological level, less than 1 percent of the human genome accounts for visible characteristics such as skin colour. In terms of our genetic blueprint, we are more than 99 percent the same (Szalavitz, 2001).

Speak and listen with cultural sensitivity

After first speaking with someone from another culture, don't assume that you've been understood or that you fully understand the other person. The same action can have different meanings at different times, even for members of the same culture. Check it out. Verify what you think you have heard. Listen to see if what you spoke is what the other person received.

9

DIVERSITY

If you're speaking with someone who doesn't understand English well, keep the following ideas in mind:

- Speak slowly, distinctly, and patiently.
- To clarify your statement, don't repeat individual words over and over again. Restate your entire message with simple, direct language and short sentences.
- Avoid slang and figures of speech.
- Use gestures to accompany your words.
- English courses for non-native speakers often emphasize written English, so write down what you're saying. Print your message in capital letters.
- Stay calm, and avoid sending nonverbal messages that you're frustrated.

If you're unsure about how well you're communicating, ask questions: "I don't know how to make this idea clear for you. How might I communicate better?" "When you look away from me during our conversation, I feel uneasy. Is there something else we need to talk about?" "When you don't ask questions, I wonder if I am being clear. Do you want any more explanation?" Questions such as these can get cultural differences out in the open in a constructive way.

Look for individuals, not group representatives

Sometimes the way we speak glosses over differences among individuals and reinforces stereotypes. For example, a student worried about her grade in math expresses concern over "all those Asian students who are skewing the class curve." Or a white music major assumes that her Caribbean classmate knows a lot about reggae music. We can avoid such errors by seeing people as individuals—not spokespersons for an entire group.

Find a translator, mediator, or model

People who move with ease in two or more cultures can help us greatly. Diane de Anda (1984), a professor at the University of California, Los Angeles, speaks of three kinds of people who can communicate across cultures. She calls them *translators*, *mediators*, and *models*.

A *translator* is someone who is truly bicultural—a person who relates naturally to both people in a mainstream culture and people from a contrasting culture. This person can share her own experiences in overcoming discrimination, learning another language or dialect, and coping with stress.

Mediators are people who belong to the dominant or mainstream culture. Unlike translators, they might not be bicultural. However, mediators value diversity and are committed to cultural understanding. Often they are teachers, counsellors, tutors, mentors, or social workers.

Models are members of a culture who are positive examples. Models include students from any racial or cultural group who participate in class and demonstrate effective study habits. Models can also include entertainers, athletes, and community leaders.

Your school might have people who serve these functions, even if they're not labelled translators, mediators, or models. Some schools have mentor or "bridge" programs that pair new students with teachers or peers of the same race or culture. Ask your international student services or student counselling services about such programs.

Develop support systems

Many students find that their social adjustment affects their academic performance. Students with strong support systems—such as families, friends, churches, self-help groups, and mentors—are using a powerful strategy for success in school. As an exercise, list the support systems that you rely on right now. Also list new support systems you could develop.

High versus low context cultures

Cultures differ dramatically in terms of who is responsible for understanding a message, the speaker or the listener. In low context cultures such as Canada, the United States and Scandinavia, the onus is on the speaker to explicitly convey the message to the listener, whereas in high context cultures such as Japan and Mediterranean countries it is up to the listener to get the implicit message from the speaker (Dimitrov, 2009). For Canadians, this means that speakers from high context cultures will often sound vague or secretive and they might wonder why the speaker doesn't just get to the point. Speakers from high context cultures assume that the listener has the same background knowledge of the topic and therefore the listener should be able to figure out what the speaker is trying to communicate. All cultures vary on the continuum from high to low culture, and there may even be differences within a culture based on the person's age or gender. In the classroom, differences between individuals from high versus low context cultures may lead to challenges in communication between students and their instructors.

Support systems can help you bridge culture gaps. With a strong base of support in your own group, you can feel more confident in meeting people outside that group.

Be willing to accept feedback

Members of another culture might let you know that some of your words or actions had a meaning other than what you intended. For example, perhaps a comment that seems harmless to you is offensive to them. And they may tell you directly about it.

Avoid responding to such feedback with comments such as "Don't get me wrong," "You're taking this way too seriously," or "You're too sensitive." Instead, listen without resistance. Open yourself to what others have to say. Remember to distinguish between the *intention* of your behaviour and its actual *impact* on other people. Then take the feedback you receive, and ask yourself how you can use it to communicate more effectively in the future.

You can also interpret such feedback positively—a sign that others believe you can change and that they see the possibility of a better relationship with you.

If you are new at responding to diversity, expect to make some mistakes along the way. As long as you approach people in a spirit of tolerance, your words and actions can always be changed.

Speak up against discrimination

You might find yourself in the presence of someone who tells a racist joke, makes a homophobic comment, or utters an ethnic slur. When this happens, you have a right to state what you observe, share what you think, and communicate how you feel. Depending on the circumstance, you might say:

- "That's a stereotype, and we don't have to fall for it."
- "Other people are going to take offence at that. Let's tell jokes that don't put people down."
- "I realize that you don't mean to offend anybody, but I feel hurt and angry by what you just said."
- "I know that a gay person told you that story, but I still think it's homophobic and creates an atmosphere that I don't want to be in."

This kind of speaking may be the most difficult communicating you ever do. However, if you *don't* do it, you give the impression that you agree with biased speech.

In response to your candid comments, many people will apologize and express their willingness to change. Even if they don't, you can still know that you practised integrity by aligning your words with your values.

Change the institution

None of us lives in isolation. We all live in systems, and these systems do not always tolerate diversity. As a student, you might see people of colour ignored in class. You might see people of a certain ethnic group passed over in job hiring or underrepresented in school organizations. And you might see gay and lesbian students ridiculed or even threatened with violence. One way to stop these actions is to point them out.

You can speak more effectively about what you believe by making some key distinctions. Remember the following:

- *Stereotypes* are errors in thinking—inaccurate ideas about members of another culture.
- *Prejudice* refers to positive or negative feelings about others, which are often based on stereotypes.
- *Discrimination* takes places when stereotypes or prejudice gets expressed in policies and laws that undermine equal opportunities for all cultures.

The Canadian Charter of Rights and Freedoms, as well as the written policies of educational institutions, bans racial and ethnic discrimination. Most institutions have formal procedures that protect students against such discrimination. Find out what those procedures are and use them, if necessary.

In recent history, students have fuelled much social change. When it comes to ending discrimination, you are in an environment where you can make a difference. Run for student government. Write for school publications. Speak at rallies. Express your viewpoint. This is training for citizenship in a multicultural world. ✱

 Gain more strategies for building relationships across cultures @

www.bams5ce.nelson.com

DIVERSITY

9

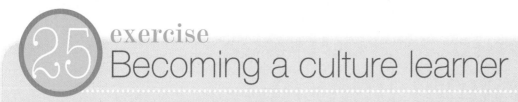

Becoming a culture learner

To learn about other cultures in depth, actively move through the cycle of learning described by psychologist David Kolb (and explained more fully in "Learning Styles—Discovering How You Learn" on page 40). This exercise, which has three parts, illustrates one way to apply the cycle of learning. Use additional paper as needed to complete each part.

Part 1: Concrete experience

Think of a specific way to interact with people from a culture different than your own. For example, attend a meeting for a campus group that you normally would not attend. Or sit in a campus cafeteria with a new group of people.

In the space below, describe what you will do to create your experience of a different culture.

Part 2: Reflective observation

Describe the experience you had while doing Part 1 of this exercise. Be sure to separate your observations—what you saw, heard, or did—from your interpretations. In addition,

see if you can think of other ways to interpret each of your observations.

Use the table at the bottom of this page for this part of the exercise. An example is included to get you started.

Part 3: Abstract conceptualization

Next, see if you can refine your initial interpretations and develop them into some informed conclusions about your experience in Part 1. Do some research about other cultures, looking specifically for information that can help you understand the experience. (Your instructor and a librarian can suggest ways to find such information.) Whenever possible, speak directly to people of various cultures. Share your observations from Part 1, and ask for *their* interpretations.

Reflect on the information you gather. Does it reinforce any of the interpretations you listed in Part 2? Does it call for a change in your thinking? Summarize your conclusions in the space below.

Observation	Your Initial Interpretation	Other Possible Interpretations
For 30 minutes starting at noon on Tuesday, I sat alone in the northeast section of the cafeteria in our student union. During this time, all of the conversations I overheard were conducted in Mandarin.	I sat alone because the Mandarin-speaking students did not want to talk to me. They are unfriendly.	The Mandarin-speaking students are actually friendly. They were just not sure how to start a conversation with me. Perhaps they thought I wanted to eat alone or study. Also, I could have taken the initiative to start a conversation.

DIVERSITY

9

Overcome stereotypes with critical thinking

CONSIDER ASSERTIONS such as "Students like to drink heavily," "People who speak English as a second language are hard to understand," and "Most of the people who live on the East Coast are on welfare."

These are examples of stereotyping—generalizing about a group of people based on the behaviour of isolated group members. Stereotypes are a potent source of intellectual error. They are signals to shift our thinking skills into high gear—to demand evidence, examine logic, and insist on accurate information.

The word *stereotype* originally referred to a method used by printers to produce duplicate pages of text. This usage still rings true. When we stereotype, we gloss over individual differences and assume that every member of a group is the same.

Stereotypes infiltrate every dimension of human individuality. People are stereotyped on the basis of their race, nationality, physical or mental abilities, ethnic group, religion, political affiliation, geographic location, job, age, gender, IQ, height, or hobby. We stereotype people based on everything from the colour of their hair to the year of their car.

Stereotypes have many possible sources: fear of the unknown, uncritical thinking, and negative encounters between individual members of different groups. Whatever their cause, stereotypes abound.

In themselves, generalizations are neither good nor bad. In fact, they are essential. Mentally sorting people, events, and objects into groups allows us to make sense of the world. But when we consciously or unconsciously make generalizations that rigidly divide the people of the world into "us" versus "them," we create stereotypes and put on the blinders of prejudice.

You can take several steps to free yourself from stereotypes.

Look for errors in thinking.

Some of the most common errors are:

- **Selective perception.** Stereotypes can literally change the way we see the world. If we assume that homeless people are lazy, for instance, we tend to notice only the examples that support our opinion. Stories about homeless people who are too young or too ill to work will probably escape our attention.

- **Self-fulfilling prophecy.** When we interact with people based on stereotypes, we set them up in ways that confirm our thinking. For example, when people of colour were denied access to higher education based on stereotypes about their intelligence, they were deprived of opportunities to demonstrate their intellectual gifts.

- **Self-justification.** Stereotypes can allow people to assume the role of a victim and to avoid taking responsibility for their own lives. An unemployed white male might believe that affirmative action programs are making it impossible for him to get a job—even as he overlooks his own lack of experience or qualifications.

Create categories in a more flexible way.

Stereotyping has been described as a case of "hardening of the categories." Avoid this problem by making your categories broader. Instead of seeing people based on their skin colour, you could look at them on the basis of their heredity. (People of all races share most of the same genes.) Or you could make your categories narrower. Instead of talking about "religious extremists," look for subgroups among the people who adopt a certain religion. Distinguish between groups that advocate violence and those that shun it.

Test your generalizations about people through action.

You can do this by actually meeting people of other cultures. It's easy to believe almost anything about certain groups of people as long as we never deal directly with individuals. Inaccurate pictures tend to die when people from various cultures study together, work together, and live together. Consider joining a school or community organization that will put you in contact with people of other cultures. Your rewards will include a more global perspective and an ability to thrive in a multicultural world.

Be willing to see your own stereotypes.

The Power Process: "Notice your pictures and let them go" can help. One belief about ourselves that many of us can shed is *I have no pictures about people from other cultures.* Even people with the best of intentions can harbour subtle biases. Admitting this possibility allows us to look inward even more deeply for stereotypes. Every time that we notice inaccurate pictures buried in our minds and let them go, we each take a personal step toward embracing diversity. ✶

 Find more examples of stereotypes and critical responses online @

www.bams5ce.nelson.com

> **Equal opportunity for people with disabilities is the law. The federal Employment Equity Act of 1995 was created to protect equal opportunity in the workplace for people with disabilities.**

Students with disabilities: Know your rights

Ask for what you want

IT USED TO be that students with disabilities faced a restricted set of choices in school. For instance, many had trouble specializing in subjects—engineering, science, or medicine—that called for using technical equipment. New technology, such as computers and calculators operated with voice commands, can change that. Students with disabilities can now choose from almost any course or program of study offered in post-secondary education.

Instructors with even the best of intentions can forget about promoting learning for people with disabilities. To protect your rights, speak up. Ask for what you want. Begin with the suggestions about being assertive in Chapter 8: Communicating, using "I" messages and listening actively. All of them can help you succeed in school. So can the following.

Use available resources

A wealth of resources already exists to support your success in education. To begin with, check into services offered by your province. Provincial governments often provide funds for education or can help you find that money. Provincial ministries of education can guide you to services. In addition, the Learning Disabilities Association of Canada (www.ldac-acta.ca/) offers help in placing employees with learning or physical disabilities. Other agencies such as the Canadian National Institute for the Blind offer those with vision loss help finding employment through CareerConnect Canada.

If you want an academic accommodation such as being allowed to have extra time on exams, first identify yourself as having a disability to your Services for Students with Disabilities office within your institution. This office is typically part of student services at

© Andersen Ross/Getty Images

most colleges or universities. If you cannot find this office, check with an admissions officer or academic counsellor. Then follow your school's procedures for getting the accommodation in place. These procedures vary across campuses. Ask for assistance even prior to admission so that you are aware of what services are in place at your school to support your success.

The services to ask about include:

- Permits that allow you to park a car closer to classrooms
- Note-taking services
- Lecture transcriptions
- Textbook-reading services and textbooks on tape
- Sign language interpreters
- Help in selecting courses and registering for classes
- Assistants for laboratory courses in science
- Shuttle buses for transportation between classes

9

DIVERSITY

- Closed captioning for instructional television programs
- TTY/TDD devices for students with hearing impairments
- Assistance with taking tests
- Accessible residence rooms.

Your school will probably ask you to document that you have a disability and need academic accommodation. This documentation might include a written evaluation from a physician, psychologist, or other professional who has worked with you.

In addition, local libraries might furnish books in Braille or on audiotapes for the visually impaired.

Speak assertively

Tell instructors when it's appropriate to consider your disability. If you use a wheelchair, for example, ask for appropriate transportation on field trips. If you have a visual disability, request that instructors speak as they write on the chalkboard. Also ask them to use high-contrast colours and to write legibly.

Plan ahead

Meet with your Counsellor for Students with Disabilities to design an educational plan—one that takes your needs into account. A key part of this plan may be choosing instructors. Ask for recommendations before registering for classes. Interview prospective instructors and sit in on their classes. Express an interest in the class, ask to see a course outline, and discuss any adjustments that could help you complete the course. Some of the services you request might take extra time to deliver. Allow for possible delays as you plan your schedule. If you have a physical disability, on a large campus consider how far apart the classrooms are and how easy it is to move from building to building in the winter.

Ask for appropriate treatment

Many instructors will be eager to help you. At times they might go overboard. For example, a student who has trouble writing by hand might ask to complete in-class writing assignments on a computer. "OK," the instructor might reply, "and take a little extra time. For you, there's no rush."

For some students this is a welcome response. For others, there is no need for more time. They can reply, "Thank you for thinking of me. I'd prefer to finish the assignment in the time frame allotted for the rest of the class."

Follow up when necessary

If the academic accommodation that you requested is not working for you, let your school know right away. Talk to the person who helped set up the accommodation or your academic counsellor. Remember that schools usually have grievance procedures for resolving conflicts about the services you're receiving. Most schools have an ombudsperson who can be a good resource on how to deal with any grievance you might have.

Take care of yourself

Many students with chronic illnesses or disabilities find that rest breaks are essential. If this is true for you, write such breaks into your daily or weekly plan. A related suggestion is to treat yourself with respect. If your health changes in a way that you don't like, avoid berating yourself. Even when you do not choose the conditions in your life, you can choose your attitude toward those conditions.

It's important to accept compliments and periodically review your accomplishments in school. Fill yourself with affirmation. As you educate yourself, you are attaining mastery. ✴

STUDENT VOICES

Before I was diagnosed with dyslexia, I was constantly frustrated whenever I had to take a test. I was never able to complete my exams because I didn't read or write as quickly as the other students in my class. When I discussed this problem with my adviser, he recommended I talk to a counsellor in the learning assistance centre. Now, I take my tests at the learning centre and have additional time to accommodate for my disability.

—IRENE CHO

9

DIVERSITY

> Sexism and sexual harassment are real. These are events that occur throughout the year at schools and workplaces. Nearly all of these incidents are illegal or violate organizational policies.

Dealing with sexism and sexual harassment

IN NORTH AMERICA today, women make up the majority of first-year students in postsecondary education, yet they still encounter bias based on gender.

This bias can take many forms. For example, instructors might gloss over the contributions of women. Students in philosophy class might never hear of a woman named Hypatia, an ancient Greek philosopher and mathematician. Those specializing in computer science might never learn about Rear Admiral Grace Murray Hopper, who pioneered the development of a computer language named COBOL. And your art history textbook might not mention the Canadian painter Florence Carlyle or the Mexican painter Frida Kahlo.

Although men also can be subjects of sexism and sexual harassment, women are more likely to experience this form of discrimination. Even the most well-intentioned people might behave in ways that discriminate against or discount women. Sexism is a factor when:

- Instructors use only masculine pronouns—*he, his,* and *him*—to refer to both men and women.
- Career counsellors hint that careers in mathematics and science are not appropriate for women.
- Students pay more attention to feedback from a male teacher than from a female teacher.
- Women are not called on in class, their comments are ignored, or they are overly praised for answering the simplest questions.
- People assume that middle-aged women who return to school have too many family commitments to study adequately or do well in their classes.

Many kinds of behaviour—both verbal and physical—can be categorized as sexual harassment. This kind of discrimination involves unwelcome sexual conduct. Examples of such conduct in a school setting are:

- Sexual touching or advances
- Any other unwanted touch
- Unwanted verbal intimacy

- Sexual graffiti
- Displaying or distributing sexually explicit materials
- Sexual gestures or jokes
- Pressure for sexual favours
- Talking about personal sexual activity
- Spreading rumours about someone's sexual activity or rating someone's sexual performance.

A brochure put out by the University of Toronto Counselling and Learning Skills Services states, "A sexual assault is any sexual act you are forced to engage in without your consent…. Contrary to the belief that sexual assault is a street crime, the majority of people are sexually assaulted by someone they know. For example, it is a sexual assault if you are out on a date and become physically close but do not wish to have sex and your date forces you into it."

The feminist movement has raised awareness about discrimination against women. We can now respond to sexism and sexual harassment and assault in the places we live, work, and go to school. Here are some specific strategies.

Point out sexist language and behaviour. When you see examples of sexism, point them out. Your message can be more effective if you use "I" messages instead of personal attacks, as explained in Chapter 8: Communicating. Indicate the specific statements and behaviours that you consider sexist.

For example, you could rephrase a sexist comment so that it targets another group, such as Jews or Blacks. People might spot anti-Semitism or racism more readily than sexism.

Keep in mind that men can also be subjected to sexism, ranging from antagonistic humour to exclusion from jobs that have traditionally been done by women.

Observe your own language and behaviour. Looking for sexist behaviour in others is effective. Detecting it in yourself can be just as powerful. Write a Discovery Statement about specific comments that could be interpreted as sexist. Then notice if you say any of these things. Also ask people you know to point out occasions when you use similar statements. Follow up with an Intention Statement that describes how you plan to change your speaking or behaviour.

You can also write Discovery Statements about the current level of intimacy (physical and verbal) in any of your relationships at home, work, or school. Be sure that any increase in the level of intimacy is mutually agreed upon.

Encourage support for women. Through networks, women can work to overcome the effects of sexism. Strategies include study groups for women, women's job networks, and professional organizations, such as Women in Small Businesses. Other examples are counselling services and health centres for women, family planning agencies, and rape prevention centres. Check your school calendar and library to see if any of these services are available at your school.

If your school does not have the women's networks you want, you can help form them. Sponsor a one-day or one-week conference on women's issues. Create a discussion or reading group for the women in your class, department, residence, union, or neighbourhood.

Set limits. Women, value yourselves. Recognize your right to an education without the distraction of inappropriate and invasive behaviour. Trust your judgment

> *Even the most well-intentioned people might behave in ways that discriminate against or discount women.*

about when your privacy or your rights are being violated. Decide now what kind of sexual comments and actions you're uncomfortable with—and refuse to put up with them.

Take action. If you are sexually harassed, take action.

Some key federal legislation protects the rights of women. The Canadian Charter of Rights and Freedoms, part of the Constitution Act of 1982, protects the interests of Canadians by providing a way to challenge abuses of basic rights and freedoms. It prohibits gender discrimination and all forms of harassment.

Since education is a provincial jurisdiction, the most direct route for students to deal with sexual harassment is through their academic institution or their provincial Human Rights Commission. These commissions administer the provincial human rights codes that provide guarantees and remedies for those who have been sexually harassed or otherwise discriminated against.

Learn your institution's procedures for enforcing these human rights codes and use them when appropriate. Your community might also offer resources to protect against sexual discrimination. Examples are public interest law firms, legal aid societies, and unions that employ lawyers to represent students. ✳

 For more information about discrimination, go online @
www.bams5ce.nelson.com

Strategies for non-sexist communication

When speaking and writing, use language that includes both women and men. Following are some ways you can do this without twisting yourself into verbal knots.

- **Use gender-neutral terms.** Instead of *policeman* or *chairman,* for example, use *police officer* or *chairperson.* In many cases, there's no need to identify the gender or marital status of a person. This fact allows us to dispose of expressions such as *female driver, male nurse,* and *lady doctor.*
- **Use examples that include both men and women.** Effective writing and speaking thrives on examples and illustrations. As you search for details to support your main points, include the stories and accomplishments of women as well as men.

- **Alternate pronoun gender.** In an attempt to be gender fair, some people make a point of mentioning both sexes whenever they refer to gender. Another method is to alternate male and female pronouns throughout a text or speech—the strategy used in this book.
- **Switch to plural.** With this approach, a sentence such as *The writer has many tools at her disposal* becomes *Writers have many tools at their disposal.*
- **Avoid words that imply sexist stereotypes.** Included here are terms such as *tomboy, sissy, office boy, advertising man, man-eater, mama's boy, old lady,* and *powder puff.*

DIVERSITY

9

© Jeff Hunter/Getty

Leadership in a diverse world

MANY PEOPLE MISTAKENLY think that leaders are only those with formal titles such as *supervisor* or *manager*. In fact, some leaders have no such titles. Some have never supervised others. Like Mahatma Gandhi, some people change the face of the world without ever reaching a formal leadership position.

No one is born knowing how to lead. We acquire the skills over time. Begin now, while you are in higher education. Campuses offer continual opportunities to gain leadership skills. Volunteer for clubs, organizations, and student government. Look for opportunities to tutor, or to become a peer adviser or mentor. No matter what you do, take on big projects—those that are worthy of your time and talents.

Statistics Canada states that, by 2031, one in three Canadians will belong to a visible minority (Friesen, 2010). Translation: Your next boss or coworker could be a person whose life experiences and views of the world differ radically from yours.

We live in a world where Naheed Nenshi, whose parents immigrated from Tanzania, became the mayor of Calgary; where Michäelle Jean, a refugee from Haiti, became the Governor General of Canada; and where Oprah Winfrey, an African American woman, could propel a book to the top of the bestseller list simply by recommending it on her television show. These people set examples of diversity in leadership that many others will follow. Prepare to apply your own leadership skills in a multicultural world.

To become more effective leaders, we can better understand the many ways we influence others. The following strategies can have a positive impact on our relationships with our children, parents, friends, teachers, employers, and employees. They can help us relate to our politicians, our places of worship, our cities, our provinces, and our planet.

Own your leadership

Let go of the reluctance that many of us feel toward assuming leadership. It's impossible to escape leadership. Every time you speak, you lead others in some small or large way. Every time you take action, you lead others through your example. Every time you ask someone to do something, you are in essence leading that person. Leadership becomes more effective when it is consciously applied.

Be willing to be uncomfortable

Leadership is a courageous act. Leaders often are not appreciated or even liked. They can feel isolated, cut off from their colleagues. This can sometimes lead to self-doubt and even fear. Before you take on a leadership role, be aware that you might experience such feelings. Also remember that none of them needs to stop you from leading.

Allow huge mistakes

The more important and influential you are, the more likely it is that your mistakes will have huge consequences. The chief financial officer for a large company can make a mistake that costs thousands or even millions of dollars. A physician's error could cost a life. The prime minister of a country can make decisions that affect thousands of lives.

At the same time, these people are in a position to make huge changes for the better—to save thousands of dollars or save lives through their power, skill, and influence.

People in leadership positions can become paralyzed and ineffective if they fear making a mistake. It's necessary for them to act even when information is incomplete or when they know a catastrophic mistake is a possible outcome.

Take on big projects

Leaders make promises. And effective leaders make big promises. These words—"I will do it. You can count on me,"—distinguish a leader.

Look around your world to see what needs to be done and then take it on. Consider taking on the biggest project you can think of—ending world hunger, eliminating nuclear weapons, wiping out poverty, or promoting universal literacy. Think about how you'd spend your life if you knew that you could make a difference regarding these overwhelming problems. Then take the actions you considered. See what a difference they can make for you and for others.

Tackle projects that stretch you to your limits—projects that are worthy of your time and talents.

Provide feedback

An effective leader is a mirror to others. Share what you see. Talk with others about what they are doing effectively—*and* what they are doing ineffectively. Keep in mind that people might not enjoy your feedback. Some would probably rather not hear it at all.

Two things can help. One is to let people know up front that if they sign on to work with you, they can expect feedback. Also give your feedback with skill. Use "I" messages as explained in Chapter 8: Communicating. Back up any criticisms with specific observations and facts. And when people complete a task with exceptional skill, point that out, too.

Paint a vision

Help others see the big picture, the ultimate purpose of a project. Speak a lot about the end result and the potential value of what you're doing.

There's a biblical saying: "Without vision, the people perish." Long-term goals usually involve many intermediate steps. Unless we're reminded of the purpose

Tackle projects that stretch you to your limits—projects that are worthy of your time and talents.

for those day-to-day actions, our work can feel like a grind. Leadership is the art of helping others lift their eyes to the horizon—keeping them in touch with the ultimate value and purpose of a project. Keeping the vision alive helps spirits soar again.

Model your values

"Be the change you want to see" is a useful motto for leaders. Perhaps you want to see integrity, focused attention, and productivity in the people around you. Begin by modelling these qualities yourself.

It's easy to excite others about a goal when you are enthusiastic about it yourself. Having fun while being productive is contagious. If you bring these qualities to a project, others might follow suit.

Make requests—lots of them

An effective leader is a request machine. Making requests—both large and small—is an act of respect. When we ask a lot from others, we demonstrate our respect for them and our confidence in their abilities.

At first, some people might get angry when we make requests of them. Over time, many will see that requests are compliments, opportunities to expand their skills. Ask a lot from others, and they might appreciate you for it.

Follow up

What we don't inspect, people don't respect. When other people agree to do a job for you, follow up to see how it is going. This can be done in a way that communicates your respect and interest—not your fear that the project might flounder. When you display a genuine interest in other people and their work, they are more likely to view you as a partner in achieving a shared goal.

Focus on the problem, not the person

Sometimes projects do not go as planned. Big mistakes occur. If this happens, focus on the project and the mistakes—not the personal faults of your colleagues. People do not make mistakes on purpose. If they did, we would call them "on-purposes," not mistakes. Most people will join you in solving a problem if your focus is on the problem, not on what they did wrong.

Acknowledge others

Express genuine appreciation for the energy and creativity that others have put into their work. Take the time to be interested in what they have done and to care about the results they have accomplished. Thank and acknowledge them with your eyes, your words, and the tone of your voice.

9

DIVERSITY

Share credit

As a leader, constantly give away the praise and acknowledgment that you receive. When you're congratulated for your performance, pass it on to others. Share the credit with the group.

When you're a leader, the results you achieve depend on the efforts of many others. Acknowledging that fact often is more than telling the truth—it's essential if you want to continue to count on their support in the future.

Delegate

Ask a coworker or classmate to take on a job that you'd like to see done. Ask the same of your family or friends. Delegate tasks to the mayor of your town, the premier of your province, and the leaders of your country.

Take on projects that are important to you. Then find people who can lead the effort. You can do this even when you have no formal role as a leader.

We often see delegation as a tool that's available only to those above us in the chain of command. Actually, delegating up or across an organization can be just as effective. Consider delegating a project to your boss. That is, ask her to take on a job that you'd like to see accomplished. This might be a job that you cannot do, given your position in the company.

Balance styles

Think for a moment about your own learning style. To lead effectively, assess your strengths, and look for people who can complement them. If you excel at gathering information and setting goals, for example, then recruit people who like to make decisions and take action. Also enlist people who think creatively and generate different points of view.

Look for different styles in the people who work with you. Remember that learning results from a balance between reflection, action, abstract thinking, and concrete experience. (For more information, see "Learning Styles: Discovering How You Learn" on page 40.) The people you lead will combine these characteristics in infinite variety. Welcome that variety, and accommodate it.

You can defuse and prevent many conflicts simply by acknowledging differences in style. Doing so opens up more options than blaming the differences on "politics" or "personality problems."

Listen

Sometimes it seems that effective leaders talk a lot. Chances are, they also listen a lot. As a leader, be aware of what other people are thinking, feeling, and wanting. Listen fully to their concerns and joys. Before you criticize their views or make personal judgments, take the time to understand what's going on inside them.

This is not merely a personal favour to the people you work with. The more you know about your coworkers or classmates, the more effectively you can lead them.

Practice

Leadership is an acquired skill. No one is born knowing how to make requests, give feedback, create budgets, do long-range planning, or delegate tasks. We learn these things over time, with practice, by seeing what works and what doesn't.

At times, leadership is a matter of trial and error and flying by the seat of your pants. As a leader, you might sometimes feel that you don't know what you're doing. That's OK. A powerful course of action can be discovered in midstream. You can act as a leader even when you don't feel like a leader. As a process of constant learning, leadership calls for all of the skills of master students. Look for areas in which you can make a difference and experiment with these strategies. Right now there's something worth doing that calls for your leadership. Take action and others will join you. ✳

 Gain more perspectives on leadership online @

www.bams5ce.nelson.com

STUDENT VOICES

As a parent, returning to college has been a positive experience for my entire family. I have had a chance to model being a good student for my children. They are eager to finish high school and continue on to college just like their dad.

—LAMONT JACKSON

DIVERSITY

9

Put It to WORK

Living in a global village, especially in Canada where immigration has skyrocketed in the past decade, your next coworker or supervisor could be a person whose life experience and view of the world differs radically from yours.

© Yuri Arcurs/Shutterstock

eert Hofstede, a Dutch psychologist and author of *Culture's Consequences: Comparing Values, Behaviors, Institutions and Organizations Across Nations,* identifies several core dimensions of cultural difference. Keeping them in mind can help you prevent and resolve conflict with coworkers on project teams.

Power-distance

If you observe teams from cultures based on high power-distance, you will see clear differences in status and power between team members. Some people will clearly function as leaders and others as followers. Compare such teams to those from low power-distance cultures, in which people function basically as equals and decisions are based on consensus. To cope with these differences, ask your team leader to clarify roles. Explain how members are expected to participate in decision making and how their performance will be evaluated.

Supervision

Some of your coworkers might do what they can to avoid uncertainty. They focus on details, expect close supervision, and prefer clearly defined tasks with specific due dates. In contrast, other team members might want less supervision rather than more, preferring to work independently. Your team can function more effectively when you look for such differences and tailor assignments to individual preferences.

Individual and collective orientations

People from many Western cultures value individual achievement, competition, and personal recognition. These workers might clash with people from Latin American and Asian cultures that emphasize group cohesion and cooperation.

If you lead a team marked by this cultural difference, take action to balance these differences. When supervising workers who are motivated by competition, acknowledge their achievements—and remind them that they are members of a group with a shared goal.

Long-term and short-term orientations

Some workers like to lift their eyes to the horizon and set goals to meet over several years or decades. Their orientation leads them to value patience, and they might be willing to make sacrifices now for long-term gains later. On the other hand, workers with a short-term orientation value immediate results and might quickly tire of long-range planning.

By recognizing this difference in orientation up front, you can make it work for you. Ask workers with a long-term orientation to craft a mission statement, list of core values, and five-year plan for your organization. Leave the details of implementing the plan to team members with a short-term orientation. These workers can focus on the month-by-month and week-by-week tasks that lead to achieving long-range goals.

chapter 9

QUIZ

■ Put It to Work
◄ ◄ ◄ ◄ ◄
■ Skills Snapshot
■ Master Student Profile

Name_____ Date____/____/____

1. Explain the differences among *stereotypes*, *prejudice*, and *discrimination* as defined in the text.

2. Give two examples of differences between individualist and collectivist cultures.

3. List three strategies for communicating across cultures.

4. Explain the difference between *self-fulfilling prophecy* and *self-justification* when it comes to detecting stereotypes.

5. Define the terms *translator, mediator,* and *model* as explained in this chapter.

6. Describe at least one way to overcome stereotypes with critical thinking.

7. Explain a strategy for taking charge of the conversations in your life.

8. You are part of a class discussion and find that one of the students responds quite tersely to a question from the instructor. When asked why we build dams for hydro electricity? The student responds: Geography. The short response may be because the student is from:
   (a) high context culture
   (b) low context culture
   (c) high power culture
   (d) low power culture

9. Rewrite the following sentence so that it is gender neutral: "Any writer can benefit from honing his skill at observing people."

10. Few of us get the chance to be leaders. True or False? Explain your answer.

Skills SNAPSHOT

Now that you've reflected on the ideas in this chapter and experimented with some new strategies, revisit your responses to the "Diversity" section of the Discovery Wheel exercise on page 37. Then complete the following sentences.

QUESTIONING ASSUMPTIONS

The racial, ethnic, and gender stereotypes that I've heard include . . .

If I talk to people who express such stereotypes, I will respond by . . .

BRIDGING CULTURES

When I meet someone whose beliefs or customs differ in a major way from mine, my first reaction is . . .

Other ways I could respond to such differences include . . .

NEXT ACTION

I'll know that I've reached a new level of mastery with diversity when . . .

To reach that level of mastery, the most important thing I can do next is to . . .

MASTER STUDENT Profile

■ Put It to Work
■ Quiz
■ Skills Snapshot
◄ ◄ ◄ ◄ ◄

chapter 9

Trey Anthony
. . . is willing to take risks

© Rene Johnston/Toronto Star/ First Light

Coming to working-class Rexdale from London, England, was a culture shock for Trey Anthony, who was 12 when she arrived with her family.

But for the creator and co-star of *Da Kink in My Hair*, a TV series, "growing up, I always had my humour to fall back on."

"Before you may laugh at me . . . I'll give you the joke first," said Anthony, whose British accent was mocked for "sounding like the Queen."

It was only through sheer tenacity, support from numerous mentors—and talent—that Anthony has been able to find success.

Despite living in a city considered by some to be the most culturally diverse in the world, Anthony said it was a struggle to get noticed by those who didn't see star qualities in a short, feisty Black woman.

"It was very hard for me to get roles as a Black actress, as a plus-size actress. A lot of people don't want to cast me, they don't see me as the perfect leading lady," Anthony, 33, said.

But there was never a time when Anthony was ready to give up. When she failed to get the part of Frenchie in a high school production of *Grease*, her grandmother had some good advice: "Don't cry, write your own play." So writing started from that place of saying, "Okay, no one is going to hire me except if I hire myself," she said.

"There was no other choice for me. I want to do this work. I come alive when I'm onstage. I come alive when I'm on camera. It's work that I just feel born to do. I live, eat and breathe this stuff. I love to entertain, I love to laugh."

A high school teacher who recognized her talent encouraged Anthony to apply to New York City's American Academy of Dramatic Arts. Her family was too poor to afford the tuition so she had to settle for the summer program. There, she was chosen as an intern and later a writing assistant on *The Chris Rock Show*, where she learned sketch comedy.

Back in Toronto, she formed her own troupe, Platform, and joined Yuk Yuk's African Nubian Comedy Nights and wrote for *After Hours with Kenny Robinson*. Her big break came in 2001 when her first play, *Da Kink in My Hair*, premiered at the Toronto Fringe Festival, a show she took on the road to New York City and San Diego. It was also adapted into a movie on Vision TV before becoming a TV series.

Anthony recently made the move to L.A., where people are still aghast when she tells them *Da Kink* is the first show to feature an all-Black cast on a major network in primetime. "When I get letters from little girls who say, 'Seeing you on TV just expands my world, I've never seen a woman that looks like you on TV,' for me, that's why it's really important."

Source: DeMara, Bruce (December 2007). "When doors closed, she hired herself." Retrieved July 5, 2011 from http://www.thestar.com/entertainment/article/282216. Reprinted with permission of Torstar Syndication Services.

(1974-) Trey Anthony was inspired to write her first play "Da Kink in My Hair" after coming out as a lesbian to her family. Hers was the first Canadian play to be put on at the Princess of Wales Theatre in Toronto and won four NAACP Theatre Awards. She is also an actress and comedian.

Find more biographical information about Trey Anthony at the Master Student Hall of Fame @

www.bams5ce.nelson.com

No matter what job you have, be as productive as possible. Look for ways to boost sales, increase quality, or accomplish tasks in less time. Every day, ask yourself how you can create value for your employer by solving a problem, reducing costs, improving service, or attracting new clients or customers.

To maximize your earning power, keep honing your job-hunting and career-planning skills. You can find a wealth of ideas on these topics in Chapter 12: What's Next?

Finally, keep things in perspective. If your job is lucrative and rewarding, great. If not, remember that almost any job can support you in becoming a master student and reaching your educational goals. ✳

 Discover more ways to increase your income @
www.bams5ce.nelson.com

Spend less money

CONTROLLING YOUR EXPENSES is something you can do right away, and it's usually easier than increasing your income. Use ideas from the following list, and invent more of your own.

Look to big-ticket items. When you look for places to cut expenses, start with the items that cost the most. Choices about where to live, for example, can save you thousands of dollars. Sometimes a place a little farther from campus, or a smaller house or apartment, will be much less expensive. You can also keep your housing costs down by finding a roommate. Offer to do repairs or maintenance in exchange for reduced rent. Pay your rent on time, and treat property with respect.

Another high-ticket item is a car. Take the cost of buying or leasing and then add expenses for parking, insurance, repairs, gas, maintenance, and tires. You might find that it makes more sense to walk, bike, use public transportation, ride a campus shuttle, and call for an occasional taxi ride. Or, carpool. Find friends with a car, and chip in for gas. Check to see if a transit or bus pass is included in your student fees—you may not need a car at all.

Use Exercise #26: "The Money Monitor/Money Plan" on page 320 to discover the main drains on your finances. Then focus on one or two areas where you can reduce spending while continuing to pay your fixed monthly bills, such as rent and tuition.

Look to small-ticket items. Reducing or eliminating the money you spend on low-cost purchases can make the difference between saving money or going into debt. For example, $3 spent at the coffee shop every day adds up to $1,095 over a year.

Ask for student discounts. Movie theatres, restaurants, bars, shopping centres, and other businesses sometimes discount prices for students. Also go to your bank, and ask whether you can open a student chequing and savings account with online banking. The fees and minimum required amounts could be lower. Go online to check your balances weekly so that you avoid overdraft fees.

Do comparison shopping. Prices vary dramatically. Shop around, wait for off-season sales, and use coupons. Check out secondhand stores, thrift stores, and garage sales. Before plunking down the full retail price for a new item, consider whether you could buy it used. You can find "preowned" clothes, CDs, furniture, sports equipment, audio equipment, and computer hardware in retail stores and on the Internet. Go online to Kijiji.ca to see what you can find—there are even things for free.

Be aware of quality. The cheapest product is not always the least expensive over the long run. Sometimes, a slightly more expensive item is the best buy because it will last longer. Remember, there is no correlation between the value of something and the amount of money spent to advertise it. Carefully inspect things you are considering buying, and see if they are well made.

Save money on eating and drinking. This single suggestion could significantly lower your expenses. Instead of hitting a restaurant or bar, head to the grocery store. Fresh fruits, fresh vegetables, and whole grains are not only better for you than processed food—they also cost less. In addition, clip food coupons. Sign up for a shopper's discount card.

job, get into the habit of putting away a portion of ev[...]
paycheque. In fact, Chilton would suggest putting as[...]
10 percent of each paycheque.

Spend less and save more. The less you spend, [...]
more money you'll have on hand. Use that money to
pay your monthly bills, pay off your credit cards, an[...]
create an emergency fund to use in case you lose you[...]
job or a source of financial aid. See "Spend Less Mo[...]
on page 328 for ideas.

Author Suze Orman recommends three actions
to show that you can reduce spending at any time:
(1) do not spend money for one day, (2) do not use
your credit card for one week, and (3) do not eat ou[...]
for one month. Success with any of these strategies [...]
open up your mind to other possibilities for spendi[...]
less and saving (Orman, 2009).

Invest only after saving. The stock market is
only for money that you can afford to lose. Before y[...]
speculate, first save enough money to live on for at
six months in case you're unemployed. Then, consi[...]
what you'll need over the next five years to finish y[...]
schooling and handle other major expenses. Save f[...]
these expenses before taking any risks with your m[...]

Think about your next job. During an econom[...]
crisis, you can get laid off even if you're a star empl[...]
Prepare for this situation now. Create a career plan [...]
describes the next job you want, the skills that you'[...]
develop to get it, and the next steps you'll take to ga[...]
those skills. Stay informed about the latest developi[...]
in your field. Find people who are already working [...]
area, and contact them for information interviews.

Take charge of your credit

A GOOD CREDIT rating will serve you for a life[...]
With this asset, you'll be able to borrow money a[...]
you need it. A poor credit rating, however, can ke[...]
from getting a car or a house in the future. You n[...]
also have to pay higher insurance rates, and you [...]
even be turned down for a job.

To take charge of your credit, borrow money [...]
when truly necessary. If you do borrow, make all [...]
payments, and make them on time. This is espec[...]
important for managing credit cards and studen[...]

Cooking for yourself doesn't need to take much time
if you do a little menu planning. Create a list of your five
favourite home-cooked meals. Learn how to prepare them.
Then keep ingredients for these meals always on hand. To
reduce grocery bills, buy these ingredients in bulk.

If you live in a residence, review the different meal
plans you can buy. Some schools offer meal plans for
students who live off campus. These plans reduce the
cost of eating while you're on campus.

Lower your phone bills. If you use a cell phone,
pull out a copy of your latest bill. Review how many
minutes you used last month. Perhaps you could get by
with a less expensive phone, fewer minutes, fewer text
messages, and a cheaper plan.

Do an Internet search on *cell phone plan comparison,*
and see if you could save money by switching providers.
Also consider a family calling plan, which might cost
less than a separate plan for each person. In addition,
consider whether you need a home phone (a land line)
and a cell phone. Dropping the home phone could save
you money right away.

Go "green." To conserve energy and save money on
utility bills, turn out the lights when you leave a room.
Keep windows and doors closed in winter. In summer,
keep windows open early in the day to invite lots of cool
air into your living space. Then close up the apartment
or house to keep it cool during the hotter hours of the
day. Leave air-conditioning set at 21°C or above. In cool
weather, dress warmly and keep the house at 19°C or
less. In hot weather, take shorter, cooler showers.

Unplug any electric appliances that are not in use.
Appliances like microwaves, audio systems, and cell
phone chargers use energy when plugged in even when
they're not in use. Also, plug computer equipment into
power strips that you can turn off while you sleep.

Find out if you have a smart meter measuring your
use of electricity. If you do, find out how the time of use
can affect your billing. It may cost almost twice as much
to run the washing machine during peak hours versus
off-peak hours.

Explore budget plans for monthly payments that
fluctuate, such as those for heating your home. These
plans average your yearly expenses so you pay the same
amount each month.

Pay cash. To avoid interest charges, deal in cash. If you
don't have the cash, don't buy. Buying on credit makes it
more difficult to monitor spending. You can easily bust
next month's money plan with this month's credit card
purchases.

Postpone purchases. If you plan to buy something,
leave your chequebook or credit card at home when
you first go shopping. Look at all the possibilities. Then

go home and make your decision when you don't feel
pressured. When you are ready to buy, wait a week,
even if the salesperson pressures you. What seems like
a necessity today may not even cross your mind the day
after tomorrow.

Notice what you spend on "fun." Blowing your
money on fun is fun. It is also a fast way to blow your
savings. When you spend money on entertainment,
ask yourself what the benefits will be and whether you
could get the same benefits for less money. You can read
magazines for free at the library, for example. Most
libraries also loan CDs and DVDs for free.

Use the envelope system. After reviewing your
monthly income and expenses, put a certain amount of
cash each week in an envelope labelled *Entertainment/
Eating Out.* When the envelope is empty, stop spending
money on these items for the rest of the week. If you use
online banking, see if you can create separate accounts
for various spending categories. Then deposit a fixed
amount of money into each of those accounts. This is
an electronic version of the envelope system.

Don't compete with big spenders. When you
watch other people spend their money, remember that
you don't know the whole story. Some students have
parents with deep pockets. Others head to Mexico
every year for spring break but finance the trips with
high-interest credit cards. If you find yourself feeling
pressured to spend money so that you can keep up with
other people, stop to think about how much it will cost
over the long run. Maybe it's time to shop around for
some new friends.

**Use the money you save to prepare for
emergencies and reduce debt.** If you apply strategies such as those listed above, you might see your savings account swell nicely. Congratulate yourself. Then
choose what to do with the extra money. To protect
yourself during tough times, create an emergency fund
(see "Money for the Future" on page 335). Then reduce
your debt by paying more than the minimum on credit
card bills and loan payments (see "Take Charge of Your
Credit" on page 331).

Spend less, and feel the power. Cutting your
spending might be challenging at first. Give it time.
Spending less is not about sacrificing pleasure. It's about
something that money can't buy—the satisfaction of
choosing exactly where your money goes and building
a secure financial future. Every dollar that you save on a
frivolous expense is a dollar you can invest in something
that truly matters to you. ✶

 Discover more cost-cutting strategies online @
www.bams5ce.nelson.com

exercise
Show me t[he]

See if you can use *Becoming a Master Student* to crea[te]
financial gain that is many times more than the cost of [this]
book. Scan the entire text, and look for suggestions tha[t]
help you save money or increase income in significant [ways,]
for example:

- Use suggestions for career planning and job huntin[g in]
  Chapter 12: What's Next? to find your next job mor[e]
  quickly—and start earning money sooner.

- Negotiate a higher salary for your next job using str[ategies]
  from the article "Use Interviews and Resumés to H[ook an]
  Employer" on page 396.

- Use suggestions for goal setting from Chapter 2: T[ime to]
  create a detailed plan for acquiring a skill that will f[acilitate]
  your getting a higher-paying job.

Managing mo[ney]
during tough t[imes]

The biggest factor in your
financial well-being is you[r]
behaviour. Taking inform[ed action is the best]
way to cut through financ[ial worries]
and move beyond fear. An[d here's the good news:]
The habits that help you s[urvive tough]
times will also help you m[ake the most]
when the economy rebou[nds.]

START BY DOING Exercise #26: The "Mone[y]
Monitor/Money Plan" on page 320. This exer[cise will]
give you the details about what you're spendi[ng and]
earning right now. With that knowledge, you [can choose]
your next strategy from among the following [options.]

---

that this investment in your future has been shown to
have significant long-term payoffs (Pachner, 2007). So
manage your money well and only borrow what you
really need.

(WWW) Find more strategies online for credit mastery @
www.bams5ce.nelson.com

STUDENT VOICES

*The "Education by the Hour" exercise made me realize that
school is costing me a lot, and everything counts when I don't
attend class or do an assignment. I couldn't believe how much
of my money I was wasting by not attending only one of my
classes.*

—LUZ LOPEZ

If you're in trouble . . .

Financial problems are common. Solve them in ways
that protect you for the future.

Get specific data. Complete Exercise #26: "The
Money Monitor/Money Plan" included earlier in this
chapter.

Be honest with creditors. Determine the
amount that you are sure you can repay each month,
and ask the creditor if that would work for your case.

Go for credit counselling. Most cities have
agencies with professional advisors who can help
straighten out your financial problems.

Change your spending patterns. If you have
a history of overspending (or under earning), change *is*
possible. This chapter is full of suggestions.

Common credit terms

Annual fee—a yearly charge for using a credit card,
sometimes called a *membership fee* or *participation fee*.

Annual percentage rate (APR)—the interest that you
owe on unpaid balances in your account. The APR equals
the periodic rate times the number of billing periods in a
year.

Balance due—the remaining amount of money that you
owe a credit card company or other lender.

Balance transfer—the process of moving an unpaid debt
from one lender to another lender.

Bankruptcy—a legal process that allows borrowers to
declare their inability to pay their debts. People who
declare bankruptcy transfer all their assets to a court-
appointed trustee and create a plan to repay some or all
of their borrowed money. Bankruptcy protects people
from harassment by their creditors and lowers their credit
scores.

Credit score—a three-digit number that reflects your history of repaying borrowed money and paying other bills
on time. This number ranges from 300 to 850. The higher
the number, the better your credit rating.

Default—state of a loan when the borrower fails to make
required payments or otherwise violates the terms of the
agreement. Default may prompt the creditor to turn the

loan over to a collection agency, which can severely harm
the borrower's credit score.

Finance charge—the total fee for using a credit card,
which includes the interest rate, periodic rate, and other
fees. Finance charges for cash advances and balance
transfers can be different than finance charges for unpaid
balances.

Grace period—a period of time when no interest is
charged on a purchase if the credit card user pays off the
entire balance due. When there is no grace period, finance
charges apply immediately to a purchase.

Interest rate—an annual fee that borrowers pay to use
someone else's money, normally a percentage of the
balance due.

Minimum payment—the amount you must pay to keep
from defaulting on an account; usually 2 percent of the
unpaid balance due.

Payment due date—the day that a lender must receive
your payment—*not* the postmarked date or the date you
make a payment online. Check your statements carefully,
as credit card companies sometimes change the due
dates.

Periodic rate—an interest rate based on a certain period
of time, such as a day or a month.

Money for the future

Start saving now

You can begin saving now even if you are in debt and living in a residence on a diet of macaroni. Saving now helps you establish a habit that will pay off in the future.

Create an emergency fund. Take some percentage of every paycheque you receive, and immediately deposit that amount in a savings account. Again, start by saving 10 percent of your income. Then see if you can increase that amount over time.

The first purpose of this savings account is to have money on hand for surprises and emergencies—anything from a big repair bill to a sudden job loss. For peace of mind, have an emergency fund equal to at least six months of living expenses. Once you have that amount in place, save for longer-term goals. Examples are a new car, a child's education, and your own retirement.

Save for retirement. It's never too early to start thinking about your retirement. Many employers offer retirement plans. Some companies will match employee contributions to these accounts. Ask your employer if this benefit is offered to you. If it is, take full advantage of it.

Invest carefully

Investing in stocks, corporate bonds, and mutual funds can be risky. Do so only if you regularly save money and pay off the full balance on your credit cards each month. Even then, only invest money that you can afford to lose.

Successful investing requires extensive homework. Educate yourself by taking a class about personal finance and getting coaching from an independent, certified financial planner. No matter how you choose to invest, put time on your side. Invest as much as you can—keeping in mind the tips above—and invest as early as you can.

Be a wise car shopper

A car is a lousy investment. The minute you drive it off the dealer's lot, it loses value. And the trade-in value will never be enough to pay off a car loan.

If you borrow money to buy a car, keep the costs as low as possible. Reduce interest charges by sticking to a three-year loan rather than extending it to four or five years. Check out certified, preowned cars. These are used cars that come with a warranty from the manufacturer, not the car dealer.

Stick to regular loans rather than leasing. Once you pay off a three-year loan, you can keep on driving the car with no monthly payments. If you lease a car for three years, you won't own the car when the lease is up, and you might find it tempting to lease another car.

Save on insurance

Protect your assets by getting insurance for your home, car, and life. If you live in an apartment, get renters' insurance.

Find an independent insurance agent who can help you with all these policies. Ask about discounts for buying more than one policy from the same insurance company. Also ask if you can lower your premiums by raising your deductibles.

There are basically two kinds of life insurance: term and whole life. Term insurance is the least expensive. It pays if you die, and that's it. Whole life is more expensive. It pays if you die, and it also accumulates money like a savings plan does. However, you'll often get a higher return on your money if you buy the lower-priced term insurance and invest your extra dollars in something other than insurance.

Many schools offer an extended health care plan (in addition to provincial coverage) for their students. Find out what's available on your campus. Keep in mind that, if you are already covered on an equivalent health care plan (such as with your parents or spouse), there usually is an opt-out date when you can withdraw from the student health care plan. You want to avoid paying twice for the same coverage. ✳

 Find more ways online to create a secure financial future @ **www.bams5ce.nelson.com**

You can pay for school

MILLIONS OF DOLLARS are waiting for people who take part in higher education. But the funds flow only to students who know how to find them.

There are many ways to pay for school. The kind of help you get depends on your financial need. In general, financial need equals the cost of your schooling minus what you can reasonably be expected to pay.

Financial aid includes money you don't pay back (grants, bursaries, and scholarships), money you do pay back (loans), and work-study programs. Most students who get financial aid receive a package that includes several examples of each type.

To find out more, visit your school's financial aid office on a regular basis.

Once you've lined up financial aid, keep it flowing. Find out the requirements for renewing loans, grants, and scholarships. Remember that many financial aid packages depend on your making "satisfactory academic progress." Plus, you may have to maintain enrolment in a minimum number of courses to continue receiving support. Also, programs change constantly. Money may be limited, and application deadlines are critical.

Scholarships, grants, and loans backed by the federal and provincial government are key sources of money for students. So are credit unions, service organizations such as Kiwanis International, and local chambers of commerce. Sometimes relatives will provide financial help. For more information on loans, refer back to the article "Take Charge of Your Credit" earlier in this chapter.

Determine how much money you need to complete your education and where you will get it. Having a plan for paying for your entire education makes it easier to finish your degree. ✳

 Discover more ways online to pay for school @ **www.bams5ce.nelson.com**

Education is worth it

Education is one of the few things you can buy that will last a lifetime. It can't rust, corrode, break down, or wear out. It can't be stolen, burned, repossessed, or destroyed. Once you have a degree, no one can take it away. That makes your education a safer investment than real estate, gold, oil, diamonds, or stocks.

Think about all the services and resources that your tuition money buys: academic advice to help you choose classes and select a major; access to the student health centre and counselling services; career planning and job placement offices that you can often visit even after you graduate; athletic, arts, and entertainment events at a central location; and a student centre where you can meet people and socialize.

If you live on campus, you also get a place to stay with meals provided, all for less than the cost of an average hotel room. And by the way, you get to attend classes. Consider how much nonstudents would have to pay for such an array of services. You can see that higher education is a bargain.

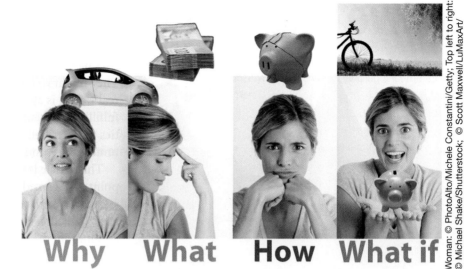

Why   What   How   What if

Your learning styles and your money

LEARNING STYLES: "Discovering How You Learn" on page 40 explains four learning styles—unique ways of perceiving and processing our experiences. You can see these different styles at work in the ways that people spend and earn money.

For example, some people buy quickly once they find a product or service that connects to something they care about deeply (*active experimentation*). Others take the time to shop around and compare prices before they spend much (*reflective observation*). Some people are curious about how the stock and bond markets work and will take the time to analyze the field (*abstract conceptualization*). Others want to jump right in and experiment with ways to make more money (*concrete experience*).

When you face a financial decision, ask the following four questions. They will help you gain the benefits of using each learning style and make a more balanced choice.

Ask: *Why* **am I considering spending this money?** We buy when we see something to be gained. This could involve a small benefit, such as spending a couple of dollars on a soft drink to satisfy your thirst. Or it could be a larger benefit, like spending thousands of dollars on a car to satisfy your desire for convenience and mobility. Before you hand over your cash or credit card, be clear about what you want to gain.

Ask: *What* **are the facts I need to know?** The answer to this question is useful even with small purchases.

In the case of a soft drink, for example, check out the ingredients on the label. Then think about whether you want to put that stuff in your body. If you're buying a car, find out exactly how much it will cost beyond the sticker price. If you plan to borrow money, research the available options. Your bank or credit union may offer a better interest rate than the car dealer. Or maybe a relative would consider giving you a no-interest loan.

Ask: *How* **would this purchase affect my life?** Many purchases come with a cost that goes beyond money. That soft drink might come with hidden costs—excess sugar and calories. Buying or renting a bigger home could tie you into higher payments. And that might require you to work more hours or see less of your family. When you spend your time, energy, and money for one purpose, those resources are not available for other purposes.

Ask: *What if* **I could get the same benefit without spending money?** You could save a couple dollars, reduce calories, *and* quench your thirst by using a water fountain instead of buying an overpriced drink. You could get around town *and* save thousands of dollars by getting a used car, or by using public transportation and paying for an occasional taxi ride. And you could gain more living space by building a small addition to your current home, or by simply cleaning out some cluttered rooms. Before you spend a dime, ask whether you can get the same benefit for no money down—or no money at all. ✱

10

MONEY

chapter 10
▪ Put It to Work
▶ ▶ ▶ ▶ ▶
▪ Skills Snapshot
▪ Master Student Profile

QUIZ

Name_____ Date____/____/____

1. List five sources of money to help students pay for their educations.

2. Describe at least three ways to decrease your expenses while you are in school.

3. How can you avoid getting into financial trouble when you use credit cards?

4. The text asserts that investing in your education is safer than investing in real estate, gold, oil, or stocks. List the reasons given for this assertion.

5. Create a list of possible expenses to go to school for one year. For three items, suggest at least one way expenses can be reduced.

6. A First Step approach to managing money is to:
   (a) Admit that you probably don't have enough money.
   (b) Admit that money management is complicated.
   (c) Tell the truth about how much money you have and how much you spend.
   (d) All of the above.
   (e) None of the above.

7. State three ways that you can ensure your credit rating remains in a healthy state as you progress through your postsecondary education.

8. Power Process: "Risk Being a Fool" suggests that sometimes you should take action without considering the consequences. True or False? Explain the answer.

9. Describe three strategies for increasing your income.

10. List three ways to make online transactions more secure.

Skills SNAPSHOT

Now that you've reflected on the ideas in this chapter and experimented with some new strategies, revisit your responses to the "Money" section of the Discovery Wheel exercise on page 37. Think about the most powerful action you could take in the near future toward financial mastery. Complete the following sentences.

MANAGING INCOME AND EXPENSES

Right now my main sources of income are . . .

My three biggest expenses each month are . . .

One monthly expense that I could reduce right away is . . .

To begin reducing this expense, I could . . .

PAYING FOR SCHOOL

I plan to graduate by (month and year) . . .

I plan to pay for my education next year by . . .

TAKING THE NEXT ACTION

I'll know that I've reached a new level of mastery with money when . . .

To reach that level of mastery, the most important thing I can do next is to . . .

MASTER STUDENT Profile

© Retna/Photoshot

Régine Chassagne & Edwin Farnham Butler

. . . are caring

Both musicians are part of the Indie Rock band *Arcade Fire* that won numerous musical awards in 2011 (Grammy, Juno, and a Brit). They are committed to giving back to others working with *Partners in Health* in Haiti.

  Find more biographical information about Régine Chassagne & Edwin Farnham Butler at the Master Student Hall of Fame @

www.bams5ce.nelson.com

Musically, Arcade Fire has always prided themselves in making it up as they go along—fidèle to the feeling, but not the rules. But there is a larger plan.

Since 2005, the group has raised more than $1 million for development work in the Western hemisphere's poorest nation. Recently, Chassagne and Dominique Anglade, a Montréal businesswoman and childhood friend, formed their own charity, Kanpe (Creole for "stand up"). Working with *Partners in Health (PIH)*, an international NGO, and Fonkoze, a Haitian micro-lending organization, Kanpe is set to launch a concerted attack on the roots of poverty in one island community, shepherding 300 families to economic and physical health. The budget for the three-year project is $2 million. The band has pledged to match every dollar raised, up to a million, from their own pockets. In March, in between award shows, they'll all travel together to Haiti to check out the work that has already begun, and get their own hands dirty.

On the surface, at least, they seem like an unlikely pair. Edwin Farnham Butler III, 30, the lanky eldest son of a blue-blood New Englander and a Joni Mitchell-style California musician, raised in Texas, and diminutive Régine Chassagne, the 33-year-old francophone

daughter of Haitian refugees who washed up on Montréal's south shore.

They met at the McGill Faculty of Music in 2000. She was studying vocals and playing recorder in a medieval ensemble. He wasn't in school—although he did study comparative Biblical Scripture for a time—just haunting the corridors, looking for a drummer for his then more-notional-than-actual band. Their paths crossed again at an art opening where Chassagne was singing with a jazz band. They got together a few nights later to play music and wrote a tune, Headlights Look Like Diamonds, that ended up on Arcade Fire's first EP in 2003, the year they married.

Chassagne taught herself to play piano at age four. Growing up in a close-knit household, song was always a part of daily life, but it was only after an undergrad degree in communications at Concordia, and her mother's untimely death, that she ever dared to breathe her dream of performing. Her parents had come to Montréal in the early 1970s, after meeting in the States. Régine's mother fled Haiti when she returned home from market one day to find her cousins and friends had been murdered. Her dad left after his father was taken away by the Tonton Macoutes and executed. As new Canadians, both worked hard to establish themselves—he taught math, she worked as a secretary and at a daycare. But Haiti remained the country of all their imaginations. "Growing up, I never went there," says Chassagne. "It wasn't a possibility financially, and especially with my mom—she still had nightmares. She wanted to forget about it."

Even before the trip, Arcade Fire had been raising money for Partners in Health, tacking on a charity surcharge—one dollar, one euro or one pound—to every ticket sold. The "biggest no-brainer thing we ever did," as Win calls it, has so far collected almost US$1 million. At shows, he gives a short spiel about the organization, and PIH volunteers are always on hand to pass out literature. During the most recent tour, 5,500 fans signed up for its "Stand with Haiti" campaign.

They still control, or as Chassagne prefers to say, "direct" their own business, paying their way in the studio, on video shoots and the road. But there have been small concessions to stardom, like the manager they share with Björk and Paul McCartney. Butler swears things haven't changed that much. "Our day-to-day life is identical, except for not sweating the electrical bill as much. We still have the same crap in our house; the old chairs, and the stool I fished out of the dumpster."

Source: "Their main act: Arcade Fire doesn't chase fame," by Jonathon Gatehouse. *Macleans*, February 21, 2011.

Master Student Map

as you read, ask yourself

what if . . .

I could meet the demands of daily life with energy and optimism to spare?

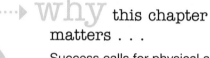

why this chapter matters . . .

Success calls for physical and emotional well-being.

what is included . . .

- Wake up to health   347
- Choose your fuel   349
- Eating well with Canada's Food Guide   350
- Choose to exercise   351
- Choose to rest   352
- Choose mental health   353
- Choose to stay safe   356
- Choose sexual health   358
- Protect against unwanted pregnancy   360
- Developing self-efficacy   365
- Emotional pain is not a sickness   366
- Suicide is no solution   367
- Alcohol, tobacco, and drugs: The truth   368
- Seeing the full scope of addiction   371
- Warning: Advertising can be dangerous to your health   373
- Power Process: Surrender   376
- Master Student Profile: Clara Hughes   380

how

you can use this chapter . . .

- Maintain your physical and mental energy.
- Enhance your self-esteem.
- Make decisions about alcohol and other drugs in a way that supports your success.

MASTER STUDENTS in action

I start every week with my Success Triangle: (1) Prioritize what needs to be done now and what can be done by others; (2) make a schedule, and check it daily (or more often as needed); and (3) reward myself—eat right, exercise, and get more rest. When I stick to my plan there's less stress in my life.

—KAREN GRAJEDA

Wake up to health

SOME PEOPLE SEE health as just a matter of common sense. These people might see little value in reading a health chapter. After all, they already know how to take care of themselves. Yet *knowing* and *doing* are two different things. Health information does not always translate into healthy habits.

We expect to experience health challenges as we age. Even youth, though, is no guarantee of good health. Over the last three decades, obesity among young adults in Canada has tripled. Twenty-seven percent of young adults smoke (Canadian Cancer Society, 2011). And the leading causes of death among 20 to 24 year olds is unintentional injuries, suicide, cancer and homicide (Public Health Agency of Canada, 2011).

As a student, your success in school is directly tied to your health. Lack of sleep and exercise have been associated with lower grade point averages among undergraduate students. So have alcohol use, tobacco use, gambling, and chronic health conditions (University of Minnesota, 2007). And any health habit that undermines your success in school can also undermine your success in later life.

People often misunderstand what the word *health* means. Remember that this word is similar in origin to *whole, hale, hardy,* and even *holy.* Implied in these words are qualities that most of us associate with healthy people: alertness, vitality, vigour. Healthy people meet the demands of daily life with energy to spare. Illness or stress might slow them down for a while, but then they bounce back. They know how to relax, create loving relationships, and find satisfaction in their work.

Perhaps *health* is one of those rich, multilayered concepts that we can never define completely. That's okay. We can still adopt habits that sustain our well-being. One study found that people lengthened their lives an average of 14 years by adopting just four habits: staying tobacco-free, eating more fruits and vegetables, exercising regularly, and drinking alcohol in moderation, if at all (Khaw, Wareham, Bingham, Welch, Luben & Day, 2008).

In the end, your definition of *health* comes from your own experience. The proof lies not on these pages but in your life—in the level of health that you create, starting now. You have two choices. You can remain unaware of habits that have major consequences for your health. Or you can become aware of current habits (discovery), choose new habits (intention), and take appropriate action.

Health is a choice you make every moment, with each action that you take. Wake up to this possibility by experimenting with the suggestions in this chapter. ✳

journal entry 30

Discovery Statement

Take a First Step about Your Health

This structured Discovery Statement allows you to look closely at your health. If you look and feel healthy, understanding your body better can help you be aware of what you're doing right. If you are not content with your present physical or emotional health, you might discover some ways to adjust your personal habits and increase your sense of well-being.

Complete the following statements in the space provided. As with the Discovery Wheel exercise in Chapter 1, the usefulness of this Journal Entry will be determined by your honesty and courage.

Eating

1. What I know about the way I eat is . . .

2. What I would most like to change about my diet is . . .

3. My eating habits lead me to be . . .

_____

_____

_____

_____

journal entry  30 —Continued

Exercise

1. The way I usually exercise is . . .
2. The last time I did 20 minutes or more of heart/lung (aerobic) exercise was . . .
3. As a result of my physical conditioning, I feel . . .
4. And I look . . .
5. It would be easier for me to work out regularly if I . . .
6. The most important benefit for me in exercising more is . . .

_____
_____
_____
_____
_____
_____
_____
_____

Substances

1. My history of cigarette smoking is . . .
2. An objective observer would say that my use of alcohol is . . .
3. In the last 10 days, the number of alcoholic drinks I have had is . . .
4. I would describe my use of coffee, colas, and other caffeinated drinks as . . .
5. I have used the following illegal drugs in the past week:
6. When it comes to drugs, what I am sometimes concerned about is . . .
7. I take the following prescription drugs:

_____
_____
_____
_____
_____
_____
_____

Relationships

1. Someone who knows me fairly well would say I am emotionally . . .
2. The way I look and feel has affected my relationships by . . .
3. My use of drugs or alcohol has been an issue with the following people . . .
4. The best thing I could do for myself and my relationships would be to . . .

_____
_____
_____
_____
_____
_____
_____

Sleep

1. The number of hours I sleep each night is . . .
2. On weekends I normally sleep . . .
3. I have trouble sleeping when . . .
4. Last night I . . .
5. The quality of my sleep is usually . . .

_____
_____
_____
_____
_____

In general

What concerns me more than anything else about my health is . . .

Looking back at my responses to this exercise, I feel . . .

_____
_____
_____
_____
_____
_____

Choose your fuel

IT'S A CLICHÉ, and it's true: You are what you eat. What you eat can have immediate and long-term effects on your performance as a student. That giant jelly doughnut can make you drowsy within minutes. A steady diet of them can affect the amount of energy you have available to meet and juggle the demands of classes, family members, jobs, extracurricular activities, and other commitments.

Start with widely accepted guidelines. There have been hundreds of books written about nutrition. One says don't drink milk. Another says the calcium provided by milk is an essential daily nutrient. Although such debate seems confusing, take comfort. There's actually wide agreement about how to fuel yourself for health.

Nutritional guidelines have been developed by Health Canada, "Canada's Food Guide." Though you might find a more healthful diet, you can do well by following these guidelines.

Avoid fad diets. If you are overweight, avoid people who make claims about a quick fix. Even if that "Lose 20 pounds in 20 days!" diet works at first, you're likely to gain the weight back.

For example, think critically about low-carbohydrate plans such as the Atkins diet. These plans can lead to significant weight loss in the short term. However, research undercuts claims for long-term benefits. The "drop-out" rate for the Atkins diet is comparable to that of other diets (Samaha, Iqbal, Seshadri et al., 2003). Many people simply find these plans too difficult to sustain. In addition, low-carbohydrate diets focus on meat and dairy products with high levels of saturated fat, which can increase the risk of heart disease and several forms of cancer. The formula for weight loss is simple, though not always easy: Eat better food, eat less food, and exercise regularly. To find safe weight loss and

© Ivonne Wierink/Shutterstock

nutrition programs, visit your doctor or student health service. Look for a program that provides peer support.

Limit fast foods. Fast foods can be tempting, especially if you're pressed for time. When eaten consistently, these foods can also expand your waistline and drain your budget. A medium pop, large order of fries, and double cheeseburger can pack over 1,500 calories and 60 grams of fat.

About 23 percent of Canadians are obese, which is significantly less than Americans, but we are quickly catching up (Tjepkema, 2011). Our love affair with fast food contributes to that figure.

To save money and promote health, prepare meals at home and centre them on whole grains, legumes, fruits, and vegetables. When you eat out, reduce portions. ✳

Discover more strategies online for fueling your body @ **www.bams5ce.nelson.com**

martial arts, kickboxing, yoga, pilates, Zumba fitness classes, or mountain climbing. Check out your school's recreational facilities to see what courses they offer.

Vary your routine. Find several activities that you enjoy, and rotate them throughout the year. Your main form of activity during winter might be dancing, step fitness class, or skiing. In summer, you could switch to outdoor sports. Whenever possible, choose weight-bearing activities such as walking, running, or stair-climbing.

Get active early. Work out first thing in the morning. Then it's done for the day. Make it part of your daily routine, just like brushing your teeth.

Exercise with other people. Making exercise a social affair can add a fun factor and raise your level of commitment.

Look for gradual results. If your goal is to lose weight, be patient. Since one pound equals 3,500 calories, you might feel tempted to reduce weight loss to a simple formula: *Let's see . . . if I burn away just 100 calories each day through exercise, I should lose one pound every 35 days.*

Actually, the relationship between exercise and weight loss is complex. Many factors—including individual differences in metabolism and the type of exercise you do—affect the amount of weight you actually lose (Brody, 2006).

When you step on the bathroom scale, look for small changes over time rather than sudden, dramatic losses.

Gradual weight loss is more healthy, anyway—and easier to sustain over the long term.

Weight loss is just one potential benefit of exercise. Choosing to exercise can also lift your mood, increase your stamina, strengthen your bones, stabilize your joints, and help prevent heart disease. It can also reduce your risk of high blood pressure, diabetes, and several forms of cancer. If you do resistance training—such as weight machines or elastic-band workouts—you'll strengthen your muscles as well. For a complete fitness program, add stretching exercises to enjoy increased flexibility (Brody, 2006).

Before beginning any vigorous exercise program, consult a health care professional. This is critical if you are overweight, in poor condition, a smoker, or if you have a history of health problems. ✳

 Discover more ways online to follow through on your exercise goals @

www.bams5ce.nelson.com

STUDENT VOICES

Staying in shape has always been important to me, so including time in my schedule for exercise is something I always try to do. It started to be the one thing I wasn't accomplishing because I had let reading or studying to prepare for class take precedence. Then I signed up for a water aerobics course that met once a week. Having a fixed time when I knew I had to be at the specific class helped me keep it a priority.

—LUPE SANTIAGO

Choose to rest

IN ADDITION TO requiring activity, human bodies need sufficient periods of rest. A lack of rest can decrease your immunity to illness and impair your performance in school

As a student, you might be tempted to cut back drastically on your sleep once in a while. All-nighters to study for exams or catch up on a lengthy reading assignment are common for some students. Unfortunately, staying up all night will leave you bleary eyed for your exam and therefore decrease your performance plus exhaust you for the other necessary work. If you find you are indulging in them often, read Chapter 2 for some time-management ideas. Depriving yourself of sleep is a choice you can avoid.

© auremar/Shutterstock

Promote sound sleep

Sometimes, getting to sleep isn't easy, even when you feel tired. If you have trouble falling asleep, experiment with the following suggestions:

- Exercise daily. For many people, this promotes sounder sleep. However, finish exercising several hours before you want to go to sleep.

- Avoid lengthy naps during the daytime.

- Monitor your caffeine intake, especially in the afternoon and evening.

- Avoid using alcohol to feel sleepy. Drinking alcohol late in the evening can disrupt your sleep during the night.

- Make tomorrow's to-do list before you go to sleep so you won't lie there worrying that tomorrow you'll forget about something you need to do.

- Develop a sleep ritual—a regular sequence of calming activities that end your day. You might take a warm bath and do some light reading. Turn off the screens (computer monitors, etc.) at least one hour before you go to bed.

- Keep your sleeping room cool.

- Sleep in the same place each night. When you're there, your body gets the message "It's time to go to sleep."

- Practise relaxation techniques while lying in bed. A simple one is to count your breaths and release distracting thoughts as they arise.

- Get up and study or do something else until you're tired.

- See a doctor if sleeplessness persists.

How much sleep is enough? Your body knows when it's tired. Also look for signs of depression, irritability, and other emotional problems. Lack of sleep can interfere with your memory, your concentration, and your ability to stay awake in class. The solution is a good night's sleep. ✳

Choose mental health

THE NUMBER OF students in higher education who have mental health problems is steadily increasing (CBC, 2011). According to the American College Health Association study, which included students from six Ontario universities, 33 to 43 percent of college students report that they have felt so depressed that it was difficult to function. Over half of the students from Ontario reported feeling hopeless and six to nine percent considered suicide within the last year before the study.

Mental health includes many factors: your skill at managing stress, your ability to build loving relationships, your capacity to meet the demands of school and work, and your beliefs about your ability to succeed. People with mental illness have thoughts, emotions, or behaviours that consistently interfere with these areas of life.

You can take simple and immediate steps to prevent mental health problems or cope with them if they do occur. Remember that strategies for managing test-related stress can help you manage *any* form of stress. (See "Let Go of Test Anxiety" on page 205.) Here are some other suggestions to promote your mental health.

Take care of your body. Your thoughts and emotions can get scrambled if you go too long feeling

© ZenShui/Alix Minde/Getty Images

hungry or tired. Follow the suggestions in this chapter for eating, exercise, and sleep.

Solve problems. Although you can't "fix" a bad feeling in the same way that you can fix a machine, you can choose to change a situation associated with that feeling. There might be a problem that needs a solution. You can use feeling bad as your motivation to solve that problem.

Stay active. A related strategy is to do something—*anything* that's constructive, even if it's not a solution to a specific problem. For example, mop the kitchen floor. Clean out your dresser drawers. Iron your shirts. This sounds silly, but it works.

11

HEALTH

The basic principle is that you can separate emotions from actions. It is appropriate to feel miserable when you do. It's normal to cry and express your feelings. It is also possible to go to class, study, work, eat, and feel miserable at the same time. Unless you have a diagnosable problem with anxiety or depression, you can continue your normal activities until the misery passes.

Japanese psychiatrist Morita Masatake, a contemporary of Sigmund Freud, based his whole approach to treatment on this insight: We can face our emotional pain directly and still take constructive action. One of Masatake's favourite suggestions for people who felt depressed was that they tend a garden (Reynolds, 1995).

Share what you're thinking and feeling. There are times when negative thoughts and emotions persist even after you take appropriate action. Tell a family member or friend about them. This is a powerful way to gain perspective. The simple act of describing a problem can sometimes reveal a solution or give you a fresh perspective.

Focus on one task at a time. It's easy to feel stressed if you dwell on how much you have to accomplish this year, this term, this month, or even this week. One solution is to plan using the suggestions in Chapter 2: Time.

Remember that an effective plan for the day does two things. First, it clarifies what you're choosing *not* to do today. (Tasks that you plan to do in the future are listed on your calendar or to-do list.) Second, an effective plan reduces your day to a series of concrete tasks—such as making phone calls, going to classes, running errands, or reading chapters—that you can do one at a time.

If you feel overwhelmed, just find the highest-priority task on your to-do list. Do it with total attention until it's done. Then go back to your list for the next high-priority task. Do *it* with total attention. Savour the feeling of mastery and control that comes with crossing each task off your list.

Manage stress. According to Dr. Richard Kadison, the chief of the Mental Health Service at Harvard University, lack of sleep is a huge issue in making college students feel stressed out. He says that most college and university students only sleep 6½ hours a night (Kadison, 2011). That is just not enough. So if you are starting to feel stressed out, check how much sleep you are getting. School environments can be especially stressful. A 2004 study of 64 universities in Canada found that 47 percent of students report experiencing psychological distress because of feeling constantly under stress (CCS, 2004), so it is important that you know ways to relax.

Stress is not always harmful. It can result from pleasant experiences as well as unpleasant ones. The excitement of a new term—new classes, new instructors, new classmates—can be fun and stressful at the same time.

Oddly enough, your body perceives excitement in almost the same way that it perceives fear. Both emotions produce rapid heart rates, increased adrenalin flow, and muscle contractions. Both emotions produce stress.

Stress, at appropriate times and at manageable levels, is normal and useful. It can sharpen our awareness and boost our energy just when we need it the most. When stress persists or becomes excessive, it is harmful.

Chances are, your stress level is too high if you consistently experience any of the following symptoms: irritability; depression; low productivity; strained relationships at work or home; health problems such as an upset stomach, frequent colds, and a low energy level; a pattern of avoiding tasks; difficulty falling asleep or staying asleep; feeling burned out at home or at work; feeling tense, nervous, or fearful.

Stress has both mental and physical components. The mental components include thoughts that promote fear and anxiety; the physical components include illnesses and muscle tension.

The fact that these elements are all part of stress points to several broad strategies for managing it:

- *Deal with the problem.* The Canadian Mental Health Association (2011) suggests that the first step is to identify what is the cause of the stress, brainstorm solutions, and take steps to solve the problem. Reducing your course load, cutting back on hours at work, getting more financial aid, delegating a task, or taking some other concrete action might solve the problem and help you feel better. With school, the issue is often mounting homework, so make sure your own procrastination isn't adding to your stress levels. Go back over Chapter 2 again to see how you can plan to get the work done. Sometimes an intense feeling of sadness, anger, or fear is related to a specific situation in your life.

- *Deal with stressful thoughts by releasing irrational beliefs.* According to Martin Seligman (1998) and other cognitive psychologists, stress results not from events in our lives but from the way we *think* about those events. If we believe that people should always behave in exactly the way we expect them to, for instance, we set ourselves up for stress. Noticing these beliefs and replacing them with more rational ones (such as *I can control my own behaviour but not the behaviour of others*) can reduce stress significantly.

- *Deal with stressful thoughts by releasing them altogether.* Meditation offers a way to release distressing thoughts. While meditating, you simply notice your thoughts as they arise and pass—without reacting to them. Eventually, your stream of thinking slows down. You might even find that it comes to a complete stop while at the same time you remain alert and aware. This is a state of deep relaxation that might also yield life-changing insights. Many religious or spiritual organizations offer meditation classes. You can also find meditation instruction through health maintenance organizations, YMCAs or YWCAs, and community centre education programs.

- *Counter the physical element of stress.* Options include breathing exercises, relaxation techniques, yoga, and therapeutic bodywork such as massage. Some schools offer classes in these subjects. Regular physical exercise is another key ingredient when you are feeling stressed (Paterson, 2002). Go for a walk or work out at the gym the next time tension causes stress.

- *Use this book.* It includes relaxation and breathing exercises. Many of the Power Processes and the techniques for letting go of test anxiety can also help you manage stress.

Find resources on or off campus. Student health centres are not just for treating colds, allergies, and flu symptoms. Counsellors expect to help students deal with adjustment to campus, changes in mood, academic problems, and drug abuse and dependence. Students with anxiety disorders, clinical depression, bipolar disorder, and other diagnoses might get referred to a psychiatrist or psychologist who works on or off campus. The referral process can take time, so seek help right away. Your tuition helps to pay for these services. It's smart to use them now.

You can find resources to promote mental health even if your campus doesn't offer counselling services. First, find a family doctor—one person who can coordinate all of your health care. (For suggestions, go to your school's health centre.) A family doctor can refer you to a mental health professional if it seems appropriate. Second, remember a basic guideline about *when* to seek help: whenever problems with your thinking, moods, or behaviours consistently interfere with your ability to sleep, eat, go to class, work, or create positive relationships. These two suggestions can also work after you graduate. Promoting mental health is a skill to use for the rest of your life.

For more information on mental health, check out the resources on this textbook's website. For instance, there you will find a depression quiz so that you can self-assess whether or not you need to seek help.

(WWW) Find more pathways to robust mental health online @
www.bams5ce.nelson.com

Is it just me who feels stressed out?

No, actually three-quarters of Canadians report they feel stressed out at least once a month and 43 percent feel really stressed more than once a week (CMHA, 2011). Luckily, stress levels do decrease as you get older, with 87 percent of 18- to 24-year-olds saying they feel stressed out at least once a month compared to only 56 percent of over 65-year-olds. Work is the major source of stress, yet many (41 percent) report that the stress from work actually has a positive impact on their performance—again reinforcing the idea that not all stress is bad. And most individuals felt that their employer was effective at dealing with workplace stress. Finally, most Canadians deal with stress through exercise or meditation rather than talking to others. So go for a bike ride or learn a new sport—stress is a part of life. It is how you deal with it that counts!

Observe Yourself

You are an expert on your body. You are more likely to notice changes before anyone else does. Pay attention to these changes. They are often your first clue about the need for medical treatment or intervention.

   Watch for the following signs:

- Weight loss of more than 10 pounds in 10 weeks with no apparent cause
- A sore, scab, or ulcer that does not heal in three weeks
- A skin blemish or mole that bleeds, itches, or changes size, shape, or colour
- Persistent or severe headaches
- Sudden vomiting that is not preceded by nausea
- Fainting spells
- Double vision
- Difficulty swallowing
- Persistent hoarseness or a nagging cough

- Blood that is coughed up or vomited
- Shortness of breath for no apparent reason
- Persistent indigestion or abdominal pain
- A big change in normal bowel habits, such as alternating diarrhea and constipation
- Pink, red, or unusually cloudy urine
- Discomfort or difficulty when urinating or during sexual intercourse
- Lumps or thickening in a breast (for men as well as women)
- Vaginal bleeding between menstrual periods.

   If you are experiencing any of these symptoms, get help. Even if you think it might not be serious, check it out. Without timely and proper treatment, a minor illness or injury can lead to serious problems. Begin with your medical health care professional, student health service or your provincial Telehealth Services (in Ontario, dial 1-866-797-0000) for free confidential health care service.

11

HEALTH

Discovery/Intention Statement

Choose to be healthy

For three minutes, brainstorm things you can do during the next month to improve the ways that you fuel, move, rest, and observe your body. Write your ideas in the space below. Use additional paper if needed.

I discovered that I . . .

_____

_____

_____

_____

Next, pick three of your ideas that you can begin to use or practise this week. Write an Intention Statement below about how and when you intend to use these ideas.

I intend to . . .

_____

_____

_____

_____

© auremar/Shutterstock

MOST SCHOOLS ARE relatively safe. While on campus, you might feel insulated from the outside world and believe that you have special protection. Yet there are people who know how to take advantage of this belief. Some criminals target students who are alone. Others monitor residence activity. They know that rooms are often unlocked and stashed with computers and other valuables.

Take general precautions

Three simple actions can significantly increase your personal safety. One is to always lock doors when you're away from home. If you live in a residence, follow the policies for keeping the front doors secure. Don't let an unauthorized person walk in behind you. If you

Choose to stay safe

commute to school or have a car on campus, keep your car doors locked.

The second action is to avoid walking alone, especially at night. Many schools offer a foot patrol service where students will walk with you to your car or residence. Use them. As a backup, carry enough spare cash for a taxi ride.

Third, plan for emergencies. Look for emergency phones along the campus routes that you normally walk. If you have a cell phone, you can always call 911 for help.

Also, be willing to make that call when you see other people in unsafe situations. For example, you might be at a party with a friend who drinks too much and collapses. In this situation, some underage students might hesitate to call for help. They fear getting charged with illegal alcohol possession. Don't make this mistake. Every minute that you delay calling 911 puts your friend at further risk.

Lesbian, Gay, Bisexual, Transgendered, Queer (LGBTQ) Students

If you are an LGBTQ student, you are more at risk for **_homophobic bullying_** and hate crimes. Statistics Canada recently found that youth are most likely to be involved in hate crimes than other age groups, and that more

11

HEALTH

than half the hate crimes motivated by sexual orientation were violent (Toronto Police Service, 2011). Many schools have a "Positive Space" program (Algonquin College, 2011) in which volunteers (including students, staff, and faculty) provide support to LGBTQ campus members. One of the goals of the program is to make us all more aware of the **transphobia, heterosexism,** and **homophobia** that occur in our schools and society. Positive Space Program volunteers participate in training and typically identify themselves by placing a sticker on their office or residence room doors. Find out if your school has such a program and, if not, consider starting one. Whether you are gay or straight, we all are responsible for creating a safe school environment.

There are many organizations available to support LGBTQ members from PFLAG Canada (www.pflagcanada.ca) to the LGBT Youth Line (www.youthline.ca) which provides peer counselling.

 Find more information on how to stay safe, go online @
··
www.bams5ce.nelson.com

Prevent sexual assault

You need to know how to prevent sexual assault while you're on campus. This problem could be more common at your school than you think. People often hesitate to report rape for many reasons, such as fear, embarrassment, and concerns that others won't believe them.

- Both women and men can take steps to prevent rape from occurring in the first place:

- Get together with a group of people for a tour of the campus. Make a special note of danger spots, such as unlighted paths and unguarded buildings. Keep in mind that rape can occur during daylight and in well-lit places.

- Ask if your school has a foot patrol service for people taking evening classes. If you do take an evening class, ask if there are security officers on duty before and after the class.

- Take a course or seminar on self-defence and rape prevention. To find these courses, check with your student counselling service, community education centre, or local library.

If you are raped, get medical care right away. Go to the nearest rape crisis centre, hospital, student health service, or police station. Also arrange for follow-up counselling. It's your decision whether to report the crime. Filing a report does not mean that you have to press charges. And if you do choose to press charges later, having a report on file can help your case.

Date rape—the act of forcing sex on a date—is a common form of rape among college students. Date rape is rape. It is a crime.

Drugs such as Rohypnol (flunitrazepam) and GHB (gamma-hydroxybutyrate) have been used in date rape. These drugs, which can be secretly slipped into a drink, reduce resistance to sexual advances and produce an effect similar to amnesia. People who take these drugs might not remember the circumstances that led to their being raped. To protect yourself when you are out, don't leave your drinks unattended, and don't let someone else get drinks for you.

Take further steps to protect yourself from sexual assault. Decide what kind of sexual relationships you want. Then set firm limits, and communicate them clearly and assertively. Make sure that your nonverbal messages match your verbal message. If someone refuses to respect your limits, stay away from that person.

Also make careful decisions about using alcohol or drugs. Be wary of dates who get drunk or high. Consider providing your own transportation on dates. Avoid going to secluded places with people you don't know well. Forcing someone to have sex is *never* acceptable. You have the right to refuse to have sex with anyone—dates, your partner, your fiancée or fiancé, or your spouse.

Prevent accidents

Accidents due to unsafe conditions and behaviours can lead to disability and even death. Following are ways you can greatly reduce the odds of accidents:

- Don't drive after drinking alcohol or using psychoactive drugs.

- Drive with the realization that other drivers may be preoccupied, intoxicated, or careless.

- Make sure poisons are clearly labelled.

- Keep stairs, halls, doorways, and other pathways clear of shoes, toys, newspapers, and other clutter.

- Don't smoke in bed.

- Don't let candles burn unattended.

- Keep children away from hot stoves. Turn pot handles inward.

- Check electrical cords for fraying, loose connections, or breaks in insulation. Don't overload extension cords.

- Keep a fire extinguisher handy.

- Install smoke detectors where you live and work. Most run on batteries that need occasional replacement. Follow the manufacturer's guidelines.

- Watch for ways that an infant or toddler could suffocate. Put away or discard small objects that can be swallowed, old refrigerators or freezers that can act as air-tight prisons, unattended or unfenced swimming pools, kerosene heaters in tightly closed rooms, and plastic kitchen or clothing bags. ✳

 For more ways on how to stay safe, go online @
··
www.bams5ce.nelson.com

© BananaStock/Jupiter Images

Choose sexual health

SEXUAL HEALTH IS more than the absence of disease—it involves creating a state of well-being about our sexuality, not just physically but also spiritually, culturally, and psychologically. To develop healthy relationships, it is important to be able to communicate openly and clearly about sex and sexuality. This can be difficult for all students, but for LGBTQ students in particular this can be hard because they are likely to have heard negative slurs or experienced rejection. These negative experiences can lead to the need for students to hide their sexual orientation (PHAC, 2010). You still hear students saying "That's just so gay". Students who are heterosexual or straight may underestimate the impact of these words on LGBTQ students. In fact, there is a price for all these words as LGBTQ youth are more likely than their straight peers to experience bullying, depression, homophobic victimization, and substance abuse.

Recent research in the Toronto District School Board found that students who identified as non-heterosexual came out at about 15 or 16 years of age (PHAC, 2010). But college and university is still a time where we are all answering the "who am I" questions, one of which will revolve around our sexuality. Sexuality isn't simple. Some of us are predominantly heterosexual—physically and emotionally attracted to the opposite sex, some are predominantly homosexual (gay or lesbian) and some are bisexual (attracted to both men and women). Sexual orientation differs from gender identity. Orientation is about who we are are emotionally and physically attracted to whereas gender identity is about our inner sense of being male or female. Individuals who are transgendered have a gender identity that doesn't match their outward appearance. Some Aboriginal people prefer to use the term two-spirited rather than transgender, gay, lesbian or bisexual. Again sexuality is complicated. Wherever you are on the sexuality continuum, learning more about sexual minorities can help us all to create healthier communities.

Choices about sex can be life altering. Sex is a basic human drive, and it can be wonderful. In certain conditions, sex can also be hazardous to your health. It pays to be clear about the pitfalls, including sexually transmitted infections and unwanted pregnancies.

Technically, anyone who has sex is at risk of getting a sexually transmitted infection (**STI**). Without treatment, some of these diseases can lead to blindness, infertility, cancer, heart disease, or even death. Sometimes there are no signs or symptoms of an STI; the only way to tell if you're infected is to be tested by a health care professional.

STIs, which include sexually transmitted viruses, are often spread through body fluids that are exchanged during sex—semen, vaginal secretions, and blood. Some STIs, such as herpes and genital warts, are spread by direct contact with infected skin. Human immunodeficiency virus (HIV) can be spread in other ways as well.

There are more than 25 kinds of STIs, including chlamydia, gonorrhea, syphilis, genital warts, genital herpes, and trichomoniasis. Hepatitis can also be spread through sexual contact. STIs are the most common contagious diseases in North America. The two most common STIs in Canada are HPV (human papillomavirus) and Chlamydia (The Society of Obstetricians and Gynaecologists of Canada, 2010).

HPV is a sexually transmitted virus that leads to genital warts in men and women or can lead to cervical cancer in women. Often individuals with HPV have no symptoms at all. There is no cure for HPV although the warts can be removed. There is an HPV vaccine for women but it does not protect women from all types of HPV (Health Canada, 2011). Because HPV can lead to precancerous lesions and cancer of the cervix, it is imperative that women who are sexually active have regular Pap tests. It has been found in studies of university women that up to 25 percent have HPV (SOGC, 2010).

Chlamydia is also very prevalent among Canadian youth and, like HPV, often asymptomatic. However, if left undiagnosed it can cause significant health problems, such as infertility in women (SOGC, 2010). It can easily be cured with a single dose of antibiotics.

HIV is one of the most serious STIs, and it is different from the others in several respects. HIV is the virus that causes acquired immune deficiency syndrome (AIDS). AIDS is the last stage of HIV infection. A person with AIDS has an immune system that is weakened to the point of having difficulty fighting off many kinds of infections and cancers.

11

HEALTH

© Charles Thatcher/Getty Images

© Fancy/Veer/Corbis/Jupiter Images

Someone infected with HIV might feel no symptoms for months—sometimes years. Many times, those who are spreading HIV don't even know that they have it.

HIV/AIDS is not transmitted solely through unprotected sexual contact. It can be transmitted by shared needles or equipment used to inject drugs. The virus can also be passed from an infected pregnant woman to her fetus during pregnancy or delivery, or through breastfeeding after delivery.

Although gay men and men who have sex with other men are the most affected group who have HIV infections in Canada (51 percent of the estimated 58,000 living with HIV in 2005) it is becoming increasingly common among individuals who inject drugs and those who come from countries where HIV is endemic (Public Health Agency of Canada, 2011). Twenty percent of the individuals with HIV are women. In Canada, it has been found that a disproportionate percentage of those living with HIV are Aboriginal persons.

Public hysteria and misinformation about HIV/AIDS still flourish. You cannot get HIV/AIDS from touching, kissing, hugging, food, coughs, mosquitoes, toilet seats, hot tubs, or swimming pools.

Being infected with HIV is not a death sentence. There are medical treatments that can slow down the rate at which HIV weakens the immune system. Some of the illnesses associated with AIDS can be prevented or treated, although AIDS itself is not curable. Some people live with HIV for years without developing AIDS, and people with AIDS might live for years after developing the condition. As with other chronic illnesses, early detection and early entry into medical care offer more options for treatment and a longer life.

STIs other than AIDS and herpes can be cured, if treated early. Prevention is better. Remember these guidelines:

- Abstain from sex, or have sex exclusively with one person who is free of infection and has no other sex partners. This is the only way to be absolutely safe from STIs.

- Use condoms if you are sexually active. Male condoms are thin latex membranes stretched over the penis prior to intercourse that prevent semen from entering the partner's body. Both women and men can carry them and insist that they be used. Use a condom every time you have sex, and for any type of sex—oral, vaginal, or anal. Use latex condoms—not lambskin. While condoms can be effective, they are not guaranteed to work all of the time. Condoms can break, leak, or slip off. In addition, condoms cannot protect you from STIs that are spread by contact with herpes sores or warts.

- See a doctor to get checked for STIs. As part of your annual checkup, make sure you talk to your doctor about STIs. Make sure to have a Pap test if you are a sexually active woman. Both men and women can easily be checked for HIV and chlamydia. If you have sex with several different people, get checked for STIs even if you have no symptoms. The more people you have sex with, the greater your risk. You are at risk even if you have sex only once with one person who is infected.

- Talk about STIs. Ask sex partners if they have an STI. Tell your partner if you have one.

- Get vaccinated. Vaccines are available for HPV and Hepatitis B. Ask your doctor.

- Recognize the symptoms of STIs in yourself and others. Symptoms include swollen glands with fever and aching; itching around the vagina; vaginal discharge; pain during sex or when urinating; sore throat following oral sex; anal pain after anal sex; sores, blisters, scabs, or warts on the genitals, anus, tongue, or throat; rashes on the palms of your hands or soles of your feet; dark urine; loose and light-coloured stools; and unexplained fatigue, weight loss, and night sweats.

- Avoid injecting illegal drugs. Sharing needles or other paraphernalia with other drug users is a behaviour that can spread STIs.

- Take action soon after you have sex. Urinate soon after you have sex and wash your genitals with soap and water.

Note: Do not use spermicides containing non-oxynol-9. Also avoid lubricants, condoms, and other sex products with nonoxynol-9. At one time, researchers thought that this ingredient could help prevent STIs. New studies indicate that nonoxynol-9 can irritate the vagina and cervix, which actually increases the risk of STIs.

If you think you have an STI, call your medical health care professional, student health service, or local public health clinic. Seek counselling and further testing to find out if you are really infected. Early entry into treatment might prevent serious health problems. To avoid infecting other people, abstain from sex until you are treated and cured.

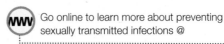 Go online to learn more about preventing sexually transmitted infections @
www.bams5ce.nelson.com

Protect against unwanted pregnancy

YOU AND YOUR partner can avoid unwanted pregnancy. This is not a complete list of options, so be sure to supplement it with information from your medical health care professional.

Total abstinence and sterilization are the most effective methods of birth control. Other methods can fail. Also, many forms of birth control do not protect against STIs.

Abstinence

Abstinence is choosing not to have intercourse. You might feel pressured to change your mind about this choice. Many people exist happily without sexual intercourse. However, remember that abstinence as a means of birth control is guaranteed only when it is practised without exception.

Hormonal Methods

Hormonal methods can be used to prevent pregnancy. These methods work by preventing ovulation, fertilization, or implantation of a fertilized egg. The *pill* is a synthetic hormone that "tells" a woman's body not to release eggs. To be effective, it must be taken as directed by your doctor or pharmacist. Birth control pills must be prescribed by a medical health care professional; the type of pill and the dose needed vary from one woman to the next. Side effects sometimes include slight nausea, breast tenderness, weight gain from water retention, and moodiness.

Some women choose not to take the pill due to increased risks of heart disease, including high blood pressure, blood clots, and breast or endometrial cancer. If you have a history of any of these conditions, see a doctor before taking the pill. If you are over age 35 and smoke, also see your doctor before using this form of birth control.

A *contraceptive injection* (Depo-Provera) into the buttocks or arm muscle is administered by a doctor or nurse every three months. This hormone prevents pregnancy by decreasing ovulation, preventing sperm from reaching the egg, and preventing a fertilized egg from implanting in the uterus. Unlike the pill, this method requires little effort: Women simply need an injection every three months. Side effects can include irregular periods, weight gain, and breast tenderness.

The *hormonal vaginal contraceptive ring* (NuvaRing) releases the hormones progestin and estrogen from a ring placed inside the vagina and around the cervix. A woman removes the ring during her period and then puts in a new ring.

The *patch* is a new method available by prescription in Canada since 2004 (SOGC, 2010). Similar to the birth control pill, it stops women's ovaries from releasing eggs. The advantage of this method is that a new patch only needs to be administered weekly rather than daily like the Pill. You put on a new patch each week for three consecutive weeks and then have a patch-free week prior to starting the cycle again. Some negatives are side effects like skin irritation, and no protection against STIs. However, for women who have trouble remembering to take the pill daily, the patch may be a good alternative.

Barrier Methods

Several methods of birth control create barriers that prevent sperm from reaching a woman's egg. When used carefully and consistently, *male condoms* offer a safe method of birth control. Latex condoms work the best for reducing the risk of STIs. Do not use condoms with oil-based lubricants such as petroleum jelly, lotions, or baby oil, all of which can lead to breakage.

Another method is the *sponge*. This is a soft disk made of polyurethane that contains nonoxynol-9—a spermicide (chemical that kills sperm). To use a sponge, a woman runs it under water and then places it inside her vagina to cover the cervix (the opening to the womb). If you choose to use the sponge, ask your doctor for instructions on when to remove it after you have intercourse. This method is not very effective on its own and should only be used with other birth control methods such as condoms. Keep in mind that non-oxynol-9 can irritate tissue in the vagina and anus with frequent use. This makes it easier for STIs to enter the body. Remember also that some women are sensitive to nonoxynol-9 so the sponge is not an option for them.

Another barrier method is the *diaphragm*. A diaphragm is a shallow rubber dome that is covered with a spermicide (sperm-killing cream) and inserted in the vagina. It fits over the cervix, which is the opening of the uterus, and prevents sperm from getting to the egg. A trained medical health care professional must measure and fit the diaphragm. It must be inserted before intercourse and left in place for six to eight hours after intercourse. It is more than 80 percent effective.

The *cervical cap* is a soft rubber cup that fits snugly around the cervix. Available by prescription only, it is also used with spermicide. Wearing it for more than 48 hours is not recommended due to a low risk of toxic shock syndrome.

Foams, creams, tablets, suppositories, and *jellies* are chemicals that are placed in the vagina before intercourse and prevent sperm from getting to the egg.

Female condoms are made of polyurethane. They are lubricated and placed inside the woman's vagina. Carefully follow the instructions about when to insert the female condom. Use a new condom each time you have sex. Do not use a female condom and a male condom at the same time.

Implants

An *intrauterine device* (IUD) is a small metal or plastic device that is inserted in the uterus and left there for 1 to 10 years. It prevents fertilized eggs from developing. Side effects might include heavier menstrual flow, anaemia, pelvic infection, perforation of the cervix or uterus, increased risk of pelvic inflammatory disease, abnormal bleeding, cramps, or septic abortion.

Calendar Method

This is often called the *rhythm method.* It involves avoiding intercourse during ovulation. The problem with this method is that it is difficult to know for sure when a woman is ovulating. There are no side effects to this method, but as it is often difficult to predict ovulation, it is more likely to lead to pregnancy than the other methods that were discussed.

Emergency contraceptives

When women have vaginal sex without using birth control, or when they use birth control that fails, they can take "morning-after" pills. These pills are taken in two doses, 12 hours apart. The pills release hormones that stop ovulation or stop sperm from fertilizing an egg. This method works best when the pills are taken within 72 hours after sex.

Permanent methods

Some birth control methods are only for people who do not want to have children, or want to stop having children. One method is surgical sterilization. For women this means clipping shut, or cutting and cauterizing the fallopian tubes (where eggs travel to the uterus to implant). Men get a vasectomy, which prevents sperm from entering the penis by severing and sealing the vas deferens (the tubes from the testes). Remember that sperm can stay in a man's body for about three months after surgery. Use another form of birth control during this time, and until a fertility test verifies no presence of sperm.

Women can also be sterilized without surgery. The doctor inserts an implant (Essure) that causes scar tissue to form in the fallopian tubes. Until the scarring appears—usually in about three months—another form of birth control is needed.

Where to get birth control

You can buy condoms, sponges, and spermicides over-the-counter at a store. The morning after pill is also available as an over-the-counter drug in all provinces except Saskatchewan, where it is kept behind the counter; and Québec, where a prescription is required (Canada Citizen, May 2008). Other birth control devices require a prescription.

Note: Withdrawal does not work

Withdrawal happens when a man takes his penis out of the woman's vagina before he has an orgasm. Don't rely on this method for birth control. It requires extraordinary self-control. In addition, men can release some sperm before they have an orgasm. This can lead to pregnancy. The withdrawal method also does not prevent the spread of infection from an STI.

Evaluate birth control methods

Be sure you know how to use your chosen method of birth control. A doctor might assume that you already have this knowledge. If you don't, ask questions freely. Remember that some methods require practice and special techniques. For example, male condoms have an inside and outside surface, and they work best when there's a little space left at the tip for fluid.

The chart on the following page summarizes the effectiveness of various birth control methods and possible side effects. However, effectiveness rates can only be estimated. The estimates depend on many factors—for example, the health of the people using them, their number of sex partners, and how often they have sex. *Remember, the best method is the one you consistently use.* ✳

 Learn more about preventing pregnancy online @
www.bams5ce.nelson.com

HEALTH

for balance. Tell the truth about the times you set a goal and miss it. Also take the time to write and speak about the goals you meet and what works well in your life.

People with a strong sense of self-efficacy attribute their failures to skills that they currently lack—and that they can acquire in the future. This approach chooses not to look on failures as permanent, personal defects. Rather than saying "I just don't have what it takes to become a skilled test taker," say "I can adopt techniques to help me remember key facts even when I feel stressed."

Interpret stress in a new way

Achieving your goals might place you right in the middle of situations in which you feel stress. You might find yourself meeting new people, leading a meeting, speaking in public, or doing something else that you've never done before. That can feel scary.

Remember that stress comes in two forms—thoughts and physical sensations. Thoughts can include mental pictures of yourself making mistakes or being publicly humiliated, and statements such as "This is the worst possible thing that could happen to me." Sensations can include shortness of breath, dry mouth, knots in the stomach, tingling feelings, headaches, and other forms of discomfort.

The way you interpret stress as you become aware of it can make a big difference in your sense of self-efficacy. During moments when you want to do well, you might rely on a stream of personal impressions to judge your performance. In those moments, see if you can focus your attention. Rather than attaching negative interpretations to your experience of stress, simply notice your thoughts and sensations. Release them instead of dwelling on them or trying to resist them. As you observe yourself over time, you might find that the physical sensations associated with your sense of stress and your sense of excitement are largely the same. Instead of viewing these sensations as signs of impending doom, see them as a boost of energy and enthusiasm that you can channel into performing well.

Compare yourself to yourself

Our own failures are often more dramatic to us than the failures of others, and our own successes are often more invisible. When we're unsure of ourselves, we can look in any direction and see people who seem more competent and more confident than we do. When we start the comparison game, we open the door to self-doubt.

There is a way to play the comparison game and win: Instead of comparing yourself to others, compare yourself to yourself. Measure success in terms of self-improvement rather than of triumphs over others. Take time to note any progress you've made over time toward your goals. Write Discovery Statements about that progress. Celebrate your success in any area of life, no matter how small that success might seem.

There is a way to play the comparison game and win: Instead of comparing yourself to others, compare yourself to yourself.

Soak in the acknowledgments of others

Instead of deflecting compliments ("It was nothing"), fully receive the positive things that others say about you ("Thank you"). Also take public credit for your successes. "Well, I was just lucky" can change to "I worked hard to achieve that goal." ✳

Emotional pain is not a sickness

Emotional pain has gotten a bad name. This type of slander is undeserved. There is nothing wrong with feeling bad. It's OK to feel miserable, depressed, sad, upset, angry, dejected, gloomy, or unhappy.

IT MIGHT NOT be pleasant to feel bad, but it can be good for you. Often, the appropriate way to feel is bad. When you leave a place you love, sadness is natural. When you lose a friend or lover, misery might be in order. When someone treats you badly, it is probably appropriate to feel angry. Our feelings are what make us human and the goal of good mental health is not to suppress our feelings but, in fact, to be open to them.

Feeling bad for too long can be a problem. If depression, sadness, or anger persists, get help. Otherwise, allow yourself to experience these emotions. They're usually appropriate and necessary for personal growth.

In fact, feeling rotten can be a cue to us that something is wrong in our lives that we need to address.

When a loved one dies, it is necessary to grieve. The grief might appear in the form of depression, sadness, or anger. There is nothing wrong with extreme emotional pain. It is natural, and it doesn't have to be fixed.

When feeling bad becomes a problem, it is usually because you didn't allow yourself to feel bad at the outset. So the next time you feel rotten, go ahead and feel rotten. It will pass—and probably more quickly if you don't fight it or try to ignore it.

Allowing yourself to feel bad might even help you get smart. Harvey Jackins (1991), a psychotherapist, bases his work on this premise. Jackins believes that when people fully experience and release their emotions, they also remove blocks to their thinking and clear a path for profound personal insights. And Daniel Goleman (1997), author of *Emotional Intelligence,* asserts that being attuned to feelings can lead to sounder personal decisions. Following are some good ways to feel bad.

Don't worry about reasons. Sometimes we allow ourselves to feel bad only if we have a good reason. For example: "Well, I feel very sad, but that is because I just found out my best friend is moving to Europe." It's all right to know the reason why you are sad, and it is fine not to know. You can feel bad for no apparent reason. The reason doesn't matter.

Connect with people. Talking to people is a way of healing. Do things with other people. Include old friends. Make new friends. If friends and family members can't help, see a counsellor at your campus health centre.

Reassure others. Sometimes other people—friends or family members, for example—have a hard time letting you feel bad. They might be worried that they did something wrong and want to make it better. They want you to quit feeling bad. Tell them you will. Assure them that you will feel good again, but that for right now, you just want to feel bad.

Remember that pain passes. Emotional pain does not last forever. Often it ends in a matter of weeks. There's no need to let a broken heart stop your life. Although you can find abundant advice on the subject, just remember a simple and powerful idea: This, too, shall pass. ✳

Suicide is no solution

WHILE PREPARING for and entering higher education, people typically face major changes. The stress that they feel can lead to an increase in depression, anxiety and, very occasionally, attempted suicide. So let's talk about the danger signals for suicide.

Recognize danger signals

- *Talking about suicide.* People who attempt suicide often talk about it. They might say, "I just don't want to live anymore." Or "I want you to know that no matter what happens, I've always loved you." Or "Tomorrow night at 7:30 I'm going to end it all with a gun."
- *Planning for it.* People planning suicide will sometimes put their affairs in order. They might close bank accounts, give away or sell precious possessions, or make or update a will. They might even develop specific plans on how to kill themselves.
- *Having a history of previous attempts.* Some estimates suggest that up to 50 percent of the people who kill themselves have attempted suicide at least once before.

- *Dwelling on problems.* Expressing extreme helplessness or hopelessness about solving problems can indicate that someone might be considering suicide.
- *Feeling depressed.* Although not everyone who is depressed attempts suicide, almost everyone who attempts suicide feels depressed.

Take prompt action

If you suspect that someone you know is considering suicide, do whatever it takes to ensure the person's safety. If you are living in residence, talk to the residence staff as it is not up to you to solve other student's problems. Let the troubled person know that you will persist until you are certain that she's safe. Any of the following actions can help.

- *Take it seriously.* Taking suicidal comments seriously is especially important when you hear them from young adults. Eleven percent of Canadian undergraduate students report having suicidal thoughts (Canadian Campus Survey, 2004). Suicide threats are more common in this age group and might be dismissed as "normal." Err on the side of being too careful rather than on the side of being negligent.

- *Listen fully.* Encourage the person at risk to express thoughts and feelings appropriately to you or, more importantly, to a trained counsellor. If she claims that she doesn't want to talk, be inviting, be assertive, and be persistent. Be totally committed to listening.

- *Speak powerfully.* Let the person at risk know that you care. Trying to talk someone out of suicide or minimizing problems is generally useless. Acknowledge that problems are serious and that they can be solved. Point out that suicide is a permanent solution to a temporary problem—and that help is available on campus and in the community.

- *Get professional help.* Suggest that the person see a mental health professional. If they resist seeking help, get others involved, including the depressed person's family, residence staff, or other school personnel.

- *Remove access to drugs, guns, and razors.* In Canada, suicide is the leading cause of premature death (Centre for Suicide Prevention, 2011).

- *Handle an emergency.* If a situation becomes a crisis, do not leave the person alone. Call a crisis hotline, 911, or a social service agency. If necessary, take the person to the nearest hospital emergency room, clinic, or police station.

Take care of yourself

If you ever begin to think about committing suicide, remember that you can apply any of the above suggestions to yourself. For example, look for warning signs and take them seriously. Seek out someone you trust and tell this person how you feel. If necessary, make an appointment to see your doctor or a counsellor and ask someone to accompany you. When you're at risk, you deserve the same compassion that you'd willingly extend to another person.

Find out more on this topic from the Centre for Suicide Prevention Web site at suicideinfo.ca. ✳

Alcohol, tobacco, and drugs: The truth

THE TRUTH is that getting high can be fun. In our culture, and especially in our media, getting high has become synonymous with having a good time. Even if you don't smoke, drink, or use other drugs, you are certain to come in contact with people who do.

For centuries, human beings have devised ways to change their feelings and thoughts by altering their body chemistry. The Chinese were using marijuana 5000 years ago. Herodotus, the ancient Greek historian, wrote about a group of people in Eastern Europe who threw marijuana on hot stones and inhaled the smoke. In the nineteenth century, customers could buy opium and morphine across the counter of their neighbourhood store. A few decades later, people were

Patrick Strattner/Getty

able to buy soft drinks that contained coca—the plant from which cocaine is derived.

Today we are still a drug-using society. Of course, some of those uses are therapeutic and lawful, including drugs that are taken as prescribed by a doctor or psychologist. The problem comes when we turn to drugs as *the* solution to any problem, even before seeking professional guidance. Are you uncomfortable? Often the first response is "Take something."

We live in times when reaching for instant comfort via chemicals is not only condoned—it is approved. If you're bored, tense, or anxious, you can drink a can of beer, down a glass of wine, or light up a cigarette. And these are only the legal options. If you're willing

We might take care of ourselves when we see that the costs of using a substance outweigh the benefits.

Some facts . . .

In Canada, substance abuse and addiction take a heavy toll on young people, including students in postsecondary education.

Among young people, alcohol is the most frequently used drug. In universities, about one-third of students drink more than 15 drinks a week, a level that puts them at greater risk of health problems and other concerns.

Eighteen percent of students reported that they had missed a class because of a hangover.

About 7.4 percent of students reported driving after drinking, plus other hazardous alcohol-related behaviour including 6 percent who engaged in unsafe sex and 14.1 percent who had unplanned sexual relations (Canadian Campus Survey, 2011).

Alcohol-related motor vehicle accidents remain a major cause of death: Among fatally injured drivers, 46 percent had some alcohol in their blood and 39 percent had over the legal blood alcohol level.

One in four students reported having been physically assaulted by a person who had been drinking.

Drinking is a factor in 54 percent of all assaults, murders, and attempted murders.

Thirty-two percent of students report using cannabis (marijuana) in the past year (Canadian Campus Survey, 2011).

Want to see how you compare to other postsecondary students? Go the textbook's website and fill out the "Check Your University Drinking Survey" to see if you have a problem.

For more information on addiction, contact the Centre for Addiction and Mental Health.

 For related weblinks, go online @
....
www.bams5ce.nelson.com

I wouldn't bet on it

When we think of gamblers, we probably picture some old guy hanging around the race track. In fact, take a look in the mirror, because the new face of gambling could be yours. Over 60 percent of undergraduates report having bet money on at least one gambling activity in the last year (Canadian Campus Survey, 2011). Types of activities that they engaged in ranged from lotteries (51 percent) to slot and video lotteries (22.7 percent) to sports betting (10.8 percent). Males are particularly likely to engage in the last activity (19.4 percent of men versus 4.0 percent of women). Over 5 percent of undergrads report gambling weekly. There are provincial differences, too, with the Atlantic provinces having the highest percentage of gamblers (72 percent) compared to British Columbia (56.8 percent).

Gambling is often seen as a low-risk activity, with even 10-year-olds being given a "scratch and win card" as a birthday present. But we know that a small percentage of students (about 6-8 percent) are at risk of developing a severe gambling problem (International Centre for Youth Gambling, 2010). Gambling problems ensue when individuals are unable to stop gambling and they are unable to set limits on the time or money devoted to this activity. Men are twice as likely as women to be at risk for gambling problems and are far more likely (six times) to have moderate to severe gambling problems (Canadian Campus Survey, 2004).

The International Centre for Youth Gambling and High Risk Behaviours at McGill University was founded because of the recent surge in compulsive gambling among youth worldwide. The growth of online gambling makes it possible to literally be gambling anytime and anywhere. If you want to see if you have a problem

© JHB Photography/Alamy

with your gambling behaviour, several inventories are available online at this textbook's website, for you to complete. If gambling is starting to interfere with getting your schoolwork done, with attending class, or if it is causing problems with friends or family, then it is time to seek help. Speak to school counsellors, or look up the many resources, such as the Ontario Problem Gambling Helpline, which has service available 24 hours a day.

 Go online to learn more about gambling additions @
....
www.bams5ce.nelson.com

to take risks, you can pick from a large selection of illegal drugs on the street.

There is a big payoff in using alcohol, tobacco, caffeine, cocaine, heroin, or other drugs—or people wouldn't do it. The payoff can be direct, such as relaxation, self-confidence, comfort, excitement, or other forms of pleasure. At times, the payoff is not so obvious, as when people seek to avoid rejection, mask emotional pain, win peer group acceptance, or reject authority.

Perhaps drugs have a timeless appeal because human beings face two perennial problems: how to cope with unpleasant moods, and how to deal with difficult circumstances such as poverty, loneliness, or the prospect of death. When faced with either problem, people are often tempted to ignore potential solutions and go directly to the chemical fix.

In addition to the payoffs, there are costs. For some people, the cost is much greater than the payoff. That cost goes beyond money. Even if illegal drug use doesn't make you broke, it can make life start to revolve around the drug rather than life being centred on living itself. You can come to care about little else except finding more drugs, and in the process neglect friends, school, work, and family.

Substance abuse—the compulsive use of a chemical in alcohol or drugs resulting in negative consequences—is only part of the picture. People can also relate to food, gambling, money, sex, and even work in compulsive ways.

Some people will stop abusing a substance or activity when the consequences get serious enough. Other people don't stop. They continue their self-defeating behaviours, no matter what the consequences are for themselves, their friends, or their families. At that point, the problem goes beyond abuse. It's addiction.

The costs of substance addiction can include overdose, infection, and lowered immunity to disease—all of which can be fatal. Long-term excessive drinking damages every organ system in the human body. Each year, 37,000 Canadians die from the effects of cigarette smoking, with the highest rate of smoking occurring in 20-24 year olds (27 percent) (Heart & Stroke Foundation, 2011).

Lectures about why to avoid alcohol and drug abuse and addiction can be pointless. Ultimately, we don't take care of our bodies because someone says we should. We might take care of ourselves when we see that the costs of using a substance outweigh the benefits. You choose. It's your body.

Acknowledging that alcohol, tobacco, and other drugs can be fun infuriates a lot of people who might assume that this is the same as condoning their use. The point is this: People are more likely to abstain when they're convinced that using these substances leads to more pain than pleasure over the long run.

29 exercise
Addiction: How do I know . . .?

People who have problems with drugs and alcohol are great at hiding that fact from themselves and from others. It is also hard to admit that a friend or loved one might have a problem.

The purpose of this exercise is to give you an objective way to look at your relationship with drugs or alcohol. There are signals that indicate when drug or alcohol use has become abusive or even addictive. This exercise can also help you determine if a friend might be addicted.

Answer the following questions quickly and honestly with "yes," "no," or "n/a" (not applicable). If you are concerned about someone else, rephrase each question using that person's name.

_____ Are you uncomfortable discussing drug abuse or addiction?

_____ Are you worried about your own drug or alcohol use?

_____ Are any of your friends worried about your drug or alcohol use?

_____ Have you ever hidden from a friend, spouse, employer, or coworker the fact that you were drinking? (Pretended you were sober? Covered up alcohol breath?)

_____ Do you sometimes use alcohol or drugs to escape lows rather than to produce highs?

_____ Have you ever gotten angry when confronted about your use?

_____ Do you brag about how much you consume? ("I drank her under the table.")

_____ Do you think about or do drugs when you are alone?

_____ Do you store up alcohol, drugs, cigarettes, or caffeine (in coffee or soft drinks) to be sure you won't run out?

_____ Does having a party almost always include alcohol or drugs?

_____ Do you try to control your drinking so that it won't be a problem? ("I drink only on weekends now." "I never drink before 5:00 p.m." "I drink only beer.")

_____ Do you often explain to other people why you are drinking? ("It's my birthday." "It's my friend's birthday." "It's the May 24 weekend." "It sure is a hot day.")

_____ Have you changed friends to accommodate your drinking or drug use? ("She's OK, but she isn't excited about getting high.")

_____ Has your behaviour changed in the last several months? (Marks down? Lack of interest in a hobby? Change of values or of what you think is moral?)

_____ Do you drink or use drugs to relieve tension? ("What a day! I need a drink.")

_____ Do you have medical problems (stomach trouble, malnutrition, liver problems, anaemia) that could be related to drinking?

_____ Have you ever decided to quit drugs or alcohol and then changed your mind?

_____ Have you had any fights, accidents, or similar incidents related to drinking or drugs in the last year?

_____ Has your drinking or drug use ever caused a problem at home?

_____ Do you envy people who go overboard with alcohol or drugs?

_____ Have you ever told yourself you can quit at any time?

_____ Have you ever been in trouble with the police after or while you were drinking?

_____ Have you ever missed school or work because you had a hangover?

_____ Have you ever had a blackout (a period you can't remember) after drinking?

_____ Do you wish that people would mind their own business when it comes to your use of alcohol or drugs?

_____ Is the cost of alcohol or other drugs taxing your budget or resulting in financial stress?

_____ Do you need increasing amounts of the drug to produce the desired effect?

_____ When you stop taking the drug, do you experience withdrawal?

_____ Do you spend a great deal of time obtaining and using alcohol or other drugs?

_____ Have you used alcohol or another drug when it was physically dangerous to do so (such as when driving a car or working with machines)?

_____ Have you been arrested or had other legal problems resulting from the use of a substance?

Now count the number of questions you answered with "yes." If you answered "yes" five or more times, talk with a professional. Five "yes" answers does not necessarily mean that you are addicted. It does point out that alcohol or other drugs are adversely affecting your life. Talk to someone with training in recovery from chemical dependency. Do not rely on the opinion of anyone who lacks such training.

If you filled out this questionnaire about another person and you answered "yes" five or more times, your friend might need help. You probably can't provide that help alone. Seek out a counsellor or a support group such as Al-Anon. Call the local Alcoholics Anonymous chapter to find out about an Al-Anon meeting near you.

Seeing the full scope of addiction

HERE ARE SOME guidelines that can help you decide if addiction is a barrier for you right now. Most addictions share some key features, such as the following:

■ *Loss of control*—continued substance use or activity in spite of adverse consequences.

■ *Pattern of relapse*—vowing to quit or limit the activity or substance use and continually failing to do so.

■ *Tolerance*—the need to take increasing amounts of a substance to produce the desired effect.

© alias/Shutterstock

■ *Withdrawal*—signs and symptoms of physical and mental discomfort or illness when the substance is taken away (American Psychological Association, 1994).

11

HEALTH

The same basic features can be present in anything from cocaine use to compulsive gambling. All of this can add up to a continuous cycle of abuse or addiction. These common features prompt many people to call some forms of addiction a disease. Some people do not agree that alcoholism is a disease or that all addictions can be labelled with that term. You don't have to wait until this question is settled before examining your own life.

If you have a problem with addiction, consider getting help. The problem might be your own addiction or perhaps the behaviour of someone you love. In any case, consider acting on several of the following suggestions.

Admit the problem. People with active addictions are a varied group—rich and poor, young and old, successful and unsuccessful. Often these people do have one thing in common: They are masters of denial. They deny that they are unhappy. They deny that they have hurt anyone. They are convinced that they can quit any time they want. They sometimes become so adept at hiding the problem from themselves that they die.

Pay attention. If you do use a substance compulsively or behave in compulsive ways, do so with awareness. Then pay attention to the consequences. Act with deliberate decision rather than out of habit or under pressure from others.

Look at the costs. There is always a trade-off. Drinking 10 beers might result in a temporary high, and you will probably remember that feeling. No one feels great the morning after consuming 10 beers, but it seems easier to forget pain. Often people don't notice how bad alcoholism, drug addiction, or other forms of substance abuse make them feel.

Take responsibility. Nobody plans to become an addict. If you have pneumonia, you can recover without guilt or shame. Approach an addiction in yourself or others in the same way. You can take responsibility for your recovery without blame, shame, or guilt.

Get help. Many people find that they cannot treat addiction on their own. Addictive behaviours are often symptoms of an illness that needs treatment.

Two broad options exist for getting help with addiction. One is the growing self-help movement. The other is formal treatment. People recovering from addiction often combine the two.

Many self-help groups are modelled after Alcoholics Anonymous. AA is made up of recovering alcoholics and addicts. These people understand the problems of abuse firsthand, and they follow a systematic, 12-step approach to living without it. This is one of the oldest and most successful self-help programs in the

You can take responsibility for your recovery without blame, shame, or guilt.

Binge Drinking

"WOW, the party started as soon as we finished our exams" Whether you call it 'getting hammered' or 'wasted,' binge drinking can take a terrible toll on your health. **Binge drinking** involves drinking alcohol quickly—four drinks if you are a woman, five if you are a man (MADD, 2011). When you drink quickly you get drunk, which leads to impaired judgment; you might engage in behaviour that will be extremely embarrassing the next day. If you are a guy, you are far more likely to engage in other reckless behaviours like driving too fast, or getting into fights. More than 40 percent of young Canadians (aged 20-24) report that they have been binge drinking 12 times or more in the last year (CAMH, 2011). And males are even more likely than females to engage in binge drinking.

Why does it matter? Well, binge drinking can lead to alcohol poisoning and can permanently damage your liver and your brain. It also increases the odds of developing cancer and becoming an addict to alcohol. Remember to drink slowly and intersperse alcohol with other non-alcoholic drinks. Regardless of how fast you drink alcohol, it still takes about an hour a drink for your body to process the alcohol. Drinking coffee won't make a difference. Chugging beer—bad idea. So before you prime to go out to a bar on Thursday, think about who you are putting at risk.

world. Chapters of AA welcome people from all walks of life, and you don't have to be an alcoholic to attend most meetings. Programs based on AA principles exist for many other forms of addiction as well.

Some people feel uncomfortable with the AA approach. Other resources exist for these people, including private therapy and group therapy. Also investigate organizations such as the Centre for Addiction and Mental Health (CAMH), Women for Sobriety, the Secular Organizations for Sobriety, and Rational Recovery Systems. Use whatever works for you.

Treatment programs are available in almost every community. They might be residential (you live there for weeks or months at a time) or outpatient (you visit several hours a day). Find out where these treatment centres are located by calling a doctor, a mental health professional, or a local hospital.

Alcohol and drug treatments are now covered by many private health insurance programs. If you don't have additional insurance, it is usually possible to arrange some other payment program. Cost is no reason to avoid treatment.

11

HEALTH

Get help for a friend or family member. You might know someone who uses alcohol or other drugs in a way that can lead to serious and sustained negative consequences. If so, you have every right to express your concern to that person. Wait until the person is clear-headed and then mention specific incidents. For example: "Last night you drank five beers when we were at my apartment, and then you wanted to drive home. When I offered to call a cab for you instead, you refused." Also be prepared to offer a source of help, such as the phone number of a local treatment centre.

 To learn more about addictions, ask your doctor or student health services. More information is available online @

www.bams5ce.nelson.com

Warning: Advertising can be dangerous to your health

The average North American is exposed to hundreds of advertising messages per day. Unless you are stranded on a desert island, you are affected by commercial messages.

ADVERTISING SERVES a useful function. It helps us make choices about how we spend our money. We can choose among cars, kitchen appliances, health clubs, books, plants, groceries, home builders, dog groomers, piano tuners, vacation spots, locksmiths, movies, amusement parks—the list is endless. Advertising makes us aware of the options.

Advertising space is also expensive, and the messages are carefully crafted to get the most value for the cost. Advertisements can play on our emotions and be dangerously manipulative. For example, consider the messages that ads convey about your health. Advertising alcohol, tobacco, and pain relievers is a big business. Much of the revenue earned by newspapers, magazines, radio, television, and websites comes from advertisements for these products.

Ads for alcohol glorify drinking. One of the aims of these ads is to convince heavy drinkers that the amount they drink is normal. Advertisers imply that daily drinking is the norm, pleasant experiences are enhanced by drinking, holidays naturally include alcohol, parties are a flop without it, relationships are more romantic over cocktails, and everybody drinks. Each of these implications is questionable.

Advertising can affect our self-image. A typical advertising message is "You are not OK unless you buy our product." These messages are painstakingly programmed to get us to buy clothes, make-up, and hair products to make us look OK; drugs, alcohol, and food to make us feel OK; perfumes, toothpaste, and deodorants to make us smell OK. Advertising also promotes the idea that buying the right product is essential to having valuable relationships in our lives.

Advertising affects what we eat. Multimedia advertisers portray the primary staples of our diets as sugary breakfast cereals, candy bars, and soft drinks. The least nutritious foods receive the most advertising money.

Another problem with advertising is the way women are commonly portrayed. The basic message is that women love to spend hours discussing floor wax, deodorants, tampons, and laundry detergent—and that they think constantly about losing weight and looking sexy. In some ads, women handle everything from kitchen to bedroom to boardroom—these women are Superwomen.

Images such as these are demeaning to women and damaging to men. Women lose when they allow their

11

HEALTH

self-image to be influenced by ads. Men lose when they expect real-life women to look and act like the women on television and in magazines. Advertising photography creates illusions. The next time you're in a crowd, notice how few people really look like people in the media.

Though advertising is making progress in representing racial diversity, it still frequently excludes people of colour. If our perceptions were based solely on advertising, we would be hard pressed to know that our society is racially and ethnically diverse. See how many examples of cultural stereotypes you can find in the ads you encounter this week.

Use advertising as a continual opportunity to develop the qualities of a critical thinker. Be aware of how a multibillion-dollar industry threatens your health and well-being. ✱

journal entry 34

Discovery/Intention Statement

Advertisements and Your Health

Think of a time when—after seeing an advertisement or a commercial—you craved a certain food or drink or you really wanted to buy something. Describe how the advertising influenced you.

I discovered that I . . .

_____

_____

_____

Now describe anything you'd like to do differently in the future when you notice that advertising affects you in the way you just described.

I intend to . . .

_____

_____

_____

practising critical thinking

11

This exercise is about clarifying the differences between behaviours and interpretations. A behaviour is factual and observable, while an interpretation is subjective and often based on observed behaviours. Understanding this distinction can help you think clearly about your behaviours—including those that affect your emotional health by influencing your key relationships.

For instance, arriving 10 minutes after a lecture starts or pulling a dog's tail are both observable behaviours. In contrast, an interpretation is a conclusion we draw on the basis of the observed behaviour: "She's either too rude or too irresponsible to get to a lecture on time." "She hates animals. Just look at how she pulled that dog's tail!" Keep in mind that other interpretations are possible. Perhaps the person's car broke down on the way to the lecture. And maybe the owner of the dog is playing a game that her pet enjoys.

Consider another example. "She shouted at me, left the room, and slammed the door" is a statement that describes behaviours. "She was angry" is one interpretation of the social significance or meaning of the observed behaviour.

With this distinction in mind, brainstorm a list of behaviours you have seen in others when they were in conflict with you. Use the space below to record your brainstorm. Afterward, review your list to see if some of the behaviours you noted are actually interpretations.

_____

_____

_____

_____

_____

_____

HEALTH

Discovery/Intention Statement

Choose a New Level of Health

Review your responses to Journal Entry 30: "Take a First Step about Your Health" on page 347. This Discovery Statement asked you to reflect on your current state of health. Review what you wrote. Then summarize your top three health concerns on a separate sheet of paper.

I discovered that . . .

If you've read the preceding articles, you've learned about ways to choose good health in a variety of areas—by eating, exercising, sleeping, protecting your mental health, and staying safe. In the space below, list some suggestions that could help you respond positively to your top health concerns:

I discovered that . . .

Next, choose one of the above suggestions that you would like to use immediately. Write an Intention Statement about turning this behaviour into a daily habit:

I intend to . . .

Finally, introduce some accountability. Share your Intention Statement with someone else. Consider asking this person to check in with you during the next month and ask how your plan to adopt a new habit is going. Alternatively, review the "Ways to Change a Habit" article, in the Introduction to this book, to help you make your intention into a new habit.

Note: You can use the above process to change your behaviour—discovery, intention, and action with accountability—and adopt *any* new habit.

Apply insights from ergonomics

The field of study called *ergonomics* focuses on ways to prevent health problems due to human behaviour and workplace conditions. Recently, specialists in ergonomics have developed many suggestions for people who work continually at computers. These people can experience health problems that range from eyestrain and lower back pain to numbness in the arms and wrists.

You can hire specialists in ergonomics to redesign your workspace. That costs money. The following suggestions are free:

- *Rest your eyes.* To prevent eyestrain caused by staring too long at a computer screen, give your eyes rest from time to time. Looking out a window or at another object that is closer or farther away can help by forcing your eyes to readjust their focus. Also, set up your computer away from windows so that you can avoid squinting as you look at the screen.
- *Take breaks.* Get away from the computer. Stretch. Move. Walk, jog, or run.

- *Pay attention to your posture.* To avoid lower back problems, pay attention to your posture as you sit at the computer. Adjust your chair so that you can sit comfortably, with your back relaxed and your spine erect. Placing a pillow or small cushion behind your lower back might help. You might want to consider a hands free headset if you are on the phone a lot.

- *Find out about technology tools.* To reduce the risk of developing carpal tunnel syndrome, consider ways to decrease your use of the keyboard, such as voice recognition software.

The idea behind each of the above suggestions is to position yourself so that you remain alert *and* relaxed while you're at the computer. Taking some simple precautions now can help you avoid feeling like a pretzel in a few years.

 For more information about ergonomics, go online @ **www.bams5ce.nelson.com**

SURRENDER

Life can be magnificent and satisfying. It can also be devastating.

Sometimes there is too much pain or confusion. Problems can be too big and too numerous. Life can bring us to our knees in a pitiful, helpless, and hopeless state. A broken relationship with a loved one, a sudden diagnosis of cancer, total frustration with a child's behaviour problem, or even the prospect of several long years of school are situations that can leave us feeling overwhelmed—powerless.

In these troubling situations, the first thing we can do is to admit that we don't have the resources to handle the problem. No matter how hard we try and no matter what skills we bring to bear, some problems remain out of our control. When this is the case, we can tell the truth: "It's too big and too mean. I can't handle it."

Desperately struggling to control a problem can easily result in the problem's controlling us. Surrender is letting go of being the master in order to avoid becoming the slave.

Many traditions make note of this idea. Western religions speak of surrendering to God. Hindus say surrender to the Self. Members of Alcoholics Anonymous talk about turning their lives over to a Higher Power. Agnostics might suggest surrendering to the ultimate source of power. Others might speak of following their intuition, their inner guide, or their conscience.

In any case, surrender means being receptive to help. Once we admit that we're at the end of our rope, we open ourselves up to receiving help. We learn that we don't have to go it alone. We find out that other people have faced similar problems and survived. We give up our

old habits of thinking and behaving as if we have to be in control of everything. We stop acting as general manager of the universe. We surrender. And that creates a space for something new in our lives.

Surrender is not "giving up." It is not a suggestion to quit and do nothing about your problems. Giving up is fatalistic and accomplishes nothing. You have many skills and resources. Use them. You can apply all of your energy to handling a situation and still surrender at the same time. Surrender includes doing whatever you can in a positive, trusting spirit. So let go, keep going, and recognize when the true source of control lies beyond you.

 Learn more about the power of this Power Process online @

www.bams5ce.nelson.com

Put It to WORK

Strategies from *Becoming a Master Student* can help you succeed in your career, as well as in school. To discover how suggestions in this chapter can apply to the workplace, reflect on the following case study.

© Image Source/Getty Images

For weeks David had been bothered by aching muscles, loss of appetite, restless sleep, and fatigue. Eventually he became so short-tempered and irritable that his wife insisted he get a checkup.

Now, sitting in the doctor's office, David barely noticed when Theresa took the seat beside him. They had been good friends when she worked in the front office at the plant. He hadn't seen her since she left three years ago to take a job as a customer service representative. Her gentle poke in the ribs brought him around. Within minutes they were talking freely.

"You got out just in time," he told her. "Since the reorganization, nobody feels safe. It used to be that as long as you did your work, you had a job. Now they expect the same production rates even though two guys are now doing the work of three. We're so backed up that I'm working 12-hour shifts 6 days a week. Guys are calling in sick just to get a break."

"Well, I really miss you guys," she said. "In my new job, the computer routes the calls, and they never stop. I even have to schedule my bathroom breaks. All I hear the whole day are complaints from unhappy customers. I try to be helpful and sympathetic, but I can't promise anything until I get my boss's approval. Most of the time I'm caught between what the customer wants and company policy. The other reps are so uptight and tense they don't even talk to one another. We all go to our own little cubicles and stay there until quitting time. No wonder I'm in here with migraine headaches and high blood pressure."

David and Theresa are using a powerful strategy to promote health—talking about how they feel with a person they trust. List three other strategies that might be useful to them:

_____

_____

_____

Imagine that you suggested those three strategies to David and Theresa. They responded, "Those are good ideas, but

we can't get relief from stress until our working conditions change. And that's up to our supervisors, not us." How would you respond to them?

_____

_____

_____

Consider these other strategies for staying healthy under pressure.

Ask for change. Use your skill with "I" messages (see Chapter 8: Communicating) to make suggestions and ask for specific changes in working conditions. If your employer conducts a survey of workers' satisfaction with their jobs, answer honestly and completely—especially if responses are kept anonymous.

Deal with depression. Untreated depression costs the economy as much as heart disease or AIDS. However, many employees don't report symptoms of depression. They worry about confidentiality in the workplace and about paying for treatment. Yet confidential and free or low-cost help is often available through employee assistance plans. Find out whether your employer offers such a plan.

Check the full range of your health benefits. In addition to screening and treatment for depression, your employee health benefits might include screenings for other conditions, paid time off for medical appointments, and massages. Set up a meeting with someone at work who can explain all the options available to you.

QUIZ

Name_____   Date____/____/____

1. Explain three ways you can respond effectively if someone you know threatens to commit suicide.

2. The strategies suggested for dealing with stress do *not* include:
   (a) Release irrational beliefs.
   (b) Use breathing and relaxation exercises included in this book.
   (c) Cut back on exercising.
   (d) Consider therapeutic bodywork such as massage.
   (e) Check with your student health service.

3. How is the Power Process: "Surrender" different from giving up?

4. A person infected with HIV might have no symptoms for months—sometimes years. True or False? Explain your answer.

5. Explain why LGBTQ students might be more at risk on campus than other students? What can you do to help?

6. List at least three dietary guidelines that can contribute to your health.

7. One of the suggestions for dealing with addiction is "Pay attention." This implies that it's OK to use drugs, as long as you do so with full awareness. True or False? Explain your answer.

8. Name at least three methods for preventing unwanted pregnancy.

9. The article "Emotional Pain Is Not a Sickness" suggests that sometimes it helps to allow yourself to feel bad for a while. What is the point behind this idea?

10. Explain two ways that an uncritical response to advertising can undermine your health.

chapter 11

Skills **SNAPSHOT**

■ Put It to Work
■ Quiz
◄ ◄ ◄ ◄ ◄
■ Master Student Profile

Now that you've reflected on the ideas in this chapter and experimented with some new strategies, revisit your responses to the "Health" section of the Discovery Wheel exercise on page 37. Think about the most powerful action you could take in the near future toward mastery in this area of your life. Complete the following sentences.

DISCOVERY

To monitor my current level of health, I look for specific changes in . . .

After reading and doing this chapter, my top three health concerns are . . .

INTENTION

My top three intentions for responding to these concerns are . . .

NEXT ACTION

I'll know that I've reached a new level of mastery with health when . . .

To reach that level of mastery, the most important intention for me to act on next is . . .

MASTER STUDENT Profile

© REUTERS/Dylan Martinez

Clara Hughes
. . . is courageous

(1972-) An extraordinary athlete who has been named an Officer of the Order of Canada. Clara is heavily involved in charity work, including Right to Play, an organization that provides youth with the opportunity to learn through sport and discover the merits of physical activity.

 Find more biographical information about Clara Hughes at the Master Student Hall of Fame @

www.bams5ce.nelson.com

Clara Hughes was already in the history books as the only Canadian to win medals in both the Summer and Winter Olympic Games. The wide-smiling former Winnipegger became the darling of the sports world (and the country) with her drive, ambition, and athletic prowess.

Now she's a hero for another reason. When Hughes decided to disclose her two-year battle with depression, she put a familiar face onto the stigma of mental illness. She, in the parlance of the business, normalized the disease.

When we spoke this week, she described her descent into despair. "I tended to internalize things," she said. "I thought I should be tough enough to deal with it."

She wasn't and she couldn't, and so she got help. She deserves kudos for her candour from the hundreds of thousands of Canadians affected by mental illness and those who love them.

"Clara has so much admiration for doing this. I think in the mental health field she deserves a medal," says Tara Brousseau, executive director of the Mood Disorders Association of Manitoba.
"She's giving strength."

Anyone who has spent time skittering their way around the edge of depression's abyss understands the strength Hughes' disclosure took. The battle back to wellness required similar guts. Hughes doesn't sugar-coat her experiences.

She felt let down after the 1996 Olympics. She attributed it to a normal post-Olympics deflation. But it didn't stop and she was crying all the time and sleeping too much and gaining weight and wanted to quit cycling.

In fact, she did quit, unsure whether she'd ever come back.

"I knew I couldn't go on like this. After I quit, I still didn't feel better. It progressed to something I had never experienced before," she said. Depression does that, disguising itself as the blues, winding tendrils of doubt and self-loathing around the sufferer. Obstacles become insurmountable. Self-worth, even for an Olympic champion, vanishes.

Hughes reached out, first to her now-husband. She talked to a doctor. She switched up her diet and changed her training schedule. She fought with the drive and single-mindedness that earned her those medals.

"I had to change my thinking. I'd look at my competitors and think they were probably training harder. I still like to revert to that to train way too hard and way too much."

She didn't require medication. She knows she's lucky there, that many people with depression need drugs and therapy and crossed fingers to get them across the abyss.

"Medication was an option," she said. "I just wanted to see if I could change things in my life. I wanted to try to get through it without being medicated. I think it's different for everyone."

She's right. It is different for everyone. And everyone with clinical depression has suffered the advice of the unknowing, people who think they should just cheer up, count their blessings, be glad it's not cancer and generally stop and smell the roses.

There are no roses when depression has you in its unforgiving grip. Depression is one of the cancers of the mind. It can be fatal, although some people insist that's a personal choice.

It's not.

Hughes came back, of course. That's why she has those extra medals in speedskating and the endorsement contracts that allow her to train and, through Bell Canada, to get the word out on mental illness. Lucky her. Lucky us.

Because if you think of [people with mental illness] as weak, as people who just need to snap out of it, look at Clara Hughes. Canadian sports has never had anyone like her, with the medals in two sports and the grit and the never-ending desire to compete.

The mental health community has never had anyone like her, either. In Hughes, they have proof illness can strike any of us, that even the strongest competitor can be felled. She has given face and voice and hope for the silently shamed.

If that's not worth a medal, I don't know what is.

Source: Reynolds, Lindor (2011) "Hughes adds new triumph: erase stigma attached to mental illness". *The Winnipeg Free Press*. February 14, 2011. Retrieved July 5, 2011 from http://www.clara-hughes.com/news/hughes-adds-new-triumph-erase-stigma-attached-to-mental-illness

Your customers or clients could be located in Ontario or China, Prince Edward Island or Panama. Your skills in thinking globally and communicating with a diverse world could help you create a new product or service for a new market—and perhaps a career that does not even exist today.

Plan by naming names

One key to making your career plan real, and ensuring that you can act on it, is naming. Go back over your plan to see that you include specific names whenever they're called for:

- *Name your job.* Take the skills you enjoy using and find out which jobs use them. What are those jobs called? List them. Note that the same job might have different names.

- *Name your company—the agency or organization you want to work for.* If you want to be self-employed or start your own business, name the product or service you'd sell. Also list some possible names for your business. If you plan to work for others, name the organizations or agencies that are high on your list.

- *Name your contacts.* Take the list of organizations you just compiled. What people in these organizations are responsible for hiring? List those people and contact them directly. If you choose self-employment, list the names of possible customers or clients. All of these people are job contacts. Don't forget that the Web has some great networking tools like *LinkedIn* (www.linkedin.com) that allow you meet others who are in industries you might be interested in.

- *Name your location.* Ask if your career choices are consistent with your preferences about where to live and work. For example, someone who wants to make a living as a studio musician might consider living in a large city such as Toronto or New York. This contrasts with the freelance graphic artist who conducts his business mainly by phone, fax, and email. He might be able to live anywhere and still pursue his career.

Now expand your list of contacts by brainstorming with your family and friends. Come up with a list of names—anyone who can help you with career planning and job-hunting. Write down each of the names in a spiral-bound notebook or in a file you keep on your computer.

Next, call the key people on your list. After you speak with them, make brief notes about what you discussed. Also jot down any actions you agreed to take, such as a follow-up call.

Consider everyone you meet a potential member of your job network, and be prepared to talk about what you do. Develop a "pitch"—a short statement of your career goal that you can share easily with your contacts.

For example: "After I graduate, I plan to work in the travel business. I'm looking for an internship in a travel agency for next summer. Do you know of any agencies that take interns?"

Describe your ideal lifestyle

In addition to choosing the content of your career, you have many options for integrating work into the context of your life. You can work full-time. You can work part-time. You can commute to a cubicle at a major corporate office. Or you can work at home and take the 30-second commute from your bedroom to your desk.

Close your eyes. Visualize an ideal day in your life after graduation. Vividly imagine the following:

- Your work setting.
- Your co-workers.
- Your calendar and to-do list for that day.
- Other sights and sounds in your work environment.

This visualization emphasizes the importance of finding a match between your career and your lifestyle preferences—the amount of flexibility in your schedule, the number of people you see each day, the variety in your tasks, and the ways that you balance work with other activities.

Consider self-employment

Instead of joining a thriving business, you could create one of your own. If the idea of self-employment seems far-fetched, consider that as a student, you already *are* self-employed. You are setting your own goals, structuring your time, making your own financial decisions, and monitoring your performance. These are all transferable skills that you could use to become your own boss. Remember that many successful businesses—including Facebook and Yahoo!—were started by college students (Toft & Ellis, 2011).

Test your career choice—and be willing to change

Career-planning materials and counsellors can help you on both counts. Read books about careers and search for career-planning websites. Ask career counsellors about skills assessments that can help you discover more about your skills and identify jobs that call for those skills. Take career-planning courses and workshops sponsored by your school. Visit the career-planning and job placement offices on campus in your first year of study—don't wait until you are graduating to make use of these excellent and free resources.

Once you have a career choice, translate it into workplace experience. For example:

- Contact people who are actually doing the job you're researching, and ask them a lot of questions about what it's like (an *information interview*). This is a great way to gain insider's knowledge about a field and also to network with potential employers after graduation.

- Choose an internship, field placement, or volunteer position in a field that interests you. Many times, employers are more willing to hire you once they have seen you on the job; and by working in the field, you have the opportunity to see if this is the correct job for you.

- Get a part-time or summer job in your career field. Obviously the more work experience you have, the more likely a potential employer will consider you for similar jobs upon graduation. So, when thinking about part-time or summer employment, look to see how the position will allow you to broaden your work skills and knowledge and not just the paycheque you will be receiving.

If you find that you enjoy meeting the people who are in your field of work or a work placement, then you've probably made a wise career choice. And the people you meet are possible sources of recommendations, referrals, and employment in the future. If you did *not* enjoy your experiences, celebrate what you learned about yourself. Now you're free to refine your initial career choice or go in a new direction.

Career planning is not a once-and-for-all proposition. Rather, career plans are made to be changed and refined as you gain new information about yourself and the world.

Career planning never ends. If your present career no longer feels right, you can choose again—no matter what stage of life you're in. The process is the same, whether you're choosing your first career or your fifth.

Remember your purpose

While digging deep into the details of career planning, take some time to back up to the big picture. Listing skills, researching jobs, writing resumés—all of this is necessary and useful. At the same time, attending to these tasks can obscure our broadest goals. To get perspective, we can go back to the basics—a life purpose.

Your life purpose is like the guidance system for a rocket. It keeps the plan on target while revealing a path for soaring to the heights.

Your deepest desire might be to see that hungry children are fed, to make sure that beautiful music keeps getting heard, or to help alcoholics become sober. When such a large purpose is clear, smaller decisions about what to do are often easier.

A life purpose makes a career plan simpler and more powerful. It cuts through the stacks of job data and employment figures. Your life purpose is like the guidance system for a rocket. It keeps the plan on target while revealing a path for soaring to the heights (Ellis, Lankowitz, Stupka & Toft, 2003). ✳

 Find more strategies for career planning online @
www.bams5ce.nelson.com

30 exercise
Create your career plan—now

Write your career plan. Now. Start the process of career planning, even if you're not sure where to begin. Your response to this exercise can be just a rough draft of your plan, which you can revise and rewrite many times. The point is to get your ideas in writing.

The final format of your plan is up to you. You might include many details, such as the next job title you'd like to have, the courses required for your major, and other training that you want to complete. You might list companies to research and people that could hire you. You might also include target dates to complete each of these tasks.

Another option is to represent your plan visually through flowcharts, timelines, mindmaps, or drawings. You can generate these by hand or use computer software.

For now, experiment with career planning by completing the following sentences. Use the space provided, and continue on additional paper as needed. When answering the

first question below, write down what comes to your mind first. The goal is to begin the process of discovery. You can always change direction after some investigation.

1. The career I choose for now is . . .

2. The major steps that will guide me to this career are . . .

3. The immediate steps I will take to pursue this career are . . .

12

exercise
Recognize your skills

This exercise about discovering your skills includes three steps. Before you begin, gather at least 100 index cards and a pen or pencil, or you might also try doing this exercise using spreadsheet software on a computer. Allow about one hour to complete the exercise.

Step 1

Recall your activities during the past week or month. To refresh your memory, review your responses to the Time Monitor/Time Plan in Chapter 2. (You might even benefit from doing that exercise again.)

Write down as many activities as you can, listing each one on a separate index card. Include work-related activities, school activities, and hobbies. Some of your cards might read "washed dishes," "tuned up my car," or "tutored a French class."

In addition to daily activities, recall any rewards you've received or recognition of your achievements during the past year. Examples include scholarship awards, athletic awards, or recognitions for volunteer work. Again, list the activities that were involved.

Spend 20 minutes on this step, listing all of the activities you can recall.

Step 2

Next, look over your activity cards. Then take another 20 minutes to list any specialized knowledge or procedures needed to complete those activities. These are your *content skills.* For example, tutoring a French class requires knowledge of that language. Tuning a car requires knowing how to adjust a car's timing and replace spark plugs. You could list several content skills for any one activity. Write each skill on a separate card and label it "Content."

Step 3

Go over your activity cards one more time. Look for examples of *transferable skills.* For instance, giving a speech or working as a salesperson in a computer store requires the ability to persuade people. That's a transferable skill. Tuning a car means that you can attend to details and troubleshoot. Tutoring in French requires teaching, listening, and speaking skills.

Write each of your transferable skills on a separate card.

Congratulations—you now have a detailed picture of your skills. Keep your lists of content and transferable skills on hand when writing your resumé or preparing for job interviews and other career-planning tasks. As you think of new skills, add them to the lists.

Sample career plans

FOLLOWING ARE SOME examples of mindmaps, pie charts, and lists that you can use to visually represent your career plan.

Sample 1

A mindmap that links personal values to desired skills that could be used in a variety of careers.

Skill:
Speaking candidly

Skill:
Listening

Skill:
Observing physical and mental states

Skill:
Resolving conflict

Love

Health

CORE VALUES

Skill:
Changing habits

Learning

Wealth

Skill:
Teaching

Skill:
Counselling

Skill:
Monitoring expenses

Skill:
Raising funds

Skill:
Creating budgets

Sample 2

A pie chart summarizing the amounts of time devoted to career-related activities.

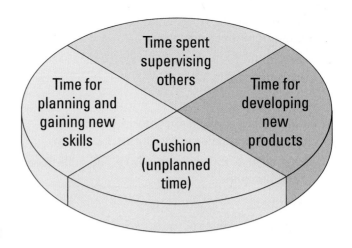

Sample 3

A list of career goals sorted by priority. In this case, each goal is assigned a number from 1 to 100. Higher numbers denote higher priority.

- Consult career services office on law school options (100)
- Prepare rigorously for LSAT and do well (100)
- Get into top-10 law school (95)
- Get position as editor on *Law Review* (90)
- Graduate in top of class at law school (85)
- Work in provincial court as a crown attorney (80)
- Use my position and influence to gain political contacts (75)
- Found private law firm focused on protection of workers' rights (70)
- Win major lawsuits in defence of human rights in the workplace (60)
- Leave law practice to travel to developing countries in aid of poor for two years (60)
- Found international agency for protection of human rights (50)
- Win Nobel Prize (30)

Find more sample career plans online @
www.bams5ce.nelson.com

Discover your employability skills

IN CHAPTER 1, we talked about how The Conference Board of Canada (2010) has produced *Employability Skills 2000+*, a list of essential skills to enter, stay in, and progress in the world of work. Review the list, assess your current skills, and consider which ones you still need to develop. Keep in mind that no matter what career you settle on, more than 70 percent of jobs require some form of postsecondary education (Ontario MTCU, 2010).

Fundamental skills
Communicate

- Read and understand information in a variety of forms.
- Write and speak so others pay attention and understand.
- Ask good questions and listen openly to other points of view.

- Share information using a range of information and communications technologies.
- Use scientific, technological, and mathematical skills to explain or clarify ideas.

Manage information

- Locate, gather, and organize information using appropriate technology and information systems.
- Access, analyse, and apply knowledge and skills from various disciplines.

Use numbers

- Decide what needs to be measured or calculated.
- Observe and record data using appropriate tools and technology.
- Make estimates and verify calculations.

Think and solve problems

- Assess situations and identify problems.
- Examine situations from a variety of perspectives.
- Identify the root cause of a problem.
- Be creative and innovative in exploring possible solutions.
- Easily use technology, science, and math as part of problem solving and decision making.
- Evaluate solutions to make recommendations or decisions.
- Implement solutions and act on opportunities.
- Review solutions to ensure that they work. and make improvements if necessary.

Personal management skills

Demonstrate positive attitudes and behaviours

- Deal with people, problems, and situations with honesty, integrity, and personal ethics.
- Exhibit good self-esteem and confidence in your abilities.
- Recognize your own and other people's good efforts.
- Demonstrate a healthy lifestyle.
- Show interest, initiative, and effort.

Be responsible

- Set goals and priorities balancing work and personal life.
- Plan and manage time, money, and other resources.
- Assess, weigh, and manage risk.
- Show accountability for your own actions and those that you work with.
- Demonstrate social responsibility and be accountable for your actions and the actions of your group.

Be adaptable

- Be innovative and resourceful, identifying alternative ways to get a job done.
- Work well individually or as part of a group.
- Be capable of multi-tasking or working on several projects at once.
- Be open to change.
- Learn from mistakes and accept feedback and change.
- Cope with uncertainty.

Learn continuously

- Assess personal strengths and areas for development.
- Embrace lifelong learning.
- Continuously assess your strengths and needs for growth.
- Set, plan, and achieve your own learning goals.
- Identify and access learning sources and opportunities.

Work safely

- Be aware of personal and group health and safety practices.
- Act in accordance with the above.

Teamwork skills

Work with others

- Recognize and respect people's diversity, individual differences, and perspectives.
- Be knowledgeable about group dynamics, ensure that you are respectful of team members and supportive of their ideas.
- Focus on clearly articulated team goals.
- Accept and provide constructive feedback to team members.
- Motivate your team to high performance.
- Contribute to a team by sharing information and expertise.
- Understand the role of conflict in a group and manage it to reach solutions.

Participate in projects and tasks

- Plan, design, and execute a project from start to finish, developing a plan with well-defined objectives and outcomes.
- Review, revise, and test plans.
- Ensure quality standards are upheld.
- Utilize appropriate technology and tools for the task at hand.
- Monitor the success of a project, seek feedback, and identify ways to improve. ✳

Employability Skills 2000+ Brochure 2000 E/F (Ottawa: The Conference Board of Canada, 2000).

12

Exercise
32 Assess Your Employability Skills

In reading the Conference Board of Canada list of employability skills, identify:

Three areas of strength that you have

1. _____
2. _____
3. _____

Three areas that you need to improve

1. _____
2. _____
3. _____

Think about how you might gain those needed skills by taking courses, through your involvement in clubs or other activities, or your volunteer work or self-study. Select three methods you will use to improve your skills.

1. _____
2. _____
3. _____

Jumpstart your education with transferable skills

When meeting with an academic advisor, some students say, "I've just been taking courses in arts and humanities. I haven't got any marketable skills." Think again.

FEW WORDS are as widely misunderstood as *skill*. Defining it carefully can have an immediate and positive impact on your career planning.

Two kinds of skills

One dictionary defines *skill* as "the ability to do something well, usually gained by training or experience." Some skills—such as the ability to repair fibre optic cables or do brain surgery—are acquired through formal schooling, on-the-job training, or both. These abilities are called *work-content skills*. People with such skills have mastered a specialized body of knowledge needed to do a specific kind of work.

However, there is another category of skills that we develop through experiences both inside and outside the classroom. We may never receive formal training to develop these abilities. Yet they are key to success in the workplace. These are *transferable skills*. Transferable skills are the kind of abilities that help people thrive in any job—no matter what work-content skills they have.

Perhaps you've heard someone described this way: "She's really smart and knows what she's doing, but she's got lousy people skills." People skills—such as

listening and *negotiating*—are prime examples of transferable skills. These are often considered to be soft skills and may be overlooked by graduates who often think that, to be successful, they need more content skills (like learning one more computer program), yet their lack of employment is probably far more related to these so-called soft skills. Other examples are listed on this page.

Succeeding in many situations

Transferable skills are often invisible to us. The problem begins when we assume that a given skill can only be used in one context, such as being in school or working at a particular job. Thinking in this way places an artificial limit on our possibilities. As an alternative, think about the things you routinely do to succeed in school. Analyze your activities to isolate specific skills. Then brainstorm a list of jobs where you could use the same skills.

Consider the task of writing an essay. This calls for skills such as:

- *Planning*—setting goals for completing your outline, first draft, second draft, and final draft
- *Managing time* to meet your writing goals

12

- *Interviewing* people who know a lot about the topic of your essay
- *Researching* using the Internet and campus library to discover key facts and ideas to include in your essay
- *Writing* to present those facts and ideas in an original way
- *Editing* your drafts for clarity and correctness.

Now consider the kinds of jobs that draw on these skills.

For example, you could transfer your skill at writing essays to a possible career in journalism, technical writing, or advertising copywriting.

You could use your editing skills to work in the field of publishing as an online magazine or book editor.

Interviewing and research skills could help you enter the field of market research. And the abilities to plan, manage time, and meet deadlines will help you succeed in all the jobs mentioned so far.

Use the same kind of analysis to think about transferring skills from one job to another job. For example, if you work part-time as an administrative assistant at a computer dealer that sells a variety of hardware and software, you probably take phone calls from potential customers, help current customers solve problems using their computers, and attend meetings where your coworkers plan ways to market new products. You are developing skills at *selling, serving customers,* and *working on teams* that could help you land a job as a sales representative for a computer manufacturer or software developer.

The basic idea is to take a cue from the word *transferable*. Almost any skill you use to succeed in one situation can *transfer* to success in another situation.

The concept of transferable skills creates a powerful link between postsecondary education and the work world. Skills are the core elements of any job. While taking any course, list the specific skills you are developing and how you can transfer them to the work world. Almost everything you do in school can be applied to your career—if you consistently pursue this line of thought.

Ask four questions

To experiment further with this concept of transferable skills, ask and answer four questions derived from the Master Student Map.

Why identify my transferable skills? Getting past the "I-don't-have-any-skills" syndrome means that you can approach job-hunting with more confidence. As you uncover these hidden assets, your list of qualifications will grow as if by magic. You won't be padding your resumé. You'll simply be using action words to tell the full truth about what you can do.

Identifying your transferable skills takes a little time. And the payoffs are numerous. A complete and accurate list of transferable skills can help you land jobs that

involve more responsibility, more variety, more freedom to structure your time, and more money.

Transferable skills also help you thrive in the midst of constant change. Technology will continue to upgrade. Ongoing discoveries in many fields could render current knowledge obsolete. Jobs that exist today may disappear in a few years, only to be replaced by entirely new ones. Your keys to prospering in this environment are transferable skills—those that you can carry from one career to another.

What are my transferable skills? Discover your transferable skills by reflecting on key experiences. Recall a time when you performed at the peak of your ability, overcame obstacles, won an award, gained a high mark, or met a significant goal. List the skills you used to create those successes.

In each case, remember that the word *skill* points to something that you *do*. In your list of transferable skills, start each item with an action verb such as *budget* or *coach* or *consult*. Or use a closely related part of speech—*budgeting* or *coaching*.

For a more complete picture of your transferable skills, describe the object of your action. Perhaps one of the skills on your list is *organizing*. This could refer to organizing ideas, organizing people, or organizing objects in a room. Specify the kind of organizing that you like to do.

How do I perform these skills? You can bring your transferable skills into even sharper focus by adding adverbs—words that describe *how* you take action. You might say that you edit *accurately* or learn *quickly*.

In summary, you can use a three-column chart to list your transferable skills. For example:

Verb	Object	Adverb
Organizing	Records	Effectively
Serving	Customers	Courteously
Coordinating	Special events	Efficiently

Add a specific example of each skill to your list, and you're well on the way to an engaging resumé and a winning job interview.

As you list your transferable skills, focus on the skills that you most enjoy using. Then look for careers and jobs that directly involve those skills.

What if I could expand my transferable skills? In addition to thinking about the skills you already have, consider the skills you'd like to acquire. Describe them in detail and list experiences that can help you develop them. Let your list of transferrable skills grow and develop as you do. ✳

 Learn more about transferable skills online @ **www.bams5ce.nelson.com**

65 transferable skills

There are literally hundreds of transferable skills. To learn more transferable skills and which occupations they match, go to the Canadian government website *Working in Canada*. On the website, fill in a checklist of your skills and knowledge and get some ideas about which occupations match up with those skill sets. If you are particularly interested in the skilled trades and technology field, go to *Skills Competencies Canada*, and check out the website of this non-profit organization. There you'll find tools for discovering your skills and matching them to specific occupations. Additional information on careers and job-hunting is available online through *Canadian Careers.com,* which is a great website that lists valuable information about labour market trends plus essential information about marketing yourself. For these and other great website URLs on careers, go to the textbook's website.

Self-discovery and self-management skills

1. Assessing your current knowledge and skills
2. Seeking out opportunities to acquire new knowledge and skills
3. Choosing and applying learning strategies
4. Showing flexibility by adopting new attitudes and behaviours

For more information about self-discovery skills, review the Introduction to this book and Chapter 1.

Time-management skills

1. Scheduling due dates for project outcomes
2. Scheduling time for goal-related tasks
3. Choosing technology and applying it to goal-related tasks
4. Choosing materials and facilities needed to meet goals
5. Designing other processes, procedures, or systems to meet goals
6. Working independently to meet goals
7. Planning projects for teams
8. Managing multiple projects at the same time
9. Monitoring progress toward goals
10. Persisting in order to meet goals
11. Delivering projects and outcomes on schedule

For more information about time-management skills, review Chapter 2.

Reading skills

1. Reading for key ideas and major themes
2. Reading for detail
3. Reading to synthesize ideas and information from several sources
4. Reading to discover strategies for solving problems or meeting goals
5. Reading to understand and follow instructions

For more information about reading skills, review Chapter 4.

Note-taking skills

1. Taking notes on material presented verbally, in print, or online
2. Creating pictures, graphs, and other visuals to summarize and clarify information
3. Organizing information and ideas in digital and paper-based forms
4. Researching by finding information online or in the library
5. Gathering data through field research or working with primary sources

For more information about note-taking skills, review Chapter 5.

Test-taking and related skills

1. Assessing personal performance at school or at work
2. Using test results and other assessments to improve performance
3. Working cooperatively in study groups and project teams
4. Managing stress
5. Applying scientific findings and methods to solve problems
6. Using mathematics to do basic computations and solve problems

For more information about this group of skills, review Chapters 3, 6, and 11.

Thinking skills

1. Thinking to create new ideas, products, or services
2. Thinking to evaluate ideas, products, or services
3. Evaluating material presented verbally, in print, or online
4. Thinking of ways to improve products, services, or programs
5. Choosing appropriate strategies for making decisions
6. Choosing ethical behaviours
7. Stating problems accurately
8. Diagnosing the sources of problems
9. Generating possible solutions to problems
10. Weighing benefits and costs of potential solutions
11. Choosing and implementing solutions
12. Interpreting information needed for problem solving or decision making

For more information about thinking skills, review Chapter 7.

Communication skills

1. Assigning and delegating tasks
2. Coaching
3. Consulting
4. Counselling
5. Editing publications
6. Giving people feedback about the quality of their performance
7. Interpreting and responding to nonverbal messages
8. Interviewing people
9. Leading meetings
10. Leading project teams
11. Listening fully (without judgment or distraction)
12. Preventing conflicts (defusing a tense situation)
13. Resolving conflicts
14. Responding to complaints
15. Speaking to diverse audiences
16. Writing
17. Editing

For more information about communication skills, review Chapters 8 and 9.

Money skills

1. Monitoring income and expenses
2. Raising funds
3. Decreasing expenses
4. Estimating costs
5. Preparing budgets

For more information about money skills, review Chapter 10.

 Find an expanded list of transferable skills online @ **www.bams5ce.nelson.com**

Use resumés and interviews to "hire" an employer

The logical outcome of your career plan is a focused job hunt.

© photos.com

MENTION THE PHRASE *job-hunting*, and many people envision someone poring through the help-wanted sections in newspapers or on websites, sending out hundreds of resumés, or enlisting the services of employment agencies to find job openings and set up interviews.

There's a big problem with these job-hunting strategies: *Most job openings are not advertised.* Many employers turn to help-wanted listings, resumés, and employment agencies only as a last resort. When they have positions to fill, they prefer instead to hire people they know—friends and colleagues—or people who walk through the door and prove that they're excellent candidates for available jobs.

Remembering this can help you overcome frustration, tap the hidden job market, and succeed more often at getting the position you want. One powerful source of information about new jobs is people. Ask around. Tell everyone—friends, relatives, coworkers, and fellow students—that you want a job. In particular, tell people who have the power to hire you. Some jobs are created on the spot when a person with potential simply shows up and asks.

Attend your campus career fairs. Most colleges and universities host career fairs for summer and permanent jobs. When you attend the fair, show that you are job-ready by wearing the appropriate clothing and having a completed resumé to submit. Many students even have business cards to distribute to potential employers so that it's easy for them to follow up your discussions at the fair.

Richard Bolles, author of *What Color Is Your Parachute? A Practical Manual for Job-Hunters and Career-Changers*, recommends the following steps in job-hunting:

- Discover which skills you want to use in your career, and which jobs draw on the skills you want to use.
- Interview people who are doing the kind of jobs you'd want to do.
- Research companies you'd like to work for, and find out what kinds of problems they face on a daily basis.
- Identify your contacts—a person at each one of these companies who has the power to hire you.
- Arrange an interview with that person, even if the company has no job openings at the moment.
- Stay in contact with the people who interviewed you, knowing that a job opening can occur at any time (Taylor, 2009).

Use resumés to get interviews. A resumé is a piece of persuasive writing, not a dry recitation of facts or a laundry list of previous jobs. It has a basic purpose—to get you to the next step in the hiring process, usually an interview.

Begin your resumé with your name, address, phone number, and email address. Then name your desired job, often called an "objective" or "goal." Follow with the body of your resumé—your skills, work experience, and education.

Write your resumé so that the facts leap off the page. Describe your work experiences in short phrases that start with action verbs: "*Supervised* three people." "*Wrote* two annual reports." "*Set up* sales calls." Also leave reasonable margins and space between paragraphs.

As you draft your resumé, remember that every organization has problems to solve. Show in your resumé that you know about those problems and can offer your skills as solutions. Give evidence that you've used those skills to get measurable results. Show a potential employer how you can contribute value and help create profits.

Resumé formats can either be chronological (by year working from the present to the past); functional or skills-based (where work or other experiences are categorized by skill, such as all work experiences that developed leadership skills); or a combination of the two. Often for students the combination format works best, as they don't have years of experience to document if they were to use the strictly chronological approach, yet the skills-based approach may not be one that employers are as familiar with. The combined approach

lets you highlight your relevant work experience but also focus on the skills you have developed through both paid and non-paid positions. For examples of these resumé formats, refer to the textbook's website.

Use interviews to screen employers. You might think of job interviews as times when potential employers size you up and possibly screen you out. Consider another viewpoint—that interviews offer you a chance to size up potential employers and possibly screen *them* out.

To get the most from your interviews, learn everything you can about each organization that interests you. Get a feel for its strong points. Learn about its successes in the marketplace. Also find out what challenges the organization faces. As in a resumé, use interviews to present your skills as unique solutions for those challenges.

Job interviewers have many standard questions. Most of them boil down to a few major concerns:

- How did you find out about us?
- Would we be comfortable working with you?
- How can you help us?
- Will you learn this job quickly?
- What makes you different from other applicants?

Before your interview, prepare some answers to these questions.

If you get turned down for the job after your interview, don't take it personally. Every interview is a source of feedback about what works—and what doesn't work—in contacting employers. Use that feedback to interview more effectively next time.

Counter bias and discrimination. During your job hunt, you might worry about discrimination based on your race, ethnic background, gender, or sexual orientation. Protect yourself by keeping records, including copies of all correspondence from prospective employers. Remember that workplace discrimination and harassment are covered by the Canadian Human Rights Act and the Employment Equity Act. Complaints about discrimination in all aspects of the workplace, from hiring to firing, can be made to the Canadian Human Rights Commission. You can contact the national office of the commission at 1-888-643-3304 and get more information through its website at www.chrc-ccdp.ca. Some employers are federally regulated, whereas others are provincial. The website for the Canadian Human Rights Commission contains important information about whether the employer is covered by the federal or provincial code. Each province or territory also has its own human rights codes. For instance, the BC human rights code protects individuals from discrimination or harassment on the basis of gender, race, sexual orientation, marital status, place of origin, mental or physical disability, and more. It is important for you to know your rights.

Give yourself a raise before you start work.
Preparing for salary negotiation can immediately increase your income by hundreds or thousands of dollars. To get the money you deserve:

- Use Exercise #26: "The Money Monitor/Money Plan" in Chapter 10 to determine how much you'll need each month to meet your expenses—and still have some money left over to save.

- Maintain flexibility by settling on a salary *range* that you want rather than a specific figure.

- Through informational interviews, library research, and Internet searches, discover typical salary ranges for jobs in your field.

- Based on your research, estimate how much the employer is likely to offer you.

- Postpone salary discussions until the end of the interview process—when you're confident an employer wants to hire you.

- Let the employer be the first to mention a salary range.

- Ask for a figure near the top of that range.

- Ask if there's room to negotiate benefits packages and vacation time as well.

Use what you have learned in becoming a master student to constantly update your skills, manage job transitions, and stay in charge of your career path. ✳

 Go online to discover more job-hunting strategies @ **www.bams5ce.nelson.com**

Looking for jobs on the Internet

On the Internet you can research companies you'd like to work for, read lists of job openings, and post your resumé and a digital recording of yourself. Through mobile phones and email, you can stay in continual contact with potential employers. High-speed Internet access has increased the number of long-distance job interviews being conducted via video conferencing or through Skype, and has increased the possibility of sending an electronic portfolio attachment with a resumé.

Although without a doubt the Internet can give you access to way more jobs than can be found in your local newspaper, there are some caveats to consider. When you're looking for a job, the strength of the Internet—the sheer density of data—can also lead to frustration:

- Job openings listed on the Internet can be heavily skewed to certain fields, such as jobs for computer professionals or people in other technical fields.

- Across all fields, the majority of job openings are not listed on the Internet (or in newspaper want ads, for that matter).

This is not meant to disparage the Internet as a tool for job-hunters and career planners. The point is that posting a resumé on a website will not automatically lead to an email in-basket that's bursting at its digital seams with job offers. For an effective job search, view the Internet as just one resource.

Also, keep in mind that employers use the Internet to find out information about job candidates. Having a Web presence can be an asset during your job search—it's an opportunity to stand out from the pack. You can show your interest in the field by posting and commenting on relevant articles using a blog or Twitter, and demonstrate skills that employers might value, such as writing or

design. But employers might use negative information they find to screen you out. Ensure that your Facebook profile is private, or remove posts and pictures that you wouldn't want potential employers to discover.

With this caveat in mind, you might choose to create a LinkedIn profile, post your resumé online or scan Internet job ads. Even if you don't choose to post a digital resumé or Web page, you can access career-planning resources on the Internet. Begin with "gateway" sites that offer organized links to many career-related pages on the Internet. For instance, the Riley Guide (www.rileyguide.com) gives an overview of job-hunting on the Internet.

Also check JobHuntersBible.com, a site maintained by Richard Bolles, author of *What Color Is Your Parachute?* This site focuses on effective ways to use the Internet. One way in which the Internet can really help you is in researching organizations before you contact them. Chances are, the company you're interested in has a website. Go to the site to gather information, discover the names of key players, and view financial data. Doing so will show potential employers that you've done your homework. That can make a favourable impression and even land you a job.

Other websites to consider are:

Your career centre's website

Service Canada's Job Bank—www.jobbank.gc.ca

CharityVillage (non-profit sector)—www.charityvillage.ca

JobPostings.ca

Brazen Careerist—www.brazencareerist.com

eluta—www.eluta.ca

indeed—www.indeed.ca

33 Do Something You Can't

Few significant accomplishments result from people sticking to the familiar. You can accomplish much more than you think you can. Doing something you can't involves taking risks. This exercise has three parts. Complete this exercise on a separate piece of paper.

Part 1

Select something that you have never done before, that you don't know how to do, that you are fearful of doing, or that you think you probably can't do.

Perhaps you've never learned to play an instrument, or you've never run a marathon. Be smart. Don't pick something that will hurt you physically, such as flying from a third-floor window.

Part 2

Do it. Of course, this is easier to say than to do. This exercise is not about easy. It is about discovering capabilities that stretch your self-image.

To accomplish something that is bigger than your self-perceived abilities, use any of the tools you have gained from this book. Develop a plan. Divide and conquer. Stay focused. Use outside resources. Let go of self-destructive thoughts.

Summarize the tools you will use.

Part 3

Write about the results of this exercise.

Creating and using portfolios

PHOTOGRAPHERS, CONTRACTORS, and designers regularly show portfolios filled with samples of their work. Today, employers and educators increasingly see the portfolio as a tool that's useful for everyone. Some schools require students to create them, and some employers expect to see a portfolio before they'll hire a job applicant. Today, many of those portfolios are created online.

When you create your portfolio, experiment with a four-step process:

1. Collect and catalogue artifacts An artifact is any object that's important to you and that reveals something about yourself. Examples include photographs, awards, recommendation letters, job descriptions for positions you've held, newspaper articles about projects you've done, lists of grants or scholarships you've received, programs from performances you've given, transcripts of your marks, or models you've constructed.

Start collecting now. Write down the kinds of artifacts you'd like to save. Think about what will be most useful to you in creating portfolios for your courses and your job search. In some cases, collecting artifacts requires follow-up. You might call former instructors

© Davis Barber/PhotoEdit Inc.

or employers to request letters of recommendation. Or you might track down newspaper articles about a service-learning project you did. Your responses to the Journal Entries and exercises in this book can also become part of your portfolio. To save hours when you create your next portfolio, start documenting your artifacts. On an index card, record the "five W's" about each artifact: *who* was involved with it, *what* you did with it, *when* it was created, *where* it was created, and *why* the artifact is important to you. File these cards and update them as you collect new artifacts. Another option is to manage this information with a computer, using word processing or database software, or using the e-portfolio

WHAT'S NEXT?

12

component of your school's course management software, if available.

2. Plan your portfolio When you're ready to create a portfolio for a specific audience, allow some time for planning. Begin with your purpose for creating the portfolio—for example, to demonstrate your learning or to document your work experience as you prepare for a job interview.

Also list some specifics about your audience. Write a description of anyone who will see your portfolio. List what each person already knows about you and predict what else these people will want to know. Answer their questions in your portfolio.

Screen artifacts with your purpose and audience in mind. If a beautiful artifact fails to meet your purpose or fit your audience, leave it out for now. Save the artifact for a future portfolio.

When you plan your portfolio, also think about how to order and arrange your artifacts. One basic option is a chronological organization. For example, start with work samples from your earliest jobs and work up to the present.

Another option is to structure your portfolio around key themes, such as your values or work skills. When preparing this type of portfolio, you can define work to include any time you used a job-related skill, whether or not you got paid.

3. Assemble your portfolio With a collection of artifacts and a written plan, you're ready to assemble your portfolio. Arranging artifacts according to your design is a big part of this process. Also include elements to orient your audience members and guide them through your portfolio. Such elements can include:

- A table of contents
- An overview or summary of the portfolio
- Titles and captions for each artifact
- An index to your artifacts.

Although many portfolios take their final form as a collection of papers, remember that this is just one possibility. You can also create a bulletin board, a display, or a case that contains your artifacts. You could even create a recording or a digital portfolio in the form of a personal website. Adobe software can be useful in creating media-rich online portfolios.

4. Present your portfolio Your audience might ask you to present your portfolio as part of an interview or oral exam. If that's the case, rehearse your portfolio presentation the way you would rehearse a speech. Write down questions that people might ask about your portfolio. Prepare some answers. Then do a dry run. Present your portfolio to friends and people in your career field, and request their feedback.

That feedback will give you plenty of ideas about ways to revise your portfolio. Any portfolio is a living document. Update it as you acquire new perspectives and skills. ✳

 For more ideas on portfolios, go online @
www.bams5ce.nelson.com

Top 10 Tips to Help
Ensure a Successful Job Search

1. Access your school's career centre.
   - Attend career counselling workshops, employer recruitment events, career fairs, and opportunities for skill development.
2. Start early.
   - Don't wait until the term before graduation to begin. Career planning is a process and it can't be done successfully overnight.
   - The earlier you start thinking about your career goals and planning for employment after graduation, the more successful you will be in getting the job you want.
3. Know yourself.
   - Making good career choices requires you to have a solid understanding of your skills, interests, personality, and values.
   - If you aren't clear on who you are and what your needs are in terms of your career, consider taking a career assessment, which can help clarify some of these areas.
4. Do your research.
   - Learn all that you can about the industries, companies and job roles that are part of the labour market. Start by browsing company or government websites.
   - Talk to people who are doing the type of work that you are interested in. This is called *information interviewing* and is a highly effective way to assess your fit for different roles and organizations.
5. Get away from the computer.
   - Do not restrict your job search to the Internet and online job search postings.

- Approximately 20 percent of employment opportunities are posted, which means that 80 percent are part of the hidden job market.
- So spend 20 percent of your time looking for opportunities online and the remaining 80 percent of your time actually meeting people.

6. Network, network, network.
- A successful job search begins with networking, and is the primary way to access the hidden job market.
- Talk to everyone about your job search

7. Think broadly.
- Don't let your major dictate or limit the type of work that you consider; even if a job isn't directly related to your degree or diploma, there is a good chance that you will be able to demonstrate to an employer that you do, in fact, have the skills necessary to do the work.

8. Customize your resumé and cover letter.
- Use the job posting to customize your documents according to the specific skills requested, and show a potential employer why you're the best candidate for the job.

9. Practise, practise, practise.
- Successfully interviewing is a skill and, like any skill, it is perfected through practise.
- Ask if your career centre provides opportunities for students to practise their interview skills. If not, you can also practise on your own with friends or family, or even in front of a mirror.

10. Be strategic.
- All experience is good experience, but being *strategic* about the activities you participate in as a student is even better.
- Think about where you want to go career-wise, and then actively participate in paid and unpaid opportunities that will help you develop the *skills* necessary for your career choice.

Kim Miller
Career Counsellor

 For more information on the career search, go online @
www.bams5ce.nelson.com

Surviving your first day on a new job

YOU'VE LANDED a new job. Congratulations! Now prepare to walk into the office and make a place for yourself. Well-meaning people may advise you to "just be yourself" when you show up for your first day of work. The following checklist offers more specifics.

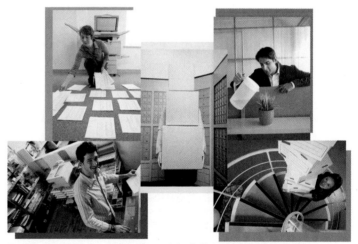

Top left: © Phil Boorman/Getty; Bottom left: © Christopher Robbins/Getty; Middle: © Somos/Veer/Getty; Top right: © John Lund/Sam Diephuis/Getty; Bottom right: © Anthony Marsland/Getty Images

Dress the part. To make a positive impression, put special effort into looking your best on your first day. Some students cultivate an eclectic wardrobe, and that won't pass the test for a new job. Even employers with "casual days" prefer to meet new employees in standard business attire. Think back to what people in the office were wearing when you showed up for your job interview. Then dress at that level or slightly above it.

Arrive early. Don't underestimate the power of this simple suggestion. Arriving late for your first day of work sends mixed messages. To you, it may be a simple mistake. Your supervisor might interpret it as being careless or having an "attitude." Remove all possibility of misunderstanding by showing up with at least 15 minutes to spare.

Notice your "nonverbal." Remember to shake hands firmly and say hello in a friendly voice. Make eye contact and smile. Also be aware of your other nonverbal messages. In meetings, for example, check to see if your posture says, "I'm here now, and I am paying attention to what you say." Make sure your cell phone is turned off or on vibrate.

Start decoding the culture. Even if you graduated from school with a straight-A average—a real accomplishment—your new coworkers are not likely to know or care. Unless you're working in education, prepare for a business rather than an academic environment. Your job on your first day is to start adapting to this environment rather than remaking it. (Remaking might come later—*after* you pay some dues.)

Keep your eyes open. Notice when people arrive for work, how they greet each other, when they leave for lunch, how often they take breaks, how they make requests, and when they go home. Look for clues to the workplace culture: the unwritten rules that seem to shape peoples' behaviour.

Take notes. During your first day, you'll cover lots of details. First, there's the obvious stuff—where to sit, where to park, where to eat, where to make photocopies, where to take breaks, where to go to the bathroom. Then there's higher-level stuff, such as phone numbers, and user IDs and passwords for Internet access. Be prepared with paper and a pen so you can write this information down. Besides aiding your memory, taking notes gives you something to do with your hands if you feel nervous.

Pack a briefcase. Companies just love to push paper at new employees—brochures, forms, maps, manuals, and more. When you receive these things, look at them for a few seconds. This communicates in a small and significant way that you pay attention to details. Then place the papers in a professional-looking folder or briefcase.

Do not say these words. Avoid saying, "Wow, that's not how we did things at my last job!" This invites an inevitable response: "Well, then why did you leave that job?" Expect procedures to differ from job to job. Look for chances to suggest improvements in the future—but not right away.

Go easy on yourself. Notice whether there's a self-critical voice in your head that's saying something like this: "You're not fooling anyone—you really have no idea what you're doing here." No one else hears that voice. And no one expects you to perform to perfection on your first day.

Remember that your boss has already scoped out your qualifications. Since she hired you, she's probably confident that you can handle job tasks now, or learn to do them within a reasonable period. To really shine as a new employee, focus on your people skills. If you demonstrate that you're willing to listen and learn, you'll have done good work on your first day. ✳

Choosing schools . . . again

Changing to a different school involves making a decision that will have a major impact on your education. This is true at many points in postsecondary education—such as when you're transferring from a community college to a university, or when you're choosing a graduate school or a post-degree diploma at a college.

© Photolibrary

WHAT'S NEXT?

CHANCES ARE YOU will attend more than one postsecondary institution throughout your life, whether you choose to return to school to acquire new career skills or because you just want to continue to expand your mind. Lifelong learning is the norm for Canadians, with more and more of them engaging in furthering their education after high school. Selecting the school that has the best fit for you requires that you learn a bit more about what is out there. The options today are endless—from face-to-face classes, to online programs to hybrid courses. Figuring out what works best for you means taking the time to learn more about the postsecondary opportunities that are available.

Know key terms

As you begin researching schools, take a few minutes to review some key terms

Undergraduate university degree program. Offers three- or four-year academic studies at university that lead to degrees such as Bachelor of Arts (B.A.), Bachelor of Science (B.S.), or Bachelor of Commerce (B.Comm.) degrees.

Four-year applied college degree program. Offers the best of both worlds: the practical, technical strengths of a college education and the theoretical foundation of a bachelor's degree.

Joint college/university collaborative program. Offers a collaborative learning environment that involves taking courses at both the college and university levels.

Post-diploma/post-graduate/post-certificate program. Builds on knowledge and experience gained through previous postsecondary study and may result in an additional diploma, certificate, or degree. Often includes some hands-on experience in the workplace through internships or practicum.

Co-op program. Offers in-school training through scheduled periods of employment in related industries within the academic year, often paid and required for graduation. These programs are offered at both colleges and universities.

Apprenticeship program. Provides provincial certification in a trade after completing provincial training requirements; usually includes 75 to 90 percent learning time on-the-job and the remaining 10 to 25 percent in the classroom (Ontario College Guide, 2004).

Gather information

To find out more about your new school, you need to do research. Go online and look at the school websites and write to request the school's viewbook. Go to www.campusstarter.com/ to get a complete list of college and university programs in Canada plus links to the school websites. The *Globe Campus* at www.globecampus.ca provides in-depth articles on Canadian colleges and universities. Talk to the school's recruitment officers, academic counsellors, and other staff members. If you can talk to students who have gone to the school you are considering, that is another great source of information.

Find out if there are any college fairs happening in your city. In Toronto, the *Ontario University Fair* happens annually in September and is a great way to comparison shop on the spot. Both *Maclean's* magazine through its annual rankings of universities, and *The Globe and Mail*'s University Report Card can give you

more information to consider in making your choice. The *Globe Campus* allows you to directly compare two different colleges or universities, plus gives you information about the size of school, tuition, etc.

You might also want to check to see if the institution has participated in the *National Survey of Student Engagement (NSSE)*. NSSE measures students' participation in activities, both inside and outside the classroom, that lead to deep learning (Pascarella, Seifert & Blaich, 2010). Take a look and see whether students feel there is a high degree of student-faculty interaction or opportunities for experiential education. This again could provide an important benchmark for you to use to compare institutions you might be considering attending. Institutions that have participated in NSSE often list their outcomes on their websites. Finally, take the time to visit your top two or three picks and look for the place that feels right to you. Use your research to find out more about key factors such as the following:

- **Number of students.** Large Canadian universities can have a full-time student body numbering 50,000 or more. Smaller universities, colleges, and vocational schools might have fewer than 1,000 students, with most somewhere in between. According to the University Report Card, a survey produced annually by *The Globe and Mail*, larger universities are often considered impersonal and lacking in school spirit. Smaller colleges often score higher with students in terms of personal attention and quality of education, but are criticized for problems with student services and poor campus facilities, such as inadequate libraries.

- **Class sizes.** Large educational institutions might enrol 800 in an introductory course. At smaller institutions, classes might number between 20 and 30 people, especially in specialized courses. Don't be swayed by the average class size in the printed materials, as within a single school class sizes can vary between course levels and departments. Ask how often you can expect to have smaller classes, particularly in the upper-year courses.

- **Contact with instructors.** Schools vary about who they have teaching their classes. At some educational institutions, the instructors are faculty members who are dedicated to teaching full-time, while others employ experts in the field who teach part-time. Or you could take most of your classes from associate or full professors while other schools have graduate teaching assistants in the classrooms. In other academic institutions, professors focus mainly on teaching graduate students and performing research. If you value close contact with your instructors, this

12

is a crucial factor to investigate, especially at the graduate level.

- **Admissions criteria.** Some educational institutions are highly competitive, admitting only a small percentage of the students who apply each year. Other educational institutions are relatively open, admitting most students with high school diplomas.

- **Availability of degrees.** Community colleges and vocational-technical schools commonly offer diplomas or certificates. For university grads, community college diplomas are often a way for them to gain applied skills that lead directly to employment (Belford, 2009). Most college programs include some type of experiential education component such as internships or co-op placement that employers value. Other colleges and universities generally offer four-year degrees, such as the Bachelor of Arts (B.A.) or Bachelor of Science (B.S.). Many larger educational institutions also offer graduate programs, leading to master's and doctoral degrees, or specialized degrees in law, medicine, or dentistry. If you want to make only one transfer, the availability of such degrees can have an impact on your decision.

- **Costs.** Tuition fees at Canadian colleges and universities vary, with an average cost at about $5,200 per year for a full-time student; however, professional degrees such as dentistry tend to have significantly higher fees. Other costs include books, materials, housing, health insurance, student fees, and laboratory fees.

- **Location.** The educational institution you choose might be nestled in an idyllic rural setting or thrive in the heart of a large city, and the differences between these two settings can greatly colour your experience of postsecondary education. Take this opportunity to try something new and to explore Canada.

- **Diversity.** This term can apply to faculty members as well as students. Today most large Canadian universities have a highly diverse student body in terms of race, nationality, religion, culture, language, and sexual orientation. Also consider the mix between full-time and part-time students; students who live at the college or university, and those who commute; and graduate and undergraduate students.

- **Opportunities for Experiential Education.** Find out what the opportunities are for you to have work-integrated learning experiences such as co-op, internships, service learning, or field placements. Opportunities to apply what you learn in the classroom can greatly enhance your educational

experience. The availability of study abroad programs can also greatly deepen the learning experience. Schools should also be able to tell you if the work experiences are paid or unpaid, or for study abroad, if bursaries are available.

Dig up other key facts

Gather the facts about your current academic profile. This includes marks, courses completed, degrees attained, and grade point average (GPA). Check course equivalents at your new institution with a registrar or an admissions office. Since no two educational institutions offer the same curriculum, determining which of your courses are accepted is often a matter of interpretation. Keep a folder of syllabuses from your courses; they can be useful when transferring credits.

After totalling the costs of attending an educational institution, check on the financial aid that is available to you.

Choose your new school

If you follow the above suggestions, you'll end up with stacks of publications and pages of notes. As you sort through all this information, remember that your impressions of a school will go beyond a dry list of facts. Also pay attention to your instincts and intuitions—your "gut feelings" of attraction to one school or hesitation about another. These impressions can be important to your choice. Allow time for such feelings to emerge.

You can also benefit from putting your choice of schools in a bigger context. Consider the purposes, values, and long-term goals you've generated by doing the exercises and Journal Entries in this book. Consider which school is most likely to support the body of discoveries and intentions that you've created.

As you choose your new school, consider the needs and wishes of your family members and friends. Ask for their guidance and support. If you involve them in the decision, they'll have more stake in your success.

At some point, you'll just choose a school. Remember that there is no one "right" choice. You could probably thrive at many schools—perhaps even at your current one. Use the suggestions in this book to practice self-responsibility. Take charge of your education no matter which school you attend.

Succeed at your new school

Be willing to begin again. Some students approach a transfer with a "been there, done that" attitude. Having enrolled in higher education before, they assume that they don't need the orientation, advising, or other student services available at their new school.

Consider an alternative. Since your tuition and fees cover all these services, you might as well take advantage of them. By doing so, you could uncover opportunities that you missed while researching schools. At the very least, you'll meet people who will support your transition.

Your prior experience in higher education gives you strengths. Acknowledge them, even as you begin again at your new school. While celebrating your past accomplishments, you can explore new paths to student success.

Connect to people. At your new school, you'll be in classes with people who have already developed social networks. To avoid feeling left out, seek out chances to meet people. Join study groups, check out extracurricular activities, and consider volunteering for student organizations. Making social connections can ease your transition to a new academic environment. ✳

Contributing:
The art of selfishness

© Leland Bobbe/Getty Images

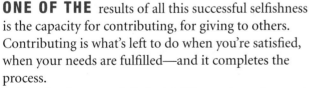

This book is about contributing to yourself—about taking care of yourself, being selfish, and fulfilling your own needs. The techniques and suggestions in these pages focus on ways to get what you want out of school and out of life.

ONE OF THE results of all this successful selfishness is the capacity for contributing, for giving to others. Contributing is what's left to do when you're satisfied, when your needs are fulfilled—and it completes the process.

People who are satisfied with life can share that satisfaction with others. It is not easy to contribute to another person's joy until you experience joy yourself. The same is true for love. When people are filled with love, they can more easily contribute love to others.

Our interdependence calls for contributing. Every day we depend on contributing. We stake our lives on the compassion of other people. When we drive, we depend on others for our lives. If a driver in an oncoming lane should cross into our lane, we might die. We also depend upon the sensibilities of world leaders for our safety. People everywhere are growing more interdependent. A plunge in the U.S. stock market reverberates in markets around the planet. A decrease in oil prices gives businesses everywhere a shot in the arm. A tsunami in Japan can cause widespread devastation and lead to the slowing down of automobile manufacturing in Canada.

In this interdependent world, there is no such thing as win/lose. If others lose, their loss directly affects us. If we lose, it is more difficult to contribute to others. The only way to win and to get what we want in life is for others to win, also.

Besides, contributing means getting involved with other people. This is one way to break the ice in a new community and meet people with interests similar to your own. If you want to build community, then contribute.

You can start to experience the advantages of contributing right now. Don't wait for disasters such as a terrorist attack, flood, or hurricane to motivate your volunteerism. The world will welcome your gifts of time, money, and talent.

A caution. The idea of contributing is not the same as knowing what is best for other people. We can't know. There are people, of course, who go around "fixing" others: "I know what you need. Here, do it my way." That is not contributing. It often causes more harm than good and can result in dependence on the part of the person we are "helping."

True contributing occurs only after you find out what another person wants or needs and then determine that you can lovingly support his having it.

How you can begin contributing. When you've made the decision to contribute, the next step is knowing how. There are ways to contribute in your immediate surroundings. Visit a neighbour, take a family member to a movie, offer to tutor a roommate, or participate in an alternative spring break program where you volunteer abroad. Check online for local sites in your area (search for "volunteer" and your city). Volunteering gives you a way to both contribute to society and allows you to explore possible career choices. Consider the following organizations, for starters.

You can mentor younger students through involvement in Girl Guides and Boy Scouts. The Canadian Environmental Network, Greenpeace, World Wildlife Fund, and similar organizations are dedicated to protecting the environment and endangered species.

Amnesty International investigates human rights violations. It assists people who are imprisoned or tortured for peacefully expressing their points of view. You can participate in letter-writing campaigns.

Museums and art galleries need interested people to conduct tours and provide supervision. Performing arts organizations, such as local theatre groups or ballet companies, are always in need of volunteers for everything from set decoration to ticket sales.

Hospitals and hospice programs often depend on volunteer help to supplement patient care provided by the professional staff. Nursing homes welcome visitors who are willing to spend time listening to and talking with residents. Most communities have volunteer-based programs for people living with HIV infection or AIDS that provide daily hot meals to men, women, and children too ill to cook for themselves. Political parties, candidates, and special interest groups need volunteers to stuff envelopes, gather petition signatures, and distribute literature. The Canadian Red Cross provides disaster relief. Local community care centres use volunteers to help feed homeless people, and food banks often need volunteers to sort and portion food.

Political parties often need volunteers to make phone calls, canvass houses and stuff envelopes. It's also a great way to become better informed about the issues that shape the world we live in.

Community service organizations such as Kiwanis, Lions, and Rotary Clubs want members who are willing to serve others. Tutoring centres offer opportunities for competent students to help non-English-speaking people, primary and high school students, and illiterate adults. Places of worship of all denominations want volunteers to assist with projects for the community and beyond. World hunger groups want you to help feed starving people and to inform all of us about the problems of malnutrition, food spoilage, and starvation. These groups include Oxfam, CARE, and The Hunger Project.

Considering the full scope of our international problems reminds us that there are plenty of opportunities for contributing. For instance, there are still enough nuclear warheads on the planet to end human life. And according to the *Human Development Report 2003,* commissioned by the United Nations, 1,242 million people in the world live on less than one dollar per day (Center for Human Resources, 2009).

If they remain unused, the techniques and strategies in this book make no difference in all this. However, *you* can make a difference. By using these techniques to work with others, you can choose a new future for our planet. Remember, you want to "Be the Change" you want to see in the world. ✳

Service-learning: The art of learning by contributing

© Douglas Keddy, The University of Western Ontario

AS PART OF a community service-learning project for a sociology course, students volunteer at a community centre for older adults. For another service-learning project, history students interview people in seniors' residences about their immigration to Canada.

Meanwhile, arts students work collaboratively on a community-based cultural production. Photography students facilitate digital photography workshops for inner city teens. Other students learn about nutritional health issues and youth and then create a curriculum that can be delivered in the classroom to youth.

These examples of actual projects from the Canadian Alliance for Community Service-Learning demonstrate the working premise of service-learning—that volunteer work and other forms of contributing can become a vehicle for postsecondary education.

Service-learning generally includes three elements: meaningful community service, a formal academic curriculum, and time for students to reflect on what they learn from service. That reflection can include speeches, journal writing, and essays.

Service-learning creates a win/win scenario. For one thing, students gain the satisfaction of contributing. They also gain experiences that can guide their career choices and help them develop job skills.

At the same time, community service-learning adds a valuable resource with a handsome return on investment to the community.

When you design a service-learning project, consider these suggestions:

- Work with a community agency that has experience with students. Make sure that the agency has liability insurance to cover volunteers.

- Handle logistics. Integrating service learning into your schedule can call for detailed planning. If your volunteer work takes place off campus, arrange for transportation and allow for travel time.

- Reflect on your service-learning project with a tool you've used throughout this book—the Discovery and Intention Journal Entry system explained in the Introduction. Write Discovery Statements about what you want to gain from service learning and how you feel about what you're doing. Follow up with Intention Statements about what you'll do differently for your next volunteer experience.

- Include ways to evaluate your project. From your Intention Statements, create action goals and outcome goals. *Action goals* state what you plan to do and how many people you intend to serve, for instance, "We plan to provide 100 hours of literacy tutoring to 10 people in the community." *Outcome goals* describe the actual impact that your project will have: "At the end of our project, 60 percent of the people we tutor will be able to write a resumé and fill out a job application." Build numbers into your goals whenever possible. That makes it easier service-learning to evaluate the success of your project.

- Create a way to build long-term impact into your project. One potential pitfall of is that the programs are often short-lived. After students pack up and return to campus, programs can die. To avoid this outcome, make sure that other students or community members are willing to step in and take over for you when the semester ends.

- Celebrate mistakes. If your project fails to meet its goals, have a party. State—in writing—the obstacles you encountered and ways to overcome them. The solutions you offer will be worth gold to the people who follow in your footsteps. Sharing the lessons learned from your mistakes is an act of service in itself. For more on service-learning, go to this textbook's website. ✳

STUDENT VOICES

Community service learning (CSL) has allowed me to engage with academic material in a way I never believed possible. After participating in CSL, I was able to direct my education toward careers I could directly name, rather than an ambiguous hope to one day make the world a better place. I was able to tailor my schedule with courses that supported my interest in the field of disaster and emergency management—an interest that grew specifically out of my CSL experience.

—LUCAS BAILEY

WHAT'S NEXT?

12

One key way to choose what's next in your life is to define your values. Values are the things in life that you want for their own sake. Values influence and guide your choices, including your moment-by-moment choices of what to do and what to have. Your values define who you are and who you want to be.

Define your values, align your actions

SOME PEOPLE ARE guided by values that they automatically adopt from others or by values that remain largely unconscious. These people could be missing the opportunity to live a life that's truly of their own choosing.

Investing time and energy to define your values is a pivotal suggestion in this book. In fact, *Becoming a Master Student* is based on a particular value system that underlies suggestions given throughout the book. This system includes the values of:

- Focused attention
- Self-responsibility
- Integrity
- Risk-taking
- Contributing

You'll find these values and related ones directly stated in the Power Processes throughout the text. For instance:

Discover what you want is about the importance of living a purpose-based life.

Ideas are tools points to the benefits of being willing to experiment with new ideas.

Be here now expresses the value of focused attention.

Love your problems (and experience your barriers) is about seeing difficulties as opportunities to develop new skills.

Notice your pictures and let them go is about adopting an attitude of open-mindedness.

I create it all is about taking responsibility for our beliefs and behaviours.

Detach reminds us that our core identity and value as a person does not depend on our possessions, our circumstances, or even our accomplishments.

Find a bigger problem is about offering our lives by contributing to others.

Employ your word expresses the value of making and keeping agreements.

Choose your conversations and your community reminds us of the power of language, and that we can reshape our lives by taking charge of our thoughts.

Risk being a fool is about courage—the willingness to take risks for the sake of learning something new.

Surrender points to the value of human community and the power of asking for help.

Be it is specifically about the power of attitudes—the idea that change proceeds from the inside out as we learn to see ourselves in new ways.

In addition, most of the study skills and life skills you read about in these pages have their source in values. The Time Monitor/Time Plan exercise, for example, calls for focused attention. Even the simple act of sharing your notes with a student who missed a class is an example of contributing.

As you begin to define your values, consider those who have gone before you. In creeds, scriptures, philosophies, myths, and sacred stories, the human race has left a vast and varied record of values. Be willing to look everywhere, including sources that are close to home. The creed of your local place of worship might eloquently describe some of your values—so might the mission statement of your school, company, or club. Another way to define your values is to describe the qualities of people you admire.

Also translate your values into behaviour. Although defining your values is powerful, it doesn't guarantee any results. To achieve your goals, take actions that align with your values. ✴

34 The Discovery Wheel— coming full circle

This book doesn't work. It is worthless. Only you can work. Only you can make a difference and use this book to become a more effective student.

The purpose of this book is to give you the opportunity to change your behaviour. The fact that something seems like a good idea doesn't necessarily mean that you will put it into practice. This exercise gives you a chance to see what behaviours you have changed on your journey toward becoming a master student.

Answer each question quickly and honestly. Record your results on the Discovery Wheel on page 412 and then compare it with the one you completed in Chapter 1.

The scores on this Discovery Wheel indicate your current strengths and weaknesses on your path toward becoming a master student. The last Journal Entry in this chapter provides an opportunity to write about how you intend to change. As you complete this self-evaluation, keep in mind that your commitment to change allows you to become a master student. *Your scores might be lower here than on your earlier Discovery Wheel*. That's OK. Lower scores might result from increased self-awareness and honesty, and other valuable assets.

Note: The online version of this exercise does not include number ratings, so the results will be formatted differently than described here. If you did your previous Discovery Wheel online, do it online again. This will help you compare your two sets of responses more accurately.

5 points	This statement is always or almost always true of me.
4 points	This statement is often true of me.
3 points	This statement is true of me about half the time.
2 points	This statement is seldom true of me.
1 point	This statement is never or almost never true of me.

1. _____ I enjoy learning.

2. _____ I understand and apply the concept of multiple intelligences.

3. _____ I connect my courses to my purpose for being in school.

4. _____ I make a habit of assessing my personal strengths and areas for improvement.

5. _____ I am satisfied with how I am progressing toward achieving my goals.

6. _____ I use my knowledge of learning styles to support my success in school.

7. _____ I am willing to consider any idea that can help me succeed in school—even if I initially disagree with that idea.

8. _____ I regularly remind myself of the benefits I intend to get from my education.

_____ **Total score (1) Attitude**

1. _____ I set long-term goals and periodically review them.

2. _____ I set short-term goals to support my long-term goals.

3. _____ I write a plan for each day and each week.

4. _____ I assign priorities to what I choose to do each day.

5. _____ I plan regular recreation time.

6. _____ I adjust my study time to meet the demands of individual courses.

7. _____ I have adequate time each day to accomplish what I plan.

8. _____ I plan review time so that I don't have to cram before exams.

_____ **Total score (2) Time**

1. _____ I am confident of my ability to remember.

2. _____ I can remember people's names.

3. _____ At the end of a lecture, I can summarize what was presented.

4. _____ I apply techniques that enhance my memory skills.

5. _____ I can recall information when I'm under pressure.

6. _____ I remember important information clearly and easily.

7. _____ I can jog my memory when I have difficulty recalling.

8. _____ I can relate new information to what I've already learned.

_____ **Total score (3) Memory**

1. _____ I preview and review reading assignments.

2. _____ When reading, I ask myself questions about the material.

3. _____ I underline or highlight important passages when reading.

4. _____ When I read textbooks, I am alert and awake.

5. _____ I relate what I read to my life.

6. _____ I select a reading strategy to fit the type of material I'm reading.

7. _____ I take effective notes when I read.

8. _____ When I don't understand what I'm reading, I note my questions and find answers.

_____ **Total score (4) Reading**

1. _____ When I am in class, I focus my attention.

2. _____ I take notes in class.

3. _____ I am aware of various methods for taking notes and choose those that work best for me.

4. _____ I distinguish important material and note key phrases in a lecture.

5. _____ I copy down material that the instructor writes on the chalkboard or overhead projector.

6. _____ I can put important concepts into my own words.

7. _____ My notes are valuable for review.

8. _____ I review class notes within 24 hours.

_____ **Total score (5) Notes**

1. _____ I use techniques to manage stress related to exams.

2. _____ I manage my time during exams and am able to complete them.

3. _____ I am able to predict test questions.

4. _____ I adapt my test-taking strategy to the kind of test I'm taking.

5. _____ I understand what essay questions ask and can answer them completely and accurately.

6. _____ I start reviewing for tests at the beginning of the term.

7. _____ I continue reviewing for tests throughout the term.

8. _____ My sense of personal worth is independent of my test scores.

_____ **Total score (6) Tests**

1. _____ I have flashes of insight and often think of solutions to problems at unusual times.

2. _____ I use brainstorming to generate solutions to a variety of problems.

3. _____ When I get stuck on a creative project, I use specific methods to get unstuck.

4. _____ I see problems and tough decisions as opportunities for learning and personal growth.

5. _____ I am willing to consider different points of view and alternative solutions.

6. _____ I can detect common errors in logic.

7. _____ I construct viewpoints by drawing on information and ideas from many sources.

8. _____ As I share my viewpoints with others, I am open to their feedback.

_____ **Total score (7) Thinking**

1. _____ I am candid with others about who I am, what I feel, and what I want.

2. _____ Other people tell me that I am a good listener.

3. _____ I can communicate my upset and anger without blaming others.

4. _____ I can make friends and create valuable relationships in a new setting.

5. _____ I am open to being with people I don't especially like in order to learn from them.

6. _____ I can effectively plan and research a large writing assignment.

7. _____ I create first drafts without criticizing my writing, then edit later for clarity, accuracy, and coherence.

8. _____ I know ways to prepare and deliver effective speeches.

_____ **Total score (8) Communicating**

1. _____ I am aware of my biases and am open to understanding people from other cultures, nationalities, and ethnic groups.

2. _____ I build rewarding relationships with people from other backgrounds.

3. _____ I can point out examples of discrimination and sexual harassment and effectively respond to them.

4. _____ I am learning ways to thrive with diversity—attitudes and behaviours that will support my career success.

5. _____ I can effectively resolve conflict with people from other cultures.

6. _____ My writing and speaking are free of sexist expressions.

7. _____ I can recognize bias and discrimination in the media.

8. _____ I am aware of the changing demographics in my country and community.

_____ **Total score (9) Diversity**

1. _____ I am in control of my personal finances.

2. _____ I can access a variety of resources to finance my education.

3. _____ I am confident that I will have enough money to complete my education.

4. _____ I take on debts carefully and repay them on time.

5. _____ I have long-range financial goals and a plan to meet them.

6. _____ I make regular deposits to a savings account.

7. _____ I pay off the balance on credit card accounts each month.

8. _____ I can have fun without spending money.

_____ **Total score (10) Money**

1. _____ I have enough energy to study and still fully enjoy other areas of my life.

2. _____ If the situation calls for it, I have enough reserve energy to put in a long day.

3. _____ The food I eat supports my long-term health.

4. _____ The way I eat is independent of my feelings of self-worth.

5. _____ I exercise regularly to maintain a healthful weight.

6. _____ My emotional health supports my ability to learn.

7. _____ I notice changes in my physical condition and respond effectively.

8. _____ I am in control of any alcohol or other drugs I put into my body.

_____ **Total score (11) Health**

1. _____ I see learning as a lifelong process.

2. _____ I relate school to what I plan to do for the rest of my life.

3. _____ I learn by contributing to others.

4. _____ I have written a career plan and update it regularly.

5. _____ I am gaining skills to support my success in the workplace.

6. _____ I take responsibility for the quality of my education-and my life.

7. _____ I live by a set of values that translates into daily actions.

8. _____ I am willing to accept challenges even when I'm not sure how to meet them.

_____ **Total score (12) Purpose**

Filling in your Discovery Wheel

Using the total score from each category, shade in each section of the Discovery Wheel below. Use different colours, if you want. For example, you could use green to denote areas you want to work on. When you have finished, complete Journal Entry #37 on page 413.

WWW Complete this exercise online @ **www.bams5ce.nelson.com**

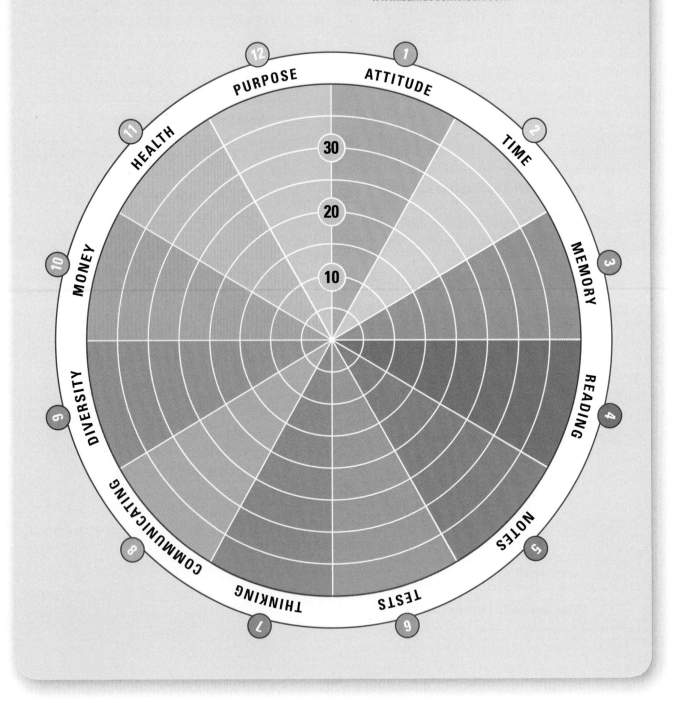

Discovery/Intention Statement

Revisiting your Discovery Wheels

The purpose of this Journal Entry is to (1) review both of the Discovery Wheels you completed in this book, (2) summarize your insights from doing them, and (3) declare how you will use these insights to promote your continued success in school.

Again, a lower score on the second Discovery Wheel does not necessarily indicate decreased personal effectiveness. Instead, the lower score could result from increased honesty and greater self-awareness.

	Chapter 1	Chapter 12
Attitude		
Time		
Memory		
Reading		
Notes		
Tests		
Thinking		
Communicating		
Diversity		
Money		
Health		
Purpose		

Comparing the Discovery Wheel in this chapter with the Discovery Wheel in Chapter 1, I discovered that I . . .

_____

_____

_____

_____

_____

_____

_____

In the next six months, I intend to review the following articles from this book for additional suggestions I could use:

_____

_____

_____

_____

_____

_____

_____

_____

---

35 exercise
This book shouts, "Use me!"

Becoming a Master Student is designed to be used for years. The success strategies presented here are not likely to become habits overnight. There are more suggestions than can be put into action immediately. Some of what is discussed might not apply to your life right now, but might be just what you could use in a few months.

Plan to keep this book and use it again. Imagine that your book has a mouth. (Visualize the mouth.) Also imagine that it has arms and legs. (Visualize them.)

Now picture your book sitting on a shelf or table that you see every day. Imagine a time when you are having trouble in school and struggling to be successful as a student. Visualize your book jumping up and down, shouting, "Use me! Read me! I might have the solution to your problem, and I know I can help you solve it."

This is a memory technique to remind you to use a resource. Sometimes when you are stuck, all you need is a small push or a list of possible actions. At those times, hear your book shout, "Use me!"

WHAT'S NEXT?

12

Create your next semester or term

This exercise offers a chance to celebrate your successes during the past term—and to think in specific ways about what you want to create next term.

Part 1: Update your First Step

Looking back on this past semester or term, you might be surprised at how quickly it went by. You might also be surprised at how much you learned, both inside and outside the classroom.

In the space below, list three things that you did well during the current term. Perhaps you took the initiative to meet a new person or created an effective way to take notes in class. Write down any success that you find personally significant, no matter how small it might seem to others. Use additional paper as needed.

1. _____

2. _____

3. _____

Now take a moment to write about three things that did not go as well as you wanted during the past term. Give yourself permission to explore whatever comes to mind—anything from a simple embarrassment to a major mistake. If you missed a class because you set your alarm for 7 p.m. instead of 7 a.m., you can write about that. If you failed a test, you might describe that experience as well.

As you practise truth-telling, remember to keep it light. It's fine to acknowledge breakdowns and to laugh at yourself as you do.

1. _____

2. _____

3. _____

Part 2: Determine what you want next

You've come a long way since first setting foot on campus. Now consider where you want to go next term. Brainstorm some intentions in several areas of your life. Then channel them into some new behaviours.

Do this activity by building on the writing you did in Part 1 of this exercise. Reflect on ways to maintain or expand on the successes you listed. Also consider ways to change or prevent some of the experiences you didn't like.

Determine what you want from academics. For instance, you could set a goal to raise your average to a specific number, or to declare your major by a certain date. Complete the following sentence.

In my academic life, I want to . . .

_____

_____

_____

Now consider your social life. Perhaps you want to resolve a conflict with an instructor or roommate. Or you might want to deepen a connection with someone you already know and make this person a friend for life. Put such goals in writing by completing the following sentence.

In my social life, I want to . . .

_____

_____

_____

Finally, brainstorm a list of specific actions you can take to meet the goals you just described. Write these actions below. Reflect on which ones might work best for you and record them in your calendar or to-do list. For more suggestions on goal setting, see Chapter 2.

_____

_____

_____

_____

_____

_____

_____

_____

_____

BE IT

Use this Power Process to enhance all of the techniques in this book.

Consider that most of our choices in life fall into three categories. We can do the following:

- Increase our material wealth (what we have).
- Improve our skills (what we do).
- Develop our "being" (who we are).

Many people devote their entire life-time to the first two categories. They act as if they are "human havings" instead of human beings. For them, the quality of life hinges on what they have. They devote most of their waking hours to getting more—more clothes, more cars, more relationships, more degrees, more trophies. "Human havings" define them-selves by looking at the circumstances in their lives—what they have.

Some people escape this materialist trap by adding another dimension to their identities. In addition to living as "human havings," they also live as "human doings." They thrive on working hard and doing everything well. They define themselves by how efficiently they do their jobs, how effectively they raise their children, and how actively they participate in clubs and organizations. Their thoughts are constantly about methods, techniques, and skills.

In addition to focusing on what we have and what we do, we can also focus on our being. That last word describes how we *see* ourselves.

All of the techniques in this book can be worthless if you operate with the idea that you are an ineffective student. You might do almost everything this book sug-gests and still never achieve the success in school that you desire.

Instead, picture yourself as a master student right now. Through higher education, you are simply gaining knowl-edge and skills that reflect and reinforce this view of yourself. Change the way you see yourself. Then watch your actions and results shift as if by magic.

Remember that "Be It" is not positive thinking or mental cheerleading. This Power Process works well when you take a First Step—when you tell the truth about your current abilities. The very act of accepting who you are and what you can do right now unleashes a powerful force for personal change.

If you can first visualize where you want to be, if you can go there in your imagination, if you can *be* it today, then you set yourself up to succeed.

If you want it, be it.

 Learn more about this
Power Process online @
....
www.bams5ce.nelson.com

Put It to **WORK**

Plan for change

Even the most brilliant people can fall flat when predicting trends in business and the workplace. Case in point: Thomas Watson, founder of IBM, said, "I think there's a world market for about five computers" (Isaac, 2007).

Still, you can benefit from making predictions about changes in the workplace that affect your own employment opportunities. Keep up-to-date with breaking changes as you decide what's next in your career. This is easier to do than ever before, thanks to resources mentioned throughout this book:

- *The Internet.* Use your skills in searching the Internet to find websites devoted to your field. Start by keying your job title into a search engine such as Google or Yahoo! Also search for career-related listservs—programs that distribute email messages to groups of people with similar interests.
- *Periodicals.* Read the business sections of *The Globe and Mail* and *The Wall Street Journal,* for example. Most news-papers also have online editions, as do general interest magazines such as *Maclean's* and *Business Week.*
- *Professional associations.* People in similar jobs like to band together and give each other a heads-up on emerging trends—which is one reason for professional associations. These range from the Canadian Medical Association to the Certified General Accountants Association of Canada. There's bound to be one for people in your field. Ask colleagues and search the Internet. **Note:** Many associations post websites and publish newsletters or trade magazines.
- *Conferences and conventions.* Many professional associations sponsor annual meetings. Here's where you can meet people face-to-face and use your networking skills. Print and online publications are powerful sources of news, but sometimes nothing beats plain old schmoozing.

Consider coaching

Consider receiving life coaching as a way to continue the cycle of discovery, intention, and action you started in this

© HENG KONG CHEN/iStockphoto

book. A life coach is someone with training in counselling or a related field who meets with clients several times per month in person or over the phone. Life coaches can help you define your personal values, align your daily life with those values, write goals and action plans, and create projects that allow you to contribute to others. With the support of a life coach, you can start now to envision the jobs you want to have in 5 years, 10 years, and 20 or more years into the future. You can set comprehensive, long-term goals in every other area of your life as well. Like other professionals, life coaches charge for their services. Fees vary widely. Consider life coaching even if you can afford only a few hours of this service a year.

You can also meet with friends to offer each other free coaching. Start by repeating the exercises and Journal Entries in this book, sharing the results, and inventing new exercises of your own. The results can be dramatic.

Continue the conversation about success

As you begin your life beyond this student success course, continue to engage in a conversation about what you want from your life and how you intend to get it. You can experience success as you define it and live the life of your dreams.

QUIZ

chapter 12

- Put It to Work
◀ ◀ ◀ ◀ ◀
- Skills Snapshot
- Master Student Profile

Name_____   Date____/____/____

1. According to the text, you can create a career plan through the process of "naming names." True or False? Explain your answer.

2. Explain how work *content skills* and *transferable skills* differ. Give one example of each kind of skill.

3. Explain how career planning can be a process of choosing instead of a process of discovery.

4. List three suggestions for designing an effective service-learning project.

5. Describe the three main types of life choices explained in the Power Process: "Be It."

6. List at least three strategies for negotiating a starting salary during the interview process.

7. If your scores are lower on the Discovery Wheel the second time you complete it, that means your study skills have not improved. True or False? Explain your answer.

8. Contributing to others does *not* involve:
   (a) telling people what is best for them
   (b) finding out what people want or need
   (c) determining if you can help people get what they want
   (d) giving your time, talent, or money
   (e) making sure that you experience satisfaction, as well.

9. Describe a flaw associated with the typical job-hunting strategy of looking through help wanted advertisements. Suggest an alternative approach to job-hunting.

10. List at least four ways that you can continue on your path of becoming a master student after completing this book.

Skills SNAPSHOT

Jerry Seinfeld told one aspiring comedian that "the way to be a better comic was to create better jokes and the way to create better jokes was to write every day" (Isaac, 2007). Seinfeld also revealed his own system for creating a writing habit: He bought a big wall calendar that displayed the whole year on one page. On each day that he wrote jokes, Seinfeld marked a big red "X" on the appropriate day on the wall calendar. He knew that he'd established a new habit when he looked at the calendar and saw an unbroken chain of "Xs."

So much of success boils down to changing habits. Take a snapshot of your habits as they exist today, after reading and doing this book. Then take the next step toward mastery by committing to a specific action in the near future.

DISCOVERY

During this course, it has been my intention to change the following habits . . .

I would describe my skill at changing those habits as . . .

INTENTION

Three habits that I am committed to changing in the future are . . .

NEXT ACTION

Of the three habits listed above, the one I would like to focus on next is . . .

To experience a new level of mastery at making this habit change, I will . . .

MASTER STUDENT Profile

chapter 12

■ Put It to Work
■ Quiz
■ Skills Snapshot
◄ ◄ ◄ ◄ ◄

Craig and Marc Kielburger

. . . are change leaders

© Rajzman/Free the Children

M arc Kielburger apologizes for the mess as he moves stacks of files, unopened mail, and brochure material off an old sofa. With posters tacked to the walls and mismatched furniture, the space feels more like student digs than the downtown Toronto office of the executive director of Free the Children (FTC), a $4-million charity. And Marc, in blue jeans with a couple of unopened sub sandwiches sitting beside his laptop, looks more like a young intern who's just getting his feet wet than the boss of this successful organization. But appearances can be deceiving.

As social activists with a string of accomplishments between them, Marc and his more famous brother, Craig, have been meeting and exchanging views with celebrities, world thinkers and thousands of kids and adults on children's rights issues as well as peace-building and volunteering initiatives since they were young teens growing up in Thornhill, Ont. FTC, an international network that has built more than 400 schools in developing countries, was launched by Craig when he was just 12. Its sister organization, Leaders Today, offers leadership programs and volunteer opportunities to young people abroad.

Big accomplishments

These days, Marc, a former Rhodes Scholar with degrees from Harvard and Oxford, oversees the various facets of the brothers' good works while Craig has taken on the role of full-time student at the University of Toronto. While he clears

a spot on his office couch, Marc talks about the "amazing" (a trademark expression) time he and his partner, Roxanne Joyal, had the night before. They were in Santa Barbara, Calif., for an FTC meeting and had lunch with the American journalism titan Walter Cronkite, an honorary adviser to the organization. "He gave us the most incredible history lesson," says the [then] 27-year-old, with obvious excitement. As soon as he could, Marc got on the phone to tell his younger brother, Craig, all about the eventful night.

Craig, [then] 21, was a tad jealous. Instead of rubbing shoulders with a media icon in balmy California, he took time away from his studies to take on the less glamorous—but equally important—task of wading through an early snowfall in Red Deer, Alberta, to give a speech on behalf of FTC (one of 70 he gives a year) and hand out awards to rural kids involved in farming. One recipient was being honoured for his innovative idea for saving threatened farms. "It was worth the trip," says Craig sincerely.

And the award goes to . . .

The two brothers have received a slew of awards for their work. Craig has been nominated twice for the Nobel Peace Prize, and Marc was named one of Canada's Top 40 under 40 in 2003. Given all that they've accomplished, you can't help but wonder before you meet this pair just what you're in for. Can two brothers, still in their 20s, who

Marc (1977–) and Craig (1982–) are authors and children's rights activists. When Craig was 12, he founded Free The Children International, an organization of children helping children who are the victims of poverty and exploitation. Marc was recently selected by the World Economic Forum as one of the 250 Young Global Leaders. They are cofounders of "Me to We."

Find more biographical information about Craig and Marc Kielburger at the Master Student Hall of Fame @

www.bams5ce.nelson.com

have experienced so much and achieved so much for so many, still be just a couple of nice normal guys?

Fortunately, yes. Both Marc and Craig are as down-to-earth as they come; they're both warm, friendly and quick to laugh. And both brothers will modestly tell you they believe that everyone, in his or her own way, can do what they both do. "We're both accidental activists," says Marc, adding they slowly got hooked on the joys of helping others.

Where it all began

Craig's role model for getting involved in social change was brother Marc. At 13, Marc became interested in environmental issues and eventually developed environmentally friendly cleaning products for a high school science project. He started collecting names on petitions for various environmental initiatives and enlisted his little brother, Craig, to help out. "He'd get me to go up and ask the girls to sign. They always would because I was so cute," says Craig, laughing.

So the seed of social consciousness was already planted when at age 12 Craig read with great dismay in the morning paper about the killing of another 12-year-old, Iqbal Masih, a freed child labourer from Pakistan. Indeed, he was so moved by Iqbal's struggles to end child labour and his eventual murder that he couldn't stop thinking about it. "I was shocked, and then I thought, What can I do? I'm only one person."

They caught the charity bug

But then Craig recalled Marc's zeal in raising people's awareness of environmental issues and that struck a chord. "I remember thinking, If he could do it, I can, too." A few weeks later, with the help of his school librarian, Craig had gathered enough information and mustered up the courage to talk to his Grade 7 class about child labour and ask if other kids wanted to join a group to fight against it. That first step back in 1995 eventually led to the participation of hundreds of thousands of children in 35 countries.

Craig and Marc remain each other's biggest supporters, and their latest joint endeavour—*Me to We: Turning Self-Help on Its Head*, the book the two have cowritten—is their most ambitious collaboration to date, and one that they unabashedly hope will spark a social movement. Since Craig started FTC as a child with other kids, detractors have argued that the organization's work wasn't appropriate for children, that it took away from their youth to be so immersed in the major problems of the world. But the critics missed the main point: the kids were being driven by the success of their projects and they were having a good time at the serious business of helping others. Now Marc and Craig want to help adults learn the same lesson. "This is what we do for fun," says Craig. "It's not a job. We do it because we love it."

Source: Excerpts from Christine Langlois, "The Accidental Activists: Craig and Marc Kielburger." Article originally published by *Canadian Living*. Found at http://www.canadianliving.com/life/community/the_accidental_activists_craig_and_marc_kielburger.php. Reprinted with permission.

Glossary

Acronyms Words created from the initial letters of a series of words. Can be used as a mnemonic device. p. 125

Affirmation Making positive assertions. p. 60

Analogy A similarity between two things or events. p. 237

Assertion A complete sentence that directly answers a key question. p. 227

Binge Drinking The consumption of large quantities of alcohol over a short time period—four drinks for women and five for men at least once in the past two weeks. p. 372

Bulimia An eating disorder where normal or near-normal weight adults eat excessively and then use methods such as self-induced vomiting or laxatives to prevent weight gain. p. 350

Cognition Everything that goes on inside your brain—thinking, perceiving, and learning. p. 53

Communication The process of creating shared meaning. p. 255

Communication Orientation See public speaking simply as an extension of one-to-one conversation. p. 283

Concept Map A diagram in which you draw circles or boxes in a hierarchical fashion and then create links between related ideas. These cross links are particularly important. The starting point is often a focus question from which you can branch off. Concept maps are an elaborative study strategy which we know supports effective encoding, particularly when they are developed along with materials you are trying to learn. p. 116

Convergent Thinking A narrowing-down process in choosing the most reasonable viewpoint on an issue or solution to a problem. p. 231

Cultural Competence Gaining skills in understanding people from cultures other than your own and using these skills in everyday life. p. 293

Culture A set of learned behaviours and beliefs that characterize a particular group. p. 295

Decode Memories are not really "stored." Instead, remembering is a part of the memory process in which you *encode* information as links between active neurons that fire together, and *decode*, or reactivate, neurons that wired together in the past. p. 109

Deductive Reasoning Reasoning from the general to the particular. p. 47

Discovery Statements A record of what you are learning about yourself as a student—both strengths and weaknesses. Discovery Statements can also be declarations of your goals, descriptions of your attitudes, statements of your feelings, transcripts of your thoughts, and chronicles of your behaviour. p. 8

Divergent Thinking (also called creative thinking.) The process of generating as many solutions/ideas as possible. p. 231

Diversity Differences of any type. p. 293

Eating Disorder Serious disturbances in eating behaviours such as overeating or extreme reduction of food intake. p. 350

Elaboration Consciously encoding new information. p. 115

Emotional Intelligence An ability to validly reason with emotions and to use emotions to enhance thought. Recognizing and responding to feelings in skilful ways. Often referred to as "people skills." p. 263

Encode Memories are not really "stored." Instead, remembering is a process in which you *encode* information as links between active neurons that fire together and *decode*, or reactivate, neurons that wired together in the past. p. 109

Fallacies Common mistakes in logic. p. 236

Graphic Organizers Visual representations of ideas or concepts. p. 116

Heterosexism A system of attitudes, bias, and discrimination that favours heterosexual relationships. p. 357

Homophobia Describes a range of negative attitudes including prejudice, fear, and antipathy toward lesbian and gay, and sometimes bisexual and transgendered people. p. 357

Homophobic Bullying Describes bullying that is based on negative beliefs or prejudices towards people who are perceived to be or who are actually gay. p. 356

"I" Messages A technique for communicating when strong emotions might get in the way of the message. Replace "you . . ." accusations with "I feel" messages that report your own thoughts and feelings. p. 259

Intention Statements Your commitment to do a specific task or take a certain action. An intention arises out of your choice to direct your energy toward a particular goal. p. 8

Kinesthetic Learning People who prefer learning through physical activity (also referred to as bodily intelligence). p. 51

Learning Styles Describes differences in how people prefer to perceive and process information. p. 40

Loci A synonym for place. Describes a system to create visual associations with familiar locations. p. 126

Lower- and Higher-Order Thinking Skills Lower-order thinking is receiving or reciting factual information or using rules and algorithms. Higher-order thinking requires manipulation of information and ideas in ways that transform their meaning and implications. For example, synthesizing or hypothesizing to arrive at a conclusion. p. 121

Mastery Attaining a level of skill that goes beyond technique. p. 54

Mediator In cross-cultural communication, someone who is committed to cultural understanding and who belongs to the dominant or mainstream culture. p. 299

Metacognition Thinking about thinking, learning about learning. The ability to stand "above" your mental processes—to observe them and to take conscious control of them. p. 53

Mindmaps Visual patterns that can serve as a framework for recalling information. They work on both verbal and nonverbal levels, contain lists and sequences, and show relationships. They can also provide a picture of a subject. p. 170

Mnemonic Devices Tricks that can increase your ability to recall information. p. 125

Model In cross-cultural communication, a model is a member of a culture who is a positive example. p. 299

Motivation Describes the willingness to do something, and the reasons a person has for behaving a certain way. p. 57

Multiculturalism Racial, ethnic, and other kinds of diversity. p. 295

Multiple Intelligences Gardner's theory of intelligences states that people have different kinds of intelligences. People do not have just one, but use many different intelligences including musical, interpersonal, spatial-visual, and linguistic intelligences. p. 48

Netiquette Common courtesy guidelines for online interpersonal relationships. p. 272

Neural Traces Paths in the brain. p. 111

Neuron A specialized cell that makes up the body's nervous system. p. 109

Noise A term used in communication theory to refer to any internal or external factor that distorts meaning. p. 256

Performance Orientation Belief that the speaker must captivate the audience by using formal techniques that differ from normal conversation. p. 283

Plagiarism Using another person's words or pictures without giving proper credit. p. 182, 280

Primacy-recency Effect Suggests that we remember most easily the first and last items in any presentation. p. 142

Procrastination Putting off doing something, delaying an action until a later time. p. 59

Proposition A relationship between two or more concepts. p. 117

Reflection Listening, then summarizing what the person says. p. 258

Selective Perception The tendency to notice only the stereotypes that support our opinion. p. 302

Self-actualization Realizing your talents and potentials. p. 18

Self-discipline Controlling your feelings in order to overcome weaknesses. The ability to reject instant gratification in service of a greater goal. p. 57

Self-efficacy Belief in your ability to determine the outcomes of events, especially outcomes that are strongly influenced by your own behaviour. p. 365

Self-fulfilling Prophecy The error in thinking about people such that we set them up in ways that confirm common stereotypes. p. 302

Self-justification The tendency in stereotypical thinking for someone to assume the role of a victim and avoid taking responsibility for their own lives. p. 302

Self-regulation People who set specific goals, monitor their progress toward those goals, and regularly change their behaviour to produce the desired results. These people have a clear idea of their objectives and their capabilities. p. 14

Serendipity The ability to see something valuable that you weren't looking for. p. 233

Short-term Memory The system in your brain that works to temporarily store and manage information. p. 114

Stereotype The assumption that every member of a group is the same. p. 302

STI Sexually Transmitted Infection. p. 358

Synthesis Combining individual facts into a meaningful whole. An aspect of metacognition. p. 142

Translators In cross-cultural communication, a "bicultural" person—someone who relates naturally to people in a mainstream and a contrasting culture. p. 299

Transphobia Discrimination against transsexual or transgender people. p. 357

Willpower The inner strength to make decisions and carry out tasks, regardless of resistance. p. 57

References

A

Adler, M., & Van Doren, C. (1972). *How to read a book: The classic guide to intelligent reading.* New York, NY: Simon and Schuster.

Agency for Healthcare Research and Quality. (2003). *Men, stay healthy at any age.* Retrieved from http://www.ahrq.gov/ppip/healthymen.htm/

Algonquin College. (n.d.). *Positive space program.* Retrieved from http://www.algonquincollege.com/studentservices/counselling/current_students/pshome.html/

Allen, D. (2001). *Getting things done: The art of stress-free productivity.* New York, NY: Penguin.

Alzheimer's Association. (2009). *Brain health.* Retrieved from http://www.alz.org.brainhealth/overview.asp/

American Psychological Association. (1994). *Diagnostic and statistical manual of psychoactive substance abuse disorders.* Washington, D.C.: American Psychological Association.

Anonymous. (n.d.). Sexuality and U.ca. *Birth control: hormonal methods.* Retrieved from http://sexualityandu.ca/en/birth-control/birth_control_methods_contraception/hormonal-methods

B

Bandura, A. (1994). Self-efficacy. In V. S. Ramachaudran (Ed.), *Encyclopedia of Human Behavior* (vol. 4, pp. 71–81). New York, NY: Academic Press.

BBC. (n.d.). *Afghanistan timeline.* Retrieved from http://news.bbc.co.uk/2/hi/1162108.stm/

Beck, B. L., Koons, S. R., & Milgrim, D. L. (2000). Correlates and consequences of behavioural procrastination: The effects of academic procrastination, self-consciousness, self-esteem and self-handicapping. *Journal of Social Behavior and Personality, 15*(5) 3–13.

Belford, T. (2009, November 16). *Cultivating the new work force.* Retrieved from www.globecampus.ca/in-the-news/globecampusreport/cultivating-the-new-work-force/

Bohart, A.(2005). *Master student guide to academic success.* Boston MA: Houghton Mifflin.

Bolles, R. N. (2005). *What color is your parachute? A practical manual for job-hunters and career-changers.* Berkeley, CA: Ten Speed Press

Brescani, M. J., Duncan, A. J., & Hui Cao, L. (2010). Embracing the ambiguity: Twelve considerations for holistic time management. *About Campus, 15*(5), 17–21.

Brownlow, S., & Reasinger, R. D. (2000). Putting off until tomorrow what is better done today: Academic procrastination as a function of motivation toward college work. *Journal of Social Behavior and Personality, 15*(5), 15–34.

Brody, J. (2006, September 12). Exercise = weight loss, except when it doesn't. *New York Times.* Retrieved from www.nytimes.com/2006/09/12/health/nutrition/12brody.html/

Buzan, T. (1991). *Use both sides of your brain.* New York, NY: Dutton.

C

CBC. (n.d.) *Mental illness rises on campus: studies.* Retrieved from http://www.cbc.ca/health/story/2010/08/12/mental-illness-college.html/

Calaprice, A. (Ed.). (2000). *The expanded quotable Einstein.* Princeton, NJ: Princeton University Press.

Canada Citizen (2008, May 16). *Morning after pill approved for over the counter sales.* Retrieved from http://www.canada.com/ottawacitizen/news/story.html?id=eb9a322c-0b86-414c-8a28-a21d22c8c6a3/

Canadian Campus Survey. (n.d.). Retrieved from http://www.camh.net/Research/Areas_of_research/Population_Life_Course_Studies/CCS_2004_report.pdf

Canadian Cancer Society. (n.d.). Retrieved from http://www.cancer.ca/quebec/about%20us/media%20centre/qc-media%20releases/qc-quebec%20media%20releases/qc_taux_tabagisme.aspx

Canadian Council on Learning. (n.d.). Retrieved from http://www.ccl-cca.ca/CCL/Reports/PostSecondaryEducation/Archives2006/PSEChapter9.html

Canadian Mental Health Association. (2011, February 10). *2001 Canadian Mental Health Survey.* Retrieved from http://www.cmha.ca/bins/content_page.asp?cid=5-34-212-213&lang=1/

Canadian Mental Health Association. (n.d.). Retrieved from http://www.cmha.ca/bins/content_page.asp?cid=2-28

Carlzon, J. (1989). *Moments of truth.* New York, NY: HarperCollins.

Carter, C. (2008). *Keys to effective learning: developing powerful habits of mind* http://webcat2.library.ubc.ca/vwebv/holdingsInfo?searchId=734009&recCount=20&recPointer=0&bibId=3705951&searchType=7. Upper Saddle River, N.J: Pearson Prentice Hall.

Center for Human Resources. (1999, July). *National evaluation of learn and serve America,* Retrieved from www.cpn.org/topics/youth/k12/pdfs/Learn_and_Serve1999.pdf/

Centre for Addiction and Mental Health. (n.d.). Retrieved from http://www.sano.camh.net/infoline/tp13.htm/

Centre for Addiction and Mental Health. (n.d.). Retrieved from http://www.camh.net/About_Addiction_Mental_Health/Drug_and_Addiction_Information/binge_drinking.html/

Centre for Suicide Prevention. (n.d.). Retrieved from http://www.suicideinfo.ca/csp/assets/FacingtheFacts.pdf/

Cheney, T. A. R. (1990). *Getting the words right: How to rewrite, edit and revise.* Cincinnati, OH: Writer's Digest Books.

Conference Board of Canada. (2010, November 10). Retrieved from http://www.conferenceboard.ca/topics/education/learning-tools/employability-skills.aspx/

Conway-Smith, E. (2004, July 16). Toronto second in proportion of foreign-born. *The Globe and Mail.*

Covey, S. R. (1989, 1990). *The seven habits of highly effective people: Restoring the character ethic.* New York: Simon & Schuster.

CTV. (n.d.). Retrieved from http://www.ctv.ca/CTVNews/World/20050804/afghanistan_timeline_050804/

Cuseo, J. (n.d.). *Academic-support strategies for promoting student retention and achievement during the first year of college.* University of Ulster Office of Student Transition and Retention. Retrieved from http://www.ulst.ac.uk/star/data/cuseoretention .htm#peestud

D

de Anda, D. (1984). *Bicultural socialization: Factors affecting the minority experience.* Washington, DC: National Association of Social Workers.

Dewey, J. (1910). *How we think.* Boston, MA: Heath.

Dimitrov, N. (2009). *Western guide to mentoring graduate students across cultures.* London, ON: Teaching Support Centre Purple Guides.

E

Elbow, P. (1981). *Writing with power: techniques for mastering the writing process.* New York, NY: Oxford University Press.

Ellis, D. (2006). *From master student to master employee.* Boston, MA: Houghton Mifflin.

Ellis, D. (2006) *Master student guide to academic success.* Boston, MA: Houghton Mifflin.

Ellis, D. (1998). *Creating your future.* Boston, MA: Houghton Mifflin Company.

Ellis, D., Lankowitz, S., Stupka, E., & Toft, D., (2003). *Career planning* (3 ed.). Boston, MA: Houghton Mifflin Company

Ellis, D., & Lankowitz, S. (1995). *Human being: a manual for happiness, health, love, and wealth.* Rapid City, SD: Breakthrough Enterprises.

F

Facione, P. A. (n.d.) *Critical thinking: What it is and why it counts.* California Academic Press. Retrieved from http://www .calpress.com/critical.html

Fleming, N. (2009, February 13). *VARK: A guide to learning styles.* Retrieved from www.vark-learn.com/

Fordcarz.com. (n.d.). *Henry Ford Quotations.* Retrieved from www .fordcarz.com/henry_ford_quotes.htm/

Friesen, J. (2010, March 9). The changing face of Canada: booming minority populations by 2031. *The Globe and Mail.* Retrieved from http://www.theglobeandmail.com/news/national/the-changing-face-of-canada-booming-minority-populations-by-2031/ article1494651/

Fried, C. B. (2008). In-class laptop use and its effects on student learning. *Computers and Education, 50,* 906–914.

G

Gardner, H. (1993). *Frames of mind: The theory of multiple intelligences.* New York, NY: Basic Books.

Gates, G. S. (1917). Recitation as a factor in memorizing. *Archives of Psychology, 6*(40).

Glater, J. D. (2006, May 18). Colleges chase as cheats shift to higher tech. *New York Times.* Retrieved from http://www.nytimes .com/2006/05/18/education/18cheating.html/

Goleman, D. (1995). *Emotional intelligence: Why it can matter more than IQ.* New York, NY: Bantam.

Ibid. (1997).

Government of Canada. (2006). *The Human Face of Mental Health and Mental Illness in Canada.* Retrieved from

http://www.phac-aspc.gc.ca/publicat/human-humain06/pdf/ human_face_e.pdf/

Gu, W. & Wong, A. (n.d.). Estimates of human capital in Canada: The lifetime income approach. *Statistics Canada.* Retrieved from www.statcan.gc.ca/pub/11f0027m/11f0027m2010062-eng.pdf/

H

Hallowell, E. (2006). *CrazyBusy: Overstretched, overbooked, and about to snap!* New York, NY: Ballantine.

Harvard Medical School. (2008, October 14). *HEALTHbeat: 20 no-sweat ways to get more exercise.* Boston, MA: Harvard Health Publications.

Hatch, C. W. (2008). *Pass that test: A guide to successful test taking.* Columbia, SC: Institute for Evidence-Based Decision-Making in Education.

Hayes, Steven C. (2004). *Get out of your mind and into your life: The new acceptance and commitment therapy.* Oakland, CA: New Harbinger.

Health Canada. (n.d.). http://ezinearticles.com/?Talking-Mental-Health-In-College--Q-and-A-with-Richard-Kadison-M.D.-of-Harvard-University&id=506696/

Health Canada. (n.d.). *Human papilloma virus.* Retrieved from http://www.hc-sc.gc.ca/hl-vs/iyh-vsv/diseases-maladies/hpv-vph-eng.php

Heart and Stroke Foundation. (n.d.). Retrieved from http://www .heartandstroke.com/site/c.ikIQLcMWJtE/b.3483991/k.34A8/ Statistics.htm#smoking/

Howe, N., & Strauss, W. (2000). *Millennials rising: The next great generation.* Toronto, Canada: Random House.

Hyden, H. (1969). Biochemical aspects of learning and memory. In Karl H. Pribram (Ed.), *On the Biology of Learning.* New York, NY: Harcourt, Brace & World.

I

International Centre for Youth Gambling. (n.d.). Retrieved from http://youthgambling.mcgill.ca/en/Adolescents/lesjeuxdargent .htm/

Isaac, B. (2007). Jerry Seinfeld's productivity secret. *Lifehacker.* Retrieved from http://www.lifehacker.com/software/motivation/ jerry-seinfelds-productivity-secret-281626.php/

J

Jackins, H. (1991). *The Benign Reality.* Seattle, WA: Rational Island.

Jourard, Sidney. (1971). *The Transparent Self.* New York, NY: Van Nostrand.

K

Kabat-Zin, J. (2001). *Full catastrophe living: How to cope with stress, pain and illness using mindfulness meditation.* London, UK: Piatkus Books.

Karpicke, J. D., & Blunt, J. R. (2011, January 20). Retrieval practice process produces more learning than elaborative studying with concept mapping. *Science Express* (2011), 1–10. Retrieved from www.sciencemag.org

Kay-Tee, K. Wareham, N., Bingham, S., Welch, A., Luben, R., & Day, N. (2008). Combined impact of health behaviours and mortality in men and women: The EPIC-Norfolk Prospective Population Study. *PLoS Medicine. 5*(11). Retrieved from www.plosmedicine.org/article/info:doi/10.1371/journal .pmed.0050012/

Knowles, M. (1984). *Andragogy in action*. San Francisco, CA: Jossey-Bass.

Koestler, A. (1964). *The act of creation*. New York, NY: Dell.

Kolb, D. A. (1984). *Experiential learning: Experience as the source of learning and development*. Englewood Cliffs, NJ: Prentice-Hall.

L

LaFasto, F. (2002, July). The Zen of brilliant teams. *Center for Association Leadership*. Retrieved from www.asaecenter.org/PublicationsResources/articledetail.cfm?ItemNumber=13295/

Lakein, A. (1973, 1996). *How to get control of your time and your life*. New York, NY: New American Library.

Lee, D. (1959). *Freedom and culture*. Englewood Cliffs, NJ: Prentice-Hall.

Life Literacy Canada. (2011, March 7). *Adult Literacy Facts*. Retrieved from http://abclifeliteracy.ca/en/adult-literacy-facts/

M

MADD. (2011, February 14). Retrieved from http://www.madd.ca/english/research/maddusa_stats_youth/

Mager, R. (1975). *Preparing instructional objectives*. Belmont, CA: Fearon.

Marshall, S. M. (2009). The student leadership challenge: Five practices for exemplary leaders. *Journal of College Student Development, 50*, 245–247.

Maslow, A. H. (1971). *The farther reaches of human nature*. New York, NY: Viking.

Mayo Clinic. (2007, September 11). *Generalized anxiety disorder*. Retrieved from www.mayoclinic.com/health/generalized-anxiety-disorder/DS00502/DSECTION=symptoms/

McGill University. (2006, December 16). Retrieved from http://www.mcgill.ca/mentalhealth/edp/campus/

McGregor, J., Symonds, W. C., Foust, D., Brady, D., & Herbst, M., (2006, July 10). How failure breeds success. *Business Week*. Retrieved from http://www.businessweek.com/magazine/content/06_28/b3992001.htm/

McKinney, M. (2000–2011). *Overcome procrastination*. Retrieved from http://www.successfulacademic.com/index.htm/

McLaren, D. (2009, November 16). *On campus it's hip to be mature*. Retrieved from http://www.globecampus.ca/in-the-news/globecampusreport/on-campus-its-hip-to-be-mature/

Miller, V. A. (1979). *Guidebook for international trainers in business and industry*. New York, NY: Van Nostrand Reinhold.

Mind Tools. (n.d.). *Understanding SMART goal setting*. Retrieved from http://www.mindtools.com/pages/article/newHTE_87.htm/

MySpace. (n.d.). *Safety Tips*. Retrieved from www1.myspace.com/misc/safetyTips.html/

N

National Committee for Latin and Greek. (2006, March 5). Retrieved from www.promotelatin.org/Default.htm#famous/

Nielsen, J. (1997, October 1). *How users read on the web*. Retrieved from www.useit.com/alertbox/9710a.html/

Novak, J., & Gowin, D. B. (1984). *Learning how to learn*. Cambridge, UK: Cambridge University Press.

O

O'Malley, M. (2008). *Educating undergraduates on using credit cards*. Retrieved from www.nelliemae.com/library/cc_use.html/

Ontario Colleges. (n.d.). *2004–2005 Ontario College Guide*. Retrieved from http://www.ontariocolleges.ca

Ontario Ministry of Training, Colleges and Universities. (2010). *Change your world: Achieve your dreams*. Retrieved from www.tcu.gov.on.ca/yourfuture/index.html

Orman, Suze (2009). *Suze Orman's 2009 action plan*. New York, NY: Spiegel & Grau.

P

Pachner, Joanna. (2007, June 11). *Personal debt: Coping strategies for the scholarly tab*. Retrieved from www.cbc.ca/news/background/personalfinance/studentdebt2.html

Pascarella, E. T., Seifert, T. A., & Blaich, C. (2010). How effective are the NSSE benchmarks in predicting important educational outcomes? *Change, 42*(1), 16–22.

Pascarella, E. T., & Terenzini, P. T. (2005). *How college affects students: Volume 2, a third decade of research*. San Francisco, CA: Jossey-Bass.

Paterson, R. J. (2002). *Your depression map*. Oakland, CA: New Harbinger Publications.

Pauk, W., & . Owens, R. J. Q. (2005). *How to study in college* (8 ed.). Boston, MA: Houghton Mifflin.

Perry, W. G. Jr. (1970). *Forms of intellectual and ethical development in the college years: A scheme*. New York, NY: Holt, Rinehart, & Winston.

Pintrich, P. R., Smith, D. A., Garcia, T., & McKeachie, W. J. (1993). Reliability and predictive validity of the motivated strategies for learning questionnaire (MSLQ). *Educational and Psychological Measurement, 53*, 801–813.

Prochaska, J. O., Norcross, J. C., & DiClemente, C. C. (1994). *Changing for Good*. New York, NY: Avon.

Progoff, Ira. (1975). *At a journal workshop*. New York, NY: Dialogue House.

Public Health Agency of Canada. (n.d.). Retrieved from http://www.phac-aspc.gc.ca/publicat/lcd-pcd97/table1-eng.php/

Public Health Agency of Canada. (n.d.). *Populations at risk*. Retrieved from http://www.phac-aspc.gc.ca/aids-sida/populations-eng.php/

Public Health Agency of Canada. (2010). *Questions and answers: Sexual orientation in schools*. Retrieved from http://www.phac-aspc.gc.ca/publicat/qasos-qose/index-eng.php/

Pychyl, T. A. (2010). *The procrastinator's digest: A concise guide to solving the procrastination puzzle*. Canada: Howling Pines Publishing.

Pychyl, T. A. , Morin, R. W., & Salmon, B. R. (2000). Procrastination and the planning fallacy: An examination of the study habits of university students. *Journal of Social Behavior and Personality, 15*(5), 135–150.

R

Raimes, A. (2004). *Universal keys for writers*. Boston, MA: Houghton Mifflin.

Reynolds, D. (1995). *A handbook for constructive living*. New York, NY: Morrow.

Rico, G. (1983). *Writing the natural way*. Los Angeles, CA: J. P. Tarcher.

Rogers, C. (1969). *Freedom to learn*. Columbus, OH: Merrill.

Rogers, C. (1961). *On becoming a person.* Boston, MA: Houghton Mifflin.

Roseman, E. (2009, December 16). *Roseman Carney's debt warning a shot of common sense.* Retrieved from http://www.yourhome.ca/homes/realestate/article/739287/

Rosnow, R., & Robinson, E. (1967). *Experiments in persuasion.* New York, NY: Academic Press.

S

Samaha, F. F., Iqbal, N., & Seshadri, P. et al. (2003). A low-carbohydrate as compared with a low-fat diet in severe obesity. *New England Journal of Medicine, 348*(21), 2074–2081.

Sandman, D., Simantov, E. & An, C., (n.d.). Out of touch: American men and the health care system. *The Commonwealth Fund, 2000.* Retrieved from www.commonwealthfund.org/Content/Publications/Fund-Reports/2000/Mar/Out-of-Touch-American-Men-and-the-Health-Care-System.aspx/

Sapadin, Linda with Jack Maguire. (1997). *It's about time! The six styles of procrastination and how to overcome them.* New York, NY: Penguin.

Saskatchewan Indian. (n.d.). The impact of Saskatchewan's growing aboriginal community. *Saskatchewan Indian.* Retrieved from http://www.sicc.sk.ca/saskindian/a00spr18.htm/

Schacter, D. L. (2001). *The seven sins of memory: How the mind forgets and remembers.* Boston: Houghton Mifflin.

Schreiner, L. (2010). Thriving in the classroom. *About Campus, 15*(3), 2–10.

Schreiner, L. (2010). Thriving in community. *About Campus, 15*(4), 2–11.

Seligman, M. E. P. (2002). *Authentic happiness: Using the new positive psychology to realize your potential for lasting fulfillment.* New York, NY: Simon and Schuster.

Seligman, M. E. P. (1998). *Learned optimism.* New York, NY: Pocket Books.

Sexuality and U. (n.d.). *What are the most commonly sexually transmitted infections affecting youth?* Retrieved from http://sexualityandu.ca/pdfs/CTR_CommonSTIs.pdf/

Siegel, D. J. (2001). Memory: An overview. *Journal of the American Academy of Child and Adolescent Psychiatry, 40*(9) 997–1011.

Skinner, B. F. (1965). *Science and human behavior.* Boston, MA: Free Press.

Solly, R., & Lloyd, R. (1989). *Journey notes: Writing for recovery and spiritual growth.* Center City, MN: Hazelden.

Statistics Canada. (n.d.). *Adult obesity in Canada: Measured height and weight.* Retrieved from http://www.statcan.gc.ca/pub/82-620-m/2005001/article/adults-adultes/8060-eng.htm#5/

Statistics Canada. (2011, May 25). *Canadians in context—People with Disabilities.* Retrieved from http://www4.hrsdc.gc.ca/.3ndic.1t.4r@-eng.jsp?iid=40/

Statistics Canada (2010, March 9). *Study: Projections of the diversity of the Canadian population.* Retrieved from www.statcan.gc.ca/daily-quotien/100309/dq10039a-eng.htm

Statistics Canada (2009, September 22). *Population, urban and rural, by province and territory.* Retrieved from http://www40.statcan.ca/l01/cst01/demo62k-eng.htm/

Statistics Canada (2009, August 21). *Gay pride . . . by the numbers.* Retrieved from http://www42.statcan.gc.ca/smr08/2008/smr08_118_2008-eng.htm/

Statistics Canada. (2008, April 2). *2006 Census: Ethnic origin, V=visible minorities, place of work and mode of transportation.* Retrieved from http://www.statcan.gc.ca/daily-quotidien/080402/dq080402a-eng.htm/

Statistics Canada (2001). *Selected religions, for Canada, provinces and territories.* Retrieved from http://www12.statcan.ca/english/census01/products/highlight/religion/Page.cfm?Lang=E&Geo=PR&View=1a&Code=62&Table=1&StartRec=1&Sort=2&B1=Canada&B2=1/

Svinicki, M. D. (2004). *Learning and motivation in the postsecondary classroom.* Bolton, MA: Anker Publishing.

Szalavitz, M. (2001, March 2). *Race and the genome. Howard University Human Genome Center.* Retrieved from www.genomecenter.howard.edu/article.htm/

T

Taylor, L. C. (2009, March 09). Bad English barrier to job: survey. *The Star.* Retrieved from www.thestar.com/printarticle/598636

Taylor, P. (2011, January 13). Writing about fears before the tests boosts students' grades, study. *The Globe and Mail.* Retrieved from http://license.icopyright.net/user/viewFree.act?fuid=MTE0MTc5Nzk%3D/

Thayer, L. (1968). Communication—Sine qua non of the behavioral sciences. In David L. Arm (Ed.), *Vistas in Science.* Albuquerque, NM: University of New Mexico.

Toft, D. & Ellis, D. (2011). *From master student to master employee* (3rd ed.). Boston MA: Wadsworth.

Toronto Police. (2011, February 12). *Report homophobic violence period.* Retrieved from http://www.torontopolice.on.ca/rhvp/

Tracy, E. (2006). *Student's guide to exam success.* Berkshire, UK: Open University Press.

Tjepkema, M. (2011, May 17). Statistics Canada. *Adult obesity in Canada: Measured height and weight.* Retrieved from http://www.statcan.gc.ca/pub/82-620-m/2005001/article/adults-adultes/8060-eng.htm#5/

U

University of Minnesota. (2007). *Health and academic performance: Minnesota undergraduate students.* Retrieved from www.bhs.umn.edu/reports/HealthAcademicPerformanceReport_2007.pdf/

University of Waterloo. (n.d.). *RIM founder named chancellor.* Retrieved from http://newsrelease.uwaterloo.ca/news.php?id=2764/

W

Wurman, R. S., Leifer, L., & Sume, D. (2001). *Information anxiety #2.* Indianapolis, IN: Que.

Wurman, R. S., (1989). *Information anxiety.* New York , NY: Doubleday.

Y

York University's Learning Skills. (2010, December 16). *University time management.* Retrieved from http://www.yorku.ca/cdc/lsp/skillbuilding/timemanagement.html#cycle/

Z

Zúñiga, X. (n.d.). Fostering intergroup dialogue on campus: Essential ingredients. *Diversity Digest.* Retrieved from www.diversityweb.org/Digest/W98/fostering.html/

AA (Alcoholics Anonymous), 372
Aariak, Eva, 160–161
ABC daily to-do list, 81–82
About.com, 386
Abstinence (from sex), 360
Abstract conceptualization, 40, 43, 45
Academic counsellor/advisor, 13, 16–17, 18
Acceptance, 208
Access resources, 13
Accident prevention, 357
Acronym, 125
Acrostics, 125
Action goals, 407
Active experimentation, 40, 43
Active voice, 277
Act of Creation, The (Koesler), 234
Addiction, 368–373
Ad populum fallacy, 237
Adrenalin, 383
Advertising, 373–374
Advice, 258
Aerobic exercise, 207
Affirmation, 60, 276
"Aha!" experience, 231
AIDS, 358–359
Alcohol addiction, 368–373
Alcoholics Anonymous (AA), 372
Aldinger, Tauni, 108
Allen, David, 96
All-or-nothing thinking, 237
Almanacs, 149
Alumni organizations, 18
Alzheimer's Association, 122
Amnesty International, 406
Amygdala, 114
Analogy, 237
Analytical ability, 230
Annual fee, 334
Annual percentage rate (APR), 334
Anorexia nervosa, 350
Answers.com, 152
Anthony, Scott, 215
Anthony, Trey, 317
Anxiety. *See also* Stress
    math tests, 209–210
    public speaking, 282–283, 284
    tests, 205–208
    writing, 279
APA Publication Manual, 278
Appealing to authority, 236
Appealing to "the people," 237
Appealing to tradition, 237
Apprenticeship program, 403
APR, 334
Arcade Fire, 344
Armstrong, Lance, 123
Artifact, 399
Arts organizations, 20

Arts resources, 18–19
Asking questions, 245, 246, 258
Assertion, 227
Assistance, 19
Association, 112–113
Assumptions, 238–239
Athletic facilities, 19
Atkins diet, 349
Atkinson, Mike, 3
Atlases, 149
Attacking the person, 236
Attend class, 3, 14, 166, 334
Attention deficit-hyperactivity disorder
    (ADHD), 120
Attitude
    adopt new behaviours, 46
    affirmation/visualization, 60
    critical thinker, 230
    exercise, 62
    memory technique, 115
Attitude replacements, 61
Auditory learning, 52
Auto brokers, 387
Automobile shopping, 335
Awards office, 19

Bailey, Luca, 407
Balance due, 334
Balance transfer, 334
Bandura, Albert, 365
Bankruptcy, 334
Barrier methods of birth control, 360–361
Barriers to communication, 260–261
Basic life processes, 255
Beatles, 123
Becoming a Critical Thinker (Ruggiero), 227
Beech, Terry, 68–69
Beethoven, Ludwig, 123
Begging the question, 237
Beginner's mind, 296
Behaviour, 374
"Be here now," 102, 270
"Be it," 415
Bellows, Keith, 82
Bibliography, 181
Binge drinking, 372
Biographical sketches. *See* Master student profiles
*Biography Index: A Cumulative Index to
    Biographical Material in Books and
    Magazines,* 148
Birth control methods, 360–363
Birth control pills, 360, 362, 363
Bisexuality, 358
Blackboard, 278
Blackhall, Kaitlin, 385
Bodily/kinesthetic intelligence, 48, 49
Body language, 45
Bolles, Richard, 398

Boyle, Susan, 123
Boyle's law, 114
Boy Scouts, 406
Brain, 122, 170
Brain-healthy diet, 122
Brainstorming, 118, 232, 273
Brazen Careerist, 398
Browser extensions, 185
Brumfield, Sue, 154
Bulimia, 350
Bursaries, 326
Butler, Edwin Farnham, 344–345
Buying a car, 335
Buzan, Tony, 170

Caffeine, 207
Calendar, 83, 97–99
Calendar method of birth control, 361, 363
Campus career fairs, 396–397
Canada's Food Guide, 350–351
Canada Student Loan, 333
Canadian Charter of Rights and Freedoms,
    300, 306
Canadian Environmental Network, 406
Canadian Human Rights Commission, 397
Candid speaking, 261
CanLearn, 333
Capsule biographies. *See* Master student profiles
CARE, 406
Career and job placement services, 326
Career fairs, 396–397
Career Handbook, The, 387
Career plan, 21
Career planning, 386–390. *See also* Job hunting
    be specific, 388
    career goals, list of, 390
    choices, 387–388
    exercise, 389
    mind map, 390
    pie chart, 390
    self-employment, 388
    take action, 388–389
    your ideal lifestyle, 388
Career services, 19
Carlyle, Florence, 305
Carlzon, Jan, 250
Car-pooling map, 19
Car shopping, 335
Cause-and-effect relationship, 235
Cell phone, 329
Centre for Addiction and Mental Health
    (CAMH), 372
Centre for Suicide Prevention, 365
Cervical cap, 361
Chapel, 19
CharityVillage, 398
Charter of Rights and Freedoms, 300, 306
Chassagne, Régine, 344–345

Cheating, 204–205
Cheat sheet, 174
Chicago Manual of Style, 278
Child care, 19, 20
Children underfoot, studying with, 153–154
Chilton, David, 330
Chlamydia, 358
Cho, Irene, 304
Choosing schools, 402–405
CIA World Factbook, 149
Ciccone, Daniella, 292
Citation information, 181
Citation management software, 181
Citations, 278, 280
Classroom observation skills, 164–166
Class size, 403
Coca-Cola, 215
Coffee houses and cafés, 20
Collaboration, 270
Collectivist cultures, 298, 314
Combination pill, 360, 363
Commitment, 7
Communication, 254–291
    barriers to, 260–261
    candid speaking, 261
    collaborating for success, 270
    complaints, 269
    criticism, 368
    defined, 255
    essay. *See* Essay/report writing
    group presentations, 278, 283
    "I" message, 259–260
    listening, 257–259
    non verbal messages, 260
    plagiarism, 280
    public speaking, 281–284
    questions that are not questions, 260
    required skills, 396
    saying "no," 267–268
    sexism, 305, 306
    social networking, 271–272
    speaking up, 261
    styles, 262
    workplace application, 287
Communication orientation, 283
Community college diplomas, 404
Community education classes, 20
Community information services, 20
Community resources, 20
Community service learning (CSL), 407
Community service organizations, 406
Comparison shopping, 328
Competence, 55
Complaints/complaining, 46, 261, 269
Compliments, 268
Computer-based source, 181
Computer-graded tests, 201
Computer lab, 19
Computers, ergonomics, 375
Concentration cheat sheet, 120
Concept map, 117
Concrete experience, 40, 43
Condom, 359–361, 363
Conferences and conventions, 416

Conflict management, 264–267
Consolidation, 115
Constructive criticism, 269
Consumer credit counselling, 20
Contact managers, 83
Context clues, 145
Contraception, 360–363
Contraceptive injection (Depo-Provera),
    360, 362
Contributing, 405–406
Convergent thinking, 231
Cooperative learning (study groups),
    197–199
Co-op placement, 404
Co-op program, 403
Cornell system of note-taking,
    169–170
Cost-benefit analysis, 58
Counselling, 384–385
Counselling centre, 20
Counselling services, 19
Courage, 56
Course evaluation, 176
Course management platforms, 278
Covey, Stephen R., 92
Creative serendipity, 233
Creative thinking
    "aha!" experience, 231
    brainstorming, 232
    creating while you sleep, 234
    decision making, 241
    focusing and let go, 232–233
    following through, 231, 234
    groups, 233
    idea files, 233–234
    serendipity, 233
    success strategies, 234
    trusting the process, 234–235
Creativity, 56
Credit cards, 331–332
Credit counselling, 334
Credit management, 331–334
Credit report, 332
Credit score, 332, 334
Credit terminology, 334
Critical thinking. *See also* Practising
        critical thinking
    assertion, 227
    attitudes, 230
    benefits, 225–226
    changing perspectives, 230
    considering the source, 228
    defining terms, 227
    different points of view, 227, 228
    hot spots, 229
    journal writing, 179
    logic and evidence, 229
    "spreadsheet," 229
    thorough thinking, 226
    tolerance, 228
    uncertainty, 229
    understanding before criticizing, 229
Critical Thinking: What It Is and Why It Counts
        (Facione), 63

Critical thinking "spreadsheet," 229
Criticism, 368
CSL (community service learning), 407
Cue column, 169
Cultural competence, 294
Cultural differences. *See also* Diversity
    conflict management, 266
    ESL students, 151–152
    time management, 92
Culture, 295
*Culture's Consequences: Comparing Values,
    Behaviors, Institutions and Organizations
    Across Nations* (Hofstede), 314
Cuseo, Joe, 197, 198
Cut costs, 328–329

Daily reviews, 194
Daily to-do list, 81–82
Date rape, 357
Dave's ESL Café, 152
da Vinci, Leonardo, 54
Dean, Lea, 192
de Anda, Diane, 299
Decision making, 240–241
Decode, 109
Decreasing options technique
    (DOT), 250
Default, 334
Defiers, 86
Delegation
    adult learner, 17
    leadership, 309
    time management, 92
    up and across the organization, 309
Denizard, Alex, 382
Depo-Provera, 360, 362
Depression, 377
Desire2Learn, 278
Desk dictionary, 144
Detachment, 208, 217
Devil's advocate, 233
DEVONThink, 185
Dewey, John, 241
Diaphragm, 361
Dickinson, Emily, 123
DiClemente, Carlo, 25
Dictionary, 144, 149
dictionary.canadaspace.com, 144
Dictionary of Canadian Biography, 148
Dictionary of the Social Sciences, 149
Dieting, 349
Digital recorder, 169, 177
Disabilities, students with, 19, 303–304,
    312, 333
Discomfort, 10, 46, 56, 57
Discovery and intention journal entry system
    See also Discovery/intention statements,
    Discovery statements, Intention Statements
    guidelines, 10–11
    overview, 8–9
Discovery/intention statements
    advertisements and your health, 374
    barriers to communication, 310
    communication, 255

communication styles, 262
discovery wheel, 39, 413
diversity, 294
first step, 33
health, 356, 374, 375
lectures, 166
major, choosing a, 248
memory, 109
money management, 319
money monitor/money plan, 325
muscle reading, 143
note-taking, 163
reading, 137
relationships, 266
test-taking, 193
thinking, 225
time management, 71
wants, desires, 383
Discovery statements, 5, 10
beginning to write, 279
conversations, 311
health, 347–348, 364
learning style inventory, 42
memory skills, 123
purpose, 27
recalling excellence, 11
review habits, 174
test anxiety, 210
time management, 78
Discovery wheel, 35–38, 409–412
Discrimination, 295–296, 300, 397
Disease. *See* Health
Disney, Walt, 123
Distracting from the real issue,
    237–238
Distress hotline, 20
Distribute learning, 119
Divergent thinking, 231
Diversity, 292–317. *See also* Cultural differences
beginner's mind, 296
Charter, 300, 306
defined, 293
disabilities, students with, 303–304, 312
discrimination, 295–296, 300
individualist *vs.* collectivist cultures, 298
leadership, 307–309
low *vs.* high context cultures, 299
racism, 296
relationship building, 297–300
school, at, 404
sexism/sexual harassment, 305–306
statistics, 293
stereotyping, 302
synergy, 296
translator, mediator, model, 299
workplace application, 314
Document your sources, 181
DOT, 250
Downtime, 96
Dreamers, 86
Dropbox, 83
Drug abuse, 368–373
Dry run, 196
Dual degrees, 243

Eating disorders, 350
Ebbinghaus forgetting curve, 174
E-books, 149, 150
Edison, Thomas, 233
Education
aim, 383
higher. *See* Postsecondary education
value of, 336
eduFire, 386
Egocentric thinking, 239
Einstein, Albert, 123
Elaboration, 115–118
Elbow, Peter, 273
eluta, 398
Email, 247
Emergency contraceptives, 361, 363
Emergency fund, 335
Emotional intelligence, 263
*Emotional Intelligence: Why It Can Matter More
    Than IQ* (Goleman), 263
Emotional pain, 366–367
Emotions
acceptance, 208, 263
emotional intelligence, 263
express, 263
logical fallacy, 237
naming, 263
test anxiety, 208
Employability skills, 391–392, 393
Employability Skills 2000+, 391
Employer's wish list, 47
Employment interview, 397
Encode, 109
Encyclopedia Britannica, 148
Encyclopedia of Asian History, 148
Encyclopedia of Psychology, 148
Encyclopedia of the Biological Sciences, 149
Encyclopedia, 148
EndNote, 181, 274
Energy drinks, 207
English as a second language (ESL), 151–152
Envelope system, 329
Ergonomics, 375
ESL students, 151–152
Essay questions, 201–202, 203
Essay/report writing, 273–280
active *vs.* passive voice, 277
citations, 278, 280
cut and paste, 277
first draft, 275–276
format/presentation, 278
generating ideas, 273–274
initial research, 274
outline, 274
phases, 273
plagiarism, 280
proofreading, 278
purpose, 274
required skills, 393–394
research, 274–275
revising the draft, 276–278
selecting a topic, 274
specificity, 278
starting up, 275

thesis statement, 274
verbosity, avoid, 278
Essure, 361, 362
Event planners, 387
EverNote, 185
Evidence, 228
Exams. *See* Test taking
Exercise aerobically, 207
Exercises
addiction, 370–371
attitude, 62
calendar, 97
career plan, 389
commitment, 7
communication (sending and
    receiving), 256
cost of school, 333
culture learner, 301
discovery wheel, 35–38, 409–412
employability skills, 393
first step, 34
goals, 80, 183
goals, translating, into action, 248
hot spots, 235
"I" message, 261
increase income/save money, 330
lifeline, 79
major, choosing a, 244
math success (learning styles), 214
mnemonic devices, 127
multiple intelligences, 48–50
next semester, 414
problems and solutions, 129
Q-cards, 121
relax, 145
skills, 390, 393
textbook reconnaissance, 5
things I like to do, 209
time, where does it go, 79
time monitor/time plan process, 72–74
trying something new, 399
TV note-taking, 178
using *Becoming a Master Student*, 413
Experiential education, 404
Extracurricular activities, 21
Extroversion, 262
Eye contact, 257, 284
Eye strain, 145
Eyestrain, 375

Facebook, 271
Facione, Peter A., 63
Fact *vs.* opinion, 237
Fad diets, 349
Failure, 123
Fallacies, 236. *See also* Logical fallacies
False cause, 236
Fast foods, 349
Faulty analogy, 237
Feedback
changing habits, 26
leadership, 308
online learning, 185
portfolio, 400

FeedDemon, 386
Feeling bad, 366–367
Feelings, 13
"F" grade, 202
Field placement, 404
File-synching, 83
Finance charge, 334
Finances. *See* Money management
Financial aid, 19, 326, 336
Financial aid office, 331
Firefox, 147
First day on the job, 401–402
5pm, 199
Fixed blocks of time, 84
Flash cards, 127
Flashcards, 195
Fleming, Alexander, 233
Flunitrazepam, 357
Foams, creams, tablets, suppositories, 361
Focus, 55, 94–96, 206, 232
Follow through, 231, 234
Follow up, 308
Food, 349–351
Food banks, 331
Fool (risk being, by trying new things), 340
Footnotes, 181
Ford, Henry, 326
Forgetting, 174
43Things, 83
Four-year applied college degree program, 403
Franklin, Benjamin, 234
Frederick, Cathy, 385
Freedom and Culture (Lee), 92
Free fun, 338
Free Mind, 171
Free writing, 273–274
Fulford, Robert, 231
Fun
   free, 338
   tests, 209
   time management, 85
Fundamental skills, 47, 391–392

Gambling, 369
GAMES, 130
Gamma-hydroxybutyrate (GHB), 357
Gandhi, Mahatma, 307
Gardner, Howard, 48
Gender identity, 358
Gender-neutral terms, 306
Generalist, 55
Getting Things Done: The Art of Stress-free Productivity (Allen), 96
GHB, 357
Ghomeshi, Jian, 253
Giblin, Lindsey, 136
Girl Guides, 406
Gliffy, 278
Globe and Mail's University Report Card, 403
Globe Campus, 403
Goals
   action, 407
   brainstorming and evaluation, 80
   categories, 78

   exercises, 80, 183
   major, choosing a, 243
   outcome, 407
   reflection ("spot checks"), 78
   SMART, 78
   specificity, 77
   time frames, 77
Going "green," 329
Goleman, Daniel, 263, 366
Google Calendar, 83
Google Docs, 83, 199, 278
Google Reader, 247, 271, 386
Google Scholar, 147
Gordon, Thomas, 259
Gowin, D. Bob, 117
Grace period, 334
Grajeda, Karen, 346
Graphic organizer, 116–117
Greenpeace, 406
Grindrod-Millar, Kathleen, 328
Group presentations, 278, 283
Group think, 233
Gubb, 83
Guided imagery, 207
Guy, Amy, 9

Habit, 25–26
Habitat for Humanity, 384
Hallowel, Edward, 264
Hasty generalization, 235
Health, 346–381
   accident prevention, 357
   advertising, 373–374
   alcohol addiction, 368–373
   anxiety. *See* Anxiety
   brain, 122
   eating disorders, 350
   emotional pain, 366–367
   ergonomics, 375
   food, 349–351
   gambling, 369
   men, 364
   mental, 353–355
   observing yourself, 355
   physical exercise, 207, 351–352
   pregnancy, unwanted, 360–363
   safety, 356–357
   self-efficacy, 365–366
   sexual, 358–360
   sexual assault, 357
   sleep, 352–353
   STIs, 358–360
   stress. *See* Stress
   substance abuse, 368–373
   suicide, 367–368
   workplace applications, 377
Health care centres and clinics, 20
Hebb, Donald, 109
Herbert, Richard, 127
Herodotus, 368
Heterosexuality, 358
High context cultures, 299
Higher education. *See* Postsecondary education
Highlighting, 141

High-tech cheating, 205
HIV/AIDS, 358–359
Hofstede, Geert, 314
Homophobic bullying, 356
Homosexuality, 356–357, 358
Hopper, Grace Murray, 305
Hormonal methods of birth control, 360
Hormonal vaginal contraceptive ring (NuvaRing), 360, 363
Hospice programs, 406
Hospitals, 406
Hot spots, 229, 235
How to Get Control of Your Time and Your Life (Lakein), 81
How to Read a Book (Adler/Van Doren), 228
HPV, 358
Hughes, Clara, 380–381
Human papillomavirus (HPV), 358
Human rights, 397
Hypatia, 305

"I create it all," 186
Idea files, 233–234
Ideas, 64
Identity theft, 327
Idioms, 152
"I" message, 259–260
"I'm lost" signal, 168
Implanon, 362
Implantable rod (Implanon), 362
Implants (contraception), 361, 362
Increase income, 326–328
Indeed, 398
Indexes and databases, 149
Indigenous services, 19
Individualist cultures, 298, 314
Information Anxiety (Wurman), 112
InfoTrac, 149
Inquiry-based learning, 245
Inquisitiveness, 55, 230
Instructor, 175–177
Insurance, 335
Intellectual property, 280
Intention statements, 5, 10–11
   excuses, 210
   habits and health, 364
   plan for transition, 13
Interdependence, 405
Interest rate, 334
International Centre for Youth Gambling and High Risk Behaviours, 369
Internet. *See also* Technology
   cell phone plan comparison, 329
   evaluate the sources, 247
   job hunting, 398
   job-related use, 416
   lifelong learning, 386
   online scams, 327
   search techniques, 147
   social networking, 271–272
   time management tools, 83
Internet Archive, 271
Internship, 404

Interpretation, 374
Interruptions, 91
In their own words. *See* Student voices
Intrapersonal intelligence, 48, 50
Intrauterine device (IUD), 361, 362
Introversion, 262
Intuition/intuitive, 56, 241
Investing, 335
IPMAT, 125
Isdell, E. Neville, 215
IUD, 361, 362

Jackins, Harvey, 366
Jackson, Lamont, 309
Jacquez, Macheala, 127
Jean, Michäelle, 307
Jellies (contraception), 361
Jenner, Edward, 233
Job hunting, 396–398. *See also* Career planning
    discrimination, 397
    first day on the job, 401–402
    job interview, 397
    salary negotiation, 398
    searching on the Internet, 398
    steps in process, 397
    tips/pointers, 400–401
Job interview, 397
JobHuntersBible.com, 398
JobPostings.ca, 398
Joint college/university collaborative
        program, 403
Joint Contact, 199
Jones, Kimani, 154
Jordan, Michael, 123
Jourard, Sidney, 261
Journal, 233, 384
Journal entries. *See* Discovery and intention
        journal entry system
Journal writing, 178–180
Jumping on the bandwagon, 237
Jumping to conclusions, 236

Kadison, Richard, 354
Kahlo, Frida, 305
Keeping up/networking, 416
Keynote, 282
Key words
    Internet search, 147
    mind mapping, 170
    note taking, 167, 173
Khan Academy, 386
Kielburger, Craig and Marc, 419–420
Kinesthetic learning, 52
Kiwanis, 406
Knowles, Malcolm, 18
Koestler, Arthur, 234
Kolb, David, 40
Korsakoff's syndrome, 122
Kuczmarski, Thomas D., 215

Laboratory work, 212, 214
LaFasto, Frank, 270
Lakein, Alan, 81
Laptop computer, 174

Laraque, Georges, 221–222
Larson, Carl, 270
Lazaridis, Mike, 327
Leadership skills, 284
Learning
    attitude, 46
    cycle of, 42 (LSI–6)
    defined, 26
    and inquiry, 245
    learn from any instructor, 46
    modes of, 41
    perceiving and processing, 40–41
    VARK system, 53
    VAK system, 51–53
Learning cycle, 42(LSI–6)
Learning Disabilities Association of Canada, 303
Learning skills and effective writing centre, 19
Learning style
    accommodating different styles, 44, 45
    activity (sentence to complete), 42(LSI–1,
        LSI–2, LSI–5)
    clues to another person's style, 45
    flexible learner, 41
    inventory, 42–42(LSI–3)
    journal writing, 179
    math success, 214
    money management, 337
    preferences, 42(LSI–8)
    success, and, 43–46
    theory, 42(LSI–7)
    work, and, 65
Learning style graph, 42(LSI–5)
Learning style inventory, 42–42(LSI–3)
LearnOutLoud.com, 386
Lee, Dorothy, 92, 295
Lee, Spike, 123
Left brain *vs.* right brain, 170
Legal aid services, 20
Lesbian, gay, bisexual, transgendered, queer
        (LGBTQ) students, 356–357
Letting go, 232
Lexis-Nexis Academic Universe, 149
LGBTQ students, 356–357
LGBT Youth Line, 357
Librarian, 148
Library
    almanacs, atlases, 149
    biographies, 148
    catalogue, 148
    community resource, as, 20
    computer resources, 149
    critical works, 148
    dictionaries, 149
    e-books, 149
    encyclopedias, 148
    evaluate the materials, 149
    indexes and databases, 149
    librarian, 148
    periodical articles, 149
    school resource, as, 19
    statistics and government documents, 149
    where to study, 90
Library and Archives Canada, 149
Library catalogue, 148

Life coaches, 387
Life coaching, 416
Life insurance, 335
Lifeline, 79, 103
Lineberger, Lynn, 245, 296
LinkedIn, 271, 398
Lions Clubs, 406
Listening, 257–259
Lists, 179
Literacy, 150
Lloyd, Roseann, 179
Local newspapers, 20
Local places of worship, 20
Local residents, 20
Loci system, 126
Locke, Edwin, 78
Logic, 228
Logical fallacies, 236–238
    all-or-nothing thinking, 237
    appealing to authority, 236
    appealing to "the people," 237
    appealing to tradition, 237
    attacking the person, 236
    begging the question, 237
    confusing fact and opinion, 237
    distracting from the real issue,
        237–238
    emotion, basing arguments on, 237
    false cause, 236
    faulty analogy, 237
    jumping to conclusions, 236
    red herring, 237
    slippery slope fallacy, 238
    straw man fallacy, 237
Long-term goals, 77, 243
Long-term orientation, 314
Long-term planner, 100–101
Low-carbohydrate diets, 349
Low context cultures, 299
Lucas, Deondré, 32

Maclean's annual rankings of universities, 403
Mager, Roger, 10
Mahmoud, Yahja, 147
Major, choosing a, 242–244
Major reviews, 194–195
Male condom, 359, 360, 363
Managing conflict, 264–267
Marking up the text, 140–141
Masatake, Morita, 354
Maslow, Abraham, 18
Master assignment list, 100
Mastering technology. *See* Technology
Master monthly calendar, 97–99
Master student, 54–56
Master student map, 6
Master student profiles
    Aariak, Eva, 160–161
    Anthony, Trey, 317
    Beech, Terry, 68–69
    Butler, Edwin Farnham, 344–345
    Chassagne, Régine, 344–345
    Ghomeshi, Jian, 253
    Hughes, Clara, 380–381

Master student profiles (*continued*)
  Kielburger, Craig and Marc, 419–420
  Laraque, Georges, 221–222
  Moubouyi, Gwenaelle, 190–191
  Pasricha, Neil, 290–291
  Petitclerc, Chantal, 106–107
  Suzuki, David, 135
Mastery situations, 365
Matching tests, 201
Mathematical/logical intelligence, 48, 49
Math tests, 211–213
Maturity, 230
*McGraw-Hill Encyclopedia of Science and
  Technology,* 148
Mediator, 299
Meetings, 103
Meeting with your instructor, 176
Memory, 108–135
  acrostics, 125
  associations, 112–113
  brain, 114–118
  categorize, 112
  combine techniques, 118
  concept map, 117
  distribute learning, 119
  Ebbinghaus forgetting curve, 174
  elaboration, 115–118
  loci system, 126
  mnemonic devices, 125–126
  names, remembering, 124
  organize, 112–113
  overlearn, 118
  peak energy, 119
  peg system, 126
  pictures, 114
  Q-cards, 121
  recite and repeat, 113–114
  relax, 113
  rhymes and songs, 125–126
  short-term, 118–119
  technology, 127
  write it down, 114
Memory jungle, 110–111
Men's health, 364
Mental crutch, 46
Mental health, 353–355
Mentor, 385, 406
Merriam-Webster Online, 152
Metacognition, 53
Meta-search engine, 147
Meyer, Courtney, 126
Microblogging sites, 271
Mid-term goals, 77
Miller, Kim, 401
Mills, Tricia, 335
Mind mapping, 170–171
Mindmap summary sheets, 195
MindMeister, 199
Mindomo, 171, 199
MindTools.com, 386
Minimum payment, 334
Mini-review, 146
MinMeister, 171
Mirena, 362

Missing class, 166
Mistakes, 215–216
Mistakes in logic. *See* Logical fallacies
MLA Handbook for Writers of Research Papers, 278
Mnemonic devices, 125–126
Moalim, Mohamed, 154
Model, 299
Money management
  common credit terms, 334
  core ideas, 339
  credit management, 331–334
  financial aid, 326, 336
  free fun, 338
  future needs, 335
  increase income, 326–328
  learning styles, 337
  money monitor/money plan, 320
  new way of thinking, 338
  online scams, 327
  paying for school, 336
  reduce expenses, 328–329
  required skills, 396
  sources of money, 336
  student loans, 332–333
  tough times, 330–331, 334
  workplace applications, 341
Money monitor/money plan, 320
Monthly calendar, 97–99
Mood metre, 263
Morning-after pills, 361, 363
Morrison, Toni, 244
Mosher, Deeanna, 70
Motivation, 57–59
Motley, Michael, 283
Moubouyi, Gwenaelle, 190–191
Multicultural centre, 20
Multiculturalism, 295. *See also* Diversity
Multiple choice questions, 200–201
Multiple intelligences, 48–50
Multi-tasking, 103
Murphy's law of computer crashes, 184
Murray, Laurie, 87
Muscle reading, 137–142. *See also* Reading
  e-books, 150
  leaner approach (shorter variation), 142
  overview, 138
  step 1 (preview), 139
  step 2 (outline), 139
  step 3 (question), 139
  step 4 (read), 140
  step 5 (underline), 140–141
  step 6 (answer), 141
  step 7 (recite), 141
  step 8 (review), 141
  step 9 (review again), 141
Musical/rhythmic intelligence, 48, 50
Myers-Briggs Type Indicator, 42(LSI-7)
myGoals.com, 83
myNoteIt, 83, 185
MySpace, 272

Names, remembering, 124
National Survey of Student Engagement
  (NSSE), 403

Naturalist intelligence, 48, 50
Negative self-talk, 180
Nenshi, Naheed, 307
Netiquette, 272
NetNewsWire, 271
Neural traces, 111
NewsGator, 386
Newspapers, 20, 416
Newsreader, 386
New York Times Almanac, 149
Noise, 256
Noise distractions, 91
Nonoxynol-9, 360, 361
Non-verbal behaviour, 258, 260, 284
Non-verbal communication, 284
Non-verbal messaging, 260
Non-verbal listening, 257–258
No-period pill, 363
Norcross, John, 25
Notable failures, 123
Note-taking, 162–191
  abbreviations, 168
  blank space, 168
  colours, 168
  combining formats, 172
  Cornell format, 169–170
  digital recorder, 169, 177
  edit the notes, 173
  graphic signals, 168–169
  "I'm lost" signal, 168
  keywords, 167
  laptop computer, 174
  mind mapping, 170–171
  observe, 164–166
  one side of a piece of paper, 168
  online classes, 184–185
  outlining, 171–172
  paragraphs, 167–168
  pictures and diagrams, 167
  plagiarism, 181–182
  PowerPoint presentation, 182
  reading, while, 180–182
  required skills, 395
  research notes, 180–181
  review, 173–174
  review notes, 180
  special cases, 182
  summaries, 174
  three-part process, 163
  three-ring binder, 168
  typing up your notes, 174
  when instructor talks fast, 177
Note-taking groups, 197–198
Note-taking skills, 395
Novak, Joseph, 117
NSSE, 403
Nursing homes, 406
Nutritional guidelines, 349
NuvaRing, 360, 363

Observation skills, 164–166
OCLC FirstSearch, 149
Ombudsperson, 176
Online banking services, 320

Online classes, 184–185
Online communities, 271–272
Online dictionary, 144
Online newspapers, 416
Online notebooks, 185
Online scams, 327
Online tests, 202
Ontario Problem Gambling Helpline, 369
Ontario University Fair, 403
Open-book tests, 201
Open-mindedness, 230
OpenOffice, 83
Oral contraceptives, 360, 362, 363
Organize by alphabet, 112
Organize by category, 112
Organize by continuum, 112
Organize by location, 112
Organize by time, 112
Organizing, principles for ideas, facts, objects, 112-113
Orman, Suze, 331
Ortho Evra, 360, 363
Outcome goals, 407
Outlining, 171–172
Outlining feature (word processing program), 127
Overdoers, 86
Overlearn, 118
Oxfam, 406
Oxford Companion to Classical Literature, 149
Oxford Companion volumes, 148
Oxford English Dictionary, 149

Paradox, 55–56
ParaGard, 362
Paraphrasing, 180
Part-time jobs, 327
Pasricha, Neil, 290–291
Passive voice, 277
Passphrase, 327
Password, 327
Patch, 360, 363
Pauk, Walter, 169
Pay attention, 120
Payment due date, 334
Peer-mentoring programs, 385
Peg system, 126
Penguin Dictionary of Literary Terms and Literary Theory, 149
People skills, 393
Perfectionist, 59
Perfectionists, 86
Performance orientation, 283
Perimeter Institute, 327
Periodical articles, 149, 181
Periodic rate, 334
Permanent methods of birth control, 361, 362
Perry, William, 230
Personal experiences. *See* Student voices
Personal finance software, 320
Personal information managers, 185
Personal management skills, 47, 392
Personal relationship managers, 83
Petitclerc, Chantal, 106–107

Pet psychologists, 387
PFLAG Canada, 357
Phishing, 327
Phone bills, 329
Physical exercise, 207, 351–352
Pill, birth control, 360, 362, 363
Plagiarism, 181–182, 280
Plan B, 361, 363
Planning
    long-term planner, 100–101
    strategies, 84–85
Political parties, 20
Portfolio, 399–400
Positive Space Program, 357
Post-diploma/post-graduate/post-certificate program, 403
Postsecondary education
    benefits/payoffs, 22
    community resources, 20
    delegate tasks, 17
    differences, 12
    extracurricular activities, 21
    get to know younger students, 17
    planning, 17
    "publish" your schedule, 18
    school resources, 18–19
    study habits, 17
    what to do, 13–14
Posture, 375
Power-distance, 314
PowerPoint, 282
PowerPoint presentation, 182
Power processes
    agreements/promising, 286
    be here now, 102
    "be it," 415
    conversations, 313
    detachment, 217
    discover what you want, 29
    "I create it all," 186
    ideas, 64
    pictures, 156
    problems, 249
    problems/barriers, 131
    risk being a fool, 340
    surrender, 376
Practice, practice, practice, 26
Practising critical thinking. *See also* Critical thinking
    asking questions, 246
    audience's attitude system, 285
    behaviour *vs.* interpretation, 374
    bias/stereotyping, 311
    concept map, 119
    enjoyability of learning, 128
    master student profiles, 63
    money management, 339
    multiple choice test, 216
    newspaper editorial, 155
    procrastination, 88
Praise yourself, 206
Pregnancy, unwanted, 360–363
Prejudice, 239, 300

Presley, Elvis, 123
Preventing accidents, 357
Problem solving, 241–242
Prochaska, James, 25
Procrastination, 59, 86–88, 103, 185
Procrastination style, 86
Professional associations, 416
Professional organizers, 387
Professor (instructor), 175–177
Profiles of successful students. *See* Master student profiles
Project Gutenberg, 152
Proofreading, 278
Public speaking, 281–28
"Publish" your schedule,
Punctuality, 15
Pychyl, Tim, 59, 90, 93

Q-cards, 121
Questions, 245, 246, 258
Quicken, 320

Racism, 296
Rape, 357
Rational Recovery Systems, 372
Read for pleasure, 150
Reading, 136–161. *See also* Muscle read
    children underfoot, with, 153–154
    context clues, 145
    dictionary, 144, 149
    e-books, 149, 150
    essential words, 146
    highlighting, 141
    literacy, 150
    marking up the text, 140–141
    math tests, 212
    mini-review, 146
    note-taking, 180–182
    re-read, 146
    required skills, 395
    skip around, 146
    stand up, 146
    tutor, 147
    underlining, 140
    vocabulary, 144–145
    workplace application, 157
Reading groups, 198
Reading skills, 395
Reality condom, 363
Recitation, 114
Recreation centre, 19
Red herring, 237
Redoing the book, 385
Reduce expenses, 328–329
Reference librarian, 148
Reflection, 258
Reflective observation, 40, 43
RefWorks, 181, 274–275
Registrar's office, 19
Relaxation, 113
Remember the Milk, 83
Repetition, 113
Report writing. *See* Essay/report writing
Re-read, 146

Research groups, 198
Research notes, 180–181
Resources
    community, 20
    online, 39
    school, 18–19
Respect, 15–16
Responsibility, 55
Restivo, Julian, 21
Review notes, 180
Reward yourself, 11
Rhymes and songs, 125–126
Rhythm method of birth control, 361, 363
Rico, Gabrielle, 170
Right brain *vs.* left brain, 170
Riley Guide, 398
Risk being a fool, 340
Risk taking, 55
Rogers, Carl, 56, 258
Rohypnol, 357
Roommates, conflicts with, 267
Rotary clubs, 406
Rowling, J. K., 123, 244
Roy G. Biv, 125
Royles, Belle, 276
RSS feeders, 386
RSS reader, 271
Rueda, Mauricio, 162
Ruggles, Kristine, 238

Safari, 147
Safety, 356–357
Salary negotiation, 398
Salerno, Cat, 254
Santiago, Lupe, 352
Sapadin, Linda, 86
Saying "no," 90, 267–268
Schacter, Daniel, 115
School calendar, 19
School resources, 18–19
Schools, choosing, 402–405
School security services, 19
Science courses, 214
Screensucking, 264
Secular Organizations for Sobriety, 372
Seinfeld, Jerry, 123
Selective perception, 302
Self-actualization, 18
Self-awareness, 55
Self-confidence, 230
Self-discovery, 243
Self-discovery and self-management skills, 395
Self-efficacy, 365–366
Self-esteem, 365
Self-fulfilling prophecy, 302
Self-handicapping, 59
Self-justification, 302
Self-regulation, 14
Seligman, Martin, 354
Serendipity, 233
Service Canada's Job Bank, 398
Service-learning, 407
Services for students with disabilities, 19
7-day antiprocrastination plan, 87

Sexism, 305
Sexist language, 305, 306
Sexual assault, 305, 357
Sexual harassment, 305, 306
Sexual health, 358–360
Sexually transmitted infection (STI), 358–360
Sexual orientation, 358
Short-answer/fill-in-the-blanks tests, 201
Short-term goals, 77
Short-term memory, 114–115
Short-term orientation, 314
Silence, 257
Skills. *See also* Skills snapshot
    communication, 396
    fundamental, 47, 391–392
    money, 396
    note-taking, 395
    people, 393
    personal management, 47, 392
    self-discovery, 395
    teamwork, 47, 392
    test-taking, 395
    thinking, 395
    time-management, 395
    transferable, 393–396
    work-content, 393
Skills snapshot. *See also* Skills
    applied thinking, 252
    balance, 105
    communication, 289
    conflict management, 289
    creative and critical thinking, 252
    cultural diversity, 316
    daily planning, 105
    flexibility, 67
    goals, 105
    habit change, 379
    health, 379
    learning style, 67
    listening, 289
    memory, 134
    money management, 343
    note-taking, 189
    paying for school, 343
    procrastination, 105
    public speaking, 289
    reading y, 159
    self-awareness, 67
    stereotyping, 316
    test anxiety, 220
Skinner, B. F., 26
Skin patch (Ortho Evra), 360, 363
Slang, 152
Sleep, 352–353
SlideShare, 199
Slippery slope fallacy, 238
SMART goals, 78
Social networking
    netiquette, 272
    time management, 90–91
    unwanted encounters, 271
Solly, Richard, 179
SOS, 199

Sources, 181
Space planners, 387
Speakers (on campus), 384
Speaking notes, 282
Specialty clubs and organizations, 20
Specific goals, 77
Spermicide, 360, 363
Sponge with spermicide, 360–361, 363
Spontaneous, 56
Stage fright, 282–283, 284
Stand-up desk, 235
STAR, 77
Starting and stopping time, 84
Statistics and government documents, 149
Statistics Canada, 149
Stereotype, 300
Stereotyping, 302
Sterilization implant (Essure), 361, 362
Sterilization surgery, 361, 362
STIs, 358–360
Strauss, Malte, 213
Straw man fallacy, 237
Stress. *See also* Anxiety
    cheating, 204
    journal writing, 180
    managing, 354–355
    statistics (prevalence), 355
Student bursaries, 326
Student discounts, 328
Student government, 19
Student health services, 19
Student loans, 332–333
Student organizations, 19
Students Offering Support (SOS), 199
Student success course, 24
Students with disabilities, 19, 303–304, 312, 333
Student unions, 19
Student voices
    adult student, 309
    alternative spring break, 21
    attending class, 334
    community service learning (CSL), 407
    cost of school, 334
    creative thinking, 226
    critical thinking, 245
    dictionary, 147
    discovery and intention statements, 9
    diversity, 296
    dyslexia, 304
    fear, 128
    goal of making it to college, 335
    goal setting, 82
    leadership opportunities, 284
    list making, 87
    mnemonic devices, 126
    part-time work, 328
    putting pointers from textbook into
        action, 385
    repeat the material within 24 hours, 128
    report writing, 275
    staying in shape, 352
    studying with children nearby, 154
    successful, how to be, 276
    test preparation, 213

Study checklists, 195
Study group, 212
Study groups, 197–199
Style guides, 278
Substance abuse, 368–373
Suggestion box, 233
Suicide, 208, 367–368
suicideinfo.ca, 365
Supervision, 314
Support group, 20, 385
Suppositories, 361
Surgical sterilization, 361, 362
Surrender, 376
Suspend judgment, 10, 55
Suzuki, David, 135
Svinicki, Marilla, 130
Sweeten the task, 57
Swidler, Lauren, 224
Synergy, 296
Systematic, 230
Szaefer, Joel, 284

Table of contents, 180
Take an unrelated class, 384
Taking notes. *See* Note-taking
Talks on campus, 384
Tangram, 231
Teamwork, 270
Teamwork skills, 47, 392
Technology. *See also* Internet
    browser extensions, 185
    disabilities, students with, 312
    email, 247
    group projects, tools, 278
    high-tech cheating, 205
    memory, 127
    money, protect it, 327
    networking, 271
    online notebooks, 185
    online resources, 39
    personal information managers, 185
    screensucking, 264
    searching the Internet, 147
    virtual study groups, 199
    Web-based time management tools, 83
TED talks, 386
Telehealth Services, 355
Telephone bills, 329
Tell the truth, 10, 25, 33
Terminology
    credit terms, 334
    essay questions, 203
Term insurance, 335
Test anxiety, 205–208
    breathe, 207
    detachment, 208
    dispute your thoughts, 206
    emotions, 208
    focus, 206
    get help, 208
    guided imagery, 207
    physical exercise, 207
    praise yourself, 206
    scan your body, 207

symptoms, 206
    visualization, 206
Test review groups, 197
Test taking, 192–222
    cheating, 204–205
    computer-graded tests, 201
    copies of old exams, 196
    daily reviews, 194
    dry run, 196
    essay questions, 201–202, 203
    flashcards, 195
    fun, 209
    major reviews, 194–195
    matching tests, 201
    math tests, 211–213
    mindmap summary sheets, 195
    multiple choice questions, 200–201
    online tests, 202
    open-book tests, 201
    post-test activities, 203–204
    predicting test questions, 196–197
    short-answer/fill-in-the-blanks tests, 201
    study checklists, 195
    study groups, 197–199
    test anxiety, 205–208
    true/false questions, 201
    weekly reviews, 194
Test-taking and related skills, 395
Textbook. *See Becoming a Master Student*
Textbook reconnaissance, 5
Text message etiquette, 272
Thayer, Lee, 255
The Hunger Project, 406
Thesis statement, 274
Thinking, 224–253
    assumptions, 238–239
    convergent, 231
    creative. *See* Creative thinking
    critical. *See* Critical thinking
    egocentric, 239
    logical fallacies, 236–238
    major, choosing a, 242–244
    required skills, 395
Thinking skills, 395
30 Boxes, 83
Three-ring binder, 168
Time boxing, 84–85
Timelines, 11
Time management, 70–107
    best time of day, 89
    calendar, 97–99
    changes in workload, 85
    delegation, 92
    downtime, 96
    fixed blocks of time, 84
    flexibility and fun, 85
    focus, 94–96
    get things done, 96
    handling the rest of the world, 90
    interruptions, 91
    involve others where appropriate, 85
    long-term planner, 100–101
    noise distractions, 91
    procrastination, 86–88

promise it, 93
    required skills, 395
    saying "no," 90
    social networking sites, 90–91
    starting and stopping time, 84
    time boxing, 84–85
    time monitor/time plan process, 72–76
    to-do list, 81–82
    waiting time, 90
    Web-based tools, 83
    when to study, 89–90
    when you get stuck, 91–93
    where to study, 90
    workplace application, 103
Time-management cycle, 85
Time-management skills, 395
Time monitor/time plan process, 72–76
Today sponge, 360–361, 363
To-do list, 81–82
Tolerance, 228
Toms, Forrest, 296
Topic-point-details chart, 116
Tourism office, 20
Transferable skills, 393–396
Transgendered persons, 358
Transition to higher education.
        See Postsecondary education
Translator, 299
Transparency, 261
Travel, 384
Trial run, 21
Trobriand Islands, 92
True/false questions, 201
Truth, 10, 25, 33
Truth-seeking, 230
Tuition fees, 404
Turner, Ted, 244
Tutor/tutoring, 19, 147
TV note-taking, 178
12-step program (AA), 372
Twitter, 271
Two-spirited persons, 358

Unabridged dictionary, 144
Uncertainty, 229
Undergraduate university degree
        program, 403
Underlining, 140
Understanding before criticizing, 229
Unemployment benefits, 331
University Report Card, 403
Unknowns, 13
Unwanted pregnancy, 360–363

Vaccination, 359
Vaginal ring, 360, 363
Vague goal, 77
VARK system, 53
VAK system, 51–53
Values, 408
Vasectomy, 361, 362
Venn diagram, 116, 117
Verbal/linguistic intelligence, 48, 49
Verbal listening, 258

Virtual office hours, 39
Virtual study groups, 199
Visualization, 60–61, 95, 206, 276
Visual learning, 52
Vocabulary, 144–145
Volunteering, 406

Waiting time, 90
Walpole, Horace, 233
Watermen, Pat, 275
Watson, Thomas, 416
Wealthy Barber, The (Chilton), 330
Web-based time management tools, 83
Weekly reviews, 194
*What Color Is Your Parachute? A Practical Manual
        for Job-Hunters and Career-Changers*
        (Bolles), 397
When Teams Work Best (LaFasto/Larson), 270
Whole life insurance, 335
Who's Who, 148
Wiggio, 199, 278
Wiki, 278
Wikipedia, 247
Williams, Scooter, 226

Willingness to change, 55
Women for Sobriety, 372
Word stack, 144
Work-content skills, 393
Working on-campus, 327
Work-integrated learning
        experiences, 404
Workplace applications, 23–24
        communicating, 287
        cooperative learning skills, 218
        creative and critical thinking, 250
        cultural differences, 314
        health, 377
        keeping up/networking, 416
        learning styles, 65
        life coaching, 416
        money management, 341
        names, remembering, 132
        note-taking, 187
        reading, 157
        test-taking strategies, 218
        time management, 103
Workplace financial literacy, 341
Workplace stress, 355

Workshop, 384
World Almanac and Book of Facts, 149
World Wildlife Fund, 406
Worriers, 86
Writing
        anxiety, 279
        conflict management, and, 266
        essays. *See* Essay/report writing
Writing anxiety, 279
Writing centre, 278
Wurman, Richard Saul, 112
www.campusstarter.com, 403
www.ted.com/talks, 386

Yahoo, 83
Yojimbo, 185
"You" messages, 259
Young, Aubrey, 9

Zoho, 83
Zoho Notebook, 185
Zoho Writer, 199
Zotero, 185, 274
Zucker, Jake, 318